THE COURT OF JUSTICE
OF THE
EUROPEAN COMMUNITIES

Volume One

JURISDICTION AND PROCEDURE

BY THE SAME AUTHOR

The Court of Justice of the European Coal and Steel Community (1955)

JOINT EDITOR: Common Market Law Reports (1962–   )

AUSTRALIA

The Law Book Co. of Australasia Pty. Ltd.
Sydney : Melbourne : Brisbane

INDIA

N. M. Tripathi Private Ltd.
Bombay

ISRAEL

Steimatzky's Agency Ltd.
Jerusalem : Tel Aviv : Haifa

NEW ZEALAND

Sweet & Maxwell (N.Z.) Ltd.
Wellington

PAKISTAN

Pakistan Law House
Karachi

U.S.A. AND CANADA

Fred B. Rothman & Co.
South Hackensack, N.J.

The Court of Justice

of the

European Communities

VOLUME ONE

JURISDICTION AND PROCEDURE

BY

D. G. VALENTINE, M.A., LL.B.(Cantab.), Dr.Jur.(Utrecht)

*of the South-Eastern Circuit and Lincoln's Inn, Barrister-at-Law; Senior Lecturer,
London School of Economics and Political Science; sometime Freelance Translator
to the E.E.C. Commission*

*Human nature does not change, but when nations and men accept the same
rules, and the same institutions to make sure that they are applied, their behaviour
towards each other changes. This is the process of civilisation itself.*

Jean Monnet,
First President of the High Authority.

LONDON   *SOUTH HACKENSACK, N.J.*

STEVENS & SONS   FRED B. ROTHMAN & CO.

1965

*Published in the United Kingdom
in 1965 by Stevens and Sons
Limited of 11 New Fetter Lane
London.*

*Published in the
United States of America in 1965
by Fred B. Rothman and Co.
of 57 Leuning Street, South
Hackensack, New Jersey.*

*Printed in Great Britain
by The Eastern Press Limited
of London and Reading.*

*Library of Congress Catalog
Card Number 65-12432.*

X 76 0276519

FOREWORD

by

Judge A. M. DONNER,
President of the Court of Justice of the European Communities

By presenting Anglo-Saxon lawyers with a translation of and commentary on the judgments which were given between 1954 and 1960, by the Court of Justice of the European Coal and Steel Community and its successor since 1958, the Court of Justice of the European Communities, Dr. Valentine has done a very valuable work.

Since 1961 the publication of the Common Market Law Reports ensures a regular reporting of the Court's jurisprudence. But this left a gap for the period prior to 1961, which Volume II of this work aims to fill.

It is no exaggeration to state that the judgments the Court gave in the first years of its functioning remain of enduring importance. Not in view of the subject-matter, which was often of ephemeral interest, but because they determined some of the basic principles of interpretation of the European law and settled once and for all in which way the judiciary approaches the fundamental problems involved. Many a point that in later judgments is passed over practically without comment has been exhaustively treated in those first years and the lawyer who wants to understand the apparently tacit position of the Court is obliged to consult the judgments rendered in that period.

On reading once again the judgments published in Volume II one is struck by the great unity they present. It was the Court's fortune that the comparatively small number of cases offered an opportunity to consider its first decisions very thoroughly and thus to lay the foundations of a coherent and balanced jurisprudence which gave each of the texts and principles of the Treaty law its due importance. It would be contrary to Continental usage to specify the various merits of the sitting judges and so I must abstain from mentioning names. Those who have known the Court in the years 1954–60 will be able to determine themselves whom I have in mind.

Foreword

The presentation of the Court's judgments does not make them easily accessible to the Anglo-Saxon lawyer. It is conditioned by the judicial traditions of the six member-countries and these differ from the Anglo-Saxon tradition, more perhaps with regard to the exterior forms of justice and the administration of justice than in their substance. We should therefore be very grateful to Dr. Valentine who went to the trouble of editing the judgments published in this work in a way designed to make them accessible to the Anglo-Saxon lawyer. Only those who compare Volume II with the original judgments of the Court can evaluate the time and reflection this must have demanded. In undertaking it, the editor has put under an obligation both the Anglo-Saxon lawyer and all of those who have the development of the European Communities at heart.

In concluding I express my fervent hope that this publication may contribute to an increasing and well-informed interest in the extremely important experiment which the establishment of a tribunal with such extensive powers as those conferred upon the Court of Justice constitutes. A proverb in my own country says " unknown, unloved "; and so— though it may be somewhat eccentric to suppose that judicial decisions could ever be loved—may this book contribute to the growth of that mutual appreciation the European Communities and the Community law need to attain their full development.

PREFACE

THE purpose of this work is twofold: first, to provide a detailed analysis of the jurisdiction and working of the European Court, and secondly, to present the judgments of that Court not merely in an accessible form, but in a manner in which they reveal the fascinating legal battles fought out during the first years of the European Communities' existence.

VOLUME I

In Volume I, I have first, very briefly, outlined the history of the present Court of Justice, which succeeded the earlier Court of Justice of the European Coal and Steel Community, which was dissolved when the Common Market and Euratom Communities were formed. I have turned then to the organisation and procedure of the Court, and, in addition to studying the Rules, I have tried, by reference to the judgments, to show how, in its practice, the Court has applied these Rules—for example, the Rules concerning the bringing of an action and those concerning costs.

The bulk of Volume I, however, is an analysis in three chapters of every Article in the three Community Treaties which confers jurisdiction upon the Court. In order to make this analysis I was forced to break these Articles down into sentences or phrases, and, in some cases, even into individual words, and then, by illustrations from the judgments, to show what interpretation has been given to these by the Court, either expressly or by implication.

Following this, I have attempted to make what, with such a young Court, must necessarily be a tentative survey of the process by which the Court approaches its task of deciding cases. I have tried to show what are the assumptions that the Court is making; how it sets about interpreting an ambiguous document; whether, to use popular terms, it is concerned with the economic and social effects of its judgments, and whether it is pro-Community or pro-Member States or indeed, pro-anything.

As a final chapter I have included a brief description of what the three Communities are, and what are the powers of the various institutions which figure so often in this work. I have done this because from my own experience I know that there is nothing more annoying than constantly to read about, say, the High Authority, without being able readily to find out exactly what it is and what it does.

At the end are set out the full texts of the Statutes of the Court, its Rules, the Instructions to the Registrar, and other relevant documents.

VOLUME II

Volume II contains a translation of all of the judgments given by the Coal and Steel Community Court between 1954, when it gave its first judgment, and 1958, when it was dissolved, as well as those of the present Court, delivered after its creation in October 1958, until the end of 1960. I have also included brief notes of all cases withdrawn before judgment.

Rather than place the judgments in chronological order, they have been grouped in chapters according to their subject matter. The judgments themselves, however, are not fully intelligible without there being available the wording of the relevant administrative acts being challenged. I have therefore translated these acts, mainly Decisions of the High Authority, and this is the first occasion on which the majority of these Decisions have appeared in English.

Rather than leave the reader to make the best he can of these documents, each chapter is preceded by a Background, setting out briefly the factual situation, summarising the relevant Decisions of the High Authority, and showing how the cases arose and in what way, for example, after an adverse judgment, the High Authority took action to comply with the judgment given. The Background is intended to be read: the documents are intended only to be referred to.

The Court's official publications of the judgments are issued in the four languages of the Communities—French, German, Italian and Dutch. Each judgment is divided into two sections: the first sets out all the procedural stages with their dates, and gives a summary of the facts and of the arguments; the second part contains the *Motifs* which comprise the ruling and the reasoning of the Court. Rather than merely translate the first section, I have omitted the mass of procedural detail except where this is relevant. I have set out in my own words the facts of the case, obtained not only from this first section of the judgments but from the submissions of the Advocate

General, augmented where appropriate from the Annual Reports of the Communities and from the pleadings of the parties.

After these facts I have set out the arguments of the parties, trying wherever possible to state the plaintiffs' case in one paragraph and the defendants' answer immediately afterwards. I have given a summary of each judgment immediately before the actual text of it: these summaries do not appear in the official reports, but I hope they may assist the reader.

It will be noted that the judgments themselves are often set out in unusually short paragraphs. This is because the originals are set out in this way. This means that at any time the reader can make a direct comparison, paragraph by paragraph, between my translation and the official versions in any of the four languages: the ability to do this seemed to me a conclusive reason for not editing or altering the judgments in any way.

The Court's official reports of the judgments include the Advocate General's submissions in full. In these submissions the Advocate General outlines the facts, analyses the arguments of the parties and suggests what the judgments of the Court should be. This statement of the facts I have incorporated with additions into my statement of the facts; I have relied upon this analysis of the arguments when setting out my summary of the arguments: I have, therefore, not translated this part of the submissions. The recommendation for the judgment, which is of particular interest when compared with the judgment actually given, I have set out in a direct translation. The rest of the submissions I have reluctantly had to omit. What finally decided me to do this was the extreme length of these submissions. In the cases here set out, they run to over 1200 pages in the original. Volume II would, therefore, have been about 1200 pages longer if the submissions had been included and so vastly more expensive.

ACKNOWLEDGMENTS

During the six years that I have been writing this work, I have been helped and encouraged by many people. I wish particularly to thank Judge A. M. Donner, the President of the Court of Justice, for doing me the honour of writing the Foreword; Judge Riese, for his suggestions concerning my translations; M. Albert van Houtte, the Registrar of the Court, for his patience with me and for his promptitude in replying to my queries, and M. Michel Gaudet, Director General of the joint Legal Service of the Communities, with whom I have had several opportunities of discussing the Court and its judgments. My colleagues at the London School of Economics, and particularly Professor Otto Kahn-Freund, have been of far greater assistance to me than they will ever realise: my thanks are due to all of them.

I am indebted also to Miss Jan Cochran, Barrister-at-Law, for the very many hours she has devoted to helping me with the translations. She very willingly made the first drafts of most of the judgments: the errors that remain are in no way due to her. The Index to Volume I has been largely compiled by Mr. Roger Bell, Barrister-at-Law, and that to Volume II by Mr. Neville March Hunnings, Barrister-at-Law: they each took a great weight off my mind.

During the years, I have worked through six typists, in both senses of that phrase, and they assisted me a great deal, but the bulk of the misery of typing has been borne by Mrs. Sybil Rang of the firm of Sybil Rang & Ap Simon of Hampstead; of her efforts I cannot speak too highly.

I wish also to mention the annual grant that I have received from the Ford Foundation, which has been of tremendous help. Without it the costs perpetually being incurred in a work of this nature would have frightened and probably deterred me. The assistance I have received from my wife has not been of a technical nature: it has been far more valuable, and far more feminine.

D. G. VALENTINE.

22, Old Buildings,
    Lincoln's Inn,
        London, W.C.2.

January 1, 1965.

NOTE. After the text of this book went to press the following changes in the composition of the Court took place: in October 1964 Riccardo Monaco, Professor of Law at Rome University and legal adviser to the Italian Ministry of Foreign Affairs, was elected to replace Judge Trabucchi. The two Advocates General are at present Herr Karl Roehmer and M. Joseph Gand, who was elected in 1964 in place of M. Lagrange.

This amends the composition of the Court as set out on pages 8 and 9.

CONTENTS OF VOLUME I

Contents of Volume I

3. The Procedure of the Court—*continued*

4. The Jurisdiction of the Court under the European Coal and Steel Community Treaty 109

5. The Jurisdiction of the Court under the European Economic Community Treaty 268

NOTE ON TRANSLATIONS

No official English translation exists of the three Community Treaties or the Rules of the Court and its Statutes. Most of these documents, however, have been unofficially translated by Her Majesty's Stationery Office.[1] I, therefore, naturally hoped to use these translations: however, on examination they were found to be too full of errors and omissions for this to be possible.

Thus for example:—

" *Les recours formés devant la cour n'ont pas d'effet suspensif* " is translated " The institution of proceedings shall not cause a judgment to be suspended." [2]

" *La reqûete doit être formée dans le delai d'un mois* " is translated " Proceedings must have been instituted within a period of two months." [3]

" *Si la réplique ou la duplique* " is translated " If the reply . . ." [4]

" *Ils [les rapporteurs adjoins] sont nommés par le conseil.*" This sentence is omitted.[5]

"*l'application du présent article* " is translated " The interpretation of this Article." [6]

Indeed, on one occasion the Stationery Office placed in brackets the French word *"acte"* which it has translated as " act." [7] Reference to the French, however, shows that the word in the original is " *decision* " and not " *acte.*" It is thus pretty clear that that part of the translation being printed as the E.C.S.C. Statute of the Court is, in fact, the somewhat similar E.E.C. Statute [8] where the word " *acte* " does appear.

Again, one cannot copy the Stationery Office when Articles of the Rules of the Court which, in the original, contained two paragraphs, are printed by the Stationery Office as only one paragraph.[9]

---

[1] The Stationery Office has not translated the Amendment to the Instructions to the Registrar, and so the Instructions are printed by them in their unamended form.
[2] E.C.S.C. Treaty, Art. 39, para. 1.
[3] E.C.S.C. Statute, Art. 40, see p. 461 below.
[4] Rules, Art. 44, para. 1 (a), see p. 505 below.
[5] E.C.S.C. Statute, Art. 16, para. 2, see p. 449 below. Further examples of omissions are:
"*l'agent peut être assisté d'un conseil ou d'un advocat* " is translated " the agent may be assisted by a legal adviser "—E.E.C. Statute, Art. 17, see p. 467;
" *la suite de la procedure sur la demande est orale* " " the remainder of the proceedings shall be oral "—Rules, Art. 91, para. 3, see p. 528;
" *Prononcée à l'encontre d'un membre de la communauté* " and " *dans la monnaie* " are omitted from the Stationery Office translation of the Regulation on Emoluments of the Court, Arts. 16–19, see pp. 568–569 below.
[6] E.C.S.C. Statute, Art. 19, para. 3, see p. 451 below.
[7] E.C.S.C. Statute, Art. 22, para. 2, see p. 454 below.
[8] Art. 19, para 2, see p. 469 below.
[9] See Rules, Art. 32, para. 2 (a) and Art. 57, see pp. 498 and 514 below. Further examples of errors are:
" *Au depot* " is not " the deposit in advance "—Rules, Art. 47, para. 3, see p. 509;
" *peut ordonner* " is not " shall order "—Rules, Art. 48, para. 2, see p. 510;
" *paragraph précedent* " is not " the previous Article "—Instructions to the Registrar, Art. 21, para. 2, see p. 553; " *Les noms et domicile du requérant* " is not " the full names and domicile of the plaintiff "—Rules, Art. 38, para. 1 (a), see p. 501.
On occasions the Stationery Office will add words which are not in the original. Thus: " *non susceptible de recours* " becomes " which may not be appealed

Note on Translations

Each of the three Community Treaties empowers the Court to examine the validity of administrative acts upon the same four grounds.[10] It is essential, therefore, that an English translation of the Treaties should show this. However, one of these four grounds

> *Violation des formes substantielles*

appears alternatively as

> Violation of basic procedural rules [11] or as,
> Substantial violations of basic procedural rules.[12]

Another of these grounds is

> *Violation du traité*

By the Stationery Office this is translated as

> Violation of the Treaty,[13] and
> Infringements of this Treaty.[14]

For these reasons I have been forced to discard the Stationery Office's translations and, therefore, before discussing any Article of any of the Treaties, I have set out what, in my submission, is the closest translation to the original texts, but for the reader I have included in footnotes both the original French and the Stationery Office translation. In documents such as the Statutes and the Rules of the Court, which I set out in full at the end of this volume, on any occasion where I have differed from the Stationery Office, I have set out the original French, together with the Stationery Office translation which I have discarded with my reason for so doing, unless it is reasonably obvious.

Certain French terms, however, have been retained in the original, such as *"détournement de pouvoir"* and *"faute de service."* This is because an English translation of the former as "abuse of power" or some similar translation tends to make an English lawyer think in terms of the English meaning of that phrase, which is not the same as the concept being referred to.[15] To translate *"faute de service"* as "administrative failure" or even as "wrongful act performed on behalf of the Community", as does the Stationery Office, is not, it is suggested, of any real assistance.[16]

In translating the judgments in Volume II, I would have wished to have been able to translate from the original Dutch those cases where the judgment was given in Dutch: from the original German, those judgments given in German, and similarly for Italian. My sole reason for not doing so is, in the words of Dr. Johnson, "ignorance, sheer ignorance." I have, therefore, been forced to translate from the French, which of course for all cases

---

against or otherwise impugned "—Rules, Art. 86, para. 1, see p. 526 below; the words "except where otherwise provided for in this Treaty" are inserted into Euratom Treaty, Art. 157, see p. 368 below.

[10] E.C.S.C. Treaty, Art. 33, para. 1; E.E.C. Treaty, Art. 173, para. 1; Euratom Treaty, Art. 146, para. 1.

[11] E.C.S.C Treaty and Euratom Treaty.

[12] E.E.C. Treaty.

[13] E.C.S.C. Treaty.

[14] E.E.C. and Euratom Treaties. Further examples of inconsistency are: *"les conclusions"*, translated both as "the relief sought" and "the arguments" —Euratom Treaty, Art. 20, para. 1, and E.C.S.C. Statute, Art. 20, para. 1, see pp. 479 and 452; *"l'intérêt de la procédure,"* translated as "the proper conduct of the proceedings" and "the interest of the proceedings"—Rules, Art. 34, para. 2, and Art. 34, para 1, see p. 499; *"garanties nécessaire,"* translated as "guaranties necessary" and "privileges required"—E.C.S.C. Statute, Art. 20, para. 3, and E.E.C. Statute, Art. 17, para. 3, see pp. 452 and 467.

[15] Indeed, French lawyers are finding that the European Courts' use of the term *"détournement de pouvoir,"* bringing in as it does concepts derived from Italian and German law, is not the concept which the use of that French term leads them to think it is—see, for example, *ASSIDER* v. *The High Authority* (Case 3–54), Vol. II, and p. 138 below.

[16] See E.C.S.C. Treaty, Art. 40, para. 1, and p. 217 below.

coming from France, Luxembourg and, in practice, Belgium, was the procedural language.

Where necessary I have checked the French translation against the original in the procedural language.[17] What this procedural language was is stated at the beginning of each judgment.

[17] I have, of course, omitted the " *attendu que* " which precedes every paragraph in the French.

TABLE OF CASES—Alphabetical

Page references in **bold** refer to Volume II.
Case names in *italics* refer to cases withdrawn before judgment.

Table of Cases—Alphabetical

TABLE OF CASES—Numerical

Page references in **bold** refer to Volume II.
Case numbers in *italics* refer to cases withdrawn before judgment.

Table of Cases—Numerical

TABLE OF TREATIES

Page references in **bold type** refer to pages where the terms of the relevant Article are set out and discussed; page references in *italics* refers to pages where the terms of the relevant Article are set out.

Table of Treaties

European Economic Community Treaty—*continued*

European Economic Community Treaty—Protocol on the Statute of the Court of Justice

European Economic Community Treaty—Protocol on Privileges and Immunities

European Atomic Energy Community Treaty—*continued*

Euratom Community Treaty—Protocol on the Statute of the Court of Justice

TABLES OF RULES OF COURT

Page references in *italics* refer to pages where the terms of the relevant Article are set out.

Old Rules of the Court of Justice of the European Coal and Steel Community

Article 5	..	25	Article 41	..	26, 67
6	..	20. 50	42	..	63
9	..	30	43	..	32, 73
10	..	35	46	..	23
11	..	40	48	..	23, 32, 73
12	..	36	53	..	74
19	..	41	54	..	32–33
20	..	42	57	..	33
23	..	43	63	..	213
25	..	33, 44	69	..	24, 60, 61
27	..	3, 46, 47	71	..	58, 60
28	..	47	72	..	79
29	..	50	75	..	77
31	..	53	86	..	77
34	..	26	79	..	234
38	..	26, 64	80	..	61
39	..	32	81	..	62
34	..	21	83	..	105
35	..	62	85	..	100, 193
36	..	71			

Old Rules of the Court on Agents and Advocates

Article 4	..	48	Article 10	..	71
9	..	26			

The Rules of the Court of Justice of the European Communities

Article 1	..	*484*	Article 16	..	37, *490*
2	..	18, *484*, 487	17	..	39, *490*
3	..	4, 18, 30, 35, *484–485*, 487, 488, 492	18	..	*490*
			19	..	21, 36, *490–491*
4	..	3, 18, 44, 45, 350, *485*, 486, 487, 493, 494	20	..	36, *491*
			21	..	47, *491*
			22	..	21, 45, *491*
5	..	30, 38, *485*, 487, 490	23	..	41, *491–492*
6	..	19, 20, 25, *485–486*, 488	24	..	16, 21, 26, 44, 486, *492–493*, 493
7	..	20, 26, 350, *486*, 526, 528	25	..	22, 26, 43, *493*
			26	..	22, 26, 44, 90, *493*
8	..	30, 38, *487*	27	..	33, 38, 41, 44, 45, 490, *494–495*
9	..	30, *487*			
10	..	21, 30, 31, 34, *487*	28	..	22, 26, 45, *495*
11	..	21, 31, 35, 40, *487–488*	29	..	3, 32, 38, 46, 47, 74, *496*, 498
12	..	40, *498*	30	..	32, 38, 47, 75, *497*
13	..	21, *489*	31	..	47, *498*
14	..	21, 488, *489*, 545, 560	32	..	39, 49, *498*, 499, 550
			33	..	39, 48, *499*, 549
15	..	21, 39, *489–490*, 519, 545, 555	34	..	49, *499*

The Rules of the Court of Justice of the European Communities—*continued*

TABLE OF ADMINISTRATIVE ACTS

Decisions of the High Authority

CHAPTER
1

THE HISTORY OF THE COURT

THE ESTABLISHMENT OF THE COURT

THE Court of Justice of the European Communities has its origins
in an earlier Court, which was established under the European Coal
and Steel Community Treaty. Although signed on April 18, 1951, the
E.C.S.C. Treaty was first conceived of less than a year earlier. On
May 9, 1950, Robert Schuman, who was then the Foreign Minister
of France, spoke at a Press Conference in Paris, and outlined the idea of
establishing a Community within Europe to control the production of
coal and steel. He stated:

> The French Government propose to place the whole of the Franco-
> German production of coal and steel under a common high authority [1]
> within an organisation open to the participation of other countries of
> Europe . . . This will form the first concrete step towards a European
> Federation, which is indispensable for peace.[2]

Apart from the specific reference to a high authority, this statement
did not mention any proposed organs of such a Community, and, indeed,
at that time no idea of the Community's structure existed.

Six weeks later, a conference composed of the six States which were
to form the Coal and Steel Community [3] met in Paris under the presidency of M. Monnet.[4] This conference continued its work " con-
sciencieux et discret, rue Martignac " until March 1951.[5]

The first reference which was made to a judicial organ to control
the activity of the Community was contained in the document submitted
by the Commissariat général du Plan.[6] When compared with the
provisions eventually embodied in Articles 33 and 37 of the Treaty,
which impose very rigid restrictions upon the power of the Court, this
reference clearly reveals the transition of opinion that occurred during

---

[1] The term was given in small letters as a description rather than as a title.
[2] Bulletin Quotidien, May 11, 1950.
[3] Belgium, France, Germany, Italy, Luxembourg and the Netherlands.
[4] For details of this conference, see the lecture of M. Schuman, published in Les
Cahiers de Bruges, 1953, p. 280 et seq.
[5] Loc. cit., 282.
[6] Bulletin Quotidien, June 28, 1950.

1

the discussions preceding the drafting of the Treaty. The relevant section, which is here translated in full, is as follows:

> It is proposed that the general responsibility of the [High] Authority shall be ensured by the organisation of a system of appeals normally open to States, and to enterprises in the exceptional case where decisions affect them individually. To the right of demanding a second examination [of a particular matter by the High Authority] should be added the means of bringing an appeal before an arbitral tribunal which shall have not only judicial authority but which shall also be able, in the case where a decision appears to affect the economic expansion or the international standing of a State, to request the High Authority to modify its decision.

It is to be regretted that no record of the *travaux préparatoires* of the Treaty exists so that only two glimpses can be obtained of the preliminary discussions. The first comes from the Report of the French Delegation [7] which declared:

> It was quite clear that the actions of the High Authority must be exercised with a respect for law, and especially for the rules set out in the Treaty. That is why the necessity of subjecting the High Authority to a judicial control was at once recognised.

The second glimpse comes from the *Exposé des Motifs* of the Luxembourg Government [8] which indicated that it was only " despite certain hesitations " that it was decided to institute a Court rather than an arbitral tribunal.

The next step that can be recorded is the signing of the draft Treaty and its attached Protocols in Paris on April 18, 1951.[9] After this followed the ratification debates in the Parliaments of the six countries concerned.[10] In accordance with Article 99, para. 2, the Treaty came into force on the day when the deposit with the French Government of its instrument of ratification had been made by the last signatory State.

Following this, a further conference of the six States was held on July 24 and 25, 1952, at which certain matters were discussed. It was decided, first, that the Court of Justice would commence its duties on August 10, 1952, and that the names of the President and members would be the subject of a special statement before that date.[11] The second matter discussed was the question of where the Court was to be established. The final communiqué of the conference declared that

---

[7] *Rapport de la Délégation Française sur le Traité instituant la C.E.C.A.*, published by the French Ministry of Foreign Affairs, October 1951.
[8] *Compte Rendu, Session ordinaire*, 1951–52, p. 127.
[9] By Messrs. Adenauer for Germany; van Zeeland and Meurice for Belgium; Schuman for France; Sforza for Italy; Bech for Luxembourg; Strikker and van den Brink for the Netherlands.
[10] An analysis of these debates, as far as they concerned the Court, is to be found in Valentine, D. G., *The Court of Justice of the European Coal and Steel Community*, Nijhoff (1954).
[11] *Le Monde*, July 26, 1952.

the choice of the provisional seat of the Court had been referred to the next conference of the Ministers of Foreign Affairs of the six Member States and that until that decision the Court was to start work in Luxembourg.[12] The third matter discussed was the question of the official languages to be adopted. *Le Monde* implied a great deal when it wrote [13]:

> Despite everything, the conference has this morning discussed the question of the language of the Court of Justice. Agreement has been reached on this point. The procedural language and the language of the judgment of the Court will be that of the plaintiff, whether an independent institution or a State.[14]

This followed a decision taken earlier in the conference that within the Community there were to be four official languages—French, German, Italian and Dutch.[15]

On December 1, 1952, the Council of Ministers reached an agreement upon the composition of the Court of Justice, and the following were elected:

Massimo Pilotti, of Italy, sometime joint Secretary-General of the League of Nations and a member of the Permanent Court of Arbitration, was appointed President of the Court. The other judges in order of seniority were [16]:

P. J. S. Serrarens, of the Netherlands, for over thirty years Secretary-General of the International Federation of Christian Trade Unionists, and sometime deputy member on the I.L.O. Governing Body: the only member of the Court who was not a lawyer.

Otto Riese, of Germany, sometime Professor of Law at Lausanne University, and *Senatspräsident* of the High Court of Karlsruhe.

Jacques Rueff, of France, Professor of Economics at the *Institut des Sciences Politiques,* Paris, and sometimes Deputy Governor of the Bank of France.

Louis Delvaux, of Belgium, Minister of Agriculture, 1954, and sometime Legal Adviser to the *Banque Nationale de Belgique.*

---

12 M. Schuman, when referring to this declaration, stated: " It was at six o'clock in the morning, owing to the general exhaustion, that an outsider won this Derby—Luxembourg," see *Les Cahiers de Bruges,* 1953, p. 283.
13 *Le Monde,* July 26, 1952.
14 See Old Rules, Art. 27, para. 2: New Rules, Art. 29, para. 2.
15 *Le Monde,* July 28, 1952. The discussion on what should be the official language was carried out entirely in French.
16 As all the judges were elected at the same time their order of seniority after the President was determined according to age—Rules, Art. 4.

Charles-Leon Hammes, of Luxembourg, sometime Professor of Law at Brussels University and member of the Luxembourg Council of State.

Adrianus van Kleffens, of the Netherlands, sometime Deputy Director General of the Netherlands Foreign Trade Bureau.

On December 10, 1952,[17] in the *Grande Salle du Palais de Conseil* in the presence of high officials both of the Coal and Steel Community and of the Grand Duchy of Luxembourg,[18] the seven judges took the oath of office [19] and the Court was thereupon established.[20]

After the swearing in of the judges, Judge Pilotti, the President, in a short speech declared:

> The task imposed upon this Court is extensive and difficult—our task is to guarantee to the parties concerned, whether they be States, enterprises, or humble individuals, protection against encroachment beyond those limits within which the organs of the Community must act.[21]

This was followed by a short statement by M. Monnet, the first President of the High Authority, in which he said:

> The formation of the Court marks the supreme authority of law in the Community. . . . For the first time there has been created a sovereign European Court. I foresee in it also the prospect of a supreme federal European Court.[22]

In the following March 1953, the Court appointed **Albert van Houtte** as its Registrar. The Court also appointed two Advocates General, **Maurice Lagrange,** France, and **Karl Roemer,** Germany, to be attached to the First and Second Chambers.[23]

The first case [24] was submitted to the Court in April 1953, and challenged the High Authority's prohibition of certain special concessions allowed by collieries to German railway, electricity and gas companies.[25] This case, however, was subsequently withdrawn as were three other cases submitted during that year. As judgment in the first case to be decided [26] was not given until December 1954,

---

[17] The postponement of the establishment of the Court from the proposed date of August 10 was on account of illness.

[18] *Le Monde,* December 11, 1952.

[19] Four of the judges having refused to swear before God, the oath adopted was:
" I swear to fulfil my obligations with complete impartiality and not to divulge any secrets of the Court."
This may be compared with the oath later adopted—see Rules, Art. 3, para. 1.

[20] For a study of the working and jurisdiction of this Court, see Valentine, D. G., *The Court of Justice of the European Coal and Steel Community* (Nijhoff, 1954).

[21] *Chronique de Politique Etrangère,* January 1953.

[22] *Ibid.*

[23] *Journal Officiel,* May 4, 1953.

[24] *Union des Armateurs Allemands and others* v. *The High Authority,* Vol. II, below.

[25] By Decision 25-53, Art. 2 (a).

[26] *French Government* v. *The High Authority* (Case 1-54), Vol. II, below.

there was, and perhaps naturally, a certain amount of newspaper comment suggesting that the seven new judges in Luxembourg were being very highly paid for doing nothing at all.

PROPOSED EXTENSIONS OF THE COURT'S JURISDICTION

During 1954, however, it was being suggested that the jurisdiction of the Court should be widened, and that it should become not only the Court of Justice of the European Defence Community, but also the Court of the European Political Community. Although the Defence Community Treaty was killed by the refusal of the French Parliament to ratify it,[27] and although the Political Community Treaty has not even got as far as ratification, it may be useful to consider the proposals suggested.

(A) UNDER THE EUROPEAN DEFENCE COMMUNITY TREATY

Under the European Defence Community Treaty,[28] the Court was to have possessed jurisdiction to annul the decisions, recommendations or *délibérations* of the Commissariat—the projected central organ of that Community, similar to the High Authority—on any of the four classic grounds,[29] in any action brought by the Council of Ministers, the Assembly or a Member State.[30] On the same grounds, the *délibérations* of the Council could have been challenged by the Commissariat, the Assembly or by Member States[31]: whereas *délibérations* of the Assembly could have been annulled only on the grounds of incompetence or violation of a substantial procedural requirement.[32]

An additional right to challenge action of the Commissariat was to have existed when a Member State believed that such action was of the nature to cause fundamental and persistant disturbance in its affairs.[33] Also, and again directly copying the E.C.S.C. Treaty, a right of action was to have been given to the Council and to the Member States to challenge the inaction of the Commissariat when that body was either required or empowered to take action.[34]

---

27 The vote of August 30, 1954, was 319 against to 264 in favour.
28 E.D.C. Treaty, Art. 54, para. 1.
29 Namely, incompetence, violation of a substantial procedural requirement, violation of the Treaty, and of any rule of law concerning its application, or for *détournement de pouvoir.*
30 *Cf.* E.C.S.C. Treaty, Art. 33, para. 1.
31 E.D.C. Treaty, Arts. 54 and 57, para. 1; *cf.* E.C.S.C. Treaty, Art. 38.
32 *Cf.* E.C.S.C. Treaty, Art. 38.
33 " *En ce qui le concerne* "—E.D.C. Treaty, Art. 56, para. 2: *cf.* E.C.S.C. Treaty, Art. 37, para. 3.
34 E.D.C. Treaty, Art. 55: *cf.* E.C.S.C. Treaty, Art. 35.

5

In addition to this, the Court was intended to have international jurisdiction in disputes between Member States concerning the application of the Treaty.[35]

The most interesting proposals, however, related to criminal jurisdiction. Under the Treaty,[36] various Local Compensation Commissions were to have been set up, each composed of three members.[37] These Local Commissions were to have heard claims for compensation brought against the Community in respect of its activities under the Treaty, which would have covered the activities of the European military forces themselves. The first task of a Commission would have been to have sought an amicable settlement, but, failing this, the Commission was itself, by a majority vote, to give a reasoned award setting out the compensation due.[38]

In order to hear appeals from these Local Commissions, the Court of Justice was to have been divided up into several sections each known as a Regional Section. One judge of the Court was to have been assigned to each Regional Section, and he was to sit with four judges of the State in which the relevant Local Commission was established. To one of these Regional Sections of the Court a final appeal against the award of a Local Commission might have been brought either by the claimant or by the Commissariat.[39]

However, where a case involved a demand for compensation in excess of 3,000 American dollars, the appeal could have been referred to the Court of Justice itself either by the Regional Section, or by its President in any case which involved " a question of principle," a term which was not defined.[40] In cases concerning an amount less than 3,000 dollars such a reference to the Court could only have been made by the Commissariat and then only " in the interests of the law." [41]

---

[35] E.D.C. Treaty, Art. 65, para. 1: *cf.* E.C.S.C. Treaty, Art. 89, para. 1, Other powers of the Court were to have been: to suspend the execution of any decisions or recommendations challenged—Art. 59, para. 2; to control the members of the Commissariat—Art. 23. The Court's powers could have been extended either by a law of a Member State—Art. 65, para. 2—or by a jurisdiction clause in any contract, entered into by the Community or on its behalf—Art. 63—or by a *compromis* between Member States—Art. 65, para. 2.
[36] E.D.C. Protocol, on Jurisdiction, Art. 10, para. 2.
[37] A President appointed by the Commissariat, possessing the nationality of the State where the Local Commission was established; one member also appointed by the Commissariat, being a national of another Member State, and one member of the European Defence Forces, appointed by the Local European Military Authority.
[38] E.D.C. Treaty, Art. 10, para. 32.
[39] *Ibid.* Art. 12, para. 3.
[40] *Ibid.* Art. 13, para. 1.
[41] *Ibid.*

6

(B) UNDER THE EUROPEAN POLITICAL COMMUNITY TREATY

Under the European Political Community Treaty, signed by the same six Member States, the Court of Justice was intended to have been greatly enlarged. The number of judges was to have been increased from the existing number of seven to a maximum of fifteen.[42] Instead of their appointments being made by agreement among the governments of the Member States, the election was to be made by a proposed European Executive Council with the approval of the proposed Senate from a double list of candidates nominated by the Member States and by any of the groups composing the Permanent Court of Arbitration.[43]

The Court was to have had jurisdiction to annul the decisions or recommendations of the European Executive Council or of any of the administrative authorities subordinated to it, on the four classic grounds.[44] Further, the Court was to have been given two important additional powers. First, jurisdiction to determine any dispute arising out of a decision, or any measure whatsoever, of one of the organs of the Political Community which infringed any of the rights granted by the European Convention on Human Rights and Fundamental Freedoms,[45] although after the establishment of the Human Rights Court, and the Human Rights Commission, the Court of Justice was to have postponed its own decision in any case involving a question of principle concerning the interpretation or the extent of the obligations under that Convention until the Commission or the Court had given its ruling.[46] Secondly, it was set out that the decisions or judgments of " subordinate tribunals " of the Community were to be brought before the Court either by way of appeal or by way of " revision." [47] Although it was not set out what these " subordinate tribunals " were, it appears that the municipal courts of the Member States were being referred to and that the Court of Justice was at that time intended to have been indeed the Supreme Court of Europe.

THE REPLACEMENT OF THE COAL AND STEEL COMMUNITY COURT

In the European Economic Community Treaty,[48] and in the Euratom Community Treaty, a Court of Justice is established to control each of these Communities. A Convention in identical wording was, therefore,

---

42 E.P.C. Treaty, Art. 39, para. 1.1.
43 E.P.C. Treaty, Art. 39, para. 1.1.
44 E.P.C. Treaty, Art. 43. For these grounds, see note 29, p. 5, above.
45 E.P.C., Art. 45, para. 1.
46 E.P.C., Art. 41, para. 2.
47 E.P.C., Art. 41, para. 2.
48 Known popularly either as the Common Market Treaty, or the Treaty of Rome.

attached to each of these Treaties setting out that the two Courts were in fact one,[49] and further that this new Court, referred to as "the single Court of Justice" was to replace the Court provided for under the E.C.S.C. Treaty, but that the new Court was "to exercise the jurisdiction conferred upon that Court by the said Treaty." [50]

Because the earlier Court was being abolished and replaced, instead of the alternative possibility of having additional jurisdiction given to it, the judges, upon ratification of these two new Treaties found themselves without a Court to sit in and they were also rendered judges no longer. More than this, the two new Treaties amended the wording of the E.C.S.C. Treaty, so that for appointment to the new Court it was no longer adequate, as before, to possess "recognised independence and competence." [51] It was now required that the judges should be chosen from

> persons whose independence can be fully guaranteed and who fulfil the conditions required for the exercise of the highest judicial functions in their respective countries or who are legal experts of universally recognised and outstanding ability.[52]

As a result of this change of wording Judge Serrarens was no longer eligible.

In the appointments made to the new Court, Judge Pilotti was not re-elected, but his place in the Court and as President was taken by **A. M. Donner,** of the Netherlands, Professor of Constitutional Law in the Free University of Amsterdam, and Judge van Kleffens was replaced by **Nicola Catalano,** sometime lecturer at Rome University, Legal Adviser to the High Authority and subsequently Legal Adviser to the Italian delegation at the drawing up of the Economic and Euratom Community Treaties.

On March 8, 1962, **Alberto Trabucchi,** sometime Professor of the Universities of Venice and Padua, and an advocate before the Court in the *Meroni* case,[53] took over from Judge Catalano. On May 18, 1962, **Robert Lecourt,** former French Minister of Justice and Minister of State for overseas territories, replaced Judge Rueff. On January 24,

---

49 Convention Relating to Certain Institutions Common to the European Communities, Art. 3.
50 *Ibid.* Art. 4.1.
51 E.C.S.C. Treaty, Art. 32, para. 1.
52 E.E.C. Treaty, Art. 167, para. 1; Euratom Treaty, Art. 139, para. 1. As there is no condition concerning nationality, it will be observed that even without Britain acceding to the Treaties an English solicitor is eligible to be appointed.
53 *Meroni e C. Industrie Metallurgiche S.p. A.* v. *The High Authority* (Case 9–56), Vol. II, below.

1963, Judge Riese retired and his place has been taken by **Walter Strauss,** Secretary of State at the German Ministry of Justice from 1949.[54]

THE TYPES OF JURISDICTION OF THE COURT

The Court of the European Communities possesses more varied jurisdiction than any other court ever established—at one end of the scale it is an international court settling disputes between the Member States; it is also in part a *Conseil d'Etats,* and it can also deal with the contracts of employment of Community typists and with running down actions brought against E.E.C. chauffeurs.

1. INTERNATIONAL JURISDICTION

Under each of the three Community Treaties, any Member State which considers that another Member State has failed to fulfil one of its obligations under any of those Treaties, may refer the matter to the Court.[55] Further, the Court has jurisdiction to settle any dispute between Member States in connection with the purposes of the Treaties when such dispute is submitted to it by virtue of an arbitration agreement.[56]

Under the Economic Community Treaty, any Member State may refer to the Court the failure of another Member State, within the time specified by the Commission, to cease granting aid or applying state resources in a manner not compatible with that Community.[57] It may also cite before the Court another Member State which, it alleges, is improperly using its power to withhold essential information relating to security, or is failing to consult with the other Member States upon how best to prevent serious international tension, etc., from affecting the common market.[58]

Under the Euratom Treaty, if any Member State fails to comply with the Euratom Commission's directives concerning the level of radio-activity in the atmosphere, in water or in the soil, any other Member State may immediately refer the matter to the Court.[59]

---

[54] The present composition of the Court is, therefore: Judge A. M. Donner, President; Judges L. Delvaux, R. Rossi, Ch. L. Hammes, A. Trabucchi, R. Lecourt and W. Strauss.
[55] E.C.S.C. Treaty, Art. 89, para. 1; E.E.C. Treaty, Art. 170, para. 1; Euratom Treaty, Art. 142, para. 1.
[56] E.C.S.C. Treaty, Art. 89, para. 2; E.E.C. Treaty, Art. 182; Euratom Treaty, Art. 154.
[57] E.E.C. Treaty, Art 93, para. 2.2.
[58] E.E.C. Treaty, Art. 225, para. 2.
[59] Euratom Treaty, Art. 38, para. 3.

2. JURISDICTION OVER THE LEGAL VALIDITY OF THE EXECUTIVE ACTION OF THE ORGANS OF THE THREE COMMUNITIES

Under the three Treaties, the various executive institutions, namely the High Authority, the two Commissions, the three Councils of Ministers, the European Investment Bank and to a limited extent, the Common Assembly, are empowered to pass executive acts, known variously as Regulations, Directives, Decisions and Recommendations. The legal validity of these, but not, of course, the political or economic desirability, can be challenged before the Court. In various circumstances these actions may be brought either by another organ of the relevant Community or by Member States, enterprises, association of enterprises, other legal persons or by individuals.

(A) ACTIONS BROUGHT BY ORGANS OF THE COMMUNITIES

Thus, under the E.C.S.C. Treaty, actions may be brought by the Council of Ministers for the annulment of the Decisions and Recommendations of the High Authority,[60] whether these are express or are implied by the two months' inactivity of the High Authority.[61] The High Authority may also seek the annulment of the *délibérations* of the Council of Ministers or of the Common Assembly.[62] Under the E.E.C. Treaty, the Council of Ministers may challenge the Regulations, Directives and Decisions of the Commission, and similarly the Commission may challenge those of the Council.[63] This right of appeal also applies both to express acts of the Council and of the Commission and to those that are implied as a result of two months' inactivity on the part of those organs.[64]

Similar powers are given under the Euratom Treaty to the Euratom Council of Ministers and to the Euratom Commission.[65]

The E.E.C. Commission may also challenge the decisions of the Board of Governors of the European Investment Bank [66] or challenge the decisions of the Board of Directors of the Bank.[67]

---

[60] E.C.S.C. Treaty, Art. 33, para. 1. Annulment can be sought on the classic grounds of incompetence, violation of a substantial procedural requirement, violation of the Treaty, or of any rule of law concerning its application or *détournement de pouvoir*—*ibid.*

[61] *Ibid.* Art. 35, para. 1.

[62] *Ibid.* Art. 38, para. 1. The sole grounds that may here be alleged are incompetence or violation of a substantial procedural requirement—*ibid.* para. 3.

[63] E.E.C. Treaty, Art. 173, para. 1. The grounds of appeal are those set out in note 60, above.

[64] *Ibid.* Art. 175, para. 1.

[65] Euratom Treaty, Arts. 146 and 148.

[66] E.E.C. Treaty, Art. 180 (b). The grounds of appeal are those set out in note 60, above.

[67] *Ibid.* Art. 180 (c). The only grounds of appeal are breaches of procedural requirements.

(B) ACTIONS BROUGHT BY MEMBER STATES

Under the three Treaties, the Member States may challenge the admini-
trative acts of the High Authority and of the two Commissions [68] and of
the three Councils of Ministers [69]; they may also challenge the inaction
of the High Authority, the Commissions or of the Councils of Ministers
of the E.E.C. and the Euratom Community, because, after the specified
period of two months from a request to the relevant body to take action,
this inaction is deemed to amount to a Decision refusing to take such
action and that implied Decision is open to appeal.[70] Under the
E.C.S.C. Treaty, the Member States may also challenge the *délibérations*
of the Common Assembly.[71] Under the E.E.C. Treaty, the Member
States can challenge the decisions of the Board of Governors and
of the Directors of the European Investment Bank, on the same grounds
as can the organs of that Community.[72]

(C) ACTIONS BROUGHT BY ENTERPRISES, ASSOCIATIONS OF ENTERPRISES,
OTHER LEGAL PERSONS AND BY INDIVIDUALS

Under the E.C.S.C. Treaty, enterprises and associations of enterprises [77] may appeal against express or implied individual Recommendations and Decisions of the High Authority concerning them, and against
express or implied general Decisions which they believe to be vitiated
by a *détournement de pouvoir* with respect to them.[78]

Under the other two Treaties, any natural or legal person may
challenge any decision of either of the two Commissions or of the two

---

[68] E.C.S.C. Treaty, Art. 33, para. 1; E.E.C. Treaty, Art. 173, para. 1; Euratom Treaty,
Art. 146, para. 1. These appeals may be brought on the grounds set out in note 60,
above.

[69] E.C.S.C. Treaty, Art. 38, para. 1, and Art. 35, para. 1; E.E.C. Treaty, Art. 173,
para. 1; Euratom Treaty, Art. 146, para. 1. Appeals against acts of the E.C.S.C.
Council of Ministers are limited to the grounds set out in note 62 above, the other
appeals may allege the grounds set out in note 60, above. Power of Member States
to challenge action of the High Authority that is likely to cause fundamental and
persistent disturbances in their economy is given by E.C.S.C. Treaty, Art. 37, para. 1.

[70] E.C.S.C. Treaty, Art. 35, para. 1; E.E.C. Treaty, Art. 175, para. 1; Euratom Treaty,
Art. 148, para. 1. Power of a state to challenge the lack of action of the High
Authority that is likely to cause fundamental and persistent disturbances in its
economy is given by E.C.S.C. Treaty, Art. 37, para. 1.

[71] E.C.S.C. Treaty, Art. 38, para. 1. A similar power is, for some reason, not included
in the other two Treaties.

[72] E.E.C. Treaty, Art. 180 (b) and (c).

[77] This right is, however, limited to those associations which either permit the properly
chosen representatives of the workers and consumers to participate in the direction
of the associations or in consultative committees attached to them, or in any other
way give a satisfactory place in their organisation to the expression of the workers'
and consumers' interests—E.C.S.C. Treaty, Art. 33, para. 2 and Art. 48, para. 3.

[78] *Ibid.* Art. 33, para. 2 and Art. 35, para. 1.

Councils of Ministers which is addressed to him or it, or, although addressed to someone else, is of direct and specific concern to him or it.[79] These natural or legal persons may also make complaint to the Court that one of the institutions of the two Communities has failed to pass a legislative act concerning them.[80]

Further, under the E.C.S.C. Treaty, the High Authority may order the separation of illegal monopolies, and any person who is directly affected by this order may appeal to the Court[81]; so also may any person who has been fined in respect of activities of illegal monopolies.[82]

3. JURISDICTION ARISING OUT OF ENFORCEMENT OF THE THREE TREATIES

The institutions primarily responsible for ensuring that the Community Treaties are carried out by all concerned are the High Authority and the two Commissions: although naturally it is the Member States which have the main responsibility for carrying out the Treaties, enterprises and even individuals can be proceeded against for violations. Actions arising out of this enforcement procedure come before the Court.

Thus, by the E.C.S.C. Treaty, if the High Authority considers that a Member State has failed in one of its obligations under the Treaty it may set out this failure in a reasoned decision.[83] The Member State may appeal to the Court against this Decision.[84] If the Member State continues in breach, the High Authority may impose sanctions upon it,[85] and the Member State may also appeal against these.[86]

Under the E.E.C. Treaty, offences by Member States are dealt with more specifically. If the Commission considers that a Member State is granting financial aid or using its resources in a way which is not compatible with that Community, or that it is using aid in an improper manner, it must set out this default in a Decision and state the time within which this default is to be ended. If a State does not comply with this, the Commission may refer the matter to the Court,[87] as it may also do if it believes that a State is abusing the right to withhold such information as will protect its essential interests, or is not assisting

---

79 E.E.C. Treaty, Art. 173, para. 2; Euratom Treaty, Art. 146, para 2. The grounds of these appeals are those set out in note 60, above.
80 E.E.C. Treaty, Art. 175, para. 3; Euratom Treaty, Art. 148, para. 3.
81 E.C.S.C. Treaty, Art. 66, section 5.2.
82 *Ibid.* Art. 66, section 6.2 and Art. 36, para. 2.
83 *Ibid.* Art. 88, para. 1.
84 *Ibid.* Art. 88, para. 2.
85 *Ibid.* Art. 88, para. 3.
86 *Ibid.* Art. 88, para. 4.
87 E.E.C. Treaty, Art. 93, para. 2.2.

in taking measures to prevent serious disturbances from affecting the common market.[88] Further, if a Member State does not comply with an opinion declaring that it has failed to fulfil any of its other Treaty obligations, the Commission may refer the matter to the Court.[89]

If the Directors of the European Investment Bank consider that a Member State has failed to observe any of the obligations arising under the Statute of that Bank, they may record that failure and require it to be rectified. If the Member State concerned does not comply with this requirement the Directors may refer the matter to the Court.[90]

Under the Euratom Treaty, if a Member State refuses to grant a licence for the exploitation of patents or refuses to cause a patent to be granted, or fails to make a statement concerning its granting, the Euratom Commission may refer the matter to the Court.[91]

Again, if a Member State fails to comply with a directive of the Commission concerning the level of radio-activity in the atmosphere, water or soil, the Commission may immediately refer the matter to the Court.[92] If a Member State fails to comply with a Directive of the Commission instructing it to cease diverting nuclear materials to purposes other than those for which they were intended, the Commission may refer the breach to the Court.[93]

If when the Commission cannot lawfully sanction a person or enterprise directly for a breach of the Treaty, and the Member State having such jurisdiction does not itself impose penalties, the Commission may refer the matter to the Court.[94]

Similarly, as under the E.E.C. Treaty, the Euratom Commission can refer to the Court any failure of a Member State to comply with an opinion setting out that the State has failed to carry out any of its obligations under the Treaty.[95]

Enforcement against enterprises, associations, other legal persons or against individuals is effected by the High Authority or the relevant Commission passing a Decision which may impose a fine which is open to immediate execution. Appeals to the Court are then open to those concerned.[96]

[88] *Ibid.* Art. 225, para. 2.
[89] *Ibid.* Art. 169, para. 2.
[90] *Ibid.* Art. 180 (a) and Art. 169.
[91] Euratom Treaty, Art. 21, para. 3.
[92] *Ibid.* Art. 38, para. 3.
[93] *Ibid.* Art. 82, para. 4.
[94] *Ibid.* Art. 145, para. 2.
[95] *Ibid.* Art. 141, para. 2.
[96] E.C.S.C. Treaty, Art. 36, para. 2; E.E.C. Treaty, Art. 173, para. 2; Euratom Treaty, Art. 146, para. 2.

4. ADVISORY OPINIONS IN CONNECTION WITH
THE THREE TREATIES

The Court is required to give its advisory opinion upon certain matters; namely, if unforeseen difficulties are revealed by experience in the methods of carrying out the E.C.S.C. Treaty or a profound change in the economic and technical conditions directly affecting the common market for coal and steel should require an amendment of the powers of the High Authority, these amendments must be submitted to the Court, which, with full powers to review any matters of law and fact, is to give its advisory opinion upon whether these amendments may be passed to the Common Assembly for approval or whether they conflict with the fundamental aims of the Community [97] or alter the relationship between the High Authority and the other institutions of the Community.[98]

The E.E.C. may enter into agreements with one or more non-Member States or with an international organisation, but the Council, the Commission or any Member State may, as a preliminary, request the advisory opinion of the Court upon the compatibility of the contemplated agreement with the provisions of that Treaty.[99] If the Court gives a negative opinion the agreement, instead of being concluded by the Council, may be entered into only by being ratified by all of the Member States.[1]

Any Member State of the Euratom Community which wishes to enter into an agreement with a non-Member State, or international organisation or national of a non-Member State, must submit that agreement to the Commission. If the Commission disallows any part of the agreement on the grounds that it is incompatible with the provisions of the Treaty, the Member State may request the Court to give an opinion upon whether the proposed agreement is indeed incompatible.[2]

5. APPELLATE JURISDICTION

An appeal against a Decision of the Euratom Arbitration Committee lies to the Court, which may determine upon the regularity

---

[97] As set out in E.C.S.C. Treaty, Arts. 2, 3 and 4.
[98] E.C.S.C. Treaty, Art. 95, para. 4. There is no corresponding power given to the Court under the other two Treaties. Amendments to those Treaties may be made provided they are ratified by all the Member States concerned—E.E.C. Treaty, Art. 236, para. 3; Euratom Treaty, Art. 204, para. 3.
[99] E.E.C. Treaty, Art. 228, para. 2.
[1] *Ibid.* Arts. 228, paras. 1 and 2 and Art. 236, para. 3.
[2] Euratom Treaty, Art. 103, para. 3. A similar right of appeal to the Court is given to the Commission to test the compatibility of any agreement entered into by a person or enterprise of a Member State, with a non-Member State, international organisation, or national of a non-Member State: *ibid.* Art. 104, para. 3.

of form of the decision and upon the interpretation given by the Committee to the provisions of the Euratom Treaty.[3]

6. SOLE JURISDICTION TO DETERMINE UPON COMMUNITY MATTERS WHEN THESE FIGURE IN CASES BEFORE CERTAIN MUNICIPAL COURTS

The Communities' Court is in no way a court of appeal from municipal courts, but reciprocally these municipal courts have only limited powers to determine upon matters relating to the Community Treaties. Thus under the E.C.S.C. Treaty, the Court has sole jurisdiction to determine, as a preliminary issue, in any case brought before a municipal court upon the validity of the *délibérations* of the High Authority and of the Council of Ministers [4]; under the other two Treaties, the Court, as a preliminary issue, may determine not only upon the validity but also upon the interpretation of the acts of the institutions of those Communities in any action where these matters are brought into issue before a municipal court.[5] This power is held jointly with the municipal courts, except that where the matter is pending before a municipal court from which there is no appeal, the Communities' Court possesses sole jurisdiction.[6]

Under these same two Treaties, the Court, when determining a preliminary issue, can also make a declaration concerning the interpretation of the two Treaties [7]; this power, however, is not expressly given in the E.C.S.C. Treaty.[8]

It is this Court, sworn in on October 7, 1958, possessing this unique jurisdiction and being the successor to the earlier Court of the European Coal and Steel Community [9] which is the subject-matter of the following chapters.

---

3 *Ibid.* Art. 18, para. 2.
4 E.C.S.C. Treaty, Art. 41.
5 E.E.C. Treaty, Art. 177, para. 1 (b); Euratom Treaty, Art. 150, para. 1 (b).
6 E.E.C. Treaty, Art. 177, para. 3; Euratom Treaty, Art. 150, para. 3.
7 E.E.C. Treaty, Art. 177, para. 1 (a): Euratom Treaty, Art. 150, para. 1 (a).
8 The power might be implied, however, from E.C.S.C. Treaty, Art. 31, by which the Court is to ensure the rule of law in the interpretation of the Treaty.
9 For the declaration of the existence of the present Court see *Journal Officiel*, October 19, 1958, p. 453.

CHAPTER
2

THE ORGANISATION OF THE COURT

THE COURT

THE Court of Justice of the European Communities is composed of seven judges who were elected by common agreement of the Governments of the six Member States.[1]

The Court is required to sit in plenary session when hearing appeals brought by any of the Member States or by one of the institutions of the three Communities,[2] or where the Court is dealing with the validity of acts of one of the Community institutions where this validity has been referred to it by a municipal court.[3]

A sitting in plenary session requires a minimum of five judges,[4] but as the Court must always sit with an uneven number,[5] the only other valid sitting is one of the entire seven judges.

THE CHAMBERS OF THE COURT

The Court is empowered, but not obliged, to create within itself two Chambers each consisting of three or five judges each,[6] but the Rules declare that the Court shall create these two Chambers.[7]

---

[1] E.C.S.C. Treaty, Art. 32, para. 1; E.E.C. Treaty, Art. 167, para. 1; Euratom Treaty, Art. 139, para. 1.

[2] E.C.S.C. Treaty, Art. 32, para. 3, as amended by Art. 4, para. 2, of the Convention relating to certain Institutions common to the European Communities of March 25, 1957; E.E.C. Treaty, Art. 165, para. 3; Euratom Treaty, Art. 137, para. 3. Under the earlier provision in the E.C.S.C. Treaty, it was only appeals by the Council of Ministers, which were expressly required to be heard in plenary session, and not, for example, appeals by the High Authority challenging the validity of *délibérations* of the Council or of the Assembly under Art. 38. This omission has thus now been rectified.

[3] *Ibid.* These appeals are brought under the E.C.S.C. Treaty, Art. 42; E.E.C. Treaty, Art. 177; Euratom Treaty, Art. 150.

[4] E.C.S.C. Statute, Art. 18, para. 2; E.E.C. Statute, Art. 15; Euratom Statute, Art. 15.

[5] *Ibid.* If six judges are available to sit, the most junior judge, determined by the precedence of judges, abstains from sitting; see p. 18, below.

[6] E.C.S.C. Treaty, Art. 32, para. 2, as amended by Art. 4 of the Convention relating to certain Institutions common to the European Communities of March 25, 1957; E.E.C. Treaty, Art. 165, para. 2; Euratom Treaty, Art. 137, para. 2. The reference to five judges per Chamber is looking to a possible increase in the number of judges to 11.

[7] Rules, Art. 24, para. 1, but, expressly, only to undertake the Instruction in cases which are entrusted to them.

The principal function that is given to a Chamber is that of hearing appeals brought by an official or other servant of one of the institutions of the Communities against that institution,[8] and the Court is required to appoint one Chamber each year to hear these cases,[9] but the Chamber may nevertheless remit such a case to the Court as a whole.[10]

Where a case brought by an official or servant also claims some interim measures, this claim, on general principle,[11] is brought before the President, but he may nevertheless refer a decision upon these measures to the competent Chamber.[12]

The other function assigned to a Chamber is that of carrying out the Instruction of a case,[13] which is considered below.

THE JUDGES

Under the E.C.S.C. Treaty, it is laid down [14] that the judges shall be selected from persons " of recognised independence and competence." This provision was not interpreted as meaning legal competence exclusively, and, thus, at the original election in 1952, Heer Serrarens, a Dutch Catholic Trade Unionist, was elected a judge of the Court. Such a breath of fresh lay air, however, is no longer permitted, for in the two later Treaties it is expressly provided that the judges shall be chosen from among persons who fulfil the conditions required for the exercise of the highest judicial functions in their respective countries or who are legal experts of universally recognised and outstanding ability.[15]

There is no mention in the Treaties of any rules or machinery for nominating candidates, nor, most important of all, is there any requirement of nationality, so that, unlike the members of the High Authority [16] or of the Commissions,[17] a judge of the Court can be drawn from

---

8 Rules, Art. 95, para. 1.1.
9 *Ibid.* There is no provision that this duty shall be placed upon the two Chambers alternately. The First Chamber was appointed in 1961 to hear appeals of officials for the subsequent three years—*Journal Officiel,* October 28, 1961.
10 Rules, Art. 95, para. 2.
11 See pp. 85–87, below.
12 Rules, Art. 96, para. 2. Although this provision states that, instead of referring the decision upon the request for these measures to the Court, the President may refer the decision to " the competent Chamber," this must be read together with Rules, Art. 95, para. 1, which states that appeals of the official or other servant shall be judged by a Chamber " unless they concern a request for interim measures." It appears, therefore, that the President cannot refer an appeal for such measures to a Chamber.
13 E.C.S.C. Treaty, Art. 32, para. 2, as amended by Art. 4, para. 2, of the Convention relating to certain Institutions common to the European Communities of March 25, 1957 ; E.E.C. Treaty, Art. 165, para. 3 ; Euratom Treaty, Art. 137, para. 3.
14 E.C.S.C. Treaty, Art. 32, para. 1.
15 E.E.C. Treaty, Art. 167, para. 1 ; Euratom Treaty, Art. 139, para. 1.
16 E.C.S.C. Treaty, Art. 9, para. 3.
17 E.E.C. Treaty, Art. 157, para. 1.3 ; Euratom Treaty, Art. 126, para. 1.2.

persons of a nationality other than that of one of the Member States. There would be difficulties, however, in the way of the election of such a judge because the non-Member State would not have agreed to grant to him the immunities set out in the three Treaties and which would be enjoyed by his fellow judges.

Before entering upon his duties, each judge is sworn in in open court,[18] and the oath may be taken in the manner prescribed by the municipal legislation applicable to the judge for such an act.[19]

In addition, the Statutes contained in the Economic Community Treaty and in the Euratom Treaty have introduced a new requirement, that when taking up their duties the judges shall give a solemn undertaking that both during their period of office and after its termination they will respect the obligations imposed upon them, and, in particular, the duty to exercise honesty and discretion as regards the acceptance after their term of office of certain posts or of certain benefits.[20] The judges are required to sign a declaration to this effect immediately after they have been sworn in.[21]

The order of precedence of the judges is governed by their seniority of office,[22] or, where this is the same for two or more judges, they are to take precedence according to their seniority of age.[23] If a judge is re-appointed, his term of office continues to be reckoned from his original appointment.[24]

A partial re-election of the judges occurs every three years, when alternately three and four seats are to be filled.[25] The three judges who are to retire at the first partial re-election are to be decided by lot,[26] but all judges may be re-elected.[27]

---

[18] E.C.S.C. Statute, Art. 2; E.E.C. Statute, Art. 2; Euratom Statute, Art. 2. The oath of office of the Court runs: " I swear to perform my duties conscientiously and with complete impartiality; I swear to divulge nothing of the Court's consideration of its judgments."—Rules, Art. 3, para. 1.

[19] Rules, Art. 3, para. 2.

[20] E.E.C. Statute, Art. 4, para. 3; Euratom Statute, Art. 4, para. 3.

[21] Rules, Art. 3, para. 3.

[22] Rules, Art. 4, para. 1. The period of office of a judge commences from the date laid down in his appointment, or if none is stated there, then from the date of that document itself—Rules, Art. 2.

[23] Rules, Art. 4, para. 2.

[24] Rules, Art. 4, para. 3. The case of a judge being re-elected after a period of years during which he was not a member of the Court is not provided for.

[25] E.C.S.C. Treaty, Art. 32, para. 2; E.E.C. Treaty, Art. 167, para. 2; Euratom Treaty, Art. 139, para. 2.

[26] E.C.S.C. Treaty, Art. 32, para. 2; E.E.C. Treaty, Art. 167, para. 2; Euratom Treaty, Art. 139, para. 2.

[27] E.C.S.C. Treaty, Art. 32, para. 3; E.E.C. Treaty, Art. 167, para. 4; Euratom Treaty, Art. 139, para. 4.

Although the Treaties provide only for seven judges to be elected this number can be increased by the unanimous vote of the Council of Ministers upon a proposal from the Court itself.[28]

The Treaties introduce a very commendable new principle in international adjudication when they state that a party may not invoke either the nationality of a judge, or the absence from the Court or from one of its Chambers of a judge of its own nationality, in order to ask for a change in the composition of the Court or of one of its Chambers.[29]

The judges are required to reside at the place where the Court has its seat.[30] Their salaries and pensions are decided upon by the Council of Ministers.[31]

THE PRESIDENT OF THE COURT

The President of the Court is elected by the judges from among themselves for a period of three years.[32] Although it is nowhere stated that the President is eligible for re-election, H.E. Signor Pilotti, the President of the earlier European Coal and Steel Community Court, was re-elected for a second term.[33] If the President should cease to be a

---

28 E.C.S.C. Treaty, Art. 32, para. 4; E.E.C. Treaty, Art. 166, para. 3; Euratom Treaty, Art. 137, para. 4. This proposal can presumably be made by a simple majority. Once the number of judges has been increased, the provisions concerning the re-election of three and four judges alternately, and the provision concerning the number of judges required to form a Chamber of the Court, of necessity have also to be amended, although this was not provided in the original E.C.S.C. Treaty. Both the E.E.C. Treaty and the Euratom Treaty require a further amendment to be made to the provision that the Court is to hear cases in plenary session where such cases are submitted by a Member State or by an institution of the Community. What the required amendment of this provision may be is not apparent. However, as the provision that the Court shall consist of seven judges is not one of those that is required to be amended, it is suggested that a mistake in the numbering of the paragraphs has been made—see E.E.C. Treaty, Art. 165, para. 4, and Euratom Treaty, Art. 137, para. 4. Once the number of judges has been increased, there appears to be no machinery for reducing the Court to the original number of seven.

29 E.C.S.C. Statute, Art. 19, para. 4; E.E.C. Statute, Art. 16, para. 4; Euratom Statute, Art. 16, para. 4. This provision may be compared with the rules for appointing *ad hoc* judges to the International Court of Justice.

30 E.C.S.C. Statute, Art. 9; E.E.C. Statute, Art. 13; Euratom Statute, Art. 13.

31 E.C.S.C. Statute, Art. 5; E.E.C. Treaty, Art. 154; Euratom Treaty, Art. 123. As to these, see pp. 561–571, below. In the case of the Coal and Steel Community, the Council was to act upon a proposal of a Committee of the Presidents of the four institutions. This provision is not repeated in the case of the other two Treaties.

32 Rules, Art. 6, para. 1. Judge A. M. Donner has been elected President for the period October 8, 1961–October 7, 1964—*Journal Officiel*, October 28, 1961. The election is by secret ballot. If no judge obtains an absolute majority, a second ballot is taken. After this ballot, the judge with the greatest number of votes is elected. In case of equality of voting, the elder judge is elected—Rules, Art. 6, para. 4. The election of the first President of the present Court, who took over from the President of the previous Court of Justice of the European Coal and Steel Community, however, took place by agreement between the Governments—E.E.C. Treaty, Art. 244, para. 1; Euratom Treaty, Art. 212, para. 1.

33 This election took place on December 1, 1955, and was effected by the unanimous vote of the other judges.

19

member of the Court, either because of his death or resignation,[34] a further appointment is made for that period of office still unexpired.[35] In the absence of the President of the Court, or if he is unable to attend or if the office of President is vacant, his functions are taken over by the senior of the two Presidents of the Chambers.[36]

The main duty of the President is to direct the work and the running of the Court.[37] In addition, he has important powers granted to him by the Statutes by which he can himself order a stay of execution of a Decision or Recommendation issued by any institution of the Coal and Steel Community or of any Directive, Regulation or Decision issued by an institution of the other two Communities.[38] By the same provision, the President may also order any other provisional measures which he may think necessary.[39] However, these emergency powers of the President have only a provisional character and in no way prejudice the decision of the Court in determining upon the principal action.[40]

In his administrative capacity, the President can lift the immunity of the Registrar, and of the officials and employees of the Court.[41] The President is the Chairman of the Committee set up under the E.C.S.C. Treaty to determine, among other things, the number of officials that are to be employed by the Community as well as upon their salaries and pensions.[42]

---

[34] Under E.C.S.C. Statute, Art. 6, para. 1; E.E.C. Statute, Art. 6, para. 1; Euratom Statute, Art. 6, para. 1; see p. 29, below.

[35] E.C.S.C. Statute, Art. 8; E.E.C. Statute, Art. 7; Euratom Statute, Art. 7, and Rules, Art. 6, para. 3.

[36] Rules, Art. 7, para. 2.1. Under the previous Rules of the Court, the President of the First Chamber was appointed to the Presidency of the Court in preference to the President of the Second Chamber, the latter being called upon only if the President of the First Chamber was prevented from undertaking the task or if there was a vacancy in that Presidency as well—old Rules, Art. 6, para. 2.1. The new Rules have presumably been adopted to underline the fact that the two Chambers of the Court are of equal standing, and that the First Chamber is first in name only. In a case where the President of the Court and the Presidents of both the Chambers are unable to attend, or where their offices are simultaneously vacant, the Presidency is undertaken by one of the other judges, determined according to the order of seniority established by Art. 4 of the Rules—Rules, Art. 7, para. 2.2. On Art. 4, see p. 18, above.

[37] Rules, Art. 7, para. 1. For his control of the proceedings during a session, see below.

[38] E.C.S.C. Statute, Art. 33, para. 1; E.E.C. Statute, Art. 36, para. 1; Euratom Statute, Art. 37, para. 1. The procedure is governed by Arts. 83–90 of the Rules; see pp. 87–89, below.

[39] E.C.S.C. Statute, Art. 33, para. 1; E.E.C. Statute, Art. 36, para. 1; Euratom Statute, Art. 37, para. 1.

[40] E.C.S.C. Statute, Art. 33, para. 3; E.E.C. Statute, Art. 36, para. 3; Euratom Statute, Art. 37, para. 3.

[41] E.C.S.C. Statute, Art. 16, para. 3; E.E.C. Protocol on Immunities, Art. 17, para. 2, and Art. 20; Euratom Protocol on Immunities, Art. 17, para. 2, and Art. 20.

[42] E.C.S.C. Treaty, Art. 78, para. 3.2 A similar Committee has not been set up under the other Treaties.

The most important of his remaining functions may be summarised as follows:

APPOINTMENTS

1. The President, on the joint proposal of the Advocates General, may appoint for a particular case the other Advocate General and not the one attached to the Chamber concerned with the case in question.[43]

2. The President informs the judges and the Advocates General of the candidates whose names have been submitted for the post of Registrar fourteen days before the Court makes the appointment.[44]

3. In the event of the absence of the Registrar and the Deputy-Registrars, or of their inability to attend or when their posts are simultaneously vacant, the President appoints the official who for the time being is to carry out the duties of the Registrar.[45]

4. The officials of the Court are required to take the oath of office before the President.[46]

ADMINISTRATION

5. The President is to initial entries in the Register of the Court.[47]

6. Instructions determining the duties of the Registrar were established by the Court on a proposal of the President.[48]

7. The administration of the Court, its financial management and the keeping of the Court's accounts are to be undertaken by the Registrar, with the assistance of an administrative assistant, both acting under the authority of the President.[49]

PROCEDURE

8. Following the filing of the Request, the President assigns the case to one of the Chambers and appoints one of the judges of that Chamber to be the *juge rapporteur*.[50]

9. If during the proceedings, the *juge rapporteur* is appointed to the other Chamber, he still continues to act, subject to any contrary decision of the President.[51]

[43] Rules, Art. 10, para. 1.2.
[44] Rules, Art. 11, para. 1.2.
[45] Rules, Art. 13.
[46] Rules, Art. 19, para. 2.
[47] Rules, Art. 15, para. 1.
[48] Rules, Art. 14. As to these, see p. 545, below.
[49] Rules, Art. 22.
[50] Rules, Art. 24, para. 2. Under the old Rules (Art. 34, para. 1), the *juge rapporteur* was not appointed until the end of the written proceedings.
[51] Rules, Art. 24, para. 2.2.

10. The dates and times of the sittings of the Court are fixed by the President.[52]

11. If in one of the Chambers the quorum of three judges is not present, the President of that Chamber is required to inform the President of the Court who then appoints another judge to take the place of the judge who is unable to attend.[53]

12. During legal vacations, the President is to keep in touch with the Registrar or he is to request a President of a Chamber or another judge to undertake this duty for him.[54]

13. During these vacations, the President, in case of urgency may convene the judges and the Advocates General.[55]

14. The President sets the dates by which the procedural documents must be submitted.[56]

15. If during the course of the written proceedings, one of the parties raises a fresh argument based upon contentions of law or of fact which have come to light during those proceedings, the President, upon the expiry of the normal procedural time limits, may grant to the other party a time limit within which to reply to this ground.[57]

16. If at the end of the written proceedings, the Court decides to open the oral proceedings without holding an Instruction, the President sets a date for that opening.[58]

17. If an Instruction is held, the Court may grant to the parties a period of time within which to present their written submissions upon it. In this case, the President, after the end of this period, sets the date for the opening of the oral proceedings.[59]

18. If no such period is granted, the President will fix the date for the opening of the oral proceedings after the completion of the measures of instruction.[60]

19. If the parties to a case whose Instruction has been completed, jointly request the postponement of the hearing, the President may

---

[52] Rules, Art. 25, para. 1.
[53] Rules, Art. 26, para. 3. This Rule elaborates the provisions of E.C.S.C. Statute, Art. 18, para. 2; E.E.C. Statute, Art 15 and Euratom Statute, Art 15. This provision refers only to the possibility of one judge being absent. This may mean that if two judges were away from a Chamber, they would not be replaced as then the majority of judges would be drawn from the other Chamber.
[54] Rules, Art. 28, para. 1.2.
[55] Rules, Art. 28, para. 2.
[56] Rules, Art. 41, para. 2.
[57] Rules, Art. 42, para. 2.2.
[58] Rules, Art. 44, para. 2.2.
[59] Rules, Art. 54, para. 2.
[60] Rules, Art. 54, para. 1.

accede to their request. If the parties are not in agreement, the President must refer the matter to the Court for a decision.[61]

20. During the Instruction, the Registrar, under the direction of the President, is required to draw up a record of the deposition of each witness. After it has been read aloud, this record is signed by the witness, the Registrar and the President or the *juge rapporteur*.[62]

21. During the proceedings, the President may put questions to the agents, legal advisers or counsel of the parties.[63]

22. After hearing the submissions of the Advocate General, the President declares the oral proceedings closed.[64]

23. The President signs the record of every judgment.[65]

24. If a party requests free legal aid, the President appoints a *juge rapporteur* if one has not already been appointed, and the Chamber of which that *juge* is a member will decide whether aid is to be granted wholly or in part or whether it is to be refused.[66]

25. When any party requests the suspension of the execution of any Decisions, etc., of any institution of the three Communities,[67] or if any party requests the Court to make any interim order,[68] the President decides whether there is any need to order the opening of an Instruction.[69]

26. When either of the above requests is made, the President grants to the institution concerned a short time limit within which it may present its written or oral observations.[70]

27. The suspension of this execution or the interim order requested may be granted by the President himself,[71] and even before the other party has presented its observations to the Court.[72]

---

[61] Rules, Art. 55, para. 2. Under the old Rules (Art. 46, para. 3), if the parties were not in agreement the President had a discretion either himself to decide whether to grant a postponement or to refer the matter to the Court for its decision. This discretion has now been removed.

[62] Rules, Art. 47, para. 6.

[63] Rules, Art. 57, para. 1. Under the old Rules (Art. 48, para. 1), the President was expressly empowered in addition to asking questions in order to seek clarifications. It is suggested that there can be no intention here of reducing the President's powers, as clarification can only be sought by the asking of questions.

[64] Rules, Art. 59, para. 2.

[65] Rules, Art. 64, para. 2.

[66] Rules, Art. 76, para. 3.

[67] Requests submitted under E.C.S.C. Treaty, Art. 39, para. 2; E.E.C. Treaty, Art. 185, and Euratom Treaty, Art. 157.

[68] Requests submitted under E.C.S.C. Treaty, Art. 39, para. 3; E.E.C. Treaty, Art, 186, and Euratom Treaty, Art. 158.

[69] Rules, Art. 84, para. 2.

[70] Rules, Art. 84, para. 1.

[71] Rules, Art. 85, para. 1.

[72] Rules, Art. 84, para. 2.2.

28. The President possesses the same powers in relation to a request for the suspension of a judgment of the Court itself or of a Decision or Recommendation of the High Authority,[73] or of the Commission or Councils of the Economic and Euratom Communities.[74]

29. If a party applies to the Court to determine upon a preliminary objection or upon a preliminary issue of fact, without undertaking a consideration of the merits of the case, the President fixes a time limit for the other party to submit its case and its submissions in writing.[75]

30. If the Court rejects the application or joins it to the merits of the case, the President fixes new time limits for the continuation of the case.[76]

31. Where a third party has intervened in a dispute, the President fixes the time limit by which that party may state in writing the arguments supporting its submissions, and the time limit within which the parties to the principal action may reply.[77]

32. When a legal adviser or counsel has been barred from the proceedings during the course of an action, the proceedings are adjourned until the expiration of a period set by the President in order to allow the party concerned to appoint another legal adviser or counsel.[78]

33. If within the time limit laid down, the defendants fail to reply to the plaintiffs' Request by filing their Defence, and the plaintiffs request the Court to give judgment in their favour, the President fixes the date for the opening of the oral proceedings.[79]

34. Where a judgment of the Court has been given in default of appearance of the defendants, and an application is subsequently made to set the judgment aside, the President fixes the time for the other party to submit its written observations.[80]

35. Where a request has been made for an opinion of the Court upon whether a proposed agreement between the Commission of the Economic Community and a State or international organisation is compatible with the terms of that Treaty,[81] the President fixes the time within which the institution of the Community and the State concerned are to submit their written observations.[82]

---

[73] Submitted under E.C.S.C. Treaty, Arts. 44 and 92, para. 3.
[74] Submitted under E.E.C. Treaty, Arts. 187 and 192, para. 3 and Euratom Treaty, Arts. 159 and 164, para. 3—Rules, Art. 89, para. 1.
[75] Rules, Art. 91, para. 2. This is a new power given to the President; under the old Rules (Art. 69, para. 4) the fixing of the time limits was left to the Court itself.
[76] Rules, Art. 91, para. 4.2.   [77] Rules, Art. 93, para. 5.2.
[78] Rules, Art. 35, para. 2.   [79] Rules, Art. 94, para. 1.2.
[80] Rules, Art. 94, para. 5.1.
[81] This request is submitted under E.E.C. Treaty, Art. 228, para. 2.
[82] Rules, Art. 106, para. 1.2.

36. Following this request, the President appoints the *juge rapporteur* [83] and signs the Court's opinion.[84]

37. The President has the same powers as above when a request has been made for an advisory opinion upon whether proposed amendments of the rules for the exercise by the High Authority of its power conforms to the aims of the European Coal and Steel Community as set out in that Treaty.[85]

38. There is a new provision set out in the Statutes contained in the two new Treaties that the President is to arrange the list of cases.[86]

39. The President has power to issue a warrant to enable inspectors of the Euratom Commission to have access to all places, data and to all persons connected with special fissile material.[87]

40. During the first five years of its existence, the President is to be one of the three arbitrators if an arbitration is held under the 1961 Agreement of Association between Greece and the E.E.C.[88]

THE PRESIDENTS OF THE CHAMBERS

A President of each of the Chambers is to be elected for a period of one year.[89] The method of election, which is by secret ballot, is the same as that for the President of the Court.[90] Should the President of a Chamber cease to hold his position [91] before the end of the normal period of office, the Court appoints a replacement for the remaining period.[92] It would appear that the choice of a successor is not limited to judges of the same Chamber as the one in which the President sat.

The main task of the Presidents is to open and direct the hearings before the Chambers and conduct the proceedings.[93] Although most of the incidental administrative decisions are taken by the Chamber

---

[83] Rules, Art. 107, para. 1.

[84] Rules, Art. 107, para. 3.

[85] Rules, Art. 108, para. 2. The request is submitted under E.C.S.C. Treaty, Art. 95, para. 4.

[86] E.E.C. Statute, Art. 31; Euratom Statute, Art. 32.

[87] Euratom Treaty, Art. 81, para. 3. If there is no time for this warrant, the President can authorise a forced inspection which has already occurred—*ibid.* para. 4.

[88] Agreement of July 9, 1961, Art. 67, section 4.

[89] Rules, Art. 6, para. 2. The old Rules (Art. 5, para. 2) declared that the Presidents of the Chambers were to be elected for one judicial year, that is to say, for the year which commences on January 1. It appears, therefore, that the period of office is now intended to run from the date of election. The Rules make no mention of whether the Presidents may be re-elected, but it is inevitable that one judge will be President on more than one occasion during his six years of office.

[90] Rules, Art. 6, para. 4. See p. 19, note 32, above.

[91] Described in the Stationery Office's translation of the Rules as " termination of the mandate."

[92] Rules, Art. 6, para. 3.

[93] Rules, Art. 46, para. 2 and Art. 56, para. 1.

as a whole,[94] certain of them are made by the Presidents alone. Thus:

The dates and times of the sittings of the Chambers are fixed by the respective President.[95]

If a Chamber does not comprise the requisite number of three judges, the President must inform the President of the Court who then appoints another judge to replace the one who is unable to attend.[96]

In addition to this, the Presidents of the Chambers may be called upon to deputise for the President of the Court in his absence, or if he is unable to attend, or if the office of President is vacant,[97] or during the vacations of the Court.[98]

THE JUGE RAPPORTEUR [99]

Under the old Rules, the President was not required to appoint the *juge rapporteur* in a particular case until the end of the written proceedings.[1] Now, however, the *juge* is to be appointed as soon as the Request has been filed with the Court.[2] His main task is to make a preliminary report on the question of whether the case requires an Instruction,[3] the final decision being left to the Court itself.[4]

If it is decided to hold an Instruction, instead of it being held before the Court or a Chamber, it may be entrusted to the *juge rapporteur* alone.[5] Under the old Rules, when the *juge rapporteur* was entrusted with the Instruction, he controlled the proceedings in the same way as would the President of the Chamber. He was required to inform the witnesses and experts that they must give their evidence on oath [6] and might take the same measures against defaulting witnesses as might the Court or one of the Chambers. As all these provisions have been

---

[94] *E.g.*, determining the measures of instruction believed necessary (Rules, Art. 45, para. 1, read with Art. 46, para. 1) and specifying the facts which witnesses are to prove (Art. 47, para. 1, read with Art. 46, para. 1).

[95] Rules, Art. 25, para. 2.

[96] Rules, Art. 26, para. 3, see page 22, note 53, above.

[97] Rules, Art. 7, para. 2.

[98] Rules, Art. 28, para. 1.2.

[99] As this position does not exist in English courts, no translation has been attempted.

[1] Old Rules, Art. 34, para. 1.

[2] Rules, Art. 24, para. 2.1.

[3] Rules, Art. 44, para. 1. The old Rules (Art. 34, para. 2), expressly stated that the *juge* in his report was not to make submissions upon the merits of the case. The omission of these words in the present Rules, however, is not, one assumes, intended to have altered the situation.

[4] Rules, Art. 44, para. 1. The decision is also, presumably, left to a Chamber if that Chamber is dealing with the case.

[5] Rules, Art. 45, para. 3.1. Under the old Rules (Art. 38), it could only be so entrusted if there was no objection by the parties. As the provision has not been incorporated into the present Rules, it appears that the parties can no longer object.

[6] Old Rules, Art. 41, para. 7, and old Rules on Agents and Advocates, Art. 9, para. 2.

excluded from the present Rules, it is now quite unclear what powers the *juge* possesses, but the fact that he needs to possess some powers is self-evident.

DISQUALIFICATIONS

Once a judge has been elected, it is set out [7] that he may not hold any political or administrative office, nor is he allowed to engage in any occupation or profession whether paid or unpaid, unless as an exception he obtains an exemption granted by a two-thirds majority of the Council.[8] It is further stated that they may not acquire or hold, directly or indirectly, any interest in any businesses related to coal or steel during their term of office and during a period of three years thereafter.[9] However, in matters regarding the Economic and Euratom Communities, the respective Treaties are far vaguer,[10] merely requiring the judges to respect the obligations imposed upon them and in particular the duty to exercise honesty and discretion as regards the acceptance, after their term of office, " of certain posts or of certain benefits," a term which is in no way made more specific. Further, no judge is allowed to take part in the settlement of any case in which he has previously participated as agent of, or legal adviser to, or counsel for, one of the parties, or in which he has been called upon to decide as a member of a tribunal, of a commission of inquiry, or in any other capacity.[11] In the event of difficulty in the application of this rule, the Court is to decide.[12]

IMMUNITIES

In order to ensure that once they are elected the judges shall not be prevented from acting with entire impartiality, the Treaties endow them with certain specific immunities. First, the judges of the Court are granted immunity from legal action in respect of any acts done by

[7] E.C.S.C. Statute, Art. 4, para. 1; E.E.C. Statute, Art. 4, para. 1; Euratum Statute, Art. 4, para. 1.
[8] The requirement as to the two-thirds majority is found only in E.C.S.C. Statute, Art. 4, para. 2, the other two Statutes merely referring to exemption being granted by the Council. It is suggested, however, that the provision cannot be less rigorous under one Treaty than it is under another.
[9] E.C.S.C. Statute, Art. 4, para. 3.
[10] E.E.C. Statute, Art. 4, para. 3; Euratom Statute, Art. 4, para. 3.
[11] E.C.S.C. Statute, Art. 19, para. 1; E.E.C. Statute, Art. 16, para. 1; Euratom Statute, Art. 16, para. 1. If, for some special reason, a judge considers that he should not take part in the judgment or in the examination of a particular case, he must inform the President of the Court. Simililarly, where the President considers that a judge, for some special reason, should not sit in a particular case, he shall give notice to the judge concerned. E.C.S.C. Statute, Art. 19, para. 2; E.E.C. Statute, Art. 16, para. 2; Euratom Statute, Art 16, para. 2.
[12] E.C.S.C. Statute, Art. 19, para. 3; E.E.C. Statute, Art. 16, para. 3; Euratom Statute, Art. 16, para. 3.

them in their official capacity—which includes anything that they have spoken or written—and this immunity continues after the ending of their period of office.[13]

The judges enjoy in each of the Member States exemption from any national tax on their salaries[14] or emoluments paid by the Communities.[15] In addition, neither they, nor their wives and dependants, are to be subject to any immigration restrictions, or registration formalities, and, in respect of currency or exchange regulations, the judges are to be accorded the same facilities as are accorded by custom to the officials of international organisations.[16]

Further, they are to enjoy the right to import, free of duty, from the country of their last residence, or from the country of which they are nationals, their furniture and effects at the time of first taking up their office, and are also to enjoy the right to re-export such property free of duty when they cease to hold office, subject, however, in both cases to such conditions as are deemed necessary by the government of the country in which the right is exercised.[17]

Finally, by the Economic Community and Euratom Treaties the judges are granted the right, which they did not expressly possess before, of importing their motor cars for their personal use free of duty, and of similarly re-exporting them, but subject on both occasions to such conditions as are deemed necessary by the government of the country concerned.[18]

---

[13] E.C.S.C. Statute, Art. 3, para. 1; E.E.C. Statute, Art. 3, para. 1; Euratom Statute, Art. 3, para. 1.

[14] For the extent of this exemption see *Jean-E Humblet* v. *The Belgian State* (Case 6–60), Vol. II, below.

[15] E.C.S.C. Protocol on Immunities, Art. 11 (b); E.C.C. Protocol on Immunities, Art. 12, para. 2 and Art. 20; Euratom Protocol on Immunities, Art. 12, para. 2 and Art. 20. It is set out in the Economic Community and Euratom Treaties that the Council of Ministers is to lay down procedures for the taxing by those two Communities of salaries and emoluments for the benefit of those Communities— Protocol on Immunities, Art. 12, para. 1. As such a provision does not appear in the E.C.S.C. Treaty, a brave judge might argue that only two-thirds of his salary could be taxed.

[16] E.E.C. Protocol on Immunities, Art. 11 (c); Euratom Protocol on Immunities, Art. 11 (c). This is a new provision not included in the original E.C.S.C. Protocol on Immunities.

[17] E.E.C. Protocol on Immunities, Art. 11 (d); Euratom Protocol on Immunities, Art. 11 (d). This provision is an enlarged and modified version of the one contained in E.C.S.C. Protocol on Immunities, Art. 11 (d).

[18] E.E.C. Protocol on Immunities, Art. 11 (e); Euratom Protocol on Immunities, Art. 11 (d). Prior to the coming into force of these Treaties, judges had to rely upon the contention that the term " furniture and effects " was wide enough to cover their cars. In respect of income tax, capital tax, death duties and the avoidance of double taxation, the judges who, solely by reason of the exercise of their office, establish their residence in the territory of a Member State other than their " home " State, are to be considered in both States as having maintained the residence in their " home " State, provided that such " home " State is a member of the Communities. This also applies to a judge's wife, provided that she is not exercising her own

The immunity from jurisdiction may be suspended by the Court sitting in plenary session.[19] If it is so suspended, and subsequently a criminal action is brought against a judge, the case is justiciable within any of the Member States only by a court competent to judge members of " the highest municipal court." [20] This provision is limited to penal actions, so that it would appear not to apply to civil actions, such as for breach of contract or for defamation.

TERMINATION OF OFFICE

Apart from the termination of office at the end of six years,[21] a seat may also become vacant by the death or resignation of a member of the Court.[22] However, if a judge gives notice of his resignation,[23] he continues to sit until his successor enters upon his duties.[24] This successor holds office during the unexpired period of his predecessor's term.[25]

A judge may be removed from office only if in the unanimous opinion of the other judges and of the Advocates General of the Court [26] he no longer fulfils the required conditions or meets the obligations resulting from his office.[27] Before the Court can take this decision, the President

professional activities, and to dependent children—E.E.C. Protocol on Immunities, Art. 13, para. 1; Euratom Protocol on Immunities, Art. 13, para. 1. There is no similar provision in the E.C.S.C. Protocol.

19 E.C.S.C. Statute, Art. 3, para. 2; E.E.C. Statute, Art. 3, para. 2; Euratom Statute, Art. 3, para. 2. In the present case this will mean five judges, as presumably the judge concerned would be barred from judging, and a plenary session must consist of an uneven number of judges—E.C.S.C. Statute, Art. 18, para. 2; E.E.C. Statute, Art. 15; Euratom Statute, Art. 15.

20 E.C.S.C. Statute, Art. 3, para. 3; E.E.C. Statute, Art. 3, para. 3; Euratom Statute, Art. 3, para. 3.

21 Three seats were also to become vacant after an initial period of three years— E.C.S.C. Treaty, Art. 32, para. 2; E.E.C. Treaty, Art. 167, para. 2; Euratom Treaty, Art. 139, para. 2

22 E.C.S.C. Statute, Art. 6, para. 1; E.E.C. Statute, Art. 5, para. 1; Euratom Statute, Art. 5, para. 1. At the end of a six-year period a judge is eligible for re-election— E.C.S.C. Treaty, Art. 32, para. 2; E.E.C. Treaty, Art. 167, para. 4; Euratom Treaty, Art. 139, para. 4.

23 This is effected by a letter addressed to the President of the Court for forwarding to the President of the Council. The seat becomes vacant from this notification —E.C.S.C. Statute, Art 6, para. 2; E.E.C. Statute, Art. 5, para. 2; Euratom Statute, Art. 5, para. 2. " This notification " is presumably to be taken as implying the receipt of the letter by the President of the Council.

24 E.C.S.C. Statute, Art. 6, para. 3; E.E.C. Statute, Art. 5, para. 3; Euratom Statute, Art. 5, para. 3.

25 E.C.S.C. Statute, Art. 8; E.E.C. Statute, Art. 7; Euratom Statute, Art. 7.

26 This provision concerning the Advocates General is new in the sense that it was not contained in the E.C.S.C. Treaty—see E.C.S.C. Statute, Art. 7, para. 1.

27 E.C.S.C. Statute, Art. 7, para. 1; E.E.C. Statute, Art. 6, para. 1; Euratom Statute, Art. 6, para. 1. The judge concerned does not take part in these deliberations—_ibid._ If a judge is thus deprived of office, the Registrar informs the Presidents of the High Authority, of the two Commissions, of the Assembly and of the Councils of Ministers —_ibid._ para. 2. The E.E.C. and Euratom Statutes appear to imply that only upon notification to the Council of Ministers does the seat become vacant—_ibid._ para. 3.

must invite the judge concerned to appear at a private session of the Court to present his comments.[28] From this session of the Court the Registrar is excluded.[29]

THE ADVOCATES GENERAL

The Court is assisted by two Advocates General[30] whose duty it is to present publicly, and with complete impartiality and independence, their oral reasoned submissions—*conclusions*—upon the cases submitted to the Court.[31] They are to be appointed for six years by the Governments of the Member States acting in common agreement and they are to be selected from persons of recognised independence who fulfil the conditions required for the exercise of the highest judicial functions in their respective States or who are legal experts of universally recognised and outstanding ability.[32] Their seniority is determined in the same way as that of the judges, and they take precedence immediately after the judges themselves.[33]

There is to be a partial renewal every three years, and the Advocate General who was to retire first was designed by lot,[34] the retiring Advocate being eligible for re-election.[35]

Upon election, the Advocates General are required to take the same oath as that prescribed for the judges[36] and to give the same solemn undertaking concerning the acceptance of certain offices or of certain advantages both during their period of office and after its termination.[37] After the formation of the two Chambers, the Court assigned one Advocate General to each of them.[38] The number of Advocates can be

---

28 Rules, Art. 5.
29 *Ibid.*
30 E.C.S.C. Statute, Art. 10; E.E.C. Treaty, Art. 166, para. 1; Euratom Treaty, Art. 138, para. 1.
31 *Affaires soumises à la Cour*—E.C.S.C. Statute, Art. 11; E.E.C. Treaty, Art. 166, para. 2; Euratom Treaty, Art. 138, para. 2. That this phrase is accepted in the Rules of the Court as being wider than to cover only cases of litigation is shown by Art. 107, para. 2 and Art. 108, para. 1 of the Rules which extends it to cover the giving of advisory opinions.
32 E.C.S.C. Statute, Art. 12; E.E.C. Treaty, Art. 167, para. 1; Euratom Treaty, Art. 139, para. 1.
33 Rules, Art. 9. For the determining of the seniority of the judges see p. 18, above.
34 E.C.S.C. Statute, Art. 12; E.E.C. Treaty, Art. 167, para. 3; Euratom Treaty, Art. 139, para. 3.
35 E.C.S.C. Statute, Art. 12 and E.C.S.C. Treaty, Art. 32, para. 3; E.E.C. Treaty, Art. 167, para. 4; Euratom Treaty, Art. 139, para. 4.
36 Rules, Art. 8 and Art. 3, para. 1. As to this oath, see note 18, p. 18, above. This may be done according to the procedure prescribed by the municipal legislation applicable to that Advocate—Rules, Art. 8 and Art. 3, para. 2.
37 E.E.C. Statute, Art. 8 and Art. 4, para. 3; Euratom Statute, Art. 8 and Art 4, para. 3.
38 Rules, Art. 10, para. 1.1. Under the old Rules (Art. 9, para. 1), this allocation was to be made at the beginning of each judicial year.

increased by the unanimous decision of the Council of Ministers acting upon a proposal of the Court.[39] However, if this is done, the interpretation of many of the articles relating to these Advocates will become difficult, as these articles have been drawn up on the assumption that there were merely to be two Advocates General. Thus, the Rules require the Court to appoint one Advocate General to each of the Chambers,[40] and where one Advocate General is absent or unable to attend, the President of the Court may call on the other Advocate.[41] What the position should be under these articles if, at any time, there were three Advocates General and only two Chambers, is unclear.

The Advocates General enjoy immunities identical to those granted to the judges [42]; they are subject to the same prohibition concerning holding political and administrative offices and the engaging in any paid or unpaid profession or occupation [43] and acquiring or retaining directly or indirectly any interest in any businesses related to coal or steel [44] or the acceptance after the termination of their period of office of certain posts or of certain benefits connected with the Economic Community or Euratom.[45] Their salaries and pensions are also determined in the same way as those of the judges.[46] Similarly, they are required to reside at the place where the Court has its seat.[47]

The part in the proceedings before the Court which is played by the Advocates General is set out in various provisions of the Rules and may be summarised as follows:

1. They must be heard by the Court before it appoints a Registrar.[48]

2. The Advocate General is heard by the Court before it decides whether the failure of a Request to comply with the requirements of the Rules must lead the Court to refuse to entertain it as being bad in form.[49]

---

39 E.C.S.C. Statute, Art. 12 and Treaty, Art. 32, para. 4; E.E.C. Treaty, Art. 166, para. 3; Euratom Treaty, Art. 138, para. 3. The E.E.C. and Euratom Treaties both set out, *ibid.*, that if the number of Advocates General is increased, the Council is to amend Art. 167, para. 3 and Art. 139, para. 3 respectively, which state that there shall be a partial renewal every three years. As the Advocates hold office for six years, it is presumed that if their number is increased to three, partial elections will be held every two years.
40 Rules. Art. 10, para. 1.1.
41 Rules, Art. 10, para. 2.
42 E.C.S.C. Statute, Art. 13, para. 1 and Art. 3; E.E.C. Statute, Art. 8 and Art. 3 and Protocol on Immunities, Art. 20; Euratom Statute, Art 8 and Art. 3 and Protocol on Immunities, Art. 20.
43 E.C.S.C. Statute, Art. 13, para. 1 and Art. 4, paras. 1 and 2; E.E.C. Statute, Art. 8 and Art. 4, paras. 1 and 2; Euratom Statute, Art. 8 and Art. 4, paras. 1 and 2.
44 E.C.S.C. Statute, Art 13, para. 1 and Art. 4, para. 3.
45 E.E.C. Statute, Art. 8 and Art 4, para. 3; Euratom Statute, Art. 8 and Art. 4, para. 3.
46 E.C.S.C. Statute, Art. 13, para. 1 and Art. 5; E.E.C. Treaty, Art. 154; Euratom Treaty, Art. 123. As to these see pp. 561–571, below.
47 E.C.S.C. Statute, Art. 9; E.E.C. Statute, Art. 13; Euratom Statute, Art. 13.
48 Rules, Art. 11, para. 1.1.
49 Rules, Art. 38, para. 7.

3. If in the course of the written proceedings in a case, one of the parties raises a fresh argument based upon contentions of law or fact which came to light during those written proceedings, the President, after he has heard the Advocate General, may grant to the other party a time limit within which to reply to this argument.[50]

4. The Advocate General must be heard by the Court before it gives a ruling on a preliminary objection or upon a preliminary issue of fact or joins them to the merits of the case.[51]

5. If there is to be an Instruction, the Advocate General concerned with the case must be heard by the Court about what measures of instruction are necessary and what facts are to be proved.[52]

6. The Advocate General concerned is to be heard by the Court before it orders the proof of certain facts to be made by witnesses.[53]

7. The Advocate General concerned can request the hearing of a particular witness.[54]

8. He can require the Registrar to have anything said or written during the proceedings before the Court or a Chamber translated into any of the official languages.[55]

9. The Advocate is also to be heard by the Court before it decides to authorise the total or partial use as the procedural language in a case of one of the official languages other than the one determined by the Rules.[56]

10. During the oral proceedings, the Advocate General may put questions to the agents, legal advisers or counsel of the parties.[57]

11. Immediately before the closing of the oral proceedings, the Advocate General presents his oral reasoned submissions.[58]

---

[50] Rules, Art. 42, para. 2.2. This provision was not contained in the old Rules.
[51] Rules, Art. 91, para. 4.1.
[52] Rules, Art. 45, para. 1.
[53] Rules, Art. 47, para. 1.1.
[54] Rules, Art. 47, para. 1.2. Under the old Rules (Art. 39, para. 2.2), the Advocate could also request the hearing of an expert.
[55] Rules, Art. 30, para. 1. The Advocates General were previously given the express right of access to any transcript or report and the right to obtain a copy of it—old Rules, Art. 43, para. 2. This right is now in terms limited to the parties to a case—Rules, Art. 53, para. 2.
[56] Rules, Art. 29, para. 2 (c). As to determining the procedural language see p. 46, below.
[57] Rules, Art. 57, para. 2. The provision in the old Rules (Art. 48, paras. 1 and 2) that they could also request clarifications has been omitted, presumably because clarifications are obtained by means of questions. Previously, the Advocates were required to give notice to the President of their intention to ask questions—*ibid.* para. 2.
[58] Rules, Art. 59, paras. 1 and 2. This provision elaborates the requirement set out in E.C.S.C. Statute, Art. 21, para. 4; E.E.C. Statute, Art. 18, para. 4 and Euratom Statute, Art. 18, para. 4. The judgment of the Court must set out that the Advocate General has been so heard—Rules, Art. 63. Under the old Rules (Art. 54)

12. If there is a dispute about costs, the Advocate General is heard by the Chamber to which the dispute has been assigned.[59]

13. The Advocate is also heard by the Court before it condemns the party which caused them to pay costs incurred by the Court where they could have been avoided.[60]

14. The Advocate General concerned with the case is heard by the Court before it corrects any judgment on the grounds of clerical or arithmetical errors or obvious inaccuracies.[61]

15. Where one party alleges that the Court has failed to determine upon a particular point in the submissions or to decide upon costs, the Advocate General concerned is heard by the Court before it determines upon the admissibility and the well founding of the allegation.[62]

16. If a request for the suspension of the execution of a Decision, etc., of the High Authority or of the Commissions of either the Economic Community or of Euratom is submitted to the Court by the President,[63] the Advocate General must be heard by the Court before it decides whether to accede to the request.[64]

17. Before the Court can declare upon whether a Member State's draft agreement or convention with non-Member State is compatible with the Euratom Treaty, the Advocate General is to be heard at a private session.[65]

18. When the Court is deliberating upon administrative matters, the Advocates General take part and each is given a vote.[66]

the judgment was expressly required to set out the Advocate General's submissions themselves. In practice, the publication of these submissions has only been omitted in one case.

[59] Rules, Art. 74, para. 1.

[60] Rules, Art. 72 (a).

[61] Rules, Art. 66, para. 3. Previously (old Rules Art. 57, para. 3) the Advocate presented his written observations to the Court. The present Rule thus speeds up the poceedings.

[62] Rules, Art. 67, para. 3. This duty was not included in the old Rules.

[63] The President himself has power to suspend the execution summarily—E.C.S.C. Statute, Art. 33, para. 1; E.E.C. Statute, Art. 36, para. 1; Euratom Statute, Art. 37, para. 1.

[64] Rules, Art. 85, para. 3. It is not clear which of the two Advocates General is here being referred to. In all previous cases where the singular is used it has naturally referred to that Advocate who has been concerned with the case. But here the Court may well have to come to a decision concerning the suspension before the request for the annulment of the Decision or Recommendation of the High Authority of the Coal and Steel Community has been allocated to one of the Chambers, or, if the case is brought by a State or by the Council of Ministers, the whole court will hear the case—E.C.S.C. Statute, Art. 18, para. 3.

[65] Rules, Art. 104, para. 4.1.

[66] Rules, Art. 27, para. 7. The right to possess a vote was not enjoyed under the old Rules (Art. 25, para. 7.1).

33

19.   Before the Court or a Chamber excludes from the proceedings any legal adviser or counsel of one of the parties on account of his conduct before it, or before a municipal judge, or because he has made use of the rights which he possesses by reason of his position for purposes other than those for which they were intended, the Advocate General must be heard.[67]

20.   The Advocates General, like the judges of the Court, may not take part in the settlement of any case in which they have previously participated in any capacity.[68]   Further, if for some special reason one of the Advocates considers that he should not take part in the judging or in the examination of a particular case, he is required to inform the President, who may, independently of this, decide that the Advocate should not take part in a particular case.[69]

21.   Should one of the Advocates General be absent or unable to fulfil his duties, in a case of urgency, the President may call upon the other Advocate to act.[70]   This rule will naturally be relied upon when one of the Advocates General is disqualified from acting in a particular case.   In the normal way, however, the Advocate General appointed is the one attached to the Chamber of which the *juge rapporteur* is a member, although on the joint proposal of both Advocates General the President of the Court may appoint the other Advocate.[71]

When the office of Advocate General becomes vacant through the death or resignation of the holder, the Advocate General appointed to replace him holds office for the unexpired period of his predecessor's term.[72]

On the question of the dismissal of an Advocate General, the provisions of the various Treaties are in direct conflict.   The Statute of the E.C.S.C. Treaty sets out [73] that the decision to dismiss one of them is to be taken by the unanimous vote of the Council of Ministers acting upon the advice of the Court.   The two later Treaties, however, each state [74] that an Advocate General may be deprived of office only if in the unanimous opinion of the judges and of the other Advocate General, he no longer fulfils the required conditions or satisfies the obligations

---

[67] Rules, Art. 35, para. 1.1.
[68] E.C.S.C. Statute, Art. 19, para. 1; E.E.C. Statute, Art. 16, para. 1; Euratom Statute, Art. 16, para. 1.
[69] E.C.S.C. Statute, Art. 19, para. 2; E.E.C. Statute, Art. 16, para. 2; Euratom Statute, Art. 16, para. 2.
[70] Rules, Art. 10, para. 2.
[71] Rules, Art. 10, para. 1.2.
[72] E.C.S.C. Statute, Art. 13, para. 1 and Art. 8; E.E.C. Statute, Art. 8 and Art. 7; Euratom Statute, Art. 8 and Art. 7.
[73] E.C.S.C. Statute, Art. 13, para. 2.
[74] E.E.C. Statute, Art 8 and Art. 6, para. 1; Euratom Statute, Art. 8 and Art. 6, para. 1.

resulting from his office. It would appear, therefore, that the requirement of the participation of the Council of Ministers has been repealed.[75]

THE REGISTRY

The Registry of the Court is open to the public except on official holidays on Mondays to Fridays from 10 a.m. to 12 noon and then, after three hours for lunch, from 3 p.m. to 6 p.m. It is also open on Saturdays from 10 a.m. to 12 noon.[76] However, when the Court or a Chamber is holding a public sitting, the Registry is always open 30 minutes before the sitting is due to begin.[77]

When the Registry is closed, procedural documents may properly be placed in the Court's letter box which is cleared daily when the Registry is opened.[78]

THE REGISTRAR

The Court, after having heard the Advocates General, proceeds to appoint a Registrar from among candidates previously nominated.[79] The appointment is for a period of six years.[80] The mode of election is the same as for the President of the Court or of the President of either of the Chambers,[81] and he is eligible for re-election.[82]

Before taking up office, the Registrar is required to take the same oath as the judges and to give the same solemn undertaking.[83] He enjoys

---

[75] The alternative view is that there are now two alternative methods of dismissal. If this is so it should be noted that under the method set out in the E.C.S.C. Statute only the advice of the Court is required, and that there is no requirement that the advice should be unanimous, and further that the other Advocate General plays no part in the proceedings.

[76] Instructions to the Registrar, Art. 1, para. 1.1. For these official holidays see p. 543, below.

[77] *Ibid.* Art. 1, para. 2.

[78] *Ibid.* Art. 1, para. 1.2.

[79] Rules, Art. 11, para. 1. Under the old Rules (Art. 10, para. 1.2) it was expressly declared that candidates were to be nominated by the judges. The nominations must be accompanied by full details of the candidate's age, nationality, university degrees, linguistic knowledge, past and present occupations, and of his experience in the judicial and international fields—Rules, Art. 11, para. 2. On March 17, 1953, the Court of the European Coal and Steel Community appointed M. Albert van Houtte as Registrar for a period of six years. He was subsequently re-appointed Registrar for a further six years, by the Court of Justice of the European Communities on October 7, 1958.

[80] Rules, Art. 11, para. 4.

[81] Rules, Art. 11, para. 3. As to this procedure, see p. 19, above.

[82] Rules, Art. 11, para. 4.

[83] E.C.S.C. Statute, Art. 14, para. 1; E.E.C. Statute, Art. 9; Euratom Statute, Art. 9—Rules, Art. 11, para. 5 and Art. 3, para. 3. For this oath and undertaking see p. 18, above. The present Registrar, M. Albert van Houtte, took the oath of office as Registrar of the Court of Justice of the European Coal and Steel Community on March 26, 1953, and as Registrar of the Court of Justice of the European Communities on October 7, 1958.

the same immunity as do the judges and Advocates General.[84] There is a conflict, however, between the Treaties as to how this immunity can be lifted. In the case of the judges, it can only be lifted by the Court sitting in plenary session.[85] This provision is extended to cover also the Advocates General,[86] but it is not made to cover the Registrar. It appears, therefore, that his case is regulated in the same way as is the lifting of the immunity of any of the other servants or agents of the Community, and in the case of the E.C.S.C. Treaty, the sole person empowered to suspend his immunity is the President of the Court.[87] In the case of the other two Communities, however, it is set out that it is the relevant institution of the Community which is so empowered,[88] and in this case, that institution is the Court as a whole. It appears, therefore, that the President has now lost his previous power in this matter.[89]

The functions that are to be performed by the Registrar are set out in the Statutes of the Court that are contained in the three Treaties and in the Court's Rules of Procedure. His principal functions may briefly be summarised as follows:

1. The Registrar draws up the plan for the organisation of the Court administrative services, and submits these for the approval of the Court. He may subsequently submit modified plans.[90]

2. The Registrar is to be present when officials are sworn in before the President of the Court.[91]

---

84 E.E.C. Protocol on Immunities, Art. 20; Euratom Protocol on Immunities, Art. 20. Under the E.C.S.C. Statute (Art. 14, para. 2) his immunities differed from those of the judges and Advocates General, in that the Registrar's were expressly made subject by E.C.S.C. Protocol on Immunities, Art. 11(a) to E.C.S.C. Treaty, Art. 40, para. 2. The effect of this is apparently expressly to give the Court jurisdiction over any case for damages arising out of the Registrar's personal fault, and also, in certain circumstances, to make the Community liable. As to E.C.S.C. Treaty, Art. 40, para. 2, see p. 217, below.

85 E.C.S.C. Statute, Art. 3, para. 2; E.E.C. Statute, Art. 3, para. 2; Euratom Statute, Art. 3, para. 2.

86 E.C.S.C. Statute, Art. 13; E.E.C. Statute, Art. 8; Euratom Statute, Art. 8.

87 E.C.S.C. Protocol on Immunities, Art. 13, para. 2, read with E.C.S.C. Statute, Art. 14, para. 2.

88 E.E.C. Protocol on Immunities, Art. 17, para. 2. Euratom Protocol on Immunities, Art. 17, para. 2.

89 In any event, the immunity may only be lifted when it would not be against the interests of the Communities to do so—E.C.S.C. Statute, Art. 14, para. 2 and Protocol on Immunities, Art. 13, para. 2; E.E.C. Protocol on Immunities, Art. 17, para. 2 and Euratom Protocol on Immunities, Art. 17, para. 2.

90 Rules, Art. 20.

91 Rules, Art. 19, para. 2. In the old Rules (Art. 12, para. 2) these officials were described as " officials of the Registry ": the use of this phrase has not been continued.

3. The Registrar, acting under the directions of the President, is responsible for receiving, sending and preserving all documents as well as for making the notifications required in carrying out the Rules of the Court.[92]

4. The Registrar assists the Court, its constituent Chambers, the President and the judges in all their official duties.[93]

5. Proceedings are instituted before the Court by means of a request addressed to the Registrar.[94] The Registrar is to ask the party concerned to produce any further documents needed in order that the request may comply with the requirements of the Statutes[95] or of the Rules.[96]

6. The Registrar is responsible for seeing that all communications relating to the written proceedings of a case are made to the parties concerned, as well as to the organs of the Community whose Decisions[97] are in dispute, in the sequence and within the time limits fixed by the Rules of Procedure.[98]

7. Where the Court is requested by a domestic court or tribunal to give a decision upon a preliminary question of the interpretation of the Economic Community or Euratom Treaties,[99] the Registrar notifies this request to the parties in the case, to the Member States and to the Commission of the relevant Community. He also notifies the relevant Council of Ministers if the validity or the interpretation of an act of that Council is in issue.[1]

8. Before each public sitting of the Court or Chamber, the Registrar draws up a cause list in the procedural language of the case in question.[2]

[92] Rules, Art. 16, para. 1. These include notifying the parties of the dates for the submission of documents in the written proceedings, the summoning of witnesses, etc. The Registrar is required to serve all documents on the person concerned at his chosen address at the place where the Court has its seat—Rules, Art. 79, para. 1.1. Copies of all original documents are certified correct by the Registrar—Rules, Art. 79, para. 1.2.
[93] Rules, Art. 16, para. 2.
[94] E.C.S.C. Statute, Art. 22, para. 1; E.E.C. Statute, Art. 19, para. 1; Euratom Statute, Art. 19, para. 1.
[95] E.C.S.C. Statute, Art. 22, para. 2; E.E.C. Statute, Art. 19, para. 2; Euratom Statute, Art. 19, para. 2. See further, p. 50, below.
[96] Rules, Art. 38, para. 7 and Instructions to the Registrar, Art. 5. When the request is an appeal against the decision of the Arbitration Committee set up under the Euratom Treaty, the Registrar invites the Registry of the Committee to forward to the Court the file of the case concerned—Rules, Art. 101, para. 2.
[97] The term " Decision " is here being used loosely; it presumably covers Regulations, Directives and Recommendations as well.
[98] E.C.S.C. Statute, Art. 21, para. 3; E.E.C. Statute, Art. 18, para. 3; Euratom Statute, Art. 18, para. 3.
[99] This appeal is brought under E.E.C. Treaty, Art. 177 or Euratom Treaty, Art. 150.
[1] E.E.C. Statute, Art. 20, para. 1; Euratom Statute, Art. 21, para. 1.
[2] This list contains: the date, hour and place of the sitting; particulars of the cases to be called; the names of the parties; the names and status of the agents, legal advisers and counsel of the parties—Instructions to the Registrar, Art. 7, para. 2. This cause list is put up at the entrance to the court room—*ibid*, Art. 7, para. 3.

9. The Registrar attends the deliberations of the Court when administrative matters are being decided unless the Court decides otherwise.[3]

10. The Registrar is required to ensure that at the request of one of the judges or of the Advocates General or of one of the parties, a translation into the official language of the Court chosen by them is made of anything said or written during the proceedings before either the Court or a Chamber.[4]

11. He is also to ensure that any evidence given by a witness or expert in a language other than one of the official languages is translated into the procedural language.[5]

12. The Registrar draws up a record of the deposition of each witness. After it has been read aloud, this record is signed by the witnesses, the President or by the *juge rapporteur*, and the Registrar.[6]

13. The Registrar also prepares a record of each hearing of the Court, whether held during the Instruction or during the oral proceedings.[7] This record is signed by the President and the Registrar.[8]

14. The Registrar, together with the President and the *juge rapporteur*, is required to sign the record of the judgment of the Court.[9]

15. The Registrar is in charge of the publication of official law reports of all the judgments of the Court.[10]

16. He also has wide powers to reduce any advance claimed from the Court Pay Office by witnesses or experts for their travel and subsistence, or advances claimed by way of free legal aid, or by counsel assigned to an assisted person by way of an advance of his expenses or fees.[11] It is also the Registrar who subsequently claims recovery of these sums advanced, from the party required to pay them by way of costs.[12]

---

[3] Rules, Art. 27, para. 7. The Registrar is excluded from the deliberations of the Court on all other matters—Rules, Art. 27, para. 2—and from the hearing itself when either a judge or an Advocate General is accused of no longer fulfilling the conditions or no longer satisfying obligations inherent in his position—Rules, Arts. 5 and 8.

[4] Rules, Art. 30, para. 1.

[5] Rules, Art. 29, para. 4.

[6] Rules, Art. 47, para. 6.

[7] This record is to contain: the date and place of the hearing; the names of the judges, Advocates General and Registrar present; particulars of the case; the names of the parties; the names and status of the agents, legal advisers, and counsel of the parties; the name, forenames, status and address of the witnesses or experts heard; particulars of documents produced by the parties during the hearing; the decisions of the Court or Chamber or of the President of the Court or Chamber given at the hearing—Instructions to the Registrar, Art. 7, para. 2.2.

[8] Rules, Art. 53, para. 1 and Art. 62, para. 1. These Rules elaborate E.C.S.C. Statute, Art. 27; E.E.C. Statute, Art. 30 and Euratom Statute, Art. 31.

[9] E.C.S.C. Statute, Art. 31; E.E.C. Statute, Art. 34; Euratom Statute, Art. 25.

[10] Rules, Art. 68.

[11] Instructions to the Registrar, as amended, Art. 21, para. 2.1 and 2 and para. 4.

[12] Instructions to the Registrar, as amended, Art. 22, paras. 1 and 2.

17.   The Registrar informs the Presidents of the Council of Ministers, the High Authority, the Commissions of the Economic and Euratom Communities and of the Assembly when one of the judges has been found no longer to fulfil the required conditions for being a member of the Court.[13]

18.   The Registrar, acting under the authority of the President, directs the officials and employees of the Court.[14]

19.   The Registrar is responsible for keeping the register of the Court in which are recorded all the steps in the procedure and all the exhibits submitted in support of them.[15]

20.   Reference to this entry in the register is made by the Registrar on the originals of all documents and, at the request of the parties to a dispute, on the copies as well.[16]

21.   The Registrar is responsible for the Court archives and for the publications of the Court. He also has the custody of the seals.[17]

22.   In case of dispute arising as to what papers and documents relate to proceedings before the Court, so as to be exempt from search and confiscation, the customs officials or police may seal them and they are then to forward them immediately to the Court in order that they may be examined in the presence of the Registrar.[18]

23.   In order that agents may benefit from the privileges, immunities and facilities granted to them,[19] an official document certifying their status issued by the State or the institution of the Community which they are representing must be sent to the Registrar.[20]

24.   In order that legal advisers, counsel or senior university teachers may also benefit from these privileges, etc., credentials certifying their status must be drawn up and signed by the Registrar.[21]

The Registrar may be relieved of his office only if he no longer fulfils the required conditions for holding it or if he no longer fulfils the

---

[13] E.C.S.C. Statute, Art. 7, para. 2; E.E.C. Statute, Art. 6, para. 2; Euratom Statute, Art. 6, para. 2.

[14] E.C.S.C. Statute, Art. 16, para. 1; E.E.C. Statute, Art. 11; Euratom Statute, Art. 11.

[15] Rules, Art. 15, para. 1; Instructions to the Registrar, Arts. 11 and 14. Registration is effected immediately after the document has been filed with the Registry—*ibid*. Art. 15, para. 2.1.   The entry in the register shall contain the necessary information for identification of the document and in particular: the date of entry; particulars of the case and the nature and date of the document—*ibid*. Art. 15, para. 3.1   These entries are made in the procedural language—*ibid*. Art. 15, para. 3.2.

[16] Rules, Art. 15, para. 2.

[17] Rules, Art. 17.

[18] Rules, Art. 32, para. 2a.2.

[19] Rules, Art. 32, para. 1.

[20] Rules, Art. 33(a).

[21] Rules, Arts. 33 and 36; Instructions to the Registrar, Art. 9, para. 2.

duties of his position.[22] Whether he should be so relieved is decided by the Court, after it has heard the Advocates General and allowed the Registrar the opportunity of presenting his comments.[23]

Should the Registrar cease to hold office before the end of the six-year period for which he was elected, the Court appoints his successor for a period of six years and not merely for the unexpired portion of his predecessor's term of office.[24]

The salary, allowances and pension of the Registrar are fixed by the Council of Ministers, acting by means of a qualified majority vote.[25]

DEPUTY REGISTRARS

The Court at any time may appoint one or more deputies to assist the Registrar.[26] The Rules specify [27] that they are to be appointed " following the procedure laid down for the Registrar." This clearly means that their mode of nomination and the manner of voting for them is to be the same as if a Registrar were being elected.[28] It is assumed that a deputy Registrar would be required to take the same oath and to give the same written undertaking as the Registrar, although it is suggested this does not fall within the above wording, as it has nothing to do with their election.[29]

Further, the Rules are silent upon how many deputies may be appointed, for how long they are to serve and how, once they are appointed, they can be dismissed. It is presumed that the provisions relating to the Registrar would apply, but the Rules have carefully avoided clarifying the position.

THE ASSISTANT *RAPPORTEURS*

At the present time there are no provisions for the appointment of assistant *rapporteurs*, but the Council of Ministers, acting by means of a

---

22 Rules, Art. 11, para. 6. As to these conditions and obligations, see p. 35, above.
23 Rules, Art. 11, para. 6.
24 Rules, Art. 11, para. 7.
25 E.C.S.C. Statute, Art. 5; E.E.C. Treaty, Art 154; Euratom Treaty, Art. 123. For this salary, etc., see pp. 561–571, below. In the case of the Coal and Steel Community, the Council was to act upon a proposal of a Committee of the Presidents of the four institutions. This provision has not been repeated in the case of the other two Treaties.
26 Rules, Art. 12.
27 *Ibid.*
28 See Rules, Art. 11, paras. 1 and 2, p. 35, above.
29 Under the old Rules (Art. 11, para. 1), it is expressly set out that the requirement of taking the oath applies both to the Registrar and to any deputy Registrars. Under the present Rules—Art. 11, para. 5—although it is set out that the Registrar must take the oath, all mention of the deputy Registrars doing so is for some reason omitted.

unanimous vote, on a proposal of the Court, may provide for their appointment [30] and lay down their terms of employment.[31]

The E.C.S.C. Treaty set out no qualifications which had to be fulfilled by these *rapporteurs*. This omission has now been remedied in the two later Treaties, which state that they are to possess every guarantee of independence and possess the necessary legal qualifications [32] —a term which is not defined. They are to be appointed by the Council of Ministers,[33] and, if appointed, they will be required principally to assist the President when he is considering the suspension of the execution of Decisions, etc., of the High Authority or of one of the two Commissions, and also to assist the *juges rapporteurs* in their tasks.[34] They will take part in the deliberation of the Court in any case in which they have been connected.[35]

Before taking up their duties, the assistant *rapporteurs* will be required to take the same oath as the judges,[36] and in the exercise of their duties they will be responsible to the President of the Court, the President of one of the Chambers or a *juge rapporteur*, according to which of these they are assisting.[37]

The *rapporteurs* will enjoy the same immunity from legal action as the judges, the Advocates General and the Registrar, as well as the same additional immunities from taxation and from immigration regulations for themselves and their family and the same exemption from import and export duties on their furniture and their car.[38] As in all other

[30] E.E.C. Statute, Art. 12, para. 1; Euratom Statute, Art. 12, para. 1. It was provided in the E.C.S.C. Statute (Art. 16, para. 2) that the conditions of the appointment of assistant *rapporteurs* were to be set out in the (old) Rules of the Court. These Rules, however, failed to do this.
[31] E.C.S.C. Statute, Art. 16, para. 2; E.E.C. Statute, Art. 12, para. 1; Euratom Statute, Art. 12, para. 1.
[32] E.E.C. Statute, Art. 12, para. 2; Euratom Statute, Art. 12, para. 2.
[33] E.C.S.C. Statute, Art. 16, para. 2; E.E.C. Statute, Art. 12, para. 2; Euratom Statute, Art. 12, para. 2.
[34] Rules, Art. 23, para. 2. Under the old Rules (Art. 19, para. 2) it was set out that they would also be required to assist the Court or one of the Chambers.
[35] Rules, Art. 27, para. 2.
[36] Rules, Art. 23, para. 4. For this oath, see note 18, p. 18, above. It is not stated, however, that they are also to take the solemn undertaking not to accept certain functions and advantages as is required of every other Court official. This omission it is suggested, is clearly an error.
[37] Rules, Art. 23, para. 3. This provision is the same as old Rules, Art. 19, para. 3, where the reference to the President of a Chamber had meaning in view of the fact that under those Rules the *rapporteurs* were expressly intended to assist a Chamber— see note 30, above. Either the reference to the President of the Chamber should have been removed from this paragraph, or the reference to assisting the Chambers should have been retained in Art. 23, para. 2.
[38] E.C.S.C. Statute, Art. 16, para. 3; E.E.C. Protocol on Immunities, Art. 20; Euratom Protocol on Immunities, Art. 20. See p. 27, above.

41

cases, this immunity is granted in the interest of the Community.[39] It may be lifted by the Court[40] if this may be done without injury to that interest.[41]

There are no provisions governing the dismissal of the assistant *rapporteurs.*

THE ATTACHÉS TO THE COURT

In addition to the above officials, the old Rules[42] set out that the Court might appoint, upon nomination of the President, the judges or the Advocates General, persons to be their *attachés*. It was further specified that the *attachés* were required to possess adequate legal training and that before entering upon their duties they were required to take an oath before the President of the Court. These persons, for some reason, are now no longer specifically mentioned.

---

39 E.C.S.C. Statute, Art. 16, para. 3 and Protocol on Immunities, Art. 13, para. 1, E.E.C. Protocol on Immunities, Art. 17, para. 1 and Art. 20; Euratom Protocol on Immunities, Art. 17, para. 1 and Art. 20.
40 See p. 29, above.
41 E.C.S.C. Statute, Art. 16, para. 3 and Protocol on Immunities, Art. 13, para. 2; E.E.C. Protocol on Immunities, Art. 17, para. 2 and Art. 20; Euratom Protocol on Immunities, Art. 17, para. 2 and Art. 20. The E.C.S.C. Statute (Art. 16, para. 3) also makes Art. 12 of the E.C.S.C. Protocol on Immunities applicable to the assistant *rapporteurs*. These provisions, however, create a difficulty. Their joint effect is that the President of the Court is to determine to which officials the immunities set out in the Protocol are to apply, and, if so, to what extent, and he is then to submit the list of these immunities to the Council of Ministers and also to inform the Governments of all the Member States. As, however, the extent to which the assistant *rapporteurs* enjoy immunity is set out in the E.C.S.C. Statute, the President can clearly not determine this himself. The only effect, therefore, of making Art. 12 of the Protocol applicable to the assistant *rapporteurs* would appear to be to require the President of the Court to inform the Council and the Governments of the Member States who are the *rapporteurs* who enjoy the immunities set out by the Treaty. The giving of this information, which in the E.C.S.C. Statute is done by the President of the Court, is in the other two Treaties to be done by the respective Commissions— E.E.C. Protocol on Immunities, Art. 15, para. 1; Euratom Protocol on Immunities, Art. 15, para. 1. It is thus not clear who now is supposed to perform it, unless the Commissions win by two Treaties to one.
42 Art. 20.

CHAPTER

3

THE PROCEDURE OF THE COURT

THE procedure of the Court is almost entirely laid down in its Rules which have been drawn up by the Court itself and unanimously approved by the Council of Ministers.[1]

The dates and times of the sittings of the Court are fixed by the President of the Court,[2] while those of the two Chambers are determined by their respective Presidents.[3] Both the Court itself and the Chambers, for one or more given sittings, may choose a place other than that where the Court has its seat.[4]

SESSIONS AND DELIBERATIONS OF THE COURT

The hearings of the Court are public.[5] However, under the E.C.S.C. Statute it is stated that the Court, for substantial reasons, may decide otherwise,[6] and the Statutes in the two later Treaties add that this decision may be taken either by the Court of its own motion or at the request of the parties.[7]

The Statute of the Court of Justice of the E.C.S.C. Treaty sets out [8] that appeals brought by States or by the Council of Ministers and disputes between the Member States, must in all cases be heard in

---

1 This approval was given on February 2, 1959 by the Councils of the Economic and Euratom Communities, and on March 2, 1959, by the Council of Ministers of the Coal and Steel Community. These Rules were published in the *Journal Officiel* of March 21, 1959, but were found to contain over 25 printing and other errors so that the entire Rules had to be re-published in the *Journal Officiel* of January 18, 1960, and even now they have not been adequately proof-read. In addition, certain " Instructions to the Registrar " were agreed upon by the Court on June 23, 1960, and amended by the Court on April 6, 1962: Supplementary Rules were agreed upon on March 9, 1962. A translation of all of the above is to be found on pp. 483–561, below. It should be noted that the Stationery Office has published the Instructions in their *un*amended form.

2 Rules, Art. 25, para. 1.

3 Rules, Art. 25, para. 2.

4 Rules, Art. 25, para. 3. Under the old Rules (Art. 23, para. 3) it was only the Chambers and not the Court as a whole which possessed this peripatetic power. It has never yet been used.

5 E.C.S.C. Statute, Art. 26; E.E.C. Statute, Art. 28, Euratom Statute, Art. 29.

6 Art. 26.

7 E.E.C. Statute, Art. 28; Euratom Statute, Art. 29. It is not clear whether this means that the parties are to be in agreement before they can make this request or whether this provision should read " at the request of one of the parties."

8 E.C.S.C. Statute, Art. 18, para. 3 and Art. 41, para. 3.

plenary session. Even although this provision is not repeated so as to cover similar cases arising under the other two Treaties, in practice the procedure has been the same in respect to them as well.

A hearing in plenary session means a hearing either by seven or by five judges, as the Court may validly sit only with an uneven number of judges [9] and the presence of five of them is required to constitute a quorum.[10] If this required number is not present, the President must adjourn the sitting until a quorum is present.[11] If after seven judges have heard a case, one of the seven is unable to take part in the consideration of the judgment, the most junior judge abstains from taking part in this consideration in order to create the required uneven number.[12]

The deliberations of the two Chambers of the Court require the presence of three judges.[13] If one of the judges is not present [14] the President of that Chamber informs the President of the Court who then appoints another judge to replace him.[15]

The Court and the two Chambers consider their judgments in private,[16] and only the judges who were present at the oral proceedings and, if required, the assistant *rapporteur* entrusted with the study of the case, take part in this consideration.[17] During this, each judge is required to express his opinion and set out the reasons upon which it is based.[18] A judge may require that any question to be decided shall be formulated in the official languages selected by him and communicated in writing to the Court or to the Chamber before being put to a vote.[19] In the event of a difference of opinion on the purpose, purport or upon the order of the questions it is decided by the Court or the Chamber, according to whichever is trying the case.[20]

---

[9] E.C.S.C. Statute, Art. 18, para. 2; E.E.C. Statute, Art. 15; Euratom Statute, Art. 15.

[10] *Ibid.*

[11] Rules, Art. 26, para. 2.

[12] Rules, Art. 26, para. 1. For the determination of the seniority of the judges, see Art. 4, p. 18, above.

[13] E.C.S.C. Statute, Art. 18, para. 2; E.E.C. Statute, Art. 15; Euratom Statute, Art. 15.

[14] Each Chamber only consists of three judges—Rules, Art. 24, para. 1.

[15] Rules, Art. 26, para. 3.

[16] Rules, Art. 27, para. 1.

[17] Rules, Art. 27, para. 2. Under the old Rules (Art. 25, para. 2) there was no limitation specifying that the judges must have attended the oral proceedings. It was clearly wrong, however, that a judge should have been able to take part in the decision of a case when he had not heard the evidence. In addition, under the old Rules (Art. 25, para. 2) other persons, by virtue of a special decision of the Court or of a Chamber, could be invited. This rule has been repealed.

[18] Rules, Art. 27, para. 3.

[19] Rules, Art. 27, para. 4. In practice the judges use French during their considerations.

[20] Rules, Art. 27, para. 6.

The decision of the Court [21] is arrived at by a majority vote, and the voting is done individually by each judge starting with the most junior and continuing in the reverse order of their seniority.[22] Any dispute about the interpretation of the voting is decided by the Court or the Chamber.[23]

When the Court is deciding upon "administrative matters," a term which presumably means administrative matters relating merely to the Court and not to the Communities,[24] the Advocates General take part and each has a vote. The Registrar of the Court is also required to attend unless the Court decides otherwise.[25]

THE VACATIONS OF THE COURT

By its Statutes, the Court sits permanently [26] but, unless by a special decision it should decide otherwise,[27] the Court does not sit from December 18 to January 10, or from the Sunday next before Easter to the second Sunday after Easter, or from July 15 to September 15.[28]

During these legal vacations, the control of affairs at the place where the Court has its seat is exercised by the President himself, who keeps in touch with the Registrar, but he may request one of the Presidents of the two Chambers or another judge to take his place.[29] However, at any time during these vacations, the President in a case of urgency may convene the judges and the Advocates General.[30]

In addition to this, the Court observes the official public holidays of the place where it has its seat.[31]

21 This rule presumably also covers the decisions of the Chambers, although it is nowhere stated that these speak for the Court as a whole.
22 Rules, Art. 27, para. 5. The seniority of the judges is set out in Art. 4 of the Rules—see p. 18, above.
23 Rules, Art. 27, para. 6.
24 Most administrative matters are either decided upon by the President, such as finance under Art. 22 of the Rules, or by the Registrar. It is doubted whether the raising of the immunity of the judges can strictly be called administrative.
25 Rules, Art. 27, para. 7. When the Registrar is excluded by the Court, and minutes of the proceedings are required, the task of taking them is entrusted to the junior judge present, and the record is signed by him and by the President—Rules, Art. 27, para. 8.
26 E.C.S.C. Statute, Art. 17; E.E.C. Statute, Art. 14; Euratom Statute, Art. 14.
27 The vacations of the Court are to be fixed subject to the exigencies of its business. E.C.S.C. Statute, Art. 17; E.E.C. Statute, Art. 14; Euratom Statute, Art. 14.
28 Rules, Art. 28, para. 1. It is not stated whether these dates are inclusive, though it may be assumed that they are.
29 Rules, Art. 28, para. 1.2.
30 Rules, Art. 28, para. 2. This power of convening the Court is not stated to be transferred to those who are deputising for the President during the vacations. It would appear to be tenable that by the strict letter of the Rules only the President can do this, or alternatively that his substitute can, as temporarily exercising his powers.
31 Rules, Art. 28, para. 3, and Appendix I, p. 543, below.

THE OFFICIAL LANGUAGES OF THE COURT

At a special conference of the six Member States, after an all-night session, it was decided that there should be four official languages for the Court—Dutch, French, German and Italian.[32] The choice of the language to be used for a particular case is basically the language chosen by the plaintiffs.[33] This is subject, however, to three exceptions. First, that if the defendant is a Member State, or a natural or legal person subject to the jurisdiction of a Member State, the procedural language is the official language of that State[34]; secondly, on the joint request of the parties concerned, the Court may authorise the use of another official language as the procedural language; thirdly, and notwithstanding the above, at the request of one party, and after the other party and the Advocate General have been heard, the Court or a Chamber may authorise the total or partial use of another official language as the procedural language.[35] This right, however, is not extended to any of the institutions of the Communities,[36] so that in every case in which they are the defendants, the language of the procedure will be that selected or agreed to by the plaintiffs.

Where a municipal court refers any matter relating to the interpretation of the Treaties or the validity of any acts done by the institutions of the Communities for the decision of this Court,[37] the language of the procedure is that of the municipal court itself.[38]

---

[32] This is now incorporated in the Rules, Art. 29, para. 1. The discussions upon the choice of an official language were carried on entirely in French.

[33] Rules, Art. 29, para. 2.1.

[34] Rules, Art. 29, para. 2.1. (a). Where there exists more than one official language of a State, the plaintiff has the option to choose whichever language suits him—*ibid.* This provision is inserted to cover the situation in Belgium where both French and Dutch (Flemish) are official languages. Under the old Rules (Art. 27, para. 4), the choice between these two languages was not left to the plaintiff, but the language to be employed was to be determined according to the Belgian law on the matter.

[35] Rules, Art. 29, para. 1.2 (c). The procedural language governs the language in which the original request and the other pleadings are to be made, as well as the language of any attached papers or documents, the written record of the proceedings and the decision of the Court—Rules, Art. 29, para. 3.1. Where any exhibits or documents are submitted in a language other than that of the procedure, they must be accompanied by a translation into that language—Rules, Art. 29, para. 3.2. However, in the case of bulky exhibits and documents, translations of extracts only may be submitted. However, at any time, the Court or a Chamber, either of its own motion or at the request of one of the parties, may require a more complete or a verbatim translation—Rules, Art. 29, para. 3.3.

[36] Rules, Art. 29, para. 2 (c).

[37] These matters are referred for the preliminary decision of the Court under E.C.S.C. Treaty, Art. 41; E.E.C. Treaty, Art. 177, para. 2 and Euratom Treaty, Art. 150, para. 2.

[38] Art. 29, para. 2.2. This language will of course be one of the official languages of the Communities Court.

As it is natural that the judges and others of the Court are not necessarily able to speak all four of the official languages, it is provided that the President of the Court, or the President of a Chamber, when directing the proceedings, as well as the *juge rapporteur* when presenting his report, and the judges and the Advocates General when they ask questions, and the Advocates General when they present their submissions, may all use an official language other than that of the procedural language.[39]

Further, any of the judges, or the Advocate General dealing with the case or one of the parties may request the Registrar to provide a translation into any of the official languages of anything said or written during the proceedings before the Court or before a Chamber.[40]

Again, the Court is required to authorise the use of another language, and not necessarily an official language, for those witnesses or experts who declare that they cannot adequately express themselves in one of the four official languages.[41]

In case of a dispute concerning different texts, the text in the procedural language is taken as authoritative except in the case of witnesses and experts heard in another language other than that of the procedure, when the copy in the language used by the witness or the expert is authoritative.[42]

The judgment of the Court as well as its publications are issued in all four official languages.[43]

In order to carry out all these numerous translations, the Court is required to set up a translation department of experts with an appropriate legal knowledge and an extensive knowledge of several of the official languages of the Court.[44]

REPRESENTATION

Member States and the institutions of the Community are required to be represented before the Court by an agent appointed for each case. According to the E.C.S.C. Statute,[45] these may be assisted by

---

39 Rules, Art. 29, para. 5. The Registrar has to ensure that there is a translation into the procedural language—*ibid.*
40 Rules, Art. 30, para. 1.
41 Rules, Art. 29, para. 4.
42 Rules, Art. 31. Under the old Rules (Art. 28, para. 4), only the translation of the witnesses' or experts' evidence into the procedural language was authoritative—one can now go behind this translation.
43 Rules, Art. 30, para. 2.
44 Rules, Art. 21. Under the old Rules (Art. 27, para. 5), the translators were required to have a perfect knowledge—*une connaissance parfaite*—of the languages. The Rules have compromised with reality when now there is merely required *une connaissance étendue.*
45 E.C.S.C. Statute, Art. 20, para. 1.

a counsel—*un avocat*—who must have been called to a Bar of one of the Member States.[46] In the two later Statutes, however, it is stated that in addition to this counsel, these parties may also be represented by a legal adviser—*un conseil*—who, it appears, need not be a member of a Bar.[47] Enterprises and other legal persons are in practice often represented by an agent,[48] although the right to such representation is not expressly set out in the Statute: however, unlike Member States and the institution of the Community, enterprises and other legal persons and all natural persons must be represented by a counsel from a Bar of one of the Member States.[49] They cannot be represented by a legal adviser. Senior university teachers of the Member States may plead before the Court on the same footing as counsel when the laws of their own State grant to them a right of audience in Court.[50] In that case such teachers, when appearing before the Court, enjoy the same privileges as those granted to counsel.[51]

IMMUNITIES OF THOSE APPEARING BEFORE THE COURT

The Statutes of the Court grant to agents, legal advisers and counsel such legal rights and guarantees as are necessary for the independent performance of their functions. The Rules elaborate this when they provide that not only agents representing States or institutions of the Community, but also legal advisers and counsel appearing before the

---

[46] E.C.S.C. Statute, Art. 20, para. 1; E.E.C. Statute, Art. 17, para. 1; Euratom Statute, Art. 17, para. 1. The distinction between an agent and a counsel as used in the present context is that an agent possesses the full legal power in relation to the proceedings to undertake commitments that are binding upon his principal, whereas a counsel does not have this power. The practical advantage of agents representing Member States and the organs of the Community is thus immediately apparent.

[47] E.E.C. Statute, Art. 17, para. 1; Euratom Statute, Art. 17, para. 1. The French states: " *L'agent peut être assisté d'un conseil ou d'un avocat inscrit à un barreau de l'un des états membres.*" It is, thus, not clear whether *inscrit* qualifies merely *avocat* or *conseil* as well. However, it is suggested that it does not, because any person who has been *inscrit* must be an *avocat*. The effect of this new provision, if it were ever to be applied to the United Kingdom, would seem to be that solicitors could appear before the Court if representing the British Government or, for example, one of the Commissions, although they could not appear for anyone else.

[48] The agent is usually a director of the plaintiff enterprise.

[49] E.C.S.C. Statute, Art. 20, para. 2; E.E.C. Statute, Art. 17, para. 2; Euratom Statute, Art. 17, para. 2. Counsel assisting or representing a party are required to deposit with the Registry a certificate that they are members of a Bar of one of the Member States—Rules, Art. 38, para. 3. Under the old Rules (Additional Rules on Agents and Advocates, Art. 4), such counsel could not take part in any act of procedure before this certificate had been produced.

[50] E.C.S.C. Statute, Art. 20, para. 5; E.E.C. Statute, Art. 17, para. 5; Euratom Statute, Art. 17, para. 5. It is assumed that this refers only to senior university teachers who, by virtue of their university position, are granted the right to plead in Court; if the United Kingdom acceded to the Statute, an English professor who was also a solicitor would thus appear not to have the right of audience before the Communities Court by virtue of this provision.

[51] Rules, Art. 36.

Court or before a judicial authority appointed by it, by virtue of a *commission rogatoire,* shall enjoy immunity from jurisdiction in respect of words spoken and writing produced by them in relation to the case or to the parties.[52] Further, all papers and documents relating to the proceedings are exempt from search and confiscation.[53] Agents, legal advisers and counsel have the right to be granted the currency and enjoy such freedom of movement as may be necessary for the carrying out of their tasks.[54] However, all these privileges, immunities and facilities are granted solely in the interest of the proceedings before the Court,[55] and the immunity can be waived by the Court when it considers that such waiver is not inconsistent with that interest.[56]

The Court by its Statutes is granted such powers of control over the counsel who appear before it as are normally accorded to courts and tribunals.[57] These powers are further defined in the Rules. These state[58] that any legal adviser or counsel whose conduct before the Court or a Chamber or a municipal judge is incompatible with the dignity of the Court, or who makes use of the rights which they enjoy by reason of their position for purposes other than those for which they were intended, may at any time be barred from the proceedings by an order of the Court or the particular Chamber, after it has heard the opinion of the Advocate General and after the defence of the legal adviser

---

52 Rules, Art. 32, para. 1.
53 Rules, Art. 32, para. 2 (a). Should there be any dispute, the customs or police officials may seal the papers and documents in question which must then be sent without delay to the Court in order that they may be verified in the presence of the Registrar and of the party concerned—*ibid.*
54 Rules, Art. 32, para. 2 (b) and (c).
55 Rules, Art. 34, para. 1.
56 Rules, Art. 34, para. 2. In order to enjoy the privileges, immunities and facilities set out above, agents must first prove their status by means of an official document issued by the State or the institution which they are representing; a copy of this is immediately to be sent to the Registrar of the Court by that State or institution—Rules, Art. 33 (a). Legal advisers, counsel and senior university teachers having the right to appear before the Court must prove their status by credentials signed by the Registrar of the Court. The validity of these credentials, which are issued for a fixed period, may be extended or shortened according to the length of the proceedings—Rules, Art. 33 (b) and Art. 36, and Instructions to the Registrar, Art. 9, para. 2. Should this be necessary for the smooth running of the proceedings, these credentials are to be transmitted to the legal adviser, counsel or senior university teacher as soon as the date for the opening of the oral proceedings has been set, or, at the request of the party concerned, at any other time following the filing with the Registry of the authority containing his appointment—Instructions to the Registrar, Art. 9, para. 1.
57 E.C.S.C. Statute, Art. 20, para. 4; E.E.C. Statute, Art. 17, para. 4; Euratom Statute, Art. 17, para. 4. The E.C.S.C. Statute, however, is expressly limited to counsel; the term "legal adviser" has only been introduced in the later Treaties.
58 Rules, Art. 35, para. 1.1.

or counsel has been ensured.[59]   Such an order is immediately enforceable.[60]   When the Court exercises this power, the proceedings are adjourned for a period set by the President in order to allow the party concerned to appoint another legal adviser or counsel.[61] This disciplinary measure may subsequently be repealed by the Court.[62]

THE WRITTEN PROCEEDINGS

PLEADINGS

The Statutes of the Court set out that in a case before the Court the proceedings shall be in two stages—one written, and the other oral.[63]

A case is instituted before the Court by means of a request addressed to the Registrar.[64]   This request [65] must contain the name and address of the plaintiff [66] and the status of the party signing the request, the name of the party against whom the request has been brought,[67] the subject-matter of the action,[68] the submission [69] and a short summary

---

59 Where a legal adviser or counsel is accused of such conduct before a municipal judge, it appears, on a strict interpretation, that either the Court or a Chamber can take the action set out. Alternatively, the judicial authority concerned can presumably impose penalties. In the original draft of this provision there was no mention of a municipal judge which made interpretation simpler.
60 Rules, Art. 35, para. 1.2. Under the old Rules (Art. 6, para. 2), the Court could also, under the same conditions, deprive counsel of the right of appearing before it for any period not exceeding two years.
61 Rules, Art. 35, para. 2.
62 Rules, Art. 35, para. 3. The provisions on disciplinary measures set out above are expressly made applicable to senior university teachers entitled to plead before the Court —Rules, Art. 36.
63 E.C.S.C. Statute, Art. 21, para. 1; E.E.C. Statute, Art. 18, para. 1; Euratom Statute, Art. 18, para. 1.
64 E.C.S.C. Statute, Art. 22, para. 1; E.E.C. Statute, Art. 19, para. 1; Euratom Statute, Art. 19, para. 1. For the opening times of the Registry, see p. 35, above. On request a receipt can be obtained—Instructions to the Registrar, Art. 4, para. 1. When the request is registered, a serial number shall be ascribed to the case, followed by the year and accompanied by mention either of the plaintiff's name or the subject-matter of the request—Instructions to the Registrar, Art. 12, para. 1. Cases are to be referred to by this number—*ibid.* E.g., the first case tried by the Court was Case 1–54, *French Government* v. *The High Authority.*
65 For Rules applying to every act of procedure, see p. 500, below.
66 In the E.C.S.C. Statute, this is stated in French as " *la demeure de la partie* "; in the two later Statutes as " *le domicile du requérant* "—E.C.S.C. Statute, Art. 22, para. 1 ; E.E.C. Statute, Art. 19, para. 1; Euratom Statute, Art. 19, para. 1.
67 This requirement was omitted in the E.C.S.C. Statute, Art. 22, para. 1.
68 " The Court . . . accepts the ability of a single appeal to embrace three decisions "— *French Government* v. *The High Authority* (Case 1–54) Vol. II. " The Statute (Article 22) and the Rules of the Court (Article 29, paragraph 3) do not require a plaintiff to cite the articles upon which he relies. It is sufficient that ' the facts and grounds and the submissions of the plaintiff' should be set out "—*Mlle Dineke Algera and others* v. *The Common Assembly* (Joint cases 7–56 and 3–57 to 7–57) Vol. II.   This is a reference to the old Rules: the present equivalent provision is Rules, Art. 38, para. 1.1, see p. 501, below.
" A general reference to what has been stated in another action is not sufficient in order that the request should comply with [Article 22 of the Statute and Article 38

---

69 See note on next page.

of the grounds relied upon.[70] However, if the request is not drawn up in the procedural language,[71] the Registrar will refuse to accept it or will immediately return it by registered post.[72]

Every procedural document must be dated [73] and the original must be signed by the agent or counsel of the party concerned.[74] Such documents must be submitted together with two copies for the Court and one further copy for each of the parties to the action.[75] In addition to this, the institutions of the Communities must produce translations into the other official languages of every procedural document, within the time limits fixed by the Court.[76]

Where the case concerns a request for the annulment of an explicit Decision of the High Authority or of an act of either of the two Commissions or of one of the three Councils of Ministers, a copy of this Decision or act must be attached.[77] Where the challenge is being

of the Rules], and even less when the reference . . . has been made without at the same time a request for the joining of the actions "—*Société des Charbonnages de Beeringen and others* v. *The High Authority* (Case 9–55) Vol. II.

[69] " Nothing prevents a plaintiff in one and the same action from presenting subsidiary submissions to cover the case where his main submissions are rejected "—*Mlle Dineke Algera and others* v. *The Common Assembly* (Joint Cases 7–56 and 3–57 to 7–57) Vol. II.

[70] E.C.S.C. Statute, Art. 22, para. 1 ; E.E.C. Statute, Art. 19, para. 1 ; Euratom Statute, Art. 19, para. 1. " The words ' a short summary of the grounds ' as used in these texts mean that the request must set out what the grounds are on which the appeal is based. It is necessary, therefore, that the grounds relied upon should be supported by the facts in the form in which they have been set out "—*Société Fives Lille Cail and others* v. *The High Authority* (Joint cases 19–60, 21–60, 2–61 and 3–61). In addition to the requirements set out in the Statutes, the request must contain an outline of the evidence, if any—Rules, Art. 38, para. 1 (e)—as well as the plaintiff's choice of address at the place where the Court has its seat and the name of the person who is authorised and who has agreed to accept service of all documents—Rules, Art. 38, para. 2. For further conditions governing the request, see note 79, p. 52, below.

[71] As to this procedural language, see p. 46, above.

[72] Instructions to the Registrar, Art. 4, para. 2. The President of the Court may, however, expressly authorise its receipt—*ibid.*

[73] Rules, Art. 37, para. 3.

[74] Rules, Art. 37, para. 1.1.

[75] Rules, Art. 37, para. 1.2. The duplicate copies must be certified correct by the party submitting them—*ibid.*

[76] Rules, Art. 37, para. 2. The term " every procedural document " is wide enough to require the institutions to translate the pleadings of their opponents, presumably free of charge. It appears that if documents are bulky, only one copy need be deposited with the Registry and the Registrar after consulting the *juge rapporteur* informs the parties that this copy may be seen at the Registry—Instructions to the Registrar, Art. 3, para. 3.3.

[77] E.C.S.C. Statute, Art. 22, para. 2 ; E.E.C. Statute, Art. 19, para. 2 ; Euratom Statute, Art. 19, para. 2, and Rules, Art. 38, para. 4. This provision has to be read, however, together with Rules, Art. 38, para. 2, see p. 502, below. The word used in the E.C.S.C. Statute is " Decision," and no mention is made of the case of requests for the annulment of Recommendations. In the two later Statutes this defect is corrected, with respect to those Statutes, by the substitution of the word " act " for the word " Decision." It is not essential that the request should state which one or more of the four classic grounds of appeal are being relied upon to

made against an implied Decision,[78] documentary evidence of the date
of the making of the request for action submitted to the institution
concerned must also be included.[79] Where the request is for the
annulment of an act of one of the institutions of the E.C.S.C. Community, that institution is required to transmit all relevant documents
to the Court.[80]

Where the Court is given jurisdiction in a particular matter by virtue
of a clause to that effect in any contract concluded by the Community
or on its behalf under either public or private law,[81] or where Member
States in a dispute connected with the application of any of the three
Treaties submit the case to the Court,[82] then the request must be
accompanied either by a copy of the clause conferring jurisdiction,
or of the submission agreement reached between the Member States
concerned.[83]

Finally, where the plaintiff is an enterprise or other legal person in
private law [84] there must be sent with the request the memorandum and
Articles of Association, together with proof that the powers granted to
counsel have been properly conferred by a representative authorised
to do so.[85]

justify the annulment. " The presentation of these grounds for bringing appeals
may be allowed by virtue of their substance rather than of their legal classification,
on condition, however, that it is sufficiently clear from the request which of the
grounds referred to in the Treaty is being relied upon "—*Société Fives Lille Cail
and others* v. *The High Authority* (Joint Cases 19–60, 21–60, 2–61 and 3–61).

78 Under E.C.S.C. Treaty, Art. 35, para. 3; E.E.C. Treaty, Art. 175, para. 3;
Euratom Treaty, Art. 148, para. 3.

79 E.C.S.C. Statute, Art. 22, para. 2; E.E.C. Statute, Art. 19, para. 2; Euratom
Statute, Art. 19, para. 2. The prior request to the High Authority is required
by E.C.S.C. Treaty, Art. 35, paras. 1 and 2, and the request to the other institutions
by E.E.C. Treaty, Art. 175, para. 2, and Euratom Treaty, Art. 148, para. 2. If the
required documents have not been annexed to the request, the Registrar is to ask
the party concerned to produce them within a reasonable period, but a case may
not be struck out even where the request is regularised after the expiration of the
time limit for appealing—E.C.S.C. Statute, Art. 22, para. 2; E.E.C. Statute, Art. 19,
para. 2; Euratom Statute, Art. 19, para. 2.

80 E.C.S.C. Statute, Art. 23. Strangely enough this provision is not repeated in the
other two Statutes so as to apply to the Commissions or the Councils of the
Economic or Euratom Communities.

81 By virtue of E.C.S.C. Treaty, Art. 42; E.E.C. Treaty, Art. 181, or Euratom Treaty,
Art. 153.

82 By virtue of E.C.S.C. Treaty, Art. 89; E.E.C. Treaty, Art. 182, or Euratom Treaty,
Art. 154.

83 Rules, Art. 38, para. 6.

84 The distinction between public and private law, fortunately, does not yet exist in
English law.

85 Rules, Art. 38, para. 5. This provision was not included in the old Rules. The
Court of its own motion will ensure that the above provisions are complied with
" because the requirements governing the form of requests do not merely affect
the interests of the parties, but also the means for the Court to exercise its legal
control "—*Société Fives Lille Cail and others* v. *The High Authority, supra.*

Within one month of being served with the plaintiff's request, the defendants are required to submit their defence.[86] However, this time limit may be extended by the President on the request of the defendants upon good cause being shown.[87] The defence must set out the facts and the law that are being relied upon, the submissions of the defendants and an outline of their evidence.[88] Under the old Rules,[89] it was an express requirement that the defence should contain an admission or denial of the facts alleged by the plaintiff. This requirement, for no apparent reason, is no longer set out in the Rules. It can hardly be believed, however, that such admission or denial is not intended to be made any more, for without it the issue between the parties can never be narrowed down.

The original request and the defence having been submitted, the plaintiff may then submit his reply and the defendants may answer this in their rejoinder.[90] The President of the Court sets the dates by which these acts of procedure shall be submitted.[91]

In the reply and the rejoinder, the parties may put forward further evidence in support of their arguments, but if they do, reasons must be given for the delay in this presentation.[92]

After the submission of the rejoinder, the President fixes the date on which the *juge rapporteur* is to present his preliminary report upon whether the case requires the holding of an Instruction.[93] The Court, after hearing the Advocate General, decides whether to proceed to measures of instruction.[94] If, however, the Court should decide against this, it proceeds straight to the oral proceedings,[95] the President setting a date for it to be held.[96]

---

[86] Rules, Art. 40, para. 1. Procedural documents and documents relating thereto shall be served on the parties—Instructions to the Registrar, Art. 3, para. 3.1.
[87] Rules, Art. 40, para. 2.
[88] Rules, Art. 40, para. 1. The defence must also set out the name and address of the defendants, their choice of address at the place where the Court has its seat and the name of the person who has been authorised to accept service of all documents and who has agreed to do so. Further, if the defendant is a legal person in private law, the defence must have attached to it the defendant's memorandum and articles of association, and proof that the powers granted to counsel have been properly conferred by a representative authorised to do so—Rules, Art. 40, para. 1.2.
[89] Old Rules, Art. 31, para. 1.
[90] Rules, Art. 41, para. 1.   [91] Rules, Art. 41, para. 2.
[92] Rules, Art. 42, para. 1. This provision was not included in the Rules of the previous Court of the E.C.S.C.
[93] Rules, Art. 44, para. 1.1. If no rejoinder or no reply has been submitted within the time limit fixed by the President, or if the party concerned states that it is waiving its right to submit either of these pleadings, the President, either after the end of the time limit, or after the renunciation, will fix the above mentioned date—Rules, Art. 44, para. 1.2.
[94] Rules, Art. 44, para. 1.1.
[95] Rules, Art. 44, para. 2.2.
[96] *Ibid.*

53

AMENDMENT OF THE PLEADINGS

If the request does not comply with the above conditions, the Registrar fixes a reasonable period for the plaintiffs to regularise the request or to produce any necessary further documents.[97] If the plaintiffs do neither of these two things the Registrar refers the matter to the President[98] and the Court, after hearing the Advocate General, decides whether as a result of the non-compliance with these conditions, it must refuse to entertain the request as being bad in form.[99]

NEW GROUNDS OF APPEAL

Although in their reply and rejoinder the parties may put forward further evidence in support of their arguments, the submission of fresh arguments is prohibited unless these arguments are based upon points of law or of fact which have come to light during the written proceedings.[1] If the submission of such arguments is made, the President, acting on the report of the *juge rapporteur*, and after hearing the Advocate General, may grant to the other party a time limit within which to reply.[2] Apart from this one exception, there can be no submission of fresh arguments after the filing of the request or the defence respectively.[3] However, the Court has drawn a distinction between what is a new ground of appeal, which is inadmissible, and an extension or elaboration of an existing ground. This may be illustrated by the following extract from a judgment.[4]

> The plaintiffs did not at first dispute that the trading regulations embodied in their agreement constituted a restriction of competition requiring to be authorised. It was only for the first time in their

---

[97] Rules, Art. 38, para. 7. The Registrar fixes the time limit by registered letter with an acknowledgment of receipt—Instructions to the Registrar, Art. 5, para. 1.2. Where the original request is amended or further documents are supplied, notice of this is sent to the defendants—Rules, Art. 39.

[98] Instructions to the Registrar, Art. 5, para. 1.3.

[99] Rules, Art. 38, para. 7.

[1] Rules, Art. 42, para. 2.1. It is difficult to see what is meant by a new point of law coming to light during the written proceedings. It should also be noted that, in terms, this provision does not distinguish between a new fact occurring and a previously existing fact " coming to light."

[2] Rules, Art. 42, para. 2.2. The decision upon the admissibility of the fresh argument is reserved until the final judgment—Rules, Art. 42, para. 2.3.

[3] " Under no circumstances can the grounds of an appeal be modified in the reply even in a subsidiary manner "—*De Gazamenlijke Steenkolenmijnen in Limburg* v. *The High Authority* (Case 17–57), see Vol. II, below. " The plaintiff's . . . subsidiary contentions have, moreover, been presented only in their reply, that is to say, after the time limits stated in Article 22 of the Statute and Article [38, para. 1] of the Rules of the Court, and are already inadmissible for this reason "—*Friedrich Stork et Cie* v. *The High Authority* (Case 1–58) Vol. II. See also *Charbonnages de Beeringen and others* v. *The High Authority* (Case 9–55) Vol. II.

[4] " *Geitling* " *and others* v. *The High Authority* (Case 2–56) Vol II.

reply that they alleged that the clause in question did not of itself impose any restriction and that it did not, therefore, require to be authorised.

This contention is valid as a development of the claim of violation of Article 65 alleged in the request and it should not be regarded as an independent ground of appeal liable to be rejected under Article 22 of the Statute of the Court as being out of time.[5]

However, although plaintiffs may not have pleaded a particular contention in their request, so that it cannot subsequently be raised, it appears that if the contention involves the public interest, the Court, of its own motion, will consider that contention. As yet this has only occurred in one case.[6] The Court declared:

In a memorial submitted on November 11, 1957, the plaintiffs have, for the first time, based their appeal upon the ground of violation of a substantial procedural requirement on account of the insufficient reasoning of the Decision challenged.

By the terms of Article 22 of the E.C.S.C. Statute of the Court and of Article [38, para. 1] of its Rules, the request must contain a summary of the arguments alleged.

The provisions involve the inadmissibility of a ground of appeal which has not been set out in the request.

The Court rejects, furthermore, the plaintiffs' argument by which the general ground of discrimination, on which the appeal is based, includes the ground of violation of a substantial procedural requirement. In fact, this has nothing in common with, or even any resemblance to, the latter.

However, the obligation to give reasons for Decisions which Article 15 of the E.C.S.C. Treaty imposes upon the High Authority is provided not only for the benefit of the parties concerned but also with a view to placing the Court in a position freely to exercise the legal control which the Treaty confers upon it.

In consequence, a possible failure to give reasons which prevents this legal control may be and must be considered by the Court of its own motion.[7]

5 For a further consideration of the difference between a new ground of appeal and an elaboration of a ground also made, see *Compagnie des Hauts Fourneaux de Chasse* v. *The High Authority* (Case 2–57) Vol. II, below. In one request a claim for "compensation for giving up office, with all legal consequences" was held by the Court to have been "intended to take into account all the pecuniary consequences" so that it was permissible for the plaintiff's reply to specify what these were, including a claim for interest on the sums claimed—*Alberto Campolongo* v. *The High Authority* (Joint Cases 27–59 and 34–59), see Vol. II, below. Where in their request, plaintiffs claimed compensation for an injury caused to them by the High Authority, the Court declared: "It is not necessary to add to the subject-matter of the claim . . . legal arguments relied upon to show the existence of a *Faute de service*, because these arguments can be completed and developed during the proceedings"—*Société Commerciale Antoine Vloebergs* v. *The High Authority* (Joint Cases 9 and 12–60).
6 *Nold K.G.* v. *The High Authority* (Case 18–57) Vol. II.
7 *Ibid.* Vol. II. Author's italics.

Even if a claim is not pleaded in the request, and there exists no element of public interest, the Court may not be restricted by the pleadings if the Court is exercising its power in *pleine juridiction*.

Thus in a case in *pleine juridiction*, the plaintiffs had not expressly requested the reduction of a fine which had been imposed upon them, but had set out that their enterprise was only of a modest size. The Court stated:

> Even in the absence of any formal request, the Court is authorised to reduce the amount of an excessive fine, *when to do so would not go beyond the limits of the request, but on the contrary would have the result of partially amplifying the request.*[8]

This limitation was not referred to in a later case where the Court declared [9]:

> The plaintiff asks that the defendant may be condemned to pay damages for loss of reputation. In accordance with Article 38, para. (1) (d) of the Rules of Procedure of the Court of Justice of the European Communities the submissions of the plaintiff must be contained in the request.
>
> The aforesaid submission was presented for the first time in the written observations of the plaintiff in connection with the Instruction ordered by the Court on June 20, 1960, and is not impliedly contained in the submission set out in the request. Thus this submission must be considered as out of time, and therefore inadmissible.
>
> However, as the present instance concerns an appeal in *pleine juridiction*, the Court, even in the absence of valid submissions, is invested with a power not only to annul, but also, if there are grounds, of its own motion, to condemn the defendant to pay damages for the loss of reputation caused by its *faute de service.*

JOINDER OF ACTIONS

At any time the Court, after it has heard the parties and the Advocate General,[10] may join two or more actions pending where these actions relate to the same subject.[11] This joinder may be for the written or oral proceedings [12] or for the final judgment. Once joined, a case may nevertheless be once more separated.[13]

---

[8] *Acciaierie Laminatoi Magliano Alpi (A.L.M.A.)* v. *The High Authority* (Case 8–56) Vol. II. Author's italics.

[9] *R. P. M. Fiddelaar* v. *The Commission of E.E.C.* (Case 44–59) Vol. II.

[10] In the Rules this is phrased in the singular, but both Advocates General may have to be heard where both are concerned in one or more cases affected by the proposed joinder.

[11] Rules, Art. 43.

[12] It appears clear that the term " oral proceedings " is here being used to cover the Instruction. See further p. 72, note 51, below.

[13] Rules, Art. 43.

THIRD PARTY INTERVENTION

Under the E.C.S.C. Treaty, any natural or legal person [13a] is granted the right to intervene in any action provided that he can show that he has an interest in the result of the case,[14] although the Court has expressly limited the right of enterprises to intervene.[15] Of the reason for this provision the Court has declared:

> In the interest of an efficient administration of justice and of definite legal relations it is necessary to prevent as much as possible persons interested in the outcome of a case pending before the Court asserting this interest after the judgment has been pronounced and the issue has been settled.
>
> It is precisely in order to meet this requirement that Article 34 of the Protocol of the Statute of the Court allows all those who have a valid interest in the result of a case before the Court to intervene voluntarily in that case, provided their submissions seek either to support or reject the submissions of a party to the dispute.[16]

What will amount to " an interest " is not defined, and will necessarily differ according to the nature of the particular case.

> Although it cannot be denied that every Member State, by being a signatory to the Treaty and responsible for its application, is interested in the compliance with the principle of free circulation, it is equally true that the general interest in the observance of the Treaty would not justify voluntary intervention in any particular case. Indeed, the interest in intervening in an action before the Court must be justified both in relation to the nature of the case in which the intervener wishes to take part and in relation to the submissions of one of the parties which the intervener must either support or reject.[17]

The two later Treaties, however, limit the equivalent right in respect of the Economic and Euratom Communities by setting out that while Member States and the institutions of these two Communities may intervene in cases before the Court, natural and legal persons may not intervene in any case between Member States themselves, between the

---

13a The term " any person " has been held wide enough to include the *Assemble permanente des président de chambres d'agriculture,* an unincorporated body—see Order of the Court in *Confédération Nationale des Producteurs de Fruit et Légumes and others* v. *The Council of E.E.C.* (Joint Cases 6 and 17–62).

14 E.C.S.C. Statute, Art. 34, para. 1. " Contrary to the contention advanced by the defendants in the principal action, nothing . . . justifies the view that the interest of the intervening party must be distinct from that of the party which they support " —Order of the Court in *Confédération Nationale des Producteurs de Fruit et Légumes and others* v. *Council of E.E.C., supra.*

15 See p. 401, below.

16 *Belgian Government* v. *Antoine Vloebergs and the High Authority* (Request to modify judgment in Joint Cases 9–60 and 12–60) [1963] C.M.L.R. 44 at p. 56.

17 *Ibid.* at pp. 56–57. The above statement was repeated in *Breedband N.V.* v. *Société des Acieries du Temple and the High Authority* (Joint Cases 42–59 and 49–59) [1963] C.M.L.R. 60 at p. 70.

institutions of those Communities or between Member States and institutions of those two Communities.[18]

Requests for leave to intervene [19] must be submitted to the Registry before the opening of the oral proceedings.[20]

Where a party is intervening under its right to do so contained in the E.C.S.C. Treaty, it may seek in its request either to support or to reject the arguments of a party to the action,[21] but where the intervention is being made under either of the other two Treaties, the intervening party is expressly limited to supporting the arguments of one of the parties.[22]

By the Rules, the intervening party must accept the case as it finds it at the time of its intervention.[22a] In one case,[22b] the German Government intervened to support the High Authority who were the defendants; its request to intervene, however, was only lodged after the written pleadings in the main case had been closed. The plaintiffs, relying not only upon the fact that, by the above Rule, the Government was required to accept the case at the stage that it had reached, but also upon the fact that by the Rules additional arguments not outlined in the defence cannot be admitted,[22c] contended that the Government as an intervening party could not raise any new arguments either. Indeed, in the case in question, the German Government sought to support the High Authority by maintaining an argument from which that Authority expressly wished

---

[18] E.E.C. Statute, Art. 37, paras. 1 and 2; Euratom Statute, Art. 38, paras. 1 and 2.

[19] Request for leave to intervene must contain, in addition to the submissions being made, particulars of the case and of the parties, the name and address of the intervening party, a summary of the reasons establishing the interest of the intervening party in the outcome of the case and an outline of its evidence and documents in support. It must also state the intervening party's chosen address at the place where the Court has its seat—Rules, Art. 93, para. 2.

[20] Rules, Art. 93, para. 1. Under the old Rules (Art. 71, para. 1) requests had to be submitted before the closing of the written proceedings. This change in the wording will give a considerably extended time for intervention, especially if an Instruction is held, as an Instruction is held after the written proceedings are closed and before oral proceedings are opened.

[21] E.C.S.C. Statute, Art. 34, para. 2. The Court has expressly left open the question of whether the intervening party can advance arguments that the principal action is inadmissible—*Groupement des Industries Sidérurgiques Luxembourgeoises* v. *The High Authority* (Joint Cases 7–54 and 9–53) Vol. II.

[22] E.E.C. Statute, Art. 37, para. 3; Euratom Statute, Art. 38, para. 2. There would appear to be no reason for this distinction between the three Treaties. The provision in the E.E.C. and Euratom Treaties appears to enable the intervening party to argue for the rejection of the contentions of one of the parties, provided that he is thereby *supporting* an argument already advanced, but that if he advanced new arguments these would not be accepted as they would be arguments for rejection and not arguments in support of a rejection. This appears to be a most unprofitable distinction, but one forced upon the Court by this provision.

[22a] Rules, Art. 93, para. 5.1.

[22b] *De Gazamenlijke Steenkolenmijen in Limburg* v. *The High Authority* (Case 30–59), Vol. II.

[22c] Rules, Art. 42, para. 2.1, see p. 54, above.

to disassociate itself. The plaintiffs' contention was dismissed by the Court: It stated:

The request to intervene submitted by the Government of the Federal Republic of Germany was declared admissible by Order of the Court dated February 18, 1960.

The plaintiffs consider that because Article 93, para. 5 of the Rules of Procedure requires the intervening party to accept the action at the state at which it was at the time of its intervention, the intervening party was not free, at the time when it made its intervention, which was after delivery of the rejoinder, to put forward a basic argument contrary to those of the party which it is seeking to support.

The plaintiffs, however, refrain from relying upon Article 93, (para. 5), in order not to prevent the Court from examining the arguments set out in the request.

The question must be examined by the Court of its own motion.

By the terms of Article 34 of the Protocol on the Statute of the Court of Justice, the submissions of a request to intervene may have no other object than the support of the submissions of one of the parties or their rejection.

The Government of the Federal Republic of Germany in its intervention supports the defendant's submissions and the arguments on which it relies, and although these are different from those of the defendants, they seek the rejection of the plaintiffs' submissions.

It would deprive the intervention procedure of all meaning if the intervening party were prevented from advancing any argument which had not been employed by the party which it supports.

In these circumstances, the arguments put forward by the Government of the Federal Republic of Germany in its intervention are admissible.[22d]

In order to draw the attention of parties, who might wish to intervene, to the fact that a particular case has been submitted, the Court publishes in the *Journal Officiel* the name and address of the parties, the subject of the action and the particular grounds of appeal, such as violation of the Treaty, etc., which are being relied upon, but without specifying any of the arguments or facts being alleged.[23]

[22d] *Ibid*. Vol. II.
[23] This provision was only accepted by the Court in 1954—*Journal Officiel*, July 20, 1954. Before then, there had been an unfortunate duplication of actions. Thus, the French Government, the Italian Government, ASSIDER and I.S.A. all appealed against the same decision of the High Authority—see Cases 1–54, 2–54, 3–54 and 4–54, Vol. II.

When a request to intervene has been received, it is served on the parties to the principal action, who are then enabled to submit their written or oral observations concerning the request.[24] Following this, the Court, after it has heard the Advocate General, gives a ruling upon the admissibility by means of an order.[25]

If the Court allows the intervention, the intervening party receives from the Court a copy of all the procedural documents that have already been served on the parties,[26] and the President fixes a time limit by which the intervening party may set out in writing the arguments supporting its submissions, and also the time within which the original parties to the case may reply.[27]

PRELIMINARY OBJECTIONS [28]

If a party wishes to request the Court to determine upon a preliminary objection without undertaking a consideration of the merits of the case, it must make its application in a document separately from the other pleadings.[29]

Under the old Rules,[30] the bringing of such a request was expressly declared to suspend the procedure upon the merits generally. This provision has not been carried over into the new Rules, but it is perhaps to be implied, because, upon the introduction of a preliminary objection, the President specifies the time within which the other party is to present its defence and its submissions, and that other party can hardly be expected to fight both the objection and the main action at the same time.[31] The Court in this matter is not limited to the contentions raised by the parties, but can at any time,[32] of its own motion, examine whether the request should be rejected on the grounds of public policy.[33]

---

[24] Rules, Art. 93, para. 3. Under the old Rules (Art. 71, para. 3), these observations could not have been made orally. The time within which observations were to be made was, under the old Rules, to be decided upon by the Court—*ibid.* This provision is not repeated in the present Rules, but is presumably to be implied.

[25] Rules, Art. 93, para. 3.   [26] Rules, Art. 93, para. 4.

[27] Rules, Art. 93, para. 5.2. Under the old Rules (Art. 71, para. 4), the request to intervene was to be examined by the Court, but if the parties had not disputed the right to intervene the Court might decide that an oral hearing should not take place. These provisions have not been included in the present Rules, but it appears that something similar is implied by Art. 93, para. 3.

[28] *Exceptions.*

[29] Rules, Art. 91, para. 1.1. This application must contain a summary of the main legal and factual arguments upon which it is based, as well as the relief sought and, annexed, thereto, the documents relied upon in support—Rules, Art. 91, para. 1.2.

[30] Old Rules, Art. 69, para. 4.

[31] It would appear, however, that the omission of the provision providing for suspension does mean that the time periods for the main case continue to run despite the raising of this objection.

[32] It is assumed that the phrase " at any time "—*à tout moment*—does not mean even after it has once given a decision upon the admissibilty of the objection.

[33] Rules, Art. 92. This provision is new. No definition of public policy is given.

After the Court has heard the parties [34] and the Advocate General, it gives a ruling on the application, or joins it to the merits.[35] If the Court accepts a preliminary objection, the case before the Court is automatically ended,[36] but if it rejects it, or joins it to the merits, the President fixes new time limits for the continuation of the case.[37]

Further, at any time, one of the parties may apply to the Court for a ruling upon a preliminary issue of fact,[38] and if this should occur all the above provisions apply as if the application had raised a preliminary objection.[39]

THE WITHDRAWAL OF A CASE

Under the old Rules,[40] in any action other than one seeking the annulment of an administrative act, where, before the Court had given judgment, the parties reached an agreement out of Court on the solution to be given to their dispute, and informed the Court that they renounced all claims against each other, the Court, it was stated, would give effect to their agreement,[41] and would order the case to be struck off the Register. The present Rules, however, when repeating this Rule, omit the phrase that the Court will give effect to their agreement, and the Court is now in terms merely required to strike the case off the Register.[42]

---

[34] Unless the Court decides to the contrary, the remainder of the proceeding upon these applications is to be oral—Rules, Art. 91, para. 3.

[35] Rules, Art. 91, para. 4.1. For an example of an objection being joined to the merits of a case, see *Société Metallurgique de Knutange* v. *The High Authority* (Joint Cases 15–59 and 29–59) Vol. II.

[36] This was specifically stated in the old Rules (Art. 69, para. 6.2). For an example, of a case thus ended see *Confédération Nationale des Producteurs de Fruits et Légumes and others* v. *The Council of E.E.C.* (Joint Cases 16–62 and 17–62) [1963] C.M.L.R. 160.

[37] Rules, Art. 91, para. 4.2.

[38] *Incident.*

[39] Rules, Art. 91, para. 1.1.

[40] Old Rules, Art. 80, paras. 1 and 2.

[41] *La Cour leur donne acte de leur accord.* The exact significance of this provision was not clear, but it seems plain that the compromise was in no way given the force of a Court judgment.

[42] Rules, Art. 77, para. 1. Under the old Rules this provision did not apply to actions for annulment of administrative acts. Presumably, therefore, the present Rule was similarly intended not to apply to such actions. However, there has been an oversight in the wording of Rules, Art. 77, para. 2. The old Rule provided: "The provisions of the present article shall not apply to appeals for annulment." The present Rule states: "This provision shall not apply to proceedings referred to in Articles 33 and 35 of the E.C.S.C. Treaty, Articles 173 and 175 of the E.E.C. Treaty, and Articles 146 and 148 of the E.A.E.C. Treaty." Although these provisions in the two later Treaties govern actions for the annulment of express or implied acts not only of the Commissions but of the two Councils of Ministers, the articles cited of the E.C.S.C. Treaty are not the equivalent ones, as they deal only with appeals against the High Authority—appeals against the Council of Ministers of that Community are dealt with under Art. 38, and, therefore, unintentionally slip through this provision.

Where a party is seeking the annulment of an administrative act, it may at any time unilaterally give written notice to the Court that it wishes to discontinue its action and the Court then orders the case to be struck out from the Register.[43]   The same provision applies in any other action as an alternative to a joint submission of a compromise.[44]

THE INSTRUCTION

After the submission of the rejoinder by the defendants, the written proceedings are concluded,[45] and the President of the Court fixes the date on which the *juge rapporteur* is to present his preliminary report upon whether the case requires an Instruction.[46]   After the Court has heard the Advocate General, it decides whether it is necessary to proceed to measures of instruction.[47]

If an Instruction is decided upon, it is held either before the Court or before one of the Chambers,[48] or the Court may even entrust it to the *juge rapporteur* himself.[49] Before the Instruction is so held, however, the Court, after it has again heard the Advocate General, determines by means of an order what are the facts which are to be proved, and this order is served on the parties.[50]

The measures of instruction include the personal appearance of the parties, the request for information and for the production of documents, the evidence of witnesses, the compiling of an experts' report [51] and a visit to the site.[52]

HOLDING THE INSTRUCTION BEFORE THE COURT

Where the Court decides to hold the Instruction before itself, witnesses are subpoenaed by an order of the Court specifying in outline the

[43] Rules, Art. 78.   As to costs incurred prior to the withdrawal, see p. 97, below.
[44] *Ibid.* Under the old Rules (Art. 81, para. 2), this withdrawal could not have been made after the defendant had filed either its defence or raised a preliminary objection—the desirability of removing that rule appears self-evident.
[45] If the party concerned has renounced its right of presenting a reply or a rejoinder, or if these have not been submitted within the prescribed time limits, the written proceedings are concluded at the date of the renunciation or of the expiry of the time limit, and the President may exercise his power as from that date—Rules, Art. 44, para. 1.2.
[46] Rules, Art. 44, para. 1.1.   [47] Rules, Art. 44, para. 1.1.
[48] Rules, Art. 44, para. 2.1.   Under the old Rules (Art. 35, para. 1), it was merely a Chamber of the Court that decided upon whether an Instruction was to be held.
[49] Rules, Art. 45, para. 3.1.   [50] Rules, Art. 45, para. 1.
[51] *Une expertise*, see p. 69 below.
[52] Rules, Art. 45, para. 2.   It is assumed, despite the wording of this provision—*les mesures d'instruction comprennent*—that not all these measures of instruction will be required in each case.   Under the old Rules (Art. 35, para. 2.1.), the ordering of the only two measures of instruction there specified, namely, the supplying of information and the personal appearance of the parties, was made optional upon the Chamber—*la Chambre peut ordonner.*

facts upon which the witnesses are to be heard.[53] After verification of the identity of the witnesses, the President informs them that they will be required to give their evidence on oath.[54] The witnesses are heard by the Court after notice has been given to the parties to be present.[55] After they have given their evidence, the President, either for himself or at the request of one of the parties, may put questions to the witness,[56] as also may each of the other judges and the Advocate General.[57]

If the Court should order an expert's report, an order of the Court is drawn up appointing the expert, specifying his terms of reference and fixing a time limit within which his report is to be presented.[58] A copy of this order is given to the expert together with all necessary documents.[59] The expert is placed under the orders of the *juge rapporteur*, who may be present during the investigations involved in the report, and who is required to be kept informed of the progress of the expert in the task assigned to him.[60]

If the expert so requests, the Court may decide to hear witnesses, and if so, they are summoned and heard in the manner set out above.[61]

After the expert has presented his report,[62] the Court may order that the expert should be heard, after notice has been given to the parties to attend.[63] This hearing of the expert, however, may take place before a *commission rogatoire*, either if the Court so decides or if the parties so request.[64]

[53] Rules, Art. 47, para. 2.1(b). For the full provisions concerning the calling of witnesses, see pp. 66–69, below.
[54] Rules, Art. 47, para. 4.1. The oath itself, however, is not taken until after the evidence has been given—Rules, Art. 47, para. 5.1.
[55] Rules, Art. 47, para. 4.2 and Art. 46, para. 3.
[56] Rules, Art. 47, para. 4.2.
[57] Rules, Art. 47, para. 4.3. Under the old Rules (Art. 42), the agents or counsel of the parties, with the permission of the President, could cross-examine the witnesses. This provision has been repealed, and all such examination has now to be carried out via the President.
[58] Rules, Art. 49, para. 1.
[59] Rules, Art. 49, para. 2.
[60] Rules, Art. 49, para. 2.
[61] Rules, Art. 49, para. 3. As Art. 47 of the Rules, which required notice to be given to the parties to the grant before witnesses are heard, is expressly made to apply to this hearing, it is clear that it is not intended that the witnesses should be heard by the expert alone. In fact, on a strict reading of the Rules, the expert has no right to ask any questions or request that any particular question be asked—see Rules, Art. 49, para. 3 and Art. 47, para. 4.3 and para. 4.4.
[62] This must deal only with the points which were expressly put to him—Rules, Art. 49, para. 4.
[63] Rules, Art. 49, para. 5. After presenting his report the expert must take the following oath: " I swear that I have carried out my task conscientiously and with full impartiality." This oath may be in the form laid down by the expert's national law. The Court, however, with the agreement of the parties, may excuse him from taking the oath—Rules, Art. 49, para. 6.
[64] Rules, Art. 52. On these *Commissions*, see p. 71, below.

There are no Rules governing the summoning of the parties to take part in the measures of instructions, nor concerning any visit to the site.

HOLDING THE INSTRUCTION BEFORE A *Juge Rapporteur*

Instead of the Court itself undertaking the measures of instruction, it may entrust them to the *juge rapporteur*.[65] Under the old Rules, however, this could only have been done if neither of the parties objected.[66] The removal of this restrictive provision shows, it is suggested, that greater use was intended to be made of the *juge rapporteur* in this capacity. From the Rules, however, it is by no means clear what role the *juge rapporteur* is to play, or what powers he is to possess.

The present Rules specify that when an Instruction is to be held by a Chamber and not by the Court, those provisions relating to witnesses and to experts etc. shall apply, and that the Chamber shall exercise the powers there given to the Court, and that the powers of the President of the Court shall be exercised by the President of the Chamber.[67] There is, however, no provision making these provisions apply to the *juge rapporteur* or conferring on him the powers of the President of the Court.

For the want, therefore, of any provision upon this matter, it is impossible to say anything concerning the manner of holding an Instruction before a *juge rapporteur* and it is probably fruitless to speculate.

HOLDING THE INSTRUCTION BEFORE A CHAMBER

The Court, instead of undertaking the Instruction itself, or entrusting it to the *juge rapporteur*, may assign it to a Chamber.[68] If it does so, the procedure is virtually identical with what it would have been if the Court had been holding the Instruction, except that the Chamber will draw up the order setting out the facts upon which the witnesses are to be heard.[69]

It is the President of the Chamber who informs witnesses that they must give their evidence on oath,[70] and the Chamber as a whole has

[65] Rules, Art. 45, para. 3.1.
[66] Old Rules, Art. 38.
[67] Rules, Art. 46, paras. 1 and 2.
[68] Rules, Art. 44, para. 2.1.
[69] Rules, Art. 46, para. 1 and Art. 45, para 1. By Art. 46, para. 1 all the powers of the Court in Art. 45 are given to the Chamber, and by Art. 45, para. 3 the Court, instead of holding the Instruction can entrust it to the *juge rapporteur*. It would appear therefore, that the Chamber can so entrust it as well, yet if the Court had desired this to occur it would itself have entrusted the *juge* with the matter. It would seem strange if a Chamber could circumvent the desires of the Court as a whole.
[70] Rules, Art. 46, para. 1 and Art. 47, para 4.1.

the same powers as the Court to take action against defaulting witnesses.[71] The Chamber also has similar powers to the Court to require an expert examination and to appoint and hear the expert.[72]

DISCOVERY OF DOCUMENTS AND THE OBTAINING OF INFORMATION

The Court may at any time request the parties to produce all documents and to supply all information which the Court considers desirable.[73] Further, under the E.C.S.C. Statute,[74] but not under the two later Statutes, it is provided that where an appeal has been lodged against a decision taken by one of the institutions of that Community, the institution concerned is to transmit to the Court all documents relating to the case. Under the E.C.S.C. Statute,[75] the Court in addition possesses power to request the representatives or agents of the parties to produce *all* documents, so that it might appear that even counsel's opinions could be requested. This latter reference, however, has been omitted in the two later Statutes,[76] and because presumably the Court's procedure is intended to be uniform, it is suggested that this power has in effect now been abandoned.

The Court also has power to request information from a Member State even although it is not a party to the case concerned.[77] Under the two later Statutes, an additional power has been given to the Court also to request information, but not documents, from the institutions of the E.E.C. and Euratom Communities.[78]

In one case before it, the Court ordered the High Authority to produce the relevant minutes and opinions of the Consultative Committee, while reserving to itself the right to decide later upon the possible production of the minutes of the Council of Ministers and of the High Authority. The Court also stated that at the request of the High Authority it would

---

[71] Rules, Art. 46, para. 1 and Art. 48, paras. 2 and 3—on these powers, see pp. 67 and 68, below.
[72] Rules, Art. 46, para. 1 and Arts. 49 and 50. On the Court's powers in this matter, see pp. 69–72, below.
[73] E.C.S.C. Statute, Art. 24; E.E.C. Statute, Art. 21, para. 1; Euratom Statute, Art. 21, para. 1. It should be noted that there is thus no automatic obligation to make full discovery, nor is there any guarantee that documents will be available before the oral proceedings. It is presumed that a party desiring discovery of a document could request the Court to ask the other party to produce it, but the Court would only do so if it also regarded the production as desirable.
[74] Art. 23.
[75] E.C.S.C. Statute, Art. 24.
[76] E.E.C. Statute, Art. 21, para. 1; Euratom Statute, Art. 21, para. 1.
[77] E.C.S.C. Statute, Art. 24; E.E.C. Statute, Art. 21, para. 2; Euratom Statute, Art. 22, para. 2.
[78] E.E.C. Statute, Art. 21, para. 2; Euratom Statute, Art. 22.

have been prepared to authorise the suppression of the names of all the speakers recorded in the minutes and if necessary would have ordered a session *in camera* for the discussion of these documents.[79] Each of the Statutes in the three Treaties states that if the parties refuse to supply the documents or the information requested " the Court shall take judicial notice thereof." [80] Under the E.C.S.C. Statute,[81] the Court is also to take judicial notice of the refusal of a Member State, which is not a party to the case, to supply documents or information: under the two later Statutes there is no such provision to this effect.[82]

WITNESSES [83]

The Court, either of itself, or on the request of one of the parties,[84] and after hearing the Advocate General may order the proof of certain facts by means of witnesses.[85] If it does so, the Court issues an order setting out the particular facts to be established.[86]

The witnesses are summoned by the Court either of its own motion, or at the request of one of the parties [84] or of the Advocate General.[87]

When it is the Court that requires the hearing of a witness, the Court itself advances the necessary money.[88] However, the Court may make the summoning of those witnesses requested by one of the parties

---

[79] *Italian Government* v. *The High Authority* (Case 2–54) Vol. II.
[80] E.C.S.C. Statute, Art. 24; E.E.C. Statute, Art. 21, para. 1; Euratom Statute, Art. 22, para. 1. In one case, the Court respecting the intervening party's claim that a particular contract was " extremely confidential," did not order its production: in default of the document, however, the Court held that there was no evidence to support the intervening party's case—*Société nouvelle des usines de Pontlioue—Acieries de Temple (S.N.U.P.A.T.)* v. *The High Authority* (Joint Cases 42 and 49–59).
[81] Art. 24.
[82] This is because in E.C.S.C. Statute, Art. 24, the provision concerning taking judicial notice comes at the end of the article and governs all before it. In the two later Statutes this provision concerning judicial notice appears at the end of para. 1, so that it does not in terms govern the information which may be requested under para. 2.
[83] On these, see also " The Instruction," pp. 63–65, above.
[84] The Rules, Art. 47, para. 1 state " at the request of the parties," but this presumably cannot mean on the joint request of the parties. Where a party requests the hearing of a witness, it must specify precisely the facts on which the witness is required to be heard and the reasons justifying his being heard—Rules, Art. 47, para. 1.3.
[85] Rules, Art. 47, para. 1. For an example of witnesses being heard by the Court, see *R. P. M. Fiddelaar* v. *The Commission of E.E.C.* (Case 44–59) Vol. II.
[86] *Ibid.*
[87] Rules, Art. 47, para. 2. The order of the Court subpoenaing them must contain (a) the surname, christian names, occupation and address of the witness, (b) an outline of the facts on which the witness is to be heard and (c) where applicable, mention of the arrangements made by the Court for reimbursing expenses claimed by the witnesses and of the penalties to which defaulting witnesses are liable—Rules, Art. 47, para. 2.1. This order is served on the parties and on the witness concerned—Rules, Art. 47, para. 2.2.
[88] Rules, Art. 47, para. 3.2. The witnesses when applying for this money from the Court pay office shall give the Registrar details of the expenses in respect of which this money is required—Instructions to the Registrar, Art. 21, para. 1.

conditional upon the depositing with the Court pay office of a sum to cover the witnesses' taxed expenses.[89] The amount of this sum is fixed by the Court itself.[90]

If one of the parties objects to a witness on the grounds of incompetence, lack of qualification to give evidence or of any other reason or if the witness refuses to swear the oath, the Court gives a ruling upon the validity of this objection.[91] It must be made, however, within fourteen days from the service of the order which summoned the witness,[92] and must be made in a document containing the grounds of the objection and the matters relied on in support.[93]

When a witness has been duly served with a subpoena, he is required to obey the summons and to present himself at the hearing.[94] If he does not so appear or without a good reason refuses to give evidence or to take the oath, the Court may impose a fine upon him not exceeding 250 E.P.Us,[95] and if he did not appear, may order him to pay the costs of a fresh service of the summons.[96] If, however, the witness subsequently produces valid reasons to the Court, he may be relieved of the fine.[97]

When a witness has appeared before the Court, his identity is first verified, and the President [98] then informs him that his evidence will have to be given on oath,[99] unless the Court, with the agreement of the parties, excuses the witness from this requirement.[1]

A witness is heard by the Court after notice has been given to the parties to be present.[2] After he has given his evidence, the President,

---

[89] Rules, Art. 47, para. 3.1.
[90] *Ibid.*
[91] Rules, Art. 50, para. 1.
[92] It will, however, obviously be impossible to comply with this time limit if the ground of object is the witness's refusal to swear the oath. Such a contingency is thus not provided for.
[93] Rules, Art. 50, para. 2.
[94] Rules, Art. 48, para. 1.
[95] 1 E.P.U. equals one American dollar.
[96] Rules, Art. 48, para. 2, paras. 1 and 3. A similar provision is also, entirely redundantly, contained in Rules, Art. 50, para. 1. The payment of the fine is enforced in the same manner as are the judgments of the Court itself—Rules, Art. 48, para. 4, see p. 80, below. This provision imposing a fine has been enacted under power given in E.C.S.C. Statute, Art. 28, para. 5; E.E.C. Statute, Art. 24 and Euratom Statute, Art. 25.
[97] Rules Art. 48, para. 3.
[98] Under the old Rules (Art. 41, para. 1), the *juge rapporteur* was also empowered to inform the witnesses of this.
[99] Rules, Art. 47, para. 4.1. The witness takes the oath after he has given his evidence. The words of the oath are: " I swear that what I have said is the truth, the whole truth and nothing but the truth "—Rules, Art. 47, para. 5.1. The oath may be taken in the form laid down by the national law of the witness—Rules, Art. 47, para. 5.2. and E.E.C. Statute, Art. 25; Euratom Statute, Art. 26.
[1] Rules, Art. 47, para. 5.3.
[2] Rules, Art. 47, para. 4.2.

either of his own motion or at the request of the parties, may put questions to him.[3]

Witnesses are entitled to reimbursement of their expenses for travel and subsistence.[4] An advance to cover these expenses may be granted to them from the Court pay office.[5] They are also entitled after they have fulfilled their duties to compensation for loss of earnings.[6] If, however, the Registrar considers the sums requested under either of the above heads to be excessive, he may reduce them on his own authority or spread payment over a period.[7]

If a witness before the Court gives false testimony under oath,[8] the Court, after hearing the Advocate General, may decide to report the matter to the Minister of Justice of that Member State whose criminal courts can prosecute.[9] This decision shall set out the facts and circumstances on which the allegation of perjury is based[10] and the Registrar is responsible for transmitting this decision of the Court to the Minister concerned.[11]

Under the Statutes of the Court in the E.E.C. and Euratom Treaties, the Court is granted the powers possessed by courts of law as regards defaulting witnesses and may " impose such pecuniary penalties as are laid down in the Rules of Procedure."[12] Further, where the Court orders that a witness is to be heard by the judicial authority of his place of residence rather than by the Court itself, it is provided[13] that each Member State is to regard any violation of an oath of that witness as if the same offence had been committed before a municipal court or

---

3 *Ibid.* It is assumed that this provision should read " at the request of *one* of the parties."
4 Rules, Art. 51, para. 1.
5 *Ibid.* When applying for this advance, the witness must give the Registrar details of the expenses in respect of which the advance is requested—Instructions to the Registrar, Art. 21, para. 1.1. Payment out is made against a signed receipt or proof of transfer—*ibid.* Art. 21, para. 2.1.
6 Rules, Art. 51, para. 2. Witnesses are required to provide documentary evidence of this loss of earnings—Instructions to the Registrar, Art. 21, para. 1.2. Payment out is made against a signed receipt or proof of transfer—*ibid.* Art. 21, para. 2.1.
7 Instructions to the Registrar, Art. 21, para. 2.2. There appears to be no appeal against this action of the Registrar.
8 Supplementary Rules, Art. 6. It appears that if, under Rules, Art. 47, para. 5.3, a witness is excused taking the oath, no proceedings for violation of that oath can subsequently be instituted, and there are no provisions allowing a witness to make an affirmation instead of taking an oath. Under the E.C.S.C. Statute, however, no reference is made to the violation of an oath and the witness can be proceeded against when it is established that he has " concealed or falsified the facts upon which he has given evidence "—Art. 28, para. 4. It is suggested that the position of witnesses should be the same under all three Treaties.
9 Supplementary Rules, Art. 6.
10 *Ibid.* Art. 7, para. 2.
11 *Ibid.* Art. 7, para. 1.
12 E.E.C. Statute, Art. 25; Euratom Statute, Art. 25.
13 E.E.C. Statute, Art. 27; Euratom Statute, Art. 27.

tribunal dealing with a case in civil law. The Member State concerned is required to prosecute the offender before the competent municipal court or tribunal.[14] No such duty is imposed in relation to coal and steel cases by the Statute contained in the E.C.S.C. Treaty by which the Court was merely empowered to refer the violation to the Minister of Justice of the State to which the witness belongs "with a view to sanctions being imposed upon him" by his municipal law.[15] It is suggested that the variation in wording will make no difference in practice.

EXPERTS

The Court has power to order an expert's report.[16] If it decides to exercise this power,[17] the Court by an order appoints the expert, specifies his terms of reference and fixes a time limit within which his report is to be presented.[18] Alternatively, the Court at any time may entrust the inquiry or the making of the report to a particular body, office, commission or organ of its own choice.[19]

The expert once appointed receives a copy of the Court's order as well as all the documents necessary for carrying out his task,[20] and he is placed under the orders of the *juge rapporteur*.[21] If, during the making of his examination, the expert requires to hear witnesses, they are heard, not by him alone, but by the Court after notice has been given to the parties to attend.[22]

14 E.E.C. Statute, Art. 27; Euratom Statute, Art. 28.
15 E.C.S.C. Statute, Art. 28, para. 4.
16 *Une expertise.*
17 In one case the Court held that it was only by an expert examination that it could discover the amount owing from an enterprise in respect of its levy to the fund to subsidise the cost of imported scrap—*Meroni & Co. Industrie Metallurgiche S.P.A.* v. *The High Authority* (Case 9-59) Vol. II.
18 Rules, Art. 49, para. 1.
19 E.C.S.C. Statute, Art. 25; E.E.C. Statute, Art. 22; Euratom Statute, Art. 23. Under the E.C.S.C. Statute, the Court may draw up a list of persons or organisations qualified to serve as experts—Art. 25. This power, curiously enough, is not repeated in the two later Statutes.
20 The Registrar is to ensure that the expert or organisation entrusted with making a report possesses all necessary means for the performance of their duties—Instructions to the Registrar, Art. 8.
21 Rules, Art. 49, para. 2.
22 Rules, Art. 49, para. 3. This Rule states that the witnesses shall be heard "in accordance with the provisions set out in Article 47 of the present Rules." Art 47, para. 4.2, however, provides that questions may be put to witnesses only by the President either of his own motion or at the request of the parties, and that the same right is possessed by the judges and the Advocate General. It is assumed that in practice, however, the expert would be allowed to ask questions or at least require questions to be asked, or the whole proceedings lose their point.

The expert then presents his report [23] following which he is required to take an oath affirming that he has carried out his duties conscientiously and with complete impartiality.[24]

Following this presentation, the Court may order that the expert should himself be heard by the Court after notice has been given to the parties to attend.[25] Alternatively, it appears the Court may authorise the parties to put written questions to the expert.

As with witnesses before the Court, experts may be objected to on the grounds of lack of ability, lack of qualification or on any other ground.[26] An objection may also be raised if he refuses to take the oath.[27] The Court rules on these objections.[28]

Experts are entitled to reimbursement of their expenses for travel and subsistence. An advance [29] to cover these expenses may be granted to them from the Court pay office.[30] They are also entitled after they have fulfilled their duties to fees for their work.[31] If, however, the Registrar considers the sum requested under either of the above heads to be excessive, he may reduce them of his own authority or spread payment over a period.[32]

If an expert in his report to the Court makes a false statement, which must presumably mean *knowingly* makes a false statement, under oath the same provisions apply for referring the matter to the Minister of Justice of the Member State whose criminal courts can prosecute as apply to a witness who has violated his oath.[33] The same duty to prosecute in respect of this violation is imposed upon the Member State concerned.[34]

23 Rules, Art. 49, para. 5. This report must be limited to the matters which are expressly submitted to him in the order appointing him—Rules, Art. 49, para. 4. For the terms of one report of an expert—the Director of the Central Office of International Rail Transport, Berne—see *Chambre Syndicale de la Sidérurgiche de l'Est de la France and others* v. *The High Authority* (Joint Cases 24–58 and 34–58) Vol. II.
24 Rules, Art. 49, para. 6.1. This oath may be taken in the form prescribed by the municipal legislation applicable to the expert—para. 6.2, or the Court may, with the agreement of the parties, release the expert from swearing the oath—para. 6.3.
25 Rules, Art. 49, para. 5.
26 Rules, Art. 50, para. 1; compare p. 67, above.
27 Rules, Art. 50, para. 1; compare p. 67, above.
28 *Ibid.*
29 Rules, Art. 51, para. 1.
30 *Ibid.* When applying for this advance, the expert must give the Registrar details of the expenses in respect of which the advance is requested—Instructions to the Registrar, Art. 21, para. 1.1. Payment out is made against a signed receipt or proof of transfer—*ibid.* Art. 21, para. 2.1.
31 Rules, Art. 51, para. 2. Experts are required to provide the Registrar with a note of these fees—Instructions to the Registrar, Art. 21, para. 1.2. Payment out is made against a signed receipt or proof of transfer—*ibid.* Art. 21, para. 2.1.
32 Instructions to the Registrar, Art. 21, para. 2.2. There appears to be no appeal against this action of the Registrar.
33 As to these provisions, see p. 68, above.
34 See p. 68, above.

COMMISSIONS ROGATOIRES

Under the Statute of the Court contained in the E.E.C. and Euratom Treaties,[35] the Court may order that a witness or an expert [36] shall be heard by a judicial authority of his place of residence.

Under the Statute in the E.C.S.C. Treaty, no such provision is made.[37] However, under the Supplementary Rules of Procedure [38] it is stated that *commissions rogatoires* are to be issued by means of a Court order [39] which the Registrar is to forward to the Minister of Justice of the Member States on whose territory the witnesses or experts are to be heard.[40] Upon receipt of this order, the Minister of Justice is required to transmit it to the judicial authority competent under its domestic law.[41] This authority must then carry out the *commission* in accordance with the provisions of the relevant law.[42] When this has been done, the authority forwards to the Minister of Justice the records of the hearing and a statement of costs.[43] The Minister then forwards these documents to the Registrar of the Court.[44] The Court then itself pays the costs of the *commission* subject to its right where applicable to order such costs to be repaid by the parties.[45]

It is important to note that under the Statute of the Court in the E.C.S.C. Treaty, no provision is made for these *commissions rogatoires*. They were provided for, however, in the old Rules themselves.[46] As the

---

[35] E.E.C. Statute, Art. 26, para. 1; Euratom Statute, Art. 27, para. 1.

[36] The term " expert " as here used does not mean an expert witness, but a person or body etc. entrusted with the carrying out of an expert examination. On this, see p. 69, above.

[37] Under the old Rules (Art. 36 and Rules on Agents and Advocates, Art. 10, para. 1 and 2), however, reference was made to such hearings. When these old Rules were repealed, power to issue *commissions* was not included in the new Rules, so that until the Supplementary Rules came into force on May 5, 1962, it appears that in relation to coal and steel matters these *commissions* could not have been set up.

[38] See pp. 556–559, below.

[39] Supplementary Rules, Art. 1.1. This order shall contain the names, forenames, occupations and addresses of the witnesses or experts, state the facts on which the witnesses or experts are to be heard, name the parties, their agents, counsel or legal advisors, together with their address for service and set out briefly the subject of the dispute—*ibid*.

[40] *Ibid*. Art. 2, para. 1. Where applicable this order is to be accompanied by a translation into the one or more official languages of the Member State to which it is sent—*ibid*. Notice of this order is served on the parties by the Registrar—*ibid*. Art. 1.2.

[41] *Ibid*. Art. 2.1. [42] *Ibid*. Art. 2.2.

[43] *Ibid*. The authority is also required to forward the original order of the Court ordering the *commission*.

[44] *Ibid*. The Registrar then ensures that these documents are translated into the procedural language—*ibid*. Art. 2.2.

[45] *Ibid*. Art. 3. Although Art. 3 refers to repayment by the parties in the plural, it is assumed that on general principle it will be the losing party which will pay.

[46] Old Rules, Art. 36 and Rules on Agents and Advocates, etc., Art. 10, paras. 1 and 2. These provisions were virtually identical with those now contained in the Statute of the E.E.C. and Euratom Treaties—see above.

71

Rules of the Court are subordinate to its Statutes, the legality of these provisions could well have been challenged. Presumably to avoid such a challenge, the relevant provisions relating to *commissions* have now been embodied in the Statutes of the Economic Community and Euratom Treaties and taken out of the Rules. The result is that, so far as the E.C.S.C. Treaty is concerned, *commissions rogatoires* are now neither mentioned in the Statute of the Court nor in the Rules of Court, so that, it is suggested, they could not be instituted in respect of cases brought under that Treaty.

WRITTEN OBSERVATIONS ON THE INSTRUCTION

After the ending of the Instruction, whether held before the Court or a Chamber or the *juge rapporteur*, the Court decides whether to grant to the parties a time limit for them to present their written observations upon the matters brought out in the Instruction.[47] If such a time period is given, the President of the Court sets the date of the opening of the oral proceedings at the end of this time limit.[48] If the parties are not granted this right to present written observations, the President fixes the time for the opening of the oral proceedings at a date after the ending of the Instruction.[49]

THE ORAL PROCEEDINGS

After the Instruction, as outlined above, has been completed, the Court decides whether to give the parties a further time in which to present their written observations. If it does, the President fixes the date for the opening of the oral proceedings at the end of this further time,[50] or, if no such time is given, the President fixes the date for the opening of the oral proceedings after the completion of the measures of instruction.[51]

The order in which several cases pending before the Court are to be heard depends upon the order in which their Instruction was completed or, where the Instructions in a number of cases have been completed simultaneously, the order is determined by the date of entry of the request in the Court Register.[52] The President, however, in view of

---

[47] Rules, Art. 54, para. 1.
[48] Rules, Art. 54, para. 2. This provision is ambiguous. It is suggested, however, that the opening of the oral proceedings is to occur at the end of the time limit in question, and that the date for that opening is to be determined only after that time limit has ended.
[49] Rules, Art. 54, para. 2.
[50] Rules, Art. 54, para. 2.
[51] Rules, Art. 54, para. 1. Although the Rules deal with the hearing of witnesses and with the expert examination, etc., as part of the Instruction, and distinct from the oral proceedings, they are strictly part of it—see E.C.S.C. Statute, Art. 21, para. 4; E.E.C. Statute, Art. 18, para. 4; Euratom Statute, Art. 18, para. 4.
[52] Rules, Art. 55, para. 1.1.

special circumstances, may decide to give priority to the hearing of a particular case.[53] Precedence is, however, always given to the consideration of requests for a stay of execution of acts of the institutions of the Communities, if these are referred to the Court by the President.[54]

The parties to a case, however, may always jointly request that the oral proceedings shall be postponed, in which case the President is empowered to accede to this request. In default of agreement between the parties on this point, however, the President is required to refer the matter to the Court for a decision.[55]

During the oral hearing, the President directs the proceedings, and has full control over their conduct.[56] The parties may plead only through their agent, legal adviser or counsel [57] and the President, as well as the judges and the Advocate General, may put questions to them.[58]

At any time during the proceedings, the Court may order any measure of instruction to be undertaken, or may require the re-opening or amplification of any part of the Instruction.[59] The Court may entrust the carrying out of any of these to a Chamber or to the *juge rapporteur*.[60]

At the conclusion of the case, the parties are entitled to address the Court by way of closing speeches. Nothing is stated in the Rules concerning this, nor concerning the order of speeches. In practice, however, the plaintiff's counsel delivers the first speech: if there is more than one plaintiff, the speeches of counsel follow in the order in which the plaintiffs are named in the cause list. The defendant's counsel then replies. If a third party has intervened in a case, that party has the right to address the Court immediately following the party whose case it is seeking to support.

If the Court wishes to put questions to counsel, these are usually asked after the defendant's speech [61]; whether or not these are asked, all the plaintiffs have a right of reply, after which, and unlike English

---

53 Rules, Art. 55, para. 1.2. This power was previously given to the Court as a whole, and not to the President.
54 Rules, Art. 55, para. 1.1. For the procedure governing such requests, see pp. 85–87, below.
55 Rules, Art. 55, para. 2. Under the old Rules, the President had a discretion as to whether there was need to consult the Court—old Rules, Art. 43, para. 3.
56 Rules, Art. 56, para. 1.
57 Rules, Art. 58.
58 Rules, Art. 57, paras. 1 and 2. Under the old Rules, the judges and the Advocate General had to inform the President of their intention to put questions—old Rules, Art. 48, para. 2.
59 Rules, Art. 60. The provision enabling new measures of instruction to be undertaken is new.
60 *Ibid.*
61 It is noteworthy that in practice the Court is extremely loath to interrupt counsel or engage in any running discussion with them which is such a marked feature of English courts.

procedure, the defendant has a right to a second speech, as also has the intervening party.[62]

After all of these speeches, the Advocate General orally presents his reasoned submissions,[63] after which the President declares the oral proceedings to be closed.[64] However, the Court may subsequently order their re-opening.[65]

The Registrar is required to draw up a record of every hearing, which is signed by the President and by himself and constitutes an official record.[66]

THE JUDGMENT OF THE COURT

The Court's deliberations upon what its judgment shall be are secret.[67] The final reasoned judgment of the Court,[68] signed by the President, by the *juge rapporteur* if relating to coal and steel matters, and by the Registrar, is read in a public session of the Court [69] after notice has been given to the parties to attend.[70] It must state the names of the judges who took part in the deliberations,[71] except that judgments on coal and steel matters must give the names of the judges who heard the case even if subsequently they did not take part in the deliberations. The judgment is given in the procedural language [72] and is subsequently

---

62 In practice, the right to these second speeches is often waived.
63 Rules, Art. 59, para. 1.
64 Rules, Art. 59, para. 2.
65 Rules, Art. 61.
66 Rules, Art. 62, para. 1. Under the old Rules, it was specified that to this record should be annexed a shorthand note of the proceedings and, where they occurred, the oral translations made by the interpreters—old Rules, Art. 53, para. 2.
67 E.C.S.C. Statute, Art. 29; E.E.C. Statute, Art. 32; Euratom Statute, Art. 33. This provision also presumably covers the Court's rulings upon preliminary objections although these are nowhere referred to as judgments—see Rules, Art. 91, and p. 60, above.
68 E.C.S.C. Statute, Art. 30; E.E.C. Statute, Art. 33; Euratom Statute, Art. 34.
69 E.C.S.C. Statute, Art. 31; E.E.C. Statute, Art. 34; Euratom Statute, Art. 35. An entry in the procedural language is to be made at the foot of the record that the judgment has been read in open Court—Instructions to the Registrar, Art. 6, para. 1.
70 Rules, Art. 64, para. 1. The record of the judgment is sealed and deposited in the Registry of the Court, and a certified copy of it is sent to each one of the parties—Rules, Art. 64, para. 2.
71 E.C.S.C. Statute, Art. 30; E.E.C. Statute, Art. 33; Euratom Statute, Art. 34. The judgment must also state that it was delivered by the Court, and set out the date when it was pronounced, the name of the Advocate General, and of the Registrar, particulars of the parties to the dispute, the names of their agents, legal advisers or counsel, the submissions of the parties, reference to the fact that the Advocate General has been heard, a brief summary of the facts, the grounds on which the judgment is based, the order of the Court, which is to include the decision on costs—Rules, Art. 63.
72 Rules, Art. 29, para. 3—as to the determination of this language, see p. 46, above.

published by the Registrar [73] in all the official languages.[74] It is binding from the date when it is pronounced.[75]

JUDGMENTS UPON PRELIMINARY ISSUES REQUESTED BY MUNICIPAL COURTS

Where under the E.C.S.C. Treaty,[76] a municipal court refers to the Communities' Court the question, as a preliminary issue, of the validity of the resolutions of the High Authority or of the Council of Ministers, the decision so to refer the matter is served on the parties in the case, on the Member States, on the High Authority and on the Council of Ministers.[77]

Within two months of this service, any of the entities concerned have the right to submit their written statements or observations.[78] As soon as these have been submitted, or if they have not been submitted, at the end of the two months, the Court continues with the reference as if it were an ordinary case before it and the written proceedings had just been closed.[79]

The procedure is similar where a reference is made to the Court by a municipal court or tribunal by virtue of the provisions of either the Economic Community or the Euratom Treaties.[80] This reference of the matter to the Court is notified by the Registrar to the parties to the principal action, to the Member States, to the relevant Commission, and also to the relevant Council of Ministers if the act whose validity or interpretation is in dispute originates from one of these Councils.[81]

[73] Rules, Art. 68.
[74] Rules, Art. 30, para. 2.
[75] Rules, Art. 65. It is important to note that the Rules make a clear distinction between the date when a judgment is pronounced—*prononcé*—and the date when it is delivered—*rendu*. The date when it was pronounced must be set out in the judgment by Rules, Art. 63; the date when it was delivered is set out by the Registrar on the record of the judgment. Thus in one case judgment was pronounced on July 6, 1959, but not delivered until July 17, 1959: *Société nouvelle des usines de Pontlieue-Aciéries du Temple (S.N.U.P.A.T.)* v. *The High Authority* (Joint Cases 32–58 and 33–58), see Vol. II. The effect of the above provision is that this judgment was binding ten days before the parties knew about it.
[76] E.C.S.C. Treaty, Art. 41, see p. 234, below.
[77] Rules, Art. 103, para. 2.1.
[78] Rules, Art. 103, para. 2.2.
[79] Rules, Art. 103, para. 2.3. That is to say, the Court hears the *juge rapporteur* upon whether an Instruction is necessary. If one is not, the Court proceeds straight to the oral proceedings—see Rules, Art. 44, discussed on p. 62, above.
[80] By these Treaties, application may be made to the Court for judgment upon the preliminary issue of the interpretation of the two Treaties, the validity and interpretation of acts of the institutions of the two Communities, or of the interpretation of the Statute of any bodies set up by an act of the Council, where such Statutes so provide—E.E.C. Treaty, Art. 177, para. 1; Euratom Treaty, Art. 150, para. 1, see pp. 303 and 365, below.
[81] E.E.C. Statute, Art. 20, para. 1; Euratom Statute, Art. 21, para. 1.

These parties, the Member States and, where appropriate, the Council, are similarly entitled to present their written statements or observations within a period of two months.[82]

CORRECTIONS OF A JUDGMENT

Within fourteen days from the pronouncement of a judgment,[83] the Court, either of its own motion, or on the request of one of the parties, may correct any clerical errors in a judgment or arithmetical errors [84] or obvious inaccuracies in it.[85]   The parties, having been duly notified by the Registrar, may submit their written observations within the time limit fixed by the President,[86] after which the decision is taken by the Court at a private session after hearing the Advocate General.[87]

Further, if the Court has omitted to give a ruling either upon a particular point in the submissions or upon costs, the Rules state that the party " intending to rely upon this " may bring the matter before the Court by means of a request made within one month of the date of the notification of the judgment.[88] This presumably means that the party adversely affected is the party to bring the request. Indeed, if the Court has omitted to condemn the losing party in costs, it is only that losing party who in any intelligible sense could " rely " upon the omission, and that party is unlikely to be over keen to approach the Court for a correction.

The request when made is served on the other party, and the President sets it a time limit in which it may present its written observations.[89] After these have been presented, the Court having heard the Advocate General decides upon the admissibility of the request, and if admissible determines upon whether it is well founded.[90]

---

[82] E.E.C. Statute, Art. 20, para. 2; Euratom Statute, Art. 21, para. 2. In the first case submitted to the Court under E.E.C. Treaty, Art. 177, written statements were submitted by the Commission and by the German, French, Belgian and Netherlands Governments—*Société Kledingver koopbedrijt de Geus en Uitdenbogerd* v. *Société de Droit Allemand Robert Bosch G.m.b.H. and another* (Case 13–61) [1962] C.M.L.R. 1.

[83] The date of the pronouncement of a judgment is not the same as that of the delivery of a judgment, see note 75, above.

[84] The obvious arithmetical error in one judgment where the Court made 1 year plus 2 months plus 4 months = 16 months passed without notice—to the financial detriment of the plaintiff—see *M. Antoine Kergall* v. *The Common Assembly* (Case 1–55), Vol. II.

[85] Rules, Art. 66, para. 1. This correction is made by means of an Order of the Court. For an example of such an Order, see the correction of *Mannesmann AG and others* v. *The High Authority* (Joint Cases 4–59 to 13–59), Vol. II.

[86] Rules, Art. 66, para. 2.

[87] Rules, Art. 66, para. 3. When a judgment is rectified, the record of the order making the correction is annexed to the record of the judgment and a note of this order is made in the margin of the record of the judgment corrected—Rules, Art. 66, para. 4.

[88] Rules, Art. 67, para. 1.   [89] Rules, Art. 67, para. 2.

[90] Rules, Art. 67, para. 3.

REVISION OF A JUDGMENT

Revision of a judgment may be requested from the Court only by reason of the discovery of a fact likely to exercise a decisive influence, and which, before the pronouncement of the judgment, was unknown both to the Court [91] and to the party which requests the revision.[92] This request for revision must be brought within ten years from the date of the judgment [93] and within three months from the day when the applicant had knowledge of the new fact.[94]

Apart from the ordinary requirements that must be satisfied when a request is submitted to the Court,[95] a request for the revision of a judgment must specify the judgment objected to [96]; indicate the points on which the judgment is being objected to; set out the facts on which the request is based, and that these facts justify a revision and evidence that the prescribed time limit has been observed.[97]

Without prejudicing its decision upon the merits of the request, the Court, after hearing the Advocate General,[98] and after considering the written observations of the parties, gives a ruling upon the admissibility of the request by means of a judgment delivered in private session.[99] The request, however, cannot in this judgment be declared admissible, except following an express finding of the Court that the alleged new fact exists and recognising that it possesses the characteristics justifying a revision.[1]

[91] In one case the Court declared: " The documents in question were deposited with the Registry before the end of the oral proceedings and, in consequence, were known by the Court before it delivered its judgment. From the fact of the production of a document written in one of the official languages of the Community, not only its physical existence but also its contents are brought to the knowledge of the Court "—*Acciaieria Ferriera di Roma (F.E.R.A.M.)* v. *The High Authority* (Case 1–60), Vol. II.

[92] E.C.S.C. Statute, Art. 38, para. 1; E.E.C. Statute, Art. 41, para. 1; Euratom Statute, Art. 42, para. 1. No mention is made of the case where a party was negligent in not knowing of these facts before judgment was pronounced.

[93] E.C.S.C. Statute, Art. 38, para. 3; E.E.C. Statute, Art. 41, para. 3; Euratom Statute, Art. 42, para. 3. It is not clear whether " the date of the judgment " implies the date of the pronouncement of the judgment, or the date of the delivery of the judgment, or the date of the service of the judgment, see further note 75, p. 75, above.

[94] Rules, Art. 98.

[95] See p. 50, above.

[96] Previously a copy of the judgment had to be enclosed—old Rules, Art. 75, para. 2.

[97] Rules, Art. 99, para. 1. This request is brought against all the parties bound by the original judgment—Rules, Art. 99, para. 2.

[98] Which Advocate General is here being referred to is not stated: the one concerned with the original hearing of the case may well have been replaced.

[99] Rules, Art. 100, para. 1. Under the old Rules (Art. 76, para. 1), this ruling was given merely by an order. Why it is desired that the judgment should be delivered in private is not clear.

[1] E.C.S.C. Statute, Art. 38, para. 2; E.E.C. Statute, Art. 41, para. 2; Euratom Statute, Art. 42, para. 2.

If the Court declares the request to be admissible, it proceeds, " in accordance with the provisions of these Rules," with the consideration of the merits and gives a ruling by means of a judgment.[2] From this it would appear that where necessary the Court has full powers to institute a completely new trial with an Instruction and written and oral procedings.

THE INTERPRETATION OF A JUDGMENT

In case of difficulty [3] as to the meaning or scope of a judgment, the Court may interpret it upon the request of a party [4] or of an institution of the Community showing an interest in such interpretation.[5] This request must comply with the general requirements for requests [6] and must specify, in addition, the particular provisions of the judgment of which interpretation is sought.[7]

Concerning what are the particular provisions of a judgment which can be interpreted, the Court has held:

> From all appearances, it can only be those [provisions] which express the judgment of the Court in the dispute which has been submitted for its final decision and those parts of the reasoning upon which this decision is based and which are, therefore, essential to it . . . On the other hand, the Court does not have to interpret those passages which are incidental to and which complete or explain that basic reasoning.[8]

After it has given an opportunity to the parties to present their observations, and after hearing the Advocate General, the Court gives a ruling upon the request for this interpretation by means of a judgment,[9] and

---

2 Rules, Art. 100, para. 2.

3 " The expression ' difficulty ' is general: it is less limited than the expression ' *contestation* ' which is found in the French text of Article 60 of the Statute of the International Court of Justice. For a request for interpretation to be admissible, it is sufficient that the parties in question give different meanings to the text of that judgment "—*Associazione Industrie Siderurgiche Italiane (ASSIDER)* v. *The High Authority* (Case 5–55), Vol. II.

4 " In the event of several appeals being brought against the same decision of the High Authority, if the decision is annulled [in one appeal], the plaintiffs in the other appeals may be considered as ' parties ' to the action within the meaning of Article 37 of the Statute of the Court, but subject to the express condition that the plaintiff in its earlier appeal has invoked the same ground as that on which the judgment to be interpreted has annulled the decision or . . . has declared the appeal well founded "—*ibid.* Vol. II.

5 E.C.S.C. Statute, Art. 37; E.E.C. Statute, Art. 40; Euratom Statute, Art. 41.

6 *I.e.*, with the provisions of Rules, Arts. 37 and 38, above.

7 Rules, Art. 102, para. 1.1.

8 *Associazione Industrie Siderurgiche Italiane (ASSIDER)* v. *The High Authority* (Case 5–55), Vol. II. It may be noted that in one case, without being requested to do so, the Court gave reasons why the German Government's interpretation of a particular judgment was inaccurate and, thus, to a certain extent itself interpreted that judgment—*German Government* v. *The High Authority* (Case 3–59), Vol. II.

9 Rules, Art. 102, para. 2.1.

orders that the record of this interpretative judgment shall be annexed to the record of the judgment interpreted. A reference to the interpretative judgment is made in the margin of the record of the judgment interpreted.[10]

JUDGMENTS AGAINST A DEFAULTING PARTY

If, in a case brought under the E.C.S.C. Treaty in which the Court possesses powers in *pleine juridiction*,[11] or in any cases at all under the two later Treaties, the defendant, having been duly notified, fails to file its written submissions, judgment is required to be given against it by default.[12] The Rules, which of course apply also to coal and steel cases, extend the provision in the E.C.S.C. Treaty to cover all cases before the Court where the defendant does not " reply to the request," [13] that is to say the defendant does not reply to the plaintiff's request in the form and in the time limit laid down.[14] The Rules do not, as did the old Rules,[15] also cover delays in submitting the reply or the rejoinder.[16] Further, the old Rules enabled the Court to give judgment by default when one of the parties, duly notified, failed to attend the oral hearing.[17] It can now only be assumed that the Court has deprived itself of its earlier powers.

Before giving judgment against the defaulting party, the Court, after hearing the Advocate General, considers the admissibility of the request [18] and verifies that the procedural formalities have been properly observed and that the plaintiff's contentions appear to be based on good grounds.[19] To do this, the Court may order measures of Instruction to be carried out.[20]

The party against whom judgment has been given by default may within one month from the service of the judgment make an application

---

10 Rules, Art. 102, para. 2.2.
11 See E.C.S.C. Treaty, Art. 36, para. 2, p. 193, below.
12 E.C.S.C. Statute, Art. 35; E.E.C. Statute, Art. 38; Euratom Statute, Art. 39.
13 Rules, Art. 94, para. 1.1. There is little practical point in considering whether the Court had competence thus to increase its jurisdiction.
14 Although E.C.S.C. Statute, Art. 35 refers to " written submissions," a term which is clearly wide enough to cover the defendant's rejoinder, there is no obligation to submit a rejoinder—Rules, Art. 41, para. 1 and Art. 44, para. 1.2 (b).
15 Old Rules, Art. 72, para. 1, which was expressed to be independent of the power contained in Art. 35 of the Statute.
16 Under the present Rules, if either or both of the reply and the rejoinder are not submitted within the time fixed, the Court proceeds with the case on the strength of the request and the reply alone—Rules, Art. 44, para. 1.2 (a). This is presumably also so even if the reply raises a counterclaim against the plaintiffs. It, therefore, might appear that this counterclaim need never be answered in the written pleadings.
17 Old Rules, Art. 72, para. 1.
18 This part of the provision is new. *Cf.* old Rules, Art. 72, para. 2.
19 Rules, Art. 94, para. 2.
20 *Ibid.*

to have it set aside.[21]   If such an application is made,[22] the President fixes the time limit within which the other side may submit its written observations,[23] and after the Court has considered them, it gives a ruling upon the application by means of a judgment which is not open to challenge.[24]

It is curious, however, that it is nowhere specified what are the grounds upon which a defendant may apply to set aside a judgment given in default against him, although it is assumed that some adequate explanation of the original failure to defend must be offered.   Further, if the application is granted, it is assumed that the original action is re-opened, and that the defendants are given a time in which to file their defence and that the case continues as it would have done previously.

A judgment given in default is executory.[25]   However, the Court may stay execution until it has given a ruling on an application to set the judgment aside, or the Court may make execution conditional upon the giving of a recognisance, the amount and nature of which are fixed having regard to the circumstances.[26]   This recognisance is subsequently released if no such application is made on it or if it is rejected.[27]

EXECUTION OF JUDGMENTS

Where an appeal has been brought challenging the validity of an act of a Community institution, the Court in its judgment will either uphold that validity or will annul the act.[28]   If it upholds that validity, the act is lawful and can therefore be lawfully operated by the institution concerned.   The judgment of the Court is itself, therefore, never required to be enforced.   If the act is annulled, the institution cannot lawfully

---

[21] Rules, Art. 94, para. 4.1 and 2.

[22] This application must be submitted in the same form and set out the same facts as must a request—Rules, Art. 94, para. 4.2.   As to the mode of presenting a request, see p. 50, above.

[23] Rules, Art. 94, para. 5.1.

[24] Rules, Art. 94, para. 6.1.   The record of this judgment is annexed to the record of the judgment given by default.   Reference to the judgment given on the application to set aside is made in the margin of the record of judgment by default—Rules, Art. 94, para. 6.2.

[25] Rules, Art. 94, para. 3.   This provision is new.

[26] Rules, Art. 94, para. 3.   This provision is new.

[27] *Ibid.*   This provision is new.

[28] The Court can also annul only part of an act, or, although annulling a regulation, it may declare that some part of the annulled regulation shall remain in force. E.E.C. Treaty, Art. 174, para. 2—see p. 295, below.   For the obligation upon the institution concerned when one of its acts has been annulled, see E.C.S.C. Treaty, Art. 34, p. 176, below, E.E.C. Treaty, Art. 176, p. 301, below and Euratom Treaty, Art. 149, p. 362, below.

operate it, so that, again, the judgment of the Court requires no enforcement in order to be effective.[29]

Where the Court has upheld the validity of a Decision of the High Authority setting out that a Member State has failed in one of the obligations incumbent upon it by virtue of the E.C.S.C. Treaty, this amounts to a finding by the Court that the alleged breach in fact exists. Constraint upon the Member State to end the breach can be imposed not by the Court but by the High Authority with the agreement of the Council of Ministers deciding by a two-thirds majority.[30] This constraint may amount either to the High Authority in effect fining the State by the simple process of withholding payment of the sums which it may owe to the State in question by virtue of the E.C.S.C. Treaty,[31] or to the High Authority taking, or authorising other Member States to take, measures to re-impose, for example, duties and restrictions upon the import of goods from the defaulting State, and the export of goods to it.[32]

Under the two later Treaties, there is no repetition of the above provision, so that where a State has been found by the Court to have failed to fulfil any of its Treaty obligations,[33] there are no means of coercing the defaulting State. It is merely declared in each of the two Treaties that:

> If the Court of Justice finds that a Member State has failed in one of the obligations incumbent upon it by virtue of the present Treaty, this State is required to take the measures which comprise the execution of the judgment of the Court.[34]

Where it is not a Member State but for example an enterprise or other legal or natural person which has violated one of the three Treaties, the High Authority or the appropriate commission may, among other sanctions,[35] fine the party concerned. The party concerned may then appeal in *pleine juridiction* to the Court.[36] If the Court approves the

29 The Court has no physical means of preventing an institution from attempting to operate an annulled act, but all of the daughter acts under an annulled parent act will be invalid and open to annulment—*cf. Meroni e C.* v. *The High Authority* (Case 9–56), Vol. II.

30 Art. 88, para. 3. If the Member State has not appealed to the Court against the High Authority's Decision setting out its breach, these measures may be taken without any reference to the Court.

31 *Ibid.* para. 3 (a).

32 *Ibid.* para. 3 (b). As to the above, see the discussion of Art. 88, p. 249, below.

33 The Court's power is contained in E.E.C. Treaty, Arts. 169 and 170; Euratom Treaty, Arts. 141 and 142.

34 E.E.C. Treaty, Art. 171; Euratom Treaty, Art. 143. For a discussion of Art. 171, see p. 281, below.

35 The High Authority, for example, might also order the separation of company assets illegally concentrated, E.C.S.C. Treaty, Art. 66, section 5, para. 2.

36 E.C.S.C. Treaty, Art. 36; *cf.* E.E.C. Treaty, Art. 172; Euratom Treaty, Art. 144 (b).

fine,[37] the Decision or other act which imposed it can lawfully be enforced. Enforcement of this administrative act proceeds in accordance with the relevant Treaty provisions.

Under the E.C.S.C. Treaty it is provided, first that the fine may be enforced by the High Authority suspending settlement of sums which it may owe to an enterprise up to the amount of the fine,[38] or secondly the High Authority's Decision may itself be enforced by the levying of execution. It is declared:

> Enforcement on the territory of Member States shall be carried out by means of the legal procedure in effect in each State, after the order for enforcement in the form in use in the State on whose territory the Decision is to be carried out has been stamped on the Decision.[39]

Under the two later Treaties, it is further provided that enforcement shall be governed by the rules of civil procedure in force in the State in whose territory it is to take place [40] and further that the party seeking the enforcement may proceed to such enforcement by applying directly to the authority which is competent by municipal law.[41]

Where the Court gives judgment against one of the institutions of the Communities, for example, in respect of a breach of contract,[42] a *faute de service*,[43] or in respect of tortious liability,[44] the winning party has no means of enforcing that judgment. The institution, however, is required to make good any damage caused [45] and it need hardly be considered that the institution would not comply with the judgment. If there were a delay in such compliance, however, the matter could be brought into prominence by the winning party commencing proceedings for the annulment of the implied Decision refusing to take action.[46]

---

[37] The Court has accepted that it has jurisdiction to reduce or quash the fine—see *Acciaceria Laminatoi Magliano Alpi (A.L.M.A.)* v. *The High Authority* (Case 8-56), Vol. II.

[38] Art. 91.

[39] Art. 92, para. 2. This stamping to be done without more verification than that the Decision is authentic. Each Government is to designate a Minister to be responsible for carrying out these formalities—*ibid*.

[40] E.E.C. Treaty, Art. 192, para. 2; Euratom Treaty, Art. 164, para. 1.

[41] E.E.C. Treaty, Art. 192, para. 3: Euratom Treaty, Art. 164, para. 2. The proper method of enforcement is declared to be a matter for the municipal courts—*ibid*. paras. 4 and 3.

[42] By virtue of E.C.S.C. Treaty, Art. 42; E.E.C. Treaty, Arts. 179 and 181; Euratom Treaty, Arts. 152 and 153.

[43] E.C.S.C. Treaty, Art. 40.

[44] E.E.C. Treaty, Art. 178; Euratom Treaty, Art. 151.

[45] E.E.C. Treaty, Art. 215, para. 2; Euratom Treaty, Art. 188, para. 2; *cf.* E.C.S.C. Treaty, Art. 40.

[46] Under E.C.S.C. Treaty, Art. 35; E.E.C. Treaty, Art. 175, para. 3; Euratom Treaty, 148, para. 3. For the enforcement of penalties against defaulting witnesses etc. see pp. 67–68, above.

REQUEST FOR A STAY OF EXECUTION OF A JUDGMENT

It is provided in each of the three Treaties that a judgment of the Court shall be enforced within the territory of a Member State by means of the legal procedure in effect in that State.[47] It is then declared that the execution of such a judgment can be suspended only by a decision of the Court.[48] The old Rules of the Court, which, of course, only regulated procedure under the E.C.S.C. Treaty, made no reference to a request for a stay of execution of a judgment. The present Rules, however, set out that such requests are to be governed by the same rules as apply both to a request for a stay of the execution of an administrative act of one of the institutions of the Community, and to a request for interim measures.[49] Some of these rules, however, are quite clearly inapplicable,[50] but, as appears from the remaining rules, the request for this stay of execution must set out the circumstances which give rise to urgency, as well as the grounds of fact and of law which prima facie show the justification for the granting of this stay.[51]

A request for a stay can be brought not only by one of the parties to the original action, but by a third party who challenges the final judgment on the ground that it prejudices his rights.[52]

If the request is acceded to, the order embodying the Court's decision must fix the date on which this stay ceases to have effect.[53]

THIRD PARTY PROCEEDINGS FOR SETTING ASIDE OR MODIFYING A JUDGMENT

Under the Statute of the E.C.S.C. Treaty, natural or legal persons as well as the institutions of that Community may bring third party proceedings to set aside or modify a judgment which has been given without their having been notified of the fact that the action had been brought.[54] The two later Treaties in their similar provisions [55] expressly mention

---

[47] E.C.S.C. Treaty, Arts. 44 and 92, para. 2; E.E.C. Treaty, Arts. 187 and 192, para. 2; Euratom Treaty, Arts, 159 and 164, para. 2.
[48] E.C.S.C. Treaty, Art. 92, para. 3; E.E.C. Treaty, Art. 192, para. 4; Euratom Treaty, Art. 164, para. 4.
[49] Rules, Art. 89, para. 1. As to those Rules, see pp. 85–87, below.
[50] Thus Rules, Art. 83, para. 1, states that a request for a stay of execution of an administrative act of one of the institutions of the Communities can be brought only where an appeal against that act has also been lodged. No appeal against a judgment of the Court itself can ever be brought before the Court.
[51] Rules, Art. 89, para. 1 and Art. 83, para. 2. As to the further procedural rules governing this request, see p. 86, below.
[52] The latter case is to be inferred from Rules, Art. 97, paras. 2 and 3, p. 84, below.
[53] Rules, Art. 89, para. 2. This provision is included in order to prevent the stay being indefinite and, therefore, acting as an appeal against the judgment itself. It is not stated, however. whether a request for a further stay may be brought.
[54] E.C.S.C. Statute, Art. 36.
[55] E.E.C. Statute, Art. 39; Euratom Statute, Art. 40.

that Member States may bring these proceedings [56] but that no one may bring them unless the judgment is prejudicial to their rights.[57]

Besides having to conform to the normal provisions governing the submission of a request to the Court,[58] a request by a third party to set aside a judgment must in addition specify the judgment objected to; indicate in what way the judgment objected to prejudices that third party's rights, and, by Article 91 (1) (c) it must indicate the reasons why the third party was not able to take part in the principal case.[59]

The Court has declared on this that:

> One must interpret Article 91 (1) (c) of the Rules of Procedure as admitting, on the one hand, the third party who, after notification of the case, was unable to take part in it for valid reasons, and on the other hand, all those who were not able to intervene in the case in accordance with Article 34 of the Protocol of the Statute of the Court and 93 of the Rules of Procedure.[60]

It would thus appear that no party which should have realised that it ought to have intervened in a case before the Court can seek to set aside or modify the judgment given.[61]

If it can be brought, the request seeking to set aside or modify a judgment may also request a stay of execution of the judgment concerned.[62] The request for a stay is treated in the same manner as such a request coming from one of the parties, and a ruling is given upon

---

[56] Member States, however, are presumably covered by the wording in the earlier Treaty " any legal person."

[57] E.E.C. Statute, Art. 39; Euratom Statute, Art. 40.

[58] Rules, Art. 97, para. 1.1. These provisions are set out in Rules, Arts. 37 and 38, see p. 50, above.

[59] Rules, Art. 97, para. 1 (a) (b) (c). If the judgment has been published in the *Journal Officiel*, the request must be submitted within two months of that publication—Rules, Art. 97, para. 1.3. Nothing is stated concerning the position where the judgment has not been so published. It might be argued, by analogy with appeals against Decisions of the High Authority and the Commissions etc., that the request is to be made within one or two months of the service of the judgment—see E.C.S.C. Treaty, Art. 33, para. 3; E.E.C. Treaty, Art. 173, para. 3; Euratom Treaty, Art. 146, para. 3. As, however, the parties concerned will not necessarily see the judgment within this time, it would appear that a more logical provision would be a time limit of one or two months from the time when the third party was in fact aware of the judgment.

[60] *Belgian Government* v. *Antoine Vloebergs and The High Authority* (Request to modify judgment in Joint Cases 9–60 and 12–60) [1963] 2 C.M.L.R. 44 where the Court held that where notice of an action seeking damages brought, under Art. 40 of the E.C.S.C. Treaty, by a Belgian enterprise against the High Authority had been published in the *Journal Officiel*, this notice was not sufficient to enable the Belgian Government to realise that it should have intervened in the case, so that after judgment had been given, the Government, when seeking to set aside the judgment by means of third party proceedings, could show reasons why it had not taken part in the principal case.

[61] As to intervention, see pp. 57–60, above.

[62] This is nowhere expressly stated in the Rules, but is to be inferred from Rules, Art. 97, paras. 2 and 3.

the matter by the President himself or by the Court, if he refers the decision to it.[63]

Concerning the request for the amendment of the judgment itself, however, the Rules, surprisingly enough, are quite silent. All that is stated is that the request for amendment is brought against all the parties to the principal case.[64] From this, it is suggested that it can only be assumed that all the parties to the original action are in effect made defendants.[65] What rights they have, however, of presenting their contentions and whether orally or in writing is not stated. Nor is it set out whether the third party can orally support the statements set out in its request, or call expert witnesses. All that is revealed is that the judgment challenged is amended to the extent to which " the third party's request is allowed." [66]

The record of the judgment given in pursuance of the request is annexed to the original of the judgment challenged. Reference to that judgment is made in the margin of the record of the judgment objected to.[67]

REQUESTS FOR A STAY OF EXECUTION OF ADMINISTRATIVE ACTS, AND FOR THE ORDERING OF PROVISIONAL MEASURES [68]

Appeals to the Court against Regulations, Decisions, etc, of the institutions of the Communities do not as a general rule have any suspensive effect.[69] However, if the Court believes that the circumstances so require, it may order the stay of execution of the administrative act that is being challenged, and may prescribe all necessary provisional measures that are to be taken.[70] Further, the President on his own may

---

[63] Rules, Art. 97, para. 2 and Art. 85, para. 1. For the procedure governing requests for stays of execution of a judgment, see p. 83, above.
[64] Rules, Art. 97, para. 1.2.
[65] This is what in effect occurred in *Belgian Government* v. *Antoine Vloebergs and The High Authority* (Request to modify judgment in Joint Cases 9–60 and 12–60) [1963] C.M.L.R. p. 44.
[66] Rules, Art. 97, para. 3.1. If a judgment is to be amended, it would seem only right that the parties should be allowed to submit their views, especially if an amendment will affect either or both of them.
[67] Rules, Art. 97, para. 3.2.
[68] *Du sursis et des autres mesures provisoires par voie de référé.*
[69] E.C.S.C. Treaty, Art. 39, para. 1; E.E.C. Treaty, Art. 185; Euratom Treaty, Art. 157. An exception to this general rule is, for example, E.C.S.C. Treaty, Art. 66, para. 5 (a) concerning the separation of concentrations.
[70] E.C.S.C. Treaty, Art. 39, paras. 2 and 3; E.E.C. Treaty, Arts. 185 and 186; Euratom Treaty, Arts. 157 and 158. For an example of the considerations taken into account when determining whether a Decision should be suspended, see the orders issued in *Firma J. Nold K.G.* v. *The High Authority* (Case 18–57), Vol. II, and in *Barbara Erzbergbau AG and other* v. *The High Authority* (Joint Cases 3–18, 25 and 26–58), Vol. II.

rule by means of a summary procedure upon submissions either for obtaining the stay of execution of administrative acts of the institutions of the Communities or for the applications for provisional measures.[71] A request for a stay of execution of an administrative act is admissible only where the applicant has challenged this particular act in an appeal before the Court.[72] Further, a request for one of the other provisional measures is admissible only if it is made by a party to an action which has been brought before the Court and if the request for these measures relates to that action.[73]

Both requests for a stay and for provisional measures must be brought in the standard manner,[74] and must set out the circumstances giving rise to urgency and the legal and factual grounds showing prima facie justification for the granting of the measures requested.[75]

On this provision, the Court has stated:

> In principle it is for the plaintiff to judge of the desirability of bringing a request for the suspension of execution and to decide at what stage of the procedure this request should be made.
>
> However, there are obvious objections to granting such a request when it has been introduced after the closing of the written proceedings and after the oral proceedings relating to the merits, and at a time when the Court has already started its deliberations upon the merits.[76]

The request when submitted is served on the other party, and the President sets a short time limit within which that party may make written or oral observations.[77] The President may also decide whether there is any need to order the opening of an Instruction.[78] In a case of urgency, however, the President may grant the request even before the other party has presented its observations, in which case the President's ruling may subsequently be modified or revoked, even by the President acting of his own motion.[79]

---

[71] E.C.S.C. Statute, Art. 33, para. 1; E.E.C. Statute, Art. 36, para. 1; Euratom Statute, Art. 37, para. 1.
[72] Rules, Art. 83, para. 1.1.
[73] Rules, Art. 83, para. 1.2.
[74] Rules, Art. 83, para. 3. The standard manner is set out in Rules, Arts. 37 and 38, see p. 50, above.
[75] Rules, in Art. 83, para. 2.
[76] *Barbara Erzbergbau AG* v. *The High Authority* (Joint Cases 3–18, 25 and 26–58), Vol. II.
[77] Rules, Art. 84, para. 1. It is assumed that these oral observations are made to the President himself, if he is deciding the matter, or to the whole Court if the case is referred to it under Rules, Art. 85, para. 1.
[78] Rules, Art. 84, para. 2. It is also assumed that this Instruction may be held entirely before the President, in which case the Rules governing an Instruction will have to be modified accordingly. See also preceding note.
[79] Rules, Art. 84, para. 2.2.

If there is no such urgency, the President [80] may determine upon the request himself, or he may refer the matter to the Court for decision.[81] If the matter is so referred, the Court leaving all other business and, having heard the Advocate General, gives a ruling.[82]

The ruling on the request either by the President or by the Court is given by means of a reasoned order which is not open to appeal.[83] The order is immediately served on the parties concerned.[84]

Even if this ruling rejects the request, it is still open to the party concerned to present a further request based upon fresh facts.[85]

The enforcement of this order may be made subject to the provision of security by the person bringing the request, the amount and the nature of which are fixed having regard to the circumstances.[86]

The order itself is only temporary in nature and in no way prejudices the Court's decision upon the principal action.[87] Further, the order may be modified or revoked at any time on the application of one of the parties by reason of a change in circumstances.[88]

REQUESTS FOR A STAY OF EXECUTION OF DECISIONS OF THE EURATOM ARBITRATION COMMITTEE

Where a party to an action before the Arbitration Committee set up under the Euratom Treaty [89] wishes to appeal to the Court against that decision [90] the request to the Court is to be sent by registered letter with

---

[80] If the President is absent or unable to attend, his place is taken by the senior of the two Presidents of the Chambers—Rules, Art. 85, para. 2, in accordance with E.C.S.C. Statute, Art. 33, para. 2; E.E.C. Statute, Art. 36, para. 2; Euratom Statute, Art. 37, para. 2. Where, however, a request for provisional measures has been brought by an official or other employee of an institution against that institution, the person to deputise for the President of the Court is the President of the Chamber designated to hear appeals by employees—Rules, Art. 96, para. 1.

[81] Rules, Art. 85, para. 1. Where such a request is brought by an official or other employee of an institution of the Communities against the institution, the President may refer the matter to the Chamber designated to hear appeals by employees—Rules, Art. 96, para. 2, see p. 89, below.

[82] Rules, Art. 85, para. 3. It is further provided by this article that " The provisions of the preceding article shall apply." This is a reference to Art. 84 by which the President can decide whether there is need to order an Instruction, and may grant the request even before the other party has presented its observations. These powers are thus possessed by the Court when the matter is referred to it.

[83] Rules, Art. 86, para. 1.

[84] *Ibid.*

[85] Rules, Art. 88.

[86] Rules, Art. 86, para. 2.

[87] Rules, Art. 86, para. 4. The order may itself appoint the date from which the measure is to cease to be applicable; if it does not do so, the measure automatically ceases to have effect from the pronouncement of the judgment in the principal action— Rules, Art. 86, para. 3.

[88] Rules, Art. 87.

[89] Euratom Treaty, Art. 18, para. 1: as to this Committee, see p. 442, below.

[90] This appeal involves a suspension of the operation of the decision—Euratom Treaty, Art. 18, para. 2.

acknowledgment of receipt [91] and must be lodged within one month after the notification of the decision.[92]

This request must contain the name and address of the applicant, the status of the signatory who drew up the request, particulars of the decision of the Arbitration Committee which is being appealed against, particulars of the parties, a brief summary of the facts and the grounds of appeal and submissions of the applicant.[93] A certified copy of the decision must be annexed to the request.[94] If the plaintiff is not a legal person in private law,[95] there must, in addition, be attached to the request the relevant Memorandum and Articles of Association and proof that the powers granted to counsel have been properly conferred by a representative authorised to do so.[96]

After this request has been lodged, the Registrar requires the Registry of the Arbitration Committee to forward the file on the case to the Court.[97] The request is then served on the other party to the arbitration [98] which within the following month must submit its defence.[99] After this, the oral proceedings are opened.[1]

In judging this appeal, the only matters which the Court may take into consideration are procedural defects in the giving of the decision, and

[91] Instructions to the Registrar, Art. 5, para. 2.1.
[92] Rules, Art. 101, para. 1.
[93] *Ibid.*
[94] Rules, Art. 101, para. 2.2. This request is dated by the Court with the date of its being filed in the Registry—Rules, Art. 101, para. 2.1, and Art. 37, para. 3. There must also be annexed to the request a file containing the papers and documents relied upon in support of the request, and a memorandum of these—Rules, Art. 101, para. 2.1, and Art. 37, para. 4. This file will be returned to the Registry of the Arbitration Committee after the Court has pronounced judgment or after the case has been struck off the Court Register—Instructions to the Registrar, Art. 5, para. 2.2. The request must also contain an address chosen at the place where the Court is sitting, and the name of the person who is authorised and who has consented to accept service of all documents—Rules, Art. 101, para. 2.1, and Art. 38, para. 2.
[95] The division into public and private does not exist in English law.
[96] Rules, Art. 101, para. 2, and Art. 38, para. 5.
[97] Rules, Art. 101, para. 3.
[98] Rules, Art. 101, para. 4, and Art. 39. If the request when originally submitted does not comply with the conditions of the Rules, the request is served as soon as it has been regularised or the Court has agreed to entertain it—*ibid.*
[99] Rules, Art. 101, para. 4, and Art. 40, para. 1.1. This defence must contain the name and address of the defendant, the factual and legal arguments that are relied upon, the defendant's submissions and an outline of the evidence—*ibid.*; and, as with the request, the defence must set out the choice of an address for service at the place where the Court has its seat, and, if the defendant is a legal person in private law, there must be attached to the defence the defendant's memorandum and articles of association and proof that the powers granted to the defendant's counsel have been properly conferred by a representative authorised to do so—Rules, Art. 101, para. 4, and Art. 40, para. 1.2.
[1] Rules, Art. 101, para. 4, and Art. 55. As to these proceedings see pp. 72–74, above. If no defence is submitted, judgment may be given by default, in accordance with the procedure discussed, pp. 79–80, above.

the interpretation given by the Arbitration Committee to the provisions of the Euratom Treaty.[2] The appeal is finally disposed of by means of a judgment.[3]

If this judgment annuls the decision of the Arbitration Committee, the Court refers the case back to that Committee if this should be necessary.[4]

REQUESTS FOR MANDATORY INJUNCTIONS

The only occasion when the Court has power to grant a mandatory injunction to require a party to carry out its duty under a Treaty is contained in the Euratom Treaty. By this, where a Member State of the Euratom Community hinders the carrying out of an inspection within its territory to ensure that no ores, source materials or special fissionable materials are diverted from their intended uses, or that agreements between the Community and non-Member States are observed, the Euratom Commission shall request the President of the Court for a warrant to enforce the carrying out of the inspection.[5] When this request is made, it must specify the name and address of the persons and enterprises subject to inspection and an indication of the object and aim of the inspection.[6] The President gives a ruling by means of an order [7] and is required to give his decision within three days.[8]

If, however, there is danger in delaying even for these three days, the Euratom Commission may itself issue a warrant in the form of a Decision to the effect that the inspection is to be carried out.[9] Such a warrant is to be submitted without delay to the President for his subsequent approval.[10]

APPEALS BROUGHT BY EMPLOYEES OF THE COMMUNITIES

Where an appeal is brought by an official or other employee of an institution of one of the Communities against that institution, the case is to be judged by a Chamber of the Court which is to be appointed each

---

2 Euratom Treaty, Art. 18, para. 2. The effect of this provision is that there is an appeal on a point of law, but not of fact.
3 Rules, Art. 101, para. 5.
4 *Ibid.*
5 Euratom Treaty, Art. 81, para. 3, and Art. 77 (a) and (b).
6 Rules, Art. 90, para. 1 (a) and (b).
7 Rules, Art. 90, para. 2.1. Art. 86 of the Rules is expressly made to apply to this order, as to which, see p. 87, above.
8 Euratom Treaty, Art. 81, para. 3. In the event of the absence of the President or where he is unable to attend, his place is taken by the senior of the two Presidents of the Chambers—Rules, Art. 90, para. 2.2, and Art. 7, para. 2.
9 Euratom Treaty, Art. 81, para. 4.
10 *Ibid.* Nothing is stated about what is to occur if the President does not approve the Commission's warrant.

year for this purpose, unless the appeal contains a request for interim measures.[11] Where a case is so referred to a Chamber, the powers of the President of the Court are exercised by the President of that Chamber.[12] However, the Chamber may remit the case to the Court as a whole.[13]

ADVISORY OPINIONS

UPON THE VALIDITY OF AMENDMENTS OF THE POWERS OF THE HIGH AUTHORITY

Under the E.C.S.C. Treaty,[14] the Court is required to examine any joint proposals of the High Authority and the Council of Ministers which have been drawn up for the amendment of the rules governing the exercise by the High Authority of the powers conferred upon it.[15]

The request to the Court to give its opinion upon these amendments is brought jointly by the High Authority and the Council of Ministers.[16] The Court, having heard both the Advocates General, gives its reasoned opinion in a private session.[17] This Opinion is subsequently notified to the High Authority, the Council of Ministers and to the Assembly.[18]

UPON THE COMPATIBILITY OF INTERNATIONAL AGREEMENTS TO BE ENTERED INTO BY THE ECONOMIC COMMUNITY

The Economic Community is empowered to conclude agreements with one or more States or with international organisations. Before these agreements are signed, however, the Council, the Commission or any Member State may obtain the preliminary opinion of the Court as to

---

[11] Rules, Art. 95, para. 1.1. As to interim measures, see pp. 85–87, above.

[12] Rules, Art. 95, para. 1.2. The provisions of the Rules are expressly made to apply to the proceedings before the Chamber—*ibid.* The case will thus have a written and an oral proceedings and Instruction, witnesses may be called, etc.

[13] Rules, Art. 95, para. 2. For an example of an employee's case being remitted to the whole Court see *Gabriel Simon* v. *The Court of Justice* (Case 15–60). Because the case concerned the validity of a ruling made by the President, he did not himself sit, and in order that the required uneven number of judges should be present the most junior judge did not sit either—see Rules, Art. 26, para. 1.

[14] E.C.S.C. Treaty, Art. 95, para. 4.

[15] The Court is to determine whether these amendments modify the basic aims of the Treaty as set out in Arts. 2, 3 and 4, or the relationship between the powers of the High Authority and those of the other institutions of the Community—E.C.S.C. Treaty, Art. 95, para. 3. On this see *Re Amendment Procedure under Article 95, paras. 3 and 4 of the E.C.S.C. Treaty*, Vol. II, below; Opinion 1–60, Vol. II, below, and *Re Amendment of Article 65 of the E.C.S.C. Treaty* (Opinion 1–61).

[16] Rules, Art. 108, para. 1.

[17] Rules, Art. 108, para. 2, and Art. 107, para. 2. The Opinion is signed by the President, the judges who took part in the deliberations and by the Registrar—*ibid.*

[18] Rules, Art. 108, para. 2.

the compatibility of the contemplated agreements with the provisions of the Economic Community Treaty.[19]

The President fixes a time limit within which the institution and the Member States on whom the request has been served may present their written observations,[20] and he further appoints the *juge rapporteur*.[21]

After the Court has heard both of the Advocates General, it gives its reasoned opinion in a private session,[22] and this is served on the Council, the Commission and on the Member States.[23]

UPON THE COMPATIBILITY WITH THE TERMS OF THE EURATOM TREATY OF A MEMBER STATE'S DRAFT AGREEMENT OR CONVENTION

A Member State is required to communicate to the Euratom Commission any draft agreement or convention to be entered into with a non-Member State, an international organisation, or a national of such a non-Member State to the extent to which such agreement or convention concerns the field of application of the Euratom Treaty.[24] If the Commission finds that the proposed agreement or convention is not compatible with the Treaty, it is to inform the State of this fact.[25] The State may challenge this finding of the Commission by appealing to the Court.[26]

Four certified copies of the request must be presented [27] and must be accompanied by the draft agreement or convention in question, by the observations addressed by the Commission to the State concerned, as well as by any other documents in support of the appeal.[28] The request is served on the Commission,[29] which is required to present its observations to the Court within ten days, but this time limit, however, may be

---

19 E.E.C. Treaty, Art. 228, para. 1.1. If the request is brought by the Council, it is served on the Commission; if it is brought by the Commission it is served on the Council and on the Member States; if the request is brought by one of the Member States, it is served on the Council, the Commission and the other Member States—Rules, Art. 106, para. 1.1.
20 Rules, Art. 106, para. 1.2.   21 Rules, Art. 107, para. 1.
22 Rules, Art. 107, para. 2.
23 Rules, Art. 107, para. 3. The Opinion is signed by the President, the judges who took part in the deliberations and by the Registrar—*ibid*. If the opinion of the Court is that the agreement is not compatible with the provisions of the Treaty, or that the Community or the particular institution which is seeking to conclude it is incompetent to do so, the agreement may only enter into force if ratified by all the Member States—E.E.C. Treaty, Art. 228, para. 1.2 and Art. 236, para. 3; Rules, Art. 106, para. 2.
24 Euratom Treaty, Art. 103, para. 1.
25 *Ibid*. Art. 103, para. 2.
26 *Ibid*. Art. 103, para. 3. For discussion of the Court's competence under this provision, see p. 14, above.
27 Rules, Art. 104, para. 1
28 Rules, Art. 104, para. 2. Following the submission of the request, the President appoints the *juge rapporteur*—Rules, Art. 104, para. 3.
29 Rules, Art. 104, para. 1.

extended by the President, after he has heard the State concerned in respect of such extension.[30] A certified copy of these observations is served on this State,[31] and either the State or the Commission may be heard by agents or legal advisors, if it so requests.[32] The decision is taken at a private session after the Advocates General have been heard.[33]

Upon the Compatibility with the Terms of the Euratom Treaty of a Member State's concluded Agreement or Convention

Where, after the date of entry into force of the Euratom Treaty,[34] a Member State concludes an agreement or convention with a non-Member State, an international organisation, or a national of such a non-Member State, the Commission may require from the State concerned all relevant information for the purpose of ascertaining whether such agreement or convention contains clauses impeding the application of the Treaty.[35]

Upon a request by the Commission, the Court shall rule upon the compatibility of the agreement or convention with the provisions of the Treaty.[36] This request, when received, is served on the State concerned.[37] There are then written proceedings, an Instruction and oral proceedings as in normal litigation before the Court.[38]

COSTS

By the Rules, every judgment must include a decision concerning costs.[39] The actual proceedings before the Court itself, however, are declared to be free in all their stages,[40] but there are two exceptions to this. First, a party must reimburse to the Court any expenses which the Court

30 Rules, Art. 104, para. 2.2.
31 Rules, Art. 104, para. 2.3.
32 Rules, Art. 104, para. 4.2.
33 Rules, Art. 104, para. 4.1. It is not clear which Advocate General is here being referred to.
34 January, 1, 1958.
35 Euratom Treaty, Art. 104, para. 2.
36 *Ibid.* Art. 104, para. 3. On this competence of the Court, see further p. 14, above.
37 Rules, Art. 105, para. 2.
38 Rules, Art. 105, para. 1. The Court also had similar jurisdiction in respect of agreements and conventions concluded between the time of the signing of the Treaty, April 17, 1957, and its entry into force, January 1, 1958—Euratom Treaty, Art. 105, para. 2. Identical Rules applied to these actions—Rules, Art. 105, para. 1. These provisions are now spent. No cases were brought under them.
39 Rules, Art. 63. If the judgment omits to do so, the party which finds itself affected thereby may bring the matter before the Court by means of a request brought within a month of the notification of the judgment—Rules, Art. 67, para. 1, see p. 76, above.
40 Rules, Art. 72, para. 1.

has had to bear if these could have been avoided,[41] and secondly, a party must pay the costs of all copying or of translation carried out at its request, which is considered by the Registrar to have been excessive.[42]

The basic rule of the Court is that the winning party can recover its costs if application is made to this effect.[43] However, where plaintiffs have claimed more damages than the Court finally awards them, they will be penalised by being required to pay part of the costs.[44] Similarly, where the defendants win, but they have pleaded that the action was inadmissible and have lost on this plea, they will be required to pay some part of the plaintiff's costs.[45]

The costs that the winning party can claim are: first, all sums owing to witnesses in respect of travelling and subsistence and loss of earnings[46]; secondly, sums due to experts in respect of travelling and subsistence and the fees for their work[47]; thirdly, necessary costs incurred by the parties for the purposes of the proceedings and in particular the travelling subsistence and remuneration of an agent, legal adviser or counsel[48]; fourthly, costs which have been caused by the other party

---

[41] Rules, Art. 72 (a). The Advocate General is heard by the Court before a party is ordered to pay these costs—*ibid.*

[42] Rules, Art. 72 (b). The scale of charges are:
  (a) For a copy of a judgment or order, a copy of a procedural document or of minutes of proceedings, an extract from the Court register, a copy of the Court register—30 Luxembourg francs per page of a maximum of 40 lines.
  (b) For a translation—200 Luxembourg francs per page of a maximum of 40 lines. Each subsequent copy is charged at 5 Luxembourg francs per page or part of a page—Instructions to the Registrar, Art. 20.

[43] Rules, Art. 69, para. 2.1. This is subject to what is set out below. If there is more than one losing party, the Court may apportion costs between them—Rules, Art. 69, para. 2.2.

[44] See, *e.g.*, *M. Antoine Kergall* v. *The Common Assembly* (Case 1–55), Vol. II, and *Fiddelaar* v. *The Commission of E.E.C.* (Case 44–59), Vol. II, both of whom were required to pay one-third of their own costs although each had a valid claim against the defendants.

[45] See, *e.g.*, *Compagnie des Hauts Fourneaux de Chasse* v. *The High Authority* (Case 15–57), Vol. II. This case may be compared with the earlier action brought by the same plaintiffs (Case 2–57) where the High Authority lost on the challenge of the admissibility of some of the plaintiffs' arguments, but nevertheless were awarded their full costs, see Vol. II, below. Where both the plaintiffs and the defendants lost on their submissions concerning admissibility each was required to pay its own costs—*Groupement des Industries Sidérurgiques Luxembourgeoises* v. *The High Authority* (Case 9–54), Vol. II. [46] Rules, Art. 73 (a) and Art. 51, paras. 1 and 2.1.

[47] *Ibid.* In one case where the Court ordered an expert examination, costs in respect of it were apportioned as to half to each party:
The Court declared:
  The defendants have in part lost on the first ground of the submissions in their request. The expert report, ordered by the Second Chamber of the Court on June 26, 1959, concerned the facts referred to under this head.
  It is necessary, therefore, to apportion the costs of the expert's report equally.
Chambre Syndicale de l'Est de la France and others v. *The High Authority* (Joint Cases 24–58 and 34-58), Vol. II.

[48] Rules, Art. 73 (b). It is not clear whether there is any significance in the fact that the fees of only one advocate, etc., are referred to. It is suggested, however, that the costs must cover those of both a leader and a junior.

and which the Court regards as thrown away or vexatious [49]; and finally any expenses which the winning party has been forced to incur for the purposes of execution of the judgment.[50]

Vexatious costs were awarded to plaintiffs in one case [51] where the High Authority had written a letter to the plaintiffs setting out that a particular application of theirs concerning investment would be refused: two months later the High Authority passed a Decision formally refusing that application. The plaintiffs in order to be cautious appealed in two separate actions, first against the letter and secondly against the Decision. The Court declared:

> The plaintiffs were led by the defendants' behaviour to bring two appeals, whereas if the letter . . . had not been prematurely issued a single appeal would have sufficed.
>
> The costs incurred by the plaintiffs in connection with [the first appeal] thus constitute vexatious costs caused to the plaintiffs by the defendants.[52]

In another case,[52a] certain Italian steel works had appealed against Decisions of the High Authority which set out how much they owed by virtue of a particular levy upon every ton of scrap purchased. During the course of the written proceedings, the High Authority repealed the Decisions, but the plaintiffs nevertheless carried on with their actions. The Court declared:

> Expenses incurred by the parties since the notification of the repeal of the challenged Decisions could have been avoided had the plaintiffs discontinued as from that time.
>
> The plaintiffs when informed of the repeal of the Decisions in issue were not obliged to discontinue their appeals.
>
> However, they no longer had any further interest in the continuance of the proceedings; a better appreciation of their interests should have encouraged them not to have continued.
>
> By reason of this absence of interest, costs incurred after the notification of the withdrawal of the decisions must be regarded as " thrown away " within the meaning of Article 69, paragraph 2 (3), of the Rules of Procedure and must, therefore, be borne by the plaintiffs.[52b]

---

[49] Rules, Art. 69, para. 3.2. These costs are those that any party, even the winning one, must pay to the other side—*ibid.*

[50] Rules, Art. 71. These charges are determined in accordance with the tariff in force in the State where the execution has occurred—*ibid.*

[51] *Société Métallurgique de Knutange* v. *The High Authority* (Joint Cases 15–54 and 29–59), Vol. II.

[52] *Ibid.* Vol. II. For a case where the Court refused to hold a particular action reckless or vexatious, see *M. René Bourgaux* v. *The Common Assembly* (Case 1–56), Vol. II.

[52a] *Meroni & Co. and others* v. *The High Authority* (Joint Cases 5, 7 and 8–60).

[52b] *Ibid.*

The Court may reduce the costs claimable by the winning party or
hold that no costs are claimable at all, if that party has itself lost on one
or more counts,[53] or if there are exceptional reasons.[54]

As an example of exceptional reasons reference may be made to one
case where the plaintiffs brought an action for the annulment of the
reasoning supporting a Decision of the High Authority because such
reasoning had been,

> expressed so clearly in an imperative manner that it naturally gave
> the impression that it amounted there and then to the acceptance of a
> final standpoint and, therefore, to an actual Decision.[55]

As the High Authority was responsible for this wording, the Court held
that although the High Authority won the action it should be condemned
to pay one third of the plaintiffs' costs.

Special rules cover the situation where an appeal is brought by an
official or other employee against an institution of the Communities.
Here, if the individual wins his case, he will obtain his costs as set out
above, and if that individual has been granted free legal aid, either in
whole or in part, these costs will include a reimbursement to the Court
of such aid paid out by it.[56] If, however, the individual loses, he will
not be required to pay the costs incurred by the institution,[57] but will,
of course, have to meet his own costs.

---

[53] In order to avoid this result, in one case in 1957 the High Authority
   " without expressly declaring that the action is inadmissible, asks whether the
   plaintiffs ought not to have challenged the system of payments to the subsidy
   fund at the time that the payments were made obligatory, that is to say in 1954."
   Although the Court declared that " this question must receive a negative answer," the
   High Authority was awarded its full costs because it had not lost on any formal claim
   concerning inadmissibility—*Compagnie des Hauts Fourneaux de Chasse* v. *The
   High Authority* (Case 2–57), Vol. II.

[54] Rules, Art. 69, para. 3.1. This provision is an elaboration of that set out in the
   statutes that the Court is to determine upon costs—E.C.S.C. Statute, Art. 32; E.E.C.
   Statute, Art. 35; Euratom Statute, Art. 36.

[55] *" Geitling," " Mausegatt " and " Präsident " and others* v. *The High Authority*
   (Joint Cases 16–59, 17–59 and 18–59), Vol. II. In the normal way, of course,
   reasoning supporting a Decision cannot itself be another Decision.

[56] See *Mlle. Miranda Mirossevich* v. *The High Authority* (Case 10–55), Vol. II. As to
   legal aid, see p. 98, below.

[57] Rules, Art. 70. The provision, however, concerning paying to the other party the
   costs which it has caused and which the Court regards as thrown away or vexatious
   still applies to actions brought by individuals against institutions—Rules, Art. 70
   and Art. 69, para. 3.2. It is suggested that the individual will also have to pay
   to the Court under Rules, Art. 72 (a) and (b) those expenses which could have been
   avoided, as well as the costs of excessive translations. This is not clear, however,
   because Art. 70 states: " Costs incurred by the institutions shall be borne by them,
   without prejudice to the provisions of Article 69, paragraph 3, second sub-paragraph
   of these Rules." This may mean that no other provisions except Art. 69, para. 3.2
   concerning thrown away and vexatious expenses are to apply. If this is so, the Court
   would itself have to pay for translations, however lengthy.

Where a third party intervenes in an action and supports the arguments of the plaintiffs solely on one or more heads of claim and the plaintiffs subsequently lose on those heads, either the plaintiffs must pay the costs of the third party [58] or these costs must be paid for by that party itself.[59] However, there does not appear to be any clear principle to determine how the Court exercises its discretion in this matter. If the plaintiffs win, however, the defendants must pay the costs of the third party, in accordance with general principles.

In assessing costs, the Court keeps distinct from the costs of the principal action any costs incurred, for example, in a request for the suspension of execution of a Decision and in a request for provisional measures. The party losing in these requests is required to pay the costs.[60] In one case where an expert report was ordered by the Court, the costs of this were divided equally between the parties.[61]

Where a municipal court of one of the Member States has submitted a request to the Court for a preliminary ruling upon the interpretation of the E.E.C. or Euratom Treaties [62] or of acts passed by the institutions of those Communities, the parties, the Member States, the Commission and, where appropriate, the Council of Ministers have the right to submit a statement or written observation to the Court.[63] Where these observations are so submitted, it appears that any costs involved must be paid by the Commission or the Council of Ministers and by the Member States themselves: the costs of the application to the Court are left to the municipal court to apportion, and it would appear that they become costs in the cause in the normal way.[64]

---

[58] *Groupement des Industries Sidérurgiques Luxembourgeoises* v. *The High Authority* (Joint Cases 7–54 and 9–54), Vol. II and others.

[59] *Chambre Syndicale de la Sidérurgie de l'Est de la France and others* v. *The High Authority* (Joint cases 24–58 and 34–58), Vol. II. In a more recent case the intervening party was required by the Court to pay not only its own costs but those incurred by the defendants as a result of the intervention whereas the Advocate General had submitted that the plaintiffs should pay the intervener's costs—*Confédération Nationale des Producteurs de Fruits et Légumes and others* v. *The Council of E.E.C.* (Joint Cases 16 and 17–62) [1963] C.M.L.R. 160.

[60] As to the costs of a Request for the suspension of the execution of a Decision, see *e.g.*, " *Geitling*," " *Maussegatt* " and " *Präsident* " v. *The High Authority* (Joint Cases 16–59 and 18–59), Vol. II, and *Eva von Lachmüller and others* v. *The Commission of E.E.C.* (Joint Cases 43–59, 45–59 and 48–59), Vol. II. As to costs in a request for provisional measures see *R. P. M. Fiddelaar* v. *The Commission of E.E.C.* (Case 44–59), Vol. II.

[61] *Chambre Syndicale de la Sidérurgie de l'Est de la France* v. *The High Authority* (Joint Cases 24–58 and 34–58), Vol. II.

[62] Under E.E.C. Treaty, Art. 177 and Euratom Treaty, Art. 150, see pp. 303 and 365, below.

[63] E.E.C. Statute, Art. 20, para. 2; Euratom Statute, Art 21, para. 2.

[64] *Robert Bosch G.m.b.H. and others* v. *Kleding-Verkoopbedrijf de Geus en Uitdenbogerd* (Case 31–61) [1962] C.M.L.R. 1 at p. 30, and *N.V. Algemene Transport- en Expeditie Onderneming van Gend en Loos* v. *Nederlandse Tariefcommissie* [1963] C.M.L.R. 105 at p. 132.

However, if there is no application for costs, no order will be made, so that each party will pay its own costs.[65]

A party which discontinues its action is required to pay the costs of both sides unless the discontinuance was justified by the conduct of the other party.[66] In the event of there being nothing upon which to adjudicate, the Court determines freely upon costs.[67]

If a dispute arises concerning the amount of costs recoverable, the dispute is assigned to one of the two Chambers.[68] After this Chamber has heard the observations of the other party and the submissions of the Advocate General, it decides by making an order which is not subject to appeal.[69]

Once costs have been finally determined, execution for them may be levied in accordance with the provisions of the Treaties.[70] Where sums have been paid out by the Court itself,[71] these are claimed by means of a registered letter signed by the Registrar, from the party which is required to pay them.[72] If the provisions of this letter are not complied with, the Registrar is required to ask the Court to make an executory order which he then requires to be enforced as a judgment [73] and recovery can be made by way of execution.[74]

Where money is to be paid into the Court itself, as for example to meet the costs of excessive translations,[75] or to guarantee the costs incurred by witnesses,[76] this is done in the currency of the country of origin of the party which is making the payment.[77] Where, alternatively,

---

[65] Rules, Art. 69, para. 4.2.
[66] Rules, Art. 69, para. 4.1.
[67] Rules, Art. 69, para. 5.
[68] There are no Rules setting out how such cases are to be assigned to a Chamber, or even stating that they are to be assigned, but this is to be inferred from Rules, Art. 74, para. 1. The Chamber concerned is presumably the one to which the judge previously appointed as *juge rapporteur* belongs.
[69] Rules, Art. 74, para. 1.
[70] E.C.S.C. Treaty, Arts. 44 and 92; E.E.C. Treaty, Arts. 187 and 192; Euratom Treaty, Arts. 159 and 164. For the purpose of levying this execution the parties may request a copy of the order—Rules, Art. 74, para. 2.
[71] In respect of free legal aid—Rules, Art. 76, para. 5.1; on the costs of a *commission rogatoire*—Instructions to the Registrar, as amended, Art. 22, para. 2.2., or as an advance to witnesses or experts—Rules, Art. 47, para. 3.2 and Art. 51, para. 1; or to the counsel assigned to an assisted person—Instructions to the Registrar, as amended, Art. 22, para. 2.2; or costs which might have been avoided—Rules, Art. 72 (a).
[72] Instructions to the Registrar, Art. 22, para. 1.1. This letter must specify, in addition to the amount to be reimbursed, the method of payment and the time limit allowed for such reimbursement—*ibid*.
[73] Art. 22, para. 2.1—see further, note 2, p. 100, below.
[74] Art. 22, para. 2.2.   [75] Under Rules, Art. 72 (b).
[76] Under Rules, Art. 47, para. 3.1.
[77] Rules, Art 75, para. 2. The rate of exchange is that ruling on the day of payment in the country where the Court has its seat—Rules, Art. 75, para. 3.

the Court is paying out money, as for example where the Court is advancing payment in respect of a witness's travel or subsistence expenses,[78] this is made in the currency of the country where the Court has its seat,[79] or, at the request of the party concerned, these payments may be made in the currency of the country in which he incurred the recoverable costs or carried out the acts giving rise to the reimbursement.[80]

LEGAL AID

If a party to an action [81] finds himself unable in whole or in part to meet the costs of proceedings he may at any time apply for free legal aid.[82] This application must be accompanied by full information showing that the party concerned is in need, such as a certificate from a competent authority certifying his lack of means.[83]

If the application is made prior to the proceedings which the requesting party intends to institute, it must give a brief account of the object of those proceedings.[84]

Upon the receipt of such an application, the President appoints a *juge rapporteur*.[85] The Chamber of which that *juge* is a member, after it has studied the written observations of the other party [86] and heard the Advocate General, decides whether the grounds of the proceedings which have been brought or which it is intended to bring are manifestly ill founded. If they are not, the Chamber may grant free legal aid wholly or in part or it may refuse it.[87] The Chamber decides by means

78 Under Rules, Art. 51, para. 1.
79 Rules, Art. 75, para. 1.1.
80 Rules, Art. 75, para. 1.2. The acts here being referred to include, for example, witnesses appearing before *commissions rogatoires*, under Rules, Art. 52, or experts preparing their reports.
81 It seems to be implied in the Rules that the party being referred to is a natural person; it is nowhere expressly stated, however, that an enterprise of limited means could not also apply for aid.
82 Rules, Art. 76, para. 1.1. For an example of a plaintiff being granted free legal aid, see *Mlle. Miranda Mirosevich* v. *The High Authority* (Case 10–55), Vol. II.
83 Rules, Art. 76, para. 1.2. No indication is given of what authorities are here being referred to.
84 Rules, Art. 76, para. 2.1. The application for legal aid need not be drafted by counsel—Rules, Art. 76, para. 2.2.
85 Rules, Art. 76, para. 3.1. The duties of this judge are not specified.
86 There are no Rules governing the submission of these observations. So it is unknown within what time limit they must be submitted; whether the applicant's financial position is notified to the other side and whether the summary of the grounds of the action contemplated are also revealed. There is no authority either, what matters the observations may deal with, whether evidence concerning the applicant's financial position, or submissions upon the manifestly ill founded nature of the action are allowed or not.
87 Rules, Art. 76, para. 3.1.

of an order without giving reasons.[88] There is no appeal against this order.[89]

If free legal aid is granted, the Court Pay Office will advance the necessary funds,[90] but the applicant must supply the Registrar with details of the expenses in respect of which the legal aid is requested.[91] If, however, the Registrar considers the sum to be excessive, he may reduce it of his own authority or spread payment over a period.[92]

In the order of the Court [93] in which it decides to grant free legal aid, the Court is to require that counsel shall be appointed to assist the party concerned.[94] The Court is also required to decide upon the expenses and fees of a counsel which will be paid by the Court and, on request, the President may order that such counsel shall receive an advance.[95]

If the assisted party does not himself indicate his choice of counsel, or if the Court considers that his choice should not be endorsed,[96] the Registrar is required to forward a copy of the Court's order and a copy of the original request for legal aid to the competent authority in the State concerned.[97] Having regard to the proposals transmitted to it by that authority, the Court itself appoints counsel to assist the party.[98]

[88] Rules, Art. 76, para. 3.2.
[89] *Ibid.* If the application for legal aid is made after an action has been commenced, the position is not entirely clear. It would appear that the application is submitted to the Chamber to which the *juge rapporteur*, who has probably been nominated, belongs, and that that Chamber follows the same procedure as set out above, except, of course, that the Chamber may possibly not now be concerned with the well founding of the action, according to how far that action has proceeded. It follows from this that if a defence to the action has been submitted, the observations of the other party, to be considered by the Chamber, must relate solely to the validity of the application for legal aid.
[90] Rules, Art. 76, para. 5.1. These funds include the payment of all Registry charges in respect of translations, etc.—Instructions to the Registrar, Art. 19. Application for these funds is made to the Court Pay Office in the normal way—*ibid.*
[91] Instructions to the Registrar, Art. 21, para. 1.1. Payment is made against a signed receipt or proof of transfer—*ibid.* Art. 21, para. 2.1.
[92] Instructions to the Registrar, Art. 21, para. 2.2.
[93] The Supplementary Rules describe this as an Order of the Court, but, as seen above, it is a Chamber, on behalf of the Court, which issues the orders.
[94] Supplementary Rules, Art. 4, para. 1.
[95] *Ibid.* Art. 5, paras. 1 and 2. The Registrar shall order payment by the Court Pay Office of this advance but if he considers that the sum requested is excessive he may reduce it of his own authority or spread payment over a period—Instructions to the Registrar, as amended, Art. 21, para. 4. It is suggested that by this provision the Registrar is not being given power to overrule the President of the Court, but rather that the President, under Art. 5, para. 2 above, approves an advance in principle, and the Registrar regulates the amount of that advance so approved.
[96] No grounds for this possible veto are set out. It is suggested that they can relate only to the specialisation of the counsel concerned and to the importance of the case in question.
[97] Supplementary Rules, Art. 4, para. 2 and Appendix I. Their authorities are:
Germany: Bundesrechtsanwaltskamer;
Belgium, France, Italy and Luxembourg: the Minister of Justice.
Netherlands: Algemene Raad van de Nederlandse Orde van Advocaten.
[98] *Ibid.* Art. 4, para. 2. The Rules in their present form make no reference to the employment of legal advisers as well as counsel.

In the final judgment of the Court, the decision as to costs shall order a deduction to be made in favour of the Court of the sum disbursed as free legal aid.[99] It is then provided that the Registrar is to recover these sums from the party ordered to pay them.[1] If this party does not pay within the time limit specified by the Registrar, the latter is required to request the Court to issue an executory order. The Registrar then requires this to be enforced in the same manner as a judgment.[2]

PROCEDURAL TIME LIMITS

Where a time limit is specified either for the bringing of an action or for completing any of the procedural stages of an action, these periods apply only to parties habitually resident in Luxembourg. For those resident in Belgium these periods are increased by two days; for those in Germany, Metropolitan France and the Netherlands, by six days; for those in Italy, by ten days; for those in other European countries fourteen days and for those in all other countries, by one month.[3]

In reckoning these time limits, however, the day on which the particular act occurred from which time begins to run is not itself counted as a day,[4] and furthermore in reckoning the time limit for the bringing of an appeal against an act of an institution of the Communities, time begins to run, in the case where that act has been notified to the plaintiff, only from the day following that on which the party concerned received notice of the act in question, and in the case where that act

---

[99] Rules, Art. 76, para. 5.2. If, however, the assisted party loses, this provision clearly cannot apply.

[1] Rules, Art. 76, para. 5.3. On general principles this party is the one who loses—Rules, Art. 69, para. 2. These sums are claimed by a registered letter signed by the Registrar. The letter shall specify, in addition to the sum to be reimbursed, the method and time limit allowed for such reimbursement—Instructions to the Registrar, Art. 22, para. 1.1.

[2] Instructions to the Registrar, Art. 22, para. 2.1. " Enforcement on the territory of Member States shall be carried out by means of the legal procedure in effect in each State, after the order for enforcement in the form in use in the State on whose territory the decision is to be carried out has been stamped on the decision; this shall be done without more verification than that the decision is authentic. These formalities shall be carried out under the responsibility of a Minister designated for this purpose by each of the Governments."—E.C.S.C. Treaty, Art. 92; E.C.C. Treaty, Art. 192; Euratom Treaty, Art. 164.

[3] Rules, Appendix II, Art. 1 and Rules, Art. 81, para. 2. These extensions appear to be largely arbitrary as no one will suggest that an airmail letter from Rome to Luxembourg takes ten days, or from New York to Luxembourg, one month. Under the old Rules (Art. 85, para. 2) these periods were: Belgium, one day; Germany, Metropolitan France and the Netherlands, three days; Italy, five days; other European countries: one month. Other countries: two months. It will be seen that some of these periods have been doubled and some halved. It might be inferred from this that the term " one month " is being used to mean 28 days—*i.e.*, twice 14 days, and not a calendar month.

[4] Rules, Art. 80, para. 1.1.

has been published, from the fourteenth day after the publication of the act in the *Journal Officiel des Communautés européennes.*[5]

These time limits continue to run during Court vacations,[6] but if the day on which they end is a Sunday or a public holiday, the expiry is postponed until the end of the next working day.[7] It is set out, however, that all the time limits fixed by virtue of the Rules may be extended by the authority which laid them down.[8] The meaning of this provision is not quite clear, but it presumably means, for example that where the President of the Court has power to fix time limits,[9] he can extend these times once fixed.[10]

Finally, it is set out that where a party has failed to comply with any of these time periods, it shall not thereby lose any of its rights provided that it can prove the existence of an unforeseeable circumstance or *force majeure.*[11]

TIME LIMITS FOR BRINGING ACTIONS BEFORE THE COURT

The following are the time limits specified for bringing actions in the Court [12]:

1. Appeals against Decisions and Recommendations of the High Authority—one month from the date of notification or publication, as the case may be.[13]

2. Appeals against Regulations, Directives or Decisions of the Commissions of the Economic and Euratom Communities—two months from the notification or publication thereof, as the case may be, or failing that, from the day on which the plaintiff had knowledge of the Regulation, Directive or Decision.[14]

3. Appeals for damages against the High Authority for failing within a reasonable time to take the measures necessary to give effect to a judgment of annulment [15]—no time specified.

---

5 Rules, Art. 81, para. 1.
6 Rules, Art. 80, para. 1.2. As to these vacations, see p. 45, above.
7 Rules, Art. 80, para. 2.1. For these legal holidays, see p. 543, below.
8 Rules, Art. 82.
9 As, for example, the time within which the Reply and the Rejoinder must be submitted —Rules, Art. 41, para. 2.
10 For a list of time limits and the authority which can fix them, see pp. 106–108, below.
11 E.C.S.C. Statute, Art. 39, para. 3; E.E.C. Statute, Art. 42, para. 2; Euratom Statute, Art. 43, para. 2.
12 All the time periods here specified are subject to the possibility of extensions set out above.
13 E.C.S.C. Treaty, Art. 33, para. 3.
14 E.E.C. Treaty, Art. 173, para. 3; Euratom Treaty, Art. 146, para. 3.
15 E.C.S.C. Treaty, Art. 34, para. 2.

4. Appeals for damages against the Commissions and Councils of the Economic and Euratom Communities for failing to take measures required for giving effect to a judgment of the Court[16]—no time specified.

5. Appeals for the annulment of negative Decisions or Recommendations of the High Authority which are implied following upon its inaction for a period of two months after being requested to take action —one month.[17]

6. Appeals for the annulment of negative acts of the Commissions or the Councils of the Economic or Euratom Communities which are implied following upon their inaction for a period of two months after being requested to take action—two months.[18]

7. Appeals against Decisions of the High Authority imposing pecuniary sanctions and daily penalties—one month from the notification or publication of the Decision, as the case may be.[19]

8. Appeals against penalties imposed by the Commission of the Economic Community—within a time to be specified by the Council of Ministers in Regulations which may confer jurisdiction upon the Court in such matters.[20]

9. Appeals brought by persons or enterprises against penalties imposed upon them by the Euratom Commission[21]—no time specified.

10. Appeals against a Decision of the High Authority recognising the existence of a situation likely to cause fundamental and persistent disturbances in the economy of a State, or against explicit or implied Decisions refusing to recognise such a situation—one month from the publication of an explicit Decision[22]; presumably also one month from the time when the High Authority's inaction creates an implied Decision refusing to act.[23] When this occurs is not stated.

11. Appeals against the *délibérations* of the Assembly or of the Council of the E.C.S.C.—one month from the publication of the *délibérations* of the Assembly, or from the notification of such *délibération* of the Council to the Member States or to the High Authority.[24]

---

[16] E.E.C. Treaty, Art. 176, para. 1, Art. 215, para. 2 and Art. 178; Euratom Treaty, Art. 149, para. 1. Art. 188, para. 2 and Art. 151.
[17] E.C.S.C. Treaty, Art. 35, para. 3.
[18] E.E.C. Treaty, Art. 175, para. 2; Euratom Treaty, Art. 148, para. 2.
[19] E.C.S.C. Treaty, Art. 36, para. 2 and E.C.S.C. Statute, Art. 39, para. 1.
[20] E.E.C. Treaty, Art. 172. These regulations have not yet been drawn up.
[21] Euratom Treaty, Art. 144 (b) and Art. 83.
[22] E.C.S.C. Treaty, Art. 37, para. 3 and E.C.S.C. Statute, Art. 39, para. 1.
[23] E.C.S.C. Treaty, Art. 37, para. 3 and E.C.S.C. Statute, Art. 39, para. 1 by analogy with E.C.S.C. Treaty, Art. 35, para. 3.
[24] E.C.S.C. Treaty, Art. 38, para. 2.

12. Disputes between Member States relating to the object of any of the three Treaties, that are submitted to the Court by virtue of an arbitration agreement [25]—presumably governed by the particular arbitration agreement.

13. Disputes among Member States concerning the application of the E.C.S.C. Treaty [26]—no time specified.[27]

14. Appeals brought by one Member State against another Member State alleging that that other has failed to fulfil one of its obligations under either the Economic or Euratom Treaties [28]—no time specified.

15. Appeals by a Member State against a Decision of the High Authority declaring that it has failed in one of the obligations incumbent upon it by virtue of the E.C.S.C. Treaty—two months from the notification of the Decision.[29]

16. Appeals against sanctions imposed by the High Authority against a Member State which, after being declared to be in default, has failed to take steps to fulfil its obligations under the E.C.S.C. Treaty—two months from the notification of the sanctions.[30]

17. Appeals alleging non-fulfilment by a Member State of the obligations arising under the Statute of the European Investment Bank [31] —no time specified.

18. Appeals for the annulment of the resolutions of the Board of Directors of the European Investment Bank—two months from the publication of the resolution or its notification to the plaintiff or, failing that, from the day on which the plaintiff had knowledge of it.[32]

19. Appeals by the Euratom Commission against a Member State for the purpose of establishing that a person or enterprise under that State's jurisdiction has infringed the Euratom Treaty [33]—no time specified.

---

25 E.C.S.C. Treaty, Art. 29, para. 2; E.E.C. Treaty, Art. 182; Euratom Treaty, Art. 154.
26 E.C.S.C. Treaty, Art. 89, para. 1.
27 Such a dispute can be submitted regardless of whether there is an express clause conferring jurisdiction or not.
28 E.E.C. Treaty, Art. 170, para. 1; Euratom Treaty, Art. 142, para. 1. Before a State brings such an action it must refer the alleged default to the appropriate Commission. If that Commission fails to give an opinion within three months, it is provided that reference to the Court " shall not thereby be prevented "—*ibid.* para. 4. For a discussion of the meaning of this provision, see pp. 277–281, below.
29 E.C.S.C. Treaty, Art. 88, para. 2.
30 E.C.S.C. Treaty, Art. 88, para. 4.
31 E.E.C. Treaty, Art. 180 (a)
32 E.E.C. Treaty, Art. 180 (b) and Art. 187, para. 3; and E.E.C. Treaty, Art. 180 (c) and Art. 187, para. 3.
33 Euratom Treaty, Art. 145, para. 2.

20. Appeals against one of the Communities for injury resulting from a *faute de service* of that Community [34]—no time specified.

21. Appeals against an official or employee of one of the Communities for injury resulting from a *faute personnel* of such official or employee [35]—no time specified.

22. Disputes submitted to the Court pursuant to an arbitration agreement contained in a contract concluded under private or public law by or on behalf of one of the Communities [36]—presumably governed by the particular arbitration agreement.

23. Disputes between the Economic or Euratom Communities and their employees—as laid down in the relevant Statute of Service or conditions of employment.[37]

24. Requests from municipal tribunals for a preliminary decision upon:

    (1) the interpretation of the Economic or Euratom Treaties;

    (2) the validity or interpretation of the acts of the institutions of the Economic or Euratom Communities;

    (3) the validity of acts of the High Authority or Council of Ministers of the Coal and Steel Community;

    (4) the interpretation of the Statutes of any body set up by an act of the Councils of the Economic or Euratom Communities [38]—no time specified.

25. Requests for Advisory Opinions upon the compatibility with the relevant Treaty of:

    (1) amendments of the power of the High Authority [39]—no time specified;

    (2) agreements between the Economic Community and one or more States or an international organisation [40]—no time specified;

    (3) agreements between a Member State and a non-Member State, international organisation or a national of a non-Member State—at any time after the State has received the comments of the Euratom Commission [41];

[34] E.C.S.C. Treaty, Art. 40, para. 1; E.E.C. Treaty, Art. 178 and 215, para. 2; Euratom Treaty, Art. 151 and 188, para. 2.
[35] E.C.S.C. Treaty, Art. 40, para. 1; E.E.C. Treaty, Art. 178 and 215, para. 2; Euratom Treaty, Art. 151 and 188, para. 2.
[36] E.C.S.C. Treaty, Art. 42; E.E.C. Treaty, Art. 181; Euratom Treaty, Art. 153.
[37] E.E.C. Treaty, Art. 179, Euratom Treaty, Art. 152.
[38] E.C.S.C. Treaty, Art. 41; E.E.C. Treaty, Art. 177; Euratom Treaty, Art. 150.
[39] E.C.S.C. Treaty, Art. 95, para. 4.
[40] E.E.C. Treaty, Art. 228, para. 2.
[41] Euratom Treaty, Art. 103, para. 3.

(4) agreements between persons or enterprises and a non-Member State or an international organisation or a national of a non-Member State [42]—no time specified.

26. Requests to the Court to settle suitable conditions for the grant by the Euratom Commission of licences and sub-licences for the use of patents, etc.[43]—no time specified.

SERVICE OF DOCUMENTS

All service of documents referred to in the Rules is effected under the direction of the Registrar at the address at the seat of the Court which has been chosen by that party.[44] Service is effected by delivery against a receipt,[45] or by dispatch of a copy of the relevant document by registered post with acknowledgment of its receipt.[46]

---

[42] Euratom Treaty, Art. 104, para. 3. A similar right to obtain an advisory opinion existed in the case of agreements concluded between the signing of the Euratom Treaty and its entry into force. These have now expired.
[43] Euratom Treaty, Art. 144 and Art. 12, para. 4.
[44] Rules, Art. 79, para. 1.1. For the necessity to choose this address, see note 70, p. 51 and note 88, p. 53, above.
[45] Under the old Rules (old Rules, Art. 83, para. 1.1) copies of these documents could only be sent through the post and not delivered by hand.
[46] Rules, Art. 79, para. 1.1. These copies of the originals are prepared and certified as accurate by the Registrar, except where the parties themselves are required to forward certified duplicate copies for the other parties concerned—under Rules, Art. 37, para. 1.2. The acknowledgments of receipt are annexed to the original of the documents concerned—Rules, Art. 79, para. 2.

TIME LIMITS FOR THE PROCEDURAL STAGES OF AN ACTION

Stage	Time
Submission of the defence	One month from the service on the defendant of the request.[47]
Defendant's observations upon request for a stay of execution or for interim measures.	Brief period as fixed by the President.[48]
Submission of the plaintiff's reply.	As fixed by the President.[49]
Submission of the defendant's rejoinder.	As fixed by the President.[50]
Answer by a party to a new ground of appeal advanced by the other side during the written proceedings.	The previous time as extended by the President.[51]
Joinder by the Court of two or more actions	Any time.[52]
Giving by the *juge rapporteur* of his report upon whether the case needs an Instruction.	As fixed by the President.[53]
Presentation of a report by an expert.	As fixed by the Court.[54]
Challenge of the capacity, etc., of a witness or of an expert.	Fifteen days from the service of the Order summoning the witness or nominating the expert.[55]
Observations of the parties upon the Instruction.	As fixed by the President.[56]
Request for judgment upon a preliminary objection or upon a particular matter.[57]	No time specified.
Presentation of written submissions by the other side upon this request.	As fixed by the President.[58]
Third party's request to intervene.	Before the the opening of the oral proceedings.[59]
Reply to this request to intervene.[60]	No time specified.
Submissions of the party intervening.	As fixed by the President.[61]
Reply to such submissions.	As fixed by the President.[62]
Opening of the oral proceedings.	As fixed by the President.[63]
Discontinuance by agreement of an action other than a challenge of an act of the High Authority, the Commissions or the Council of the Economic and Euratom Communities,	Any time before judgment.[64]
Application for leave to defend where judgment has been given against a defendant in default.	One month from the service of the judgment on the defendant.[65]
Plaintiff's observations upon this application.	As fixed by the President.[66]

infringes a third party's rights.	the *Journal Officiel des Communautés européennes*.[69]
Submission of the observations of the parties to the case which gave rise to that judgment.	A brief period as fixed by the President.[70]
Challenge of the costs awarded in a case.[71]	No time specified.
Presentation of oral submissions by the other side upon this challenge.[72]	No time specified.
Requests for the interpretation of a judgment.[73]	No time specified.
Submission of the observations of the parties subject to this judgment upon this request for interpretation.[74]	No time specified.
Request for the revision of a judgment on the grounds of the discovery of new facts.	Three months from the day on which the party concerned discovered the new facts[75] provided that this three months is within 10 years from the date of the judgment.[76]
Observations of the other side upon this request.[77]	No time specified.
Applications for legal aid.	At any time.[78]

[47] Rules, Art. 40, para. 1. This time limit may be extended by the President at the defendants' request and for good cause shown—*ibid.* para. 2.
[48] Rules, Art. 84, para. 1.
[49] Rules, Art. 41, para. 2.
[50] Rules, Art. 41, para. 2.
[51] Rules, Art. 42, para. 2.
[52] Rules, Art. 43.
[53] Rules, Art. 44, para. 1.
[54] Rules, Art. 49, para. 1.
[55] Rules, Art. 50, para. 2.
[56] Rules, Art. 54, para. 1.
[57] Rules, Art. 91, para. 3.
[58] Rules, Art. 91, para. 2.
[59] Rules, Art. 93, para. 1. As to whether the Instruction is part of the oral procedure see p. 72, note 51, above.
[60] Rules, Art. 93, para. 3.
[61] Rules, Art. 93, para. 5.2.
[62] Rules, Art. 93, para. 5.2.
[63] Rules, Art. 44. para. 2 and Art. 54, para. 2.
[64] Rules, Art. 77, para. 1.
[65] Rules, Art. 94, para. 4.2.
[66] Rules, Art. 94, para. 5.1.
[67] Rules, Art. 66, para. 1.
[68] Rules, Art. 67, para. 1.
[69] Rules, Art. 97, para. 1.3.
[70] Rules, Art. 92, para. 2 and Art. 84, para. 1.
[71] Rules, Art. 74, para. 1.
[72] Rules, Art. 74, para. 2.
[73] Rules, Art. 102, para. 1.1.
[74] Rules, Art. 102, para. 2.1.
[75] Rules, Art. 98.
[76] E.C.S.C. Statute, Art. 38, para. 3; E.E.C. Statute, Art. 41, para. 3; Euratom Statute, Art. 42, para. 3.
[77] Rules, Art. 100, para. 1.
[78] Rules, Art. 76, para. 1.1.

Stage	Time
Observation of the other party upon this application.[79]	No time specified.
Observations by the parties, Member States, the High Authority or the Council of Ministers of the Coal and Steel Community upon a request for a preliminary decision upon the validity of the acts of the High Authority or the Council of Ministers, submitted by a national tribunal.	Two months from the service of the request on the party concerned.[80]
Observations by the parties, Member States, the Commissions or the Councils of Ministers of the Economic or Euratom Communities upon a request for a preliminary decision upon the interpretation of the Treaty, etc., submitted by a domestic court or tribunal.	Two months from the service of the request to the party concerned.[81]
Observations of Member States and the international organisations concerned upon the validity of proposed agreements between the Economic Community and one or more States or an international organisation.	As fixed by the President.[82]
Observations of the Euratom Commission upon proposed agreements between a Member State and a non-Member State.	Ten days, presumably from the receipt by the Commission of the request, and all other documents to which it is entitled.[83] This period may be extended after the State concerned has been heard.[84]

[79] Rules, Art. 76, para. 3.1.
[80] Rules, Art. 103, para. 2.2.
[81] E.E.C. Statute, Art. 20, para. 2; Euratom Statute, Art. 21, para. 2.
[82] Rules, Art. 106, para. 1.1.
[83] Rules, Art. 104, para. 2.2.
[84] *Ibid.*

108

CHAPTER
4

THE JURISDICTION OF THE COURT UNDER THE EUROPEAN COAL AND STEEL COMMUNITY TREATY

ARTICLE 10, Para. 10

In all cases provided for in the present Article where a member [of the High Authority] is appointed by the governments by a five-sixths majority or by vote of the members of the High Authority, each government shall have a right of veto under the following conditions :

If a government has used its right of veto with respect to two persons in the case of an individual appointment and of four persons in the case of a general or biennial renewal of membership, any other exercise of that right on the same occasion may be referred to the Court by another government; the Court may declare the veto null and void if it considers the right of veto has been abused.[1]

Article 10 sets out the method to be adopted in the election of the members of the High Authority. Three types of election may occur:

(a) that to fill one seat on the death of a sitting member or upon his resignation or dismissal by the Court [2]

(b) biennial elections when three places become vacant

(c) a general re-election following a vote of censure by the Common Assembly.

---

[1] French:
" *Dans tous les cas prévus au présent article où une nomination est faite par voie de décision des gouvernements à la majorité des cinq sixièmes ou par voie de cooptation, chaque gouvernement dispose d'un droit de veto dans les conditions ci-après:*
Lorsqu'un gouvernement a usé de son droit de veto à l'égard de deux personnes s'il s'agit d'un renouvellement individuel et de quatre personnes s'il s'agit d'un renouvellement général ou biennal, tout autre exercice dudit droit à l'occasion du même renouvellement peut être déféré à la Cour par un autre gouvernement; la Cour peut déclarer le veto nul et non avenu si elle l'estime abusif."
Stationery Office:
" In all cases provided for in the present Article in which an appointment is made by a decision of the Governments by five-sixths majority or by means of co-option each Government shall have a right of veto subject to the following conditions:
If a Government has used its right of veto with respect to two persons in the case of a general or biennial renewal of membership, any further exercise of that right on the occasion of the same renewal of membership may be referred to the Court by another Government; the Court may declare the veto invalid if it considers that the right of the veto has been abused."

[2] The procedure for dismissal is set out in Art. 12, para. 2.

THE VETO

In elections of type (a) when only one seat is to be filled, members are elected alternately by the governments of the Member States and by the remaining members of the High Authority,[3] but any government has an absolute power to veto the election of any two persons. In elections of types (b) and (c) this power can be exercised in respect of four persons.[4]

Beyond this absolute power there is also a power of further veto in respect of any number of persons, subject to the right of any government to refer the matter to the Court, which may declare these further vetos null and void if it considers that there has been an unjustified use of the veto.

No cases have yet been brought to the Court under this Article, so that there is no authority upon what amounts to an injustified use of the veto. It is suggested, however, that any use of the veto for political reasons, such as keeping one country from having a member on the High Authority, or because one of a Member State's own nationals has been vetoed would be unjustified. Conversely a belief that a person does not possess general competence or is not likely to be completely independent or that he may solicit or accept instructions from a government or from an organisation [5] would justify the use of a veto.

It is not stated in this Article that the Court is bound to consult the governments whose veto is being challenged, nor is that government expressly granted any right to present its case, although it is suggested that these must be implied as the decision to be taken is a judicial one.

ARTICLE 12, Para. 2

Members [of the High Authority] who no longer fulfil the conditions required for the exercise of their functions or who have committed a serious fault may be removed from office by the Court on petition of the High Authority, or the Council.[6]

The conditions required of the members of the High Authority for the exercise of their functions are that they shall act in complete inde-

---

[3] Art. 12, paras. 9, 1 and 3. If the election is being made by the governments, a five-sixths majority is adequate, if by the other members of the High Authority five votes is adequate—*ibid.* In normal cases there will be eight remaining members of the High Authority.

[4] It appears that if three members of the High Authority were to resign or die, or be dismissed before any of them had been replaced, the election to the three seats would be classed as three individual elections so that each State could exercise six absolute vetos, whereas when three seats become vacant biennially only four such vetos are allowed.

[5] Specific requirements for the holding of office set out in Art. 9, paras. 1 and 5.

[6] French:
    " *Peuvent être déclarés démissionnaires d'office par la Cour, à la requête de la*

pendence in the general interest of the Community; that in the fulfilment of their duties, they shall neither solicit nor accept instructions from any government or from any organisation, and that they will abstain from all conduct incompatible with the impartial character of their functions.[7] Further, they are required not to exercise any business or professional activities, paid or unpaid, or acquire or hold, directly or indirectly, any interest in any business which relates to coal and steel during their term of office.[8]

Article 12 states that members of the High Authority who no longer fulfil these conditions or who have committed a serious fault may be removed by the Court. It should be noted that the wording is not that they *shall* be removed, but that they may be.

THE EXTENT OF THE COURT'S JURISDICTION

This appears to imply that the Court is to consider the case and is only to remove the member if it is itself satisfied that removal is justified. In other words, removal does not follow automatically upon a petition to that effect being brought by the High Authority or by the Council nor that it will follow automatically upon the Court judging that a member no longer fulfils the required conditions or that he has committed a serious fault.

The term " serious fault " [9] appears to be wide enough to cover both personal and official failings, for although in certain circumstances the Community accepts vicarious responsibility for faults committed by officials [10] this can in no way alter the personal responsibility of the official concerned. However, until a charge has been substantiated against the accused member either before a national tribunal or before the Court itself the member cannot in any legal sense be held to have committed a fault, but he must be held to be merely *accused* of having committed a fault.

Haute Autorité ou du Conseil, les membres de la Haute Autorité ne remplissant plus les conditions nécessaires pour exercer leurs fonctions ou ayant commis une faute grave."
Stationery Office:
" Members who no longer fulfil the conditions required for the performance of their duties or who are guilty of serious misconduct may be compulsorily retired by the Court at the request of the High Authority or the Council."
[7] Art. 12, para. 2.
[8] Art. 9, para. 5.
[9] *Faute grave.*
[10] Art. 9, para. 2.

ARTICLE 31

The Court shall ensure the respect of law in the interpretation and application of the present Treaty and of its implementing regulations.[11]

This Article defines the Court's duty. It is suggested that it does not itself grant jurisdiction—the Court being limited by the jurisdiction contained in the other Articles of the Treaty.

ARTICLE 33, Para. 1

The Court is competent to pronounce upon appeals for annulment for incompetence, violation of a substantial procedural requirement, violation of the Treaty or of any rule of law concerning its application or for *détournement de pouvoir* brought against the Decisions and Recommendations of the High Authority by one of the Member States or by the Council. However, the examination by the Court may not include an assessment of the situation resulting from the facts or economic circumstances in view of which the said Decisions or Recommendations were taken, unless the High Authority is alleged to have committed a *détournement de pouvoir* or to have patently misconstrued the provisions of the Treaty or any rule of law concerning its application.[12]

[11] French:
"*La Cour assure le respect du droit dans l'interprétation et l'application du présent Traité et des règlements d'exécution.*"
Stationery Office:
"The Court shall ensure the observance of law in the interpretation and implementation of the present Treaty and of the Regulations for giving effect to it."

[12] French:
"*La Cour est compétente pour se prononcer sur les recours en annulation pour incompétence, violation des formes substantielles, violation du Traité ou de toute règle de droit relative à son application, ou détournement de pouvoir, formés contre les décisions et recommandations de la Haute Autorité par un des Etats membres ou par le Conseil. Toutefois, l'examen de la Cour ne peut porter sur l'appreciation de la situation découlant des faits ou circonstances économiques au vu de laquelle sont intervenues lesdites décisions ou recommandations, sauf s'il fait grief à la Haute Autorité d'avoir commis un détournement de pouvoir ou méconnu d'une manière patente les dispositions du Traité ou toute règle de droit relative à son application.*"
Stationery Office:
"The Court shall be empowered to entertain applications by one of the Member States or by the Council, to quash decisions and recommendations of the High Authority on the grounds of lack of jurisdiction, violations of basic procedural rules, violation of the Treaty or of any rule of law relating to giving effect to it, or misuse of powers. However, the investigation of the Court may not cover the evaluation of the situation, resulting from economic facts and circumstances, in the light of which such decisions or recommendations were taken, except where the High Authority is accused of having misused its powers or of having patently misinterpreted the provisions of the Treaty or of any rule of law relating to giving effect to it."

112

The substance of this Article has been incorporated into both the E.E.C. and Euratom Treaties,[13] and from a lawyer's point of view this Article is one of the most important in the entire Treaty, for it sets out the jurisdiction which the Court is able to exercise over the administrative acts of the High Authority. It is not surprising, therefore, that its wording has called for much detailed and careful interpretation by the Court.[14]

THE COURT'S POWER TO CONSIDER MATTERS OF ITS OWN MOTION

The first point requiring to be resolved was whether the Court when considering an appeal for annulment brought under this Article was limited to considering merely the particular grounds of invalidity alleged by a plaintiff, or alternatively whether, of its own motion, the Court could declare a Decision or Recommendation annulled upon one of the four grounds set out in this Article even if that ground had not been pleaded.

Either of these two interpretations is tenable. It will be readily accepted that the Court is only to determine appeals actually brought before it, and that it has no power to take the initiative and itself require the High Authority to justify the legality of its Decisions—the Court, that is, is a referee and not a participant. It would appear logically to follow from this that the Court, when invoked, is to be limited to considering only the arguments submitted and not to usurp the function of counsel for the plaintiffs.

Against this interpretation, however, must be set the terms of Article 31 by which the Court is to ensure the respect of law in the interpretation and application of the Treaty. It would appear to be a violation of this provision if the Court, when asked whether a particular Decision of the High Authority was valid or not, declared it valid, because, let us say, the ground of incompetence was not alleged, while in a subsequent case holding the same Decision invalid, because the pleadings were different and did allege incompetence.

The attitude of the Court on this matter, however, has not been entirely consistent. In one case [15] it declared:

---

13 Economic Community Treaty, Art. 173, para. 1; Euratom Community Treaty, Art. 146, para. 1.
14 For a shorter version of this analysis of Art. 33, see Valentine, D. G.: " The Jurisdiction of the Court of Justice of the European Communities to Annul Executive Action," in B.Y.I.L. (1960), p. 174. For a valuable discussion of Art. 33, see Bebr, Gerhard, *Judicial Control of the European Communities* (Stevens, 1962).
15 *Groupement des Industries Sidérurgiques Luxembourgeoises* v. *The High Authority* (Cases 7–54 and 9–54), Vol. II. For the Court's interpretation of Art. 33 in its early cases see Bonaert, A. and others: *Fragen der Nichtigkeits- und Untätigkeitsklagen nach dem Recht der Europäischen Gemeinschaft für Kohle und Stahl*: Vittorio-Klostermann (1961).

In the present dispute, the plaintiffs have not accused the High Authority either of having committed a *détournement de pouvoir* or of having patently misconstrued the provisions of the Treaty, or of any rule of law relating to its application. The Court must, therefore, limit itself to examining whether, in law, [the Decision challenged] violates the Treaty or any rule relating to its application.

In the very second case that the Court heard,[16] it refused to consider whether a violation of a substantial procedural requirement had been committed when the High Authority refrained from setting out, and presumably countering, unfavourable opinions which that Authority had received concerning the advisability of taking the particular Decision being challenged. The Court gave two grounds for its refusal. First, that the violation had only been alleged in the plaintiff's reply and was therefore inadmissible by the Rules and secondly, and far more significantly, that " the public interest " did not require it.

This self imposed limitation however is in conflict with what the Court on other occasions has felt itself able to do. Thus in one action,[17] although the plaintiffs had not alleged a violation of a substantial procedural requirement, the Court examined whether such a procedural requirement had been violated,[18] and, be it noted, made no suggestion that its examination was required by public interest. In that case, also, the Court made a slightly cryptic remark when it declared:

> The other articles of Decision 2–54 have not been challenged by the plaintiffs and the Court is of the opinion that there are no grounds for their annulment.[19]

However, whether the Court intended to imply that if it had been of the opinion that there were grounds for that annulment it would have annulled them is not clear. Elsewhere,[20] the Court, of itself, undertook an investigation of whether a particular committee had been consulted by the High Authority before the latter passed the Decision that was being challenged. The High Authority objected to this, on the grounds that a failure to undertake this consultation had not been alleged by the plaintiffs. The Court, however, replied to this objection by declaring:

> The Court is of the opinion that this ground has to be examined by the Court acting of its own motion, because if it were well founded, an

---

16 *Italian Government* v. *The High Authority* (Case 2–54), Vol. II.
17 *French Government* v. *The High Authority* (Case 1–54), Vol. II.
18 The Court declared:
  " The Court of its own motion has examined the question whether Article 1 of Decision 2–54 contributes a violation of a substantial procedural requirement "—*ibid.*
19 *Ibid.*
20 *Italian Government* v. *The High Authority* (Case 2–54), Vol. II.

annulment *ex officio* on the ground of violation of the Treaty or of a substantial procedural requirement would be justified.[21]

In another case the Court stated:

> The plaintiffs have not expressly alleged the ground of illegality against Decision 2–57 and it is only with difficulty that one could admit that such an allegation had been made by implication.
>
> However, it appears unwise to allow any doubts concerning the legality of Decision 2–57 in so far as the solution of this question has a bearing on the present case.
>
> For this reason the Court considers that it is essential to examine whether this second ground of appeal is well founded.[22]

A similar situation arose in 1960 in a case where the Court appears to be saying that although for procedural reasons a particular allegation cannot be made by the plaintiffs themselves, nevertheless if adequate evidence had been furnished by them in support of the allegation, the Court would itself have considered the allegation. The Court's words were:

> The plaintiff claims that the time limits [granted by the High Authority for the modification of certain protective tariffs] are not able to prevent [serious economic disturbances].
>
> This complaint must be rejected *in limine*, because it was raised for the first time, and without any further explanation, in the reply. *Furthermore, the plaintiffs have not furnished adequate proof in law of their allegation to allow the Court to review this situation.*[23]

The present attitude of the Court, however, is well illustrated by a judgment given in 1959.[24] Here the Court held that according to the Rules of the Court, an allegation that three Decisions of the High Authority[25] had been passed in violation of a substantial procedural requirement was not acceptable, because the allegation had not been made in the original request. The Court then continued:

> The obligation to give reasons for Decisions which Article 15 of the E.C.S.C. Treaty[26] imposes upon the High Authority has been prescribed

---

21 *Ibid.*

22 *Société des Fonderies de Pont-à-Mousson* v. *The High Authority* (Case 14–59), Vol. II.

23 *Compagnie des Hauts-Fourneaux et Fonderies de Givors and others* v. *The High Authority* (Joint Cases 27–58, 28–58 and 29–58), Vol. II (Author's italics). The alternative interpretation of the words in italics might be that in any event the complaint, even if it had been admissible, did not constitute a prima facie case, so as to allow the Court to review the matter.

24 *Nold KG* v. *The High Authority* (Case 18–57), Vol. II.

25 Decisions Nos. 16–57, 17–57 and 18–57.

26 Art. 15. para. 1, states:
" The decisions, recommendations and opinions of the High Authority shall include the reasons therefor, and shall refer to the advice which the High Authority is required to obtain."

not only for the benefit of the parties concerned but also with a view to placing the Court in a position fully to exercise the legal control which the Treaty confers upon it.

In consequence, a possible failure to give reasons which prevents this legal control may be and must be reviewed by the Court of its own motion.[27]

However, the Court does impose a limitation upon its own powers to examine matters and this is illustrated by what it stated in one case in 1959 concerning exemptions which the High Authority had granted to certain steel foundries authorising them not to pay a particular levy. The Court said:

It is evident from the plaintiff's statement that they do not wish to criticise, even in a subsidiary way, the legal basis of the exemptions granted to integrated steel foundries. Hence, the Court cannot examine the legality of this exception without fear of interfering with the scope which the plaintiffs wished to give to their action.[28]

It appears, therefore, that the Court will itself consider any matters relating to the actual appeal which is before it which it regards as relevant to that appeal, but that the Court will not attempt to alter the scope of that appeal or use it as a starting point for any general survey. Finally, in two further cases [29] concerning Decisions which had been implied as a result of the inaction of the High Authority over a period of two months, the Court, of itself, examined the question of whether there had been a delay of two months, and it did this despite the fact that the High Authority itself admitted such a delay.

This power within these limits to consider matters of its own motion, which the Court has, it is submitted, now clearly accepted, may in many ways be valuable from the point of view of legal order within the Community but it may nevertheless lead to a certain difficulty. This may perhaps be illustrated by referring back to *Nold's* case which has been quoted from above.

It is accepted that unless a case is before it in which a Decision of the High Authority is being challenged, the Court cannot annul that Decision of the High Authority. In *Nold's* case the plaintiffs challenged certain Decisions of the High Authority but in their pleadings did not validly allege any grounds upon which those Decisions could have been annulled. The Court, however, of its own motion annulled the Decision

---

[27] *Nold KG* v. *The High Authority* (Case 18–57), Vol. II.

[28] *Société des Fonderies de Pont-à-Mousson* v. *The High Authority* (Case 14–59), Vol. II. If the Court had examined the exemptions it would have found them illegal, as it did subsequently, see Vol. II.

[29] *Société nouvelle des Usines de Pontlieue-Acieries du Temple (S.N.U.P.A.T.)* v. *The High Authority* (Joint Cases 32–58 and 33–58), Vol. II and *Société des Aciers fins de l'Est (S.A.F.E.)* v. *The High Authority* (Case 42–58), Vol. II.

on the ground of violation of a substantial procedural requirement. In other words, the action brought by the plaintiffs, although in itself ineffective to cause the annulment of those Decisions, nevertheless provided the means by which the Court could of itself annul them.

Now supposing the Decisions in question had been general Decisions, and not individual ones, as they actually were,[30] and suppose further that these general Decisions had also been passed by the High Authority in violation of the same substantial procedural requirement as were the actual Decisions. If the plaintiffs had challenged these general Decisions they could very well in their pleadings have alleged that the Decisions were in fact individual Decisions and have gone on to challenge their validity on the ground of a violation of a substantial procedural requirement.

On the assumption that the Court realised that the Decisions had been passed in violation of a substantial procedural requirement, it would be faced with a dilemma. It could either hold that the Decisions, being general Decisions, could not be challenged by the plaintiffs on the grounds of the existence of a substantial procedural requirement or of its own motion it could hold the Decisions void by violating a substantial procedural requirement.

If it did the former, and refused to annul the Decision, the Court would be allowing an invalid Decision to remain unannulled; if it did the latter it would, in effect, be enabling an enterprise to bring about the annulment of a general Decision on grounds which it could not itself have pleaded. This procedure appears to undermine the whole of the provisions of Article 33, para. 2.

It is suggested, therefore, that the former alternative is the one more closely in keeping with the terms of the Treaty,[31] and if this is so, then the *ex officio* power of the Court is merely to consider grounds of invalidity which could have been alleged by the plaintiffs: it is not to act as a general guardian of the respect of law.

DECISIONS AND RECOMMENDATIONS

The only acts of the High Authority which the Court can pronounce upon are Decisions and Recommendations. By the Treaty, the High Authority is required to take Decisions, formulate Recommendations and issue Opinions.[32] The difference between these is that Decisions are

---

[30] For the distinction between general and individual Decisions of the High Authority and the right of enterprises to challenge them, see Art. 33, para. 2, p. 152, below.
[31] The terms of Art. 31, however, must not be ignored. These state:
" The Court is to ensure the respect of law in the interpretation and application of the Treaty."
[32] E.C.S.C. Treaty, Art. 14, para. 1.

117

binding in every respect,[33] Recommendations are binding with respect to the objectives which they specify while leaving to the party concerned the choice of the appropriate means for attaining those objectives,[34] and Opinions are not binding.[35]

It will be noted that the above provision only lays down the different legal effect that Decisions, Recommendations and Opinions are to have; it does not state how one is to determine whether a particular act is a Decision, Recommendation or an Opinion.

This is further complicated by two factors. First, the Treaty, when it is empowering the High Authority to do certain acts sometimes states that they shall be carried out by means of a Decision [36] or by means of a Recommendation,[37] or by means of an Opinion.[38] However, more often the wording is not specific as, for example, where the Treaty states that the High Authority " shall establish a system of production quotas," [39] " shall authorise compensation schemes " [40] or, and perhaps the most general wording of all, " shall take all measures necessary." [41] The second difficulty is that although most " Decisions " of the High Authority are published by it in the *Journal Officiel* and are described as Decisions, the High Authority often proceeds merely by writing a

---

[33] Art. 14, para. 2.

[34] Art. 14, para. 3. The Court has emphasised the distinction between Decisions and Recommendations in the following way:

" By the terms of Article 14 of the Treaty, the High Authority ' in carrying out the duties assigned to it . . . shall take Decisions (and) make Recommendations. . . .'

The manner of the exercise of its executory powers is, therefore, defined and circumscribed by this provision in the sense that the exercise of the power of regulation, where the High Authority possesses such a power, is carried out by means of Decisions which are ' binding in all respects,' whereas in the case where this power of regulation is withheld and remains with the States, the High Authority, if it wishes to remind the States of their obligations, can only proceed by means of a Recommendation, without being able to impose upon them its own choice of means for complying with these obligations "—*Italian Government* v. *The High Authority* (Case 20–59), Vol. II.

[35] Art. 14, para. 4. The only occasion when an Opinion " shall have the force of a Decision as defined in Article 14 " is when the High Authority by means of an Opinion disapproves of an enterprise's financing of a project—Art. 54, para. 5. The Court, without hesitation, has declared that these Opinions can form the subject of an action for annulment, saying:

" As for Opinions, with the exception of those provided for in Art. 54, para. 5 of the Treaty, they cannot in principle form the subject of such an appeal "—*Société des Usines à Tubes de la Sarre* v. *The High Authority* (Joint Cases 1–57 and 14–57), Vol. II.

[36] For example, the method of assessing and collecting levies upon the production of coal and steel are to be fixed by a general Decision—Art. 50, para. 2.

[37] For example, if discrimination is being practised by buyers, the High Authority shall make the necessary Recommendation to the Government concerned—Art. 63, para. 1.

[38] For example, the High Authority is required to give a reasoned Opinion upon an enterprise's programme of investment—Art. 54, para. 4.

[39] Art. 58, para. 1.

[40] Art. 62, para. 1.

[41] Art. 74, para. 1. These " measures " are in this provision differentiated from " any Recommendations."

118

formal letter to the party concerned. The question arises, therefore, whether such a letter is a Decision and thus subject to challenge.[42]

The Court in dealing with the question of what constitutes Decisions has defined them in the following terms:

> An act of the High Authority constitutes a Decision when it establishes a rule capable of being applied; in other words, when in a particular act the High Authority unequivocally decides on the attitude which it will thenceforth adopt in a situation where certain conditions are operative.[43]

By applying this definition the Court has had to determine whether a letter written by the High Authority and sent to the Belgian Government on May 28, 1955, constituted a Decision. By the terms of the letter it was stated:

> It is recognised . . . that the aid granted to the Belgian coal mines by virtue of the subsidy must be accompanied by a series of measures which the Belgian Government is required to take. The High Authority considers, in particular, that the revision of the subsidy measures must be conditional upon action by the Government in the manner set out below . . .

The action then set out and lettered (a) to (d), included the granting of special credit facilities to enterprises by the reduction of interest rates and by a State guarantee, the facilitating of short-term credit, the financing of construction, or the extension of facilities in the mines, and finally, in agreement with the High Authority, the Belgian Government was to withdraw compensation from inefficient mines.

When the letter was challenged by certain Belgian enterprises [44] the High Authority alleged that the action was inadmissible on the ground that the letter was not a Decision and that therefore no action for its annulment would lie.

In its judgment the Court declared:

> In the course of the oral proceedings, the defendants posed the question of whether it was possible to regard this . . . as being a Decision which is capable of being made the subject matter of an appeal for annulment under Article 33 of the Treaty. Now, in its letter of May 28, 1955, the High Authority has recognised that the grant of compensation must of necessity be accompanied by a series of measures to be carried out by the Belgian Government. The High Authority mentioned, moreover, that the Belgian Government must carry out four measures,

---

42 See *Fédération Charbonnière de Belgique* v. *The High Authority* (Case 8–55), Vol. II.
43 *Société des Usines à Tubes de la Sarre* v. *The High Authority* (Joint Cases 1–57 and 14–57), Vol. II. The definition was also stated in *Fédération Charbonnière de Belgique* v. *The High Authority* (Case 8–55), Vol. II, and in *Société de Charbonnages de Beeringen* v. *The High Authority* (Case 9–55), Vol. II.
44 *Fédération Charbonnière de Belgique* v. *The High Authority* (Case 8–55), Vol. II.

specified as (a), (b), (c) and (d). The terms of (d) are, therefore, part of the series of measures that the Belgian Government would be required to take if the necessity arose. The High Authority has, thus, determined, in an unequivocal manner, the action from then on it had decided to take in a case where the conditions specified under the heading (d) of the letter are fulfilled. In other words, it has set out a rule capable of being applied if the need arises. It must, therefore, be seen as a Decision within the meaning of Article 14 of the Treaty.[45]

In a later case [46] the Court had to determine whether a letter written to the plaintiffs on February 27, 1957, setting out the High Authority's views upon their investment programme was an Opinion within the meaning of Article 14—and the relevant provision in the Treaty [47] states that the High Authority shall set their views out in an Opinion—or whether, as the plaintiffs alleged, the " Opinion " was a disguised Decision.

It is certain, on the one hand, that the Opinion of February 27, 1957, does not amount to a rule which is capable of being applied, for it is accepted that it does not impose upon the plaintiffs any legal obligation and, on the other hand, that nothing in the documents in this case leads one to conclude that in sending this Opinion the High Authority had specified with certainty what was the attitude which it had already decided to take towards enterprises in cases where they granted an unfavourable Opinion.

The Opinion of the High Authority of February 27, 1957, thus, cannot be regarded as a Decision within the meaning of Article 14 of the Treaty, with the result that the appeal for annulment brought against this Opinion is inadmissible as being brought against an act which cannot be subjected to the jurisdiction of the Court.[48]

From the above it will be seen that the Court is declaring that what amounts to a Decision is a matter of substance and not of form. The High Authority thus cannot disguise a Decision by hiding it in a letter or by calling it by another name.

As the Court has declared that " an act of the High Authority constitutes a Decision when it establishes a rule capable of application," it follows that if an act does not establish a rule capable of application, it cannot be a Decision.

The importance of this has recently been illustrated in a case.[49] Here the High Authority addressed a letter to the *Caisse*,[50] an organisation in Brussels which had been set up by the High Authority to run

[45] *Ibid.* Vol. II.
[46] *Société des Usines à Tubes de la Sarre* v. *The High Authority* (Joint Cases 1–57 and 14–57), Vol. II.   [47] Art. 54, para. 4.
[48] *Société des Usines à Tubes de la Sarre* v. *The High Authority* (Joint Cases 1–57 and 14–57), Vol. II.
[49] *Phoenix-Rheinrohr AG* v. *The High Authority* (Case 20–58), Vol. II.
[50] *Caisse de Péréquation des Ferrailles Importées.*

a system of subsidies, and in this letter the High Authority confirmed that two enterprises, one Italian and one Dutch, were rightly exempt from paying any tax to the Subsidy Fund. This letter was subsequently published in the *Journal Officiel* of the Community and was referred to by the Trading Division of the High Authority as a Decision.

The Court held, however, that the letter was not a Decision but rather:

> a directive of an internal nature, addressed by an administrative superior to the departments under his control and intended to guide the working of those departments.[51]

Another reason given by the Court why this and a subsequent similar letter were not Decisions was that:

> The letter does not set out a new principle, but is limited to affirming explicitly a principle which, implicitly, the administration had already applied in the carrying out of Decision 2–57.[52]

The letter itself, therefore, could not be challenged before the Court. The only means of proceeding was, thus, for the plaintiffs to challenge the Decision which had laid down the original rule or principle of which the letter was merely an application.

This judgment that for an act to be a Decision it must lay down a rule, and must not be merely the application of a pre-existing rule, is of importance for enterprises. The pre-existing rule will, in most cases, be embodied in a general Decision whereas the application of that rule, if it had been a Decision, would have been individual and could have been challenged by an enterprise on any of the four grounds in Article 33, and furthermore, as has been decided by the Court, that enterprise could also have challenged the relevant general Decision and on any of the same four grounds.[53] As it is, the enterprise can only challenge the general Decision if it is vitiated by a *détournement de pouvoir* with respect to itself.[54]

A very important ruling upon the meaning of the term " Decision " in Article 33 had to be given in a fairly recent case.[55] The facts were that the High Authority had imposed a tax upon enterprises so as to provide funds out of which a subsidy could be given to those buying imported scrap. The High Authority set up the *Caisse* referred to above,

---

[51] *Phoenix-Rheinrohr AG* v. *The High Authority* (Case 20–58), Vol. II.
[52] *Ibid.*
[53] *Meroni & Co., S.P.A.* v. *The High Authority* (Case 9–56), Vol. II.
[54] If the letter declares the existence of a duty upon the enterprise, then by not carrying out that duty the enterprise can eventually get itself fined and against this fine it can appeal under Art. 36 and can then challenge the original general Decision on any of the four grounds in Art. 33—a lengthy and unwieldy process but there is no other.
[55] *Société Nouvelle des Usines de Pontlieue-Acieries du Temple (S.N.U.P.A.T.)* v. *The High Authority* (Joint Cases 32–58 and 33–58), Vol. II.

and, by Decision No. 2–57, this *Caisse* was to notify enterprises of the amount of tax payable by them and the time within which payment was to be made. If payment was not made within the prescribed time, the *Caisse* could request the High Authority to take a Decision which had executory force.

The plaintiffs allowed their payment of tax to fall into arrears and the *Caisse,* by a letter addressed to them, specified the amount owing and demanded payment. The plaintiffs challenged the validity of this letter before the Court and the question therefore had to be determined whether this letter of the *Caisse* was to be held to be a Decision of the High Authority so that it could be challenged under Article 33.

The Court declared:

> The letter . . . constitutes a " notification " . . . creating the obligation to pay the sums stated.
>
> Under the régime of Decision 2–57, these "notifications" represented, in fact, the final word of the administration; the High Authority limiting itself, when necessary, to making them executory without claiming to re-examine them. They created an obligation for the recipient enterprise. They contained, therefore, all the requirements of a true administrative Decision.
>
> Under these conditions, it is not justified to reserve the character of a Decision to the deliverance by the High Authority of an order having executory force, especially as such a Decision is only taken when an enterprise fails to fulfil its obligations.
>
> Article 33 of the E.C.S.C. Treaty provides only for appeals for annulment against Decisions of the High Authority. It is necessary, therefore, to consider whether Decisions taken by the *C.P.F.I.*[56] are equivalent to Decisions taken by the High Authority.
>
> In this respect, one must take into consideration the fact that the *C.P.F.I.* was an organ of the financial mechanism established by the High Authority, and that it received its powers from the latter.
>
> Further, as has been stated above, the notifications by the *C.P.F.I.* constituted, in fact, the administrative decision taken at final instance, which the High Authority could have prevented if as an administrative superior it had taken action . . . against the Decisions of the organisations in Brussels.
>
> Therefore, in order not to deprive enterprises of the benefit of the protection which Article 33 of the E.C.S.C. Treaty has granted to them, it must be admitted that the Decisions taken by the *C.P.F.I.* by virtue of Article 12, paragraph 2, of Decision 2–57 are equivalent to Decisions of the High Authority and are, therefore, subject to an appeal for annulment under the conditions set out in Article 33.[57]

[56] *Caisse de Péréquation des Ferrailles Importées,* referred to in the text above as the *Caisse.*

[57] *Société Nouvelle des Usines de Pontlieue-Acieries du Temple (S.N.U.P.A.T.)* v. *The High Authority* (Joint Cases 32–58 and 33–58), Vol. II. For details of the powers of the *Caisse* and the whole working of the subsidy system, see Vol. II.

When, therefore, Article 33 states that actions for annulment can be brought against " Decisions of the High Authority," this expression includes Decisions which were not taken by the High Authority itself but by subordinate bodies to which the High Authority has delegated certain of its powers.

A further interpretation of the word " Decision " had to be made in a case in 1957 [58] where the High Authority took the point that a Decision meant a complete Decision, and not merely one provision in a Decision. The grounds of this contention were not linguistic, but based upon Article 34 of the Treaty. Annulled Decisions have to be referred back to the High Authority and that Authority, as distinct from the Court, is required to take the necessary measures to give effect to the judgment. It was contended, therefore, that if certain words only could be annulled in a Decision, the remaining words might amount to an entirely different Decision and one which, in effect, had been brought into being by the Court and not the High Authority. The Court declared:

> This contention is not well founded because by the terms of Article 34, a judgment in no way prejudices the measures which the High Authority is required to take in order to amend the Decision, regard being had to the annulment.[58a]

THE FOUR GROUNDS OF APPEAL

The four grounds of appeal granted by Article 33 of the Treaty are the same as the grounds which may be alleged in the French *Conseil d'Etat* against a French administrative act.[59] They are also virtually the same as those which can be alleged in Belgium and in Italy before the national courts of those countries. This fact has been widely recognised and in the ratification debates of the Coal and Steel Community Treaty it was often mentioned. Speakers thus made such statements as: " If I wished to define this new organ in a single word, I would say that it is a *Conseil d'Etat* " [60]: " The principles of our French public law are the basis of . . . the Court of Justice " [61]: " The Court of Justice is organised upon the model of the French *contentieux*

---

[58] " *Geitling* " *and others* v. *The High Authority* (Case 2–56), Vol. II.
[58a] *Ibid.*
[59] For extreme French satisfaction in this fact, see L'Huillier, " Une conquête du droit administratif français: le contentieux de la C.E.C.A.," in *Recueil Dalloz* (1953).
[60] M. Coste-Floret, *Rapporteur* of the Foreign Affairs Commission, *Assemblée Nationale*, Official Reports, 1951, p. 8855, col. 1.
[61] *Ibid.*

administratif," [62] and the Belgian Government declared that the role of the Court " is similar in many respects to that of our *Conseil d'Etat.*" [63]

This being so, it may be of value to consider the manner in which the Court has applied these four grounds of appeal.

INCOMPETENCE

When the Treaty speaks of the High Authority as being incompetent to do a particular act, it refers to it not having been empowered by the Treaty to do the act concerned—that is to say, it refers to its lack of legal competence.[64]

In two cases in 1960, the Court held that, by the terms of the Treaty, the High Authority was incompetent to pass particular Decisions.[65]

In the Chapter of the Treaty dealing with transport it is declared that:

> Rates, prices and tariff provisions of all kinds applied to the transport of coal and steel within the interior of each Member State and between Member States shall be published or brought to the knowledge of the High Authority.[66]

Under this provision the High Authority passed various Decisions setting out, among other things, the matters in relation to road transport tariffs which were to be brought to its knowledge, including, for example, the name and address of the sender, of the transporter, and of the purchaser, the weight of the load and the price and the distance of the journey. Both the Netherlands and the Italian Governments challenged the validity of these Decisions on the grounds that under the terms of Article 70, paragraph 3, set out above, no power was granted to enable the High Authority to take a Decision.

This contention was accepted by the Court, which declared:

> A comparison of Article 70, paragraph 3, and the provisions of Article 60, sub-paragraph 2 (a) reveals that, in a parallel matter [67] the Treaty, when imposing the obligation to publish prices which is contained in Article 60, links the power granted to the High Authority with powers concerning its application, by prescribing that this publication must be

---

[62] M. Biever, *Compte Rendu* of the Luxembourg Parliament, 1951–1952, col. 1611.

[63] *Exposé des Motifs, Senat de Belgique, Services ordinaire*, 1950–1951, no 369, p. 14. For a survey of these ratification debates, see the author's " *The Court of Justice of the European Coal and Steel Community* ", (Nijhoffs) (1954), Chap. 1.

[64] The term is, of course, not being used in the colloquial sense of signifying ineptitude. A possible translation of the term would be *ultra vires*.

[65] *Netherlands Government* v. *The High Authority* (Case 25–59), Vol. II and *Italian Government* v. *The High Authority* (Case 20–59), Vol. II.

[66] Art. 70, para. 3.

[67] Art. 60, section 2 (a), provides:
   " Price lists and conditions of sale applied by enterprises within the Common Market must be made public to the extent and in the form prescribed by the High Authority after consulting the Consultative Committee."

made " to the extent and in the form prescribed by the High Authority and after consultation with the Consultative Committee."

One can see from the fact that, as concerns the publication of rates, prices and conditions of sale applied on the Common Market, the Treaty has expressly granted a legislative power to the High Authority, providing even for control by the Consultative Committee, which is proof of the importance which it attributes to the matter and to the High Authority's control over it.

The absence of any *ad hoc* provision in Article 70 indicates conversely, that, in respect of transport, the text of the Treaty denies to the High Authority any power to take an executive decision.[68]

Later in its judgment, the Court held that the Treaty only conferred upon the High Authority such powers, formerly of course possessed by the sovereign Member States, as were expressly or impliedly mentioned in the Treaty itself. The Court declared:

> Although it is true that, by virtue of a general principle, applied moreover by Article 70 in regard to transport, control of discriminations and punitive action with regard to them devolves upon the High Authority, yet one cannot, however, deduce from this principle that the High Authority has been granted a power of decision relating to an anticipatory control by prescribing the manner of the publication of price lists or prices. Its competence, *ad hoc*, is by way of an exception and is subordinated to a renunciation by Member States, which in this instance the Treaty does not contain, either expressly or by implication.
>
> One must, therefore, deny to the High Authority any power to enforce the provisions of Article 70, paragraph 3, by means of Decisions.[69]

As the Treaty, thus, gave no power to the High Authority to pass a Decision specifying how these transport rates and prices were to be notified to it, the Decisions of the High Authority attempting to specify these matters had been passed *ultra vires* and were therefore annulled.[70]

In two other cases,[71] the ground of incompetence was alleged because under the Convention containing the Transitional Provisions [72] the High

---

[68] *Netherlands Government* v. *The High Authority* (Case 25–59), Vol. II.

[69] *Ibid*.

[70] This judgment, of course, had no effect upon the Treaty's obligation upon the Governments concerned to publish these rates and prices and bring them to the knowledge of the High Authority. The High Authority therefore passed a Recommendation addressed to the Member-States requiring them to pass legislation obliging transport enterprises to publish these rates or bring them to the knowledge of the High Authority. The validity of this Recommendation was upheld by the Court in *The Netherlands Government* v. *The High Authority* (Case 9–61) [1963] C.M.L.R. 59.

[71] *Compagnie des Hauts-Fourneaux et Fonderies de Givors and others* v. *The High Authority* (Joint Cases 27–58, 28–58 and 29–58), Vol. II, below, and *German Government* v. *The High Authority* (Case 19–58), Vol. II.

[72] Art. 10.

Authority was granted certain powers to bring to an end discriminatory practices in the transport of coal and steel. This Convention expired at midnight on February 9, 1958.[73] The plaintiffs alleged that a Decision notified only on February 12, 1958, should be annulled on the grounds of the High Authority's incompetence to pass it. In the actual cases, the Court found that the Decisions had been agreed upon in all their details during the evening of February 9, but had this not been so, the Decision would have had to have been annulled.

VIOLATION OF A SUBSTANTIAL PROCEDURAL REQUIREMENT

It is clear that because all the procedure requirements which have to be observed by the High Authority have been laid down in the Treaty, a violation of any of them, whether it be substantial or not, amounts to a violation of the Treaty.

Nevertheless the two heads of violation of the Treaty and violation of a substantial procedural requirement are set out in Article 33 as being distinct. It is surprising, therefore, that the Court has on occasions failed to keep that distinction clear. Some examples will illustrate this.

By Article 36 of the Treaty, before the High Authority may fine an enterprise, " it shall enable the party concerned to state its case." [74] In 1956, the High Authority imposed a fine of 800,000 lire upon an Italian enterprise. In its appeal against this fine, the enterprise declared that it had never been given an opportunity to state its case in accordance with Article 36. The Court would appear to be regarding such an omission if it had occurred as not falling within the heading of a violation of the Treaty—although clearly Article 36 would have been violated—but as a violation of a substantial procedural requirement. The Court declared, however:

> Without needing to examine whether this allegation amounts to a violation of a substantial procedural requirement, the Court holds that it is not well founded.[74a]

In another case [75] it was alleged that a particular Decision of the High Authority concerning price lists was invalid because before its enactment the Consultative Committee had not been consulted. The Court, however, when dealing with this, clearly did not know whether this

---

[73] Art. 1, para. 4 provides:
" The transitional provision shall begin on the date on which the Common Market is established and shall end five years after the Common Market for coal was set up."
[74] For the terms of Art. 36, see p. 193, below.
[74a] *Acciaierie Laminatoi Magliano Alpi (A.L.M.A.)* v. *The High Authority* (Case 8–56), Vol. II. The Decision of the High Authority was dated October 24, 1956: it was unnumbered. [75] *Italian Government* v. *The High Authority* (Case 2–54), Vol. II.

defect, if it had existed, would have amounted to a violation of the Treaty or to a violation of a substantial procedural requirement.

The Court stated:

> The ground that the Consultative Committee has not been consulted in accordance with the legal requirements.
>
> The defendants request the Court to declare this ground inadmissible because it has not been pleaded in the request.[76] The Court is of the opinion that this ground has to be examined by the Court acting of its own motion, because if it were well founded an annulment *ex officio* for violation of the Treaty or for *violation* of a *substantial procedural requirement* would be justified.[77]

In a later case [78] the High Authority by a particular Decision [79] had declared that the plaintiffs owed a sum of over 54m. lire to the fund set up to compensate the Belgian coal and steel industries. The plaintiffs alleged that the Decision was based on incorrect facts and was not supported by reasons.

The Court, in annulling the Decision, declared:

> The insufficiency of the reasoning and the failure to publish the data upon which the decision of October 24, 1956, has been based *constitute of themselves violations of the Treaty* such as to require the annulment of that Decision.[80]

The confusion existing is in no way decreased when one finds that the plaintiffs had used the fact of this lack both of reasoning and of data to support a claim not of the violation of a substantial procedural requirement, nor even of a violation of the Treaty, but of a *détournement de pouvoir*.[81]

It is suggested, however, that there does exist a clear distinction between these two heads of appeal and that it is possible to conceive of a Decision which in its wording and effect is in full compliance with the Treaty, yet during the stages preceding its enactment procedural requirements have not been observed. The Decision, on its wording alone, could not therefore be challenged; it is only the manner of its enactment that in such a case is open to attack.

This distinction between the stages of enactment and the end product was illustrated in the very same case as that mentioned above when the

---

76 The plaintiffs first raised it in their Reply.
77 *Ibid.*, Vol. II.
78 *Meroni & Co., Industrie Metallurgiche S.P.A.* v. *The High Authority* (Case 9–56), Vol. II.
79 The Decision was taken on October 24, 1956: it was not given a number.
80 *Meroni & Co., S.P.A.* v. *The High Authority* (Case 8–56), Vol. II. (Author's italics).
81 *Ibid.* In another case, the plaintiff's arguments alleging that a particular Decision had been passed without adequate reasoning were submitted under the heading of a violation of the Treaty, see " *Präsident*," " *Geitling*," " *Mausegatt* " *and Nold KG* v. *The High Authority* (Joint Cases 36, 37, 38 and 40–59), Vol. II.

Court had to determine upon another possible ground of the Decision's invalidity. The Court took the point that if the Decision in question could be held as having been enacted under Article 60 of the Treaty, the Council of Ministers would have had to have been consulted. A failure to consult the Council therefore would have been a violation of the Treaty, but because that violation would have occurred in one of the preliminary stages prior to the final enactment of the Decision, that Decision itself would not have been void by reason of a violation of the Treaty but by reason of a violation of a substantial procedural requirement.

The Court thus declared:

> The Court of its own motion has examined the question whether Article 1 of Decision 2–54 constitutes a violation of a substantial procedural requirement.[82] By its wording, this article defines only the conditions under which the new price lists have to be published. It can be asked, however, whether this article, read in conjunction with Decision 1–54, does not in fact, in a disguised way, add to the definition of prohibited practices. If this were the case . . . the Council should have been consulted in accordance with Article 60, paragraph 1. Because such an official consultation has not taken place, and cannot be replaced by the High Authority simply informing the Council, *Article 60, paragraph 1, might have been violated.* However, the Court is of opinion that Article 1 of Decision 2–54 does not contain a complement to the definition of discriminating practices, nor an indirect definition, but is limited to regulating the system of the publication of price lists.[83]

In the above two instances the Court was in effect stating that consultations, either with the Consultative Committee or with the Council of Ministers, amounted to a substantial procedural requirement.[84] The Court has also, however, applied the term substantial procedural requirement in a very different sense.

By the Treaty the " Decisions, Recommendations and Opinions of the High Authority shall include the reasons therefore, and shall refer to the advice which the High Authority is required to obtain." [85]

---

82 This is loose phraseology. Art. 1 of this Decision cannot constitute a violation of a procedural requirement. The Court is intending to refer to the mode of enacting Art. 1 of this Decision and to see whether that mode of enacting violated a substantial procedural requirement.

83 *French Government* v. *The High Authority* (Case 1–54), Vol. II. (Author's italics).

84 The Court has accepted that if the High Authority in a particular case had been required to consult a Commission of Experts, a failure to do so would have amounted to a violation of a substantial procedural requirement—*Compagnie des Hauts-Fourneaux et Fonderies de Givors and others* v. *The High Authority* (Joint Cases 27–58, 28–58 and 29–58), Vol. II.

85 Art. 15, para. 1.

Of this provision, the Court has stated:

> The general provisions of Articles 5 [86] and 15 of the Treaty require the High Authority to support its Decisions with reasons and to publish those reasons. No definition has been given, however, either as to the form or as to the extent of this obligation.
>
> When interpreted in a reasonable manner, the provisions require the High Authority to set out in the reasons supporting its Decisions what are those essential elements of the existing situations upon which depend the legal justification for the measure in question.[87]

A failure to observe the requirements of those provisions amounts in the opinion of the Court to a violation of a substantial procedural requirement.[88]

As an example of this may be taken the case where an enterprise [89] appealed against a Decision of the High Authority passed on October 24, 1956, by which a fine was imposed upon it. The grounds of the appeal were that the Decision did not adequately set out the reasons for the Decision having been taken. The reasons stated were:

> That [the plaintiffs] . . . have failed as from April 1, 1954, to pay to the *Caisse de Péréquation des Ferrailles Importées* the contributions due from them in conformity with the Decisions set out below;
>
> That the contributions due for the period from April 1, 1954, to June 30, 1956, amounted to the sum of 54,819,656 lire.[90]

Of this Decision, the Court stated:

> These two paragraphs do not amount to a statement of those considerations both of law and of fact upon which the Decision of October 24, 1956, was based.
>
> This Decision thus lacks the necessary requirements to enable any legal control to be properly exercised over it.
>
> The Decision of October 24, 1956, therefore, does not comply with the requirements of Article 15 of the Treaty by which " Decisions . . . of the High Authority are to be supported by reasons." [91]

In another case,[92] the High Authority by three Decisions [93] authorised an agreement between three Ruhr sales organisations not to sell coal to

---

[86] Art. 5, para. 2 also provides that " The Community shall . . . publish the reasons for its actions."
[87] *Netherlands Government* v. *The High Authority* (Case 6–54), Vol. II.
[88] In one case, however, the Court declared that the obligation to give reasons for an express Decision passed under Art. 88, setting out that a State was in breach of the Treaty did not apply to an implied Decision. " Consequently," it declared, " the absence of reasons in the implied negative Decision *does not constitute a violation of . . . the Treaty* ": *Groupement des Industries Sidérurgiques Luxembourgeoises* v. *The High Authority* (Joint Cases 7–54 and 9–54), Vol. II.
[89] The right of enterprises to appeal is granted by Art. 33, para. 2, see p. 152, below.
[90] *Meroni & Co., S.P.A.* v. *The High Authority* (Case 9–56), Vol. II.
[91] *Ibid.*
[92] *Nold KG* v. *The High Authority* (Case 18–57), Vol. II.
[93] Decisions 16–57, 17–57 and 18–57, see Vol. II.

any wholesaler who had not sold in the previous year within the Common Market at least 60,000 tons of coal mined within the Community.[94] When these Decisions were challenged, the plaintiffs alleged that they had been passed in violation of a substantial procedural requirement in that they did not set out the reasons why this agreement had been authorised. This contention was accepted by the Court and the Decisions were annulled. The Court stated:

> The absence of any justification for the quantitative limits intro-duced, fails to establish that in taking the Decisions challenged, the High Authority has also examined whether the said limits are of a more restrictive character than was required for the substantial improvement in distribution, which was the aim and object of Article 65, section 2 (b).
>
> Under these conditions the reasoning of Decisions 16–57, 17–57 and 18–57 do not specify . . . in a sufficient and adequate manner the factual and legal considerations upon which the Decisions taken have been based.
>
> They, therefore, do not permit of legal control, particularly upon the question of whether the High Authority has observed Article 65, section 2.[95]

In other judgments, the Court has amplified this requirement that Decisions shall be supported with reasons. It has thus stated:

> The Treaty does not require [the High Authority] to set out—and much less to refute—the dissenting opinions expressed . . . by consulta-tive organisations or by certain of their members.[96]
>
> The High Authority is not required to discuss every conceivable objection which might be brought against the Decision.
>
> Generally speaking, it was not necessary to support with reasons, exhaustively and independently, the article being challenged where that article merely forms part of a complex Decision. Sufficient supporting reasons may be inferred from all the grounds that are relied upon in support of the Decision as a whole.[97]
>
> The legal reasoning supporting the Decision of October 24, 1956 [which imposed a fine of over 54m. lire upon an Italian enterprise], requires a precise and detailed breakdown of the heads of the debt to which that Decision is giving executory force.
>
> Only such a breakdown can allow any legal control to be exercised over that Decision.[98]

---

94 By the Treaty, the High Authority is required to authorise agreements to engage in joint selling of specified products if it finds *inter alia*, (a) that the joint selling will contribute to a substantial improvement in the distribution of the products in question; and (b) that the agreement in question is essential to achieve these results, and is not more restrictive than is necessary for that purpose—Art. 65, section 2.

95 *Nold KG* v. *The High Authority* (Case 18–57), Vol. II.

96 *Netherlands Government* v. *The High Authority* (Case 6–54), Vol. II, and *Industrie Sidérurgiche Associate* v. *The High Authority* (Case 4–54), Vol. II.

97 " *Geitling* " *and others* v. *The High Authority* (Case 2–56), Vol. II.

98 *Meroni & Co., S.P.A.* v. *The High Authority* (Case 9–56), Vol. II.

A statement of reasons must be considered adequate, in relation to Articles 14 and 33 of the Treaty, when it enables the interested parties as well as the Court to discover the essential elements of the High Authority's reasoning.[98a]

In a later case the High Authority had allowed certain rail tariff concessions to two German enterprises on account of their geographical position. Because in a Decision refusing tariff concessions to the plaintiffs, their geographical position had not been distinguished from that of the two other enterprises, the plaintiffs alleged that the Decision had not been adequately reasoned. The Court rejected this on the grounds that

> The allegation appears to require that, having accepted a reason for granting a special tariff for one individual case, the High Authority must be obliged to specify in all other cases the grounds why it has not accepted this reason.
>
> This requirement cannot be justified from the point of view of giving sufficient reasons, and must, therefore, be rejected.[98b]

Once recently the Court has held:

> The statement of the reasons of public interest justifying an administrative action must be set out in a precise manner and one capable of being challenged; otherwise the official concerned would be placed in a position where it was impossible to ascertain whether his legitimate interests had been respected or violated, and, moreover, the review of the legality of the Decision would be impeded.[99]

In 1962, the High Authority argued that this obligation to support Decisions with reasons did not apply to Decisions dismissing employees on the grounds, first, that dismissal was an entirely discretionary matter, and secondly

> that such an obligation would have undesirable consequences both for the administration and for the employee, since it would require the former, in certain cases, to set out unpleasant facts about the employee.[99a]

The Court rejected this.

> The actions of the authorities, in the administrative sphere as well as in the contractual sphere, are still required to respect the public

---

[98a] *Koninklijke Nederlandsche Hoogovens Staalfabrieken N.V.* v. *The High Authority* (Case 14–61) [1963] C.M.L.R. at p. 73.

[98b] *German Government* v. *The High Authority* (Case 19–58) Vol. II. See also *Barbara Erzbergbau A.G. and others* v. *The High Authority* (Joint Cases 3 to 18, 25 and 26–58), Vol. II.

[99] *Eva von Lachmüller and others* v. *The Commission of E.E.C.* (Joint Cases 43, 45 and 48–59), Vol. II.—a judgment given under the E.E.C. Treaty.

[99a] *Leda De Bruyn* v. *European Parliamentary Assembly* (Case 25–60)—a case brought under E.E.C. Treaty Art. 179 and Euratom Treaty, Art. 152, see pp. 312 and 367, below.

interest; thus, every Decision of dismissal must be supported by reasons relating to the interests of the department and must exclude anything arbitrary.

This requirement exists from the time of the creation of a legal relationship between the administration and its employees.[1]

Although the Court in nearly all its judgments has assumed that a failure to give supporting reasons means that a substantial procedural requirement has been violated, one case throws certain doubts upon this. In the case in question an Italian enterprise alleged that a particular Decision of the High Authority was vitiated by a *détournement de pouvoir*. The reason the plaintiffs alleged was that the Decision violated the rules of good administration by not reporting the dissenting opinions which had been given when the Decision had been discussed in the various consultative committees before it had been passed.

The Court declared:

> The plaintiffs see a breach of the rules of good administration and, therefore, grounds establishing a *détournement de pouvoir* in the fact that the High Authority, in setting out the reasons for the Decisions which are now being challenged, has omitted to comment upon the dissenting opinions expressed in the consultative bodies. . . .
>
> However, the Treaty does not require it to set out—and much less to refute—the dissenting opinions expressed by consultative organisations or by some of their members.
>
> Thus the omission which is alleged cannot be considered as proof, or even as the mere beginning of proof, in support of a claim of a *détournement de pouvoir*.[1a]

It will be noted that the Court here, instead of declaring that this failure would, if anything, go to establish a violation of a substantial procedural requirement held instead, that because the High Authority was not required to set out these dissenting opinions, therefore this allegation did not prove a *détournement de pouvoir*. This statement presumably has the converse that if these opinions had been required to be stated, a failure to state them would have amounted to a *détournement de pouvoir*.[2]

---

[1] *Ibid.*

[1a] *Industrie Sidérurgiche Associate* v. *The High Authority* (Case 4–54), Vol. II.

[2] In a later case the Court went so far as to state:

"The High Authority must give reasons for its Decision, and if it fails to give legal reasons, *it would violate the Treaty* "—*Acciaieria e Tubificio di Brescia* v. *The High Authority* (Case 31–59), Vol. II. The Court made confusion a little worse when later in the same case it declared:

"The arguments presented to support the allegations of ' error and incongruity ' in the reasoning supporting the Decision, which, therefore, *would violate substantial procedural requirements*, is really the contention *that there has been a violation of the Treaty* "—*Ibid.* Vol. II.

In all these cases it is being assumed by the Court that a violation of a substantial procedural requirement forms merely one ground for declaring the annulment of a Decision or Recommendation. This implies, presumably, therefore, that if not challenged and therefore not annulled the Decision or Recommendation will stand and be valid. One case, however, throws grave doubts upon this assumed situation.

In that case [3] an enterprise [4] had submitted its investment plan to the High Authority for its approval. By the Treaty it is stated that if the High Authority disapproves of such an investment plan it shall do so not by means of a Decision but by means of an Opinion, which nevertheless is to have the force of a Decision and, as an exception to Article 33, an appeal can be brought against this Opinion.[5]

The High Authority by a letter dated December 19, 1956, and addressed to the plaintiffs declared:

> The High Authority has examined your investment plan dated July 28, 1956. In the present circumstances the High Authority had no other alternative but, following Article 54, paragraph 4, of the Treaty, to reply to your investment plan by an unfavourable response.

The plaintiffs appealed against this Opinion, on the ground that it did not comply with the requirements of Article 15 of the Treaty which specifies that, like Decisions and Recommendations, Opinions must also be supported with reasons.

In its judgment the Court declared:

> As for supporting reasons, the Court holds, accepting the submission of the Advocate General, that these are non-existent. The words " in the present circumstances " cannot, indeed, be considered as setting out the essential elements of a finding of fact upon which the legal justification of the measure must depend.
>
> Several of the conditions imposed by the Treaty have, thus, not been complied with. Although certain of these conditions are formalities which cannot affect the nature or the existence of the act, it appears that the giving of reasons for an opinion is not only laid down by Articles 5, 15 and 54, paragraph 4, of the Treaty, but that *it constitutes an essential, indeed a constitutive element of such an act. The absence therefore of supporting reasons entails the non-existence of the act.* Hence the letter of December 19, 1956, does not constitute an opinion within the meaning of Article 54, paragraph 4, of the Treaty and Case 1–57 is inadmissible for lack of subject-matter—the acts which it challenges being non-existent in law.[6]

[3] *Société des Usines à Tubes de la Sarre* v. *The High Authority* (Joint Cases 1–57 and 14–57), Vol. II.
[4] Appealing under Art. 33, para. 2; for the terms of which see p. 152, below.
[5] Art. 54, para. 5
[6] *Société des Usines à Tubes de la Sarre* v. *The High Authority* (Joint Cases 1–57 and 14–57), Vol. II, Author's italics.

Now this finding is extremely far-reaching. The Court, in this action has not sought to make any distinction between an Opinion having the force of a Decision, and a Decision within the meaning of Article 33, and indeed, what applies to a mere Opinion must *a fortiori* apply to a Decision. Article 33 allows Decisions to be challenged on the ground of violation of a substantial procedural requirement, and such a violation, it has held, occurs when a Decision is not adequately supported by reasons. The Court now appears to have implied that where a Decision is not adequately supported by reasons it does not in law exist at all, so that an appeal need not be brought against it—or rather that, as in the above case, an appeal so brought is inadmissible as there is nothing against which it can be brought.

If this is correct, that is to say, if the Court is not going to limit its ruling to the case of Opinions issued disapproving of investment plans, it is difficult to see why its reasoning should not also apply to cases where Decisions of the High Authority are challenged upon the other grounds set out in Article 33—and indeed, with greater force. If the High Authority purports to pass a Decision on a matter over which it has no legal competence, that " Decision " must surely *ab initio* be void and of no effect so that, as in the present case, an appeal against it is inadmissible as being against a legally non-existing act.[7]

VIOLATION OF THE TREATY OR OF ANY RULE OF LAW CONCERNING ITS APPLICATION

Violation of the Treaty

The overlap has already been mentioned which exists between a violation of a substantial procedural requirement and a violation of the Treaty. There exists also, in theory, a difficulty in determining the boundary between the heads of incompetence and violation of the Treaty.

Thus if the High Authority finds that the Community is faced with a period of manifest crisis it is required by the Treaty to establish a system of production quotas.[8] If when the Community is so faced with such a crisis, the High Authority, instead of establishing these production quotas passed a Decision authorising States to impose import quotas instead, it would appear that this Decision could be annulled for violation of the Treaty—the Treaty requiring the High Authority to do one thing and the Authority doing another. It would also appear that

---

[7] The paradox of this is that unless such an inadmissible appeal is brought, the Court will have no occasion on which it can declare the particular act to be non-existent.
[8] Art. 58, para. 1.

this Decision could be annulled on the ground of incompetence, as the High Authority has done an act which by the Treaty it is not empowered to do.

In practice the Court has also met with the further difficulty of delimiting violation of the Treaty from *détournement de pouvoir*.

In an early case [9] the Italian Government challenged a Decision of the High Authority on the grounds that it violated one of the Transitional Provisions annexed to the Treaty. The Court declared:

> The plaintiffs request the annulment of Articles 1, 2 and 3 of Decision 2–54 for violation of Article 30 of the Convention containing the Transitional Provisions. . . .
> Article 30 prohibits an extension to the Italian market of the system of deviations from price lists. Since Decision 2–54 has not taken this prohibition into account, it violates a rule of law concerning the application of the Treaty.[10]

The decision was, therefore, annulled by the Court on the ground of violation of the Treaty.

In two subsequent cases [11] this same Decision was challenged by two Italian enterprises.[12] Under Article 33, paragraph 2, however, associations can only challenge a general Decision, such as was the one here in question, on the grounds of *détournement de pouvoir* affecting them. The plaintiffs therefore alleged a *détournement de pouvoir* by arguing that there had been a violation of Article 30 of the Convention containing the Transitional Provisions. One of the plaintiffs thus declared:

> The decision challenged robs this Article of all practical meaning. The provision is intended to protect the Italian steel industry and especially the small and medium sized enterprises which are grouped within the plaintiffs' association.[13]

The plaintiffs argued, therefore, that a violation of this provision, while clearly being a violation of the Treaty, which, being an enterprise they were not allowed to allege, also amounted to a *détournement de pouvoir*.

The Court when considering the admissibility of the appeal took no point on this but merely made the factual statement:

---

[9] *Italian Government* v. *The High Authority* (Case 2–54), Vol. II.

[10] *Ibid.* For the terms of Decision 2–54, see Vol. II.

[11] *Associazione Industrie Siderurgiche Italiane (ASSIDER)* v. *The High Authority* (Case 3–54), Vol. II, below, and *Industrie Siderurgiche Associate (I.S.A.)* v. *The High Authority* (Case 4–54), Vol. II.

[12] The reason for this application was that the Court in its early days refused to publish information concerning what requests had been received, a practice which was reversed in July 1954—see *Avis* of the Court, *Journal Officiel*, July 20, 1954.

[13] *Associazione Industrie Siderurgiche Italiane (ASSIDER)* v. *The High Authority* (Case 3–54), Vol. II.

In the present action, the plaintiffs alleged, with supporting arguments, a *détournement de pouvoir* with respect to the enterprises which they represent. This *détournement de pouvoir* is alleged to exist in relation to Article 30 of the Convention containing the Transitional Provisions. . . .[14]

The arguments of the plaintiffs in these cases were not considered by the Court in any detail because the Decisions being challenged had already been annulled, so that there was no discussion of the validity of these arguments. However, the contention was held by the Court as being admissible.

These cases show, therefore, that a particular contention when made by the Italian Government was accepted by the Court as revealing a violation of the Treaty, and that the same violation of the Treaty when alleged by associations of Italian enterprises was accepted, at any rate as prima facie evidence of a *détournement de pouvoir*.

Violation of any Rule of Law Concerning the Application of the Treaty

A Decision or Recommendation of the High Authority may be annulled, not only on the grounds of a violation of the Treaty itself, but also on the ground of violation of any rule of law concerning its application.

Nothing is stated in the Treaty about the nature of the rule of law here being referred to, but the Court has declared that it is solely a breach of " a general and impersonal rule of law " and not, as in the case in question, a breach of an undertaking made on behalf of the High Authority to certain enterprises which fall within this term.[15] Defined in this way, the Court has accepted that this ground of annulment gives it a wide jurisdiction to test the legality of Decisions and Recommendations. Two examples will illustrate this.

In one case the High Authority by various Decisions had demanded the payment back from certain steel enterprises of subsidy payments which had been wrongly paid. The Court, when reviewing the validity of these Decisions, decided that the High Authority was competent to pass these Decisions, because power to do so was to be implied from the terms of the Treaty. However, the Court recognised the existence of a general proposition of law to the effect that the payment back of money could only be demanded when there existed some element of unjustified enrichment on the part of the party being required to pay. The Court then went on to declare:

14 *Ibid.*
15 *Société Fives. Lille Cail and others* v. *The High Authority* (Joint Cases 19–60, 21–60, 2–61 and 3–61).

136

In effect, the subsidy was aimed at reducing the difference in price between imported scrap which is more expensive, and scrap coming from within the Common Market.

This additional cost, according to the very principles upon which the subsidy is based, ought to be borne, not by the plaintiffs, by reason of the supplies of imported scrap received by them, but by all of the consumers of scrap. . . .

The payment of the subsidy did not, therefore, constitute an enrichment for the plaintiffs by reason of a payment which benefited them directly, but was the result of an operation which aligned the price of the scrap delivered, to the price on the domestic market. . . .

The conditions for an unjustified enrichment requiring repayment, therefore, do not exist in this case.

Under these circumstances, the Decisions [demanding such repayment], by violating the rules of law concerning the application of the Treaty, must be annulled.[16]

As there was thus no enrichment of the plaintiffs, unjust or otherwise, they were not by law obliged to repay anything to the High Authority. The Decisions demanding this repayment had, therefore, been passed in violation of a rule of law concerning the application of the Treaty, and thus were required to be annulled. In this case, therefore, the rule of law being referred to was a general principle of law: in another case [17] the Court has given a rather different meaning to this provision.

The relevant facts were that under the system, referred to above, of subsidising imported scrap which had been set up by Decision 2–57, enterprises were not required to pay the money to the subsidy fund in respect of any scrap which they obtained from their " own resources." In 1957 the High Authority defined this term in a letter to the *Office commun,* which was the organisation charged with running the subsidy system. Challenges of this definition, however, were rejected by the Court [18] on the grounds that the definition had not been embodied in a Decision of the High Authority but only in a directive of an internal nature, which was not open to review. Enterprises, therefore, found themselves unable to challenge the definition directly.

Later, however, after a particular enterprise had failed to pay the levy in respect of certain scrap which it alleged came from its " own resources," the *Caisse,* another of the organisations set up to run the subsidy system, acting on behalf of the High Authority, passed a

[16] *Mannesmann AG and others* v. *The High Authority* (Joint Cases 4 to 13–59), Vol. II.
[17] *Société Nouvelle des Usines de Pontlieue-Acieries du Temple (S.N.U.P.A.T.)* v. *The High Authority* (Cases 32–58 and 33–58), Vol. II.
[18] *Phoenix-Rheinrohr AG* v. *The High Authority* (Case 20–58), Vol. II: *Felten und Guilleaume Carleswerk Eisen und Stahl AG and another* v. *The High Authority* (Case 21–58), Vol. II; *Bochumer Verein für Güssstahlfabrikation AG and others* v. *The High Authority* (Case 22–58), Vol. II and *Mannesmann AG* v. *The High Authority* (Case 23–58), Vol. II.

Decision demanding a certain sum as the levy due. When the plaintiffs challenged the validity of this Decision,[19] the Court found itself able to consider the High Authority's definition of "own resources" contained in its letter sent to the *Office commun* whereas in the earlier cases it had not been able to do so. The reason for this change was that in the earlier cases the challenge was being made against a particular letter of the High Authority and this letter the Court had held was not a Decision. Now the challenge was being made against a demand for money and this demand was a Decision, and the validity of that Decision depended upon whether the High Authority's definition of "own resources" was correct or not. As the Court phrased it:

> From the time when the principles set out in the above-mentioned letters were applied by the administration, they became part of the framework of the interpretation and application of Decision 2–57.
> The interpretation of the High Authority affected the plaintiffs' rights from the moment when the departments, to which the letters . . . were addressed, applied this interpretation in respect to them.
> It is, thus, necessary to examine whether the interpretation of Decision 2–57, which appears from the letters . . . is legal.[20]

This examination was undertaken by the Court under its power to examine whether the Decisions being challenged had been passed in violation of a rule of law. The rule of law here being referred to was, presumably, the rule giving the true interpretation of the phrase "own resources." In the previous case the law being referred to was the general principle of law governing unjustified enrichment. In both cases the Court was considering something very much wider than the terms of the Treaty itself. The Court is seen, therefore, to have given a broad scope to its power under this provision, and it does not seem appropriate to suggest limitations upon it.[20a]

DÉTOURNEMENT DE POUVOIR

The Court itself has never expressly defined the term *détournement de pouvoir* but has impliedly accepted a definition on several occasions.[21] Thus the Court did not dissent from the definition given in classical terms by the High Authority, when it declared:

---

19 *Société Nouvelle des Usines de Pontlieue-Aciéries du Temple (S.N.U.P.A.T.)* v. *The High Authority* (Cases 32–58 and 33–58), Vol. II.
20 *Ibid.* Vol. II. For the terms of Decision 2–57, see Vol. II.
20a Where a plaintiff alleges that there has been a violation of a rule of law, the rule in question must be set out in the plaintiff's Request—see *Société Fives Lille Cail and others* v. *The High Authority.*
21 For a discussion of *détournement de pouvoir* in European municipal laws, see Laun: " Bemerkungen zum freien Ermessen und zum *détournement de pouvoir* im staatlichen und in Völkerrecht," *Festschrift für Herbert Kraus* (1954), p. 128.

There is a *détournement de pouvoir* when an administrative act is objectively in accordance with the rule of law but subjectively vitiated by reason of the aim being pursued by the administrative authority.[22]

This definition has been re-stated by the Court itself in the following terms:

The powers . . . granted to the High Authority . . . become divorced (*détourné*) from their legal objectives if it appears that the High Authority in dealing with circumstances with which it is faced has used them with the sole purpose, or at any rate with a dominant purpose, of avoiding a procedure specially provided by the Treaty [*i.e.*, for an improper purpose].[23]

Later in the same case the Court considered the terms of the actual Decision of the High Authority which was being challenged. This Decision had set up a system to subsidise the price of scrap and although ostensibly the Decision had been taken under Article 53 (b)—which empowers financial arrangements to be set up—the plaintiffs alleged that in fact the Decision fell within the terms of Article 59, by being an allocation of resources. To act in this way, they alleged, constituted a *détournement de pouvoir*.

Of the proof necessary for such an allegation, the Court declared:

Even on the assumption that this system [set up by the Decision in question] might possess certain characteristics of an indirect allocation, it would be necessary to prove that the aim of these challenged provisions was to make such an allocation by means of Article 53 (b) under cover of a financial arrangement and contrary to their expressed aim. . . . Further, proof would have to be made that the High Authority had allowed itself to be influenced by the desire to avoid Article 59, or that by a serious misinterpretation that Authority had mistakenly believed that the system challenged was equivalent to the system set out in Article 59.[24]

No Decision or Recommendation of the High Authority has yet been annulled upon the ground of *détournement de pouvoir,* but in the course of its judgments the Court has given some examples of facts which would have justified such an annulment had they been established. A mention of some of these may be of value.

---

[22] The High Authority's defence in *Fédération Charbonnière de Belgique* v. *The High Authority* (Case 8–55), Part I, published in *Recueil de la Jurisprudence de la Cour,* Vol. II, at p. 211. This definition was repeated by the High Authority in *Société des Charbonnages de Beeringen* v. *The High Authority* (Case 9–55), *Recueil,* Vol. IV at p. 335.

[23] *Groupement des Hauts Fourneaux et Aciéries Belges* v. *The High Authority* (Case 8–57), Vol. II.

[24] *Ibid.* Vol. II.

Examples of Détournement de Pouvoir

(1) By Article 59 of the Treaty, if the High Authority finds that the Community is faced with a serious shortage of coal or steel, it must bring the situation to the attention of the Council of Ministers and must make proposals for allocating such resources as exist.

By Article 53 (b), the High Authority may at any time create any financial arrangement common to several enterprises as it considers necessary.

Of these two provisions the Court has said:

> It must be recognised that a *détournement de pouvoir* would have occurred if the High Authority, finding itself faced with a situation which necessitated the application of the procedure set out in Article 59, had nevertheless, in order to avoid the guarantees of Article 59, proceeded under Article 53 (b) and the financial arrangements which it contains.[25]

The Court gives no reasons for this statement but the *détournement* would appear to occur because although the High Authority's action would objectively be valid within the terms of Article 53 (b), yet it would be vitiated because the provisions of that Article were not intended to be used in a situation which is expressly provided for by Article 59.

(2) By Article 26 of the Convention containing the Transitional Provisions, the High Authority was empowered during the years 1951 to 1958, which were known as the transitional period, to subsidise the price of Belgian coal by means of a system of compensation payments. The aim of this compensation was declared by the Convention to be " to make it possible to bring the price of Belgian coal to all consumers in the Common Market as close as possible to prices in the Common Market generally, so as to reduce Belgian prices to a level near that of the estimated costs of production at the end of the transitional period." [26] Of this provision the Court said:

> There could be no question of a *détournement de pouvoir* when the sole measure which the High Authority had taken with a view to achieving the aims of Article 26 was precisely that which consisted in the lowering of the price of Belgian coal. In default of proof that the level of prices which the High Authority had fixed by means of its Decision 22–55 was different from the level obtained by a correct fixing of the prices by application of Article 26, paragraph 2 (a), of the Convention, the Decision in question could not be vitiated by *détournement de pouvoir*.[27]

---

[25] *Compagnie des Hauts Fourneaux de Chasse* v. *The High Authority* (Case 2–57), Vol. II.

[26] Convention containing the Transitional Provisions, Art. 26, para. 2 (a).

[27] *Fédération Charbonnière de Belgique* v. *The High Authority* (Case 8–55), Part II, Vol. II.

A little later the Court stated:

> If the High Authority—as the plaintiffs allege—had fixed prices with the sole aim of equalising them with the prices of the Common Market, and had completely ignored the level of foreseeable costs of production at the end of the transitional period, this Decision would be vitiated by a *détournement de pouvoir* and would have to be annulled.[28]

In both these statements the Court is interpreting the wording of Article 26, paragraph 2a, of the Convention, set out above, as meaning that the High Authority possessed the power to fix the price of Belgian coal at the price reigning in the Common Market generally, with the object of reducing Belgian prices to a level near to that of the costs of production at the end of 1958. If, therefore, the High Authority exercised its power, but did not bear in mind the object lying behind the use of that power, it would commit a *détournement de pouvoir*.

(3) By Article 61 of the Treaty, if the fixing of maximum prices becomes necessary in order to keep prices at their lowest possible level, the High Authority, in certain circumstances, may fix such prices for coal and steel.[29]

In a case where it was alleged that the High Authority when making a decision in exercise of this power had committed a *détournement de pouvoir,* the Court declared:

> This ground [of appeal] requires one to judge whether, when fixing maximum prices by virtue of Article 61 of the Treaty, the High Authority sought not so much the objectives which it stated, particularly a lowering of prices, but in reality that it sought to act against agreements and concentrations of enterprises.
>
> It would thus have used the powers which were given to it by Article 61 for a purpose other than the one for which those powers were given.[29a]

This appears to be a clear instance and calls for no comment.

How Détournement de Pouvoir may be proved

As it is clear from the definition of *détournement de pouvoir* given by the High Authority and set out above, that the vitiating elements in a Decision annulled on this ground are the subjective intentions of the High Authority, the question arises of how those intentions are to be established.

On this the Court has not regarded itself as in any way limited and has consulted *travaux préparatoires,* and these it has taken to include

---

28 *Ibid.*
29 Art. 61, para. 1 (a).
29a *Netherlands Government* v. *The High Authority* (Case 6–54), Vol. II.

the minutes of the Council of Ministers and of the Consultative Committee, where these bodies were required to be consulted before a Decision was taken.[30]   The Court has also, on occasion, referred both to the report of the Mixed Commission set up to consider the subsidising of the Belgian coal industry,[31] and to the High Authority's own preliminary calculations [32] and has recognised that a comparison between prices previously existing within the Common Market and those prescribed by the particular Decision in question, may also be a guide.[33]

Main and Subsidiary Motives for a Decision

To establish a *détournement de pouvoir,* a plaintiff has to establish the existence of a wrongful intention on the part of the administrative body concerned.   What is the Court's attitude to be, therefore, if the motives of the High Authority are many and some of them are proper and some improper?

This particular problem presented itself in the first case that the Court had to judge.[34]   In that case enterprises had been selling at prices below those stated in their price lists and the High Authority subsequently passed a Decision allowing this price variation within certain narrow limits.   It was alleged by the French Government that the Decision was void as the ground for taking it was so that enterprises in selling below their published price lists would no longer be acting illegally and therefore the High Authority would not be under a duty to fine them.

The Court stated:

> Even if the Decisions in question have been partially inspired by the desire to introduce a new system more likely to be observed by enterprises than the previous one, one cannot conclude from this that it was intended to legalise infractions previously committed. . . . Even if an unjustified motive, namely the desire to avoid sanctioning defaulting enterprises, is present together with motives which, of themselves, justify the action of the High Authority, the Decisions would not, on this account, be vitiated by a *détournement de pouvoir, provided that they do not infringe upon the essential aim,* which is the prohibition of unfair competitive practices and discriminations.[35]

The Court in this case, therefore, distinguished between what may be called main and subsidiary motives, and held that where merely subsidiary motives were wrongful this did not vitiate the Decision provided

---

[30] As to this see further, Chap. VII, at p. 370, below.
[31] *Fédération Charbonnière de Belgique* v. *The High Authority* (Case 8–55), Part II, Vol. II.   [32] *Ibid.*
[33] *Netherlands Government* v. *The High Authority* (Case 6–54), Vol. II.
[34] *French Government* v. *The High Authority* (Case 1–54), Vol. II.
[35] *Ibid.*   Author's italics

that these subsidiary motives " did not infringe upon the essential aim," which presumably means that they must not make that essential aim unlawful as well.

In a later case,[36] a Decision of the High Authority relating to the compensation system for Belgian coal was challenged. Under the relevant provision of the Treaty [37] the purpose of this compensation system was set out to be to lower the high price of Belgian coal and to enable the Belgian steel industry to compete in the Common Market. The plaintiffs alleged, however, that the real aims of the High Authority when passing a Decision lowering the price of Belgian coal were to bring about structural changes in the Belgian coal industry and to avoid difficulties in selling high priced coal.

The Court although it found these allegations unjustified, applied the same criterion as has been set out above and declared:

> Even if an unjustified motive has been joined to motives which themselves justified the action of the High Authority, the Decision would not from this fact be vitiated by *détournement de pouvoir* provided that it did not affect the essential aim of Article 26 of the Convention.[38-9]

Allegations which support a claim of Détournement de Pouvoir

In order to prove the existence of a *détournement de pouvoir* a plaintiff has to compare on the one hand the purpose for which a particular power was given to the administrative authority, and on the other the purpose with which that power has been used.[40]

In one of the early cases,[41] the plaintiffs were an Italian enterprise. They alleged that the Decision of the High Authority allowing enterprises to sell below the prices set out in their price lists [42] had been

---

[36] *Fédération Charbonnière de Belgique* v. *The High Authority* (Case 8–55), Vol. II.
[37] Convention concerning the Transitional Provisions, Art. 26, para. 2.
[38-9] *Ibid.* Vol. II.
[40] The grounds giving rise to the *détournement* must be specifically set out and proved— a general allegation will not be accepted. Thus the Court has declared:
" The plaintiffs maintain that by the Decision which has been taken [concerning a demand to inspect the books of a company], the High Authority improperly wanted to transform the right to obtain information and, above all, the right to proceed to verifications, into a procedure of an inquisitional character, with the aim of extending its powers beyond the limits prescribed by the Treaty so that it would have thus pursued an aim other than the one which the Treaty empowered it to attain.
" This argument is not relevant, because it does not specify in any way what are the aims, *ultra vires* of those of the Decision, which are allegedly being sought by the High Authority. Furthermore, it has not been supported by any proof or offer of proof.
" It must, therefore, be rejected "—*Acciaieria e Tubificio di Brescia* v. *The High Authority* (Case 31–59), Vol. II.
[41] *Associazione Industrie Siderurgiche Italiane (ASSIDER)* v. *The High Authority* (Case 3–54), Vol. II.
[42] Decision 2–54, see Vol. II.

taken so as to avoid the need to impose fines upon enterprises who were doing this. In their pleadings, the plaintiffs declared:

> The High Authority has failed to impose the sanctions prescribed in Article 64 against the enterprises which, prior to the Decision here challenged, were selling at prices below their price lists. It had, however, a duty to do this. *This failure constitutes a manifest injustice and therefore a détournement de pouvoir* with respect to those enterprises which have observed the Treaty.[43]

The plaintiffs by alleging this manifest injustice—*manifesta ingiustizia*—as substantiating a claim of *détournement de pouvoir* were adopting an argument which has been accepted by the Italian *Consiglio di Stato* as being adducible to establish incompetence—*eccesso di potere*[44]—but never as a means of establishing *détournement de pouvoir—suiamento di potere.* However, the Court, although it did not expressly rule on this point, because the Decision being challenged had already been annulled in a previous case, gave no indication that it did not accept a contention of manifest injustice as, at least prima facie, going to show a *détournement de pouvoir.*[45]

Further, when challenging a later Decision of the High Authority[46] which required enterprises to make reports to the High Authority twice a week setting out all sales which were at prices other than those stated in the enterprises' price lists, the plaintiffs in their pleadings declared:

> The system for giving information which is introduced by Decision 3–54 is impracticable and therefore illogical. Consequently the system is vitiated by a *détournement de pouvoir.*[47]

The same type of argument was advanced in a more recent case[48] when the plaintiffs stated:

---

[43] *Ibid.* Author's italics.

[44] See Galeotti: *The Judicial Control of Public Authorities in England and Italy,* pp. 147 and 150.

[45] If manifest injustice of a Decision were to support a claim of *détournement de pouvoir* it could do so only on the reasoning that the purpose of the powers given to the High Authority was so that it should ensure justice, and the High Authority had here acted with another intention. It could, of course, equally well be argued that a manifestly unjust Decision could be annulled on the grounds of incompetence, by implying that the High Authority was only authorised to do actions that would lead to just results; alternatively that such a Decision violated the Treaty, by implying the same term as before. In the present case, it should be noted that the plaintiffs were not alleging that the particular Decision being challenged was manifestly unjust, but that the failure of the High Authority in the past to fine certain enterprises was unjust, so that the relevance of the contention is, in any event, dubious.

[46] Decision 3–54, see Vol. II.

[47] *Associazione Industrie Siderurgiche Italiane (ASSIDER)* v. *The High Authority,* Vol. II.

[48] *Phoenix-Rheinrohr AG and another* v. *The High Authority* (Case 20–58), Vol. II.

It is a generally recognised principle of law that an administrative authority can only exercise its powers by taking clear, coherent, sensible and comprehensive Decisions. By using its powers to take an obscure, contradictory, absurd and unintelligible Decision, the High Authority has gravely misconstrued the legal purpose behind its powers: it has committed a *détournement de pouvoir.*[49]

An Italian enterprise in another case [50] sought to base a *détournement de pouvoir* upon what they alleged was a breach of the rules of good administration, and also upon the fact that the High Authority when giving reasons for the particular Decision had failed to refute the dissenting opinions of consultative bodies. The validity of these arguments has been considered above.[51]

In a case decided in 1958,[52] the plaintiffs challenged a Decision of the High Authority [53] by which they were required to pay a sum exceeding 54m. lire to the fund set up to subsidise the higher cost of imported steel scrap. The plaintiffs alleged the existence of a *détournement de pouvoir* and supported this by alleging, first, that the Decision had been based upon insufficient reasoning and upon inaccurate calculations, secondly, that the High Authority had disregarded certain suggestions which the Council of Ministers had made at the time when they approved the setting up of the machinery for the compensation system, and, thirdly, that the High Authority by a Decision No. 14–55 had wrongfully delegated certain of its own powers to organisations in Brussels which were to run the compensation system.

Of these grounds, the Court declared, as to the first:

> The insufficiency of the reasoning and the failure to publish the data upon which the decision of October 24, 1956, has been based constitute of themselves violations of the Treaty such as to require the annulment of this Decision.[54]

As to the second, having stated that the suggestions of the Council of Ministers had been embodied in six principles and published in a General Report, the Court declared:

> It is not necessary for the purpose of the present action to consider the legal consequences which these principles, published under these conditions, might involve because the Decision of October 24, 1956, is required to be annulled for the above-mentioned reasons.[55]

49 *Ibid.*
50 *Industrie Sidérurgiche Associate (I.S.A.)* v. *The High Authority* (Case 4–54), Vol II.
51 See p. 130, above.
52 *Meroni & Co., S.p.A.* v. *The High Authority* (Case 9–56), Vol. II.
53 The Decision was taken on October 24, 1956; it was not given a number.
54 *Ibid.* Insufficiency of reasoning is usually regarded by the Court as a violation of a substantial procedural requirement—see pp. 126–134, above.
55 *Ibid.*

As to the High Authority's delegation of its powers, the Court on the particular facts held:

> The delegation of powers granted to the organisations in Brussels by Decision 14–55 gave to them a freedom of assessment which involved a large discretionary power and cannot be held compatible with the terms of the Treaty.
>
> The Decision of October 24, 1956, is based upon a general Decision improperly taken with regard to the Treaty, and for that reason also it must be annulled.[56]

It would appear, therefore, although the Court does not say so, and although in its judgment it considers these allegations under the heading of "Third Ground: *Détournement de Pouvoir*" that the Court is holding that *détournement de pouvoir* cannot be proved by such allegation as these and, in this, it is suggested, it is correct.

Finally, there is another way in which a plaintiff has sought to prove *détournement de pouvoir* and this was by proving the existence of incompetence, violation of a substantial procedural requirement and violation of the Treaty, thereby ending any distinction between the various heads of appeal.

On this the Court declared:

> The plaintiffs believe . . . that they may prove the other grounds of annulment set out in Article 33 to establish a *détournement de pouvoir*. In their opinion, the Treaty established a legal system by which private enterprises could only admissibly allege the sole ground of *détournement de pouvoir* with regard to them. It would be illogical, therefore, they contend to interpret this ground as being merely exceptional and subsidiary.[57]

Not unnaturally the Court summarily rejected this contention.[58]

The Standard of Proof to establish a Détournement de Pouvoir

As has been stated already, no Decision of the High Authority has yet been annulled on the ground of *détournement de pouvoir,* a ground which one plaintiff has referred to as "the hardest to prove."[59] It is not thought to be of great value, therefore, to review the several sets of facts which the Court has held not to constitute a *détournement,* many of which are in any event of a somewhat complex and technical nature. One case, however, will be used to illustrate the very high standard of proof which the Court requires.

[56] *Ibid.*
[57] *Société des Charbonnages de Beeringen* v. *The High Authority* (Case 9–55), Vol II.
[58] *Ibid.*
[59] *Société Industriale Metallurgica di Napoli and others* v. *The High Authority* (Joint Cases 36, 37, 38, 40 and 41–58), Vol. II.

In December 1952, Miranda Mirossevich was accepted by the High Authority as a translator. She was given a month's trial but during this period was given only three simple passages to translate. At the end of the month the head of the Translation Department of the High Authority informed her that her work was not satisfactory and the High Authority therefore informed her by a Decision dated January 8, 1953, that she could not be offered a post as a translator. Miranda Mirossevich brought an action against this Decision of the High Authority[60] alleging, among other things, that this Decision was vitiated by a *détournement de pouvoir* on the grounds that the actual Decision to remove her had been taken by the revisor and, it was alleged, had been so taken in order that one of the revisor's friends might take her place. The Court stated:

> The plaintiff alleges that the Decision of January 8, 1953, was vitiated by *détournement de pouvoir*, the real motive for her dismissal being the desire of the revisor to replace the plaintiff by a friend.
>
> Without ignoring the fact that there exists a connection between the departure of the plaintiff and the arrival in the translation service of the revisor's friend, neither the fact that this friend effectively replaced the plaintiff, nor that the decision to dismiss and to appoint were made by one and the same person, the Court holds that the proof of *détournement de pouvoir* has not been established to the satisfaction of the law.[61]

PATENT MISCONSTRUCTION OF THE TREATY

The second sentence of paragraph 1 of Article 33 states that the Court may not review the High Authority's evaluation of the situation based upon facts or economic circumstances except where the High Authority is alleged to have committed a *détournement de pouvoir* or to have patently misconstrued the provisions of the Treaty or of any rule of law concerning its application.[62]

As this provision stands, it might appear to mean that the Court may exercise this power of review in any case where a mere unsubstantiated allegation of *détournement de pouvoir* or of a patent misconstruction is made.

In an early case[63] in which the interpretation of this provision arose, the Court declared:

---

[60] *Mirossevich* v. *The High Authority* (Case 10–55), Vol. II. The action was brought under Art. 42 of the Treaty, see below, but the competence of the Court was nevertheless still governed by Art. 33, para. 1.

[61] *Ibid.*

[62] For a discussion of the Court's control over facts and economic circumstances see Delvaux, L., " Le contrôle de la Cour de Justice sur les faits et circonstances économiques," in *Annales de Droit et de Sciences Politiques* (1958).

[63] *Netherlands Government* v. *The High Authority* (Case 6–54), Vol. II.

It should be stressed that the contention that the provisions of the Treaty have been patently misconstrued has not been put forward by the plaintiffs as a separate ground for annulment, but only with the aim of enabling the Court to examine the evaluation of the situation based upon the facts and economic circumstances of the present case.

Article 33 does not, in respect of the allegation raised, require prior annulment of the Decision on the ground of a violation of the Treaty.

On the other hand, a mere assertion of a patent violation would not be adequate to give the Court jurisdiction over the economic evaluation, without the risk that this ground of appeal would degenerate to a mere formality.

It is necessary and sufficient that the allegation should be supported by prima facie evidence.[64]

The question of what amounts to a *détournement de pouvoir* has been discussed above; it seems necessary, therefore, only to consider what meaning is to be attached to the term " patent misconstruction of the Treaty." At first sight it would appear that if the Court is required to determine whether the High Authority has patently misconstrued the provisions of the Treaty, it is necessary for the Court, first, to construe the Treaty, and then, secondly, to see how the High Authority has construed the Treaty, and then, finally, compare the two constructions to see if the High Authority's one is patently wrong.[65] If it is, of course, then any Decisions based upon that misconstruction will be able to be annulled on the grounds either of incompetence or violation of the Treaty, or even in certain circumstances, apparently, on the grounds of a *détournement de pouvoir*.[66]

In two cases the Court has approached the matter in this way.[67] In those cases the plaintiffs challenged the validity of a Decision of the High Authority charging them with sums of 54m. and over 23m. lire respectively, payable to the compensation fund set up for the benefit of those purchasing imported steel scrap. In their actions, they alleged the existence of a patent misconstruction of the terms of the Treaty.

The plaintiffs' argument was that Article 47 of the Treaty provides that, subject to certain exceptions as to trade secrets, the High Authority

---

[64] *Ibid.*
[65] The distinction between a misconstruction and a patent misconstruction is not one that can profitably be considered in the abstract.
[66] The Court has declared that one means of proving that a subsidy system ostensibly set up under one Article of the Treaty was vitiated by *détournement de pouvoir* would be to show:
" That by a serious misinterpretation [the High Authority] had mistakenly believed that the system challenged was equivalent to the system set out in Article 59 "— *Groupement des Hauts Fourneaux et Acieres Belges* v. *The High Authority* (Case 8–57), Vol. II.
[67] *Meroni & Co. S.p.A.* v. *The High Authority* (Case 9–56), Vol. II, and *Meroni & Co. società in accomandita semplice* v. *The High Authority* (Case 10–56), Vol. II. These two judgments are identical on this point.

shall publish such data as may be useful to governments and to any other interested parties, and further, by Article 5, the High Authority is required to publish the reasons for its actions.

The plaintiffs contended that despite these requirements they had not been supplied with any of the data upon which their contributions to the compensation fund were based, and that even after waiting a year and a half they had received only provisional assessments of the amounts to be paid. They therefore alleged that the High Authority, by not observing the requirements of Articles 5 and 47 had patently misconstrued the provisions of the Treaty.

When considering this, the Court declared:

> By not making public, at least in their general aspects, the reasons for its action, and by not publishing such data which could be useful to governments or to any other interested parties, and which was not covered by the restriction regarding trade secrets . . . the High Authority has violated Articles 5 and 47 of the Treaty.[68]

From this it is clear that the Court is holding that a patent misconstruction of the Treaty means, in effect, an obvious violation of the Treaty.[69]

In an earlier case,[70] however, the Court adopted a very different interpretation of the meaning of the term " patent misconstruction of the Treaty " for there it had stated:

> The term "patent" presupposes that legal provisions have been misconstrued to such an extent that this misconstruction, when compared with the provisions of the Treaty, appears to result from an obvious error in the evaluation of that situation in the light of which the Decision has been taken.[71]

In the particular case in question, the plaintiffs were seeking the annulment of certain Decisions of the High Authority [72] which retained maximum prices for coal produced in the Ruhr and in the *Houilleres du Nord* and the *Pas-de-Calais*. The arguments alleged in an attempt to show that there had been a patent misconstruction of the Treaty were that, by the Treaty, the High Authority was only empowered to fix maximum prices " if it finds that such a Decision is necessary to attain

---

[68] *Ibid.*
[69] This appears also from the High Authority's defence to the allegations, namely that the duty to publish did not here arise because, it alleged, the information concerned was a trade secret—*Recueil de la Jurisprudence de la Cour*, Vol. IV p. 23. Although the Treaty would have empowered it to do so the Court did not here embark upon its own review of the facts and economic circumstances in the light of which these Decisions were taken; that is to say, the Court did not review whether the debts as specified in the Decisions were in fact correct.
[70] *Netherlands Government* v. *The High Authority* (Case 6–54), Vol. II.
[71] *Ibid.*
[72] Decisions Nos. 18–54, 19–54 and 20–54, Vol. II.

the objectives defined in Article 3 and particularly in paragraph (c) thereof " [73]—Article 3 (c) providing that the Community is to seek the establishment of the lowest prices. The plaintiffs then sought to show that with the conditions existing in the Common Market at the time when these Decisions were taken, minimum prices would not be achieved.

If one assumes that the plaintiffs' second contention is right, then, it is suggested, one of four alternatives may have occurred.

(a) The High Authority may honestly have believed that the fixing of maximum prices would produce minimum prices,[74] but as a matter of economics it may have been mistaken. This means that the High Authority has not misconstrued the Treaty, or in any way passed an invalid Decision, but only that it has passed a politically unsound Decision.

(b) The power of the High Authority to pass a Decision fixing maximum prices only exists, according to the wording of the Treaty, " if it finds that such a Decision is necessary to attain " minimum prices. If therefore the High Authority had not so found, it would have had no competence to pass the Decision in question, which could have been annulled on the grounds of incompetence.

(c) The Treaty may be read as granting power to the High Authority to fix maximum prices, but nevertheless that power is only to be used for a particular purpose, namely to obtain the lowest possible prices. If, therefore, the High Authority had used this power for another purpose, the decision might have been void owing to a *détournement de pouvoir*.

(d) The High Authority may have misconstrued the provisions of the Treaty, thinking for example, that the Treaty gave it other powers than in law it did. A patent misconstruction of the Treaty would have occurred and the Decision would be able to be annulled on the grounds, most probably of incompetence or of violation of the Treaty.

In the light of this discussion, it may be interesting to note what the Court itself said. It stated:

> In the present case, the " patent " misconstruction can arise only from a finding by the Court of the existence of an economic situation where, prima facie, there was no necessity for the measure which has been taken in order to achieve the aims set out in Article 3 of the Treaty, and especially in sub-paragraph (c) thereof. . . .

[73] Art. 61, para. 1 (a).
[74] It may at first sight appear illogical to fix maximum prices if one wishes to obtain minimum prices, but the necessity for so doing is soon seen if one considers what would be the effect of fixing minimum prices instead.

The plaintiffs' contention that maximum prices will in fact become minimum prices which will freeze and immobilise prices, does not, prima facie, rule out all necessity for maximum prices, and, therefore, this contention is not sufficient to establish the existence of a patent misconstruction.[75]

The Court further found, on the facts of the case, that prices in a free market were tending to rise, and held this to be additional evidence that there had not been a patent misconstruction of the Treaty.[76]

Now it appears clear that what the Court was doing here, under the power granted to it by this article, was to study the existing structure of the Common Market and from that to see whether, to use the Court's words, " prima facie, there was no necessity for the measure."

The Court was thus doing two things. It was taking the words of Article 61 of the Treaty, which state:

> the High Authority may fix . . . maximum prices within the Common Market, if it finds that such a Decision is necessary to attain

the lowest possible prices, and reading these as:

> the High Authority may fix . . . maximum prices within the Common Market if a situation therein exists such that the fixing of maximum prices is prima facie necessary to attain the lowest possible prices.

Having done this, the Court then in effect declared that if there did not exist a situation such that the fixing of maximum prices was prima facie necessary to attain the lowest possible prices, the above provision would have been patently misconstrued. It would appear, however, that in such a case what would have been misconstrued are not the provisions of the Treaty, but rather the existing economic situation.

In the light of this, the Court's interpretation of the words " patent misconstruction of the Treaty " may at first sight appear surprising, especially when compared with its rather different attitude to this expression which has been considered above. However, an interpretation of these words which holds that the High Authority's construction of the Treaty is to be compared with the Court's ignores the further provisions of this article that where the High Authority is alleged to have patently misconstrued the provisions of the Treaty, then as an exception, the Court may review the High Authority's evaluation of the economic situation. On the above interpretation this power would be unnecessary and inexplicable.

The situation is reached, therefore, that if the Court is to consider whether the Treaty itself has been patently violated, a power to review

---

[75] *Netherlands Government* v. *The High Authority* (Case 6–54), Vol. II.
[76] *Ibid.*

the economic situation is surprising; while if a review of the economic situation is made, one is not, strictly, determining whether the Treaty, but rather whether a given situation, has been misconstrued.

It is suggested that there is no way of avoiding this conflict, but that a closer approximation to the meaning of this provision would be obtained if it were conceived not as referring to a situation where there has been a patent misconstruction of the Treaty, but rather to one where a patent misapplication of the Treaty has taken place. If, in the case cited above, the Court is regarded as determining whether a provision, which can be applied to a situation in which the fixing of maximum prices is likely to lead to the lowest possible prices, has been rightly applied in a given situation or not, it follows that the first duty of the Court must be to determine the nature of the given situation. Viewed in this way the attitude and wording of the Court become explicable.

ARTICLE 33, Para. 2

The enterprises or associations referred to in Article 48 may, under the same conditions, bring an appeal against individual Decisions and Recommendations concerning them or against general Decisions and Recommendations which they consider to be vitiated by a *détournement de pouvoir* with respect to them.[77]

This provision extends the right of appeal to the Court to enterprises and associations, but this right is more limited than that given by paragraph 1 of this article to the Council and the Member States. It has, however, called forth nearly as much legal argument as paragraph 1 itself.

It might have been assumed that because by paragraph 1 appeals may be brought by Member States and the Council, and by paragraph 2, by enterprises and associations that these were the only entities authorised to bring the appeals referred to. The Court, however, has allowed the *Länder* of Germany to intervene in an action before the Court,[78] although

[77] French:
  " *Les entreprises ou les associations visées à l'article 48 peuvent former, dans les mêmes conditions, un recours contre les décisions et recommandations individuelles les concernant ou contre les décisions et recommandations générales qu'elles estiment entachées de détournement de pouvoir à leur égard.*"
  Stationery Office:
  " The undertakings or associations referred to in Article 48 may similarly appeal against individual decisions and recommendations in which they are concerned or against general decisions and recommendations which they consider to involve a misuse of powers affecting them."
[78] *Barbara Erzbergbau and others* v. *The High Authority* (Joint Cases 3–18, 25 and 26–58), Vol. II.

these *Länder* are clearly not Member States nor even legal entities in international law. More than that, their right so to intervene was not even regarded by the Court as a matter worth discussing in the judgment.

THE MEANING OF THE TERM "ENTERPRISES AND ASSOCIATIONS"

The enterprises which are here being referred to are those " engaged in production in the field of coal and steel within the European territories of the Member States, and also within those European territories [79] for whose foreign relations a Member State assumes responsibility." [80]

The terms "coal" and "steel" cover a large number of products which are listed in an Annex to the Treaty. In one case [81] the plaintiffs requested the Court to annul a Decision of the High Authority which stated that the plaintiffs could not be excused from paying contributions to the Subsidy Fund set up to subsidise the price of imported iron scrap. One of the plaintiffs' contentions was that they were not an enterprise within the meaning of the Treaty, and therefore could not be required to pay. The list in the Annex to the Treaty defining " steel," includes within the definition "foundry and other raw pig-iron." The plaintiffs, however, made iron castings, which the High Authority agreed were outside the definition of steel, yet in the manufacturing of these iron castings the plaintiffs used liquid pig-iron which they made themselves. To determine, therefore, whether the plaintiffs were an enterprise within the meaning of the Treaty the Court had to determine whether the plaintiffs' liquid pig-iron fell within the term "raw pig-iron." Having decided that it did, the Court considered whether the plaintiffs, in making liquid pig-iron as a first step in the production of iron castings could be held to be engaged in an activity of production of pig-iron. That is to say, did the term " production " mean exclusively the manufacture of a saleable product. Having held that it did not, the Court declared the plaintiffs an enterprise within the meaning of the Treaty and therefore liable to pay to the Subsidy Fund.

[79] This refers to the Saar.
[80] Arts. 80 and 79, para. 1. As concerns matters relating to concentrations and monopolies, the term " enterprises " is extended to mean any enterprise or organisation regularly engaged in distribution, other than sale to domestic consumers or to craft industries—Art. 80. For a discussion of the legal status of enterprises in the E.C.S.C. see Jerusalem; " Die Rechtslage der Unternehmen in der Montanunion," in 11 *Neu Juristische Wochenscrift* (1958), p. 410; and Vignes: " Les recours juridictionnels des entreprises privées contre les décisions de la Haute Autorité du Plan Schuman," in *Acheteurs* (1952); and Vignes: " I ricorsi giurdizionali della impresse private contrà le decisioni dell Alta Autorita del Plano Schuman," in *Rivista di Studi Politici Internazionali* (1952).
[81] *Société des Fondéries de Pont-à-Mousson* v. *The High Authority* (Case 14–59), Vol. II.

Concerning the meaning of the word " production " in the phrase " engaged in production in the field of coal and steel," the Court has held :

> The Treaty, apart from necessary implication, considers as activities of production only those activities which it expressly recognises as such.
>
> To determine whether a particular activity constitutes an activity of " production," it is necessary to refer to the nomenclature of Annex I of the Treaty.
>
> When the activity in question consists of a certain amount of transformation of the raw material, the decisive criteria is in particular that of knowing whether, within the said nomenclature, after the transforming operation the product in question falls under a different heading from that under which it had previously appeared.[82]

Paragraph 2 of Article 33 merely states that enterprises " may appeal." In one case, however, the Luxembourg Government, as an intervening party, sought to have a restriction placed upon this right of appeal. The Government's argument was fully set out and considered by the Court when it stated :

> The Luxembourg Government, however, in its request to intervene, has affirmed that " the plaintiffs, although falling, in other respects, within the competence of the Community, are not entitled to appeal to the Court having regard to the particular character of the action."
>
> The Luxembourg Government bases its contention upon the fact that because the action before the Court is solely concerned with a question relating to coal, only an enterprise producing coal, or an association of such enterprises, is qualified to bring the action. Indeed, this qualification cannot be possessed by an association of enterprises which, as in the present case, acts, and can only act, in its capacity as an association representing consumers. . . .
>
> In agreement with the submissions of the Advocate General, there is no provision in the Treaty which requires that the particular product made by the producer should be connected with the subject-matter of the dispute.
>
> The silence of the Treaty on this point cannot be interpreted in any manner which would be detrimental to enterprises and associations.
>
> Consequently, the plaintiffs' right to appeal to the Court in the present case cannot be denied.[83]

---

[82] *Société commerciale Antoine Vloebergs S.A.* v. *The High Authority* (Joint Cases 9 and 12–60). The headings in Annex I are: Hard coal; Patent fuels made from hard coal; Coke except coke or electrodes and petroleum coke; Brown coal briquettes; Lignite; Raw materials for cast-iron and steel production; Pig-iron, cast-iron and ferro-alloys; Crude and semi-finished products of iron, ordinary steel or special steel, including re-usable and re-rolled products; Hot finished products of iron, ordinary steel or special steel; End-products of iron, ordinary steel or special steel.

[83] *Groupement des Industries Sidérurgiques Luxembourgeoises* v. *The High Authority* (Joint Cases 7–54 and 9–54), Vol. II.

Although the Court here rejected the Luxembourg Government's argument, it has itself placed a restriction upon the right of appeal of an enterprise which, because it is engaged in production in the field of coal and steel, does fall within the definition in Article 80. This limitation is that the appeal brought must relate to that enterprise in its capacity of producer and not to it in any other capacity. Thus, a Belgian enterprise owned a plant which produced briquettes, which are products mentioned in Annex I of the Treaty: they also imported and exported American anthracite. This enterprise requested the High Authority to take action against the French Government because it had imposed restrictions upon the import of this anthracite into France. The High Authority passed a Decision refusing to take this action and the enterprise appealed to the Court for the annulment of this Decision. The Court held that the action was inadmissible. It stated:

> Although it is true that the plaintiffs carry on a productive activity as manufacturers of briquettes, this fact has not been taken into consideration in the present case, in which the plaintiffs have brought an appeal in their capacity of importer and exporter of coal coming from non-Member States and thus in their capacity of a trader, whereas their position as a manufacturer of briquettes plays no part at all, either directly or indirectly, in regard to the subject matter of the dispute.[83a]

The associations being referred to in Article 33 are those which " either permit the properly chosen representatives of the workers and consumers to participate in the direction of these associations, or in consultative committees attached thereto, or in any other way give a satisfactory place in their organisation to the expression of the workers' and consumers' interests." [84]

It is stated in the Treaty that the right of enterprises to form associations is not affected by the Treaty.[85] The Court has, therefore, held that the associations referred to in the expression " enterprises and associations " are associations of such enterprises as fall within the Treaty's definition of enterprise. The Court in declaring this stated:

> The associations referred to in that expression [enterprises and associations] [86] can only be associations of enterprises within the meaning of the term " enterprise " as defined by Article 80 of the Treaty for the entire Treaty.

[83a] *Société commerciale Antoine Vloebergs S.A.* v. *The High Authority* (Joint Cases 9 and 12–60).

[84] Art. 48, para. 3. It is not clear why Art. 33, para. 2 makes reference to the whole of Art. 48 as the above sentence is the only one relevant.

[85] Art. 48, para. 1.

[86] The Court was here referring to this phrase as it occured in Art. 35, para. 1, but, it is submitted, the term must be similarly defined throughout the whole Treaty.

155

Indeed, if this were not so, an association would possess a right to bring an appeal which none of its constituent members separately and on its own behalf would have been able to bring.

In the absence of any express statement to the contrary, the Treaty cannot establish any such disparity of treatment between an association and its constituent members.[87]

It follows from this, therefore, that an association composed of enterprises that are engaged in the distribution, and not in the production, of coal or steel, cannot appeal to the Court. In one case, however, the Court had to deal with the borderline case of an association composed of enterprises some of which were engaged in the production of coal, and so fell within the definition in the Treaty, and some which were not so engaged, and so fell outside that definition.[88]

The case turned upon the meaning of the word " association " in Article 35 of the Treaty, because under that article the plaintiff association had brought to the High Authority's attention that Authority's failure to make a Decision or Recommendation upon a particular matter. In the case before the Court, the same association was seeking the annulment of the Decision which the High Authority was deemed to have passed because it had failed to take action within two months.

The Court therefore had to consider whether the plaintiffs were an association who had standing to appeal to the High Authority in the first place, that is to say, whether they were an association within the meaning of the Treaty.

The Court found that the objects of the plaintiff association were " to protect and represent the interests of coal consumers . . . " and " to give advice upon questions of interest to coal consumers. . . ." The Court then declared:

> For these reasons, and without this decision prejudicing the qualifications needed to bring an appeal under other articles of the Treaty, the *Association des Utilisateurs de Charbon du Grand-Duché* is not one of the associations empowered to refer a matter to the High Authority in application of the terms of Article 35.[89]

---

[87] *Groupement des Industries Sidérurgiques Luxembourgeoises* v. *The High Authority* (Joint Cases 7–54 and 9–54), Vol. II, repeated in *Association des Utilisateurs de Charbon du Grand-Duché de Luxembourg* v. *The High Authority* (Joint Cases 8–54 and 10–54), Vol. II.

[88] *Association des Utilisateurs de Charbon du Grand-Duché de Luxembourg* v. *The High Authority* (Joint Cases 8–54 and 10–54), Vol. II. Those enterprises falling outside the definition were:

Fédération des Industries Luxembourgeois, Groupement des Negociants de Combustibles en gros, Société Nationale des Chemins de Fer Luxembourgeois, Monsieur Leon Brasseur, Engineer, representing Les Usines à gaz du Grande-Duché de Luxembourg.

The enterprise within the definition was:

Groupement des Industries Sidérurgiques Luxembourgeois.

[89] *Ibid.*

The Court further declared that the fact that one of the constituent enterprises of the association was an enterprise within the definition in the Treaty, did not alter the status of the association.[90]

It is suggested that, despite the reluctance of the Court to commit itself upon this point, as is seen from the above quotation, the term " association " must have the same meaning throughout the Treaty, and therefore that what is stated about the term in Article 35 applies equally to the term when used in Article 33. If this is so, it would appear, therefore, on the authority of this case, that the test of whether an association can appeal to the Court is, primarily, whether its Articles of Association show that it is one concerned with the production of coal and steel. If it is not, then it cannot appeal, and even if it is concerned with the production of coal and steel, it can only appeal if its constituent enterprises could themselves have appealed.[91]

When the Treaty states that " associations . . . may bring an appeal against individual Decisions and Recommendations affecting them," it might be assumed that the word " them " refers back to associations, so that only if the Decision or Recommendation in question concerned the association as a whole could that association sue. The Court has not accepted this, however, and has declared:

> In the case of an appeal brought by an association of enterprises, it is sufficient if it alleges a *détournement de pouvoir* with respect to one or more of the enterprises which are members of the association.[92]

DISTINCTION BETWEEN GENERAL AND INDIVIDUAL DECISIONS AND RECOMMENDATIONS

Where a Decision or Recommendation is an individual one concerning the plaintiff enterprise or association they may appeal against it " under the same conditions " as those set out in paragraph 1[93]: where that Decision is general, they may only bring an action against it if they believe it to be vitiated by a *détournement de pouvoir* with respect to them.

---

90 *Ibid.* The Court's words were:
   " The presence, among these members, of the *Groupement des Industries Sidérurgiques Luxembourgeois* does not alter this character [of the association], and moreover, this *Groupement* has already in its own right brought an appeal having the same object [as the present case]."
   It is suggested, however, that the latter consideration should be quite irrelevant.
91 There is no authority upon the point of how many of the constituent enterprises need to be enterprises within the meaning of the Treaty.
92 *Associazione Industrie Siderurgiche Italiane* (*ASSIDER*) v. *The High Authority* (Case 3–54), Vol. II. It is suggested that a limitation must be placed upon this right, namely, that the enterprise could itself have brought the action, for if this is not so an association, within the meaning of the Treaty, could sponsor a case on behalf of an enterprise that is not within the meaning of the Treaty.
93 For a discussion of the phrase " under the same conditions," see p. 164, below.

Because of this procedural difference it is vital that general and individual Decisions and Recommendations should be clearly distinguished.

The Treaty lays down that individual Decisions and Recommendations become binding by notification to the parties concerned, whereas general Decisions shall take effect automatically upon publication.[94] It cannot, from this, be argued, however, that every Decision that is published is general, and every one that is notified is individual. In fact, the Court has already held several published Decisions to be individual and also directives sent by letter and not published to be general Decisions.[95]

On the first occasion when the Court had to determine the nature of a particular Decision,[96] it concerned one by which the High Authority, by means of a scale of prices related to the type and grade of the coal in question, fixed the selling price of coal mined in Belgium.[97]

The Court stated:

> As respects Decision 22–55, the plaintiffs submit that it is an individual Decision. The defendants maintain, on the contrary, that it constitutes a general Decision. . . .
>
> This Decision applies to enterprises by reason only of the fact that they are producers of coal, without any other requirement. In the case of a new coal deposit being discovered in Belgium, its products would be required to be sold at the prices fixed by this Decision. On the other hand, the territorial delimitation contained in the Decision does not imply any individual character of that Decision, and is justified by the fact that the Belgian industry is in need of compensation.
>
> The fact that Decision 22–55 consists of a detailed and concrete set of rules applicable to different situations, is not contrary to the general character of the Decision. . . .
>
> The fact that the plaintiff association includes all the enterprises referred to in the Decision—and only those—does not lead in any way to a different conclusion. If it did, one would be forced to deny the general character even of a Decision applicable to all the enterprises of the Community in a situation where these had formed themselves into one and the same association. The individual or general nature of a Decision must be established by reference to objective criteria, so that it

[94] Art. 15, paras. 2 and 3. The publication is made in the *Journal Officiel*.
[95] Decisions Nos. 19 to 23–53 were published in the *Journal Officiel* of March 13, 1953, but each regulates one enterprise only. The letter of the High Authority to the Belgian Government of May 28, 1955, was held to be a general Decision—*Fédération Charbonnière de Belgique* v. *The High Authority* (Case 8–55), Part I, Vol. II.
[96] Decision 22–55 in *Fédération Charbonnière de Belgique* v. *The High Authority* (Case 8–55), Part I, Vol. II.
[97] Art. 1 of Decision 22–55 provides:
"For grades of coal set out in the schedule annexed to this Decision, coal producing enterprises in the Belgian basin when selling within the Common Market must comply with the prices therein specified." No enterprise is mentioned by name in the Decision. See further, Vol. II.

becomes impossible to make a distinction according to whether the plaintiffs are an association or an enterprise.[98]

The statement here that " the nature of a Decision must be established by reference to objective criteria " is valuable, and so is the brief statement later in the same case that " the character of a Decision does not depend upon its form but upon its content." [99] However, the Court made no attempt finally to define what the objective criteria might be.

In a later case,[1] however, the Court has given the following more general definition:

> General Decisions are quasi-legislative acts emanating from a public authority and having a normative effect *erga omnes*.[1]

This definition the Court applied when considering whether a particular Decision was general or individual, and stated:

> The general character of Decision 13–58 is directly determined by its contents which lay down many normative principles, specify in the abstract the conditions for their application and set out the legal consequences which they entail.
> Decision 13–58 establishes general organisational rules which . . . regulate in an identical manner an indeterminate number of cases.
> These rules are and will be applicable to any situation which is or which will come within the conditions specified for their application.[2]

Further, a Decision amending a general Decision is itself a general Decision.

> As the Court stated in the judgment in *Meroni & Co.* v. *The High Authority* (9–56), Decision 14–55 is a general Decision.[3]
> To the extent to which it modifies Decision 14–55, Decision 13–58 has the same character of a general Decision as has that Decision.[4]

Individual Decisions, however, are acts which, in European terminology, fall within private law. The Court declared this in the following terms:

> The High Authority . . . has limited itself to authorising sales agreements . . . and agreements for joint purchases. . . .
> The conditions of sale have been drawn up by the sales agencies for Ruhr coal and the enterprises which they serve, and the conditions of admission to the *Oberrheinische Kohlen Union* have been drawn up by

---

98 *Fédération Charbonnière de Belgique* v. *The High Authority* (Case 8–55), Part I, Vol. II.
99 *Ibid.*, Vol. II.
1 *Nold KG* v. *The High Authority* (Case 18–57), Vol. II.
2 *Società Industriale Metallurgica di Napoli* (*SIMET*) *and others* v. *The High Authority* (Joint Cases 36, 37, 38, 40 and 41–58), Vol. II. For the terms of Decision 13–58, see Vol. II.
3 For this case, see Vol. II. For the terms of Decision 14–55, see Vol. II.
4 *Società Industriale Metallurgica di Napoli* (*SIMET*) *and others* v. *The High Authority* (Joint Cases 36–58, 37–58, 38–58, 40–58 and 41–58), Vol. II.

the enterprises and wholesalers of coal in South Germany. The acts setting out these conditions have merely been authorised by the High Authority and, therefore, have not lost their character of acts in private laws. They cannot, therefore, be considered as quasi-legislative acts passed by a public authority in the exercise of its normative competence.

Therefore, the challenged Decisions [authorising these conditions] must be regarded as possessing the character of individual Decisions within the meaning of the E.C.S.C. Treaty.[5]

In a later case the Court virtually repeated this when it declared:

The Decision challenged is of an individual nature because it determines the legal validity of specific decisions taken by particular associations.[6]

Although, from the above, the distinction between general and individual Decisions appears clear, the Court appears not to have been very consistent in applying it. Thus when the Court was concerned with a Decision of the High Authority[7] setting up and regulating the joint sales organisations in the Ruhr, the plaintiffs assumed that the Decision was a general one, and this assumption was not challenged by the High Authority, and the point was not mentioned by the Court.[8] In a later action[9] when other Decisions of the High Authority further regulating these joint sales organisations in the Ruhr[10] were being considered, the Court held that "it could not be disputed" that the Decisions in question were individual. No reason for the distinction between the nature of these Decisions was stated and none readily come to mind.

An interesting variant of this problem of the nature of a Decision arose when the Court was asked to annul a Decision of the High Authority that did not exist but was implied to exist owing to the inaction of the High Authority for a period of two months after it had been requested to act.[11] The Court had, therefore, to determine whether this non-existent Decision was general or individual.

The Court solved this difficulty by seeing first what was the existing situation which the High Authority was impliedly refusing to alter and then deducing, in effect, what Decision would have been required expressly to declare this refusal. It was that Decision which was being implied and the nature of it could thus be established.

The Court stated:

---

[5] *Nold KG* v. *The High Authority* (Case 18–57), Vol. II.
[6] *Friedrich Stork et Cie* v. *The High Authority* (Case 1–58), Vol. II.
[7] Decision No. 5–56, Vol. II.
[8] " *Geitling* " *and others* v. *The High Authority* (Case 2–56), Vol. II.
[9] *Nold KG* v. *The High Authority* (Case 18–57), Vol. II.
[10] Decisions Nos. 16–57, 17–57 and 18–57, see Vol. II.
[11] Under Art. 35; see below.

The implicit negative Decision which is deemed to have resulted from the silence of the High Authority can only be considered as a refusal to take the Decision requested by the plaintiffs in their letter of July 14, 1954.

This implicit Decision is, therefore, to be deemed to have stated that there are no grounds for declaring, by means of a reasoned Decision, that the Government of the Grand Duchy failed in one of the obligations incumbent upon it by virtue of the Treaty, when by the Decree of March 8, 1954, it authorised the *Office Commercial* to increase the prices of solid fuel other than household fuel.

This Decision is an individual Decision because it relates solely to a specific activity of a public institution designated by name, *i.e.*, the *Office Commercial du Ravitaillement.*[12]

In the above cases, the appeal against an individual Decision has always been brought by the enterprise or association to which that individual Decision was addressed. In a later case,[13] however, the Court had to consider whether a Decision which was individual to one enterprise could be challenged by another enterprise adversely affected by it and, if so, whether as regards that other enterprise the Decision could be classed as an individual Decision, so that all the four grounds of appeal set out in Article 33, paragraph 1 could be alleged.

Briefly, the facts of the case were that the High Authority by three Decisions[14] had authorised an agreement between three Ruhr sales organisations by which they were to supply coal only to those wholesalers who in the previous year had themselves sold within the Common Market 60,000 tons of coal mined within the Community.

The plaintiffs in the case, however, were wholesale coal merchants established in Darmstadt who had not sold 60,000 tons of coal in the previous year as specified so that the Ruhr sales organisations, therefore, refused to supply them. The plaintiffs challenged the original Decisions of the High Authority which had authorised the agreement fixing this requirement of the sale of 60,000 tons, and alleged, *inter alia*, that the Decisions had been passed in violation of a substantial procedural requirement. This ground of appeal, however, could only be accepted by the Court if the plaintiffs were entitled to regard the High Authority's Decisions as " individual Decisions concerning them " within the meaning of Article 33, paragraph 2 of the Treaty.

The Court held first that, as regards the three Ruhr sales organisations themselves the Decisions were individual and then declared:

---

[12] *Groupement des Industries Sidérurgiques* v. *The High Authority* (Joint Cases 7–54 and 9–54), Vol. II.
[13] *Nold KG* v. *The High Authority* (Case 18–57), Vol. II.
[14] Decisions Nos. 16–57, 17–57 and 18–57, see Vol. II.

161

Owing to the silence of the Treaty on this subject, one cannot admit that a Decision, which is individual with regard to the enterprises to which it is addressed can, at the same time, be considered as general with regard to third parties.[15]

The plaintiffs could, therefore, also regard the Decisions as individual Decisions and could allege against them all the four grounds set out in paragraph 1.

RIGHT OF ENTERPRISES AND ASSOCIATIONS TO CHALLENGE GENERAL DECISIONS OF THE HIGH AUTHORITY

By Article 33, paragraph 2, although enterprises and associations may challenge individual Decisions upon any of the four grounds set out in paragraph 1, yet their right to challenge general Decisions and general Recommendations is limited to those which they believe vitiated by a *détournement de pouvoir* with respect to them.[16] This limitation upon the right of challenge of general Decisions was greatly reduced by one judgment of the Court[17] and the judgment amounts to an important piece of judicial legislation.

The facts of the case were that certain organisations had been set up in Brussels by the High Authority by a general Decision No. 14–55 and these organisations were to run the financing and distribution of a subsidy upon imported iron scrap. Enterprises were to pay a levy to these organisations but if they failed to do so the organisations could report the defaulting enterprise to the High Authority which could then pass a Decision demanding the sum owed. This Decision would be an individual Decision and would have executory force.

The plaintiffs in the case failed to pay their levy and were duly reported to the High Authority which on October 24, 1956, passed a Decision demanding the sum of nearly 55m. lire.

The plaintiffs challenged this individual Decision on three of the four grounds allowed by paragraph 1. However, the main burden of their case was that the basic policy adopted in Decision 14–55 of constituting the organisations in Brussels and empowering them to require enterprises to pay a levy to the Subsidy Fund was illegal. Decision 14–55, however, was a general Decision, and by the words of Article 33, paragraph 2, an enterprise could challenge it only on the grounds of a *détournement de pouvoir* with regard to itself, whereas the plaintiffs wished to challenge it upon other of the grounds set out in paragraph 1.

---

[15] *Ibid.*
[16] In this appeal, the plaintiffs may allege only a *détournement de pouvoir.*
[17] *Meroni & Co., S.p.A.* v. *The High Authority* (Case 9–56), Vol. II.

A further difficulty was that the time period for bringing the appeal against this general Decision had in any event long since passed.[18]
On this the Court held:

Decision 14–55 of March 26, has not been challenged directly, but only by way of an appeal against the Decision of October 24, 1956, which is of an executory nature. Whereas the Decision of October 24, 1956, is an individual Decision affecting the plaintiffs, Decision 14–55 of March 26, 1955, is a general Decision upon which the Decision of October 24, 1956, has been based.

In order to determine the ability of the plaintiffs, in support of their appeal against the individual Decision, to rely upon the irregularity of the general Decision upon which it has been based, it is necessary to discover whether the plaintiffs are able to challenge that Decision after the expiration of the time limit set out in the last paragraph of Article 33, and further, whether, in challenging that general Decision they may allege not only a *détournement de pouvoir* with respect to them, but the four grounds of annulment that are set out in the first paragraph of Article 33.

In agreement with the submissions of the Advocate General, the Court holds that a general Decision which has been taken irregularly cannot be enforced against an enterprise and money payments authorised by that Decision cannot be deducted from that enterprise.

Article 36 of the Treaty states that in support of an appeal against a Decision of the High Authority imposing pecuniary sanctions or daily penalties:

". . . the plaintiffs, under the conditions set out in the first paragraph of Article 33 of the present Treaty, may rely upon the irregularity of the Decisions and Recommendations which they are accused of having contravened."

There is no occasion to hold this provision of Article 36 to be a special provision applicable only to the case of pecuniary sanctions and daily penalties but as the application of a general principle, of which Article 36 is its application to the special case of an appeal in *pleine juridiction*.

One cannot find in the express mention made in Article 36, an argument excluding, conversely, the application of the rule there stated in any case where it is not expressly mentioned, for the Court has decided in its judgment in Case 8–55 [19] that to argue a converse is not admissible unless no other interpretation appears to be adequate and compatible with the express wording of the provision, with its context, and with its object.

Any other interpretation would render the exercise of the right of appeal granted to enterprises, and to associations mentioned in Article 48, difficult if not impossible, for it would require them to seek out in every general Decision, as soon as it was published, those provisions

---

18 By Art. 33, para. 3, appeals brought under Art. 33 must be lodged within one month of the publication or notification of a Decision.
19 *Fédération Charbonnière de Belgique* v. *The High Authority*, Vol. II.

which could possibly at some future time adversely affect them, or be considered as vitiated by *détournement de pouvoir* with respect to them.

It would encourage them to allow themselves to be subjected to those pecuniary sanctions or daily penalties prescribed by the Treaty in order to be able, by virtue of Article 36, to bring into issue the irregularity of those general Decisions and Recommendations of whose breach they would be accused.

The ability of a plaintiff, after the expiration of the period set out in the last paragraph of Article 33, to rely, in support of an appeal against an individual Decision, upon the irregularity of general Decisions and Recommendations upon which the individual Decision has been based cannot lead to the annulment of the general Decision but only of the individual Decision to which it gave rise.

The Treaties establishing the European Economic Community and Euratom expressly adopt a similar point of view when they set out in Articles 184 and 156 respectively that:

> " notwithstanding the expiration of the time limit set out in Article 173, paragraph 3 (or, in the case of Euratom, Article 146, paragraph 3), any party in an action bringing into issue a Regulation of the Council or of the Commission may rely upon the grounds set out in Article 173, paragraph 1 (or, in the case of Euratom, Article 146, paragraph 1), in order to allege before the Court of Justice the inapplicability of this Regulation."

These references, without providing a conclusive argument, support the above reasoning by showing that it is also accepted by the draftsmen of the new Treaties.

The annulment of an individual Decision upon the grounds of the irregularity of the general Decisions upon which it has been based, does not alter the effect of the general Decision except to the extent to which it has been made more specific by the individual Decision which has been annulled.

In challenging an individual Decision affecting them, any plaintiffs are entitled to allege the four grounds of annulment set out in the first paragraph of Article 33.

In these circumstances, nothing prevents a plaintiff when appealing against an individual Decision, from alleging the four grounds of annulment set out in the first paragraph of Article 33 so as to bring into issue the regularity of the general Decisions or Recommendations upon which that individual Decision has been based.[20]

MEANING OF THE WORDS: " UNDER THE SAME CONDITIONS ".

Article 33 grants to enterprises and associations the right under the same conditions to appeal against individual Decisions and Recommendations concerning them or against general Decisions and Recommendations which they believe vitiated by a *détournement de pouvoir* with respect to them.

---

[20] *Meroni & Co., S.p.A.* v. *The High Authority* (Case 9–56), Vol. II.

The phrase " under the same conditions " is a reference back to paragraph 1 of this Article which, it will be recalled, grants a right of appeal to States and the Council of Ministers upon the four grounds there specified.

It is clear, therefore, that these same four grounds can be alleged by enterprises and associations against individual Decisions concerning them. However, paragraph 1 also states that when the High Authority is alleged to have committed a *détournement de pouvoir* or to have patently misconstrued the provisions of the Treaty, the Court may review the facts and economic circumstances in the light of which the Decision in question was taken.

Two questions, therefore, arise. First, whether enterprises and associations when challenging individual Decisions concerning them can allege not only the four grounds of appeal set out in paragraph 1, but also that the High Authority when passing them has patently misconstrued the provisions of the Treaty, and secondly, if they do allege either a *détournement de pouvoir* or that the Treaty has been patently misconstrued whether the Court can review the facts and economic circumstances in the light of which the Decision was passed, as it could have done if the same case had been brought by a Member State instead of by that enterprise or association.

There is no authority upon these points, but it would appear that a choice will have to be made between the following arguments.

First, it can be contended that in the phrase " enterprises and associations may, under the same conditions, bring an appeal " the words " under the same conditions " refer only to the actual bringing of an appeal. Now the only part of paragraph 1 which governs the bringing of an appeal is its first sentence which sets out the four grounds upon which an appeal may be brought. The second sentence of paragraph 1, which refers to the Court's power in certain circumstances to review the economic situation, governs the Court's competence once an appeal has in fact been brought. It can be held, therefore, that this power, because it does not affect the actual initial bringing of an appeal, is not to be incorporated into the phrase " may, under the same conditions, bring an appeal."

Alternatively, it can be argued that the words " may . . . bring an appeal " are not to be construed so narrowly as to apply merely to the submission of the request to the Registry—which strictly is all that is required to bring an appeal—but that they must be construed as referring to all the stages of procedure. If, in fact, an enterprise brings an appeal alleging a *détournement de pouvoir* and the Court cannot consider the economic situation, as it could if another appeal on the same facts had been brought by a Member State, then, it can be contended, it is twisting the use of words to suggest that the two cases are being brought " under the same conditions."

Further than this, there are no other indications in the Treaty that enterprises and associations when challenging individual Decisions concerning them are to be placed at a disadvantage, and particularly not one which would in many cases require the enterprise's home State also to appeal on the very same facts, in which second appeal the Court could review the economic situation.

Finally, it will be recalled that when the Luxembourg Government sought to impose a limitation upon the right of enterprises to appeal to the Court by arguing that only enterprises producing coal could challenge a Decision relating to coal, the Court declared:

> The silence of the Treaty on this point cannot be interpreted in any manner which would be detrimental to enterprises and associations.

It may well be held that this statement embodies a general principle.

For these reasons it is suggested, therefore, that the phrase " under the same conditions " implies that when a *détournement de pouvoir* is alleged against an individual Decision the Court has the same power to review the economic situation as it would have in an appeal brought under paragraph 1 of this Article.

If this is so, then one has to consider whether enterprises and associations when challenging individual Decisions can also allege that the High Authority has patently misconstrued the provisions of the Treaty and by making this allegation whether they confer upon the Court the same power of making this review as it would have if the case were being brought under paragraph 1.

It must be noted first, that, although under paragraph 1 Member States and the Council can clearly allege a patent misconstruction of the Treaty, this allegation is not, in terms, one of the four grounds upon which a Decision or Recommendation can be challenged. That is to say, this allegation of a patent misconstruction is not a separate, and fifth ground of appeal, but is included within one or more of the four grounds specified.[21]

If therefore, as is submitted, the term " under the same conditions " means " on the same grounds " then it is suggested that enterprises and associations, by being empowered to allege against individual Decisions these four grounds of invalidity must, *ipso facto* be empowered also to allege a patent misconstruction of the Treaty.

---

[21] It is an attenuated form either of violation of the Treaty, or of incompetence.

Finally, if, as has been suggested, the term " under the same conditions," implies that the Court can review the economic situation when a *détournement de pouvoir* is alleged, there appear to be no logical grounds for making a distinction between the effect of making an allegation of *détournement de pouvoir* and the effect of making one of a patent misconstruction.

The phrase " under the same conditions," however, produces a still further difficulty. As paragraph 2 stands, it appears that enterprises and associations, may " under the same conditions " appeal against individual Decisions affecting them and " under the same conditions " appeal also against general Decisions which they believe vitiated by a *détournement de pouvoir* affecting them.

The plaintiffs in one case,[22] therefore argued, in effect, that because, when it refers to individual Decisions, the phrase " under the same conditions " means " on any of the four grounds set out in paragraph 1," the phrase must also have the same meaning when it refers to general Decisions alleged to be vitiated by a *détournement de pouvoir* with respect to the plaintiffs. That is to say, that as soon as such a *détournement de pouvoir* has prima facie been established, all the other grounds of appeal are also open to the plaintiffs.

The Court, however, rejected this, and declared:

> If the plaintiffs' contention were correct, enterprises would have as extensive a right of appeal as that of the States and of the Council, and it would be inexplicable why Article 33, instead of simply equating the appeals of enterprises to those of States or of the Council, has introduced a very clear distinction between individual Decisions and general Decisions, and has limited, as far as enterprises are concerned, the annulment of general Decisions to the ground of *détournement de pouvoir* with respect to those enterprises. The phrase " under the same conditions " cannot be interpreted as meaning that the enterprises, after having established a *détournement de pouvoir* with respect to them, have the right to allege the other grounds of annulment as well, because, when a *détournement de pouvoir* with respect to them has been established, the annulment of the Decision in question must follow and does not have to be pronounced on other grounds.[23]

This statement may have done one of two things. The Court may, in effect, be saying that appeals being brought against general Decisions may still be brought " under the same conditions " but that those words, as here used, do not imply " on the grounds set out in paragraph 1." Alternatively the Court may in effect have stated that the words " under the same conditions " refer only to appeals against individual Decisions.

22 *Fédération Charbonnière de Belgique* v. *The High Authority* (Case 8–55), Part I, Vol. II.
23 *Ibid.*

If the former is the case, then the words "under the same conditions" must mean something and if because of the context they do not mean "on the same grounds" then it is suggested that they must still carry their other meaning—namely that the Court is to hear the case with the same powers as if the case had been brought under paragraph 1, so that it can review the economic situation.

If the words do not apply to appeals against general Decisions, then an appeal by an enterprise or association against a general Decision deemed to be vitiated by a *détournement de pouvoir* will have to be judged by the Court with no review of economic facts. This may mean that where an enterprise has appealed against a general Decision and lost, its home State, on the self same facts and with the same allegations, may appeal and, because it is appealing under paragraph 1, and not paragraph 2, the Court will be able to review the economic situation and the State may succeed.

It is suggested that an interpretation which leads to this position cannot be correct, and that, therefore, the alternative interpretation is to be adopted.

In the light of all the above, therefore, it is submitted that under paragraph 2 enterprises and associations when challenging individual Decisions which affect them may allege any or all of the four grounds set out in paragraph 1, and if the High Authority is alleged to have committed a *détournement de pouvoir* or to have patently misconstrued the provisions of the Treaty or of a rule of law relating to its application, then the Court may review the High Authority's evaluation of the situation based on economic facts and circumstances which led to such Decision or Recommendation. Further, that enterprises and associations may appeal against general Decisions or Recommendations which they believe to be vitiated by a *détournement de pouvoir* affecting them, and that the Court when considering the appeals has the above power to review the High Authority's evaluation of the situation.

The Grounds of Appeal of Enterprises and Associations

No difficulties have been encountered concerning the right of enterprises and associations to challenge individual Decisions concerning them. When, however, they have sought to challenge general Decisions which they believe to be vitiated by *détournement de pouvoir* with respect to them, they have been met with some strange arguments from the High Authority.

The first point taken by the High Authority was that a request merely alleging, albeit with supporting evidence, a *détournement de pouvoir* was inadmissible. It thus declared in its Defence to an action brought by an association:

> The plaintiffs do not possess the right to bring an appeal because they have not set out the proof of the existence of a *détournement de pouvoir* with respect to them. It is not sufficient that the plaintiffs allege the existence of a *détournement de pouvoir* with respect to them. The appeal is only admissible if this *détournement de pouvoir* has actually been committed.[24]

This contention is not understood. One can only speak about a *détournement de pouvoir* having "actually been committed" if the Court in a judgment has declared this to be so, for without a judgment the matter has not been proved. As the bringing of a case must precede the judgment of the Court, the High Authority's argument appears to have no meaning.

The Court in its judgment rejected the High Authority's argument and held:

> By the terms of Article 33, paragraph 2, of the Treaty, enterprises or associations of enterprises "may bring an appeal . . . against general Decisions . . . which they consider to be vitiated by a *détournement de pouvoir* with respect to them." According to this provision, which is perfectly clear, it is sufficient for the admissibility of appeal that the plaintiffs formally allege a *détournement de pouvoir* with respect to them. . . .
> The Court holds that the Treaty does not provide and does not require any further condition for the admissibility of appeals, such as, in particular, the proof that a *détournement de pouvoir* with respect to the plaintiffs has actually been committed. This proof will be necessary to establish that the case is well founded—but this matter belongs to the examination of the merits and does not affect admissibility.[25]

The High Authority sought in a later case [26] to place a second restriction upon an enterprise's right to challenge a general Decision. The Court summarised its contention in the judgment:

> The views of the parties differ upon what is the exact effect of Article 33 of the Treaty concerning the admissibility of certain grounds alleged by the plaintiffs against these general Decisions.
> The defendants maintain that an enterprise can only allege a *détournement de pouvoir* with respect to them if the High Authority has disguised, under what appears to be a general administrative act, an individual Decision "with respect to" that enterprise.[27]

---

[24] *Associazione Industrie Siderurgiche Italiane (ASSIDER)* v. *The High Authority* (Case 3–54), Vol. II.

[25] *Ibid.*

[26] *Fédération Charbonnière de Belgique* v. *The High Authority* (Case 8–55), Part I. Vol. II.

[27] *Ibid.*

Of this, the Court said:

> This contention must be rejected. Indeed a disguised individual Decision remains an individual Decision. . . . The Court is of the opinion that Article 33 clearly states that associations and enterprises can challenge not only individual Decisions, but also general Decisions in the proper sense of that term.[28]

THE MEANING OF THE PHRASE: "A DÉTOURNEMENT DE POUVOIR WITH RESPECT TO THEM"

Paragraph 2 states that enterprises and associations may challenge general Decisions and Recommendations which they deem to be vitiated by a *détournement de pouvoir* with respect to them. It is necessary therefore that the words "with respect to them" should be interpreted.

The High Authority in one case when referring to this expression argued:

> The *détournement de pouvoir* here referred to presupposes that the Decision being challenged is only general in appearance while in reality it individually affects the one or more plaintiff enterprises—the High Authority having thus used its power for a purpose other than that specified by the Treaty.[29]

As the Decision being challenged in that case had already been repealed in an earlier action,[30] the Court refused to declare upon the meaning of this phrase.[31]

However, when in a subsequent case the same words again came up for consideration, the Court declared:

> The phrase "with respect to them" has no other meaning than that of the words which express it, namely, that the decision affects that enterprise which is the object, or at any rate, the victim, of the *détournement de pouvoir* which it alleges.[32]

The word "them" in the phrase, "a *détournement de pouvoir* with respect to them" refers back to the enterprises and associations. The point arose, therefore, of whether, before an association could appeal against a general Decision the *détournement de pouvoir* had to be with

---

[28] *Ibid.*
[29] *Associazione Industrie Siderurgiche Italiane (ASSIDER)* v. *The High Authority* (Case 3–54), Vol. II.
[30] *French Government* v. *The High Authority* (Case 1–54), Vol. II.
[31] Later in the judgment, however, the Court clothed the phrase with a certain mystery when it declared concerning its earlier annulment of certain Decisions of the High Authority: "No new ground has been put forward which could bring the Court to another conclusion, whatever interpretation one gives to the phrase ' *détournement de pouvoir*,' in Article 33 of the Treaty with respect to them."
[32] *Fédération Charbonnière de Belgique* v. *The High Authority* (Case 8–55), Part I, Vol. II—*ibid.* vol. II.

respect to that association as a whole or whether an association could bring a case where the *détournement de pouvoir* was merely with respect to one of its constituent enterprises.

The Court has held the latter, and has declared:

> In the case of an appeal brought by an association of enterprises, it is sufficient if [the association] alleges a *détournement de pouvoir* with respect to one or more of the enterprises which are members of the association.[33]

In the light of the above it will have been seen that paragraph 2 of Article 33 has been interpreted so that in effect it provides:

> Enterprises, or associations referred to in Article 48, paragraph 3, may bring an appeal against individual Decisions and Recommendations concerning them upon any one or more of the grounds set out in paragraph 1, and in respect of such appeals the Court shall have the same powers as if they had been brought under paragraph 1. Further, enterprises and associations may, on the sole ground of *détournement de pouvoir* bring an appeal against general Decisions and Recommendations which they believe vitiated by a *détournement de pouvoir* with respect either to themselves or to one of their constituent enterprises.

ARTICLE 33, Para. 3

The appeals provided for in the first two paragraphs of the present Article must be brought within a time limit of one month calculated, according to the case, from the notification or from the publication of the Decision or Recommendation.[34]

The existence of the time limit for bringing appeals which is contained in this paragraph has been described by the Court as " a fundamental principle of law." The Court continued:

> The strict time limit for the appeal corresponds to a generally recognised requirement, that of preventing the legality of administrative Decisions being brought into question indefinitely. This involves the prohibition upon re-opening the question after the expiration of the time limit.[35]

[33] *Associazione Industrie Siderurgiche Italiane (ASSIDER)* v. *The High Authority* (Case 3–54), Vol. II.

[34] French:
" *Les recours prévus aux deux premiers alinéas du présent article doivent être formés dans le délai d'un mois à compter, suivant le cas, de la notification ou de la publication de la décision ou recommandation.*"
Stationery Office:
" The proceedings provided for in the first two paragraphs of the present Article shall be instituted within one month from the date of notification or publication, as the case may be, of the decision or recommendation."

[35] *German Government* v. *The High Authority* (Case 3–59), Vol. II.

" WITHIN A PERIOD OF ONE MONTH " [36]

Some of the Decisions and Recommendations of the High Authority are published by it in the *Journal Officiel* the rest being notified by letter to the parties concerned. By the above provision, appeals against these must be brought within a period of one month. This period starts to run in the case where a Decision or Recommendation has been published from the fifteenth day following the date of publication.[37] In the case of notification, however, it starts to run from the day after the receipt of that notification.[38] There is also a further addition of time ostensibly to off-set the distance of the plaintiff from the Court, which varies from two days in respect of Belgium to one month in respect of non-European countries.[39]

The Court in two cases, however, has experienced great difficulty in determining when exactly the particular Decisions in question were notified to the plaintiffs. In the first of these cases [40] the Decision in question was contained in a letter dated May 12, 1958, but there was no evidence either about the date when the letter was posted or about when it was received.

The Court stated:

> The plaintiffs have their registered office in Billancourt (Seine) which is in metropolitan France. Therefore . . . the time limit granted to the plaintiffs for challenging the above-mentioned letter expires after one month and three days, to be calculated from the day following its notification.
>
> Consequently, the appeal which was filed in the Registry of the Court on June 30, 1958, has only been brought within the time limit if the letter of May 12, 1958, had not reached the plaintiffs until May 26, 1958, at the very earliest. June 29, 1958, being a Sunday, the expiration of a time limit falling on that day would be postponed until Monday, June 30.

---

[36] The term " month " presumably means " calendar month " although this is nowhere expressly stated.

[37] Rules, Art. 81, para. 1.   [38] *Ibid.*

[39] Rules, Art. 81, para. 2 and Annex II.   The calculation of this time period is apparently no easy matter.   In one case the High Authority worked it out to be September 19, 1958, the plaintiffs claimed it was September 20 and the Court held it was September 18 and all of these calculations appear either to be wrong, or else right for the wrong reason. The Decision in question (Decision No. 13–58) was published in the *Journal Officiel* on July 30, 1958.   The plaintiffs were resident in Italy and could, therefore, claim 5 extra days. The High Authority took 15 days from the day following the date of publication and reached August 14, then for some reason interpreted the word " one month " as meaning 30 days, added the five extra days and with an error in their mathematics, declared the answer to be September 19. The plaintiffs somewhere found 2 *dies non*, thus giving themselves a considerable advantage. The Court by taking one month to mean a calendar month reached September 14, to which they added the 5 extra days and gave the answer somewhat curiously, as September 18—see *Fer. Ro (Ferriere Rossi) and Acciarierie San Michele* v. *The High Authority* (Joint Cases 40 and 41–58) Vol. II.

[40] *Société Nouvelle des Usines de Pontlieue-Acieries du Temple (S.N.U.P.A.T.)* v. *The High Authority* (Joint Cases 32–58 and 33–58), Vol. II.

The explanations submitted by the parties have not made it possible to establish the date on which the plaintiffs received the above-mentioned letter, so that consequently the starting date of the time limit is uncertain.

Although it is hardly probable that a letter posted in Brussels, and bearing the date of May 12, did not arrive in Saint-Michel-de-Maurienne (Savoie) before May 26, nevertheless this possibility cannot be entirely ruled out because the date on which the letter was posted is uncertain.

Account must be taken of the fact that if the *dies a quo* of the time period in question is uncertain, this is due to the fact that the C.P.F.I.,[41] whose action is imputable to the defendants, has failed to send the letter of May 12 by registered post with an acknowledgment of receipt, and that the defendants have not been able to produce any evidence concerning the day on which the letter was posted by the department of the C.P.F.I. The benefit of the doubt, therefore, must be given in favour of the plaintiffs.

In consequence, the appeal is admissible.[42]

As a result the Court held that the letter of the High Authority had not reached the plaintiffs before May 26, 1959.

In a later similar case the Court held the other way.[43] The plaintiffs were likewise resident in metropolitan France, so that the relevant time period was one month and three days from the day following notification to them of the particular Decision.

The Court stated:

The plaintiffs have their registered office in Paris, and thus within metropolitan France. . . .

The appeal was filed in the Registry of the Court on October 20, 1958. Consequently it has been brought within the time limit only if the letter of July 31, 1958, had not reached the plaintiffs until September 17, 1958, at the earliest.

The plaintiffs, when questioned on this matter by the Court, supplied no explanation. On the other hand, the defendants formally declared that, according to its register of outgoing mail, " the said letter had been posted on August 1, 1958." This statement has not been challenged by the plaintiffs. However, the exact date on which the said letter reached the plaintiffs has not been able to be established.

However, it appears impossible that a letter posted in Luxembourg on August 1, 1958, which the plaintiffs admit having received, should not arrive in Boulogne-Billancourt, where it was addressed, before September 17, 1958. In consequence, it is established that the appeal brought against the letter of July 31, 1958, has not been brought within the time limit.

The appeal . . . is, therefore, inadmissible.[44]

---

41 *Caisse de Péréquation des Ferrailles importées*, as to which see Vol. II.
42 *Société Nouvelle des Usines de Pontlieue-Acieries du Temple (S.N.U.P.A.T.)* v. *The High Authority* (Joint Cases 32–58 and 33–58), Vol. II.
43 *Société des Aciers Fins de l'Est (S.A.F.E.)* v. *The High Authority* (Case 42–58), Vol. II.
44 *Ibid.* Vol. II.

In another case the plaintiffs had posted their request commencing their appeal one day before what they claimed was the end of the time period for bringing an action, but the request had not reached the Registry of the Court until after what all parties admitted was the end of the period. The plaintiffs then alleged that, nevertheless, the case had been correctly brought.

The Court naturally rejected this allegation and stated:

> If the plaintiffs' contentions were admitted, the time limits in respect of distance set out in paragraph 2 of Article 85 of the Rules of the Court would have no justification, because all the parties concerned, as regards postal registration, find themselves in identical positions whatever may be the distance which separates them from the Court.[45]

Paragraph 3 of Article 33 appears to have been drafted on the assumption that Decisions which are published will not be notified, and those that have been notified will not be published. If this assumption had been correct, the interpretation of this paragraph would have been easier; unfortunately the assumption is not correct and interpretation is far from easy. Two examples may illustrate this.

In one case,[46] a Decision affecting certain German sales agencies was notified to them on February 21, 1959, and was then published in the *Journal Officiel* on March 7, 1959. Earlier, in another connection, the High Authority, in December 1957, had set out in a letter that two enterprises, one in Italy and one in the Netherlands,[47] were exempt from paying a certain levy. The contents of this letter were described by one department of the High Authority as being " a Decision " [48] and if it was a Decision, it was, further, clearly an individual Decision and an appeal against it could only have been brought within one month of its notification to the enterprises concerned.

The letter, however, was subsequently published in the *Journal Officiel* on February 1, 1958. What now was to be the position? Was the right of appeal of the two enterprises who were the subject-matter of the letter to be revived for a second period of one month, this time from the publication of the Decision? There clearly appears to be no justification for this view.

A second alternative was that States and other enterprises might be granted a month from the date of publication, but as the Court has

---

[45] *Fer. Ro. (Ferriere Rossi)* v. *The High Authority* (Case 40–58), Vol. II.

[46] " *Geitling,*" " *Mausegatt* " *and* " *Präsident* " v. *The High Authority* (Joint Cases 16–59, 17–59 and 18–59), Vol. II.

[47] *Breda Siderugica S.p.A.* and *Koninklijke Nederlandsche Hoogovens en Staalfabrieken N.V.*

[48] Letter dated February 6, 1958, written by the Trading Division of the High Authority to the *Deutsche Schrottverbraucher Gemeinschaft.*

already held [49] that one particular enterprise may appeal against an individual Decision directed to a second enterprise, that particular enterprise had already had a period of one month in which to appeal, and a second period of one month may not appear justified here either.

In view of this, the correct time period would appear to be one month from the notification or publication of the Decision, whichever is the earlier.

However, the matter is complicated if one considers the position of enterprises which did not know of the Decision, notified, in all probability, by a private letter to one of their competitors, and which thus only came to know of it from the publication. There may well be other enterprises which learnt of the Decision notified only towards the end of the month following that notification and which, therefore, in practice, had not already had a month to prepare and bring their appeal.[50]

Further, even without the difficulty of a subsequent publication of a Decision which has already been notified, it is not always clear within what time limits actions can be brought.

Thus, if the High Authority passes an individual Decision affecting one enterprise and notifies that enterprise of it, it appears from the wording of paragraph 3 that no action can be brought by it after one month. However, the municipal State of that enterprise, under Article 33, paragraph 1 can clearly bring an action against this Decision. It may be queried whether time is to run against the State in a matter of which it has no knowledge, and if it is, this may appear somewhat unjust, but if it is not to run, then the insoluble question arises from when the month within which the State is to be allowed to appeal is to be calculated.

APPEALING OUT OF TIME

The High Authority, by a general Decision passed in 1955, set up certain financial machinery for the subsidising of imported iron scrap, and individual enterprises within a month of the publication of this Decision could have challenged it on the grounds of a *détournement de pouvoir* with respect to themselves. When an individual Decision was subsequently passed requiring as part of this financial mechanism a payment of over 54 m. lire from a particular enterprise, that enterprise challenged the validity of that individual Decision. The question then arose of whether the original general Decision of 1955 setting up the

---

[49] *Nold KG* v. *The High Authority*, Vol. II.
[50] In the particular instance cited, the letter of December 18, 1958, was held not to constitute a Decision, so that the above problem did not in fact arise in that instance. See *Société Nouvelle des Usines de Pontlieue* v. *The High Authority* (Cases 32–58 and 33–58), Vol. II.

financial mechanism could also be challenged, although the time period for such a challenge had long since expired. The Court's decision allowing such a challenge, and allowing it on all the four grounds set out in paragraph 1 and not merely on the ground of *détournement de pouvoir* affecting the plaintiffs, has been fully set out above and the reader is referred back to it.[51]

ARTICLE 34, Para. 1, Sentences 1 and 2

If the Court should annul a Decision or Recommendation of the High Authority, the matter shall be referred back to the High Authority. The latter is required to take the measures which comprise the carrying out of the decision of annulment.[52]

This provision illustrates the separation of powers which exist within the Community. The Court having exercised its judicial competence is expressly excluded from usurping any legislative powers which are reserved solely for the High Authority.

The reference in this Article to " a Decision or Recommendation " appears wide enough to cover not only express acts of the High Authority, but also Decisions and Recommendations which are to be implied following upon a two months' silence on the part of that Authority.[53]

By sentence 1 of this Article, reference is being made to the situation where the Court has annulled " a Decision or Recommendation." As has been noted above, the High Authority in one case [54] argued from this, that an enterprise could not challenge under Article 33, merely one Article of a Decision of the High Authority, but could only challenge the validity of a Decision as a whole. Its reasoning was that by Article 34, it was only a completely annulled Decision which must be referred back to the High Authority. It follows, therefore, it argued, that if certain words only of a Decision were annulled, leaving the remaining words still standing, the Court might be bringing into existence a Decision with an effect entirely different from the one which had originally been passed

---

[51] See p. 162, above.
[52] French:
" *En cas d'annulation, la Cour renvoie l'affaire devant la Haute Autorité. Celle-ci est tenue de prendre les mesures que comporte l'exécution de la décision d'annulation.*"
Stationery Office:
" If the Court quashes a decision or recommendation it shall refer the matter back to the High Authority. The latter shall be responsible for taking the measures required for the enforcement of the decision of annulment."
[53] These are implied under Art. 35. See p. 184, below.
[54] " *Geitling* " *and others* v. *The High Authority* (Case 2–56), Vol. II. See above.

by the High Authority. In other words, the Court would, in effect, be legislating, whereas by Article 34 it is expressly excluded from doing so. The Court rejected this and declared:

> This contention is not well founded because by the terms of the said Article 34, a judgment in no way prejudices the measures which the High Authority is required to take in order to amend the Decision, regard being had to the annulment.[55]

Measures Which "Comprise the Carrying Out of the Decision of Annulment"

When this Article speaks of the High Authority as being required to take the measures which comprise the carrying out of the Decision of annulment, it is not at all clear what measures are being referred to. The matter can be assisted, however, by seeing what measures are not being referred to.

When a Decision of the High Authority has been annulled by the Court, that Decision no longer exists, and its words have no further legal force. The High Authority is thus not required to repeal a Decision which has been annulled, because that Decision does not exist to be repealed. Similarly, if one Article of a Decision is annulled [56] that Article no longer exists although, of course, the rest of that Decision remains. If the High Authority should amend the rest of that Decision, which does remain, or if it should substitute another Decision for the one annulled, it is using its own legislative competence to do so. It is not acting under any orders from the Court.[57] The measures which comprise the carrying out of a Decision of annulment, therefore, are not measures repealing the Decision or Recommendation annulled.

One French writer,[58] when discussing the position under French law after the Conseil d'Etat has annulled an administrative act, declares that the duty upon the administrative organ concerned is to comply with the judgment.[59] This clearly is so, but to comply with the terms of a judgment is not the same thing as to take measures to carry it out: the former may be entirely passive, the latter requires active steps.

The writers submitting the *Rapport de la Délégation Française* in 1951, stated that the provision in question meant that the High Authority

---

55 *Ibid.*
56 See, *e.g., French Government* v. *The High Authority* (Case 1–54), Vol. II.
57 Even if the High Authority is under a duty by the terms of the Treaty to pass a particular Decision and the one which it has passed is annulled by the Court, it is clear that the High Authority has not yet fulfilled its duty. In subsequently fulfilling it, by passing a second, and valid Decision, the High Authority is carrying out its Treaty obligation; it is not taking measures to carry out the judgment of annulment.
58 Waline in *Droit Administratif.*
59 *Ibid.* p. 150.

was to restore the party concerned, as far as possible, to the position in which he would have been if the annulled Decision had not been passed.[60] The accuracy of this can be tested by an example. Assume that the High Authority passed a Decision fixing the levy upon the production of coal and steel,[61] and certain enterprises had paid this levy before the Court had annulled the Decision.[62] Is the High Authority required to refund the amount of the levy improperly collected? [63] The above statement in the *Rapport de la Délégation Française* would suggest that it must, for only by doing so would the enterprises, including those that were not parties to the action of annulment, be able to be restored to the position in which they would have been if the annulled Decision had not been passed. It may well be queried, here, however, whether a repayment of money to enterprises would be the taking of measures " which comprise the carrying out of the decision of annulment " and whether they would not rather be measures which are consequent upon, or incidental to, the passing of that judgment. If they are, then the fault appears to lie with the drafting of the Treaty, for it is suggested it is just such measures as this repayment which are being referred to in the text.

A less clear situation, however, arises in connection with Article 35. By that Article, certain failure of the High Authority to take action can be deemed to amount to a Decision refusing to take action. That Decision is open to annulment as is any other Decision of the High Authority. If the Treaty requires the High Authority to take action, this implied Decision refusing to take that action can be annulled for having been passed in violation of the Treaty. Following such annulment, by Article 34, the matter is referred back to the High Authority, which is to " take the measures which comprise the carrying out of the decision of annulment." It appears that what this provision means here, is that the High Authority is to take an express Decision in accordance with the Treaty requirement upon it to do so. The taking of this Decision, however, is hardly within the concept of " carrying out of the Decision of annulment." What the High Authority is doing, it is suggested, is not carrying out the

---

[60] *Rapport de la Délégation Française*, 1951, p. 39.
[61] This would be done under Art. 49.
[62] The levy must be assessed annually on the various products according to their average value; however, the rate of levy may not exceed 1 per cent. unless previously authorised by a two-thirds majority of the Council—Art. 50.2. A Decision not complying with this provision would be open to annulment on the grounds of violation of the Treaty, incompetence and also of violation of a substantial procedural requirement if the required majority in the Council had not been obtained to a levy of more than 1 per cent.
[63] The situation where the enterprise has, in addition, suffered direct and special injury is governed by sentence 3 of this Article. Damages, however, are only obtainable if the passing of the Decision in question involved a fault of a nature to involve the responsibility of the Community

decision of annulment, but rectifying the previous failure to take action which has been declared illegal in the Court's decision of annulment.

ARTICLE 34, Para. 1, Sentence 3

In the event of direct and special injury being suffered by an enterprise or group of enterprises from the existence of a Decision or Recommendation recognised by the Court as vitiated by a fault of a nature to involve the responsibility of the Community, the High Authority is required, by employing the powers granted to it by the terms of the present Treaty, to take measures adequate to ensure an equitable reparation for the damage resulting directly from the Decision or Recommendation which has been annulled and, to the extent necessary, to grant just compensation.[64]

THE DUTY TO GRANT REPARATIONS

This sentence of paragraph 1 has to be analysed with a certain care, for the duty of the High Authority to grant reparation is more restricted than perhaps at first might appear, for it does not have to compensate every injury which it has caused.

First, the only injury here being referred to is that caused by the existence of a Decision or Recommendation, the passing of which has been recognised by the Court as involving a fault of a nature to involve the responsibility of the Community.[65] What these faults may be, however, is not clear. What is clear, however, is that there are no faults which the High Authority can commit which can involve the responsibility of the Community. The Community as an entity is not vicariously

---

[64] French:
   " *En cas de préjudice direct et spécial subi par une entreprise ou un groupe d'entreprises du fait d'une décision ou d'une recommandation reconnue par la Cour entachée d'une faute de nature à engager la responsabilité de la Communauté, la Haute Autorité est tenue de prendre, en usant des pouvoirs qui lui sont reconnus par les dispositions du présent Traité, les mesures propres à assurer une équitable réparation du préjudice résultant directement de la décision ou de la recommandation annulée et d'accorder, en tant que de besoin, une juste indemnité.*"
   Stationery Office:
   " If direct and special injury is suffered by an undertaking or a group of undertakings because of a decision or recommendation, held by the Court to involve a fault of such a nature as to render the Community liable, the High Authority shall, using the powers which are conferred upon it by the provisions of the present Treaty, take suitable measures to ensure equitable redress for the injury resulting directly from the decision or recommendation which has been annulled, and, as far as may be necessary, to grant fair damages."
[65] It should be noted that it is not the injury which has been caused which is required to involve the responsibility of the Community.

liable for the acts of its constituent institutions. Any action for damages lies solely against the High Authority. Further Article 40 makes a clear distinction between *fautes de service* for which the High Authority is liable, and *fautes personnelles* for which the individual responsible is liable. The term being used in this third sentence, however, " a fault of a nature to involve the responsibility of the Community," is not " *faute de service* " or " *faute personnelle*." However, as the responsibility of the Community—*i.e.*, the High Authority—is being involved, this fault, it is suggested, is to be equated with a *faute de service*. If this is so, then, from the discussion below of what amounts to a *faute de service*, it would appear that the passing of very few Decisions or Recommendations would amount to such a *faute*.

Secondly, the right to receive compensation from the High Authority is enjoyed only by " an enterprise or group of enterprises." That is to say, no compensation can be received in respect of an injury caused to an association, or to individuals or to States. The latter must appeal, if they can at all, under Article 40. That Article, however, is declared to be " subject to the provisions of Article 34, paragraph 1."

Thirdly, the injury here being referred to is a " direct and special " injury. Any injury, therefore, the effects of which are felt generally over a particular area, would appear not to be special, but general, and as such to fall outside the present provision.

Finally, before any reparations become payable it is necessary that the Decision or Recommendation which is responsible for the injury should itself have been annulled. This means that no compensation can be claimed either for any injury suffered by an enterprise or group of enterprises by reason of a Decision or Recommendation which is no longer open to appeal because the month specified in Article 33 for such appeal has expired. Enterprises are thus, in practice, completely at the mercy of all injuries which are not virtually instantaneous with the coming into force of the Decision or Recommendation.

However, in the few cases to which this provision does apply, the strict separation of powers will against be noted.[66] It is for the Court only to recognise the existence of the fault, it is then for the High Authority to ensure an equitable reparation and, to the extent necessary, to grant just compensation. The distinction here being made between reparation and compensation appears to be that the former is to cover the cost of

---

[66] This may be compared with claims under Art. 40 where the Court itself assesses the damages against the Community.

rectifying the injury caused, while compensation is a money payment by way of amends.[67]

THE JURISDICTION OF THE COURT

There is, at the moment, very little authority upon the Court's power under the present Article. It has only been invoked in one case [68] where the plaintiffs requested the Court to recognise that an express and an implied refusal of the High Authority to grant them an exemption from a particular levy were vitiated by a fault of the nature to involve the responsibility of the Community. On this request the Court summarising the later provisions of this Article declared that such a recognition can be made only when the Court annuls the particular Decision or Recommendation in question. In the particular case no such annulment was granted so that further consideration of this Article did not arise. The question remains, however, of whether, when an enterprise is challenging a Decision of the High Authority under Article 33, the enterprise is required specifically to request the Court to recognise the existence of a direct and special injury to itself, or whether the Court's power to do so exists independently of any request in the pleadings. It may appear, however, from the wide powers already assumed by the Court to review many matters, that it would regard this as yet another matter falling within its jurisdiction.[69]

A further doubt arises if the plaintiffs challenging a Decision are not an enterprise, but an association. In such a case, can the Court recognise the existence of an injury which has been done, not to the plaintiff, for such falls outside the scope of this provision, but to a member enterprises of that association? If, however, it is accepted that in the situation just mentioned above, the Court, of its own motion, can recognise an injury when the enterprise concerned is the plaintiff, it may also be accepted that it would be prepared to recognise such an injury in the present case. If it did so, however, the Court would be determining the rights of a party that was not before the Court. If it refused to do so

---

[67] The words of the provision are " equitable reparation " not " full reparation." It was assumed by the Netherlands Government that the two phrases were synonymous—*Memorie van Toelichting* No. 2228, No. 3, 1950–1951 (p. 39, col. 1). This may be doubted first, because of the avoidance of the term " full reparation " and secondly, because as the funds at the disposal of the High Authority are obtained from the other enterprises of the Community, an equitable solution must take account of other parties than the High Authority and the injured party.

[68] *Hamborner Bergbau AG, Friedrich Thyssen AG* v. *The High Authority* (Joint Cases 41 and 50–59), Vol. II.

[69] There may be some significance in the fact that to claim the compensation under Art. 40, the injured party is expressly required to claim it, whereas no such requirement is included in Art. 34.

the Court would in effect, be compelling every enterprise in an association to bring its own action.

If the plaintiff were a Member State, or, to take a more extreme case, if it were the Council of Ministers, it may well be felt that the Court would not be prepared to issue any findings concerning an enterprise within a particular State.[70]

ARTICLE 34, Para. 2

If the High Authority fails within a reasonable time to take the measures which comprise the carrying out of a decision of annulment, an appeal for damages is open before the Court.[71]

THE HIGH AUTHORITY'S FAILURE TO TAKE MEASURES

By the second sentence of paragraph 1 of this Article, the High Authority is required to take the measures which comprise the carrying out of the decision of annulment. The third sentence of that paragraph, which appears to be an insertion into what would otherwise be a cohesive provision, provides that the High Authority is to have a further duty, apart from carrying out the decision of annulment, namely, that of granting reparation and compensation. The carrying out of this further duty, therefore, appears to be distinct from the carrying out of the decision of annulment.[72] If it is so distinct, then paragraph 2 which refers only to a failure to carry out the decision of annulment, clearly does not apply to a failure to grant reparation and compensation. If such failure should occur, therefore, an enterprise would be unable to find its remedy under Article 34 and would have to seek for it elsewhere.

The mode of procedure for such an enterprise would appear to be to request the High Authority under Article 35, paragraph 1, to take a Decision granting reparation and compensation. If the High Authority

---

[70] It would also seem that if merely certain enterprises of a group have appealed, and the rest have not, the Court would refuse to recognise any injury to those enterprises which had not appealed.

[71] French:

"*Si la Haute Autorité s'abstient de prendre dans un délai raisonable les mesures que comporte l'exécution d'une décision d'annulation, un recours en indemnité est ouvert devant la Cour.*"

Stationery Office:

"If the High Authority fails to take within a reasonable period the measures required to enforce a decision of annulment proceedings for damages may be brought before the Court."

[72] In the Common Market and Euratom Treaties, the duty upon the respective Commissions is merely to carry out the decision of annulment: they are not required in addition to grant compensation. If such is claimed it must be sought in an entirely separate action. The granting of compensation appears again, therefore, not to be a necessary part of the carrying out of a decision of annulment—see E.C.C. Treaty, Arts. 176 and 178 and Euratom Treaty, Arts. 149 and 151.

fails for a period of two months to take this Decision, an appeal may be brought within the following month for the annulment of what by that provision is deemed to be an implied Decision of refusal. If, on the other hand, the High Authority does pass an express Decision refusing compensation, whether within two months of the above request or later, an appeal is open before the Court for the annulment of this express Decision.

When an enterprise challenges the implied or express Decision of the High Authority, the defence of that Authority could not be that there had not been a direct and special injury if the Court has already recognised the existence of such an injury. Its defence will be, therefore, that such injury did not result from the original Decision or Recommendation which has been annulled, or that even if such injury did result there is no need to grant compensation.

If the action before the Court is a challenge of an implied Decision of refusal to act, the first task of the Court will be to determine whether there was a duty upon the High Authority to take a Decision granting reparation.[73] This will mean that the Court, for the first time, will have to determine what amounts to the " equitable reparation " and what constitutes the " just compensation," which is referred to in Article 34, paragraph 1. If some amount is due to the enterprise under either of these heads, the implied Decision of the High Authority refusing to pay this amount will have been " passed " in violation of Article 34, paragraph 1, and will be voidable on the grounds of violation of the Treaty. The duty upon that Authority, by the second sentence of this Article, will then be to carry out the decision of annulment, which, as has been suggested above, it can only do by paying the amounts due.

Another difficult situation arises if the High Authority, acting in accordance with its duty under paragraph 1 of Article 34, pays some reparation to an enterprise for the injury suffered, but this reparation is not regarded by the enterprise as being adequate—a situation which can arise because under that paragraph the Court has no power to specify the amount of damages to be paid.

In this situation, the enterprise concerned will be unable to proceed under Article 35, as it could have done if the High Authority had failed to pay any reparation at all, because the High Authority, by paying some reparation, has not failed to take action, it has merely failed to take adequate action. The enterprise, therefore, will be forced to challenge the individual Decision of the High Authority which ordered these reparations and seek the annulment of that Decision under Article 33.

[73] As to this, see further the discussion of Art. 35

This can be done on the ground that the Decision has been passed in violation of the obligation in the Treaty to pay equitable reparations to that enterprise.

In this action the Court will have to determine what is the extent of the Treaty obligation upon the High Authority. In other words, the Court will have to determine for itself what reparations are due, and if these have not been paid there will, of course, have been a violation of the Treaty. The Decision of the High Authority awarding inadequate reparation will therefore be annulled. The position will again be that the High Authority is required to carry out this second decision of annulment. This, as suggested above, it appears it can only do by paying the remainder of the reparation due to the enterprise concerned.

It must be noted, however, that all the above procedure assumes that the High Authority will proceed by means of Decisions to pay reparations to the enterprise concerned. If it were held that the resolution passed by the High Authority to pay a certain sum of money to an enterprise was not a Decision but, for example, merely an internal directive, the enterprise would have no legal means of obtaining redress when either no money was paid as reparation or when inadequate money was so paid.

"AN APPEAL FOR DAMAGES IS OPEN BEFORE THE COURT"

It has been suggested above that the measures which comprise the carrying out of a decision of annulment are those required to restore the party concerned as far as possible to the position in which it would have been if the annulled Decision had not been passed. The extent of the power under paragraph 2, therefore, is for the Court to award damages if these measures have not been taken within a reasonable time. As it has been further suggested that the payment of compensation for direct and special injury is not the carrying out of a decision of annulment, it follows that paragraph 2 is not a provision under which damages for the non-payment of compensation can be claimed.

ARTICLE 35

In the case where the High Authority is required by a provision of the present Treaty or by its rules of application to take a Decision or to formulate a Recommendation and does not comply with this obligation, States, the Council, or enterprises and associations, according to the case, may refer the matter to it.

The same shall be the position in the case where the High Authority is empowered by a provision of the present Treaty

or by the rules of application to take a Decision or to formulate a Recommendation, and it fails so to do, if such failure amounts to a *détournement de pouvoir.*

If at the end of a period of two months the High Authority has not taken any Decision or formulated any Recommendation, an appeal may be brought before the Court within a time limit of one month against the implied Decision of refusal to act which is deemed to result from this silence.[74]

This Article turns a two months' failure on the part of the High Authority to make a Decision or Recommendation into an implied Decision [75] so that something exists against which an appeal can be brought. This procedure is copied from that existing in French administrative law [76] and is a further example of the influence which the *Conseil d'Etat* has exercised over the whole working of the European Court.

Up to the present time four appeals have been brought under this Article [77] and the Court has been required to give its interpretation of certain parts of this provision.

[74] French:
"*Dans le cas où la Haute Autorité, tenue par une disposition du présent Traité ou des réglements d'application de prendre une décision ou de formuler une recommandation, ne se conforme pas à cette obligation, il appartient, selon le cas, aux Etats, au Conseil ou aux entreprises et associations de la saisir.*
Il en est de même dans le cas où la Haute Autorité, habilitée par une disposition du présent Traité ou des réglements d'application à prendre une décision ou à formuler une recommandation, s'en abstient et où cette abstention constitue un détournement de pouvoir.
Si, à l'expiration d'un délai de deux mois, la Haute Autorité n'a pris aucune décision ou formulé aucune recommandation, un recours peut être formé devant la Cour dans un délai d'un mois contre la décision implicite de refus qui est réputée résulter de ce silence."
Stationery Office:
" Wherever the High Authority is required by a provision of the present Treaty, or of the Regulations for giving effect to it, to take a decision or to make a recommendation and fails to fulfil this obligation the omission may be brought to its attention by the States, the Council or the undertakings and associations, as the case may be.
The same shall apply if the High Authority abstains from taking a decision or making a recommendation, when it is empowered to do so by a provision of the present Treaty or the Regulations for giving effect to it and such abstention constitutes a misuse of powers.
If at the end of two months the High Authority has not taken any decision or made any recommendation an appeal may be made to the Court, within one month, against the implicit negative decision presumed to result from such failure to act."
[75] Nothing turns on the point that a failure to make a Recommendation is turned into a Decision.
[76] See Art. 51 of the Ordinance of the French Government of July 31, 1945.
[77] *Groupement des Industries Sidérurgiques Luxembourgeoises* v. *The High Authority* (Joint Cases 7–54 and 9–54), Vol. II, below, *Association des Utilisateurs de Charbon du Grand-Duché de Luxembourg* v. *The High Authority* (Joint Cases 8–54 and 10–54), Vol. II, below; *Société Nouvelle des Usines de Pontlieue-Acieries du Temple (S.N.U.P.A.T.)* v. *The High Authority* (Joint Cases 32–58 and 33–58), Vol. II, below; and *Société des Aciers Fins de l'Est (S.A.F.E.)* v. *The High Authority*, Vol. II.

MEANING OF THE TERM " ASSOCIATIONS "

One of the first points raised before the Court concerned the meaning of the term " associations " in paragraph 1. The argument was taken that when the term " associations " is used in Article 33, paragraph 2, the associations there referred to are expressly limited to those mentioned in Article 48. As no such limitation is mentioned in Article 35 it was contended that the term " associations " in this Article must therefore have a wider meaning than the same term has in Article 33. On this the Court declared:

> Article 35 grants to " enterprises and associations " the right to appeal to the High Authority.
> The associations referred to in that expression can only be associations of enterprises within the meaning of the term " enterprise " as defined by Article 80 of the Treaty [78] in the entire Treaty.
> Indeed, if this were not so, an association would possess a right to bring an appeal which none of its constituent members separately and on its own behalf would have been able to bring.
> In the absence of any express statement to the contrary, the Treaty cannot establish any such disparity of treatment between an association and its constituent members.[79]

Where, therefore, in one case,[80] an association consisted principally of various groups of enterprises which consumed, but did not produce, coal, including the *Société Nationale des Chemins de Fer Luxembourgeois*, the Court held that the association could not bring an action. This ruling was made even although one of the constituent groups of enterprises did in fact produce steel and was thus an enterprise within the meaning of Article 80. It remains an open point, therefore, whether all the enterprises in an association must be producers before that association can appeal, or whether merely some number, more than one, must be.

MEANING OF " ACCORDING TO THE CASE "

Paragraph 1 of this Article gives a right to States, the Council, or enterprises and associations, " according to the case," to appeal to the High Authority to take action. The Court has held:

For a discussion of the Court's interpretation of this article in its early case, see Bonaert, A. and others: *Fragen der Nichtigkeits- und Untätigkeitsklagen nach dem Rech der Europäischen Gemeinschaft für Kohle und Stahl* (Vittorioklosterman, 1961).

[78] Art. 80 provides:
" The term ' enterprise,' shall for the purposes of the present Treaty mean any enterprise engaged in production in the field of coal and steel within the territories mentioned in the first paragraph of Article 79 "—see further p. 153, above.

[79] *Groupement des Industries Sidérurgiques Luxembourgeoises* v. *The High Authority* (Joint Cases 7–54 and 9–54), Vol. II.

[80] *Association des Utilisateurs de Charbon du Grand-Duché de Luxembourg* v. *The High Authority* (Joint Cases 8–54 and 10–54), Vol. II.

The expression " according to the case " in Article 35 must be understood as granting a right of appeal to the High Authority to those bodies mentioned in that Article which have an interest in the Decision which the High Authority is required to take or in the Recommendation which it is required to formulate.[81]

What will amount to such an interest is not stated in the Treaty but in the cases already brought, the Court has held that a group of Luxembourg steel producers had a sufficient interest to request the High Authority to take a Decision declaring illegal a tax imposed by the Luxembourg Government upon imported coal.[82] Later, and quite obviously, two enterprises were held to have a sufficient interest to request that they should be granted immunity from payments to the fund set up to subsidise imported scrap-iron.[83]

It is suggested that on general principle a State has a sufficient interest to appeal to the High Authority not only in respect of matters which concern it *per se* but also in respect of those which concern any of the enterprises or associations within its territory. Further, what affects more than one State, it is suggested, may well affect the Council.

EXTENSION OF THE MEANING OF THE TERM " MAY REFER THE MATTER
TO THE HIGH AUTHORITY "

Paragraph 1 of Article 35 grants only a right to refer matters to the High Authority to request it to take action. As has been seen above, however, the Court has declared that the Decisions taken by the *Caisse*— the organisation set up in Brussels to regulate the fund to subsidise the cost of imported scrap-iron—were to be regarded as Decisions of the High Authority itself and, thus, open to annulment under Article 33.[84] It followed as a corollary to this that when an enterprise had requested the *Caisse* to take a Decision which it alleged it was required to do by a rule of application of the Treaty, and the *Caisse* had failed to do so within two months, this silence should be deemed a Decision and open, therefore, to appeal under Article 35, paragraph 3. In fact, the High Authority did not even seek to argue to the contrary.[85]

---

81 *Groupement des Industries Sidérurgiques Luxembourgeoises* v. *The High Authority* (Joint Cases 7–54 and 9–54), Vol. II.
82 *Ibid.*
83 *Société Nouvelle des Usines de Pontlieue-Acieries du Temple (S.N.U.P.A.T.)* v. *The High Authority* (Joint Cases 32–58 and 33–58), Vol. II, and *Société des Aciers Fins de l'Est (S.A.F.E.)* v. *The High Authority* (Case 42–58), Vol. II.
84 See p. 122, above.
85 *Société Nouvelle des Usines de Pontlieue-Acieries du Temple (S.N.U.P.A.T.)* v. *The High Authority* (Joint Cases 32–58 and 33–58), Vol. II.

ALTERNATIVES TO APPEALS UNDER ARTICLE 35

Article 35 sets out what appears to be intended to be the general manner in which inaction on the part of the High Authority can be remedied. However, later provisions of the Treaty set up other machinery which may be used in specific circumstances. Thus, it is stated:

> If the High Authority fails to act, one of the Member States may bring the matter to the attention of the Council which, acting unanimously, may oblige the High Authority to establish a system of quotas.[86]

again:

> If the High Authority fails to act, the Council may unanimously take such a Decision upon a Government's proposal.[87]

and:

> If the High Authority should fail to act under the circumstances described above, the Government of one of the Member States may refer the matter to the Council which may, by unanimous decision, request the High Authority to fix such maximum or minimum prices.[88]

It is felt that perhaps the best way of regarding these provisions is not that they in any way derogate from the general right conferred by Article 35, but that in special cases there is a right of appeal to the Council in addition to the one to the Court already open under Article 35. In practice, however, States and enterprises in these cases would always appeal to the Council and not to the Court, because the Council can take definite action, whereas the Court can merely annul the implied Decision and refer the matter back to the High Authority.

THE APPEAL UNDER PARAGRAPH 3

On paragraph 3 of Article 35, the Court has held that the period of two months' inaction of the High Authority that is there referred to starts to run from the day after the receipt of the letter requesting action. Thus, when a letter dated March 31, 1958, was delivered on April 1, the two months' period began to run on April 2, and thus expired on June 1, 1958.[89] Further, the Court has held that even when the High Authority has not denied that no Decision has been passed within a two-month period, the Court, of its own motion, is to determine whether this is so or not.[90]

---

[86] E.C.S.C. Treaty, Art. 58, section 1.1. A similar provision is in Art. 59, section 1.1.
[87] Art. 59, section 5. A similar provision is in Art. 59, section 6.2.
[88] Art. 61, para. 3.
[89] *Société Nouvelle des Usines de Pontlieue-Acieries du Temple (S.N.U.P.A.T.)* v. *The High Authority* (Joint Cases 32–58 and 33–58), Vol. II.
[90] *Ibid.*

DETERMINING WHETHER THE IMPLIED DECISION IS GENERAL OR INDIVIDUAL

After this period of two months, the inactivity of the High Authority is deemed to be a Decision refusing to take action, and against this implied Decision an appeal lies within one month. It has been accepted by all parties that the appeal against this implied Decision is one being brought under Article 33 so that if the plaintiffs are an enterprise or an association it is necessary to investigate whether that implied Decision is general or individual, so as to be able to determine what grounds of appeal may be alleged.

On the occasion when the Court was required to make this investigation [91] it considered first what was the situation which the High Authority was impliedly refusing to alter and then the Court deduced what Decision would have been required expressly to declare this refusal. As it was that Decision which was being implied its nature was able to be established.

SUPPORTING AN IMPLIED DECISION WITH REASONS

One difficulty of the right to appeal under Article 33 has, however, been revealed. The Court has held that where a Decision has not been adequately supported by reasons it is open to be annulled on the grounds of a violation of a substantial procedural requirement.[92] Where, however, the Court is dealing with a Decision that has been implied under Article 35 it clearly has no reasons supporting it at all and the question arises, therefore, of whether it is open to be annulled as violating a substantial procedural requirement. In the particular case where this argument was advanced, the alleged duty upon the High Authority was to declare that the Luxembourg Government was in default in imposing duties upon imported coal. The Court said:

> The plaintiffs allege as a subsidiary argument that the implied negative Decision is vitiated by a violation of substantial procedural requirements in so far as it is not based upon any declared reasons.
> Article 88 of the Treaty states that: " If the High Authority considers that a State has failed in one of the obligations incumbent upon it by virtue of this Treaty, it shall set out this failure in a reasoned Decision."
> The obligation to give reasons, therefore, applies to the Decision which, in the plaintiffs' opinion, the High Authority was required to take with regard to the Government of the Grand Duchy.
> Nothing in Article 88 justifies the conclusion that this same obligation exists with regard to a refusal to take a Decision under that article.

[91] *Groupement des Industries Sidérurgiques Luxembourgeoises* v. *The High Authority* (Joint Cases 7–54 and 9–54), Vol. II.
[92] See p. 130, above.

Consequently, the absence of reasons in the implied negative Decision does not constitute a violation of Article 88 of the Treaty.[93]

It will be noted that this reasoning is applicable only to implied negative Decisions referable to Article 88, and not to implied Decisions generally. Further, the Court made no attempt to show why the clear terms of Article 15 of the Treaty did not apply when they state that " Decisions . . . of the High Authority shall include the reasons therefor." Again, the Court's reasoning was based upon a converse argument, namely, that because Article 88 requires express Decision to be supported by reasons " nothing . . . justifies the conclusion that this same obligation exists with regard to a refusal to take a Decision under that article." Now the Court has often expressed its disapproval of this manner of arguing and has declared that it is only to be employed when no other line of reasoning is appropriate.[94]

It is suggested that it would have been better if the Court, instead of arguing in this somewhat artificial way, had faced the obvious fact that no implied Decision can ever be supported by reasons, so that unless one is prepared to accept that every implied Decision is automatically to be voidable, one must hold that the requirement of giving reasons can only apply to express Decisions.

THE EXTENT OF THE RIGHT TO APPEAL

Under paragraphs 1 and 2 of Article 35, the right to request the High Authority to take action is limited, as has been seen above, to those parties which have an interest in the matter in question. Paragraph 3 merely states that after the two months' failure to take any action " an appeal may be brought before the Court." It is not clear, however, whether the party bringing this appeal must be the party which originally approached the High Authority. It is suggested, however, that no such restriction should be imposed. First, if an enterprise has approached the High Authority, there can be seen no reason why the appeal before the Court should not be undertaken either by an association of which that enterprise is a member, or even by that enterprise's home State. If such an appeal were not allowed, the only result would be that the association or home State would itself have to apply to the High Authority, and thus start the procedure of Article 35 all over again. Secondly, such a restriction would appear contrary to the general trend

[93] *Groupement des Industries Sidérurgiques Luxembourgeoises* v. *The High Authority* (Joint Cases 7–54 and 9–54), Vol. II.
[94] *Fédération Charbonnière de Belgique* v. *The High Authority* (Case 8–55), Vol. II.

of the judgments of the Court which seeks always to extend the right of appeal.[95]

The grounds alleged by a party challenging an implied Decision of refusal must be related to the reference to the High Authority. Thus on account of their difficult financial position, two plaintiffs requested the High Authority to grant them an exemption from paying a particular levy. This request was refused and the refusal was sent in an informal letter dated July 17, 1959. As the plaintiffs were not sure if this was open to appeal, on August 6, 1959, they requested the High Authority under Article 35, to take a formal Decision on their request. The High Authority, however, took no action in respect of this request for a period of two months. The question arose, and was not solved by the judgment of whether the implied Decision of refusal was to be deemed a Decision refusing to take a formal Decision—and if it was then presumably the reason for the refusal was because the letter was regarded as constituting a Decision just as much as any formal document—or alternatively, whether the Decision was to be deemed a refusal to grant the exemption requested. Be this as it may, the plaintiffs challenged the implied Decision on the ground that the imposition of the levy was in any event illegal because the Decision purporting to authorise that levy was itself illegal.

On this the Court declared:

> The defendants raise a second plea of inadmissibility by maintaining that the action does not seek the same object as did the request of July 17, 1959.
>
> By the request to take action within the meaning of Article 35, the High Authority is invited to take a stand in relation to the plaintiffs' request on the basis of precise legal grounds.
>
> The implied Decision of refusal falls within the framework of this claim and of the legal grounds relied on.
>
> It is not possible to admit, against an implied Decision of refusal, an appeal amounting to *another* claim based on *other legal grounds*.
>
> The plaintiffs in their letter of July 17, 1959, to the contents of which the letter of August 6, 1959, exclusively referred, had requested the High Authority for an *exemption* from the payment of the levy for the financial year 1959-60 *on the grounds of their difficult financial position*.
>
> On the other hand, in their request commencing the present action the plaintiffs, although formally seeking the annulment of the implied Decision of refusal, in reality request that the collection of a levy for the current financial year should be declared illegal by reason of the

---

[95] See, for example, *Groupement des Industries Sidérurgiques Luxembourgeoises* v. *The High Authority* (Joint Cases 7–54 and 9–54), Vol. II—there is no restriction preventing steel enterprises appealing on matters concerning coal, and *Meroni & Co. S.p.A.* v. *The High Authority* (Case 9–56), Vol. II—the right of appeal is to be extended so as to include the right to appeal against Decisions of organs to whom some of the powers of the High Authority have been delegated.

irregularity of Decision 33–59. This claim constitutes a profound modification both of the *claim* and of its *legal grounds*.[96]

Although this proposition is not very lucidly expressed, it is respectfully suggested that the Court is correct in its contention. If the implied Decision was one refusing merely to remould the terms of the letter of July 17 into a formal Decision, that refusal could only be challenged if, for example, it amounted to a violation of the Treaty on the grounds that the High Authority is under a duty to remould Decisions in letters into formal Decisions. Alternatively, if the implied Decision was one of refusal of the request for exemption, the only grounds of appeal would be that there was a duty upon the High Authority to grant such a request and that there had here been a breach of that duty, or that there was a power for the High Authority to grant the exception and that power had been misused so as to give rise to a *détournement de pouvoir*. However, if, as was contended by the plaintiffs, the levy was itself illegal, the correct procedure would either have been to challenge the Decision imposing that levy or to refuse to pay the levy and then to challenge the subsequent Decision demanding payment on the ground that the demand was illegal.

In one action [97] after the High Authority had failed to take a Decision for a period of two months after being requested to do so, it subsequently did take a Decision. The argument put forward was that this express Decision superseded the implied one so that the action already started against that implied one should be stayed. On this the Court held:

At the end of this time limit [in Article 35], the implied Decision of refusal referred to in this paragraph was deemed to exist and a right of appeal was unconditionally open to the plaintiffs.

Furthermore, the basis of the appeal is not the silence of the High Authority, but its refusal to take a Decision within the meaning of Article 14 of the Treaty, which in the view of the plaintiffs it was required to take.

The letter setting out the reasons for the refusal of the High Authority does not affect the existence of this refusal, which occurred once and for all at the end of the two-month time limit provided for in the third paragraph of Article 35 of the Treaty. . . .

Thus, the Court, in agreement with the submissions of the Advocate General, holds that the letter has not removed the purpose of this appeal, nor prevented the plaintiffs from pursuing their action brought under Article 35 of the Treaty.[98]

[96] *Hamborner Bergbau AG, Friedrich Thyssen Bergbau AG* v. *The High Authority* (Joint Cases 41 and 50–59), Vol. II. For the terms of Decision 33–59, see Vol. II.
[97] *Groupement des Industries Sidérurgiques Luxembourgeoises* v. *The High Authority* (Joint Cases 7–54 and 9–54), Vol. II.
[98] *Ibid.* Vol. II, Art. 14, para. 1, provides:
" In carrying out the duties assigned to it by the present Treaty and in accordance with the provisions thereof, the High Authority shall take decisions, make recommendations and issue opinions."

In other words, the right of appeal is absolute and having accrued cannot subsequently be taken away.

TIME LIMIT FOR BRINGING AN APPEAL

Paragraph 3 of Article 35 states that an appeal against the implied Decision can be brought " within a period of one month." Under the Rules of the Court the similar time period of one month specified for the bringing of appeals under Article 33 is extended according to the particular country in which the plaintiff is situated.[99] The old Rules of the Court, previously applicable to the dissolved Court of Justice of the Coal and Steel Community, expressly stated that these extensions were to apply only to appeals under Article 33,[1] so that in practice enterprises in Luxembourg had a longer period in which to appeal under Article 35 than had, say, enterprises in Sicily, who would always have to consider the postal delays.[2] The present Rules, however, have enlarged the wording of the old ones and it is now stated that the extensions of time apply not only to actions brought under Article 33 but to any time period prescribed in the Coal and Steel Community Treaty.[3]

ARTICLE 36

Before imposing one of the pecuniary sanctions or fixing one of the daily penalty payments provided for in the present Treaty, the High Authority shall enable the party concerned to state its case.

The pecuniary sanctions and daily penalty payments imposed by virtue of the provisions of the present Treaty may form the subject of an appeal in *pleine juridiction.*

In support of this appeal, the plaintiffs, under the conditions set out in the first paragraph of Article 33 of the present Treaty, may rely upon the irregularity of the Decisions and Recommendations which they are accused of having contravened.[4]

---

[99] See Rules, Art. 81, para. 2 and Annex II.   [1] Old Rules, Art. 85, para. 2.
[2] Art. 37, para. 3 of the Rules states that only the date when a document is received by the Registry of the Court is the relevant one for determining time periods.
[3] Rules, Art. 80, para. 1.
[4] French:
    " *La Haute Autorité, avant de prendre une des sanctions pécuniaires ou de fixer une des astreintes prévues au présent Traité, doit mettre l'intéressé en mesure de présenter ses observations.*
    Les sanctions pécuniaires et les astreintes prononcées en vertu des dispositions du présent Traité peuvent faire l'objet d'un recours de pleine juridiction.
    Les requérants peuvent se prévaloir, à l'appui de ce recours, dans les conditions prévues au premier alinéa de l'article 33 du présent Traité, de l'irrégularité des décisions et recommandations dont la méconnaissance leur est reprochée."

This Article regulates the powers of the High Authority to impose fines. These fines it may impose not only upon the Member States of the Community if they violate the Treaty [5] but also and principally upon enterprises if, for example, they make false returns to the High Authority [6] or if they sell above or below their price lists [7] or do not pay their prescribed levies on the production of coal and steel.[8]

In addition, the High Authority may impose fines upon individuals who have provided false or misleading information in order to induce the High Authority to authorise a concentration, or who have failed to apply for such authorisation.[9]

"MUST ENABLE THE PARTY CONCERNED TO STATE ITS CASE"

The obligation to enable the accused to state its case before being punished is one prescribed by the general concept of natural justice and

Stationery Office:
"Before imposing one the of the financial sanctions or penalties provided for in the present Treaty, the High Authority must give the party concerned an opportunity to state his case.

An appeal to the general jurisdiction of the Court may be lodged against the financial sanctions and penalties imposed under the provisions of the present Treaty.

In support of such an appeal and under the terms of the first paragraph of Article 33 of the present Treaty the plaintiffs may contest the legality of the decisions and recommendations which they are charged with violating."

[5] E.C.S.C. Treaty, Art. 88, para. 4.
[6] Art. 47, para. 3. Maximum fine is 1 per cent. of the annual turnover; maximum daily penalty payments are 5 per cent. of the average daily turnover.
[7] Art. 64. Maximum fine is twice the value of the irregular sales, or double this amount in the event of a second offence.
[8] Art. 50, para. 3. Maximum fine is a 5 per cent. increase in the levy for every three months' delay in payment. The other fines that may be imposed include: for disregarding a refusal by the High Authority to authorise an enterprise's investment programme: maximum fine, the sum spent on this investment—Art. 54, para. 6; for disregarding production quotas fixed during a period of manifest crises in the Community: maximum fine, the value of the irregular production—Art. 58, para. 4; for diverting goods from their proper use during a period of serious shortage: maximum fine, twice the value of the goods concerned—Art. 54, para. 7.

For having concluded or applied an agreement with another enterprise so as to interfere with competition in the Common Market: maximum fine, double the turnover realised. If the agreement is aimed to restrict production, this fine may be increased by 10 per cent. of the annual turnover of the enterprise, and a daily penalty payment imposed of 20 per cent. of the average daily turnover—Art. 65, para. 5.

Where a concentration has occurred without prior authorisation: maximum fine is 10 per cent. of the assets concerned. A maximum fine of half this amount is to be imposed in any case where authorisation should have been requested—Art. 66, para. 5.1.

For failing to end a concentration declared illegal: maximum daily penalty payment is one-tenth of 1 per cent. of the value of the assets in question—Art. 66, para. 5.4.

For failing to comply with a Recommendation concerning increasing abnormally low wages: maximum fine and daily penalty payments are twice the amount of the savings in labour costs—Art. 68, para. 6.
[9] Art. 66, para. 6. Maximum fines are 10 per cent. of the assets concerned.

is here only being made explicit. On one occasion before an Italian firm was fined, the Chief Inspector of the *Services de Contrôle* of the High Authority having visited the enterprise concerned allowed them 15 days in which to offer their explanations for certain alleged irregularities.[10] In another case before the Court [11] the plaintiffs alleged they had never in fact been enabled to state their case, because the registered letter from the High Authority was delivered at their registered office in Turin, but was not forwarded from there to the site of the works in Magliano Alpi. The Court naturally held that what had occurred within the plaintiffs' offices was no concern of the High Authority and that the requirements of Article 36 had been satisfied.

THE SCOPE OF THE APPEAL IN PLEINE JURIDICTION

Writing shortly after the drafting of this provision, one commentator declared that this power to proceed in *pleine juridiction* gave to the Court the widest possible powers. " It can consider," he said, " both law and fact and its decision can be either an approval of the sanction, or it may reverse it, or alter it. The Court considers the case as a court of first instance would consider a criminal case. It is only bound by facts and the Treaty, not by any measures taken by the High Authority."[12] In conformity with the above, the Court has itself stated that by virtue of an appeal in *pleine juridiction*:

> It is given the power not merely to annul but also to amend the Decision which has been taken.[13]

Further, in an appeal in *pleine juridiction* the plaintiffs are not limited in the grounds which they may allege against the sanction and in particular they are not limited to alleging one or more of the four grounds set out in Article 33. Thus, the Court has declared that:

> An appeal in *pleine juridiction* . . . involves consideration of all grounds, based not only upon law, but also upon any matters which justify an annulment.[14]

Most usually, of course, the main grounds of appeal will either be that the fine is too heavy or that an infringement of the Treaty

---

10 *Macchiolatti Dalmas & Figli* v. *The High Authority* (Case 1–59), Vol. II.

11 *Acciaierie Laminatoi Magliano Alpi (A.L.M.A.)* v. *The High Authority* (Case 8–56), Vol. II.

12 Antoine, *Revue Générale de Droit International Public*, April–June 1953, p. 242. Prof. Reuter stated that the power enabled the Court " to assess all the facts and impose any modifications that it considers equitable upon the Decision imposed by the High Authority "—*La Communauté Européene du Charbon et de l'Acier*, para. 91.

13 *Acciaierie Laminatoi Magliano Alpi (A.L.M.A.)* v. *The High Authority* (Case 8–56), Vol. II.

14 *Italian Government* v. *The High Authority* (Case 20–59), Vol. II.

has not occurred, or that the duty originally imposed upon the plaintiffs was illegal.

In practice the Court has been very liberal in its construction of the requests being made to it by plaintiffs appealing under this Article. In one case [15] the plaintiffs in terms had requested the complete annulment of the sanction and not its reduction. They had, however, in passing mentioned that they were merely an enterprise of modest size. On this the Court stated:

> Although the plaintiffs have not made any formal submissions to this effect, the Court, in agreement with the Advocate General, holds that the passage in the request which refers to the plaintiff's modest size may be interpreted as incidentally requesting such a reduction. Moreover, even in the absence of any formal demand, the Court is authorised to reduce the amount of an excessive fine, when to do so would not go beyond the limits of the request, but on the contrary, would have the result of partially amplifying the request.[16]

MATTERS TO BE CONSIDERED BEFORE APPROVING A FINE

It is clear that the fine imposed must be related to the gravity of the breach which is being sanctioned and the Court, naturally, has accepted this. Thus when an enterprise had sold products at prices above those stated in its price lists and had also discriminated against certain purchasers the Court declared:

> Although violation of the rules of non-discrimination constitutes a more serious breach than violation of the rules of publication, the latter must not be regarded as only secondary.[17]

The Court then set out the aims of the rules of non-discrimination and of the publication of prices and continued:

> The mere breach of the rules of publication involves the application of a fine which is not merely a sanction of the principle, but which is proportionate to the consequences of this breach.[18]

The Court then took into account the number of illegal transactions which had occurred, and the difference between the prices stated in the price lists and those actually charged, as well as the number of surcharges which had arbitrarily been added to the accounts of certain of that enterprise's purchasers and held the fine of 2,500,000 lire which had been imposed by the High Authority to be justified. In the second

---

[15] *Ibid.*
[16] *Ibid.* Vol. II.
[17] *Macchiorlatti Dalmas e Figli* v. *The High Authority* (Case 1–59), Vol. II.
[18] *Ibid.*

case before it, the Court also took into account the fact that the enterprise had been acting illegally for more than three years before being fined.[19]

" MAY RELY UPON THE IRREGULARITY OF DECISIONS AND RECOMMENDATIONS "

As stated above, one of the grounds upon which an enterprise may wish to challenge the imposition of a sanction upon it is that the obligation which it is alleged to have broken is itself unlawful. However, the appeal under Article 36 against the pecuniary sanction and daily penalty payments themselves must be brought within a period of the one month " provided for in the last paragraph of Article 33 of the Treaty." [20]

However, in this appeal, the plaintiffs, under the conditions set out in Article 33, paragraph 1, are expressly allowed to rely upon the irregularity of the original Decision and Recommendation which they are accused of having contravened. This reference to paragraph 1 of Article 33 enables litigants to allege any of the four grounds or invalidity set out in that paragraph and to challenge a Decision or Recommendation, even after the expiration of the one month period during which an appeal is open under Article 33 itself. More than this, enterprises and associations under Article 36 have been given the right to appeal against general Decisions of the High Authority, on any one or more of the four grounds mentioned in Article 33 paragraph 1 and not merely on the ground of a *détournement de pouvoir* affecting them, which was their only means under that Article of challenging general Decisions. The effect of this is that enterprises and associations which are unable to obtain the annulment of a general Decision because of the limitations imposed upon them by Article 33, paragraph 2, can wait until a fine is imposed upon them for breach of that Decision and then challenge that fine, and as a ground of that challenge allege the invalidity of the general Decision on any of the four grounds in Article 33, paragraph 1.

This is the very technique adopted in one case.[21]

An Italian enterprise had been charged nearly 60m. lire [22] as its contribution to the levy which the High Authority had imposed upon the

---

[19] *Acciaierie Laminatoi Magliano Alpi (A.L.M.A.)* v. *The High Authority* (Case 8–56), Vol. II.

[20] E.C.S.C. Statute, Art. 39, para. 1, see p. 460, below. The effect of this is that the period of one month runs from the publication or notification of the Decision imposing the fine, and the additional time in respect of distance, etc., are also applicable—see further, above.

[21] *Meroni & Co., S.p.A.* v. *The High Authority* (Case 9–56), Vol. II: see further, p. 162, above.

[22] £30,000 or $75,000.

consumption of scrap iron.[23] This levy was to be paid into a special Subsidy Fund set up by the High Authority to subsidise the price of scrap imported from countries outside the Common Market. The plaintiffs wished to allege that they were under no obligation to pay the levy demanded of them because, they argued, the entire subsidy system was itself illegal by the Treaty. The Court allowed them to challenge the validity of the original general Decision on grounds set out in Article 33, paragraph 1 which they could not have alleged if they had challenged that Decision during the month after its publication.

However, it must be noted that the appeal being heard by the Court under Article 36 is an appeal against the sanction being imposed. It is not an appeal against the original general Decision as such. The invalidity of the general Decision, under which the individual Decision imposing the sanction has been passed, is merely a ground for holding that individual Decision voidable: it is not a means of annulling the general Decision.

This has been stated by the Court in the following terms:

> The ability of a plaintiff, after the expiration of the period set out in the last paragraph of Article 33, to rely, in support of an appeal against an individual Decision, upon the irregularity of general Decisions and Recommendations upon which the individual Decision has been based, cannot lead to the annulment of the general Decision but only of the individual Decision to which it gave rise.[24]

In a later case,[25] referring back to this judgment, the Court attempted to correct certain misconceptions to which the judgment had given rise, namely, that under Article 36 any Decision or Recommendation by the High Authority could be challenged out of time. The Court stated:

> This judgment did not interpret the third paragraph of Article 36 as allowing plaintiffs [out of time] to invoke not only the irregularities of general Decisions and Recommendations, but also the irregularity of the Decisions and Recommendations of which they were the direct objects, and with whose breach they have been accused.
>
> Such an interpretation would, indeed, be a clear contradiction of the fundamental legal principle confirmed in the last paragraph of Article 33. The strict time limit for the appeal corresponds to a generally recognised requirement, that of preventing the legality of administrative

---

23 This was not a case of an enterprise being fined, but in its judgment the Court held: " There is no occasion to hold this provision of Article 36 to be a special provision applicable only to the case of pecuniary sanctions and daily penalties but as the application of a general principle, of which Article 36 is its application to the special case of an appeal in *pleine juridiction* "—*ibid.*, Vol. II.

24 *Ibid.*

25 *German Government* v. *The High Authority* (Case 3–59), Vol. II.

Decisions being brought into question indefinitely. This involves a prohibition upon re-opening the question after the expiration of the time limit.

. . . Article 36 does not allow a discussion of the legality of an individual Decision of the High Authority to be re-opened after the time limit for an appeal has expired.[26]

In practice, of course, the High Authority would always annul a general Decision found voidable by the Court by reason of this indirect procedure, so that Article 36 in practice provides enterprises and associations with a power as wide as that possessed by Member States or by the Council.

ARTICLE 37

When a Member State believes that, in a particular case, an action or a failure to take action on the part of the High Authority is of a nature to provoke fundamental and persistent disturbances in its economy, it can bring the matter to the attention of the High Authority.

If the situation so requires, the High Authority, after consultation with the Council, shall recognise the existence of such a situation and shall decide the measures to take, within the terms of the present Treaty, to put an end to this situation while safeguarding the essential interests of the Community.

When, under the provisions of the present Article, an appeal is brought before the Court against this Decision, or against the explicit or implied Decision refusing to recognise the existence of the above-mentioned situation, the Court may determine whether the Decision is well founded.

In the event of annulment, the High Authority is required to determine, within the scope of the judgment of the Court, the measures to take to achieve the objects set out in the second paragraph of the present Article.[27]

This Article grants a special right to Member States to enable them to protect their fundamental economic interests. If a Decision of the High Authority is passed and within one month it causes fundamental and

[26] *Ibid.*
[27] French:
" *Lorsqu'un Etat membre estime que, dans un cas déterminé, une action ou un défaut d'action de la Haute Autorité est de nature à provoquer dans son économie des troubles fondamentaux et persistants, il peut saisir la Haute Autorité.*
Celle-ci, après consultation du Conseil, reconnaît, s'il y a lieu, l'existence d'une telle situation et décide des mesures à prendre, dans les conditions prévues au

persistent disturbances, a Member State can appeal against that Decision under Article 33, and have it annulled by the Court as having been passed in violation of the Treaty.[28] If, however, the disturbances do not occur within the very limited time period under which an appeal against the offending Decision can be brought, a Member State requires some further means for obtaining legal redress. These means are provided by Article 37, by which a Member State can appeal to the High Authority to request it to recognise the likelihood of fundamental and persistent disturbances in its economy being caused by the continued existence of some Decision of that Authority, or by the High Authority's failure to take any action, and request it to take the necessary action. The Treaty, however, is careful not to upset the provisions of Article 33, so that, outside the original time limit for the bringing of actions, the existing Decision which is creating the disturbances cannot be challenged and is not able to be annulled.

ACTION OR A FAILURE TO TAKE ACTION ON THE PART OF THE HIGH AUTHORITY

When a Member State believes that an action which will usually be a Decision or a failure to take action on the part of the High Authority is of the nature to cause these fundamental and persistent disturbances in

présent Traité, pour mettre fin à cette situation tout en sauvegardant les intérèts essentiels de la Communauté.

Lorsque la Cour est saisie d'un recours fondé sur les dispositions du présent article contre cette décision ou contre la décision explicite ou implicite refusant de reconnaître l'existence de la situation ci-dessus visée, il lui appartient d'en apprécier le bien-fondé.

En cas d'annulation, la Haute Autorité est tenue de décider, dans le cadre de l'arrêt de la Cour, des mesures à prendre aux fins prévues au deuxième alinéa du présent article."

Stationery Office:

" If a Member State considers that in a given case an action of the High Authority or a failure to act is of such a nature as to provoke fundamental and persistent disturbances in its economy it may bring the matter to the attention of the High Authority.

If this is the case, the High Authority, after consulting the Council, shall make a finding to this effect and decide on the measures to be taken, under the terms of the present Treaty, to correct such a position or to put matters right, while at the same time safeguarding the Community's essential interests.

When an appeal is made to the Court under the provisions of the present Article against such a decision or against an explicit or implicit refusal to recognise the existence of the situation referred to above the Court shall consider whether the decision is justified.

If the Court annuls the decision, the High Authority shall, within the terms of the Court's decision, decide on the measures to be taken for the purposes laid down in the second paragraph of the present Article."

[28] Art. 2, para. 2 of the Treaty, requires the Community " to avoid provoking fundamental and persistent disturbances in the economies of Member States." It is suggested that a Decision which merely may cause such disturbances is not open to be annulled.

its economy, it can bring the matter to the attention of the High Authority. The Court has held, however, that the term "action," as used in
this article refers only to action already taken. The Court held:

> Concerning the applicability of Article 37, the plaintiffs [the German
> Government] have alleged, and have offered to prove that they have
> drawn the High Authority's attention, as much before as after the taking
> of the challenged Decision, to the fact that, in their opinion, the regula-
> tions proposed [which concerned transport charges] were liable to
> provoke fundamental and persistent disturbances in the German
> economy.
>
> However, it does not follow that the conditions for the admissibility
> of an appeal based on Article 37 exist in the present case. Indeed, with
> regard to the observations which the plaintiffs made to the High
> Authority *before* the taking of the Decisions being challenged, they do
> not refer to an "action" of the High Authority within the meaning
> of the first paragraph of the said article because this term must be
> interpreted as embracing only an action already taken and not a Decision
> which the High Authority proposes to take in the future.[29]

It followed, therefore, in the case in question, that communications
sent to the High Authority before the passing of the Decision which was
alleged to be causing disturbances, did not come within the terms of
Article 37, paragraph 1. A further approach after the passing of that
Decision, even if it is in identical terms with earlier approaches, is thus
required.

Further, the Court has held that under Article 37, paragraph 1, it is
the State in whose territory the actual disturbances are, or are threatened,
which can approach the High Authority. The Court phrased this in the
following terms:

> It is clear from the text of the first paragraph of Article 37 that the
> right to bring a matter to the attention of the High Authority belongs
> exclusively to the State where the disturbances have occurred or are
> likely to occur.
>
> Indeed, only the Member State concerned is in a position to assess
> whether its economic situation demands the application of Article 37.[30]

THE APPEAL BEFORE THE COURT

After the appeal has been made to the High Authority, that Authority,
after it has consulted the Council of Ministers must, if it exists, recognise
the existence of the situation which is likely to cause the disturbances,
and decide upon the measures to be taken to end it. Alternatively,

---

[29] *German Government* v. *The High Authority* (Case 19–58), Vol. II.
[30] *Niederrheinishe Bergwerks-Aktiengesellschaft Unternehmensverband des Aachener
Steinkohlenbergbauer* v. *The High Authority* (Joint Cases 2–60 and 3–60).

although it is not stated in paragraph 2 but is to be inferred from it,[31] the High Authority may either declare that in its opinion no such situation exists, or the High Authority may make no declaration one way or the other.

Paragraph 3 of Article 37 deals with the situation when an appeal is brought to the Court.[32] Three distinct appeals are possible, and these have been enumerated by the Court which declared:

> By the terms of the third paragraph of Article 37, both the Decision taken by the High Authority by virtue of the second paragraph, after the matter has been brought to its attention by the Member State concerned, as well as the express or implied Decision refusing to recognise the existence of disturbances, may be the subject of an appeal to the Court.[33]

These appeals will now be considered.[34]

APPEALS AGAINST DECISIONS REFUSING TO RECOGNISE THE LIKELIHOOD OF DISTURBANCES

Against an Explicit Decision

If the High Authority passes a Decision explicitly denying the existence of a situation of a nature to cause fundamental and persistent disturbances, this Decision is open to appeal within the normal one month of its publication or notification.[35]

It is not entirely clear from the wording of Article 37, however, who are the parties who can bring this appeal. The matter, however, has been discussed by the Court, which declared:

> The third paragraph of Article 37 does not specify who may exercise this right of appeal—
>
> In view of the silence of the text . . . it is necessary to inquire whether there is any logical reason to impose limitations upon access to the Court.
>
> It is clear that an appeal against the express . . . Decision refusing to recognise that disturbances have occurred can be brought only by the Member State concerned, as it also possesses the right to bring the

---

[31] And also from the wording of para. 3.

[32] Para. 3 refers to appeals being brought " under the provisions of the present article." Art. 37, however, lays down no provisions under which an appeal is to be brought. The right to bring one has to be implied from this reference itself and from the reference to an annulment in para. 4.

[33] *Ibid.* Vol. III.

[34] " By the terms of the first three paragraphs of Article 37, an appeal based upon this Article cannot be brought against the Decision which the State claims has provoked the said disturbances, but only against a possible subsequent Decision refusing to recognise the existence of the situation "—*German Government* v. *The High Authority* (Case 19–58), Vol. II.

[35] Art. 33, para. 1 and E.C.S.C. Statute, Art. 39. The extensions of time in respect of distance, etc., apply, see p. 100, above

matter to the attention of the High Authority and it alone, therefore, can establish an interest justifying the appeal.[36]

When judging this appeal brought by a State, the Court, by paragraph 3 of Article 37, has power itself to determine whether the alleged disturbances exist or not. If they are found not to exist, the High Authority's Decision denying their existence will have been correct and it will be affirmed. If the disturbances, however, are in fact found to exist, the High Authority, in denying their existence, will have been wrong. Its Decision expressing this denial will, therefore, be annulled.

Against an Implied Decision

After a State has appealed to the High Authority under paragraph 1 requesting it to recognise the existence of a situation of a nature to cause fundamental and persistent disturbances and to take measures to remedy that situation, the High Authority may well take no action at all and neither affirm nor deny the likelihood of disturbances. In this event, paragraph 3 of Article 37 grants a right of appeal against this implied Decision of refusal to recognise the likelihood, but just as a State is the only party which can bring an appeal against an explicit refusal to recognise this situation, so also it is only a State which can bring an appeal against an implied Decision refusing to recognise this situation.[37]

It will be noted that the reference to an appeal against an implied Decision refusing to recognise the situation is the first indication which the Treaty gives that a refusal to recognise the likelihood of disturbances is to be deemed to be a Decision refusing so to recognise it. There is, however, no provision in the Treaty which states what length of time must elapse before this negative Decision can be implied.

It will be remembered that under Article 35, a two months' silence on the part of the High Authority was there declared to amount to an implied negative Decision. It might be argued that, in order to maintain uniformity, that provision should be made to apply in the case of Article 37. On the other hand, two months is a long time for a State to wait when it believes itself faced with fundamental disturbances, particularly when one realises that implying a negative Decision is only the first step to obtaining any legal redress, and that a State has then to obtain

---

[36] *Niederrheinische Bergwerks-Aktiengesselschaft Unternehmensverband des Aachener Steinkohlenbergbauer* v. *The High Authority* (Joint Cases 2–60 and 3–60).

[37] The quotation set out above is expressly made to apply to implied Decisions. The Court stated " It is clear that an appeal against the express or *implied* Decision refusing to recognise . . . " etc.

the annulment of the implied Decision in a legal action before any allevia-
tion of the disturbances will occur. However, there is no authority on
this point, and there is clearly no advantage in speculating.[38]

The appeal under paragraph 3 is required to be brought within one
month of the date when the silence of the High Authority can be deemed
to be an implied negative Decision.[39] As that date is unknown, so also is
the time within which the appeal is to be brought.

AGAINST A DECISION RECOGNISING THE EXISTENCE OF DISTURBANCES AND SEEKING TO END THEM

If the High Authority, under paragraph 1, recognises the existence of a
situation which is likely to cause disturbances, it is then required, under
paragraph 2, after consulting the Council of Ministers, to take the
measures necessary to put an end to that situation while, at the same
time, safeguarding the essential interests of the Community.

The first question that arises is who can bring the appeal. On this
the Court has made a distinction. The Decision passed by the High
Authority to deal with the disturbances may prescribe remedies which
are regarded by the State concerned either as adequate or as inadequate.
In the latter case, the State concerned can appeal.

> The right to bring an appeal against a Decision in which the High
> Authority has incorporated measures which the Member States con-
> cerned considers to be insufficient, belongs only to that State.[40]

Where, however, the State concerned is satisfied with the measures,
it clearly will not itself appeal. The Court, however, has recognised that
other Member States may be affected by these measures and has therefore
allowed them a right of appeal.

> An appeal against a Decision taken by the High Authority by virtue
> of Article 37, which confirms the request of a Member State which
> believes that its economy is affected by fundamental and persistent
> disturbances demands an assessment of the economic situation of the
> Member States and, moreover, requires a consideration of whether, in
> view of this situation, the measures taken can be considered as necessary
> and appropriate.

---

[38] A State which appealed against a silence of less than two months because it assumed
that the silence amounted to a negative Decision, might well find, some months later,
that the Court, on a preliminary issue, ruled that there was no Decision. The State
would then have to pay the costs and start legal proceedings all over again. It is
suggested, however, that, by analogy with Art. 35, a period of more than two months
could not be required before a negative Decision can be implied.

[39] E.C.S.C. Statute, Art. 39. Extensions of time in respect of distances, etc., apply, see
p. 100, above.

[40] *Ibid.* see Vol. III.

This appeal thus brings into issue the political responsibility of the governments of the Member States and of the High Authority, and in particular that responsibility which concerns the reconciliation of the general interest of a Member State with the general interest of the Community. . . .

For the reasons set out below, the right to bring the appeal referred to in Article 37, para. 3, must be allowed not only to the Member States which brought the matter to the attention of the High Authority, but also to other Member States.

This interpretation is confirmed by the second paragraph of Article 37, which requires the High Authority before determining upon the request of the Member State concerned, merely to consult the Council of Ministers, without being bound by its advice.

Accepting the importance of the interests which may possibly be involved, this fact is explicable only if it is admitted that any Member State which does not share the opinion of the High Authority has the right to bring the matter before the Court in order to ask it to give a ruling upon the justification for and the desirability of the measures in question.[41]

It is suggested that the final words of this quotation, namely, that in an appeal under Article 37, paragraph 3, the Court is being asked to give a ruling upon " the desirability of the measures in question," are extremely important. Thus the Court, a body of legally trained persons, not one of whom is an economist, is being given power to review the economic and political desirability of action which has been decided upon by the High Authority in consultation with the political representatives of the governments of the Member States assembled in the Council of Ministers. If the Court finds such action " undesirable " it can quash it. Such power would seem to be unique in legal history.[42]

IN THE EVENT OF AN ANNULMENT

If the Court annuls either the explicit or implied decision of the High Authority refusing to recognise the existence of a situation likely to provoke fundamental disturbances, the position will be that the Court will have adjudged that such a situation exists. The High Authority is then required by Article 37 to take the measures " within the terms of the present Treaty, to put an end to this situation while safeguarding the essential interests of the Community."

[41] *Ibid.*
[42] An alternative interpretation could have given the Court much more limited power. Under para. 2, the High Authority is under a duty to end the situation which is causing or likely to cause the disturbances, but it is required to do so only " within the terms of the present Treaty " and " while safeguarding the essential interests of the Community." The Court's task might have been accepted as being merely to ensure that the measures of the High Authority were first of all ones which would end the disturbances, and secondly which would satisfy the above two requirements.

Similarly, if the High Authority has recognised the existence of the situation but its measures to remedy it have been annulled, the matter is referred back to the High Authority and, by a second effort, it is required to put an end to the situation.

No procedure is set out, however, to deal with the position where the High Authority fails to take any Decision to remedy the situation at all.

ACTION AGAINST A FAILURE TO TAKE A DECISION REMEDYING THE SITUATION

If the High Authority takes no Decision to remedy the situation, this is clearly in breach of Article 37, paragraph 3. What can be done about this breach, however, is not clear.

It will be remembered that, under Article 34, when the Court has annulled a Decision of the High Authority, it is required to refer the matter back to that Authority which is then required " to take the measures to carry out the decision of annulment." If it fails to do so within a reasonable time, an appeal in damages is open before the Court.

It will be noted that the procedure under Article 37, by which, following annulment, it is the High Authority's duty to remedy the existing situation, is similar to that under Article 34. It may well be contended, therefore, that the procedure under Article 37 is merely a specific example of the general procedure set out under Article 34. If that is so, then the appeal for damages granted by Article 34 can be claimed by a State if no action is taken within a reasonable time.

This, however, it is suggested, is pure theory. No State with unresolved economic disturbances raging will be very interested in claiming damages from the funds of the High Authority, particularly when those damages will have to be recouped by the High Authority in subsequent years from enterprises, some of whom will be within that State itself.

Under Article 35, where the High Authority is required, by a provision of the Treaty to take a Decision, and it fails to do so, a State, the Council, enterprises or associations may appeal to it. If the High Authority continues in its inactivity for two months, its silence is deemed to amount to a Decision of refusal to act.

In the situation under discussion, the obligation upon the High Authority to take a Decision is imposed by Article 37, paragraph 4. It would seem, therefore, that the machinery of Article 35 is applicable,[43]

---

[43] One would presumably have to hold that the provisions of Art. 35 allowing enterprises and associations to appeal to the High Authority are not here applicable.

and that in two months' time an action against the implied Decision of the High Authority refusing to act will lie. That implied Decision will be annulled for violation of Article 37, paragraph 4, of the Treaty, and the State concerned will be in exactly the same position as it was in when it obtained its first annulment under Article 37.

It appears, therefore, that the above situation is not one that is, or by its very nature can be, regulated by the Treaty: if the High Authority falls down on its duty, the Community is in practice at an end, and a judgment of the Court cannot prop it up again.

ARTICLE 38

The Court, at the request of one of the Member States or of the High Authority may annul the *délibérations* of the Assembly or of the Council.

The request must be brought within a period of one month calculated from the publication of the *délibération* of the Assembly or of the communication of the *délibération* of the Council to the Member States or to the High Authority.

Only the grounds of incompetence or of violation of substantial procedural requirements may be alleged in support of such an appeal.[44]

The right of appeal provided by this article is more restricted than the similar right of appeal allowed against the acts of the High Authority, for, it will be noted, the two additional grounds of violation of the Treaty and *détournement de pouvoir* are not included.[45] It was suggested at the time of the signing of the Treaty [46] that this restriction

---

[44] French:
> " *La Cour peut annuler, à la requête d'un des Etats membres ou de la Haute Autorité, les délibérations de l'Assemblé ou du Conseil.*
> *La requête doit être formée dans le délai d'un mois à compter de la publication de la délibération de l'Assemblée ou de la communication de la délibération du Conseil aux Etats membres ou à la Haute Autorité.*
> *Seuls les moyens tirés de l'incompétence ou de la violation des formes substantielles peuvent être invoqués à l'appui d'un tel recours.*"
Stationery Office:
> " On the application of a Member State or of the High Authority, the Court may quash resolutions of the Assembly or of the Council.
> Such applications shall be made within one month from the publication of such a resolution by the Assembly or the notification of such a resolution by the Council to the Member States or to the High Authority.
> The sole ground for such application shall be lack of jurisdiction or nonobservance of basic procedural rules."

[45] *Cf.* Art. 33, para. 1.

[46] *Rapport de la Délégation Française sur la Traité instituant la C.E.C.A.* published by the French Ministère des Affaires Etrangères, October 1951.

was required owing to the political character of the Assembly and the Council, and that it would be impossible to bring them under a control other than that aimed at keeping their action within the limits of their respective competence and at guaranteeing their correct functioning.[47] This statement, however, it is submitted, does not explain why the grounds of violation of the Treaty should be excluded,[48] but the restriction upon appeals clearly reflects the political nature of the two institutions.

THE DÉLIBÉRATIONS OF THE ASSEMBLY

By the European Coal and Steel Community Treaty, the Assembly is granted only two effective powers [49]: the first is to pass a motion of censure on the annual report of the High Authority,[50] and the second to approve any modifications of the powers of the High Authority.[51] In practice, therefore, a challenge of the *délibérations* of the Assembly would probably be a challenge of the manner in which they were passed, a plaintiff alleging that the rules of procedure had not been complied with or that the required majorities had not been obtained.[52]

THE DÉLIBÉRATIONS OF THE COUNCIL

In the Treaty the term "*délibérations*" is used in different senses. Thus, it is provided that when the Council is consulted by the High Authority it shall deliberate without necessarily proceeding to a vote. The *procès-verbaux* of its "*délibérations*" are to be forwarded to the High Authority.[53]

---

[47] Under the E.E.C. and Euratom Treaties the acts of the respective Councils of Ministers can be challenged on any of the four grounds—E.E.C. Treaty, Art. 173, para. 1; Euratom Treaty, Art. 146, para. 1.

[48] In practice, of course, most resolutions if passed in violation of the Treaty will be voidable on the grounds of incompetence, but violation of the Treaty and incompetence are not synonymous terms.

[49] It is also granted a power to fix its own Rules of Procedure by a vote of the majority of its total membership—Art. 25—but once fixed they are not likely to be often amended.

[50] This requires a majority of two-thirds of the members present and voting if this vote represents a majority of the total membership—Art. 24.

[51] The modifications must be approved by three-quarters of the members present and voting if this majority comprises two-thirds of the total membership—Art. 95, para. 4.

[52] A failure to obtain the required majority for a resolution which is published as having been validly passed may be regarded as voidable by reason of the violation of a substantial procedural requirement, or by reason of incompetence because the competence of the Assembly to pass such a resolution was conditional upon obtaining a prescribed majority and that condition was not fulfilled. It could also be argued that the resolution not having been properly passed does not exist and need not therefore be challenged. The period of one month for the bringing of action would thus be inapplicable.

[53] Art. 28, para. 2.

There are many occasions in the Treaty when the High Authority requires the consent of the Council before it can take certain action.[54] On other occasions, however, the High Authority is merely to consult the Council.[55] It appears that the *procès-verbaux* referred to covers both these types of *délibérations,* and that both these types are being referred to in Article 38.

By Article 41 of the Treaty it is provided that only the Court is competent to judge as a preliminary issue upon the validity of the *délibérations* of the High Authority and of the Council in a case where an action before a municipal tribunal puts this validity in issue.

Now it is clear that the *délibérations* of the High Authority being referred to are its Decisions and Recommendations, and not merely its discussions, or, to use the English term, its deliberations. It appears, therefore, that the *"délibérations"* of the Council must also include the actual Decisions of the Council.[56]

"THE REQUEST MUST BE BROUGHT WITHIN A PERIOD OF ONE MONTH"

When the request being brought to the Court concerns the executive Decisions of the Council, the existence of a time period for the bringing of that request creates no difficulty.[57] However, when the request is being brought against either the consent of the Council to action proposed by the High Authority, or against the deliberations with the Council which the High Authority has held, difficulties readily appear.

By Article 38 a Member State may challenge these *délibérations* on the ground of incompetence or of violation by the Council of a substantial procedural requirement, but only within one month of the communication to it of the *délibération.* As these communications can clearly be made to different States at different times, some States may still be able to appeal against the *délibérations* after the one month for appealing which is granted to other States has expired. Whether a State which can appeal can do so on behalf of another time-barred State, is not clear, but if the matter could at the same time in some way affect the plaintiff State, there seems no ground upon which its appeal

---

[54] *e.g.,* imposing levies upon the production of coal and steel—Art. 50, para. 2; recommending governments to establish quantitative restrictions—Art. 74, para. 2.

[55] *e.g.,* the methods of collecting levies upon coal and steel—Art. 50, para. 2; recommending means for increasing abnormally low wages—Art. 68, para. 5.1.

[56] *e.g.,* requiring the High Authority to establish a system of quotas in a period of manifest crisis—Art. 58, para. 1.2; fixing the maximum and minimum rates for export duties on coal and steel with regard to third countries—Art. 72, para. 1.

[57] As with the time period for the challenge of the Decision and Recommendation of the High Authority, the one month is extended in respect of the plaintiff's distance from the Court—Rules, Art. 81, paras. 1 and 2; see p. 100, above.

could be refused. The time period of one month, therefore, in practice may be a little artificial.

Secondly, the Court has stated that for the High Authority to fail to consult the Council when it is required to do so, and *a fortiori* to fail to obtain its consent, is a violation of a substantial procedural requirement.[58] It may be queried whether to obtain consent which would have been voidable under Article 38 is the obtaining of consent at all. If it is not consent, then the Decision of the High Authority can be annulled under Article 33 as having been passed in violation of a substantial procedural requirement, namely, the requirement to obtain valid consent: that is to say, the Court will be able to consider the validity of the *délibération* of the Council even after the expiry of the express procedural time limit for its consideration.

If on the other hand a consent of the Council can be challenged only under Article 38, a State which has been informed of that consent will only have one month in which to bring its appeal. A State wishing to protect its interests will therefore be advised to challenge what may appear to be an invalid consent without knowing whether in fact that consent is going to be acted upon by the High Authority, or even the final terms of the Decision to which consent, in broad outline, has been given.

It is suggested, however, that the latter interpretation is the correct one, and that the right of appeal granted under Article 38 is entirely distinct from that granted by Article 33, and that the terms of Article 38 cannot be circumvented by reason of an appeal against subsequent Decisions or Recommendations by the High Authority.

PROCEDURE FOLLOWING THE ANNULMENT OF A DÉLIBÉRATION

When Decisions or Recommendations of the High Authority are annulled by the Court, that Authority is required to " take the measures which comprise the execution of the decision of annulment." [59] It might appear that by analogy the *délibérations* of the Assembly or of the Council should also be referred back to the respective body.

In the case of the Assembly, it is clear that no further measures are required because the matters in issue, namely, censuring the High Authority or modifying the power of that Authority are entirely political matters. In the case of the Council, however, certain of its resolutions, such as fixing consumption priorities [60] or terminating a system of

[58] *French Government* v. *The High Authority* (Case 1–59), Vol. II.
[59] Art. 34, see p. 176, above.
[60] Art. 59, para. 2.1.

quotas,[61] will be upon matters in respect of which the Treaty imposes a duty to pass a resolution. If the High Authority were in a similar position, namely where it is required by the Treaty to act but its action has been annulled, the Treaty expressly requires a further Decision and regulates a failure to take one.[62] No such provisions are included to regulate a failure on the part of the Council, and it is suggested that it is going too far to imply by analogy the provision governing the High Authority.

ARTICLE 39

Appeals brought before the Court have no suspensive effect. However, the Court if it considers that the circumstances require it, may grant a suspension of the execution of the Decision or of the Recommendation being challenged. It may prescribe any other measures necessary.[63]

The wording of this Article is in very wide terms and the appeals here being referred to are not only those brought against Decisions and Recommendations of the High Authority [64] but also those brought against the *délibérations* of the Assembly and of the Council.[65]

APPEALS HAVE NO SUSPENSIVE EFFECT

A somewhat extreme example of the application of the provision that appeals have no suspensive effect is to be found in a recent Decision of the Court.[66] The facts were that in February 1958, the High Authority by Decisions informed the German Government that certain prices on the German railways were in violation of the Treaty and that they were therefore to be amended. The first amendments were to be made by July 1958, and further amendment by the end of November.

---

[61] Art. 58, para. 3.
[62] Arts. 34 and 35, see pp. 176 and 184, above.
[63] French:
  " *Les recours formés devant la Cour n'ont pas d'effet suspensif.*
  Toutefois la Cour peut, si elle estime que les circonstances l'exigent, ordonner le sursis à l'execution de la décision ou de la recommandation attaquée.
  Elle peut prescrire toutes autres mesures provisoires nécessaires."
  Stationery Office:
  " The institution of proceedings shall not cause a judgment to be suspended.
  The Court may, however, if it considers that circumstances so require, order that the enforcement of the decision or recommendation contested be suspended.
  The Court may prescribe any other necessary interim measures."
  This translation of para. 1 of this article is a complete misunderstanding.
[64] Under Art. 33, see p. 112, above.
[65] Under Art. 38, see p. 207, above.
[66] *German Government* v. *The High Authority* (Case 3–59), Vol. II.

211

In March 1958, the German Government appealed against these Decisions [67] and because it regarded the Decisions as being void, it naturally took no steps to amend the tariffs on the German railways. However, in December 1958, while the action against the February Decisions was still pending before the Court, the High Authority by a further Decision informed the German Government that it was in violation of the Treaty by not having complied with the February Decisions by amending its railway prices. The German Government brought a second action, this time for the annulment of the further Decision of the High Authority which set out the German Government's alleged violation of the Treaty. The grounds of the Government's case were that the February Decisions were void and secondly that having appealed against those Decisions it could not be sanctioned for failing to comply with them.

On this second ground the Court declared:

> By the terms of Article 14 of the Treaty, Decisions of the High Authority are binding in all respects and by the terms of Article 39 of the Treaty and of Article 33 of the Statute appeals brought before the Court have no suspensive effect without a contrary decision of the Court or of the President. As the plaintiffs have not requested an injunction upon the execution of the Decisions in question, they retained their binding character whatever may be the nature and effect of the appeal 19–58.[68]

Further, in order to avoid this obviously inevitable interpretation the plaintiffs had also alleged that by a general principle of law Decisions such as those passed by the High Authority in February 1958, did not come into effect until the expiration of the period during which they could be challenged, or, if so challenged, until a Court's decision had been obtained upon their validity. The present case, therefore, they argued, was not one concerning a suspension of a Decision which had previously been in force; it was a case where a Decision had never yet come into force.

The Court declared:

> This argument, although valid in certain instances in private law, cannot apply to administrative matters, where it is the rule that Decisions become binding either from the moment when they are passed, or from the date of their notification or publication.[69]

[67] *German Government* v. *The High Authority* (Case 19–58), Vol. II.
[68] *German Government* v. *The High Authority* (Case 3–59), Vol. II.
[69] *Ibid.*

" The Court May Grant a Suspension of Execution "

Paragraph 2 which grants a right to the Court to suspend the execution of a " Decision or Recommendation " appears to be referring only to Decisions and Recommendations of the High Authority, for although certain Articles [70] empower the Council of Ministers to take a Decision, the Treaty usually refers to the enactments of the Council as *" délibérations."* Further than this, the old Rules of the Court stated:

> No demand seeking to obtain by way of expedited procedure a suspension of execution as provided by Article 39, paragraph 2, of the Treaty, may be made unless the Decision or the Recommendation of the High Authority has been challenged in a principal action either previously or at least simultaneously.[71]

As an admission by the Court that despite the wording of the Treaty, this Rule was too restrictive, the present Rule declares:

> Any request for a stay of execution of *an act taken by an institution* within the terms of Article 39, paragraph 2, of the E.C.S.C. Treaty . . . shall be admissible only if the plaintiff has challenged this act in proceedings before the Court.[72]

It should be noted that Article 36, paragraph 2, refers only to a suspension " of the execution " of a Decision. Where, therefore, by its very nature a Decision of the High Authority cannot be executed, no suspension can be claimed. For example, a Decision of the High Authority taken under Article 88, paragraph 1, of the Treaty can merely set out that it considers that a State has failed in one of the obligations incumbent upon it by virtue of the Treaty. Such a Decision cannot be suspended.

On this the President of the Court in an Order declared:

> Article 88 of the E.C.S.C. Treaty, on which the Decision challenged in the principal action has been based, confers upon the High Authority only the power to set out that a State has failed in one of the obligations incumbent upon it by virtue of the Treaty, and to grant it a time limit to comply with its obligation. . . .
> Under these conditions, the provision of Article 39 of the Treaty covering suspension cannot be applied in the present case. It appears from the terms themselves of this provision that it relates only to the suspension of the measures of execution ordered either by the High Authority or, where applicable, by third persons, and taken with respect to the party concerned.[73]

In those cases where this Article is applicable, the Treaty gives no indication of the particular circumstances which were intended to

---

[70] *e.g.,* Art. 9, para. 2 and Art. 61, para. 3.
[71] Old Rules, Art. 63, para. 1.   [72] Rules, Art. 83, para. 1.1.
[73] *Italian Government* v. *The High Authority* (Case 20–59), Vol. II.

justify a suspension of execution, but two recent cases throw light upon the Court's attitude in the matter.

The basic rule would appear to be that a suspension will be granted only where the position of the party concerned will be adversely affected by the application to it of the challenged Decision [74] or, presumably where any such adverse effects can subsequently be remedied by damages.

In one case certain German enterprises requested the suspension of a Decision of the High Authority ordering certain transport tariffs to be modified—the reason for this request being that the existing unmodified tariffs were favourable to them. The Court held in an Order:

> It should be noted that the carrying out of the Decisions . . . do not involve any immediate disadvantageous consequences for certain enterprises and would only lead to partial increases in tariffs for the majority of the other enterprises.
>
> It is true that this is disadvantageous for the enterprises affected by these measures, but there is no reason why the amendments of the tariffs could not be repealed, as the plaintiffs maintain.
>
> The above considerations require the rejection of the request. . . .[75]

In a case which fell the other side of the line, the High Authority by various Decisions had required sales organisations selling Ruhr coal to specify the requirements which were to be satisfied before a wholesaler of coal could make purchases directly from these sales organisations. One particular wholesaler, who in the past had purchased coal directly, found himself in future going to be excluded, and he challenged the validity of these Decisions authorising these new requirements. In addition, so as to be able to continue in his position as a wholesaler entitled to purchase directly, he requested the Court to suspend the execution of the Decisions of the High Authority. In granting this request the Court declared:

> On the one hand, the provisional continuance of the plaintiff in his position as direct trading wholesaler can occur without danger to the coal market of the Ruhr. . . .
>
> On the other hand, it appears from the information supplied in this case, that the loss of the position of direct trading wholesaler would cause loss and a grave hardship to the plaintiffs, because the advantages enjoyed by a simple wholesaler are in no way comparable to the advantages of a direct trading wholesaler, particularly because the latter position allows the plaintiffs to satisfy the prescribed conditions of admission to membership of the [*Oberrheinische Kohlen-Union*].[76]

---

[74] " Under Art. 39 of the Treaty, it is for the party seeking the stay to establish that a refusal thereof would result in serious injury to it "—*Acciaieria e Tubificio di Brescia* v. *The High Authority* (Case 31–59), Vol. II.

[75] *Barbara Erzbergbau AG and others* v. *The High Authority* (Joint Cases 3–18, 25 and 26–58), Vol. II.

[76] *Nold KG* v. *The High Authority* (Case 18–57), Vol. II

One thus sees that the criteria for granting the suspension in this case were the damage likely to be suffered by the plaintiff if no suspension were granted and the fact that such a suspension could be granted without causing any substantial effects.

PARTIES ENTITLED TO REQUEST A SUSPENSION OF EXECUTION

Paragraph 2 provides that " the Court . . . may grant a suspension." It is assumed, however, that the Court would do so only if it had been expressly requested to grant such a suspension. It appears, also, that the only entities entitled to make this request are parties to the case challenging the validity of the Decision concerned, but the Court expressly left open the question of whether an intervening party could also make this request.[77]

The normal position under the Coal and Steel Community Treaty is that the only enterprises which may appeal to the Court are those which " carry on an activity of production in the field of coal and steel " within the Member States.[78] However, as an exception to this, under two specified Articles [79] which deal with monopolies and concentrations, enterprises and organisations which habitually exercise an activity of distribution other than that of sale to domestic consumers or to craft industries, are permitted to appeal.

The Court, however, has held that although this extended right of non-producers to appeal is, by the wording of the Treaty, limited to the situation specified in those two Articles, yet such a right exists also where, as in the case discussed immediately above, the interests of a non-producer are adversely affected not by the two Articles expressly mentioned but by an application of those Articles.[80] Being thus granted

[77] The Court stated:
" In the present proceedings it is not necessary to decide whether an intervening party is empowered to request the suspension of the execution of a Decision, and if so, under what conditions "—*Barbara Erzbergbau AG and others* v. *The High Authority* (Joint Cases 3–18, 25 and 26–58), Vol. II.   [78] Art. 80.
[79] Arts. 65 and 66, see pp. 242 and 246, below.
[80] The Courts stated:
" Although, in principle, access to the Court, according to the provisions set out in Art. 33 *et seq.* of the Treaty, is limited to enterprises ' who engage in production in the field of coal and steel,' yet by the terms of Art. 80 of the Treaty ' any enterprises or organisation regularly engaged in distribution other than sale to domestic consumers or to craft industries ' is equated with producers ' with regard to Arts. 65 and 66 of the Treaty as well as with regard to information required for their application and for appeals based upon them.'
" It follows from the text of Art. 80 that the appeals there mentioned cannot be limited merely to information required for the application of the terms of Arts. 65 and 66 and that its application should not be reduced to a discussion of the well founding or to the scope of a request for information.
" On the other hand, the terms of Art. 80 specifying ' appeals brought with regard to Arts. 65 and 66 ' refer not merely to those based upon a direct application of Arts. 65 and 66 to distributors, to groups, or to concentrations but refer also

the right to challenge the Decision of the High Authority which was affecting its interests, the plaintiff must, declared the Court, be also entitled to apply under Article 39 of the Treaty for the suspension of that Decision.[81]

The Appropriate Time for Bringing the Request for Suspension

Article 39 merely states that the Court may grant a suspension of a Decision or Recommendation which has been challenged, it does not set out the time at which this application is to be made. The Court, however, has declared:

> In principle it is for a plaintiff to judge of the desirability of making a request for the suspension of execution and to decide at what stage of the procedure this request should be made.[82]

However, arising out of the facts of that particular case, it went on to state:

> However, there are obvious objections to granting such a request when it has been introduced after both the closing of the written proceedings and of the oral proceedings relating to the merits and at a time when the Court has already started its deliberations upon the merits.[83]

In addition to this, it is suggested that unless the request for suspension is made at a fairly early stage of the proceedings, the plaintiffs are themselves weakening their own argument that the suspension is of serious concern to them.

" The Court May Prescribe Any Other Provisional Measures Necessary "

It might appear from this wording of paragraph 3 of Article 39 that the Court, of its own motion, could prescribe such provisional measures in any particular case as it declared necessary. However, the Rules of the Court make it quite plain that this is not so. The Rules provide that:

> Any request relating to one of the other interim measures referred to in Article 39, third paragraph of the E.C.S.C. Treaty . . . shall be admissible only if it is made by one of the parties in a case before the Court and if it refers to that case.[84]

No request for these provisional measures has yet been made to the Court and so there is as yet no indication of what measures the Court

---

to a case where, as in the present action, an application of these articles affects the interests of distributors." *Nold KG* v. *The High Authority* (Case 18–57), Vol. II.
[81] *Nold KG* v. *The High Authority* (Case 18–57), Vol. II.
[82] *Barbara Erzbergbau AG and others* v. *The High Authority* (Joint Cases 3–18, 25 and 26–58), Vol. II.
[83] *Ibid.* Vol. II.
[84] Rules, Art. 83, para. 1. 2.

is likely to hold fall within this provision. It is suggested, however, that any order to freeze a particular situation would be included—such, for example, as an order prohibiting the sale of specified goods or the disposal of certain funds.

ARTICLE 40, Paras. 1 and 2

Subject to the provisions of Article 34, paragraph 1, the Court shall have jurisdiction, upon the request of the injured party, to award pecuniary damages against the Community in the event of an injury caused in the execution of the present Treaty by a *faute de service* of the Community.

It shall also have jurisdiction to award damages against an employee of the Community in the event of injury caused by a *faute personnelle* of this employee in the performance of his duties. If the injured party is unable to obtain these damages from the employee, the Court may award equitable compensation against the Community.[85]

This provision introduces into the Treaty the distinction between *faute de service*—an administrative wrong, and a *faute personnelle*—a personal wrong. It is a distinction which exists in French administrative law, and provides another example of the close affinity of the jurisdiction of the Court to that of the *Conseil d'Etat*. For English trained lawyers, however, the concepts here being employed are entirely alien.[86] An English lawyer thinks automatically of personal torts of a servant and of the vicarious responsibility of the employer for that tort. Those

[85] French:
> "*Sous réserve des dispositions de l'article 34, alinéa 1, la Cour est compétente pour accorder, sur demande de la partie lésée, une réparation pécuniaire à la charge de la Communauté en cas de préjudice causé dans l'exécution du présent Traité par une faute de service de la Communauté.*
> "*Elle est également compétente pour accorder une réparation à la charge d'un agent des services de la Communauté, en cas de préjudice causé par une faute personnelle de cet agent dans l'exercice des ses fonctions. Si la partie lésée n'a pu obtenir cette réparation de la part de l'agent, la Cour peut mettre une indemnité équitable à la charge de la Communauté.*"
Stationery Office:
> "Subject to the provisions of the first paragraph of Article 34, the Court shall be competent to award pecuniary damages against the Community, on the application of the injured party, in cases where injury results from a wrongful act performed on behalf of the Community in the carrying out of the present Treaty.
> "It shall also be competent to award damages against a servant of the Community in cases where injury results from a wrongful act of that servant in the performance of his duties. If the injured party is unable to recover such damages from the servant the Court may award equitable damages against the Community."
[86] For a comparison of tortious liability under the E.C.S.C. Treaty and under American law, see Kautzar-Schroeder, " Public Tort Liability under the Treaty Constituting the European Coal and Steel Community compared with Federal Tort Claims Act " in 4 *Villanova Law Review*, p. 198.

notions, however, must here be forgotten. No vicarious responsibility is being imported by Article 40.

Speaking generally, a *faute de service* occurs when a wrong is caused, not by the fault of any one particular person, but by the inherent defects of the administrative system itself, such, for example, as a delay caused by the structure of the administration [87] or a failure to carry out its obligation.[88] If, however, a delay is deliberately caused by an employee, it is not the system which is at fault, but the employee. He is said, therefore, to have committed a *faute personnelle*.[89]

The administration is liable for its own *fautes de service*: it is the individual who is alone responsible for his *fautes personnelles*.[90]

EXAMPLES OF FAUTE DE SERVICE

The first occasion when the Court was required to consider an allegation of a *faute de service* was in a case in 1955.[91] The plaintiff had been employed by the Common Assembly for an initial period of two years and held the post of *Chef de Service aux services administratives*. However, the Common Assembly decided to discontinue that post after the expiry of the two-year contractual period. In consequence the Assembly informed the plaintiff that his contract could not be

---

[87] It is, of course, true that individuals are in fact responsible for the defects in the administrative system, but no legal liability falls upon them as individuals in respect of this responsibility.

[88] Professor Reuter found the only possible example of a *faute de service* of the High Authority to be a violation of its obligation not to divulge any professional information, especially concerning enterprises, which is imposed by Art. 47, para. 2, of the Treaty. Although a leakage of information resulting from a failure on the part of the High Authority to arrange adequate security for documents might constitute a *faute de service*, it is suggested that a leakage is more likely to be a *faute personnelle*. When Art. 47, para. 4, allows an appeal to the Court in respect of damage suffered by an enterprise, it specifies that the appeal shall be brought " under the conditions set out in Art. 40 ": it does not, however, refer specifically either to para. 1—*fautes de service*—or to para. 2—*fautes personnelles*.

[89] The distinction between these two types of wrong was first formulated by Hauriou and was based upon the degree of care employed. " *Fautes* which do not exceed the extent of negligence in practice admitted as tolerable in the administration remain administrative faults and are to some extent the responsibility of the administration. Those which exceed this extent remain personal to the employee "—Walin, *Droit Administratif*, p. 333

Duez and Debreyre state: " There is a *faute personnelle* in the case where the official has committed a fault. . . . in this case the fault is detachable from the services of the administration. . . . There is a *faute personnelle* when the faults of the official reveals a wrongful intention with regard to the party affected. The Decision has been taken . . . for motives of spite, personal rancour or private passion. . . . There is a *faute personnelle* when in certain cases the wrong is grave, implying a gross error on the part of the official either in the assessment of facts or in the extent of his legal powers "—*Traité du Droit Administratif*, pp. 694–695.

[90] Under Art. 40, para. 2, the Community can be required to pay compensation where no redress has been obtained from the individual in respect of his wrong. This makes the Community an insurer, not one vicariously liable.

[91] *Kergall* v. *The Common Assembly* (Case 1–55), Vol. II.

renewed. The plaintiff, therefore, sued and alleged that the Decision not to re-employ him had been taken improperly and constituted a *détournement de pouvoir*.[92]

The Court declared:

As for the ability of the Common Assembly to discontinue the post of Head of the Administrative Services, the Court rejects the plaintiff's submissions. The Court holds that the Bureau was empowered to organise its secretariat as it pleased in order to achieve greater efficiency and that it had full power to discontinue any post which it considers to be unnecessary.

On the other hand, the Court holds that the discontinuance of a particular post does not, of itself, involve the dismissal of the official who holds that post, and it is even less true when, as in the present case, the contract of employment does not appoint this official expressly to the post that has been discontinued. This discontinuance merely involves the release of this official to take on other duties.

It appears from the Instruction that the defendants have not taken any steps in this direction and, on the other hand, that the plaintiff would have agreed to accept not only a similar post to that which had been discontinued but that he would even have accepted a less important position.

On the basis of the above, the Court concludes that, in the circumstances that have been proved before the Court, by not extending the plaintiff's contract of employment, the Bureau of the Common Assembly has advanced in support of its Decision a ground which of itself does not justify it, and that it has not sufficiently taken account of the plaintiff's legal position.

Nevertheless, the Court holds that in taking these Decisions, and in determining the compensation referred to in Article 15 of the plaintiff's contract of employment, the Bureau of the Common Assembly ought to have taken full account of the provisions of the draft Service Regulations of the Community which govern the consequences of redundancy.

In consequence, the Court holds that the circumstances of the non-renewal of the plaintiff's contract of employment appear to be irregular and that the Bureau of the Common Assembly has committed a fault in the exercise of its functions concerning the execution of this contract. The Common Assembly is responsible for this fault and has committed a wrong to the plaintiff for which he is entitled to damages.[93]

In a later case [94] the Common Assembly was also found to have committed *fautes de service*.

---

[92] This action was brought under Art. 42 of the Treaty.
[93] *Ibid*. Vol. II.
[94] *Algera and others* v. *The Common Assembly* (Joint Cases 7–56 and 3–57 to 7–57), Vol. II.

The plaintiffs had short-term contracts of employment with the Common Assembly but before these had expired the plaintiffs applied to be admitted to the new Statute of Service which was at that time in course of being prepared by a Commission of the Presidents of the four institutions. By Decision dated December 12, 1955, the plaintiffs were so admitted: they were given new administrative gradings, and it was stated that until the Statute came into force the plaintiffs would continue to be employed in accordance with the provision of their contracts and with the existing provisional Staff Regulations. Subsequently, the plaintiffs were given new gradings by reference to the Statute of Service, but these they objected to. As a result of these objections the Common Assembly, by letter on July 12, 1956, informed the plaintiffs that the Statute would only be applied to them in their capacity of temporary employees under a one year contract. The plaintiffs appealed against the gradings given to them by the Decisions of December 12, 1955, and against the letters of July 12, 1956. The Court held that the gradings in the Decisions of December 12, 1955, had been determined without the correct procedural machinery having been adopted and were thus null, and that the letters of July 12, 1956, improperly sought to exclude the plaintiffs from admission to the Statute whereas this admission had irrevocably occurred on December 12, 1955.

On these facts, the Court found three distinct *fautes de service*. As to the first it stated:

> The defendants knew that the Commission of Presidents proposed to reach uniformity in the salaries of employees in different institutions who were doing comparable work, and the defendants had declared themselves ready to collaborate. Under these conditions, the delivery of the Decisions of December 12, 1955, on the very day on which the Commission of Presidents, at a sitting at which the President of the Common Assembly took part, had unanimously recognised the need for this uniformity, should not have been made before the results to obtain uniformity were known, even if it was prompted by a desire to create a more defined status for the plaintiffs. This premature and precipitate delivery constitutes a *faute de service* from the fact that it created a situation which is false while having the appearance of being legal.[95]

The second such *faute* arose out of the letter of July 12, 1956, by which, having once admitted the plaintiffs to the Statute of Service, the Common Assembly now sought to put the plaintiffs back onto a contractual footing. The Court held:

> The withdrawal of the admission to the Statute having been illegal, it also constituted a *faute de service*; a *faute* which gives a right, by Article 40 of the Treaty, to compensation for the injury resulting therefrom.[96]

[95] *Ibid.*   [96] *Ibid.* Vol. II.

The third *faute de service* was occasioned by the Common Assembly failing to comply with its own internal regulations.

> A *faute* here arises from the fact that the Assembly sought neither the consent nor the opinion of the Commission of Presidents, although this obligation was imposed on it both by Article 43 of its Rules and by Article 2, paragraph 4, of its internal Administrative Regulations. Moreover, this duty was set out in Article 62 of the Statute of Service in the text adopted on December 12, 1955. The Court, therefore, holds that the defendant's evasive conduct towards the plaintiffs also constitutes a *faute de service*.[97]

In a case decided in 1961 [98] the Court found the existence of *faute de service* of the High Authority. In 1954, the High Authority had set up a financial arrangement to subsidise the high cost of imported scrap and the cost of shipbreaking scrap.[99] The control of this subsidy system was given over by the High Authority to an *Office commun des consommateurs de ferraille* (O.C.C.F.) set up in Brussels. Certain enterprises within the Community, however, found that the cost to themselves of shipbreaking scrap was very high because this cost included the often very heavy charges for transporting this scrap over distances far greater than that from the nearest port, which alone would have been incurred if scrap had been imported. To encourage the use of shipbreaking scrap rather than imported scrap, the O.C.C.F. gave various promises to enterprises that it would reimburse to them the excess transport charges which they had been led to incur by their purchase of shipbreaking scrap. During the years the O.C.C.F. paid out the equivalent of half a million dollars by way of such reimbursement.

In 1960, however, the High Authority, declaring that such rebates had always been alien to the subsidy system, refused to allow the payment of any further sum on the grounds that the O.C.C.F. had possessed no authority at any time to give such promises. Certain enterprises thereupon requested the High Authority, under Article 35, paragraph 1,[1] to take a Decision authorising further payments, and, upon its failure to do so, they challenged the implied Decision of refusal, and claimed compensation for their loss of such rebate.

Of the promises to pay money and of the consequent sums paid out the Court declared:

> Such promises were made only by reason of the fact that the High Authority failed to exercise sufficient control over the functioning of

---

[97] *Ibid.* Vol. II.
[98] *Société Fives Lille Cail and others* v. *The High Authority* (Joint Cases 19–60, 21–60, 2–61 and 3–61) [1962] C.M.L.R. 251.
[99] For full details of this system, see Vol. II.
[1] See p. 184, above.

the subsidy machinery, with the result that it did not take account of the existence of practices incompatible with its policy concerning equalising transport charges. . . .

In fact, the importance of the payments made to French enterprises, under the head of equalising transport charges ($349,021), to Italian enterprises ($160,000) and to Dutch enterprises ($13,000)—in all more than half a million dollars—were certainly of a nature to have attracted attention had the High Authority exercised sufficient supervision; the more so, because it had a permanent representative on the Governing Boards of the Brussels organisations. In any event, by the very fact of having authorised the subsidy system, whatever its form, the High Authority should have kept it under its control. . . .

The High Authority, by failing to prevent [the Brussels organisations] from continuing former practices, and more particularly in October 1958, from giving guarantees to the four applicants concerning the grant of transport rebates, was—whatever the reasons for its failure—grossly negligent in its duties of supervision, which normal diligence would have imposed upon it.[2]

Such gross negligence was held by the Court to amount to a *faute de service*, and had the plaintiffs been able to establish any damages flowing from that breach, the High Authority would have been required to pay them.

ACTS NOT AMOUNTING TO FAUTES DE SERVICE

In a later case, plaintiffs alleged that the High Authority had committed two *fautes de service,* but the Court rejected these allegations.[3] The facts were that in 1955, the High Authority had set up a fund out of which subsidies were paid to enterprises which had bought scrap iron from countries outside the Community, or had purchased scrap iron obtained as a result of naval demolition. In 1957, the Netherlands Ministry of Economic Affairs certified that 22,204 tons of iron was scrap iron from naval demolitions, and on the strength of these certificates the subsidy was duly paid. It was subsequently discovered that the certificates were fraudulent. The Court held that as the official in the Netherlands Ministry was not an employee of the High Authority, the faults of that official could not be attributed to the defendants.

It was alleged, however, that the failure to discover the fraud before money was paid out amounted to a *faute de service.* The Court held:

At first sight the fact that the frauds have continued for several years appears to point towards a defective and inadequate organisation.

This conclusion, however, is not justified in this case. In effect, by leaving to the competent national authority the task of issuing the necessary certificates the defendant has followed a path which seemed

[2] *Ibid.* [1962] C.M.L.R. at pp. 281–282.
[3] *Acciaieria Ferriera di Roma (F.E.R.A.M.)* v. *The High Authority* (Case 23–59), Vol. II.

the most appropriate and the most likely to offer the surest guarantees against all abuse. . . .

The issuing of the certificates was not committed to a lower branch of the administration but to a ministry. The Netherlands regulations provided a most careful procedure for verifying the origin of the scrap in question, a procedure which must precede the issuing of the certificates. It was unforeseeable that in applying this system frauds would be able to be committed.

In these circumstances the fact of having adopted this system could not be blamed upon the defendant and could not, in any case, be held to be a *faute de service*.[4]

THE NATURE OF A FAUTE DE SERVICE

From the above, it seems that the Court accepts that a failure on the part of an institution to comply with its own regulations amounts to a *faute de service*: so also does the performance of an act which " creates a situation which is false while having the appearance of being legal," and so does the provision of an organisation which is defective and inadequate. However, it is not required that it should provide an organisation which can never fail; it must be adequate to deal with what is foreseeable: it cannot be blamed for the unforeseeable, and the standard of foreseeability appears to be that of the reasonably prudent man.

The Court, however, has raised one point and given no answer to it, namely:

> Whether a *faute de service* within the meaning of Article 40 of the Treaty presupposes deceit, or at any rate culpable negligence, or whether any illegal intention—even if not wilful—on the part of an institution may bring an action within the scope of this notion.[5]

On this, it is suggested that the whole object of Article 40 is to provide a means by which an injured person can obtain compensation for what has occurred: Article 40 is in no sense a penal section imposing a punishment upon the Community. Once the injured party has been injured he requires to be compensated and it appears irrelevant therefore to consider whether the injury was wilful or not.

---

[4] *Ibid.* The High Authority, after the discovery of this fraud declared that it would improve its system for the future. The plaintiffs argued that this was an admission that the then existing system was defective and constituted a *faute de service*. This argument was rejected by the Court.

[5] *Algera and others* v. *The Common Assembly* (Joint Cases Nos. 7–56 and 3–57 to 7–57), Vol. II.

NON-COMMUNITY ENTERPRISES CAN APPEAL TO THE COURT

By Article 40 it is provided that the Court shall have jurisdiction " upon the request of the injured party." It might very well be assumed, therefore, that the entities here being referred to are enterprises and associations, as defined by the Treaty, the Member States and individuals, for there is nothing to make one think that there is anything out of the ordinary or revolutionary in the wording being used. The Court, however, in a fairly recent judgment has interpreted the words " upon the request of the injured party " in the broadest possible manner and has held [6] that it entitles enterprises outside the jurisdiction of the Community to appear before the Court.

The facts of that case were that the plaintiffs were a Belgian enterprise at Anvers who imported both solid and liquid fuel, including a large amount of American anthracite. This it then processed and sold mainly to purchasers in France. In 1958 the French *Association technique de l'importation charbonnière* refused a licence for the import into France of this anthracite from Belgium. The plaintiffs considered that this refusal obstructed the free flow of coal within the Community [7] and therefore had requested the High Authority on many occasions from 1953 onwards to remedy the situation. Because the High Authority refused to do anything, the plaintiffs in 1960 finally brought an action under Article 40, paragraph 1, claiming damages for the injury caused to them by their inability to sell in France.

The Court first of all held that the plaintiffs, by not themselves being producers of coal, were not an enterprise within the meaning of the Treaty.[8] The Court continued:

> Because . . . the plaintiffs do not possess the status of an enterprise under Article 80 of the Treaty, it is necessary to examine whether it has the capacity to bring an appeal for damages under Article 40, paragraph 1.
>
> Article 40 does not contain the limits specified by Articles 33 and 35 concerning the status of plaintiffs.

---

[6] *Société commerciale Antoine Vloebergs S.A.* v. *The High Authority* (Joint Cases 9 and 12–60).

[7] Art. 4 provides:
" The following practices are hereby abolished and prohibited within the Community . . .:
(a) . . . quantitative restrictions upon the movement of products. . . ."

[8] Art. 80 provides:
" The term ' enterprise ' shall, for the purposes of the present Treaty, mean any enterprise engaged in production in the field of coal and steel within the territories mentioned in the first paragraph of Article 79 [the European territories of the High Contracting Parties]."

By reason of the distinction between actions challenging legality and actions concerning liability,[9] this difference of text must be considered in itself as a factor sufficient to exclude any desire on the part of the authors of the Treaty to fix, in respect of the bringing of actions concerning liability, limits similar to those which they had laid down for actions challenging liability.[10]

The Court then declared that this literal interpretation was confirmed by certain considerations.

The request for an annulment permits a direct control over the activities of the High Authority, leading, if necessary, to the annulment of illegal acts; whereas the request for damages can only lead to the High Authority being condemned to make amends for the injury caused by its conduct.

The request for annulment relates very much more to the field of the activities of the High Authority, whereas the request for damages relates only to the consequences of that action.[11]

Finally, the Court held that in respect of an action for damages:

There is no reason which can justify the withholding of all legal protection from natural or legal persons who are not subject to the jurisdiction of the Community, because when an injury has been caused by a *faute de service* committed in the execution of the Treaty, this is a matter reserved to the exclusive jurisdiction of the Court, whereas any legal or natural person, by applying to the competent municipal court can obtain redress for injuries caused by the Community institutions where these are outside the application of the Treaty (Article 40, paragraph 3).[12]

It should be noted that this judgment is limited to the case where the claim for damages arises out of the effects suffered by an enterprise as a result of inaction by the High Authority. The case thus does not put into issue the legality of that inaction or enable an enterprise which is not within the jurisdiction of the Community to challenge the validity of a Decision, an implied Decision, of the High Authority. If, therefore, the grounds of the action brought by an enterprise outside the jurisdiction of the Community had been that the very passing of the Decision itself

---

[9] The Court had previously defined this distinction in the following manner:
" As far as its object is concerned, the action for damages is seeking not the abolition of a particular measure but only compensation for an injury caused by an act or by a failure to take action constituting a *faute de service*.
" As for the grounds of appeal, which can be relied upon in support of an action for damages, only the existence of a *faute de service* can lead to the High Authority being condemned, whereas in the appeal for an annulment, the four grounds provided in Art. 33 can be alleged.
" Art. 40 is, therefore, conferring on the Court a jurisdiction which is entirely different from that which it exercises in actions concerning legality "—*Ibid.* Vol. II.
[10] *Ibid.* Vol. II.   [11] *Ibid.* Vol. II.
[12] *Ibid.* Vol. II. Art. 40, para. 3, provides:
" All other legal actions arising between the Community and third parties, outside the application of the present Treaty and of its rules of application, shall be brought before national tribunals "—see p. 233, below.

had constituted a *faute de service* [13] and that as a result of this *faute* the enterprise had been injured, the claim for damages would not have been distinct from a claim concerning the legality of the act in question, so that the Court's reasoning in the above judgment would scarcely have applied.

However, the judgment itself relates to the case of an enterprise claiming damages as a result of inaction by the High Authority. It would appear *a fortiori* to cover the case of action of that Authority and it is suggested that no distinction can be drawn between an enterprise which is not within the jurisdiction of the Community but situated in one of the Member States, as were the plaintiffs, and an enterprise situated outside the Community altogether. Further, the Court readily accepted, that " the injured party " mentioned in Article 40, paragraph 1, referred to natural or legal persons, so that it is submitted that under Article 40 not only can individuals, who are not in the employ of the E.C.S.C., appeal to the Court, but in the perhaps unlikely case of injury affecting them or their property, non-Member States could appeal as well.[14]

THE AWARD OF DAMAGES

In the *Kergall* case [15] the failure to renew the plaintiff's contract of service was held to amount to a *faute de service*. As compensation, he was awarded a sum equal to sixteen months' salary. The Court was not very specific about the manner in which this figure was calculated [16] but the factors taken into consideration were: the substantive difficulties with which the plaintiff was faced, as the head of a numerous family, after he had left the services of the Common Assembly; the expenses which he was forced to incur in seeking a new situation; the irregularity of the Common Assembly's Decision and " the facts of this particular case." [17]

In the later case of *Dineke Algera and others,* the Court considered the question of damages in greater detail. Damages were assessed under two heads, special damages and general damages.[18] When

---

[13] In *Algera and others* v. *The Common Assembly* (Joint Cases 7–56 and 3 to 7–57), the Decision contained in a letter of December 12, 1955, was held to constitute a *faute de service*, see p. 220, above.

[14] This might well cover the case of injury to the nationalised coal undertakings of non-Member States exporting coal to the Community.

[15] *Kergall* v. *The Common Assembly* (Case 1–55), Vol. II.

[16] There is an error in the Court's arithmetic when it made one year plus two months, plus four months come to sixteen months.

[17] The Court here was mainly awarding damages for breach of contract; the fact that that breach also amounted to a *faute de service* was only one aspect of the case.

[18] *Préjudice material* and *préjudice moral.* The latter term is perhaps best translated as " *salutium.*"

considering special damages the Court was careful to distinguish between the regrading of the plaintiffs by which their salaries were reduced, and the withdrawal of the plaintiffs' admission to the *Statut de Personnel*. The Court held that the Common Assembly could at any time regrade its employees, whereas the withdrawal of admission to the *Statut* constituted a *faute de service*.

Of special damages the Court stated:

> The illegal revocation of their admission to the *Statut* and their being wrongfully placed back under the temporary contract, which revocation has been annulled by the present Decision, has not caused any financial loss to the plaintiffs.
>
> The revocation of their classification deprives them of their right to the higher salary which was provided by the revoked Decisions. However, this fact is not the result of the *fautes de service* because the revocation of their classification is legal. Consequently their being deprived of it does not give rise to damages.[19]

Under general damages the matters considered by the Court appear from the following extract of the judgment:

> The defendant's wrongful attitude, namely the illegal withdrawal of the admission of the plaintiffs to the *Statut* and the fact of the precipitate delivery of the Decisions of December 12, 1955, which ought to lead to their partial subsequent withdrawal, has, however, caused moral damage to the plaintiffs.
>
> The plaintiffs, placed in the position to which their professional skill put them, and which presented to them every prospect of stability and of permanence, have found themselves, without fault on their part, before the prospect of a dismissal which would mean the end of a career on which they could legitimately have counted.
>
> The emotional stress caused by this attitude, the trouble and difficulties which resulted from it for the parties concerned, have thus caused the plaintiffs moral damage for which they require compensation.
>
> On the other hand, the Court holds that the lowering of their grading did not constitute any moral damage and should not have brought about any loss of social prestige for the plaintiffs.
>
> As to the amount which is to be awarded under the head of moral wrong, one must not lose sight of the fact that the Common Assembly's gesture in granting them, until the judgment of the Court, the material benefits of the Decisions of December 12, 1955, has only been the result of this legal action and could not remove fears concerning the future.
>
> In view of these considerations, the Court assesses the damages for each of the plaintiffs at 100 E.P.U. units of accounting.[20]

---

[19] *Algera and others* v. *The Common Assembly* (Joint Cases 7-56 and 3-57 to 7-57), Vol. II. Under this heading of special damages the Court was prepared to award a sum to cover losses resulting from offers of employment which the plaintiffs had refused because of their confidence in the promises of the Common Assembly. At the trial, however, no proof of the existence of these offers was furnished so that no sums were awarded.

[20] *Ibid.* Vol. II. 100 E.P.U. equals U.S. $100.

"SUBJECT TO THE PROVISIONS OF ARTICLE 34, PARAGRAPH 1"

The jurisdiction of the Court to grant compensation to an injured party who has suffered injury as a result of a *faute de service* of any of the institutions of the Community is expressly made " subject to the provisions of Article 34, paragraph 1." That paragraph, it will be recalled,[21] requires the High Authority to take measures adequate to ensure an equitable reparation and just compensation in respect of damage resulting directly from a Decision or Recommendation which the Court has annulled and has declared to involve " a fault of a nature to involve the responsibility of the Community."

It will be noted that that paragraph does not expressly use the term *faute de service.* The question arises, therefore, whether the phrase " a fault of a nature to involve the responsibility of the Community " is intended to mean the same thing. If it is not, it follows that the Treaty is referring to the two types of faults—those faults involving the responsibility of the Community, which are regulated by Article 34, and *fautes de service,* which, of course, also involve the responsibility of the Community, and which are regulated by Article 40. Absurd questions then arise as to whether a particular wrong is a fault or a *faute de service* or both.

If, therefore, the alternative is accepted that Article 34 is also a provision referring to *fautes de service,* as it is suggested it should be, the position is reached that where a Decision or Recommendation of the High Authority has been appealed against and the Court recognises that the Decision or Recommendation involves a *faute de service* and it annuls that Decision or Recommendation, damages must be granted by the High Authority to any enterprise or group of enterprises which has suffered a direct and special injury caused by that Decision or Recommendation.

Article 40, paragraph 1 is made " subject to the provisions of Article 34, paragraph 1." The effect of this, the Court has declared, is that

> These words prevent any possibility of reference to Article 34 and on the contrary relate to cases where Article 34 is not applicable.[22]

It appears clear from the whole tenor of the judgment of the Court, quoted above,[23] that the Court is seeing Article 34 as relating to the case where the wrongful passing of a Decision itself is the wrong giving

---

[21] For a discussion of the terms of Art. 34, para. 1, see p. 176, above.
[22] *Société commerciale Antoine Vloebergs S.A.* v. *The High Authority* (Joint Cases 9 and 12–60).
[23] See pp. 224–225, above.

rise to damages, which matter involves the prior question whether that Decision has been wrongly passed, whereas under Article 40 the only question is that of injury, regardless of whether the Decision occasioning that injury had been correctly or wrongly passed. Under Article 40, therefore, no reference to the validity of the Decision in question can be made, so that there is no difficulty arising out of the fact that the challenge of the Decision must be brought within one month,[24] whereas a claim for damages can be brought any time within five years of the injury.[25]

Further, Article 34 only requires the High Authority to compensate enterprises or groups of enterprises. If associations of enterprises or even States, who are appealing under Article 33 against a Decision or Recommendation, wish to claim compensation for an alleged *faute de service* they, unlike enterprises and groups of enterprises, must appeal under Article 40.

The effect, therefore, of these opening words of Article 40 which make this article " Subject to the provisions of Article 34, paragraph 1 " appears to be that if enterprises are appealing against a Decision or Recommendation of the High Authority [26] no separate claim need be lodged under Article 40 if compensation for injury caused by a *faute de service* is desired either by the plaintiff enterprise or by the group of which it is a member. If the appeal, however, is being brought by an association,[27] or by a Member State or by the Council, a separate claim must be lodged under Article 40 if compensation for injury caused by a *faute de service* is desired by the plaintiffs.[28] However, if at any time after the one-month period during which appeals can be brought under Article 33, plaintiffs seek compensation for injury resulting from *fautes de service,* they must proceed under Article 40.

[24] Art. 33, para. 3, see p. 171, above.
[25] E.C.S.C. Statute, Art. 40, provides:
    " Proceedings referred to in the first two paragraphs of Art. 40 of the [E.C.S.C.] Treaty shall be time barred after five years calculated from the occurrence of the act which gives rise to them."
[26] Groups of enterprises have no right of appeal as distinct from the right of each enterprise of that group. Groups of enterprises are not referred to as such in any other article of the Treaty.
[27] Including an association of which the above plaintiff enterprise is a member.
[28] It is not clear whether when an association appeals and does not claim under Art. 40, the High Authority is required under Art. 34 to compensate the enterprises constituting that association, as distinct from compensating the association itself. It appears that the wording of Art. 34 is wide enough to require this, as there is nothing to suggest that the compensated enterprise must be the plaintiff—the compensated group of enterprises can never, as such, be the plaintiffs—see note 26, above.

TIME FOR BRINGING APPEALS

It is expressly provided that the appeals allowed by Article 40 became time-barred five years from the occurrence of the acts which give rise to them.[29] The provision then continues:

> The running of time shall be interrupted either by the request brought before the Court, or by the preliminary demand which the injured party may send to the appropriate institution of the Community. In this latter case, the request must be brought within the period of one month provided for in the last paragraph of Article 33; the provisions of the last paragraph of Article 35 shall apply where appropriate.

This paragraph is extremely difficult to understand. Requests to the Court must be brought within five years, but nevertheless the running of these five years is " interrupted " by the bringing of the actual request and not merely suspended. This introduces a concept unknown in English law, namely that the bringing of the actual request wipes out all the years that time has run from the injury, so that, if the Court, without adjudicating on the merits, were to reject the request, the injured party would still possess five years from the date of that rejection in which to bring his second request.

The paragraph also refers to a " preliminary demand " to the institution concerned. It is clear that this demand is not a necessary preliminary to appealing to the Court, but in practice to make such a demand would be the obvious and cheapest thing to do. If such a demand is made, the institution, by means of an individual Decision, can either grant full compensation, so that the matter is at an end, or grant inadequate compensation, or expressly disclaim liability and refuse compensation. The institution could also fail to take any Decision at all.

It is declared that following this preliminary demand, the request to the Court must be brought within one month. The question arises, therefore, of whether in that request the injured party is challenging the Decision of the institution which grants him inadequate compensation or no compensation. The reference to the last paragraph of Article 33 might lead one to assume that this was so. However, there are two major objections to this view. First, if this were so, the injured party would be limited to alleging the grounds of appeal set out in Article 33,[30] whereas if he had appealed to the Court direct under Article 40, he would not have been so limited. Secondly, if the injury has been caused by the Council of Ministers or by the Assembly, the injured party in this appeal can only allege incompetence or a violation of a substantial procedural

---

[29] E.C.S.C. Statute, Art. 40.
[30] See p. 112, above.

requirement.[31] In other words, the legal rights of the injured party against the Community will vary according to which institution has wronged him.[32] It is suggested, therefore, that the injured party is not challenging the Decision of the institution, but is referring the matter to the Court so as to give it the same powers as if the request had been brought without a preliminary demand being made to the institution.

If the institution fails to take any Decision then " the provisions of the last paragraph of Article 35 shall apply." By these provisions,[33] the two months' silence of the High Authority is turned into an implied Decision refusing to take action and against this implied Decision an appeal can be brought before the Court. It must be assumed that it is intended that a two months' silence on the part of the Council of Ministers, the Assembly, or the Court itself, is also being turned into an implied Decision of refusal to grant compensation, although this is certainly not what the Treaty says. Further, it will be noted that Article 40 of the Statute does not merely refer to the time limit of one month which is contained in Article 35, paragraph 3, but refers to " the provisions " of that paragraph. It appears, therefore, that the request to the Court is indeed intended to be against the implied Decision of refusal, but, as set out above in relation to express Decisions, this would cause hardship in comparison with a party who had appealed to the Court direct.

It is by no means clear, if a party does make this preliminary demand to the institution, whether its right to appeal to the Court within five years continues, or whether its right of appeal becomes confined to the right to appeal merely during the prescribed month. It is suggested, however, that if the reference to an appeal within one month is to have any meaning, it must mean that outside that one month no appeal can be brought. This can only mean that the alternative right of appeal is lost.[34]

It would seem, therefore, highly undesirable to make this preliminary demand, and reduce a five-year time period to a period of one month. To avoid this result, it is submitted that in practice it will be far more desirable to commence a legal action before the institution concerned is approached. After an action has been commenced, there appears nothing to prevent the parties trying to compromise that action by

---

31 Art. 38, para. 3.

32 Further, if it is the Court which has wronged the injured party, it should be noted that there are no grounds expressly stated on which an administrative Decision of the Court can be challenged. For an action brought against the Court, see *Gabriel Simon* v. *The Court of Justice of the European Community* (Case 15–60).

33 See p. 185, above.

34 The alternative view is that the appeal to the Court against the express or implied Decision of the institution must be brought within one month and that thereafter and presumably even during that month, an appeal to the Court remains open for the full five years.

negotiations. If the institution offers inadequate compensation or none at all, the obligation to appeal within one month of that Decision, express or implied, can now freely be ignored and the pending action prosecuted.

DAMAGES AGAINST AN EMPLOYEE OF THE COMMUNITY

Under paragraph 2 of Article 40 the Court is given jurisdiction to award damages against an employee of the Community in the event of injury caused by a *faute personnelle* of this employee in the performance of his duties.[35] In the normal way, if an employee is accused of such a *faute* he will not be able to be sued in any of the national courts of the Member States because the employee will be covered by immunity.[36] Redress, therefore, will only be obtainable in the Communities' Court, unless this immunity is waived in a particular case by the President of the High Authority.[37] If, however, this Court finds that the *fautes* complained of were not done by the employee in the performance of his duties, it will have no jurisdiction. The plaintiff's only right, therefore will be to sue under municipal law.[38]

EQUITABLE COMPENSATION AGAINST THE COMMUNITY

If the Community Court has awarded damages against an employee and these damages, presumably either in whole or in part, are not recovered from that employee, the Court " may award equitable compensation against the Community."

What exactly is the intention of this provision is not stated. It may be that the Community is only intended to be a guarantor playing a part only in a case where the employee is unable to pay. An inability of the employee to pay, however, is not referred to in the provision: all that is mentioned is his failure to pay. The Community could, if it so

---

35 It would appear that in any action against an institution alleging a *faute de service*, the relevant employee, if known, should be joined in case the *faute* is declared to be a *faute personnelle*.

36 " On the territory of each of the Member States and whatever be their nationality, the members of the High Authority and the employees of the Community, (a) subject to the provisions of Art. 40, para. 2 of the Treaty, enjoy immunity from jurisdiction for acts including any oral or written statements, performed or made by them in their official capacity "—E.C.S.C. Protocol on Immunities, Art. 11.

37 Under above Protocol on Immunities—Art. 13, para. 2.

38 Art. 11 (a) of the Protocol on Immunities only covers acts done by an employee of the Community in his official capacity. It is suggested that this has the same meaning as " in the exercise of his functions " in Art. 40 of the Treaty. In respect of an act performed outside those functions an employee is thus not covered by immunity.

wished, therefore, step in and in effect accept vicarious liability.[39] However, it is suggested that the latter, although possible, is not the intended solution. The whole distinction between *fautes de service* and *fautes personnelles* is that for the latter the individual alone is responsible.[40] Further, the discretion whether to require the Community to make compensation is left to the Court, and the Community is not necessarily to be required to pay the whole of the sum unpaid by the employee.[41]

This power of the Court, however, is applicable only in the case where an employee has been originally required to pay damages by the Communities' Court itself; it does not exist in the case where immunity of that employee has been lifted and he has been required by a municipal court to pay damages and he has likewise failed to pay them.

ARTICLE 40, Para. 3

All other legal actions arising between the Community and third parties, outside the application of the clauses of the present Treaty and of its rules of application, shall be brought before national tribunals.[42]

The Coal and Steel Community in each of the Member States is granted by the Treaty the most extensive legal capacity which is afforded to legal persons of those States. The Community is expressly given the right to appear in Court.[43]

---

[39] The practice of an organisation, particularly the Crown, standing behind a defendant is well known in English law.

[40] The Community is to pay " equitable compensation ": the employee is to pay damages. It may be argued that compensation would never be equitable unless it amounts to the whole of the sum unpaid, but the concept of equitability must take into account the innocent enterprises who in fact are the ones providing the compensation money.

[41] The power of the Court to charge the Community is expressly limited by Art. 40, para. 2, to the case where the injured party has failed to obtain " these damages "— the word " these " refers to damages awarded by the Court itself.

[42] French:
"*Tous autres litiges nés entre la Communauté et les tiers, en dehors de l'application des clauses du présent Traité et des règlements d'application, sont portés devant les tribunaux nationaux.*"
Stationery Office:
" Any litigation arising between the Community and third parties, not arising out of the present Treaty and the Regulations for giving effect to it, shall be brought before the national courts."

[43] Art. 6, paras. 1 and 3, provides:
" The Community shall have legal personality. In each of the Member States, the Community shall enjoy the most extensive legal capacity granted to legal persons in that country and in particular may acquire and transfer immoveable and moveable property, and may sue and be sued in its own name."

It may be noted that in any particular action brought before a national court, it will be for that court itself, in order to determine its own jurisdiction, to decide whether the subject-matter of the action falls within or outside the application of the Treaty and to that extent it may itself, therefore, have to interpret that Treaty. If one of the parties disputes the Court's finding, an appeal lies only to a superior national court—there is no means by which the matter can be referred to the Community Court.[44]

ARTICLE 41

The Court shall have sole jurisdiction to judge as a preliminary issue upon the validity of the *délibérations* of the High Authority and of the Council in a case where an action before a national tribunal brings this validity into issue.[45]

Under the old Rules of the Court it was not made clear who was to make the submission to the Court for a ruling upon the *délibérations* of the High Authority or the Council, or what right these bodies had of presenting their views to the Court.[46]

The present Rules of the Court have been made more specific. These declare [47] that the reference to the Court is to be notified to the parties to the action, to the Member States, to the High Authority and to the Special Council of Ministers. It appears from this, therefore, that the reference is being made by the national tribunal itself, and it will naturally be for the rules of that tribunal to determine whether the reference can be made by the tribunal of its own motion, or solely at the request of one of the litigants.

The Rules further state [48] that within a period of two months from this notification all those mentioned above have the right to present

[44] By Art. 41 the Court is given jurisdiction to determine the validity of the *délibérations* of the High Authority and the Council of Ministers where their validity is challenged in a national tribunal—see immediately below; there is no provision in the E.C.S.C. Treaty by which the interpretation of the Treaty *per se* can be referred to the Court. Cf. E.E.C. Treaty, Art. 177, para. 1 (a) and Euratom Treaty, Art. 150, para. 1 (a).

[45] French:
   "*La Cour est seul compétente pour statuer, à titre préjudiciel, sur la validité des délibérations de la Haute Autorité et du Conseil, dans le cas où un litige porté devant un tribunal national mettrait en cause cette validité.*"
   Stationery Office:
   " The Court shall have sole jurisdiction to give preliminary rulings on the validity of resolutions of the High Authority and of the Council, where such validity is challenged in a suit brought before a national court."

[46] Art. 79 of the old Rules, after setting out the power of the Court to hear these, merely stated: " The provisions of the Statute and of the present Rules are applicable to the references to the Court. The Request must contain a precise statement of the subject of the litigation in question."

[47] Art. 103, para. 2.

[48] *Ibid.*

their written observations, after which, or after the two months, the Court continues as if there were an ordinary case before it and the pleadings had just been closed. However, even despite this slight elucidation, the legal position created by this Article is far from clear.

First, it must be noted that this Article granting a right of reference to the Court does not set out what are the grounds upon which that reference may be brought. It would appear, however, that the grounds, as far as the Decisions and Recommendations of the High Authority are concerned, must be those set out in Article 33, because it would be undesirable if a Decision of that Authority could be held void on an appeal under Article 41 when on the same grounds it could not be so held void by a direct appeal under Article 33.[49] If this is so, it is consistent that the reference concerning the *délibérations* of the Council should be limited to the two grounds of incompetence and violation of a substantial procedural requirement allowed by Article 38.

TIME FOR BRINGING THE REFERENCE

The second problem raised by Article 41 concerns the time within which this reference to the Court is required to be brought. Decisions and Recommendations of the High Authority and *délibérations* of the Council can only be annulled by the Court in a direct appeal to its jurisdiction within a period of one month of their publication or notification.[50]

It might be argued, therefore, that the reference to the Court under Article 41 must also be made within one month, because if the reference can be made after that one month, Decisions can be declared void by the Court by this " back door " method when they no longer are open to challenge under Article 33 or Article 38. Such a right tends to make nonsense of the stated time period, which the Court has expressly regarded as a vital provision.[51]

On the other hand, if this reference is to be made only during the period of one month, this provision will, in practice, be of very little value, because few cases are likely to have been started within that month and almost certainly they will not be sufficiently advanced for a reference by the tribunal to be made to the Community Court. Further, because the Rules of the Court allow a period of two months for a State to submit its written observations to the Court, in any

---

[49] Similarly it appears that the limitation upon the Court's power to examine the economic facts and circumstances in the light of which the Decision was taken which is included in Art. 33, must also be read into Art. 41.

[50] Art. 33, para. 3, and Art. 38, para. 3, see pp. 171 and 207, above.

[51] *German Government* v. *The High Authority* (Case 3–59), Vol. II, and see p. 171, above.

event a State has been given a right to allege the invalidity of a Decision of the High Authority after the period for such an allegation under Article 33 has expired.

It is suggested, therefore, that the right of reference granted by Article 41 is without limitation of time.

If this is accepted, the consequent legal implication has to be considered.

THE EFFECT OF A FINDING BY THE COURT

The basic matter to determine is what is the effect of a finding of the Court that, for example, a Decision of the High Authority has been passed in violation of the Treaty. It is arguable that this finding is only binding between the parties in the action before the national tribunal, and, presumably upon any other parties in matters arising out of the Decision in question in whichever one of the Member States they may be. It is not necessary to hold that the finding of the Court has any other effect. If this is so, then the High Authority, when appearing as a party before a national tribunal, will have to admit that the Decision is void, whereas when appearing before the Community Court it can rely upon the fact that the Decision stands and cannot be annulled.

If this position is regarded as being, at the very least, undesirable, the alternative must be faced, namely, that the finding of the Court on the preliminary issues has declared the Decision void for all purposes so that it cannot be relied upon by the High Authority when appearing before the Community Court itself.

If this alternative is accepted, the question arises of whether the High Authority is under an obligation to " take the measures which comprise the execution of the decision of annulment," as it would have to be if the annulment had been declared by the Court under Article 33.[52] Although it is submitted that this is in practice what would probably occur, nevertheless it is important to determine whether the High Authority is acting voluntarily or under the provisions of the Treaty. If it is acting voluntarily no redress for failure so to act is available. If the High Authority is carrying out a Treaty obligation, then upon its failure to do so a means of redress is contained in Article 35 and under that Article the Court can annul the High Authority's implied Decision of refusing to act.

It is suggested that an interpretation which holds that a Decision which has been declared void is void for all purposes is better than one which holds that such a Decision is only void in certain courts and for

---

[52] Art. 34, see p. 176, above.

certain occasions. Further, if a Decision has been held to be void, there appears, in principle, no reason why one should suggest that the procedure for dealing with just that situation should not apply.

It is suggested, therefore, that Decisions and Recommendations of the High Authority and *délibérations* of the Council can be declared void by the Court under Article 41 at any time and that if the High Authority's acts are declared void, that Authority is required by the Treaty to take measures to carry out the decision of annulment.

ARTICLE 42

The Court shall have jurisdiction to give a decision by virtue of a clause conferring jurisdiction contained in a contract in public or in private law entered into by the Community or on its behalf.[53]

The various institutions of the Coal and Steel Community have each drawn up conditions of contract for their employees, and in all of them there has been included a clause giving jurisdiction to the Court to settle any disputes. Under these clauses a relatively large number of actions have already been brought.[54]

TIME FOR BRINGING AN ACTION

One of the first questions which had to be decided by the Court was the time period during which an appeal could be brought under this Article.

When Decisions of the High Authority or of the Council of Ministers or of the Assembly are being challenged in Court, the Treaty expressly provides that the appeal must be lodged within one month of the publication or notification of the act in question.[55] It was natural, therefore, that it should be contended that appeals, which under Article 42 will also be against these same institutions, should be brought within one month, which here, naturally, would mean within one month of the alleged breach of contract.

[53] French:
  "*La Cour est compétente pour statuer en vertu d'une clause compromissoire contenue dans un contrat de droit public ou de droit privé passé par la Communauté ou pour son compte.*"
  Stationery Office:
  " The Court shall be competent to make a decision pursuant to any arbitration clause contained in a contract concluded under public or private law by or on behalf of the Community."
[54] See *Kergall* v. *The Common Assembly* (Case 1–55), Vol. II; *Mirossevich* v. *The High Authority* (Case 10–55), Vol. II; *Bourgaux* v. *The Common Assembly* (Case 1–56), Vol. II; *Algera and others* v. *The Common Assembly* (Joint Cases 7–56 and 3–57 to 7–57), Vol. II, etc.
[55] Art. 33, para. 3, and Art. 38, para. 2, see pp. 171 and 207, above.

The Court, however, has rejected this contention, and refused to apply the provisions of Article 33 by way of analogy. More than that, it was stated:

> The defendants contest the admissibility of this appeal on the grounds of the delay in bringing it. . . .
>
> The Court holds that this cannot be taken into consideration since there is no text applicable to this situation which specifies a time limit for making an appeal within the administrative structure or for bringing an appeal to the Court.[56]

THE GROUNDS OF APPEAL

By the Treaty it is provided that a Decision of the High Authority may be challenged on any one and more of four grounds.[57] The *délibérations* of the Assembly or of the Council, however, by Article 38 of the Treaty, can only be challenged for incompetence or for violation of a substantial procedural requirement. It was contested in one case, because of the terms of Article 38, therefore, that when an individual under an arbitration clause is challenging a Decision of the Common Assembly, he is also limited to alleging merely the two grounds of incompetence and violation of a substantial procedural requirement.[58]

The Court, however, rejected this contention and declared:

> The general nature of the terms of Article 42 does not allow one to impose upon an agreement to give jurisdiction to the Court any such legal limitation which, in the present case, would exclude the right to seek annulment.
>
> Appeals in administrative matters, common to the personnel of the four institutions, are entirely distinct from that legal procedure which, by Article 38 of the Treaty, is a restraint regulating the activity of the Assembly as an institution.[59]

It can be observed that in practice the Court, having declared that the restrictions of Article 38 do not apply, has allowed individuals to challenge Decisions affecting them passed by the various institutions, on any of the four standard grounds of appeal.[60]

---

[56] *Algera and others* v. *The Common Assembly* (Joint Cases 7–56 and 3–57 to 7–57), Vol. II.

[57] Incompetence, violation of a substantial procedural requirement, violation of the Treaty or *détournement de pouvoir*—Art. 33, para. 1, see p. 112, above.

[58] *Bourgaux* v. *The Common Assembly* (Case 1–56), Vol. II.

[59] *Ibid.* Vol. II. Another reason why Art. 38 would not apply is that if it did so, the employees of the Assembly and of the Council would be placed at a permanent disadvantage as compared with the employees of the High Authority who by the same reasoning could appeal under the terms of Art. 33, para. 1. This reason was not given by the Court.

[60] See, for example, *Algera and others* v. *The Common Assembly* (Joint Cases 7–56 and 3–57 to 7–57), Vol. II. It is interesting that although the two grounds of appeal allowed by Art. 38 of the Treaty are regarded by the Court as a "limitation," the grounds of appeal allowed by Art. 33 are not regarded as a limitation at all.

ARTICLE 43

The Court shall be competent to exercise jurisdiction in any other case mentioned in an additional provision of the present Treaty.

It can also exercise jurisdiction in any case relating to the object of the present Treaty where the legislation of a Member State grants such jurisdiction to it.[61]

The term " the present Treaty " has been defined [62] as meaning not only the provisions of the Treaty itself, but also those of the three annexes, the various Protocols and the Convention containing the Transitional Provisions. Under these, additional jurisdiction is granted to the Court.[63] It is suggested that nothing is gained by the insertion of this paragraph.

None of the Member States has yet passed legislation granting jurisdiction to the Court so that no matters have arisen for discussion.

ARTICLE 47, Para. 4

Any violation by the High Authority of a professional secret which causes injury to an enterprise may be made the subject of an action for damages before the Court, under the conditions prescribed in Article 40.[64]

Under the terms of Article 47, the High Authority is empowered to receive the information necessary for the carrying out of its duty.[65] It is,

---

[61] French:
> " La Cour est compétente pour statuer dans tout autre cas prévu par une dispositions additionnale du présent Traité.
> " Elle peut également statuer dans tous les cas en connexité avec l'objet du présent Traité où la législation d'un Etat membre lui attribue compétence."
Stationery Office:
> " The Court shall be competent to decide in any other case provided for by a supplementary provision of the present Treaty.
> " It may also decide in all cases relating to the purposes of the present Treaty where jurisdiction is conferred upon it by the law of a Member State."

[62] Art. 84.

[63] The provisions granting jurisdiction are: E.C.S.C. Treaty, Art. 47, para. 4; Art. 63, para. 2.2; Art. 65, para. 4.2; Art. 66, para. 5.2; Art. 88, paras. 2 and 4; Art. 89, para. 1; Art. 92, para. 3; Art. 95, para. 4; Protocol on Privileges and Immunities, Art. 1 and Art. 16. These provisions are all analysed below.

[64] French:
> " Toute violation par la Haute Autorité du secret professionnel ayant causé un dommage à une entreprise pourra faire l'objet d'une action en indemnité devant la Cour, dans les conditions prévues à l'article 40."
Stationery Office:
> " Any violation by the High Authority of trade secrecy which has caused damage to an undertaking may be the subject of a suit for damages before the Court under the conditions provided for in Article 40."

[65] Art. 47, para. 1.

239

however, expressly required not to divulge information which by its nature is covered by professional secrecy and in particular information relating to enterprises and concerning their commercial relations or the breakdown of their selling prices.[66] The above paragraph provides the remedy for any breach of this duty.

If a leakage of information occurred as a result of deficient security arrangements on the part of the High Authority, such leakage would amount to a *faute de service* and the action would lie against the High Authority.[67] If, however, the leakage were a deliberate wrong done by one of the employees of the High Authority, that Authority would be exempt from liability and the wrong would be actionable only against the employee.[68] If no satisfaction is obtained from that employee the Court can impose equitable damages, to be paid by the Community as a whole.[69]

ARTICLE 63, Section 2

To the extent to which it deems it necessary, the High Authority may decide that :—

(a) enterprises are to draw up their conditions of sale in such a manner that their purchasers and their agents are required to comply with the rules decided upon by the High Authority in application of the provisions of the present chapter;

(b) enterprises shall be held responsible for breaches of the obligations thus imposed committed by their direct agents or their dealers trading on behalf of these enterprises.

In the case of a breach committed by a purchaser of one of the obligations thus imposed, the High Authority may limit, to an extent which may, in the case of further breaches, comprise a temporary prohibition, the right of enterprises of the Community to trade with such purchaser. In this case, and without prejudice to the provisions of Article 33, an appeal shall be open to the purchaser before the Court.[70]

---

[66] *Ibid.* para. 2.
[68] *Ibid.* para. 2.
[67] Art. 40, para. 1.
[69] *Ibid.* The wording of Art. 47, para. 4, is not entirely correct, for it speaks of the injured enterprise obtaining an " *indemnité* " from the High Authority. Under Art. 40, para. 1, what would be obtained is a " *réparation pécuniaire.*" An " *indemnité equitable* " is obtained only if the action is against an employee and no satisfaction is obtained from him—see Art. 40, para. 2.
[70] French :
" *Dans la mesure où elle l'estime nécessaire, la Haute Autorité peut décider que:*
(a) *les entreprises devront établir leurs conditions de vente de telle sorte que leurs acheteurs et leurs commissionnaires s'obligent à se conformer aux règles*

If an enterprise breaks any of the obligations imposed upon it by virtue of Decisions passed by the High Authority, that enterprise can be fined, on a first offence, an amount equal to double the value of the improper transactions, and four times that amount in the event of further offences.[71]

Where a purchaser from an enterprise breaks one of these obligations, the remedy given to the High Authority is to take action against the enterprise by limiting its power to trade with the purchaser in question. No action can be taken against the purchaser directly because such a purchaser is not within the jurisdiction of the Community. As the action taken against the enterprise will inevitably affect the purchaser, that purchaser, as a special concession, is here granted the right to appeal to the Court. As, however, this right is expressly declared to be " without prejudice to the provisions of Article 33," it follows that where the High Authority does limit an enterprise's right to trade, an appeal against that Decision can also be brought by the enterprise, or by a Member State, or the Council, on any of the four grounds set out in Article 33.[72]

A PURCHASER'S RIGHT OF APPEAL

Two doubts arise out of Article 63. The first concerns the time at which a purchaser's right of appeal accrues. Paragraph 2 of this section sets out two occasions when the High Authority may limit the right of an enterprise to trade with a purchaser. These are " in the case of a breach "

posées par la Haute Autorité en application des dispositions du présent chapitre;
(b) *les entreprises seront rendues responsables des infractions aux obligations ainsi contractées commises par leurs agents directs ou les commissionnaires traitant pour le compte desdites entreprises.*
Elle pourra, en cas d'infraction commise par un acheteur aux obligations ainsi contractées, limiter, dans une mesure qui pourra, en cas de récidive, comporter une interdiction temporaire, le droit des entreprises de la Communauté de traiter avec ledit acheteur. Dans ce cas, et sans préjudice des dispositions de l'article 33, un recours sera ouvert à l'acheteur devant la Cour."
Stationery Office:
" To the extent that it finds necessary, the High Authority may decide that:
(a) undertakings must establish their conditions of sale in such a way that their customers and agents shall undertake that they will comply with the rules established by the High Authority in accordance with the provisions of this Chapter;
(b) undertakings shall be made responsible for breaches of any obligations thus entered into which are committed by their direct agents or by merchants acting on behalf of such undertakings.
In case of a breach committed by a purchaser of the obligations thus entered into the High Authority may limit the right of undertakings within the Community to deal with the said purchaser to a degree which may in case of repetition temporarily deprive him of access to the market. In this case, and without prejudice to the provisions of Article 33, the purchaser has a right of appeal to the Court."
[71] Art. 64
[72] The prohibition upon the enterprise would clearly be an individual Decision.

and " in the case of further breaches." The provision then states that
" in this case " the purchaser may appeal to the Court. It is not clear,
therefore, to which of the two cases the words " in this case " are intended
to refer. It is suggested, however, that there is here no necessity to take
a restrictive interpretation of a purchaser's right of appeal, and that,
therefore, the words " in this case an appeal shall be open to the
purchaser " should be taken as referring to the first occasion upon which
there is a breach, and not merely to the case of further breaches.

The second doubt concerns the grounds of appeal which can be
alleged by the purchaser. The above provision merely states that an
appeal shall be open before the Court. It is suggested, however, that,
without express wording, it should not be assumed that the purchaser
is to be placed in a better position than, say, the enterprise which is
prohibited from trading with him. As that enterprise can itself appeal
only on the four grounds set out in Article 33, it appears logical that
the purchaser should also be limited to those four grounds.[73]

Similarly, it is suggested that the purchaser's action, like that of the
enterprise, must be brought within one month of the publication or
notification of the Decision in question.[74]

ARTICLE 65, Sections 1, 2 and 4

**1. All agreements between enterprises, all decisions of asso-
ciations of enterprises and all joint practices which tend,
directly or indirectly to prevent, restrict or distort the normal
interplay of competition within the Common Market are forbidden, and in particular those which tend :**

(a) to fix or determine prices;

**(b) to restrict or to control production, technical develop-
ment or investment;**

**(c) to allocate markets, products, clients, or sources of
supply.**

---

[73] In practice, a purchaser who finds that enterprises are restricted in their rights to
trade with him will wish to challenge the Decision on the grounds either that he has
not committed a breach of the conditions of sale, or that he has not committed more
than one breach. If he can establish this, the Decision of the High Authority would
be annulled on the grounds either of violation of the Treaty, or incompetence. A
purchaser might also wish to allege a *détournement de pouvoir* with respect to
himself.

[74] However, see *Algera and others* v. *The Common Assembly* (Joint Cases 7–56 and
3–57 to 7–57), Vol. II, quoted at p. 238, above, where the Court held that where no
time limit is specified in the Treaty no time limit for bringing an action exists.

2. However, in respect of specified products, the High Authority shall authorise agreements to specialise, or agreements for joint buying or selling, if it finds:

(a) that this specialisation or this joint buying and selling will contribute to a substantial improvement in the production or distribution of the products in question;

(b) that the agreement in question is essential to obtain these results without being of a more restrictive character than is required to achieve its object, and

(c) that it is not capable of giving the enterprises concerned the power to determine prices or to control or limit the production or supply within the Common Market of a substantial part of the products in question, or of protecting them from effective competition of other enterprises within the common Market. . . .

3. . . .

4. The agreements or decisions prohibited by virtue of paragraph 1 of the present Article shall be null and void and cannot be invoked before any court of the Member State.

The High Authority, subject to an appeal to the Court, shall have exclusive competence to pronounce upon the conformity of the said agreements and decisions with the provisions of the present Article.[75]

---

[75] French:

1. " *Sont interdits tous accords entre entreprises, toutes décisions d'associations d'entreprises et toutes pratiques concertées qui tendraient, sur le marché commun, directement ou indirectement, à empêcher, restreindre ou fausser le jeu normal de la concurrence et en particulier:*

(a) *à fixer ou déterminer les prix;*

(b) *à restreindre ou à contrôler la production, le développement technique ou les investissements;*

(c) *à répartir les marchés, produits, clients ou sources d'approvisionnement.*

2. *Toutefois, la Haute Autorité autorise, pour des produits déterminés, des accords de spécialisation ou des accords d'achat ou de vente en commun, si elle reconnaît:*

(a) *que cette spécialisation ou ces achats ou ces ventes en commun contribueront à une amélioration notable dans la production ou la distribution des produits visés;*

(b) *que l'accord en cause est essentiel pour obtenir ces effets sans qu'il soit d'un caractère plus restrictif que ne l'exige son objet, et*

(c) *qu'il n'est pas susceptible de donner aux entreprises intéressées le pouvoir de déterminer les prix, contrôler ou limiter la production ou les débouchés, d'une partie substantielle des produits en cause dans le marché commun, ni de les soustraire à une concurrence effective d'autres entreprises dans le marché commun. . . .*

4. *Les accords ou décisions interdits en vertu du paragraphe 1 du présent article sont nuls de plein droit et ne peuvent être invoqués devant aucune juridiction des Etats membres.*

La Haute Autorité a compétence exclusive, sous réserve des recours devant la

243

THE RIGHT OF APPEAL

The opening words of this Article state that it is concerned *inter alia* with "all agreements between enterprises" and "all decisions of associations." These enterprises and associations are then given the right to appeal to the Court against a ruling by the High Authority which finds that a particular agreement, decision or joint practice violates section 1, or that if it does so, it does not satisfy the conditions set out in section 2 in order that it may be authorised. Normally by Article 80 of the Treaty, the term "enterprise" means those enterprises which engage in an activity of production within the field of coal and steel. However, as an exception, in this Article the term enterprise includes also "enterprises or organisations which habitually carry on an activity of distribution other than sale to domestic consumers or to craft industries.[76] On this the Court had held:

> The terms of Article 80 specifying appeals brought as regards Articles 65 and 66 refer not merely to those based upon a direct application of Articles 65 and 66 to distributors, to groups or to concentrations, but refer also to a case where, as in the present action, an application of these articles affects the interests of distributors.[77]

The Court virtually repeated this in a later case.[78]

Cour, pour se prononcer sur la conformité avec les dispositions du présent article desdits accords ou decisions."
Stationery Office:
    " 1.   All agreements between undertakings; all decisions by associations of undertakings and all concerted practices tending, directly or indirectly, to prevent, restrict or distort the normal operation of competition within the Common Market are forbidden, and in particular those tending:
    (a) to fix or determine prices;
    (b) to restrict or control production, technical development or investments;
    (c) to allocate markets, products, customers or sources of supply.
    2. However, the High Authority shall authorise agreements to specialise in the production of, or to engage in the joint buying or selling of, specified products if it finds:
    (a) that such specialisation or such joint buying or selling will contribute to a substantial improvement in the production or distribution of the products in question; and
    (b) that the agreement in question is essential to achieve these results and is not more restrictive than is necessary for that purpose; and
    (c) that it is not capable of giving the undertakings concerned the power to determine prices or to control or limit the production or marketing of a substantial part of the products in question within the Common Market or of protecting them from effective competition by other undertakings within the Common Market. . . .
    4. Any agreement or decision prohibited by Section 1 of the present Article shall be null and void and shall be inadmissible in evidence before any court of any of the Member States.
    The High Authority shall have exclusive competence, subject to appeal to the Court to decide whether this Article applies to any such agreement or decision."
[76] Art. 80.
[77] *Nold KG* v. *The High Authority* (Case 18–57), Vol. II.
[78] *Friedrich Stork et Cie* v. *The High Authority* (Case 1–58), Vol. II.

This right of appeal of enterprises engaged in distribution is not limited to cases where they are themselves parties to the agreement in question, but covers also the case where a Decision, which is based upon Article 65 has directly affected the sphere of interest of the plaintiff enterprises.[79]

Thus, in the case in question, the plaintiffs were coal wholesalers in Westphalia and the agreement which they objected to had been drawn up by the Ruhr coal enterprises which at that time were grouped together in an organisation known as GEORG.[80] The plaintiffs had been affected by this agreement but had been no party to it.

It was under this extended definition that a wholesaler purchasing coal from the three Ruhr sales organisations was entitled to appear before the Court, although he was not himself a producer.[81]

Under section 4 of this Article, the appeal to the Court is only referred to in parenthesis and no grounds are stated upon which the appeal can be brought. When the section provides that: " the High Authority, subject to an appeal to the Court, shall have exclusive competence to pronounce upon the conformity of the said agreements and decisions with the provisions of the present Article," it might well be assumed that the only matter open before the Court was whether, in fact, the agreements and decisions were in conformity with the provisions of the Article or not.

However, the Court has not regarded the matter in this way. In a case brought under this Article,[82] the plaintiffs alleged that a particular Decision of the High Authority authorising a joint selling agreement was void because the agreement being authorised did not facilitate distribution, so that it was not in conformity with Article 65. They also alleged, however, that the Decision granting the authorisation was itself void on the grounds of a *détournement de pouvoir* and because it violated a substantial procedural requirement. Neither the High Authority, as defendants, nor the Court, raised any objections to these allegations, and the Decision in question was annulled for violating a substantial procedural requirement.[83]

In other words, the Court appeared to be accepting that the appeal allowed by this Article is one being brought under the provisions of Article 33.

In fact the Court went so far as to state:

79 *Ibid.* Vol. II.
80 *Gemeinschaftsorganisation Ruhr Kohle*, see further Vol. II.
81 *Nold KG* v. *The High Authority* (Case 18–57), Vol. II.
82 *Ibid.*
83 *Ibid.*

> It is necessary that the appeal should satisfy the general conditions of admissibility of Article 33, paragraph 3, according to the nature of the decisions being challenged.[84]

A little later, however, the Court seemed to desire to cast doubts upon this when it declared:

> In the present case, the Court does not have to determine whether an appeal based upon Article 65, section 4, must in addition satisfy all the conditions set out in Article 33 governing an appeal for annulment, because there is no doubt that they are satisfied in the present case.[85]

It is suggested, however, that there are no reasons for treating appeals against Decisions of the High Authority which authorise certain trade agreements as appeals different in kind from those against all other Decisions of the High Authority, except those imposing sanctions, so as to take the appeal out of the conditions laid down in Article 33.

ARTICLE 66, Section 5, Para. 2

If a concentration should come into existence which the High Authority recognises cannot satisfy the general or special conditions to which an authorisation under section 2 would be subject, it shall set out in a reasoned Decision the illegal character of this concentration and after having given the parties concerned an opportunity to present their observations, it shall order the separation of the enterprises or of the assets wrongly concentrated, or the cessation of common control, and any other action which it deems appropriate to re-establish the independent operation of the enterprises or of the assets in question and restore normal conditions of competition. Any person directly affected may bring an appeal against these Decisions under the conditions set out in Article 33. Notwithstanding that Article, the Court has full competence to determine whether the operation affected has the character of a concentration within the meaning of section 1 of the present Article and of the rules taken in application of that section. This appeal is suspensive. It may only be brought after the above measures have been taken unless consent is given by the High Authority to the introduction of a separate appeal against the Decision declaring the operation illegal.[86]

---

[84] *Nold KG* v. *The High Authority* (Case 18–57), Vol. II.
[85] *Friedrich Stork et Cie* v. *The High Authority* (Case 1–58), Vol. II.
[86] French:
   " *Si une concentration vient à être réalisée, dont la Haute Autorité reconnaît qu'elle ne peut satisfaire aux conditions générales ou particulières auxquelles une*

Under section 2, a concentration may be authorised if the High Authority finds that it will not give to the persons or enterprises concerned, in relation to some or all of the products in question which are subject to its jurisdiction, the power:

> to determine prices, to control or restrict production or distribution, or prevent the maintenance of effective competition, in a substantial part of the markets for such products, or to evade the rules of competition which result from the application of the present Treaty, particularly by establishing an artificially privileged position and affording a substantial advantage in the access to sources of supply or to markets.

By section 1, any transaction which would in itself have the direct or indirect effect of bringing about a concentration is to be submitted to the prior authorisation of the High Authority. This is so whether the transaction in question is carried out by one or more individuals, or by enterprises if at least one such enterprise falls under the jurisdiction of the High Authority, or whether it concerns one or several products, whether it is brought about by a merger, acquisition of shares or assets, loans, contract or any other means of control. The term " concentration " is not defined.

> *autorisation au titre du paragraph 2 serait subordonnée, elle constate par décision motivée le caractère illicite de cette concentration et, après avoir mis les intéressés en mesure de présenter leurs observations, ordonne la séparation des entreprises ou des actifs indûment réunis ou la cessation du contrôle commun, et toute autre action qu'elle estime appropriée pour rétablir l'exploitation indépendante des entreprises ou des actifs en cause et restaurer des conditions normales de concurrence. Toute personne directement intéressée peut former contre ces décisions un recours dans les conditions prévues à l'article 22. Par dérogation au dit article, la Cour a pleine compétence pour apprécier si l'opération réalisée a le caractère d'une concentration au sens du paragraph 1 du présent article et des règlements pris en application du même paragraphe. Ce recours est suspensif. Il ne peut être formé qu'une fois ordonnées les mesures ci-dessus prévues, sauf accord donné par la Haute Autorité à l'introduction d'un recours distinct contre la décision déclarant l'opération illicite."*

Stationery Office:

> " If a concentration should occur which the High Authority finds cannot satisfy the general or special conditions to which an authorisation under paragraph 2 would be subject, it shall denounce this concentration as illegal by means of a reasoned decision; after allowing the parties concerned an opportunity to put forward any arguments they wish, the High Authority shall order separation of the undertakings or assets illegally concentrated or cessation of common control as well as any other action which it considers appropriate to re-establish the independent operation of the undertakings or assets in question and to restore normal conditions of competition. Any person directly concerned may lodge an appeal against such decisions under the conditions provided for in Article 33. Notwithstanding the provisions of the said Article, the Court shall have jurisdiction to judge whether the operation effected is a concentration within the meaning of paragraph 1 of this Article and of the Regulations issued in implementation thereof. This appeal shall be suspensive. It may not be lodged until the measures provided for above have been taken, unless the High Authority agrees to the lodging of a separate appeal against the decision holding the operations to be legal."

THE RIGHT OF APPEAL

The above paragraph grants two rights of appeal. The first is against the reasoned Decision of the High Authority that a concentration is illegal,[87] the second is against the further Decision, ordering the separation of this concentration. The right of appeal is granted to " any person directly interested." As, however, the High Authority has the power to declare illegal any concentration, one or more of whose members is an enterprise falling within the Treaty definition of an enterprise,[88] all the other members of such a concentration by this provision have the right to appeal, although they are not themselves within the scope of the Treaty. Similarly, section 1 of this Article also allows a concentration to be declared illegal when it has been brought about by one or more individuals. These also, by being " directly interested " are granted a right to appeal.[89]

TIME LIMIT FOR BRINGING AN APPEAL

The above provision sets out that the appeals that are here being allowed may be brought " under the conditions set out in Article 33." Now Article 33, besides specifying the grounds upon which an appeal may be brought, states, in paragraph 3, that an appeal must be brought within one month of the publication or notification of the Decision in question. This period of one month thus applies to appeals brought under the present Article. This, however, produces a difficulty. Article 66 expressly states that the appeal against the Decision of the High Authority declaring a concentration to be illegal may not be brought until the further Decision for the separation of that concentration has been taken, unless the consent of the High Authority is given to the introduction of a separate appeal against the Decision declaring the concentration illegal. Now it is clear that the further Decision ordering the separation of the concentration may well be taken more than one month after the Decision has been passed declaring the concentration illegal.[90] Alternatively, the High Authority may only grant permission for the bringing of an appeal against the earlier Decision more than one month after it was passed. The question arises, therefore, whether an appeal against that Decision is consequently time-barred.

---

[87] It is set out that this Decision is expressly required to be " reasoned "—every Decision of the High Authority must give reasons—Art. 15, para. 1.

[88] Art. 66, para. 1.

[89] For a discussion of the legal right of appeal of private persons see Neri: " Il ricorso dei privati davanti alla Corte di Giustizia della C.E.C.A.," in *Rivista di Studi Politici Internazionale* (1956).

[90] Before the concentration can be ordered to split up, the parties must be given an opportunity to present their observations—Art. 66, section 5.2. This could hardly be done within a month.

If the wording of Article 33 is read as it stands, it is clear that an appeal can be brought only within one month after the notification or publication of a Decision, and, therefore, in the above situations, that period of one month would have expired and no appeal could be brought. This, however, will nearly always mean that in practice there is no right of appeal.

Alternatively, however, it may be contended that the object of Article 33 is to provide a period of one month during which an appeal can be brought. If this is so, then until a party has acquired a right of appeal that period of one month during which it can be exercised clearly cannot start to run. This would mean that in the above situations, the time period must be calculated either from the date when the High Authority passed its further Decision ordering the separation of the concentration, or from the date when consent is given to the bringing of an appeal against the Decision declaring the concentration illegal. It is suggested that, although it is a straining of the words of Article 33, this second interpretation should be accepted as it is the only one which ensures a right of appeal at all.

NATURE OF THE APPEAL

The joint appeal against the Decision declaring a concentration illegal and against the further Decision ordering the separation of that concentration, which is allowed under Article 66, is declared to be suspensive.[91] That is to say, the Decision ordering the separation does not have to be complied with unless the Court rejects the appeal and then only from the date of that rejection. It is not stated whether, when the High Authority allows an appeal against the earlier Decision only, that appeal also suspends the declaration that the concentration is illegal. It is suggested, however, that the High Authority is not intended to be prevented from proceeding to order the separation of the concentration until a ruling has been obtained upon whether a concentration actually does exist or not, so that whether or not the declaration of illegality is suspended is of no practical effect.

ARTICLE 88

If the High Authority considers that a State has failed in one of the obligations incumbent upon it by virtue of the present Treaty, it shall set out this failure in a reasoned Decision after having given this State an opportunity to present its observations. It shall grant to the State concerned a time limit within which it is to provide for the carrying out of its obligation.

[91] Art. 66, section 5.2.

An appeal in *pleine juridiction* is open to this State before the Court within a time limit of two months calculated from the notification of the Decision.

If the State has not taken steps to fulfil its obligation within the time limit fixed by the High Authority, or, in the event of an appeal, if this has been rejected, the High Authority may with the agreement of the Council deciding by a two-thirds majority :

(a) suspend the payment of the sums which it may owe to the State in question by virtue of the present Treaty;

(b) take or authorise other Member States to take measures in violation of the provisions of Article 4 with a view to correcting the effects of the failure in question.

An appeal in *pleine juridiction* is open, within a period of two months calculated from their notification, against the Decisions taken in application of sub-paragraphs (a) and (b).

If the above measures should prove ineffective, the High Authority shall refer the matter to the Council.[92]

92 French:

" *Si la Haute Autorité estime qu'un Etat a manqué à une des obligations qui lui incombent en vertu du présent Traité, elle constate ledit manquement par une décision motivée, après avoir mis cet Etat en mesure de présenter ses observations. Elle impartit à l'Etat en cause un délai pour pourvoir à l'exécution de son obligation.*

Un recours de pleine juridiction est ouvert à cet Etat devant la Cour dans un délai de deux mois à compter de la notification de la décision.

Si l'Etat n'a pas pourvu à l'exécution de son obligation dans le délai fixé par la Haute Autorité ou, en cas de recours, si celui-ci a été rejeté, la Haute Autorité peut, sur avis conforme du Conseil statuant à la majorité des deux tiers:

(*a*) *suspendre le versement des sommes dont elle serait redevable pour le compte de l'Etat en question en vertu du présent Traité;*

(*b*) *prendre ou autoriser les autres Etats membres à prendre des mesures dérogatoires aux dispositions de l'article 4 en vue de corriger les effets du manquement constaté.*

Un recours de pleine juridiction est ouvert, dans un délai de deux mois à compter de leur notification, contre les décisions prises en application des alinéas (*a*) *et* (*b*).

Si les mesures ci-dessus prévues s'avèrent inopérantes, la Haute Autorité en réfère au Conseil."

Stationery Office:

" If the High Authority considers that a State has failed to fulfil any of its obligations under the present Treaty, it shall, after allowing the State in question an opportunity to present its views, take note of the failure in a reasoned decision. It shall allow the State in question a period of time within which to arrange to fulfil its obligation.

Such a State may appeal to the full jurisdiction of the Court within two months of the decision being notified.

If the State has not taken steps to fulfil its obligation within the period fixed by the High Authority or, in the case of an appeal, if its appeal has been rejected the

In the various actions which have been brought before it by the Member States, the Court has had to consider the provisions of this Article in some detail.

THE NATURE OF THE HIGH AUTHORITY'S DECISION PASSED UNDER PARAGRAPH 1

The obligations incumbent upon the Member States by virtue of the E.C.S.C. Treaty are first of all those directly imposed by that Treaty and secondly obligations resulting from Decisions and Recommendations made by the various Community institutions.[93] Not to comply with a Decision of the High Authority, therefore, is not merely to violate that Decision but to break the Treaty and thereby bring the machinery of Article 88 into force.

The Court has specified this in the following terms:

> The terms of Article 88 grant to the High Authority the power only to take note of the breach by a State of one of the obligations imposed upon it by the Treaty.
>
> This obligation must be derived either from a binding provision or from a Decision or Recommendation existing prior to the application of this article.
>
> The " reasoned Decision " referred to in Article 88, paragraph 1, may have as its object only the noting of a breach, without containing any legislative provisions.[94]

The statement of this breach must be supported by reasons.

> The supporting reasons required by paragraph 1 of Article 88 must justify the declaration of a breach and the time limit set out must specify the time within which must be carried out not the obligation imposed under this Article, but an obligation which existed before that Decision was passed.[95]

High Authority may, if it receives a confirmatory opinion from the Council and acting by a two-thirds majority:
(a) suspend the payment of sums which the High Authority may owe to the State in question under the present Treaty;
(b) adopt measures or authorise other Member States to adopt measures which would otherwise be contrary to the provisions of Article 4, so as to correct the effects of the failure in question.
An appeal to the Court's full jurisdiction may be lodged against the decisions taken under paragraphs (a) and (b) within two months of their notification.
If these measures should prove ineffective, the High Authority shall refer the matter to the Council."
93 Art. 86, para. 1, provides:
" Member States undertake that they will take all steps both general or particular, needed to discharge their obligations resulting from decisions and recommendations by the Community's institutions and that they will help the Community to carry out its duties."
94 *Italian Government* v. *The High Authority* (Case 20–59), Vol. II.
95 *Ibid*. Vol. II.

Once the Decision has been taken, the State concerned may appeal against it in *pleine juridiction* within a time limit of two months.

In this appeal the Court can undertake

a consideration of all grounds, based not only upon law, but also upon any matters which justify an annulment.[96]

However, the Decision being considered is solely the Decision setting out that there has been a breach of the Treaty; no consideration can be taken of the validity or invalidity of any prior Decision or Recommendation of the High Authority where it is alleged that these have been violated. Thus, the Court has declared:

With respect to the Decisions and Recommendations of the High Authority, the Government must accept the means of appeal in the manner and within the time limits presented by the Treaty, and may no longer, at the time when the High Authority invokes the means of execution set out in Article 88, claim *ex post facto* that these measures are irregular or void.[97]

In a case the previous year, the Court had stated virtually the same thing when it had set out that:

The appeal allowed by Article 88, paragraph 2, seeks to submit to the control of the Court the declaration made by the High Authority of the breach on the part of the Member State as well as the measures resulting from this Decision.

In contrast, the Decision taken by the High Authority in the exercise of its powers and outside the scope of Article 88 may, as a general rule, be the subject of an appeal by the terms of Article 33. . . .

Under these conditions, one must not confuse the possible appeal under the terms of Article 33—against a Decision which the High Authority subsequently alleges has not been complied with—and the appeal—under the terms of Article 88, paragraph 2—against the declaration of the breach of this Decision.[98]

Having thus drawn a distinction between the original Decision, which can be challenged under Article 33, and the further Decision setting out the breach, which can be challenged under Article 88, paragraph 2, the Court in the following terms set out what were the objects of this latter appeal namely:

(a) To obtain the annulment of the declaration of breach by showing that the Member State has complied with the obligations resulting from the Decision, with whose breach it is being accused. This excludes the possibility of contesting at the same time the legality of this Decision.

(b) To obtain the annulment or modification of the measures consequent upon the declaration of breach.[99]

96 *Ibid.* Vol. II.   97 *Ibid.* Vol. II.
98 *German Government* v. *The High Authority* (Case 19–58), Vol. II.
99 *Ibid.*

SUCH DECISION CANNOT ITSELF IMPOSE OBLIGATIONS

In its Decision passed under paragraph 1 of Article 88, the High Authority is limited to setting out the failure by a State and to granting a time limit: this Decision cannot impose any additional obligation upon the State such as specifying the manner in which compliance is to be effected. Thus where in a particular Decision [1] the High Authority set out in Article 1 that all the Member States of the Community had failed to fulfil one of the obligations under the Treaty by not publishing details of transport hauliers' contracts for the movement of coal and steel, and in Article 2 set out the manner in which these details were to be published, this latter Article was annulled on the grounds that by a Decision passed under Article 88, the High Authority was seeking to impose an obligation which could only be imposed, if at all, under Article 14. The Court held:

> If it were permissible to equate the " Decision " referred to in Article 88 with a Decision within the meaning of Article 14,[2] by which the High Authority carries out the tasks assigned to it, it would be hard to explain why a rule prescribed by virtue of Article 88 is open to an appeal in *pleine juridiction* . . . whereas Decisions passed in the form prescribed by Article 14 are subject to the rules, and are governed by the time limits for bringing an appeal, which are fixed by Article 33.[3]

APPEALS UNDER PARAGRAPH 2 ARE NOT SUSPENSIVE

A further question raised by an earlier case was whether an appeal under Article 88, paragraph 2, in any way suspended two Decisions of the High Authority of February and December, 1958, and in particular whether it suspended the duty they imposed on the German Government to amend its railway tariffs by January 31, 1959. If it did not suspend this obligation the government would be placed in the position of having a duty to comply with the February and December Decisions of the High Authority while at the same time, and even after compliance with them, it would be contending before the Court that no such duty of compliance existed. Thus if the Government were to win in its contention, the amendment, perhaps made many months before the judgment of the Court, would have been quite unnecessary.[4] Further, in this

---

[1] Decision 18–59, see Vol. II.
[2] Art. 14, paras. 1 and 2, provides:
   " In carrying out its duties assigned to it by the present Treaty and in accordance with the provisions thereof, the High Authority shall take Decisions, make Recommendations and issue opinions.
   Decisions shall be binding in all respects."
[3] *Italian Government* v. *The High Authority* (Case 20–59), Vol. II.
[4] To see the force of this argument it may be noted that the judgment in this case was not given until March 1960.

particular case, the German Government in a separate action had already appealed against the validity of the Decision of February, 1958.

The Court, however, held that an appeal under Article 88, paragraph 2, does not suspend the obligations upon the State concerned, but that the only effect of such an appeal is to prevent the High Authority under paragraph 3 of the Article from withholding payments from it, or authorising violation of the principle of free trade set out in Article 4. The Court stated:

> In fact, contrary to the opinion of the plaintiffs, Article 88, paragraph 3, only provides that the measures specified under (a) and (b) cannot be taken as long as the appeal is pending.
>
> One cannot assume that the authors of the Treaty have wished to grant a suspensive effect to the appeals mentioned in Article 88—derogation from the general principle of Article 39 cannot be presumed from the silence of this provision on this matter.
>
> Moreover, the meaning of Article 88 itself is in opposition to the view that the appeal mentioned in paragraph 2 of that Article can have a suspensive effect. Since the Decision taken by the High Authority in accordance with paragraph 1 of this Article is a declaratory act, to attribute a suspensive effect [to the appeal] would amount to a suspension . . . of the previous Decisions of the High Authority, the fulfilment of which is here in question.[5]

THE TIME LIMIT FOR COMPLIANCE WITH THE OBLIGATION

In *German Government* v. *The High Authority* a further point was raised by the plaintiffs. The Decision of the High Authority setting out a breach by the German Government was notified to that government on December 11, 1958, and gave it until January 31, 1959, to amend some offending railway tariffs. Moreover, as paragraph 2 of Article 88 allows an appeal against this Decision to be brought within two months of the notification, an appeal lay until February 11, 1959. In the present instance, therefore, the High Authority at any time after January 31 could have proceeded under paragraph 3 to impose the sanctions there set out, that is to say, even before the government's right of appeal had expired. The German Government, therefore, alleged that the time limit for amending the railway tariffs was manifestly too short. The Court, however, rejected this argument and stated:

> It does not appear from the wording of Article 88 that the time limit imposed for complying with an obligation must be at least equal to the time limit for an appeal. Such a requirement is not required by the possible interest of Member States for it clearly follows from Article 88, paragraph 3, that even in the event of the High Authority taking the measures prescribed in (a) and (b) of this paragraph before the expiration

---

[5] *German Government* v. *The High Authority* (Case 19–58), Vol. II.

of the time period for appeals, this action could be stopped by a subsequent appeal brought within the time limit.[6]

In other words, the Court is stating that if a State has not fulfilled its obligation within the time limit prescribed, the High Authority can immediately impose sanctions upon it, under paragraph 3. However, because paragraph 3 states: " If the State has not taken steps to fulfil its obligations . . . *or in the event of an appeal, if this has been rejected* . . . " the effect of bringing an appeal against the Decision passed under paragraph 1, even after the imposing of the sanction under paragraph 3 is to remove from the High Authority the power both to impose a sanction and to continue in force a sanction already imposed. This, therefore, has the effect, in practice, of suspending the sanction.

After sanctions have been imposed upon the defaulting State under paragraph 3 (a) or (b), an appeal in *pleine juridiction* may be brought under paragraph 4 against the Decisions imposing these sanctions.

APPEALS AGAINST SANCTIONS

It is suggested that in this appeal in *pleine juridiction* the Court can determine whether the State is in breach of its obligations and, if so, whether the sanction imposed is reasonable. However, as the Court has stated that appeals in *pleine juridiction* under paragraph 2 cannot question the validity of the original Decision which it is alleged has been broken, it would appear that this validity cannot be questioned in an appeal in *pleine juridiction* under paragraph 4. If this is so, Article 88 presents the following hierarchical table:

A BREACH BY A STATE OF A DECISION OF THE HIGH AUTHORITY

A Decision setting out this breach and giving a further time limit for compliance—paragraph 1.
Appeal against Decision passed under paragraph 1—paragraph 2.

BREACH OF TIME LIMIT STATED IN DECISION PASSED UNDER PARAGRAPH 1

A Decision imposing sanctions upon the State—paragraph 3.
Appeal against Decision passed under paragraph 3—paragraph 4.

Although under Article 88 itself a Member State cannot allege that the Decision which it has violated is void, nevertheless the Court has recognised that a State can challenge this Decision, even after the

---

[6] *Ibid.*

expiration of the time limit for appeals under Article 33.[7] This the State can do by appealing against the sanctions imposed upon it under Article 88, paragraph 3, and in support of that appeal it is provided in Article 36 that:

> The plaintiffs, under the conditions set out in the first paragraph of Article 33 of the present Treaty, may rely upon the irregularity of the Decisions and Recommendations which they are accused of having contravened.

It might, however, and with some force, be alleged that the only Decision the State is " accused of having contravened " is the one passed under Article 88, paragraph 1, which specified the time limit for compliance with a prior Decision, and that it is not that prior Decision which, at this juncture, the State is being accused of contravening. It is suggested, however, that such an argument would enable a Member State to be fined for having originally failed to comply with a Decision which is still existing only because it was not challenged within the original time limit of one month, but which, nonetheless has been passed irregularly. A review in *pleine juridiction* it is submitted must be wide enough to review the legality not merely of the declaratory Decision passed under Article 88, which has been broken, but of earlier Decisions referred to in that declaration Decision.

THE EXTENT OF AN ENTERPRISE'S RIGHT TO INTERVENE

By Article 34, paragraph 1, of the E.C.S.C. Statute of the Court, it is provided that:

> Legal or natural persons establishing an interest in the outcome of an action brought before the Court may intervene in such an action.

It might appear that this right was unlimited, so that an enterprise or an association, by being legal persons, could intervene in an action brought under Article 88 provided that they could show an interest in the outcome of that action. The Court, however, in line with its general interpretation that enterprises cannot be a party to State affairs,[8] has limited the right of enterprises to intervene. The Court declared:

> The Decision being challenged in the principal proceedings,[9] on the one hand sets out a failure of the Government of the Kingdom of the

---

[7] " Although . . . Art. 88 does not permit a discussion of previous Decisions, Art. 36, however, does offer this opportunity to Member States in the special circumstances which are there set out "—*German Government* v. *The High Authority* (Case 3–59), Vol. II.

[8] *Cf. Niederrheinische Bergwerks-Aktiengesellschaft Unternehmensverband des Aachener Steinkohlenbergbauer* v. *The High Authority* (Joint Cases 2 and 3–60) pp. 202–203, above.

[9] The High Authority's Decision 18–59, see Vol. II.

Netherlands to fulfil an obligation incumbent upon it by virtue of the E.C.S.C. Treaty, and on the other hand, specifies for it what are the measures necessary for carrying out that obligation.

It is, therefore, necessary to consider what are the precise provisions which the intervening parties have an interest in having annulled.

Even if it can be accepted that enterprises have an interest in intervening in an action arising under Article 88, that intervention, however, can have as its object only the mere interpretation of the Treaty, excluding any examination directed at the question of the fixing of a time limit which the High Authority might grant to the State to provide for the fulfilment of its obligations, or even the methods of execution of a possible coercive Decision of the High Authority against that State, because in these various cases the very nature of those acts, which take effect at the level of the relations between the States, which are public powers, and the High Authority, which is a Community organ, preclude the intervention of private persons. Thus discussion of these questions must occur solely between the principal parties.[10]

ARTICLE 89

Any dispute among Member States concerning the application of the present Treaty, which cannot be settled by any other procedure set out in the present Treaty, may be submitted to the Court at the request of one of the States which is a party to the dispute.

The Court also has jurisdiction to determine upon any difference between Member States in connection with the objects of the present Treaty, if this difference is referred to it by virtue of an agreement.[11]

The earlier Articles of the Treaty deal with the relationship of Member States and the various institutions of the Coal and Steel Community:

---

[10] *Netherlands Government* v. *The High Authority* (Case 25–59), Vol. II.
[11] French:

> "*Tout différend entre Etats membres au sujet de l'application du présent Traité, qui n'est pas susceptible d'être réglé par une autre procédure prévue au présent Traité, peut être soumis à la Cour, à la requête de l'un des Etats parties au différend.*
>
> *La Cour est également compétent pour statuer sur tout différend entre Etats membres en connexité avec l'objet du présent Traité, si ce différend lui est soumis en vertu d'un compromis.*"

Stationery Office:

> "Any dispute between Member States as to the implementation of the present Treaty, which cannot be settled by another procedure provided for in the present Treaty, may be submitted to the Court at the request of one of the States which are parties to the dispute.
>
> The Court shall have jurisdiction to settle any dispute between Member States related to the purpose of the Present Treaty if such a dispute is submitted to it by virtue of an arbitration clause."

this provision enables international differences between the States themselves to be settled by the Court. The necessity for this provision is seen when it is read together with Article 87 of the Treaty by which the Member States [12] " undertake not to avail themselves of any treaties, conventions or declarations existing between themselves to submit any differences concerning the interpretation or the application of the present Treaty to a mode of settlement other than those contained herein."

Having thus agreed not to rely upon any other mode of settlement, including, clearly, settlement by the International Court of Justice, the parties naturally require disputes to be settled by the Communities' Court.

INTER-STATE DISPUTES CONCERNING THE APPLICATION OF THE TREATY

Paragraph 1 of Article 89 refers to disputes " among Member States concerning *the application* of the present Treaty." It will be noted that no reference is here made to differences concerning the *interpretation* of that Treaty, so that, although in Article 87 the Member States agreed only to submit differences concerning the interpretation of the Treaty to the mode of settlement contained in the Treaty, no such mode is contained in the Treaty. It is suggested, however, that this *lacuna* is the result of bad drafting and that nothing should be made to turn upon it—indeed, it can be contended that the Court cannot proceed to determine a dispute concerning the application of the Treaty without first interpreting it, so as to determine whether the application is the authorised one or not. However, the existing wording appears to take out the possibility of applying for any advisory opinion, which would clearly be related to a matter of pure interpretation.

Paragraph 1 states that an appeal concerning the application of the Treaty may be submitted to the Court " at the request of one of the States which is a party to the dispute." This phrase appears to imply that one State by a unilateral application can refer the dispute to the Court.[13]

INTER-STATE DISPUTES CONCERNING THE OBJECTS OF THE TREATY

Whereas paragraph 1 dealt with the application of the Treaty, paragraph 2 is concerned with the objects of the Treaty. It is not entirely clear, however, what the distinction between the application of the Treaty, and the objects of that Treaty may be. The fundamental objects

---

[12] Referred to in that Article as " the High Contracting Parties." A proper co-ordination between the drafters of the Treaty does not appear to have been achieved.

[13] The alternative rendering, however, would be that one of the States may request the other to submit the dispute to the Court. This, however, would make the provisions of paragraph 1 merely permissive and make them largely overlap with those of paragraph 2.

of the Treaty are set out in its opening articles,[14] and the remaining provisions elaborate how these objects are to be obtained. One of these objects is the abolition of all import and export duties between the Member States. It may be queried, therefore, if a dispute were to arise between two States concerning such duties, whether such a dispute concerns an object of the Treaty, so that, under paragraph 2, litigation is dependent upon an arbitration agreement, or whether the dispute concerns the application of that object, so that compulsory jurisdiction can be obtained under paragraph 1.[15]

Further, a dispute concerning an object of the Treaty would arise if two States interpreted the early articles of the Treaty in different ways. The task of the Court would, therefore, be to interpret those articles. Under paragraph 2, however, this fundamental task may be done only by joint consent of the parties.

ARTICLE 92

The Decisions of the High Authority imposing pecuniary obligations shall have executory force.

The forced execution upon the territory of the Member States shall be carried out according to the legal procedure in force in each of these States . . .

The forced execution can be suspended only by virtue of a decision of the Court.[16]

The Decisions of the High Authority imposing pecuniary obligations which are here being referred to are, for example, the annual levies

---

[14] Arts. 2–5.

[15] If State A were to act upon an interpretation of the Treaty which differed from that of State B, State A would be in violation of the Treaty unless its interpretations were correct. State B, rather than attempting to proceed under Art. 89, would be better advised to request the High Authority under Art. 35, para. 1, to proceed against State A by virtue of its powers under Art. 88. If the High Authority did not proceed against State A, State B, by challenging under Art. 35 the High Authority's resulting implied Decision of refusal to act, would have the opportunity before the Court of arguing that State A's acts, based upon its interpretation of the Treaty were illegal. If State B's contention was correct, the High Authority would have been required to take action and its implied Decision would be annulled for violating Art. 88, para. 1, of the Treaty.

[16] French:
"*Les décisions de la Haute Autorité comportant des obligations pécuniaires forment titre exécutoire.*
L'exécution forcée sur le territoire des Etats membres est poursuivie suivant les voies de droit en vigueur dans chacun de ces Etats. . . .
L'exécution forcée ne peut être suspendue qu'en vertu d'une décision de la Cour."
Stationery Office:
"Decisions of the High Authority which include a pecuniary obligation on enterprises shall have the enforceability of a Court judgment.
Enforcement on the territory of Member States shall be carried out by means of the legal procedure in effect in each State. . . .
Enforcement may be stayed only by a decision of the Court."

upon enterprises producing coal and steel, and all of the fines which the High Authority may impose both upon defaulting enterprises and upon defaulting States.

RELATIONSHIP TO ARTICLE 39

It will be recalled that under Article 39 the Court, if it considers that the circumstances require it, may order the suspension of a Decision. However, this power may be exercised only provided that the plaintiff has challenged the validity of this Decision before the Court.

It is not clear from the wording of Article 92 whether the power here being given to the Court is merely a repetition of the power given by Article 39, or is a separate power. If it is a separate power, then the provisions concerning challenge of the fine itself will not apply, as those provisions are expressly limited to requests for suspension under Article 39 itself.

A party in respect of whom a Decision imposing a pecuniary obligation has been passed is granted the right by the Treaty to challenge that Decision in *pleine juridiction*.[17] It is suggested, therefore, that the Treaty adequately caters for the case of fines and sanctions being imposed and that, therefore, there is no occasion to assume that a new and distinct head of jurisdiction was being granted by the terms of this Article. It is submitted, therefore, that the jurisdiction of the Court is controlled by Articles 36 and 39 and the Rules of Court which refer to them. It would follow from this, therefore, that a party wishing to have a fine suspended will have in addition to challenge the legality of that fine. It would follow, further, that no parties can appeal to the Court when their sole request is that they should be given a longer time to pay than has been granted to them, unless they can contend that the time granted to them is unreasonable, and thus a violation of an implied provision of the Treaty that they should be granted a reasonable time, or alternatively if the failure to grant an extended time amounts to a *détournement de pouvoir*. In any event no appeal can be brought more than one month after publication or notification of the fine.[18]

ARTICLE 95, Paras. 3 and 4

If, after the expiration of the transitional period referred to in the Convention containing the Transitional Provisions,[19] unforeseen difficulties in the methods of carrying out the

---

[17] Art. 36, para. 2, see p. 211, above.
[18] E.C.S.C. Statute, Art. 39, para. 1, see p. 460, below.
[19] This period ended on February 9, 1960.

present Treaty are revealed by experience, or a fundamental change in economic or technical conditions directly affecting the Common Market in coal and steel, renders necessary an adaptation of the rules concerning the exercise by the High Authority of the powers which have been conferred upon it, appropriate amendments may be made provided that they do not alter the provisions of Articles 2, 3, and 4, or the relationship of the powers granted respectively to the High Authority and to the other institutions of the Community.

These amendments shall be made by proposals drawn by agreement by the High Authority and by the Council, determining by a majority of five-sixths of its members, and shall be submitted for the opinion of the Court. In its examination, the Court has full jurisdiction to consider all matters of fact and law. If, at the end of its examination, the Court should find that the proposals conform to the provisions of the preceeding paragraph, it shall transmit them to the Assembly and they shall come into force if they are approved by a majority of three-quarters of the votes cast representing a majority of two-thirds of the members of the Assembly.[20]

[20] French:

   " *Après l'expiration de la période de transition prévue par la Convention sur les dispositions transitoires, si des difficultés imprévues, révélées par l'expérience, dans les modalités d'application du présent Traité, ou un changement profond des conditions économiques ou techniques qui affecte directement le marché commun du charbon et de l'acier rendent nécessaire un adaptation des règles relatives à l'exercice par la Haute Autorité des pouvoirs qui lui sont conférés, des modifications appropriées peuvent y être apportées, sans qu'elles puissent porter atteinte aux dispositions des articles 2, 3 et 4 ou au rapport des pouvoirs respectivement attribués à la Haute Autorité et aux autres institutions de la Communauté.*

   Ces modifications font l'objet de propositions établies en accord par la Haute Autorité et par le Conseil statuant à la majorité des cinq-sixièmes de ses membres, et soumises à l'avis de la Cour. Dans son examen, la Cour a pleine compétence pour apprécier tous les éléments de fait et de droit. Si, à la suite de cet examen, la Cour reconnaît la conformité des propositions aux dispositions de l'alinéa qui précède, elles sont transmises à l'Assemblée et entrent en vigueur si elles sont approuvées à la majorité des trois-quarts des voix exprimées et à la majorité des deux-tiers des membres qui composent l'Assemblée."

Stationery Office:

   " If, after the transitional period, provided for in the Convention containing Transitional Provisions, has ended unforeseen difficulties, which the operation of the present Treaty has revealed, or a profound change in the economic or technical conditions directly affecting the Common Market for coal and steel, make it necessary to adapt the rules for the exercise by the High Authority of the powers conferred upon it appropriate amendments may be made provided that they do not infringe the provisions of Articles 2, 3 and 4, or the relationship between the powers of the High Authority and those of the other institutions of the Community.

   These amendments shall be jointly proposed by the High Authority and the Council, acting by a five-sixths majority of its members, and shall be submitted to the Court for its opinion. When considering the matter, the Court shall be fully competent to review all matters of fact and of law. If the Court should find

THE ARTICLE IN OPERATION

In 1959 the High Authority and the Council of Ministers jointly submitted a proposal to amend Article 56 of the Treaty.[21] That Article empowers the High Authority to grant money to compensate workers who have been rendered unemployed because " the introduction of technical processes or new equipment " has led to an exceptionally large reduction in labour requirements. If such an event occurs, the High Authority may also grant resettlement allowances and assist with the financing of the technical retraining of employees who are forced to change their employment. The amendment proposed sought to enable the High Authority until February 10, 1963, to give similar financial assistance if " profound changes in the marketing conditions of the coalmining industry make it necessary for certain enterprises permanently to discontinue, curtail or change their activities."

By the provisions of Article 95, amendments to the Treaty can only be proposed if " unforeseen difficulties are revealed by experience " or if a " fundamental change in economic or technical conditions directly affecting the Common Market in coal and steel " renders them necessary. The High Authority and the Council, therefore, referred to these unforeseen difficulties or fundamental changes. These were, first, the progressive substitution of oil firing for coal, the second was the marked reduction in freight charges, which meant that American coal could reach Europe much more cheaply than previously, and the third was the increasing importance of natural gas as a source of power. Because of these changes, it was realised that the Common Market might well be gravely affected. However, none of these changes fell within the term " the introduction of technical processes or new equipment." Under Article 56 as it stood, therefore, the High Authority would be unable to give any financial assistance should, for example, a coal mine be unable to sell its coal either because consumers were using oil or because American coal was cheaper so that it would be forced to close down. The amendment was sought, therefore, to enable assistance for a limited period to be given if " profound changes in marketing conditions of the coalmining industry make it necessary for certain enterprises permanently to discontinue, curtail or change their activities."

that the proposals conform to the provisions of the preceding paragraph they shall be forwarded to the Assembly and shall come into force if they are approved by the Assembly acting by a majority of three-quarters of the votes cast and two-thirds of the total membership."

[21] See *Opinion of the Court upon the proposed Amendment of the E.C.S.C. Treaty,* Vol. II.

The Court in its Opinion rejected this amendment as not satisfying the requirement of Article 95. First, the amendment was limited to enterprises within the coal industry. The Court declared:

> It is contrary to Articles 2, 3 and 4 and particularly to Article 4 to provide for an amendment which concerns the coal industry while leaving the steel industry in doubt of its position in the event of the conditions of the new Article 56 being extended for its benefit.[22]

Further, the amendment was expressly limited to remain in force only until February 10, 1963, which is exactly three years after the ending of the Transitional Period. The Court objected to this on two grounds. First, it declared:

> The fact of limiting the period of validity of the proposed provision to a period expiring on February 10, 1963, is scarcely reconcilable with the structure of the Treaty, the authors of which have carefully sought to separate the definitive provisions, which are destined to remain in force for fifty years, from the Transitional Provisions.
>
> From this objection . . . it appears that this limitation gives to the text submitted to the Court not the character of an amendment of the Treaty, properly so called, as is prescribed by Article 95, paragraph 3, but rather that of a prolongation of the Convention containing the Transitional Provisions.[23]

Secondly, the Court held that the limitation as to time violated Article 95 by affecting the relationship of the powers granted respectively to the High Authority and to the other institutions of the Community. It declared:

> By virtue of the fact that an extension will become necessary, the High Authority, at the time of the renewal of the extent of the powers granted by the new Article 56, will periodically be made dependent upon the consent of the special Council of Ministers and of the Parliamentary Assembly.
>
> This fact is liable to fetter the liberty of action and of discretion of the High Authority.
>
> By limiting the duration of the validity of the proposed text, the balance between the institutions of the Community as provided for in the Treaty, will be affected.[24]

Subsequently, the High Authority and the Council of Ministers submitted a revised amendment which the Court declared to be in conformity with Article 95.[25] In this second Opinion, the Court dealt

[22] Vol. II.
[23] Vol. II.
[24] Vol. II.
[25] *Amendment Procedure under Article 95, paras. 3 and 4, of the E.C.S.C. Treaty* (Opinion 1–60), Vol. II.

with one matter raised by the Council, namely, that by paragraph 3 it
is only

> an adaptation *of the rules* concerning the exercise by the High Authority
> of the powers which have been conferred upon it

which is permissible. The Council queried, therefore, whether any
alteration of the actual powers, as distinct from the rules concerning
their exercise, was possible. The Court replied:

> This view would have the result that in practice Article 95 would be
> able to be applied only for the amendment of the rules relating to the
> procedure and the requirements to be observed by the High Authority
> in the exercise of its powers . . .
> Such an interpretation of the phrase " rules for the exercise . . . of
> the powers " would reduce the means of adapting the Treaty to such
> an extent that one could not understand why its authors were able to
> consider the revision described in Article 95, paragraph 3, as an
> adequate means for placing the Community in a position to face a
> " fundamental change in economic or technical conditions."
> On the other hand, the Court interprets the above text of Article 95
> in the sense that the definition of the conditions, to which the exercise
> of the powers granted has been made subject, may itself also be
> amended.[26]

In a later Opinion [27] concerning a proposed amendment of Article 65
of the Treaty, which relates to agreements between enterprises for the
joint buying and selling of products, the Court distinguished between
a mere limited extension of an existing power possessed by the High
Authority—which is permissible—and a large and indefinite extension,
which would amount to a grant of a new power—which is not
permissible. The Court declared:

> In principle, Article 95 does not prevent an adaptation of the rules
> relating to the powers which Article 65 confers on the High Authority,
> by an amendment of section 2 of that article,[28] seeking to allow the

[26] *Ibid.*
[27] *Amendment of Article 65 of the E.C.S.C. Treaty* (Opinion 1–61).
[28] Art. 65, section 2, para. 1, provides:
" The High Authority shall authorise agreements to specialise in the production
of, or to engage in the joint buying or selling of, specified products if it finds:
  (a) that such specialisation or such joint buying or selling will contribute to a
    substantial improvement in the production or distribution of the products
    in question; and
  (b) that the agreement in question is essential to achieve these results, and is
    not more restrictive than is necessary for that purpose; and
  (c) that it is not capable of giving the enterprises concerned the power to
    determine prices or to control or limit the production or marketing of a
    substantial part of the products in question within the common market or of
    protecting them from effective competition by other enterprises within the
    common market."

High Authority to authorise either agreements of another kind than those referred to in the existing text, but having the same object, or agreements of the same kind as those referred to in the text in force, but having another object, or, finally, agreements of another kind and having other objectives.

It is, however, essential that the revised text should specify, on the one hand, the kind of agreements capable of authorisation, and, on the other hand, should clearly define the object of those agreements, because otherwise it would not be a question of the adaptation of the use of a power already conferred on the High Authority within the limited scope of the exemptions allowed by section 2 of Article 65, but of the grant of a power whose limits would be undefined. This would be such a large and indefinite extension of the present competence as to constitute a qualitative, and not merely a quantitative amendment of this competence—in other words it would be a new power.[29]

PROTOCOL ON PRIVILEGES AND IMMUNITIES OF THE COMMUNITY

ARTICLE 1

The premises and buildings of the Community shall be inviolable. They shall be exempt from search, requisition, confiscation or expropriation. The property and assets of the Community may not become the subject of any measure of administrative or judicial constraint without the authorisation of the Court.[30]

This provision does not state what are to be the grounds upon which an authorisation of the Court can be refused, although if an authorisation were automatically to be granted in every case this provision would clearly be of no value.

It would appear that a national tribunal can apply for this authorisation either before or after ordering a levy of execution or other constraint upon the property and assets of the Community, and presumably the party concerned can himself approach the Court.

[29] *Ibid.*
[30] French:
　" *Les locaux et les bâtiments de la Communauté sont inviolables. Ils sont exempts de perquisition, réquisition, confiscation ou expropriation. Les biens et avoirs de la Communauté ne peuvent être l'objet d'aucune mesure de contrainte administrative ou judiciaire sans une autorisation de la Cour.*"
　Stationery Office:
　" The premises and buildings of the Community shall be inviolable. They shall be exempt from search, requisition, confiscation or expropriation. The property and assets of the Community may not be the subject of any administrative or legal measure of constraint without the authorisation of the Court."

It may be doubted whether the Court can itself judge upon the findings of the tribunal, or withhold, permission on the grounds of differing from the judgment given, or because it regards the extent of the execution to be excessive.

ARTICLE 16

Any dispute concerning the interpretation or application of the present Protocol shall be submitted to the Court.[31]

As the jurisdiction of the Court under this Article is not specified, it appears that its powers are unlimited.

The Court has had to consider one case brought under this Article [32] concerning the immunity from taxation of the salaries of officials of the Community.[33] In its judgment the Court considered two main questions: first, whether, when he believes that one of the immunities granted by the Protocol has been violated, the Community official can himself in his own name bring an action against the party alleged to be violating the immunity, and secondly, whether if he can, that official is required to have exhausted his local remedies.

On whether an official can himself sue, the Court declared:

> By establishing a right of appeal based upon Article 16 of the Protocol, the authors of the Protocol clearly intended to guarantee respect for the privileges and immunities provided for therein, in the interest not only of the Community and its institutions, but also of persons to whom these privileges and immunities have been granted, and, moreover, in the interest of Member States and their administration which must be protected against a too wide interpretation of the said privileges and immunities.
>
> Thus it is perfectly acceptable for an individual of the Community to present himself before the Court as a plaintiff against the Government of his native country just as enterprises have already challenged before the Court arguments presented by the Government of their country when intervening on the side of the High Authority. . . .
>
> It certainly did not escape the notice of the authors of the Treaty that " disputes " likely to arise from " the interpretation or application "

---

[31] French:

 " Toute contestation portant sur l'interprétation ou l'application du présent Protocole sera soumise à la Cour."

Stationery Office:

 " Any dispute concerning the interpretation or implementation of the present Protocol shall be submitted to the Court."

[32] *Humblet* v. *The Belgian State* (Case 6–60), Vol. II.

[33] Art. 11 provides:

 " In the territory of each Member State, and regardless of their nationality, the members of the High Authority and officials of the Community:

  (b) shall be exempt from any tax on salaries and emoluments paid by the Community."

of the Protocol would result, in the first place, from controversies where persons on whom the Protocol confers privileges and immunities were in conflict with authorities having an interest in a restrictive interpretation of those privileges and immunities.

Furthermore, as has already been stated above, the privileges granted by the Protocol confer rights upon the person concerned. . . . It is natural to suppose that an actual right has as corollary the ability of the beneficiary himself to avail himself of it by a law-suit rather than by the use of a third person as intermediary.[34]

Turning to the question of whether the plaintiff before the Court was required to have exhausted his local remedies under municipal law, the Court declared:

> The Treaties establishing the European Communities did not place the Court of Justice of these Communities above national judicial proceedings in the sense that decisions taken in the proceedings could be challenged before the Court.
>
> However, the Court has exclusive jurisdiction as concerns the interpretation of the Protocol . . . The Treaties are based upon the principle of the strict separation of the powers of the Court on the one hand and municipal tribunals on the other. It follows that any overlapping of jurisdiction entrusted to these authorities is excluded.
>
> Consequently, to the extent to which the Court has jurisdiction there can be no question of a prior " exhaustion " of local judicial remedies, which would result in submitting one and the same question to the decision first of the municipal tribunals and then of the Court.[35]

[34] *Humblet* v. *The Belgian State* (Case **6–60**), Vol. **II.**
[35] *Ibid.* Vol. II.

CHAPTER
5

THE JURISDICTION OF THE COURT UNDER THE
EUROPEAN ECONOMIC COMMUNITY TREATY

ARTICLE 93, Section 2, Paras. 1 and 2

2. If, after having given notice to the parties concerned to present their observations, the Commission finds that an aid granted by a Member State or by means of the resources of a Member State is not compatible with the Common Market within the meaning of Article 92, or that this aid is being applied in an improper manner, it shall decide that the State concerned shall abolish or modify it within the time limit which it shall determine.

If the State in question has not complied with this Decision within the prescribed time limit, the Commission or any other interested State may appeal to the Court of Justice directly, notwithstanding Articles 169 and 170.[1]

By the Treaty,[2] any aid granted by a Member State, or by means of State resources in any form whatsoever, which distorts or threatens to distort competition, by favouring certain enterprises or the production of certain goods, is declared to be incompatible with the Common Market in so far as it adversely affects trade between the Member

---

[1] French:
   " 2. *Si, après avoir mis les intéressés en demeure de présenter leurs observations, la Commission constate qu'une aide accordée par un Etat membre ou au moyen des ressources d'un Etat membre, n'est pas compatible avec le marché commun aux termes de l'article 92, ou que cette aide est appliquée de façon abusive, elle décide que l'Etat intéressé doit la supprimer ou la modifier dans le délai qu'elle détermine.*
   Si l'Etat en cause ne se conforme pas à cette décision dans le délai imparti, la Commission ou tout autre Etat intéressé, peut saisir directement la Cour de Justice, par dérogation aux articles 169 et 170."
Stationery Office:
   " If, after having given notice to the parties concerned to submit their comments, the Commission find that aid granted by a State or through State resources is not compatible with the Common Market within the meaning of Article 92, or that such aid is being improperly used, it shall decide that the State concerned shall abolish or modify such aid within a time limit to be prescribed by the Commission.
   If the State concerned does not comply with this decision within the prescribed time limit, the Commission or any other interested State may, notwithstanding the provision of Articles 169 and 170, refer the matter to the Court of Justice direct."

[2] Art. 92, section 1.

States.[3] It is the duty of the Commission to make constant examination of all aids existing at any time in the Member States. The present provision deals with the situation if an aid is found to be incompatible with the Common Market, according to the definition of incompatibility set out above.

After giving notice to the State in default to present its observations, the Commission may take a Decision that the State concerned is to abolish or modify the aids.

THE APPEALS TO THE COURT

By Article 173, an appeal to the Court for the annulment of this Decision is open to the State within two months of its being passed.[4] Such an appeal, however, does not automatically suspend the Decision or the obligation to comply with it,[5] but such a suspension may be granted if circumstances require it.[6]

If compliance with the Commission's Decision is not obtained within the specified time, even if it has been appealed against under Article 173,[7] the Commission, without the necessity of setting out in a reasoned Opinion the breach complained of,[8] may appeal straight away to the Court. Similarly, any other Member State, without the usual procedure of first referring the matter to the Commission,[9] can also appeal to the Court directly. Following either of such appeals, if the Court itself finds that the State has granted aids prohibited by the Treaty, it will deliver judgment against the State which, by the Treaty,[10] is then required to take the measures which " comprise the execution of the judgment of the Court." There are no means, however, by which the State can be compelled to comply with this provision, or sanctioned if it fails to do so.[11]

---

[3] Certain aids, however, are specifically exempted from this provision, such as those to assist regions where the standard of living is abnormally low, or where there exists serious under-employment, or where the aids are to remedy damages caused by natural disasters—Art. 92, sections 2 and 3.

[4] Art. 173, paras. 1 and 3. As to these see p. 287, below.

[5] Art. 185. For argument about the suspensive effect of an appeal against a Decision under the E.C.S.C. Treaty declaring Germany to be in breach of one of her Treaty obligations, see *German Government* v. *The High Authority* (Case 19–58), Vol. II, discussed at p. 212, above.

[6] Art. 185, see p. 330, below.

[7] *Cf. German Government* v. *The High Authority*, above.

[8] The procedure required by Art. 169, para. 1, as to which see p. 274, below.

[9] The procedure required by Art. 170, para. 2, as to which see p. 277, below.

[10] Art. 171.

[11] As to this, see pp. 281–284, below.

ARTICLE 157, Section 2, Para. 3

During the term of their office, the members of the Commission may not exercise any other professional activity, whether paid or not. When taking up office, they shall give a solemn undertaking to respect, both during and after the term of their office, the obligations resulting from their position, and in particular the duty of exercising honesty and discretion as concerns the acceptance, after their term of office, of certain functions or of certain advantages. In the event of a breach of these obligations, the Court of Justice, on the application of the Council or of the Commission, may, according to the case, pronounce the dismissal from office in accordance with the provisions of Article 160, or the forfeiture of the right to a pension of the person concerned, or other advantages in lieu thereof.[12]

By the Treaty, the members of the Commission in the performance of their duties are required to act completely independently in the general interest of the Community.[13] They are neither to seek nor to accept instructions from any Government or other body, and they are to refrain from any action which is incompatible with the character of their duties.[14] They are forbidden to engage in any professional activity, whether paid or unpaid.[15] The solemn undertaking which these members are required

---

[12] French:
> "*Les membres de la Commission ne peuvent, pendant la durée de leurs fonctions, exercer aucune autre activité professionnelle rémunérée ou non. Ils prennent, lors de leur installation, l'engagement solennel de respecter, pendant la durée de leurs fonctions et après la cessation de celles-ci, les obligations découlant de leur charge, notamment les devoirs d'honnêteté et de délicatesse quant à l'acceptation, après cette cessation, de certaines fonctions ou de certains avantages. En cas de violation de ces obligations, la Cour de Justice, saisie par le Conseil ou par la Commission, peut, selon le cas, prononcer la démission d'office dans les conditions de l'article 160 ou la déchéance du droit à pension de l'intéressé ou d'autres avantages en tenant lieu.*"

Stationery Office:
> "The members of the Commission may not, during their term of office, engage in any other paid or unpaid occupation. When entering upon their duties they shall give a solemn undertaking that, both during and after their term of office, they will respect the obligations arising therefrom and in particular their duty to exercise honesty and discretion as regards the acceptance, after their term of office, of particular appointments or benefits. In the event of any breach of these obligations, the Court of Justice, on the application of the Council or of the Commission, may, according to the circumstances, order that the member concerned either be compulsorily retired in accordance with the provisions of Article 160 or forfeit his right to a pension or other benefits in lieu thereof."

[13] Art. 157, section 2.1.

[14] Art. 157, section 2.2.

[15] Art. 157, section 2.3.

to give when taking up office appears thus to impose no obligations upon them which did not already exist.

THE APPEAL TO THE COURT

For breach of these obligations, either the Commission itself or the Council can appeal to the Court.[16] Following such an appeal, the present Article provides that the Court " may, according to the case, pronounce the dismissal from office in accordance with the provision of Article 160." This reference to Article 160, however, is not understood.[17] Paragraph 1 of that Article declares that the Court at the request of the Council or of the Commission may declare a member of the Commission to be removed from office. This clearly adds nothing to the present provision. Paragraph 3 of that Article states that on the request of the Council or of the Commission, the Court may provisionally suspend such a member from his office. Now it is clear that to suspend a member from his office is not to dismiss him, so that when the present Article refers to " dismissal from office in accordance with Article 160," provisions concerning suspension clearly do not apply. This cross-reference appears, therefore, to be devoid of meaning.

In their solemn undertaking, the members of the Commission declare that even after the ending of their duties they will respect the obligations resulting therefrom,[18] and will exercise honesty and discretion in regard to the acceptance of certain functions or advantages. In the event of a breach of this obligation, a power of dismissal is clearly inappropriate because the member will by then have ceased to hold office, and instead, therefore, the Court is given the power to forfeit the member's pension, or other advantages paid to him in lieu thereof.[19]

These two powers of the Court, to dismiss from office, *or* to forfeit the right to a pension, are declared to be ones which the Court may exercise " according to the case." It appears that the meaning of these words is that a sitting member can be dismissed, and the pension of a retired member forfeited. If this is so, it would seem that the pension of the sitting member cannot be forfeited.

---

[16] The Commission's decision to appeal must be reached by a majority vote of the members—Art. 163, para. 1.

[17] For the terms of Art. 160, see p. 272, below.

[18] One of the obligations which would continue beyond the termination of office would be that of secrecy.

[19] It is not stated whether the forfeiture is retrospective so that pension money, etc., already paid becomes repayable.

ARTICLE 160

Any member of the Commission, if he no longer fulfils the conditions required for the performance of his duties or if he has been guilty of serious misconduct, may be pronounced dismissed by the Court of Justice, at the request of the Council or of the Commission.

In such a case, the Council, by a unanimous vote, may provisionally suspend him from his office and provide for his replacement until the time when the Court of Justice shall have given its ruling.

The Court of Justice may, provisionally, suspend him from his office at the request of the Council or of the Commission.[20]

By this Article the Court, at the request of the Council or of the Commission, may dismiss from office any member of the Commission who no longer satisfies the conditions required for the performance of his duties.[21] This power is merely a re-statement of the power already given to the Court by Article 157, section 2, paragraph 3,[22] except that under the present Article the Court can also declare a member of the Commission to be dismissed if he is found guilty of serious misconduct. There is no indication in the Treaty as to the meaning of this term, but because such activities as receiving instruction from particular enterprises, or passing information to a particular board room appear to be clear violations of the required conditions that a member shall be independent,[23] it is suggested that " serious misconduct " must possess

[20] French:
   " *Tout membre de la Commission, s'il ne remplit plus les conditions nécessaires à l'exercice de ses fonctions ou s'il a commis une faute grave, peut être déclaré démissionnaire par la Cour de Justice, à la requête du Conseil ou de la Commission.*
   En pareil cas, le Conseil, statuant à l'unanimité, peut, à titre provisoire, le suspendre de ses fonctions et pourvoir à son remplacement jusqu'au moment où la Cour de Justice se sera prononcée.
   La Cour de Justice peut, à titre provisoire, le suspendre de ses fonctions, à la requête du Conseil ou de la Commission."
   Stationery Office:
   " If any member of the Commission no longer fulfils the conditions required for the performance of his duties, or if he has been guilty of serious misconduct, the Court of Justice, on the application of the Council or of the Commission, may compulsorily retire him from office.
   In such a case the Council may, by a unanimous decision, provisionally suspend the member from his duties and make provision for his replacement pending the ruling of the Court of Justice.
   The Court of Justice may on the application of the Council or of the Commission provisionally suspend the member from his duties."
[21] As to the conditions, see Art. 157, p. 270, above.
[22] See p. 270, above.
[23] A condition imposed by Art. 151, section 1, para. 1.

a wider meaning, though it is mere speculation whether it would take in sexual or criminal eccentricities.

THE DISMISSAL

It is clear that the Court would only pronounce this dismissal after a full investigation of the charges against the member and, presumably, after giving the member an opportunity to present his defence. The words in paragraph 1, that the member may be declared dismissed " if he no longer fulfils the conditions required for the performance of his duties," mean, therefore, " if he in fact no longer fulfils the conditions "; they cannot mean " if he is merely accused of no longer fulfilling the conditions." Paragraph 2, however, relates to a power of suspension which the Council can exercise " in such a case." This, however, is bad drafting because the Council's power can be exercised before the member has been found in fact no longer to fulfil the conditions: the Council can act on a mere accusation, which is not the case dealt with in paragraph 1.

Following this accusation, the Council may suspend the member and provide for his replacement provided the members of the Council are unanimous. If they are not, then it appears that even by a majority vote the Council, and also the Commission, can request the Court to suspend the member, presumably without prejudice to the subsequent consideration by the Court of whether the member in fact no longer fulfils the required conditions. It may be noted, however, that this circumventing of the unanimity rule within the Council will not enable provision to be made for a replacement—this must be unanimously decided upon by the Council.

ARTICLE 164

The Court of Justice shall ensure the respect of law in the interpretation and application of the present Treaty.[24]

This article defines the Court's duty. It is suggested that it does not itself grant jurisdiction—the Court being limited by the jurisdiction contained in other articles of the Treaty.

[24] French:
" *La Cour de Justice assure le respect du droit dans l'interprétation et l'application du présent Traité.*"
Stationery Office:
" The Court of Justice shall ensure the observance of law in the interpretation and application of this Treaty."

Where the similar provision appears in the E.C.S.C. Treaty[25] mention is made of the implementing regulations of the Treaty. There appears to be no reason why reference to these has been omitted in the present article, although it seems inconceivable that any point was intended to turn on this omission.

ARTICLE 169

If the Commission considers that a Member State has failed in one of the obligations imposed upon it by virtue of the present Treaty, it shall issue a reasoned Opinion to this effect, after having given this State an opportunity to present its observations.

If the State in question does not comply with this Opinion within the period specified by the Commission, the latter may appeal to the Court of Justice.[26]

The " Reasoned Opinion " of the Commission

This provision has been based upon Article 88 of the E.C.S.C. Treaty but it differs from that Article in one very important respect. Under Article 88,[27] if the High Authority considers that a State has failed in one of its obligations under the E.C.S.C. Treaty, that Authority is required to pass a Decision setting out the breach. This Decision, like all other Decisions of the High Authority, is open to challenge before the Court on the usual four grounds of appeal.[28] Under the present Article, however, the default of a Member State under the E.E.C. Treaty is required to be set out in a " reasoned Opinion." Now, by Article 173, the Court cannot determine upon the legality of Opinions of the Commission. A Member State appears, therefore, at first sight, to

---

[25] Art. 31, see p. 112, above.

[26] French:
   " *Si la Commission estime qu'un Etat membre a manqué à une des obligations qui lui incombent en vertu du présent Traité, elle émet un avis motivé à ce sujet, après avoir mis cet Etat en mesure de présenter ses observations.*
   Si l'Etat en cause ne se conforme pas à cet avis dans le délai déterminé par la Commission, celle-ci peut saisir la Cour de Justice."
Stationery Office:
   " If the Commission considers that a Member State has failed to fulfil any of its obligations under the Treaty, it shall issue a reasoned opinion on the matter after giving the State concerned the opportunity to submit its comments.
   If the State concerned does not comply with the terms of such opinion within the period laid down by the Commission, the latter may refer the matter to the Court of Justice."

[27] For the terms of Art. 88, see p. 249, above.

[28] As to these grounds, see E.C.S.C. Treaty, Art. 33, para. 1, p. 112, above.

have no redress against the Commission even in an extreme case where, for example, that State was not granted an opportunity to present its observations, or the time given to it for compliance with the Treaty was unreasonably short.

Although Article 169 uses the term " Opinion," and an Opinion is defined in the Treaty [29] as not being binding, nevertheless in the present instance the " Opinion " of the Commission is required, first, to be reasoned and, secondly, to set out the time period within which compliance with the Opinion is to occur. If this reasoned " Opinion " is in no way binding, then, clearly by virtue of the " Opinion " there can be no obligation upon the State concerned to comply within that time period, or at all. If this is regarded as not being a tenable proposition; if it is accepted that, of course, a State is intended to be bound by the time limit specified for its compliance, then the " Opinion " must in fact be a Decision or a Regulation, and as such open to appeal under Article 173.

However, if the " Opinion " issued under the present Article is an Opinion as defined by the Treaty, as prima facie it must be, it is not open to appeal. One must, therefore, consider what redress a State possesses if, as postulated above, the Opinion in question has been issued without any adequate reasons, or if the State has not been allowed to present its observations.

In one case before it, the Court, when considering the validity of an Opinion of the High Authority declared [30];

> The giving of reasons for an Opinion . . . constitutes an essential, indeed a constitutive, element of such an act. The absence, therefore, of supporting reasons entails the non-existence of the act.[31]

It can be argued from this that an Opinion of the Commission which is issued without supporting reasons is also non-existent, so that no notice need be taken of it by the State concerned. The paradox of this, however, is that it is only the Court which can declare whether an Opinion is adequately supported by reasons or not, and to request such a declaration of the Court would be to bring an action against the Opinion, and there is no provision in the Treaty under which such an action can be brought. It appears safer, therefore, to adopt an alternative approach to the problem of appealing.

[29] Art. 189, para. 5.
[30] *Société des Usines à Tubes de la Sarre* v. *The High Authority* (Joint Cases 1–57 and 14–57), Vol. II. The Opinion in question was expressly given the force of a Decision and was, therefore, open to an appeal before the Court—E.C.S.C. Treaty, Art. 54, para. 5.
[31] *Ibid.* See also pp. 133–134, above.

By Article 169, two powers have been conferred upon the Commission. First, after having given the State in question an opportunity to present its observations, the Commission possesses the power to issue a reasoned Opinion.[32] Secondly, if the State has not complied with this Opinion within the time period specified by the Commission, that Commission has the power to appeal to the Court.[33] Now it will be noticed that this power of the Commission to appeal is dependent upon the State's failure to comply with " this Opinion," that is to say, with the reasoned Opinion issued after the State has been given an opportunity to present its observations. If, therefore, there exists no reasoned Opinion—or no Opinion adequately reasoned—or if the State concerned, has not been enabled to present its observations, the State will not have failed to comply with the obligation imposed upon it by such an Opinion, because such an Opinion as is referred to in paragraph 1 will not yet have been issued. The ability of the Commission to appeal to the Court, being dependent upon the State's failure to comply with the Opinion within the time specified therein, will, therefore, not yet have arisen. This legal inability can clearly be reviewed by the Court when the admissibility of the action brought is challenged by the State concerned. By this means, therefore, the State can ensure that it is enabled to present its observations to the Commission and that that Commission's Opinion, when issued, is reasoned.

It is suggested, however, that the procedure to ensure that the Commission acts correctly in respect of States' breaches of the Treaty is less satisfactory than the procedure under the E.C.S.C. Treaty for the control of similar breaches. First, as set out above, by the E.E.C. Treaty, the validity of the declaration of breach can only be determined after the period for compliance with that declaration has expired: whereas under the E.C.S.C. Treaty, the High Authority's declaration of breach can be challenged during the one month immediately following its publication. Secondly, the challenge of the High Authority's declaration of breach can be made on any of the usual four grounds allowed for appeals against Decisions, whereas under the present Treaty, when the validity of the declaration of the Commission can eventually be determined by the Court, it can, in effect, be challenged only for violation of a substantial procedural requirement.[34]

---

[32] Art. 169, para. 1. For examples of the use of this power, see *Commission of the E.E.C.* v. *The Italian Government* (Case 10–61) [1962] C.M.L.R. 187, and *Commission of the E.E.C.* v. *The Grand Duchy of Luxembourg and the Kingdom of Belgium* (Joint Cases 2–62 and 3–62) [1963] C.M.L.R. 199.

[33] Art. 169, para. 2.

[34] It might be argued that the words " the Commission considers " means " considers upon objectively existing grounds." If, therefore, such grounds did not exist the

A Breach of a State's Obligations under the Statute of the European Investment Bank

Under the Protocol on the Statute of the European Investment Bank, the Member States of the Community have undertaken certain duties,[35] and by the Treaty the various Protocols are declared to form an integral part of the Treaty.[36] A breach of one of the duties under this protocol is, therefore, a breach by a State of one of its Treaty obligations and, as Article 169 stands, it is able to be sanctioned by the Commission under the machinery there provided. However, Article 180 (a) provides that in respect to the carrying out by Member States of their obligations under the Statute of the Bank " the Board of Directors shall exercise the powers conferred upon the Commission by Article 169." [37] It appears reasonable, therefore, to infer that in respect of breaches of these obligations the Commission retains no power.

The Grounds of Appeal

As the sole issue before the Court, when the matter is finally brought before it, will be whether or not the defendant State is in breach of one of its obligations under the Treaty, the jurisdiction of the Court must be, first, to interpret the terms of the Treaty in order to determine the extent of the obligation in question, and, secondly, to assess whether the acts or inaction of the State concerned violated this obligation,[38] and, thirdly, where applicable, whether the State has complied with its Treaty obligations within the time granted to it by the Commission for such compliance.

ARTICLE 170

Any of the Member States may appeal to the Court of Justice if it considers that another Member State has failed to fulfil one of the obligations incumbent upon it by virtue of the present Treaty.

Before a Member State may introduce an appeal against another Member State based upon an alleged violation of the

---

Opinion could be annulled on the grounds of incompetence. It is suggested, however, that the standard can be only that the Commission is to have reasonable grounds for considering that a Member State has failed in one of its obligations, and in virtually every case these will exist so that incompetence could not be alleged.

35 For a description of these, see p. 421, below.
36 Art. 239.
37 Art. 180 (a) is discussed at pp. 318–321, below.
38 This may be compared with the jurisdiction of the Court when a State is similarly alleged to have violated the E.C.S.C. Treaty.

obligations imposed upon it by virtue of the present Treaty, it shall refer the matter to the Commission.

The Commission shall issue a reasoned Opinion after the States concerned have been given an opportunity to present their own and reply to each other's written and oral observations.

If the Commission has not issued an Opinion within a period of three months from the request, the lack of an Opinion shall be no bar to the bringing of an appeal before the Court of Justice.[39]

Under the E.C.S.C. Treaty, any dispute among Member States concerning the application of that Treaty which cannot be settled by another procedure provided for in the Treaty, may be submitted to the Court at the request of one of the States which are parties to the dispute.[40] Under the present Treaty there is no such right of immediate appeal to the Court. Instead the plaintiff State must first submit the matter to the Commission.

THE ROLE PLAYED BY THE COMMISSION

Following this submission of the matter, it is stated in paragraph 3 of this Article that the Commission shall issue a reasoned Opinion after the States concerned have each been given an opportunity to present

---

[39] French:

" *Chacun des Etats membres peut saisir la Cour de Justice s'il estime qu'un autre Etat membre a manqué à une des obligations qui lui incombent en vertu du présent Traité.*

Avant qu'un Etat membre n'introduise, contre un autre Etat membre, un recours fondé sur une prétendue violation des obligations qui lui incombent en vertu du présent Traité, il doit en saisir la Commission.

La Commission émet un avis motivé après que les Etats intéressés aient été mis en mesure de présenter contradictoirement leurs observations écrites et orales.

Si la Commission n'a pas émis l'avis dans un délai de trois mois à compter de la demande, l'absence d'avis ne fait pas obstacle à la saisie de la Cour de Justice."

Stationery Office:

" Any Member State which considers that another Member State has failed to fulfil any of its obligations under this Treaty may refer the matter to the Court of Justice.

Before a Member State institutes, against another Member State, proceedings relating to an alleged infringement of the obligations under this Treaty, it shall refer the matter to the Commission.

The Commission shall deliver a reasoned opinion after the States concerned have been given the opportunity both to submit their own cases and to reply to each other's cases both orally and in writing.

If the Commission, within a period of three months from the date on which the matter was referred to it, has not given an opinion, the absence of such opinion shall not preclude reference to the Court of Justice."

[40] E.C.S.C. Treaty, Art. 89, para. 1; see pp. 257–259, above.

their own and reply to each other's written and oral observations. This paragraph must be compared with the provisions of Article 169.[41] Under that Article, it will be recalled, an alternative procedure for remedying the default of a Member State is set out, namely, that the Commission should itself initiate action against the State concerned. However, before it may do so under that Article the Commission must request the defaulting State to present its observations. Under the present Article, the Commission must do more. It must request both the plaintiff and the defendant States to present their observations, and these observations are expressly required to be both written *and* oral and are required to set out each State's case and the reply to the case of the other side. This, it is suggested, can only mean that, in effect, a legal arbitration is to be held before the Commission. Following this hearing, the reasoned Opinion of the Commission is issued. It appears, however, that under the present Article, as distinct from Article 169, this Opinion can merely set out whether the Commission finds the alleged breach substantiated or not—it cannot, in addition, give the defaulting State a period in which to comply with the Treaty. As a result, therefore, immediately after the issuing of the Opinion of the Commission, the plaintiff State may appeal to the Court, whereas if the Commission had been acting under Article 169, the Commission could not itself have appealed to the Court until after the expiration of the time period which it had itself specified for compliance with the Treaty.

THE APPEAL TO THE COURT

If this reasoned Opinion amounts to a finding rejecting the allegations of the plaintiff State, the action before the Court will, in effect, be an appeal against the Opinion of the Commission. If, however, the reasoned Opinion finds in favour of the plaintiffs, the action before the Court will be an appeal to the highest organ of the Community for a final legal declaration of breach.[42]

BREACHES OF A STATE'S OBLIGATION NOT TO GRANT AIDS

When Article 93 (2) was discussed,[43] it was noted that if the Commission finds that a Member State has granted an aid which is not compatible with the Common Market, the Commission must give a Decision requiring the State concerned to abolish or modify the aid within a prescribed time limit. The subsequent right of appeal to the Court,

---

[41] See p. 274, above.
[42] The value of such an appeal is discussed on pp. 282–283, below.
[43] Pp. 268–269, above.

if the State fails to comply with the Decision, is declared in Article 93 to be open " notwithstanding Articles 169 and 170." The effect of the reference to Article 170 is that when a State has failed to comply with the Decision in question, any other interested State may appeal to the Court without the necessity of first referring the matter to the Commission. The object of this provision is clear, for there is obviously no need to refer a matter to the Commission when that Commission has already fully considered it and taken a Decision upon it.

The converse of this provision appears to apply, however, namely, that if it is a Member State which alleges the existence of aids granted by another Member State, the former must first refer the matter to the Commission under Article 170, paragraph 2. It would appear, however, that instead of issuing its reasoned Opinion, under paragraph 3 of this Article, the Commission, after having given notice to the parties concerned to present their observations, may instead pass a Decision under Article 93 (2), and thereby require compliance with the Treaty. If the Commission were to do this, the subsequent appeal by a State to the Court would have to be brought under Article 93 (2) and not under Article 170 because a Decision, as distinct from a reasoned Opinion, would have been issued.

BREACHES OF A STATE'S OBLIGATIONS UNDER THE STATUTE OF THE EUROPEAN INVESTMENT BANK

By Article 180 (a) [44] in matters relating to breaches by Member States of their obligations under the Statute of the European Investment Bank, the Board of Directors of that Bank exercise the powers conferred upon the Commission by Article 169. The effect of this, as discussed elsewhere,[45] is that it is the Board of Directors and not the Commission who, in a reasoned Opinion, can set out the breach by a Member State of its obligations under the Statute. Because, however, Article 180 (a) makes no reference to the powers conferred upon the Commission by the present Article, an unintended situation arises, and it is this. If a Member State breaks one of its obligations under the Statute, as, for example, by refusing to grant a loan to the Bank, the Commission possesses no power to issue an Opinion on the matter, that power residing with the Board of Directors. If, however, one of the Member States wishes to take legal action against this refusal to grant a loan, it is provided by Article 170, paragraph 2, that before appealing to the Court

[44] See p. 317, below.
[45] See p. 319, below.

the State must refer the matter to the Commission which then by paragraph 3 *can* issue a reasoned Opinion. However, it is clearly wrong that the Commission can examine and can issue a reasoned Opinion concerning the breach simply because a State has referred the matter to it, whereas the Commission could not have examined such a breach or issued any Opinion of its own motion. It is suggested, therefore, that the Commission cannot have power in the present situation and, just as in the case of Article 169, so here also, the Board of Directors exercise the powers of the Commission. The Member State, therefore, it is suggested, must refer its complaint to the Board of Directors of the Bank.

THE GROUNDS OF APPEAL

When the case comes before the Court, the issues will substantially be the same as if the case had been brought by the Commission under Article 169.[46] However, as the Commission in its Opinion issued under the present Article cannot require compliance with the obligation which it is alleged has been broken, there will be no occasion for the Court to determine upon that particular matter.

ARTICLE 171

If the Court of Justice finds that a Member State has failed in one of the obligations incumbent upon it by virtue of the present Treaty, this State is required to take the measures which comprise the execution of the judgment of the Court.[47]

This Article is to be read with Articles 169 and 170 [48] under which either the Commission or Member State can bring an action before the Court accusing another State of having failed to fulfil one of its obligations under the Treaty.[49]

Under Article 169, the Commission, before it can appeal to the Court, must have issued a reasoned Opinion specifying the breach and

---

[46] As to these, see p. 274, above.
[47] French:
  " *Si la Cour de Justice reconnaît qu'un Etat membre a manqué à une des obligations qui lui incombent en vertu du présent Traité, cet Etat est tenu de prendre les mesures que comporte l'exécution de l'arrêt de la Cour de Justice.*"
  Stationery Office:
  " If the Court of Justice finds that a Member State has failed to fulfil any of its obligations under this Treaty, such State is bound to take the measures required for the implementation of the judgment of the Court."
[48] See pp. 274–281, above.
[49] Such appeals can also be brought under Art. 93.2, see p. 268, above; Art. 180 (a), see p. 317, below, and Art. 225, para. 2, see p. 331, below.

declaring a time limit within which compliance is to occur, and this time limit must have expired without any such compliance.[50] Similarly, under Article 170, before a Member State can sue another State in the Court, the Commission must have issued a reasoned Opinion setting out its findings.[51] As the present article merely imposes an obligation upon the defaulting State to comply with the judgment given, and that judgment can itself impose no sanctions,[52] certain doubt as to the value of appealing to the Court may well be entertained.

THE VALUE OF APPEALING TO THE COURT AFTER THE COMMISSION HAS DECLARED A STATE TO BE IN BREACH OF A TREATY OBLIGATION

An example may illustrate doubts as to the value of this appeal.

The Member States of the Community are under a duty to have eliminated all customs duties between themselves within the timetable set out in the Treaty.[53] This is a duty imposed principally by Article 3. If a Member State were to retain customs duties after the permitted period, that State would be in breach of Article 3. The Commission would then be able to set out this breach in a reasoned Opinion and could give the State concerned a time limit within which to remove the offending duties. The State would then presumably be under a duty to comply with this Opinion by virtue of Article 169.[54] The position for the State would, therefore, in law, be that it was now required by the Treaty to obey both Article 3 and Article 169.

If the State were to continue to impose these customs duties, the Commission could appeal to the Court, and after judgment was given against the defaulting State, that State would then be under a duty to obey not only Article 3 and Article 169, but it would also have acquired a new duty to obey the present article. It may well be questioned, therefore, why a State should be more likely to observe an obligation specified in Article 171 when it has already failed to observe the self-same obligation when it was specified in Article 169 and originally in Article 3.

---

[50] See p. 274, above.

[51] See p. 277, above. If the Commission fails to issue this opinion within three months from the date of the request to it, the State may appeal to the Court as if an opinion had been issued—Art. 170, para. 4, see p. 278, above.

[52] This position may be compared with that under E.C.S.C. Treaty, Art. 88, where a defaulting State can be fined by the High Authority—although even under the E.C.S.C. Treaty, the Court itself can impose no sanction upon a State in respect of its breach.

[53] A time period of twelve years is stated in Art. 8.1.

[54] Opinions, however, are expressly declared not to be binding—Art. 189, para. 5, but see the discussion on this, pp. 275–276, above.

This manner of looking at the problem, however, it is suggested, is more logical than realistic. It must, of course, be immediately conceded that if, of set purpose, a State intends to defy the terms of the Treaty it will as readily defy Article 171 as Article 3. However, the Treaty has been drawn up and is in force on the assumption that the Member States are not going to intend to defy the Treaty, or certainly not to the extent of jeopardising the existence of the whole Community.

A breach of Article 3 will either be inadvertent or deliberate. If it is inadvertent, the declaration of the Commission will be adequate to cause the breach to be rectified. If the breach was deliberate, the State will have to consider whether, following the declaration of the Commission, it is going to persist in its breach and defy the Commission. Finally, after a judgment of the Court, the State will have to decide whether it will defy this final organ of the Community as well. If it does defy the Court, then clearly the assumption upon which the whole structure of the Community has been built will have been falsified, and the Community, as a group of States working together, will have come to an end. The distinction between disobeying the Commission, in breach of Article 169, and disobeying the Court, in breach of Article 171, is, it is suggested, one of degree. Admittedly, this hierarchy of obligations is based upon subjective factors: this, however, in no way detracts from the effectiveness of such a hierarchy. An appeal to the Court is recognised as the final step in the enforcement procedures. To disobey the Commission is merely to disobey the Commission: to disobey the Court is to smash the Community.[55]

LIMITATIONS UPON THE CONTENT OF THE JUDGMENT OF THE COURT

The present article declares that if the Court finds that a Member State has failed in one of its Treaty obligations, that State is to " take the measures which comprise the execution of the judgment of the Court." Now the fact that a State has failed in one of its obligations will have been set out in the judgment of the Court: the measures which comprise the execution of that judgment can, therefore, be said to have been taken only if the State in fact brings its breach to an end. There is no provision in the present article, however, by which the Court can impose any pecuniary or other sanction upon the State concerned: so that if that State has reaped advantages from its breach there are no means by which it can be deprived of these advantages. Furthermore, the Court

---

[55] It is significant that under the E.C.S.C. Treaty, the High Authority can impose financial sanctions upon the defaulting State—Art. 88, para. 3 (a) and (b). It was not thought necessary to incorporate a similar provision in the present Treaty.

in its judgment can award no relief to a State which has suffered loss because of the breach.

It follows from this that if the defaulting State has complied with its obligations at any time before the hearing before the Court, even although, if the Commission is proceeding under Article 169, that compliance must of necessity have been after the date specified for such compliance,[56] the judgment of the Court would be merely of academic value and it is doubtful, therefore, whether the Court would proceed to hear the action.[57]

ARTICLE 172

The Regulations enacted by the Council by virtue of the provision of the present Treaty may confer upon the Court of Justice power to act in *pleine juridiction* **in regard to penalties provided for in these Regulations.**[58]

The Regulations mentioned here are those referred to in Article 189 of the Treaty where it is provided:

Regulations shall have general application. They shall be binding in every respect and directly applicable in each Member State.[59]

Under the E.E.C. Treaty there are only four matters upon which the Council is empowered to enact Regulations, because the general scheme of the Treaty is that use shall mainly be made of Directives.[60] The four matters concern the promotion of a common agricultural policy and

---

56 If such compliance had been within the time specified, the Commission would have had no ability to appeal to the Court. The position stated in the text above is the same if the appeal is being brought by the Commission or a Member State under Art. 93.2, for the text of which see p. 268, above.

57 This position may be compared, however, to that in one case where the Court proceeded to consider the legal validity of a *Caisse de Compensation* in Luxembourg even after it had been abolished, because in that case the plaintiffs could show that they had suffered injury as a result of the existence of the *Caisse—Groupement des Industries Sidérurgiques Luxembourgeoises* v. *The High Authority* (Joint Cases 7–54 and 9–54), Vol. II. The question of costs incurred up to, and after, the date of the compliance will, however, be for the Court to determine—see *Meroni & Co. and others* v. *The High Authority* (Joint Cases 5, 7 and 8–60).

58 French:
" *Les règlements établis par le Conseil en vertu des dispositions du présent Traité peuvent attribuer à la Cour de Justice une compétence de pleine juridiction en ce qui concerne les sanctions prévues dans ces règlements.*"
Stationery Office:
" The regulations enacted by the Council pursuant to the provisions of this Treaty may confer on the Court of Justice full jurisdiction as to the merits in regard to the penalties provided for in these regulations."

59 Art. 189, para. 2.

60 " Directives shall be binding, in respect of the result to be achieved, upon every Member State, but the form and manner of enforcing them shall be a matter for the national authorities "—Art. 189, para. 3.

putting it into effect [61]; achieving the free movement of workers [62]; authorising certain restrictive trade practices and the breaking up of enterprises found to be improperly exploiting a dominant position within the Common Market [63] and, finally, the authorisation of certain State aid, for example, to backward regions or those suffering from natural disasters.[64] At the present time, however, the only Regulation which imposes penalties and confers jurisdiction upon the Court is Regulation 17 of 1962 passed by the Council of Ministers relating to restrictive trade practices and enterprises improperly exploiting a dominant position.[65]

By this Regulation, the Commission by a Decision may *inter alia* impose upon an enterprise or association which operates a prohibited trade agreement or practice a fine of which the minimum is 1,000 E.P.U.s [66] and the maximum 1m. E.P.U.s [67] plus 10 per cent. of the enterprise's turnover for the preceding business year. In addition there can be imposed a penalty payment of from 50 to 1,000 E.P.U.s [68] for each day that the agreement continues.[69]

THE APPEAL IN PLEINE JURIDICTION UNDER REGULATION 17

It is provided:

> The Court of Justice shall have power in *pleine juridiction* within the meaning of Article 172 of the Treaty to adjudicate upon appeals brought against the Decision by which the Commission has fixed a fine or a daily penalty; it may cancel, reduce or increase the fine or the daily penalty imposed.[70]

In the appeal in *pleine juridiction* against this penalty it will be noted that two distinct acts will be called into question: first, the actual Decision of the Commission imposing the fine or daily penalty payment,[71] and, secondly, Regulation 17 itself of the Council of Ministers, because if that Regulation is invalid, then clearly any Decisions passed under that Regulation which impose fines upon enterprises must also be invalid.

In the normal way an enterprise or association can challenge a Decision of the Commission under power given to it to do so by Article

---

[61] Art. 43.2, para. 3. A Directive can be substituted for a Regulation—*ibid.*
[62] Art. 49, para. 1. A Directive can be substituted for a Regulation—*ibid.*
[63] Art. 87.1. A Directive can be substituted for a Regulation—*ibid.*
[64] Art. 94.
[65] *Journal Officiel*, February 21, 1962, p. 204.
[66] About £360 or $1,000.
[67] About £360,000 or $1m.
[68] From about £18 or $50 to about £360 or $1,000.
[69] Regulation 17, Arts. 15 and 16.
[70] *Ibid.* Art. 17.
[71] " Decisions shall be binding in every respect upon those to whom they are directed "—Art. 189, para. 4.

173, paragraph 2.[72] Under this provision the enterprise or association, within two months, can allege that the Decision should be annulled on one or more of the four classic grounds of annulment.[73] This first appeal for annulment would be open to the enterprise or association to challenge the validity of the Decision fining it. In addition, however, the enterprise or association may appeal under Article 172 against the penalties imposed upon it by that particular Decision.[74] This second appeal is in *pleine juridiction,* and, as has been seen when the similar power of the Court in relation to penalties imposed under the E.C.S.C. Treaty was discussed,[75] in such an appeal the Court has the widest possible powers both with respect to fact and law, and can annul or amend the Decision which has been taken imposing the penalties and, as expressly set out in the German text of Article 172, can vary or suspend these penalties. The grounds of this second appeal can, of course, include any of the four grounds which could have been alleged under Article 173 in order to substantiate the first appeal; for example, that the Decision is void as not being adequately supported with reasons so that there has been a violation of a substantial procedural requirement.[76] In addition to alleging any or all of the four classic grounds of appeal, because the action is in *pleine juridiction,* the plaintiffs can allege that the fine or penalty payment is excessive or, by reliance upon allegation of fact, that the fine is not due. On this evidence the Court has an entirely free hand either to cancel, reduce, confirm or even increase the fine or daily penalties up to the maximum prescribed in Regulation 17.

In the appeal against the Decision imposing the fine or daily penalties, however, the plaintiffs may wish to allege that the power granted to the Commission by Regulation 17 to impose fines is itself illegal.[77] The difficulty here, however, is first, that under Article 173, an enterprise or an association does not possess standing to challenge a Regulation of the Council of Ministers, and, secondly, the time limit of two months for appeals under Article 173 will inevitably long since have expired.[78]

---

[72] See p. 287, below.

[73] These are set out in Art. 173, para. 1, see p. 287, below.

[74] Regulation 17, Art. 17 makes it clear that it is not merely the penalties imposed which can be challenged but the Decision itself which imposed those penalties. This is not clear from the wording of Art. 172.

[75] See Art. 36, p. 193, above.

[76] For an example of this, see *Meroni & Co., S.P.A.* v. *The High Authority* (Case 9–56), Vol. II.

[77] For an example of a similar argument in relation to a fine imposed by the *Caisse de Péréquation* set up by the High Authority under E.C.S.C. Treaty, see *Meroni & Co., S.P.A.* v. *The High Authority* (Case 9–56), Vol. II.

[78] The Regulation was published in the *Journal Officiel* on February 21, 1962.

To meet these difficulties, therefore, Article 184 of the Treaty was included which provides:

> Notwithstanding the expiration of the time limit set out in Article 173, paragraph 3, any party in an action bringing into issue a Regulation of the Council or of the Commission may rely upon the grounds set out in Article 173, paragraph 1,[79] in order to allege before the Court of Justice the inapplicability of this Regulation.

Under this article both of the above difficulties are removed and the enterprise or association can challenge the legality of the Regulation itself.

If that Regulation is held to be valid, then the authority of the Commission to impose fines and penalty payments cannot be impugned. If, however, that Regulation is declared by the Court to be invalid, no Decision passed in pursuance of that Regulation will be upheld. The Court, however, has declared that under the similar situation in the E.C.S.C. Treaty,[80] it has no jurisdiction to annul the parent Regulation [81] because of the time limit set out in the Treaty for the bringing of actions for annulment.[82] There would be an obligation upon the Council of Ministers, however, to repeal the invalid Regulation.

There is no time limit specified within which appeals under Article 172 must be brought.

ARTICLE 173

The Court of Justice shall determine upon the legality of the acts, other than Recommendations or Opinions, of the Council and of the Commission. To this end, it is competent to pronounce upon appeals for incompetence, violation of a substantial procedural requirement, violation of the present Treaty, or of any rule of law concerning its application or for *détournement de pouvoir,* **brought by a Member State, the Council or the Commission.**

Any other natural or legal person may, under the same conditions, bring an appeal against Decisions directed to him and against Decisions which, although taken under the appearance of a Regulation, or of a Decision addressed to another person, concern him directly and individually.

The appeals referred to in the present article must be brought within a period of two months, calculated, according

---

[79] These are the four classic grounds of appeal, see this page, below.
[80] Art. 36, p. 193, above.
[81] In the case of the E.C.S.C. Treaty, the parent Decision.
[82] *Meroni & Co., S.P.A.* v. *The High Authority* (Case 9-56), Vol. II.

to the case, from the publication of the act, or from its notification to the plaintiff, or in default of these, from the day when he had knowledge of it.[33]

The Change of Wording to Describe the Administrative Acts of the Council and the Commission

This article is based upon Article 33 of the E.C.S.C. Treaty, but it has also incorporated some important differences.[84] To understand the article, one must first be warned that the well-known terms employed in Article 33—namely, " Decisions " and " Recommendations," each of which may be either general or individual—do not occur in Article 173, or rather they do occur, but with entirely different meanings from those which one would expect.

Whether a Decision of the High Authority is general or individual, it is binding in every respect.[85] Both the Council and the Commission, under the E.E.C. Treaty, can issue acts which are also binding in every

---

[33] French:

" *La Cour de Justice contrôle la légalité des actes du Conseil et de la Commission, autres que les recommandations ou avis. A cet effet, elle est compétente pour se prononcer sur les recours pour incompétence, violation des formes substantielles, violation du présent Traité ou de toute règle de droit relative à son application, ou détournement de pouvoir, formés par un Etat membre, le Conseil ou la Commission.*

Toute personne physique ou morale peut former, dans les mêmes conditions, un recours contre les décisions dont elle est le destinataire, et contre les décisions qui, bien que prises sous l'apparence d'un règlement ou d'une décision adressée à une autre personne, la concernent directement et individuellement.

Les recours prévus au présent article doivent être formés dans un délai de deux mois à compter, suivant le cas, de la publication de l'acte, de sa notification au requérant, ou, à défaut, du jour où celui-ci en a eu connaissance."

Stationery Office:

" Supervision of the legality of the acts of the Council and the Commission other than recommendations or opinions shall be a matter for the Court of Justice. The Court shall for this purpose have jurisdiction in proceedings instituted by a Member State, the Council or the Commission on the grounds of lack of jurisdiction, substantial violations of basic procedural rules, infringements of this Treaty or of any rule of law relating to effect being given to it or of misuse of powers.

Any natural or legal person may, under the same conditions, appeal against a decision directed to him or against a decision which, although in the form of a regulation or a decision directed to another person, is of direct and individual concern to him.

The proceedings provided for in this Article shall be instituted within a period of two months, dating as the case may be, either from the publication of the measure concerned or from its notification to the complainant or, in default of this, from the day on which the latter learned of the said measure."

[84] The reader is referred to the discussion of Art. 33 for a consideration of some of the concepts employed in the present article; see pp. 112–176, above.

[85] E.C.S.C. Treaty, Art. 14, para. 2.

respect. If these acts are of general effect, that is to say, are the equivalent of general Decisions of the High Authority, they are termed "Regulations": if they are the equivalent of individual Decisions, they are termed "Decisions." [86]

Recommendations of the High Authority are binding with respect to the objectives which they specify, but they leave to those concerned the choice of the appropriate means for obtaining those objectives.[87] These Recommendations can be either general or individual. The acts of the Commission and Council of the E.E.C., which are equivalent to general Recommendations, are called "Directives," but there are no such things as individual Recommendations in the E.E.C. Treaty—the term "Recommendation" is employed in that Treaty, but it is used as the equivalent of an Opinion, and it has no binding force at all.

It may be of assistance to set out these somewhat confusing distinctions in a glossary, as follows:

E.C.S.C. Treaty	*E.E.C. Treaty*
General Decision	Regulation
General Recommendation	Directive
Individual Decision	Decision
Individual Recommendation	No such act
Opinion	Recommendation or Opinion

THE RIGHT TO CHALLENGE ACTS OF THE COUNCIL OF MINISTERS

The four grounds allowed by Article 173 for appealing against the administrative acts of the Council of Ministers are the same as those allowed in the E.C.S.C. Treaty for appeals against the administrative acts of the High Authority. However, it will be remembered that under the E.C.S.C. Treaty the acts of the Council of Ministers of that Community can only be challenged on two grounds, namely, incompetence and violation of a substantial procedural requirement.[88] Under Article 173, two other grounds have been added for appeals against acts of the Council of Ministers of the E.E.C., namely violation of the Treaty, or of any rule of law concerning its application, and *détournement de pouvoir*. The reason for this alteration is the greatly increased role which the Council of Ministers plays under the E.E.C. Treaty. As the members of this Council are directly controlled by the Member States,

---

[86] E.E.C. Treaty, Art. 189, paras. 2 and 4. It should be noted, however, that a binding order to one particular Member State is referred to as a Decision, and not as might be expected, as a Regulation—Art. 90, para. 3.
[87] E.C.S.C. Treaty, Art. 14, para. 3.
[88] E.C.S.C. Treaty, Art. 38, para. 3, see p. 207, above.

this is only another way of saying that the Economic Community is far less supranational than is the Coal and Steel Community.

THE RIGHT TO CHALLENGE ACTS OF THE COMMISSION

A. THE RIGHT OF APPEAL OF MEMBER STATES AND OF THE COUNCIL

The acts of the Commission—its Regulations, Directives and Decisions—can each be challenged on the four classic grounds in any action brought by a Member State or by the Council, and in view of the above discussion of these grounds,[89] it is felt that no further comment is called for.

B. THE RIGHT OF APPEAL OF ENTERPRISES

Under the E.C.S.C. Treaty, the term " enterprise " is defined, and includes only those enterprises engaged in the production of coal or steel, and for certain purposes, a few engaged in distribution.[90]

Under the E.E.C. Treaty, there is no definition of the term " enterprise." More than that, Article 173 does not expressly refer to enterprises at all, but includes them in the general term of " legal person." It is suggested that there is no limitation, therefore, upon the enterprises which can appeal. However, as enterprises are empowered to appeal only against Decisions, that is to say, against administrative acts which affect them individually,[91] there will in practice be no occasion, for example, for incorporated French shopkeepers to appeal, but their right to do so appears as complete as that of haulage contractors, banks and motor manufacturers.

Enterprises may appeal against Decisions directed to them, on any of the four grounds of appeal. They may also appeal against a Decision which " although taken under the appearance of a Regulation or of a Decision addressed to another person, concerns him directly and individually." There are two parts to this provision. It means, first, that if an act, although described as a Regulation and presumably

---

[89] See pp. 123–147, above.

[90] See p. 153, above.

[91] The Court has held:

" According to the terms of Article 173 (2) of the E.E.C. Treaty, ' legal or natural persons ' can appeal against an act, originating from the Commission or from the Council, only if this act constitutes a Decision ' directly applicable ' to such persons, or a Decision which, even though it has been taken under the guise of a Regulation or a Decision addressed to some other person, nevertheless concerns them ' directly and individually.' It follows that these persons are not entitled to bring an application for annulment against Regulations decreed by the Council or by the Commission "—*Confédération Nationale des Producteurs de Fruits et Légumes and others* v. *The Council of the E.E.C.* (Joint Cases 16–62, 17–62, 19–62, 20–62, 21–62 and 22–62) [1963] C.M.L.R. 160 at 173.

published in the *Journal Officiel* as they are required to be,[92] in fact affects an enterprise directly and individually,[93] that act is a Decision and not a Regulation.[94] Indeed, the Court has recently declared that certain provisions of a Regulation may possibly amount to a Decision so as to be open to appeal by enterprises.[95] This provision thus expressly incorporates into the E.E.C. Treaty what the Court, by its judgments, has implied into the E.C.S.C. Treaty.[96]

Secondly, enterprises may also challenge a Decision addressed to another person if that Decision concerns itself directly and individually. This provision again incorporates into the E.E.C. Treaty the legal position declared by the Court in respect of the E.C.S.C. Treaty. It will be remembered that in the *Nold* case [97] the Court held that the plaintiff enterprise was able to appeal against certain individual Decisions of the High Authority addressed, not to it, but to sales organisations of the Ruhr, because that enterprise was directly affected by the Decisions because as a result of them it was no longer enabled to continue trading with those sales organisations as a wholesaler at first hand.[98]

Enterprises under the E.E.C. Treaty can only appeal against individual enactments affecting them. They have no right to challenge general enactments or Regulations on any grounds at all.[99] This position thus differs radically from that of enterprises under the E.C.S.C. Treaty,

---

92 Art. 191, para. 1.
93 It is suggested that a Regulation does not cease to affect an enterprise directly and individually, because it also affects another enterprise in a similar way.
94 Of the distinction between a Regulation and a Decision, the Court has held:
    " The criterion for the distinction must be looked for in the general ' scope,' and not the particular application, of the act in question. The essential characteristics of a Decision arise from the limitation of the persons whom it ' designates,' while the Regulation, being of an essentially normative character, is applicable not to a limited identifiable number of designees, but rather to categories of persons envisaged both in the abstract and as a whole. Consequently, in order to determine in dubious cases whether one is concerned with a Decision or with a Regulation, it is necessary to find out if the administrative act in question is concerned with designated persons individually "—*Confédération Nationale des Producteurs de Fruits et Légumes and others* v. *The Council of the E.E.C.* (Joint Cases 16–62, 17–62, 19–62, 20–62, 21–62 and 22–62) [1963] C.M.L.R. 160 at 173–174.
95 " If an act, termed a ' Regulation ' by its author, contains provisions which are in their nature concerned with certain legal or natural persons in a manner which is not only direct but also individual, it must be admitted, without prejudicing the question whether this act concerned in its entirety can be rightly named a Regulation, that in any case these provisions do not have the character of a Regulation, and that they may be attacked by these persons according to the terms of Article 173 (2) "—*ibid.* p. 174.
96 See, *inter alia*, *Fédération Charbonnière de Belgique* v. *The High Authority* (Case 8–55), Vol. II, and generally pp. 117–123, above.
97 *Nold KG* v. *The High Authority* (Case No. 18–57), Vol. II.
98 See further, pp. 160–162, above.
99 Except where that Regulation is in fact an individual enactment: see p. 290, above.

which can challenge general Decisions of the High Authority where these are deemed to be vitiated by a *détournement de pouvoir* with respect to them. It would appear, therefore, that if a Regulation is passed, and in passing it the Commission has committed a *détournement de pouvoir* with respect to an enterprise, the only redress is for the home State of that enterprise to take up the case. Should the State refuse to do so, or not be prevailed upon to do so, within two months, the enterprise would have no redress except under Article 184 when challenging the validity of fines imposed upon it for breaches of the Regulation, if these could be imposed.[1]

C. THE RIGHT OF APPEAL OF ASSOCIATIONS

Under the E.C.S.C. Treaty, certain associations are allowed to appeal to the Court [2]; under the E.E.C. Treaty associations are not referred to as such, but they presumably fall within the term " legal person," as used in paragraph 2 of Article 173, and have the same right of appeal, therefore, as enterprises under the E.C.S.C. Treaty. However, under that Treaty it was irrelevant whether the association was incorporated or not; under the E.E.C. Treaty it is only incorporated associations which can sue, as only these are legal persons. In one case, however, without demur the Court allowed the unincorporated *Assemblée permanente des présidents de chambres d'agriculture* to intervene.[3]

D. THE RIGHT OF APPEAL OF INDIVIDUALS

No limitation is placed upon the individuals who can appeal to the Court.[4] However, as with enterprises discussed above, individuals can appeal only against Decisions directed to them, or against acts which purport to be Regulations but which are in fact Decisions, and in practice the existence of either type of Decisions would be very rare.

---

[1] It is true that where a Regulation has been passed involving a *détournement de pouvoir* with respect to an enterprise, the *détournement* will concern that enterprise directly and individually. It is suggested, however, that the Regulation still remains a Regulation despite the *détournement*. A *détournement de pouvoir* cannot turn a Regulation into a Decision, and it is only Decisions that enterprises can challenge. For the terms of Art. 184, see p. 329, below.

[2] E.C.S.C. Treaty, Art. 33, para. 2; see p. 152, above.

[3] *Confédération Nationale des Producteurs de Fruits et Légumes and others* y. *The Council of Ministers of the E.E.C.* (Joint Cases 16 and 17–62).

[4] This may be compared with the exceptional right of individuals to appeal under the E.C.S.C. Treaty—see Arts. 65 and 66, pp. 242–249, above.

THE COURT'S POWER TO EVALUATE FACTS AND ECONOMIC
CIRCUMSTANCES

Under Article 33 of the E.C.S.C. Treaty it is provided that:

> The examination of the Court cannot include an assessment of the
> situation resulting from the facts or economic circumstances in view
> of which the said Decisions or Recommendations were taken, unless
> the High Authority is alleged to have committed a *détournement de
> pouvoir* or to have patently misconstrued the provisions of the Treaty,
> or any rule of law concerning its application.

This provision has not been repeated in the E.E.C. Treaty, and the
question arises, therefore, what is the effect of its omission?

Two views appear possible. First, it can be contended that the
E.E.C. Treaty is a Treaty to be interpreted without any reference to
any other Treaty. As no provision is included in Article 173 granting
the Court power to assess the situation resulting from economic facts
and circumstances, it follows that the Court does not possess such a
power.

Alternatively, one could argue that the provision in Article 33, which
has been quoted above, is not a provision granting jurisdiction to the
Court, but rather limiting its jurisdiction to assess the situation resulting
from economic facts and circumstances to the cases where a *détournement de pouvoir* or a patent misconstruction has been alleged. If,
therefore, that restriction were removed, the Court would have this
jurisdiction without any limitations at all.

It is suggested, however, that this second view is incorrect, and that
the Court is an organ of the Community possessing no powers other
than those granted by the Treaty, for if the Court had been granted no
jurisdiction, it would clearly have possessed none. Further, it is accepted
that the Court can only review a matter in *pleine juridiction* if it is
expressly authorised to do so; it would be strange, therefore, if it could
do other things without a similar express authorisation.

If the above suggestion is correct, and the Court cannot review the
situation resulting from the facts and economic circumstances in view
of which a particular enactment was taken, the Court will be hampered
when considering allegations of *détournement de pouvoir*. One of the
ways of determining whether a *détournement* has occurred is to consider
the existing situation, then to consider the proposed remedy, and by
comparing the two to discover what must have been the intention of the
party proposing that remedy. The correctness of this intention can then
be assessed. It appears that under the E.E.C. Treaty this examination
will not be able to be made, because the Court has not expressly been
given power to consider the existing situation.

This being so, it might be contended that a power to consider the existing situation must be implied in the grant of a power to consider an allegation of *détournement de pouvoir* at all. On such a contention, however, it is hard to understand why such a power was not also able to be implied under the E.C.S.C. Treaty, and why instead it was expressly granted.

It is suggested, therefore, that under the E.C.S.C. Treaty, the Court, by being expressly granted this power of review, possesses it, and that under the E.E.C. Treaty, by not being granted it the Court possesses no power of review, however hampering this may be.

Time Limit for Bringing Appeals

Under the E.C.S.C. Treaty, the time limit for bringing an appeal against the High Authority or against the Council of Ministers is one month.[5] Under the E.E.C. Treaty, this period has been doubled and is two months.[6] This period is declared to run, according to the case:

> . . . from the publication of the act or from its notification to the plaintiff, or, in default of these, from the day when he had knowledge of it.

It is further provided in the Treaty [7] that Regulations are to be published in the *Journal Officiel,* whereas Directives and Decisions are to be notified to the parties concerned. This simple division of administrative acts into Regulations and Decisions, however, has overlooked the possibility which is mentioned in Article 173, paragraph 2, and has been discussed above, namely, that what is expressed to be a Regulation may in fact be a Decision. In this situation, the Decision being in the guise of a Regulation, it will have been published and the time period for appealing would appear, therefore, to run from the date of that publication.

The further provision that where the plaintiff has not been notified of a Decision, time shall run from his obtaining knowledge of it ends an uncertainty in the E.C.S.C. Treaty, for in that Treaty such a provision

---

[5] E.C.S.C. Treaty, Art. 33, para. 3; Art. 38, para. 2. Additional time periods are added to this month in respect of the distance of the plaintiff from the Court, etc., see pp. 100-101, above.

[6] E.E.C. Treaty, Art. 173, para. 3, see p. 287, above. The additional time periods are the same as under the E.C.S.C. Treaty, being contained in the Rules of the Court which are common to all three Communities.

[7] E.E.C. Treaty, Art. 191 provides:
"Regulations shall be published in the *Journal Officiel de la Communauté.* They shall come into force on the date provided for in them, or, failing this, on the twentieth day following their publication.
Directives and decisions shall be notified to those to whom they are addressed and shall take effect upon such notification."

is not included. The possibility, therefore, that someone other than the person named in an individual Decision should wish to appeal against it was not provided for.[8]

For the additional right to appeal out of time, reference should be made to Article 184 below.[9]

ARTICLE 174

If the appeal is well founded, the Court of Justice shall declare the act challenged to be null and void.

However, as concerns Regulations, the Court of Justice shall indicate, if it considers it necessary, those effects of the Regulations annulled which may be deemed to continue in force.[10]

THE ACT SHALL BE " NULL AND VOID "

An act which has been improperly passed by an administrative authority may either be void or voidable. If the act is void, then it is as if it had never existed; it had no effect in the past, and it can have no effect for the future. If an act is voidable, it exists as a valid act and can have legal effect. Because it is voidable, however, the Court can annul it; the only question then to be considered is whether that annulment is retrospective to the date of enactment, or whether the annulment only runs from the date of the Court's judgment.

Where there is a time limit for the bringing of an appeal against a voidable act, and no appeal is brought within that limit, the position is clear. The act which had legal effect from its inception can no longer be annulled; it will continue to have legal effect until it is repealed. Where the time limit concerns the bringing of an appeal against a void act the position is more complex. The act is void, and has always been void. The Court, in its judgment, merely declares this voidness. After the ending of the time limit for bringing an appeal, the Court can

---

[8] For a discussion of the consequent difficulties, see p. 161, above.
[9] See p. 329, below.
[10] French:

" *Si le recours est fondé, la Cour de Justice déclare nul et non avenu l'acte contesté.*

Toutefois, en ce qui concerne les règlements, la Cour de Justice indique, si elle l'estime nécessaire, ceux des effets du règlement annulé qui doivent être considérés comme définitifs."

Stationery Office:

" If the Court of Justice considers the complaint well founded, it shall declare the measure concerned to be null and void.

Provided always that if the Court declares a regulation null and void, it shall, if it considers this necessary, declare which effects of the annulled regulation shall be deemed to remain in force."

no longer declare this voidness. The effect of this is that no one can now allege that the act is void. In all respects, therefore, unless there are other provisions, that act has the same legal effects as if it were valid.[11]

Article 174 sets out that the acts of the Commission and of the Council, if successfully challenged, shall be declared null and void: following annulment, it is as if the act had never been passed, the act is void *ab initio* and not merely voidable.

CERTAIN EFFECTS OF THE REGULATION ANNULLED MAY BE CONSIDERED AS CONTINUING IN FORCE

Paragraph 2 of this Article is a saving provision, allowing the Court, if it deems it necessary, to indicate those effects of the Regulation annulled which may be deemed as continuing in force.

This provision does not occur in the E.C.S.C. Treaty, and this is presumably because it is nowhere stated there that acts annulled are to be held to have been void *ab initio*. Under the present Treaty, however, it is quite possible that before the Court has given its judgment concerning a particular Regulation the Commission or the Council may well have completed many transactions on the strength of that Regulation.[12] If all of these transactions were to be void because the Regulation was declared void, not only hardship but acute administrative difficulties might occur. Under the present provision, therefore, the Court is given power to validate these transactions.

There is no indication in the Treaty whether this power to validate transactions is one which the Court can exercise of its own motion or whether one of the parties in their pleadings must request that it should be used. As, however, the Court cannot be expected to know what transactions have occurred on the authority of the particular Regulation being challenged, it would appear inevitable that validations must be specifically requested. There is also no authority upon whether persons who are not parties to the action can request the Court to exercise its power in respect of transactions in which they have been concerned, and further, if these requests can be brought, whether they must be brought within any particular time. There appears to be little value in making private speculations upon these matters, which can only be determined by the Court itself.

---

11 In the present Treaty, Art. 184 allows plaintiffs to challenge the validity of acts dependent upon an act which could itself have been declared void, although that parent act cannot itself be annulled. For the position under the E.C.S.C. Treaty, where there is no provision equivalent to Art. 184, see *Meroni & Co. S.p.A.* v. *The High Authority* (Case 9–56), Vol. II, discussed at pp. 162–164, above.

12 Although appeals must be brought within two months of the publication of the Regulation, the judgment is not usually given until at least a year later.

Finally, it is necessary to note that this power of the Court is limited to Regulations, that is to say to those legislative acts which are binding in every respect[13]: it does not apply in respect of Directives or Decisions.[14]

ARTICLE 175

In a case where, in violation of the present Treaty, the Council or the Commission fail to pass an act, the Member States and the other institutions of the Community may appeal to the Court with a view to having this violation placed on record.

This appeal is admissible only if the institution in question has previously been requested to act. If at the expiration of two months from this request, the institution has not declared its position, the appeal can be brought within a further period of two months.

Any natural or legal person, under the conditions specified in the preceding paragraphs, may submit to the Court of Justice a complaint that one of the institutions of the Community has failed to address to him an act other than a Recommendation or an Opinion.[15]

COMPARISON WITH ARTICLE 35 OF THE E.C.S.C. TREATY

The present Article is based upon the wording of Article 35 of the E.C.S.C. Treaty, yet it contains many significant differences.   Under

---

[13] Art. 189, para. 2.
[14] For a discussion of this terminology, see p. 289, above.
[15] French:
    " *Dans le cas où en violation du présent Traité, le Conseil ou la Commission s'abstient de statuer, les Etats membres et les autres institutions de la Communauté peuvent saisir la Cour de Justice en vue de faire constater cette violation.*
    Ce recours n'est recevable que si l'institution en cause a été préalablement invitée à agir. Si, à l'expiration d'un délai de deux mois à compter de cette invitation, l'institution n'a pas pris position, le recours peut être formé dans un nouveau délai de deux mois.
    Toute personne physique ou morale peut saisir la Cour de Justice dans les conditions fixées aux alinéas précédents pour faire grief à l'une des institutions de la Communauté d'avoir manqué de lui adresser un acte outre qu'une recommandation ou un avis."
Stationery Office:
    " Should the Council or the Commission in violation of this Treaty fail to act, the Member States and the other institutions of the Community may refer the matter to the Court of Justice in order to have the said violation placed on record. No proceedings arising out of the said reference shall be heard unless the institution concerned has been called upon to act. If within two months of being so called upon, the institution concerned has not made its attitude clear, the said proceedings may be brought within a further period of two months.
    Any natural or legal person may bring proceedings before the Court of Justice, under the conditions laid down in the preceding paragraphs, on the ground that one of the institutions of the Community has failed to send him a formal document, such document not being a recommendation or an opinion."

Article 35, it will be remembered,[16] it is only inaction on the part of the High Authority which can be challenged; by the present Article the inaction both of the Commission and of the Council of Ministers is open to challenge. Secondly, in the present provision, this right of appeal is expressed to be exercisable by "the other institutions of the Community." This appears to be a mistake, for it is clear that the Court of Justice is an institution of the Community,[17] yet it cannot be suggested that the Court is intended to be able to cite the Commission and the Council before itself.

Further, it is arguable that the phrase "other institutions of the Community" includes the Economic and Social Committee, for although this committee is not listed in the chapter of the Treaty dealing with "Institutions," it is dealt with under the heading "Institutional Provisions" in the same Title of the Treaty as the Commission and the Council of Ministers. Further than that, Part Six of the Treaty contains Articles under the general heading "The Setting up of the Institutions," the second of these Articles relating to the setting up of the Economic and Social Committee.[18] Despite this, however, it is suggested that it was not intended to be one of the tasks of that Committee to challenge inactions of the Commission and the Council.

However, the Common Assembly is clearly an institution of the Community, and by Article 175 it has, therefore, been granted power to appeal to the Court. This situation is thus entirely different from that under the E.C.S.C. Treaty, where the same Assembly has no such power in respect of the inaction of the High Authority.[19]

The two other differences between Article 175 and Article 35 are far more fundamental, the one affecting the scope of an appeal to the Court, and the other the mechanism of such an appeal.

Under the E.C.S.C. Treaty, inaction on the part of the High Authority is open to challenge if that inaction is either in breach of a duty to act, or if the failure to exercise a mere power to act constitutes a *détournement de pouvoir.* By Article 175, however, recourse to the Court is allowed where "*in violation of the present Treaty,* the Council or the Commission fail to act." Now a failure to act can only amount to

[16] See p. 184, above.
[17] Art. 4 refers to the Court as an institution, and the articles of the Treaty dealing with the Court are contained in Chap. 1 "Institutions" of Title I "Institutional Provisions" of Part V of the Treaty itself entitled: "The Community's Institutions."
[18] Art. 242 provides:
"The Council shall take all appropriate measures to constitute the Economic and Social Committee within a period of three months after the first meeting of the Council."
[19] E.C.S.C. Treaty, Art. 35, para. 1, allows appeals to be brought only by Member States and by the Council, which latter is expressly referred to by name.

violation of the Treaty, if the Treaty requires action; that is to say, the inaction here being referred to must be a breach of a duty to act. As this is the sole ground upon which a challenge of inaction can be made, it follows that Article 175 does not provide for any challenge to be made against a failure to exercise a power to act, even presumably where such a failure constitutes a *détournement de pouvoir*.

The other fundamental difference between the two Articles concerns the mechanics of an appeal. Under the E.C.S.C. Treaty, at the end of the two months after the High Authority has been requested to act, its inaction, if still continuing, is deemed to constitute a Decision refusing to act, and against that Decision an appeal is open on any of the four grounds set out in Article 33. Under the E.E.C. Treaty, inaction for two months on the part of the Commission or of the Council, after they have been requested to act, is not deemed to constitute a Decision of refusal to act, so that there is no Decision which can be appealed against. Instead an alternative procedure is adopted, namely of requesting the Court to establish that the failure to act is a violation of the Treaty. This amounts to much more than a mere change of words. An implied Decision is challengeable on any of the usual four grounds,[20] just as if it were an express Decision. Under Article 175, all that the Court can examine is whether the Treaty imposes a duty to act and whether if so, that duty has not been fulfilled. The position is thus exactly as if under the E.C.S.C. Treaty, the Court could annul the implied Decision upon the sole grounds of violation of the Treaty.

THE RIGHT OF CHALLENGE OF ENTERPRISES, ASSOCIATIONS AND INDIVIDUALS

In addition to the right granted by paragraph 1 of Article 175, to Member States and the institutions of the Community to appeal to the Court, paragraph 3 allows " any natural or legal person under the conditions specified in the preceding paragraphs " to complain to the Court that " one of the institutions of the Community has failed to address to him an act other than a Recommendation or an Opinion."

It is assumed that the phrase " any natural or legal person " refers merely to enterprises, associations and individuals, although every Member State is a legal person, and so also, by the Treaty is the Community itself.[21] The institutions of the Community, as distinct from

---

[20] For challenges of an implied Decision on the grounds of violation of a substantial procedural requirement, see *Groupement des Industries Sidérurgiques Luxembourgeoises* v. *The High Authority* (Joint Cases 7–54 and 9–54), Vol. II; see also p. 189, above.
[21] Art. 210 provides: " The Community shall have legal personalty." Art. 211 provides:
" The Community shall in each of the Member States enjoy the most extensive legal capacity accorded to legal persons under their domestic law."

the Community itself, have not been incorporated by the Treaty or by the municipal laws of the Member States, but nevertheless they contract in their own names, as for example with their employees, and can hardly be held not to possess legal personality.[22]   Nonetheless, the provision of paragraph 3 of Article 175 would be largely repetitive if these legal entities were to be regarded as falling within the term " legal person."

MEANING OF " UNDER THE CONDITIONS SPECIFIED "

The legal persons referred to in paragraph 3 may submit a complaint to the Court " under the conditions specified in the preceding paragraphs." The conditions specified in paragraph 2 concern among other things, the time within which an appeal can be brought.[23]   The complaint to the Court, however, is also declared to be subject to the conditions in paragraph 1.   A difficulty arises here, however, because, strictly, there are no conditions in paragraph 1.   It is suggested, therefore, that what is meant is that just as Member States and the institutions of the Community can only challenge a violation of the Treaty, so also natural and legal persons can only challenge a violation of the Treaty, and therefore, that they also cannot challenge a mere breach of a power to act.

" AN ACT OTHER THAN A RECOMMENDATION OR AN OPINION "

The only complaints which may be submitted to the Court by the natural or legal persons being referred to are complaints in respect of failures to address to the plaintiff " an act other than a Recommendation or an Opinion." As the only acts other than Recommendations or Opinions, which can be addressed to enterprises and individuals, are Decisions,[24] the above expression appears to be a roundabout way of saying that legal persons may challenge Decisions.

THE PROCEDURE BEFORE A COMPLAINT AGAINST INACTION
CAN BE SUBMITTED

When the Commission or the Council is under a duty to act, and it fails to do so, the first step necessary to remedy this inaction is for a Member State, another institution of the Community or possibly a natural or legal person to request the institution concerned to act.   If, following this, the institution does not act within two months, a right of complaint to the Court arises, and may be exercised at any time during the

---

22 These institutions appear before the Court in their own names and not as agents of the Community.
23 See further pp. 313, 315 below.
24 Art. 189, para. 4.

following two months.[25]   This procedure, it will be noted, is the same as that under the E.C.S.C. Treaty, except that under that Treaty the period within which an appeal can be brought is only one month, and not two, as under the present Article.[26]

ARTICLE 176

The institution from which the annulled act originated, or whose failure to take action has been declared contrary to the present Treaty, shall be required to take the measures which comprise the carrying out of the judgment of the Court of Justice.

This obligation does not affect any obligation resulting from the application of Article 215, paragraph 2.[27]

THE MEASURES WHICH COMPRISE THE CARRYING OUT OF THE JUDGMENT

Paragraph 1 of this provision continues in the E.E.C. Treaty the same separation of powers as has been observed in the E.C.S.C. Treaty[28]: the duty of the Court is merely to declare upon the legality of the act brought before it under Article 173[29]; it is for the institution concerned to carry out the judgment.   Paragraph 1 is also a supplement to Article 175[30] in that after a failure to act on the part of an institution has been declared under that Article to be a violation of the Treaty, paragraph 1 of this Article expressly requires the institution concerned to take the measures which comprise the carrying out of the judgment of the Court.

It has been suggested above,[31] that where an express administrative act of an institution has been annulled, the measures which that institution are then required to take are those which restore the parties

---

[25] Art. 175, para. 2.

[26] This may be compared with the similarly extended right of appeal under E.E.C. Treaty, Art. 173, para. 3.

[27] French:
> " *L'institution dont émane l'acte annulé, ou dont l'abstention à été déclarée contraire au présent Traité, est tenue de prendre les mesures que comporte l'exécution de l'arrêt de la Cour de Justice.*
> *Cette obligation ne préjuge pas celle qui peut résulter de l'application de l'article 215, alinéa 2.*"

Stationery Office:
> " An institution responsible for a measure subsequently declared null and void or an institution whose failure to act has been declared contrary to the provisions of this Treaty shall be required to take the necessary steps to implement the judgment of the Court of Justice.
> This obligation shall not affect any obligation arising under Article 215, second paragraph."

[28] *Cf.* E.C.S.C. Treaty, Art. 39, para. 1; see p. 211, above.

[29] See pp. 287–295, above.   [30] See pp. 297–301, above.

[31] For a discussion of the similar provision in E.C.S.C. Treaty, Art. 34, concerning the High Authority, see pp. 176–179, above.

concerned into the position in which they would have been if the annulled act had never been passed. This, it is submitted, is also the duty of the Commission and of the Council of Ministers under the present provision.

Where, however, this provision goes on to state that an institution whose failure to take action has been declared contrary to the present Treaty is also required to take the measures which comprise the carrying out of the judgment of the Court, that provision, as has been discussed above,[32] appears to have another meaning, namely that the institution concerned is to bring the existing illegal situation to an end by means of passing the act which the Treaty requires it to pass.

DIFFERENCES FROM THE POSITION CONCERNING THE HIGH AUTHORITY

An important difference exists in the position when, under the present Treaty, an act of an institution has been annulled, and the position when a Decision or Recommendation of the High Authority has also been annulled. In the latter case, the High Authority in certain circumstances is required to pay compensation for direct and special injury which an enterprise or group of enterprises may have suffered.[33] No such provision has been included in the present paragraph and claims for compensation and damages, if claimable at all, have to be lodged in a separate action brought under Article 215.[34]

Further, as noted above,[35] under the present Treaty if an institution fails to take the action which the Treaty requires it to take, the appeal to the Court is an appeal against this inactivity itself. Under the E.C.S.C. Treaty, the appeal is by way of a challenge of the implied Decision of the High Authority refusing to take action. Also, under that Treaty the High Authority can be required to take a Decision or Recommendation which the Treaty merely empowered it to take, but which it is not under an express duty to take, provided that the failure to take that Decision or Recommendation amounts to a *détournement de pouvoir*.[36] No similar provision is included in the present Article, so that there are no means by which an institution can be required to exercise a mere power that has been conferred upon it.

---

[32] See p. 177, above.
[33] E.C.S.C. Treaty, Art. 34, para. 1, sentence 3; see pp. 179–182, above.
[34] See p. 310, below and the discussion of Art. 178, pp. 310–312, below.
[35] See p. 297, above.
[36] E.C.S.C. Treaty, Art. 35, para. 2, see pp. 184–193, above.

NON-CONTRACTUAL LIABILITY OF THE INSTITUTION

The present article is declared in paragraph 2 not to affect any obligation resulting from the application of Article 215, paragraph 2. That paragraph provides that:

> In the case of non-contractual liability, the Community shall, in accordance with the general principles common to the laws of the Member States, make good any damage caused by its institutions or by its servants in the performance of their duties.

This provision is discussed below under Article 178,[37] which gives the Court jurisdiction to determine cases brought by virtue of it.

ARTICLE 177

The Court of Justice shall have jurisdiction to give a preliminary ruling:

(a) on the interpretation of the present Treaty;

(b) on the validity and interpretation of acts passed by the institutions of the Community;

(c) on the interpretation of the statutes of bodies set up by an act of the Council, when these statutes so provide.

When such a question is raised before a court of one of the Member States, this court may, if it considers that a decision on this point is necessary in order to deliver its judgment, request the Court of Justice to rule on this question.

When such a question is raised in a case pending before a municipal court whose decisions are not open to appeal under municipal law, this court is required to refer the matter to the Court of Justice.[38]

---

[37] See pp. 310–312, below.

[38] French:

> " *La Cour de Justice est compétente pour statuer, à titre préjudiciel:*
>
> (a) *Sur l'interprétation du présent Traité;*
>
> (b) *Sur la validité et l'interprétation des actes pris par les institutions de la Communauté;*
>
> (c) *Sur l'interprétation des statuts des organismes créés par un acte du Conseil, lorsque ces statuts le prévoient.*
>
> *Lorsqu'une telle question est soulevée devant une juridiction d'un des Etats membres, cette juridiction peut, si elle estime qu'une décision sur ce point est nécessaire pour rendre son jugement, demander à la Cour de Justice de statuer sur cette question.*
>
> *Lorsqu'une telle question est soulevée dans une affaire pendante devant une juridiction nationale dont les décisions ne sont pas susceptibles d'un recours*

Many matters governed by the terms of the Treaty itself may come before the municipal courts of the Member States. For example, power was originally given to these municipal courts to determine what restrictive trade practices were to be permitted,[39] and certain matters relating to the contractual and tortious liability of the Community will come before these courts.[40] In such actions the interpretation to be given to the particular Treaty provisions in question will obviously be an all important point.

Further, many acts already passed by the Council of Ministers bear directly upon municipal law, such as the Regulations dealing with migrant workers,[41] restrictive trade practices[42] and food and drugs.[43] Thus, if a manufacturer were being prosecuted for violating the food and drugs Regulation of the Community, the validity and the interpretation of that Regulation would, again, be an all important point.

In order to ensure uniformity in the decisions of the municipal courts applying the Treaty and the Regulations etc. passed under it, Article 177 enables a preliminary issue to be submitted to the Court of Justice by the municipal court concerned for a ruling.

juridictionnel de droit interne, cette juridiction est tenue de saisir la Cour de Justice."

Stationery Office:

"The Court of Justice shall be competent to give preliminary rulings concerning—

(a) the interpretation of this Treaty;

(b) the validity and interpretation of acts of the institutions of the Community;

(c) the interpretation of the statutes of any bodies set up by a formal measure of the Council, where the said statutes so provide.

Where any such question is raised before any court of law of one of the Member States, the said court may, if it considers that a decision on the question is essential to enable it to render judgment, request the Court of Justice to give a ruling thereon.

Where any such question is raised in a case pending before a domestic court of a Member State, from whose decisions there is no possibility of appeal under domestic law, the said court is bound to refer the matter to the Court of Justice."

[39] Art. 88 provides:

"Until the Regulations or Directives issued in pursuance of Article 87 shall have come into force, the competent authorities shall determine to what extent to permit agreements on the improper exploitation of a dominant position in the Common Market."

[40] Art. 215, paras. 1 and 2, provide:

"The contractual liability of the Community shall be governed by the proper law of the contract in question.

In the case of non-contractual liability, the Community shall, in accordance with the general principles common to the laws of the Member States, make good any damage caused by its institutions or by its servants in the performance of their duties."

Art. 183 provides:

"Subject to the jurisdiction granted to the Court of Justice by the present Treaty, litigation to which the Community is a party shall not thereby be removed from the jurisdiction of municipal courts."

[41] Regulation No. 3–62.

[42] Regulation No. 17–62.

[43] Directive of October 23, 1962.

The Treaty makes the jurisdiction of this Court dependent solely on the existence of a Request for a preliminary decision within the meaning of Article 177. And it does so without requiring this Court to discover whether the decision of the national judge has acquired the force of *res judicata* under the national law.[43a]

This ruling may be upon any of the three matters referred to.

(i) RULING ON THE INTERPRETATION OF THE PRESENT TREATY

In the first case submitted to the Court for a ruling,[44] it was argued that the Court did not have jurisdiction because the Hague Court of Appeal which had requested the ruling was seeking an answer from the Court as to whether a particular sales agency agreement made in 1903 imposing a territorial limitation was null and void after the coming into force of Article 85 of the Treaty: this, it was suggested, did not amount to an interpretation of the Treaty. The Court held, however, that because no particular form for the request had been laid down, provided that the Court could abstract the question of interpretation it would have jurisdiction to rule upon it.

The Court declared:

> There was a further or alternative submission that the request of the Court of Appeal at The Hague could not be the proper subject of a preliminary decision in as much as the request is not restricted to a mere question of the word " interpretation " as it appears in Article 177 but on the contrary, as the content of the request discloses, calls on the Court to decide on the application of the Treaty of Rome to an actual specific case.[45]

To this the Court replied:

> The Treaty, nevertheless, has neither expressly nor merely by implication prescribed a particular form in which a national court must present its request to this Court for a preliminary decision. Moreover, since it is a question of interpretation by the national court of what is meant in Article 177 by " the interpretation of the Treaty," it is permissible for the national court to formulate its request in a simple and direct way. And the national court may do it in such a way as to impose on this Court the duty of rendering a decision on that request

43a [1962] C.M.L.R. 1 at p. 26.
44 *Robert Bosch G.m.b.H. and another* v. *Kleding-Verkoopbedrijf de Geus en Uitdenbogard* [1962] C.M.L.R. 1. For the facts, see below. For a discussion of the Bosch case, see Jean Robert in *Recueil Dalloz,* 1962, p. 359; Arved Deringer: " Gewerblicher Rechtsschutz und Urheberrecht " in *Ausländische und Internationale Teil* (1962), p. 283; Dr. W. Schlieder, " Die Anwendung der Artikel 85 und 86 des E.W.G.-Vertrages nach dem Erlass der ersten Durchführungsverordnung " in *Betriebsberater* (1962), p. 305; Fernand Charles Jeantet, *Jurisclasseur Périodique* (1962) No. 24; *Jurisprudence* 12726; Dr. Weyer, *Der Betriebsberater* (1962), p. 467, and Dennis Thompson, " The Bosch Case," in (1962) 11 I.C.L.Q. 721.
45 [1962] C.M.L.R. at p. 26.

only in so far as this Court has jurisdiction, that is to say, only in so far as the decision relates to the interpretation of the Treaty. The form of the request in the present case enables this Court without difficulty to abstract from it the question for interpretation.[46]

It was further contended in this case that because at the time when the matter was before the Hague Court of Appeal, namely in November 1960, it was the municipal courts of the Member States which had exclusive jurisdiction to determine upon the validity of restrictive trade practices,[47] it was, therefore, only these courts which could rule upon the interpretation of Article 85, and not the Communities' Court. On this the Court declared:

This argument cannot be accepted. Even on the assumption that the application of Article 85 and onwards of the Treaty was a matter for the national authorities, it is nonetheless clear that Article 177, relating to the interpretation of the Treaty, remains applicable, so that the national court is empowered, or obliged—as the case may be—to request a preliminary decision. This reasoning is supported as much by the letter as by the spirit of Article 177 for, while this Article contains no reservations relative to Article 85 and onwards, a harmonisation of interpretation—which is the purpose of Article 177—is of particular importance when the application of the Treaty is entrusted to national authorities.[48]

Further, it is no part of the Court's duty to determine whether the ruling which it is requested to give upon the interpretation of the Treaty is relevant to the case before the municipal court or not. Thus, the Court has declared:

In order to confer jurisdiction on the Court in the present case, it is only necessary that the question posed should involve interpretation of the Treaty. The considerations which may have led a national court to the choice of its questions, and the relevance which it attributes to them within the framework of the case before it, are outside the Court's jurisdiction.[49]

---

[46] [1962] C.M.L.R. at pp. 26–27.
[47] Art. 88 provides:

" Until the Regulations or Directives issued in pursuance of Article 87 shall have come into force, the competent authorities in the Member States shall determine to what extent to permit agreements. . . . The said competent authorities shall so determine in accordance with their domestic law and the provisions of Article 85 (especially para. 3) [which specifies the grounds, *e.g.*, the improvement of production or distribution of goods, on which restrictive trade practices may be allowed] . . . ."

[48] [1962] C.M.L.R. at p. 27.
[49] *N.V. Algemene Transport- en Expeditie Onderneming Van Gend en Loos* v. *Nederlandse Tariefcommissie* (Case 26–62) [1963] C.M.L.R. 105 at pp. 128–129.

(ii) RULING ON THE VALIDITY AND INTERPRETATION OF ACTS PASSED BY THE INSTITUTIONS OF THE COMMUNITY

It is clear that the acts here being referred to include the Regulations, Directives and Decisions issued by the Council of Ministers, the Commission and the Decisions passed by the Board of Governors and the Board of Directors of the European Investment Bank.[50] It presumably does not cover the Recommendations and Opinions given by the Council of Ministers or the Commission, as these have no binding force.[51] Nor, it seems, does the phrase " acts of the institutions " cover the judgments of the Court itself.[52]

It would appear that no problem arises as to the interpretation of these acts of the institutions and that the principles set out by the Court in relation to the interpretation of the Treaty itself will apply.[53] However, a problem does arise upon the question of the validity of these acts.

It will be recalled that under Article 173 " the legality of the acts, other than Recommendations or Opinions, of the Council or of the Commission " may be determined by the Court. The appeal against the legality of these acts, however, may be brought only within a period of two months from the publication or notification of the act and only by Member States, the Council, the Commission or natural or legal persons. Such an appeal may allege only one or more of the four classic grounds for annulment.[54] Under the present Article, therefore, the question arises of whether the Request for a preliminary ruling upon this validity must also be brought within two months of the notification or publication of the act, and whether only one or more of the four grounds set out in Article 173 can be alleged.

It must first be noticed that the request to the Communities' Court for a preliminary ruling upon the validity of a particular act cannot in practice be made within a period of merely two months from the notification or publication of that act, particularly if the request comes from the highest municipal court. Secondly, the request is being made by the municipal court in question and not by the parties referred to in Article 173 as being competent to challenge the validity of acts. Thirdly, under Article 177 all the municipal court is doing is seeking a ruling as to the validity of the act in question; it is not itself requesting

---

[50] As to these see the discussions of Arts. 173 and 180, p. 287, above, and p. 317, below.
[51] Art. 189, para. 5, provides: " Recommendations and Opinions have no binding force."
[52] Interpretation of judgments of the Court is governed by E.E.C. Statute of the Court, Art. 40. When E.E.C. Treaty, Art. 5, uses the phrase " acts of the institutions of the Community," it presumably does include the judgments of the Court; see note 56, below.
[53] See pp. 305–306, above.
[54] For the terms of Art. 173, see pp. 287–288, above.

the annulment of that act. The proceedings under Article 177 are thus seen to be different in kind from those governed by Article 173, so that a further question arises of whether in its consideration of the validity of the act, in pursuance of its jurisdiction under Article 177, the Court is nevertheless bound to review the legality of the act upon the only grounds which could have been alleged by a litigant if an appeal had been brought within two months under Article 173.

It is suggested that the Court is so bound. No grounds for challenging the validity of the Act are set out in Article 177 and it would be inherently wrong if a party which could not have obtained the annulment of the act in question by an appeal under Article 173 could subsequently and, as it were by the back door, obtain a declaration of invalidity under Article 177.

If, therefore, it is right that even after the expiration of the two months referred to in Article 173, a municipal court of a Member State can, and the highest municipal court must, make a request for a preliminary ruling upon the validity of a particular act,[55] the provisions of Article 173 appear to be largely superseded. Further, it should be noted that within the two months following the making of this request, the parties to the action in the municipal court, the Member States, the Commission, and where appropriate the Council of Ministers shall have the right to submit statements on written observations to the Court. These statements, it is suggested, can allege, and can only allege, such arguments as could have been brought forward in an action under Article 173.

(iii) RULING ON THE INTERPRETATION OF THE STATUTES OF BODIES SET UP BY AN ACT OF THE COUNCIL WHERE THESE STATUTES SO PROVIDE

This provision is not understood as the Treaty does not empower the Council to set up bodies.

THE LEGAL POSITION FOLLOWING THE GIVING OF A PRELIMINARY RULING

When the Court has issued a preliminary ruling concerning the interpretation of the Treaty or of an act passed by virtue of that Treaty, the matter is referred back to the municipal court whose duty it is to proceed

---

[55] It would appear that in practice this request will be made only if one of the parties, as in the *Bosch* case, requires it, or if the Court of its own motion regards such a request as desirable. It is suggested that the fact that a party in the municipal court failed to exercise its right of appeal under Art. 173, so that under " Community law " he is time-barred, does not prevent that party pressing for the municipal court to exercise its own, and distinct, power or duty to make a request to the Court.

with the case before it. Further, it appears from Article 5 of the Treaty [56] that the Member State of the municipal court must ensure that that Court is bound by the ruling given. It would also appear to follow, even if it is the lowest municipal court which originally obtained the ruling, that every higher court would also be bound by that ruling.

Further, if the Court, upon, for example, the request of a French municipal court, has given a preliminary ruling upon the interpretation of a particular Article of the Treaty, or of a particular Regulation, it would appear that the courts of all the other Member States, in addition to all French courts, will be bound by that ruling provided that it is relevant to the case coming before them.[57]

Where the preliminary ruling of the Communities' Court, however, declares that a particular act of one of the institutions of the Economic Community is not valid, a difficult situation arises. It will be remembered that when the somewhat similar position under the E.C.S.C. Treaty of an appeal by an enterprise against a particular individual Decision was being discussed [58] it was noted that the Court held:

> When after the expiration of the time limit set out in the last paragraph of Article 33,[59] a plaintiff is challenging an individual Decision, he may avail himself of the irregularity of the general Decisions and Recommendations upon which that particular individual Decision has been based. *This, however, cannot lead to the annulment of the general Decision but only of the individual Decision to which it gave rise.*[60]

That is to say, although an enterprise under the E.C.S.C. Treaty may successfully prove before the Court that a particular general Decision or Recommendation is invalid, the Court has held that, because of the provisions in Article 33, that Decision or Recommendation cannot be annulled after the expiration of the time limit of one month. Indeed, such annulment would violate what the Court has declared to be a fundamental principle of law.[61] The Court has further stated:

---

[56] Art. 5 provides:
" Member States shall take all measures, whether general or particular, appropriate to ensure the carrying out of the obligations arising out of the present Treaty or resulting from the acts of the institutions of the Community."

[57] If Art. 5 is to be interpreted in this way, interesting questions arise of whether if a municipal court fails to observe the Communities' Court's ruling, the Member State has committed, or allowed, a breach of its obligations under the Treaty, or whether such a breach can occur only if the decision of that municipal court is not reversed by a higher court. It may be noted, however, that the Member State concerned will probably have no means of instituting an appeal to obtain this reversal.

[58] See pp. 162–164, above.

[59] The time limit there is one month, under Art. 173 it is two months, but Arts. 33 and 173 are otherwise virtually identical.

[60] *Meroni & Co., S.p.A.* v. *The High Authority* (Case 9–56), Vol. II; see p. 164, above (Author's italics).

[61] *German Government* v. *The High Authority* (Case 3–59), Vol. II, see p. 198, above.

In effect the strict time limit for appeals corresponds to a generally recognised requirement, that of preventing the legality of administrative decisions being brought into question indefinitely. This involves the prohibition upon re-opening the question after the expiration of the time limit.[62]

It is suggested that an analogous situation arises in the present case. If, in its preliminary ruling, the Court finds that a particular act of an institution of the Economic Community is invalid, it is submitted that, just as the Court cannot annul a general Decision passed under the E.C.S.C. Treaty, so it cannot annul the act passed under the present Treaty, but also that, just as under the E.C.S.C. Treaty the High Authority is required to repeal the Decision in question, so, by an analogy with Article 176 of the present Treaty, the institution concerned must repeal the act.[63]

The alternative view, namely, that such a preliminary ruling of the Court would require the Court to declare the act in question null and void, or even on an extreme view that the ruling itself renders the act null and void, would completely undermine the time limit for annulment set out in Article 173 [64] and would mean that at any time an act of the institutions, however long it had been held valid and acted upon in the past, could be declared null.

Finally, reference should be made to the new Rules of Procedure, by which not only the parties themselves but Member States, the Commission and, where appropriate, the Council of Ministers can make submissions to the Court.[65]

ARTICLE 178

The Court of Justice shall have jurisdiction to hear cases concerning compensation for damage as provided for in Article 215, paragraph 2.[66]

Article 215, paragraph 2, provides:

[62] *Ibid.*
[63] Art. 176, para. 1 provides:
"An institution from which the amended act originated . . . is required to take the measures which comprise the carrying out of the judgment of the Court of Justice "—see p. 301, above. Any failure to observe this obligation can be challenged under Art. 175—see p. 297, above.
[64] See pp. 287–288, above.
[65] See pp. 469–470, below. See also the procedure in *Robert Bosch G.m.b.H. and another v. Kleding-Verkoopbedrijf de Geus en Uitdenbogard* [1962] C.M.L.R. 1.
[66] French:
"*La Cour de Justice est compétente pour connaître des litiges relatifs à la réparation des dommages visés à l'article 215, alinéa 2.*"
Stationery Office:
"The Court of Justice shall be competent to hear cases relating to compensation for any damage caused as provided for in Article 215, second paragraph."

1. As regards non-contractual liability, the Community shall, in accordance with the general principles common to the laws of Member States, make good any damage caused by its institutions or by its employees in the performance of their duties.

The present Article is conferring jurisdiction upon the Court to hear cases concerning claims for this compensation.

COMPARISON WITH THE POSITION UNDER THE E.C.S.C. TREATY

If Article 215 is compared with the provision in the E.C.S.C. Treaty under which non-contractual claims under that Treaty may be brought,[67] an interesting development is observed. It will be remembered [68] that by that Treaty, the Coal and Steel Community is liable to pay pecuniary damages to a party injured by a *faute de service* of that Community. Where the wrong in question, however, amounts to a *faute personnelle,* it is the employee himself who is declared liable to pay compensation, but if the injured party is unable to obtain these damages from the employee, the Court may award equitable compensation against the Community.[69]

In the present Treaty the terms *faute de service* and *faute personnelle* are not employed: instead the Treaty in referring to damages mentions damage " caused by [community] institutions " and damage " caused by [community] employees in the performance of their duties." The question naturally arises, therefore, of whether these two terms are intended to be synonymous with *faute de service* and *faute personnelle,* respectively.

It appears clear that damage caused by the institutions themselves can be caused solely by a *faute de service* [70]; so also, it is suggested can damage caused by employees in the performance of their duties, for the institution has no existence apart from its employees, and their acts, if within their employment, are the acts of the institution itself. If this is so, then the concept of *fautes personnelles,* which is, broadly speaking, the concept of employees acting outside the performance of their duties, finds no place in the present Treaty.[71]

---

[67] E.C.S.C. Treaty, Art. 40, see pp. 217–233, above.
[68] See pp. 226–233, above.
[69] See pp. 232–233, above.
[70] For a discussion of the meaning of this term, see pp. 217–223, above.
[71] It is suggested that this does not mean that if a *faute personnelle* should occur, the injured party is without a remedy, but only that that remedy must be sought in municipal law against the individual concerned, although regard must be had to the question of immunity.

GENERAL PRINCIPLES COMMON TO THE LAWS OF MEMBER STATES

Although the Court has at times relied upon general principles,[72] this Article is the first occasion when it has been expressly required to apply municipal law as part of Community law. The matters upon which these general principles here being referred to must relate, include, it is suggested, principally the question of remoteness of damage.

TIME FOR BRINGING CLAIMS

As no time is specified for the bringing of claims for compensation, it is suggested, in accordance with the statement of the Court concerning a similar Article,[73] that there is no limitation, and thus that appeals can be brought at any time.

ARTICLE 179

The Court of Justice shall have jurisdiction to determine actions between the Community and its employees within the limits and under the conditions laid down in Service Regulations or arising out of the system applicable to employees.[74]

Article 181[75] confers jurisdiction on the Court in respect of contracts made in public or private law where a clause in such contracts confers jurisdiction. Article 179 appears to be a specific application of that general provision to contracts made between the Community and its employees, which contracts the Court had held exist in public law.[76] It may be noted, however, that the E.C.S.C. Treaty possesses no equivalent provision: breaches of contracts with employees of that Community being brought under Article 42 of the Treaty,[77] which is in identical terms with Article 181 of the present Treaty. There appears, therefore, to have been no special need for the present Article to be included.

The " system applicable to employees " referred to in this Article was the system set out in the individual contracts with employees. These contracts have now been replaced by the terms of the Statute of Service

[72] See pp. 384–385, below.
[73] See p. 238, above.
[74] French:
    " *La Cour de Justice est compétente pour statuer sur tout litige entre la Communauté et ses agents dans les limites et conditions déterminées au statut ou résultant du régime applicable à ces dernières.*"
    Stationery Office:
    "The Court of Justice shall have jurisdiction to adjudicate in any dispute between the Community and its subordinates within the limits of and under the conditions laid down by their statute or terms of employment."
[75] See p. 324, below.
[76] *Kergall* v. *The Common Assembly* (Case 1–55), Vol. II.
[77] See p. 237, above.

issued by the Council of Ministers in June, 1962.[78] These Regulations deal with two distinct types of cases.

(i) Disputes Concerning the Validity of an Act of the Employing Authority and Financial Disputes

Article 91 of the Regulations provides:

1. Any dispute between one of the Communities and one of the persons covered by the present Service Regulations regarding the legality of any act complained of by such person shall be submitted to the Court of Justice of the European Communities. In the cases mentioned in the present Service Regulations and in disputes of a financial character between one of the Communities and one of the persons covered by the present Service Regulations, the Court of Justice shall act with *pleine juridiction*.[79]

2. All proceedings provided for by the present article shall be brought within three months from the date of publication of the act of the competent authority of the institution,[80] if the measure is of a general nature, or from the date of notification of the Decision to the person concerned if the measure is of an individual nature.

Where the competent authority announces no Decision in respect of a request or a complaint from one of the persons covered by the present Service Regulations within two months of the date of lodging of this request or complaint,[81] such omission shall be deemed to be an implied Decision of refusal[82]; any appeal against such Decision shall be lodged within two months of that date.

3. The procedure for investigating and hearing the appeals[83] shall be laid down in Rules of Procedure drawn up by the Court of Justice of the European Committees.

---

[78] E.E.C. Regulation No. 31; *Journal Officiel*, June 14, 1962, p. 1385.

[79] French:
 " *une compétence de pleine juridiction.*"
 Stationery Office:
 " full jurisdiction as to the merits."

[80] Stationery Office:
 " the date of publication by the institution's competent authority of the relevant document."

[81] French:
 " *de cette demande ou réclamation.*"
 Stationery Office:
 " thereof."

[82] French:
 " *une décision implicite de rejet.*"
 Stationery Office:
 " a tacit rejection." This translation fails to convey that this " tacit rejection " is in fact a Decision within the meaning of E.E.C. Treaty, Art. 189, para. 4, and Euratom Treaty, Art 161, para. 4.

[83] French:
 " *les recours.*"
 Stationery Office:
 " proceedings."

The persons employed by the E.E.C. and European Community to whom the above provision applies are, first, an official or *"fonctionnaire"* of those Communities, that is to say, a person appointed to a permanent post on the establishment of one of the Communities' institutions[84]; secondly, temporary staff[85]; thirdly, auxiliary staff[86] who basically are employees, whether full or part-time who are not appointed to an established position within the Communities; fourthly, special advisers[87] and finally the staff of the Joint Nuclear Research Centre.[88] These

[84] Service Regulations of Officials, Art. 1, para. 1. The official is required to have been appointed by means of a written document issued by the authority of the relevant institution which is empowered to make appointments—*ibid*. For most purposes the Economic and Social Committee is regarded as an institution of the Communities —*ibid*. Art. 1, para. 2.

[85] *Ibid*. Art. 46. " Temporary staff " means:
" (a) An employee engaged to fill a post shown in the staff plan appended to the section of the budget relating to each institution and to which the budget authorities have attached temporary status;
(b) An employee engaged to temporarily fill a permanent post included in the staff plan appended to the section of the budget relating to each institution;
(c) An employee engaged to assist a person filling an office provided for under the Treaties establishing the Communities or the elected President or Chairman of one of the Communities' institutions or agencies or of one of the political groups in the European Parliamentary Assembly, provided such person is not an official of one of the Communities "—Regulations No. 31, Conditions of Employment of other servants of the Communities, Art. 2.

[86] *Ibid*. Art. 73. "Auxiliary Staff " means:
" (a) An employee engaged in the performance, within the limits specified in Article 52, below [which provides that the term of engagement of an auxiliary employee shall not exceed the period during which the employee being replaced is unable to discharge his duties, or one year, in all other cases], of full-time or part-time duties in an institution, but who is not assigned to a post included in the staff plan appended to the section of the budget relating to that institution;
(b) An employee engaged, after the possibilities of temporary posting within the institution have been examined, in replacement of certain persons unable for the time being to discharge their duties, namely:
—officials or temporary officials in Category B, C, D of the Translation Department;
—in exceptional cases, officials or temporary employees in Category A, other than those in Grade A1 and A2 and occupying a highly specialised post,
and paid out of the global budgetary provisions for such purposes under the section of the budget relating to such institutions "—*ibid*. Art. 3.

[87] *Ibid*. Art. 83. " A special adviser " means:
"a person, who by reason of his special qualifications and notwithstanding gainful employment in another capacity, is engaged to assist one of the Communities either regularly or for a specified period and who is paid out of the global budgetary provision for the purpose, under the section of the budget relating to the institution in which he serves "—*ibid*. Art. 5.

[88] *Ibid*. Art. 97. A member of the staff means:
" a person residing at the time of his engagement in the country or in close proximity to the place where his duties are to be performed on behalf of the Joint Nuclear Research Centre, or a person equated to him under Article 95 [namely a person not residing in the country or in close proximity to the said place] and engaged with a view to occupying a permanent post in Category C [i.e., concerned with operational duties, which require a secondary educational level or equivalent experience in a practical capacity] or D, [i.e., concerned with manual or maintenance duties which require a primary education possibly supplemented by some technical training] "—*ibid*. Art. 4 and Service Regulations, Art. 5.1, paras. 4 and 5 and Appendix I.

employees can challenge the legality of any act of the relevant institution, whether that act be of a general nature, which presumably means an act affecting one or more groups of persons defined by general criteria, or of an individual character.[89] In cases brought under the E.C.S.C. Treaty, the Court has accepted without argument that the grounds which can be alleged in this appeal are the four classic grounds, set out in that Treaty in Article 33.[90] It would appear, therefore, that under the E.E.C. and the Euratom Treaties it is also these same four grounds which can be alleged.[91] Similarly, it is these same four grounds which can be alleged against the institution's implied Decision of refusal to act which it is deemed to have passed if, within the two months following a request or complaint made to it [92] no Decision is issued.[93]

Where the dispute between the Community and the employee is of a financial character, the Court is given power to act in *pleine juridiction*.[94] It will thus be able to review the actions both of the Community and of the employee so as to determine whether any wrong was in fact done as alleged. It is submitted, however, that despite this power in *pleine juridiction*, the Court will still be limited to the four classic grounds of appeal in so far as its investigations relate to the validity of any particular act of the Community concerned. Further, because there is a time limit of three months for the bringing of appeals against express acts of the Community, and a two months' time limit for appeals against implied Decisions,[94a] it would appear that if these time limits have expired, then, although, when acting in *pleine juridiction*, the Court will

---

[89] The distinction between general and individual acts may perhaps be equated to the distinction between general and individual Decisions of the High Authority, see pp. 157–162, above.

[90] See, *e.g.*, *Kergall* v. *The Common Assembly* (Case 1–55), Vol. II; and *Mirossevich* v. *The High Authority* (Case 10–55), Vol. II.

[91] These grounds are contained in E.E.C. Treaty, Art. 173, para. 1; Euratom Treaty, Art. 146, para. 1.

[92] "Any official may submit a request or a complaint to the authority empowered to make appointments in his institution. Such request or complaint shall be submitted through the official's immediate superior, except where it concerns such immediate superior, in which case it may be submitted directly to the authority next above "—Service Regulations, Art. 90, paras. 1 and 2.

[93] Service Regulations, Art. 25 provides:
   " All Decisions regarding individuals taken under the present Service Regulations shall at once be communicated in writing to the official concerned. Any adverse Decision shall be supported by reasons."
   Although from this it might appear that all Decisions which are not adverse need not be supported by reasons, nevertheless, it is suggested, Art. 190 of the E.E.C. Treaty is applicable to such Decisions by which:
   " Decisions of the Council and of the Commission shall be fully reasoned."
   Clearly an adverse Decision which is implied to exist by virtue of the two months' silence on the part of the institution, can never be reasoned. For the similar situation arising under the E.C.S.C. Treaty, see pp. 189–190, above.

[94] For a discussion of the nature of this power, see pp. 195–196, above.

[94a] Service Regulations, Art. 91, see p. 313, above.

be able to determine whether or not the acts or implied Decisions are valid, it will not be able to annul an act or Decision which is found to be invalid.[95]

(ii) DAMAGES FOR AN OFFICIAL'S SERIOUS FAUTES PERSONNELLES

It will be recalled that under the E.C.S.C. Treaty,[96] a clear distinction is drawn between *fautes de service*, for which the Community is responsible, and *fautes personnelles* for which the individual alone is liable.[97] In the E.E.C. Treaty, itself, these two concepts have ceased to be clearly differentiated,[98] but it is provided that:

> The personal liability of its servants towards the Community shall be defined in the provision establishing their statute of service.[99]

This liability has now been defined by Article 22 of the Service Regulations in the following terms:

> An official [1] may be required to make good, in whole or in part, any damage suffered by the Communities as a result of serious *fautes personnelles,* committed by him in the course of, or in connection with, the performance of his duties.[2]

It is then provided:

> A reasoned Decision shall be given by the authority empowered to make appointments, in accordance with the procedure laid down in regard to disciplinary questions.
> The Court of Justice of the European Communities shall act in *pleine juridiction* in any disputes arising under the present provision.[3]

From this it appears that by a Decision the authority concerned is to identify the *faute* committed and is to outline the evidence which places liability for that *faute* upon the accused, and that it is then to quantify the damage suffered by the Community as a result, and, finally, that the Decision is to give reasons why the person concerned is to pay either part or the whole of that damage.[4] An appeal against this Decision lies to the Court. However, it is not clear whether such appeal is only

---

[95] This may be compared with the position of challenging general Decisions of the High Authority after the expiration of the time limit for such appeals—see pp. 162–164, above.

[96] Art. 40, paras. 1 and 2, see pp. 217–233, above.

[97] For a discussion of these two concepts, see pp. 217–223, above.

[98] Art. 215, para. 2 provides:
" In the case of non-contractual liability, the Community shall, in accordance with the general principles common to the laws of Member States, make good any damage caused by its institution or by its servants in the performance of their duties."

[99] Art. 215, para. 3.

[1] For the meaning of " official," see p. 314, above.

[2] Service Regulations, Art. 22, para. 1.

[3] *Ibid.* Art. 22, paras. 2 and 3.

[4] The person concerned may also be immediately suspended—*ibid.* Art. 88, para. 1.

a particular example of the right of appeal granted under Article 91 of the Service Regulations [5] or whether it is a distinct appeal. If it is a distinct appeal, then clearly the time limit of three months for bringing it will not apply, and there will have been no time limit specified.

The arguments for holding the appeal as being within the terms of Article 91 are, first, that the appeal is being brought not only against the legality of an act of an institution, namely, against the Decision setting out the *faute* and attributing liability to the accused, and secondly, that the appeal may also involve a dispute of a financial nature, and such appeals in Article 91, as in Article 22, are to be heard in *pleine juridiction*.

Against this, however, must be set the fact that by Article 91 it is only the disputes of a financial character which the Court can hear in *pleine juridiction*, whereas the hearing of appeals challenging the validity of an act of an institution is limited to the four classic grounds of appeal. Under Article 22, however, the appeal against the finding contained in the reasoned Decision itself can be investigated by the Court acting in *pleine juridiction*. It is suggested, therefore, that the appeal under Article 22 is an appeal different in kind from that referred to in Article 91, so that the time limit set out in that Article is not applicable.

ARTICLE 180

The Court of Justice shall have jurisdiction within the following limits, to determine actions concerning:

(a) The carrying out of the obligations of Member States arising from the Statute of the European Investment Bank. The Board of Directors of the Bank shall in this respect exercise the powers conferred upon the Commission by Article 169.

(b) The *délibérations* of the Board of Governors of the Bank. Each Member State, the Commission and the Board of Directors of the Bank may bring an appeal in this matter under the conditions laid down in Article 173.

(c) The *délibérations* of the Board of Directors of the Bank. The appeals against the *délibérations* may be brought under the conditions prescribed in Article 173, only by the Member States or the Commission, and only for violation of the procedural requirements

[5] See p. 313, above.

laid down in Article 21, paragraphs 2 and 5 to 7 inclusive of the Statute of the Investment Bank.[6]

PARAGRAPH (A). REMEDIES FOR BREACHES OF A MEMBER STATE'S OBLIGATIONS UNDER THE STATUTE OF THE EUROPEAN INVESTMENT BANK

REMEDIES OPEN TO THE BOARD OF DIRECTORS

By the Statute of the European Investment Bank, certain obligations were imposed upon Member States. The first of these was to pay the Bank the agreed amount of capital in order that the Bank could be established.[7] This capital was to be paid, as to 25 per cent., by five equal instalments, and as to the remaining 75 per cent., when so required by the Board of Directors of the Bank.[8] Secondly, the Member States may be required by the Board of Governors[9] to grant to the Bank special interest-bearing loans in order to enable the Bank to finance specific projects.[10] Thirdly, the Member States undertake to make available to those who have borrowed from the Bank, the foreign

---

6 French:

" *La Cour de Justice est compétente, dans les limites ci-après, pour connaître des litiges concernant:*

(*a*) *L'exécution des obligations des Etats membres résultant des statuts de la Banque européenne d'Investissement. Le Conseil d'administration de la Banque dispose à cet égard des pouvoirs reconnus à la Commission par l'article 169;*

(*b*) *Les délibérations du Conseil des Gouverneurs de la Banque. Chaque Etat membre, la Commission et le Conseil d'administration de la Banque peuvent former un recours en cette matière dans les conditions prévues à l'article 173;*

(*c*) *Les délibérations du Conseil d'administration de la Banque. Les recours contre ces délibérations ne peuvent être formés, dans les conditions fixées à l'article 173, que par les Etats membres ou la Commission, et seulement pour violation des formes prévues à l'article 21, paragraphe 2 et 5 à 7 inclus, des statuts de la Banque d'Investissement.*"

Stationery Office:

" The Court of Justice shall be competent within the limits hereinafter set out to hear disputes concerning:—

(a) The fulfilment by Member States of the obligations arising under the Statute of the European Investment Bank. The Board of Directors of the Bank shall, in this respect, enjoy the powers conferred upon the Commission by Article 169;

(b) Decisions of the Board of Governors of the Bank. In this matter, any Member State, the Commission or the Board of Directors of the Bank may institute proceedings under the conditions laid down in Article 173;

(c) Decisions of the Board of Directors of the Bank. Appeals against such decisions, brought in accordance with Article 173, may only be brought by Member States or by the Commission, and solely upon the grounds of non-compliance with the procedure prescribed by Article 21 (2) and (5) to (7) inclusive of the Statute of the Bank."

7 Protocol on the Statute of the European Investment Bank, Art. 4. These amounts were Germany 300m. units; France 300m.; Italy 240m.; Belgium 86.5m.; Netherlands 71.5m.; and Luxembourg 2m., where one unit represents the value of 0.88867088 grammes of fine gold—*ibid*. Art. 4.1, paras. 1 and 2; see further p. 421, below.
8 *Ibid*. Art. 5.1 and 2. As to the Board of Directors, see p. 432, below.
9 As to the Board of Governors, see p. 429, below.
10 *Ibid*. Art. 6.1.

currency necessary for the repayment of the capital and interest on the sums borrowed.[11] Fourthly and lastly, the Member States have undertaken in the Treaty that they will not impose any financial regulations directing that money borrowed from the Bank has to be expended in any one specific Member State, that is to say, the borrowers are always to be free to spend the money anywhere within the Community.[12]

If a Member State fails in any of these obligations, Article 180 provides that the Board of Directors of the Bank " shall exercise the powers conferred upon the Commission by Article 169." The effect of this provision is that if the Board of Directors considers that a Member State has so failed, it is required to issue a reasoned Opinion to this effect after having given the State concerned an opportunity to present its observations. The State is then to be given a further period in which to comply with its obligations, and if it fails to do so within this period, it can be cited before the Court by the Board of Directors.[13] If the Court upholds the contention of the Board of Directors, it will give judgment against the defaulting State which is then requested " to take the measures which comprise the execution of the judgment of the Court." [14] It will be remembered that by the E.E.C. Treaty, after this judgment, there is no further action which can be taken to obtain compliance.

REMEDIES OPEN TO THE BOARD OF GOVERNORS

The above procedure under Article 180 (a) to compel a State to comply with its obligations is to be compared with the alternative procedure contained in the Statute of the Bank itself—Article 26 of this Statute providing:

> If a Member State fails to fulfil the obligations of membership resulting from this Statute and in particular the obligation to pay up its share of the subscribed capital or its special loans, or to ensure the servicing of the funds it has borrowed, the granting of loans or guarantees to that Member State or its nationals may be suspended by a decision of the Board of Governors by qualified majority vote.[15]

It will be noted that although this Article specifically mentions certain obligations of the Member States, the Article applies to any obligations imposed by the Statute and not merely those mentioned. The power

---

11 *Ibid.* Art. 25.4.
12 *Ibid.* Art. 20.4.
13 For the suggested right of the Board of Directors to exercise the powers of the Commission under Art. 170 when a Member State alleges a breach by another Member State of its obligations under the Treaty, see pp. 280–281, above.
14 Art. 171. For a discussion of this Article, see pp. 281–284, above.
15 This suspension does not release the Member State or its nationals from their obligations to the Bank—*ibid.* Art. 26, para. 2.

of the Board of Governors to suspend loans and guarantees arises, therefore, in any case where the Board of Directors could cite a Member State before the Court, and also during the earlier period when the Board of Directors are still drawing up their reasoned Opinion, and giving the State concerned a time period within which to comply.[16] Further than this, the power of suspension appears to be in no way affected by a recourse to the Court, and in any event, it can be used to sanction a failure by a Member State to comply with the Court's judgment declaring its breach. This being so, it is suggested that this alternative provision, enabling the Bank to give a defaulting State a short, sharp shock, is to be preferred to the procedure for recourse to the Court, set out in Article 180.[17]

APPEAL AGAINST THE OPINION OF THE BOARD OF DIRECTORS DECLARING A BREACH BY A MEMBER STATE

If the first of the two above alternative methods of sanctioning a State is adopted, and the Board of Directors declares in a reasoned Opinion that a Member State has defaulted in one of its obligations under the Statute of the Bank, the question arises whether this Opinion can itself be challenged before the Court.[18]

By the present Article, the powers of the Board of Directors are declared to be the same as those of the Commission under Article 169. Now it will be recalled that under that Article the Commission is required to issue an Opinion setting out the default, while by Article 173 an Opinion is not susceptible to challenge before the Court, so that it might appear that this Opinion is not susceptible of challenge either.[19] In the present instance, however, reference is to be made to paragraph (c) of the present Article, by which the " *délibérations* of the Board of Directors " may be referred to the Court. Although the term " *délibérations* " is nowhere defined in the Treaty, it would appear that a formal declaration that a State is in breach of its obligation under the Statute constitutes a " *délibération*." However, paragraph (c) only allows a " *délibération* " to be annulled for violation of certain specified

---

16 It is suggested that the contention that until the matter has come before the Court there cannot be any authoritative ruling to the effect that a State has failed to fulfil its obligations, but merely an allegation to this effect, cannot here be tenable. A breach of a financial obligation will be immediately apparent and there is here no suggestion that the Board of Governors are to act only to enforce a judgment of the Court.

17 For a discussion of how the Decision to suspend loans and guarantees can itself be challenged before the Court, see pp. 322–324, below.

18 For the somewhat similar position under the E.C.S.C. Treaty, see Art. 88, pp. 249–257, above, and *German Government* v. *The High Authority* (Case 19–58); Vol. II, discussed at pp. 251–253, above.

19 The difficulty created by this is discussed at pp. 277–281, above.

substantial procedural requirements, all of which relate to applications to the Bank for loans.[20] It appears, therefore, that the Treaty does not contemplate that the particular " *délibération* " in question should be challengeable under paragraph (c), and there is no other provision under which it can be challenged directly.[21] However, as the power of the Board of Directors is the same as that of the Commission under Article 169, it follows that just as under that Article any action brought before the Court can be struck out as inadmissible, unless prior to the action being brought a reasoned Opinion has been issued after the State concerned has been allowed to present its observations,[22] so likewise under the present Article any action brought of the Board of Directors without their also having issued a reasoned Opinion or allowed the State to present its observations will be inadmissible.

Paragraph (B). Appeals against the Délibérations of the Board of Governors of the Bank

The main function of the Board of Governors is to lay down the general credit policy of the Bank.[23] The Board can decide to require Member States to advance to the Bank special interest-bearing loans to finance specific projects,[24] and to increase the subscribed capital of the Bank.[25] The granting of loans from the Bank for investment projects, to be wholly or partly carried out in the non-European territories of the Member States, requires the sanction of the Board.[26] The power to suspend the activities of the Bank, and to appoint liquidators is also vested in the Board of Governors. In addition to this, the Board, as considered above,[27] can suspend all loans and guarantees given to a State or to its nationals, and finally, it has certain administrative duties, such as appointing and dismissing the Board of Directors and the Management Committee.

Article (b) declares that the Court can hear actions brought against the *délibérations* of the Board of Governors.

One must first note that it is unclear whether it is assumed by the Treaty that all the above acts of the Board fall within the term

---

[20] For these requirements, see pp. 322–324, below.
[21] Art. 180 (a) provides only that the Board of Directors when declaring a State to be in breach of its obligations under the Statute " shall exercise the powers conferred upon the Commission by Article 169." It does not state that the Opinion of the Board shall be equated to an Opinion of the Commission and even if it had, a right of appeal against that Opinion would be dubious, see pp. 274–277, above.
[22] See p. 276, above.
[23] For the full functions of the Board of Governors, see pp. 429–432, below.
[24] Statute, Art. 6.1.
[25] *Ibid.* Art. 4.3.
[26] *Ibid.* Art. 18.1, para. 2.
[27] See p. 319, above.

délibérations, and are thus open to appeal under this Article. If the Board of Governors dismisses a director of the Bank, or a member of the Management Committee, that dismissal will, it is submitted, have been embodied in a *délibération* of the Board. Yet such a dismissal, if improper, would constitute a breach of the contract of employment between the Bank and the individual and litigation upon such a breach is governed by the terms of Article 181. It is felt that it can hardly be argued despite the provision in Article 180 (b) that " each Member State may appeal against a *délibération* of the Board of Governors " that the home State of the dismissed person could, in addition, challenge the *délibération* before the Court. This being so, it is suggested that the true meaning of this provision is that only the *délibérations* of the Board of Governors, other than those relating to appointments and dismissals, are open to appeal under Article 180.

The appeal itself may be brought by any of the Member States, by the Commission or by the Board of Directors, but the appeal is to be brought " under the conditions laid down in Article 173." This means that the *délibérations* can be challenged on any of the usual four grounds,[28] and that the time limit for bringing appeals is as regulated by Article 173, paragraph 3. That paragraph states that appeals must be brought within two months of the publication of the act in the *Journal Officiel,* or within two months of the notification of the act to the plaintiff, or in default of either of these, within two months of the day when the act came to the plaintiff's knowledge. As, however, there is no obligation upon the Bank to publish its *délibération,* it would appear that time will normally run from notification.

PARAGRAPH (C). APPEALS AGAINST THE DÉLIBÉRATIONS OF THE BOARD OF DIRECTORS

It has already been noted that this provision allowing for appeals against the *délibérations* of the Board of Directors does not cover appeals against what are perhaps the most important *délibérations* of all, namely those by which the Board of Directors set out that a State is in breach of its obligations to the Bank.[29] The *délibérations* which are here being referred to are solely those concerned with the granting of loans by the Bank, and the appeal against these can be brought only by the Member States or by the Commission.

The grounds of appeal are limited to four specified matters.

(1) Applications for loans or for guarantees can be addressed to the Bank either by a State or by an enterprise, applying on its own

---

[28] For these, see the terms of Art. 173, para. 1, p. 287, above.
[29] See pp. 318–319, above.

behalf. Alternatively, an enterprise can apply through its home State, or through the Commission; similarly a Member State can apply through the Commission instead of applying directly.[30]

Where an application has been received, it is submitted to the Management Committee of the Bank [31] which decides by a majority vote, whether it advises that it should be granted. If the Committee does not so advise, the Board of Directors can only pass a *délibération* granting the loan, if it is unanimous.[32] If this unanimous vote has not been obtained, the *délibération* is able to be annulled on an appeal under Article 180 (c).

(2) If an application for a loan or guarantee is submitted through a Member State, and also presumably if that State is applying on its own behalf, as for example in respect of some project of a nationalised industry, the application is to be submitted to the Commission as well as to the Management Committee.[33] If the Commission gives an unfavourable Opinion,[34] the Board of Directors, as in the case above, can authorise such a loan or guarantee only by means of a unanimous vote, excluding the vote of the director nominated by the Commission itself.[35] If such a unanimous vote has not been obtained, the *délibération* is able to be annulled in an appeal under Article 180 (c).

(3) If not only the Commission but also the Management Committee advise against the grant of a loan or guarantee, the Board of Directors may not authorise it.[36] Quite surprisingly, therefore, despite this inability, it is provided that if the Board of Directors do in fact grant such a loan it is open to be annulled under Article 180 (c).

(4) Finally, if the request for a loan is brought via the Commission, it must be submitted for the opinion of the Member State in whose territory the project is to be carried out.[37] A failure on the part of the Board of Directors to make this submission is a further ground upon which a *délibération* of that Board can be annulled. Further, if the request for the loan or guarantee is made by an enterprise directly to the Bank, the Board is required to submit the request both to the Member State concerned and to the Commission, and a failure to do

---

[30] Statute, Art. 21.1.
[31] *Ibid.* Art. 13.3, para. 2 and Art. 13.4. As to this Committee, see further pp. 433–434, below.
[32] *Ibid.* Art. 21.5.
[33] *Ibid.* Art. 21.2, para. 1.
[34] A failure to give an Opinion within two months is deemed to be a favourable Opinion—*ibid.* Art. 21.2, para. 2.
[35] *Ibid.* Art. 21.6. The Commission's power to nominate one director is contained in *ibid.* Art. 11.2, para. 2.
[36] *Ibid.* Art. 21.7.
[37] *Ibid.* Art. 21.2, para. 1.

so is grounds for annulment of the *délibération* authorising such loan on guarantee.[38]

ARTICLE 181

The Court of Justice shall have jurisdiction to determine by virtue of a clause conferring jurisdiction contained in a contract in public or private law entered into by the Community or on its benefit.[39]

This Article is a re-enactment of Article 42 of the E.C.S.C. Treaty.[40] As this provision covers contracts in both public law and private law, it appears clear that if Britain became a party to the Treaty, the provision would cover not only contracts with, for example, the nationalised Electricity Board, which may perhaps be equated with contracts in " public law," but also contracts made between the institution of the Community and their employees, which contracts, in respect of the Coal and Steel Community, the Court has held to fall within the scope of public law.[41] As, therefore, Article 42 in the E.C.S.C. Treaty has been found adequate to confer the necessary jurisdiction over cases relating to employees, it is strange that the specific provision in Article 179 has been inserted in the present Treaty to confer express jurisdiction in respect of such cases.

It will be observed that no time limit is specified within which actions must be brought under this Article, nor are any grounds set out upon which the appeals are to be based. It is suggested, however, that the rulings of the Court on these topics given in relation to Article 42 [42] must also be applicable to this provision. It can be said, therefore, that there is no time limit for actions, and the grounds of appeal are the four classic grounds set out in Article 173, paragraph 1.[43]

---

[38] *Ibid.* Art. 21.2, para. 1.

[39] French:
> " La cour de Justice est compétente pour statuer en vertu d'une clause compromissoire contenue dans un contrat de droit public ou de droit privé passé par la Communauté ou pour son compte."

Stationery Office:
> " The Court of Justice shall have jurisdiction to give a decision pursuant to any arbitration clause contained in a contract concluded, by or on behalf of the Community, whether such contract be governed by public law or private law."

[40] See p. 237, above.

[41] See, *e.g.*, *Kergall* v. *The Common Assembly* (Case 1–55), Vol. II.

[42] See further, pp. 237–238, above.

[43] See p. 287, above.

ARTICLE 182

The Court of Justice shall have jurisdiction to determine upon any difference between Member States in connection with the objects of the present Treaty if this difference is referred to it by virtue of an agreement.[44]

This Article is a repetition of Article 89, paragraph 2 of the E.C.S.C. Treaty.[45] Under that Treaty, it is in addition provided that differences between the Member States concerning the application of that Treaty, which cannot be settled by any other procedure set out in that Treaty, may be submitted to the Court at the request of one of the States which is a party to the dispute.[46] That Treaty thus makes a distinction between the settlement of the differences concerning the *application* of the Treaty and differences in connection with its *objects*.

" THE APPLICATION OF THE TREATY "

The present Treaty, however, only contains the above provision concerning differences in connection with the *objects* of the Treaty, and does not contain any provision concerning differences in connection with the *application* of the Treaty. It is virtually impossible, however, to determine what cases, if any, relate solely to the application of the Treaty—and which if relating to the E.C.S.C. Treaty would have been justiciable under Article 89, paragraph 1—and those which relate solely to the objects of the Treaty—which in coal and steel matters, would have been justiciable under Article 89, paragraph 2. If, however, this distinction can be made,[47] then any matters relating solely to the application of the Treaty would appear not to be able to be brought to the Court under the present provision, or indeed under any provision.

This Article is to be read together with Article 219, which supplements it by providing:

> Member States undertake not to submit a dispute concerning the interpretation or application of this Treaty to any method of settlement other than those provided for in this Treaty.

[44] French:
"*La Cour de Justice est compétente pour statuer sur tout différend entre Etats membres en connexité avec l'objet du présent Traité, si ce différend lui est soumis en vertu d'un compromis.*"
Stationery Office:
" The Court of Justice shall be competent to decide any dispute between Member States connected with the subject of this Treaty, where the said States submit the said dispute to the Court under a special agreement beween them."
[45] p. 257, above.
[46] E.C.S.C. Treaty, Art. 89, para. 1; see p. 257, above.
[47] Unless it can there appears no necessity for the two paragraphs of E.C.S.C. Treaty, Art. 89, nor any means of determining whether a dispute in relation to coal and steel can be brought merely at the request of one party—under Art. 89, para. 1— or only by virtue of an express agreement—Art. 89, para. 2.

As the Treaty provides no method of settlement in disputes concerning the application of the Treaty, it might be contended on a strict reading that the Member States are unrestricted in the choice of settlement open to them. In practice, however, it is suggested, some interpretation of necessity would be adopted to restrain this freedom.

ARTICLE 183

Subject to the jurisdiction conferred upon the Court of Justice by the present Treaty, legal action to which the Community is a party shall not, for that reason, be excluded from the jurisdiction of municipal courts.[48]

By this Article, the mere fact that the Community is a party to a legal action does not of itself mean that the action cannot be heard in a municipal court of one of the Member States.

Indeed, it is set out in the Treaty that the Community is to possess in each of the Member States " the most extensive legal capacity accorded to legal persons under their domestic law "[49] and further that:

> it may, in particular, . . . sue and be sued in its own name. For this purpose the Community shall be represented by the Commission.[50]

Finally, in the service Regulations[51] it is set out that:

> Any dispute between the institution and local employees shall be a matter for the courts having jurisdiction in the place where the employee performs his duties.[52]

CONTRACTUAL ACTION AGAINST THE COMMUNITY

By the Treaty, the contractual liability of the Community is to be governed by the proper law of the contract in question.[53] Thus, if this

---

[48] French:
   " *Sous réserve des compétences attribués à la Cour de Justice par le présent Traité, les litiges auxquels la Communauté est partie ne sont pas, de ce chef, soustraits à la compétence des juridictions nationales.*"
   Stationery Office:
   " Subject to the powers conferred in the Court of Justice by this Treaty, cases to which the Community is a party shall not for that reason alone be excluded from the jurisdiction of national courts."
[49] Art. 211.
[50] *Ibid*.
[51] E.E.C. Regulation, No. 31, Conditions of Employment of other Servants of the Communities, Art. 81.
[52] " Local employee " means:
   " an employee engaged according to local practice for manual work or to serve in a post not shown in the staff plan appended to the section of the budget relating to each institution and paid out of the global budgetary provision made for this purpose under that section of the budget "—*ibid*. Art. 4, para. 1.
[53] Art. 215, para. 1. French: " *par la loi applicable au contrat en cause.*" Stationery Office: " by the law applying to the contract in question."

proper law is, for example, French, it is, basically, French courts which will possess jurisdiction. However, if the contract expressly grants jurisdiction to the Communities' Court, that Court and that Court alone will possess jurisdiction.[54]

On this, it may be noted that in practice the greatest number of contracts made by the E.E.C. Community will be contracts of employment, and by the Statute of Service now in force and applicable to them, it is the Court of Justice which has been given jurisdiction.[55] Furthermore, express jurisdiction in these matters is conferred on the Court by Article 179.[56] Again, even if a particular contract does not possess a clause conferring jurisdiction, nevertheless the municipal court having jurisdiction will be empowered, and the highest municipal court will be required to refer the case to the Communities' Court for a preliminary ruling upon the validity or interpretation of the contract if either of these matters is raised before the municipal court.[57]

Tortious Actions against the Community

By Article 215, paragraph 2, it is provided:

> As regards non-contractual liability, the Community, in accordance with the general principles common to the laws of Member States, shall pay compensation for damage caused by its institutions or by its employees in the exercise of their duties.

By Article 183, therefore, the mere fact that the Community is being sued for a tort does not exclude the relevant municipal court.[58] However, by Article 178 [59]:

> The Court of Justice shall have jurisdiction to determine actions concerning compensation for damage as provided for in Article 215, paragraph 2.

The question, therefore, arises of whether both the municipal court and the Communities' Court possess jurisdiction under Article 183 and Article 178 respectively, or whether, because the Communities' Court has jurisdiction, no other court can have such jurisdiction: in other words, whether the phrase " shall have jurisdiction " means " shall have exclusive jurisdiction."

---

54 Art. 181, see p. 324, above.
55 See the cases concerning contracts of employment, Vol. II, Chap. 9.
56 See p. 312, above.
57 Art. 177. It is suggested that the power of the Communities' Court to rule upon " the validity and interpretation of acts of the institution of the Community " include power to rule upon the validity and interpretation of *contracts* entered into by the Community. The term " act " is not defined in the Treaty, even in Art. 189.
58 The determination of which municipal court would have jurisdiction involves the question of where the tort actually occurred.
59 See p. 310, above.

On this, it is suggested that two considerations are relevant. First, in all other Articles where the expression " the Court of Justice shall have jurisdiction " occurs [60] it appears clear that exclusive jurisdiction is being conferred. For example, by Article 180 the Court " shall have jurisdiction " to determine actions concerning the *délibérations* of the Board of Governors and Board of Directors of the Bank, and it appears clear that this jurisdiction is not intended in any way to be shared.

Secondly, in one decided case, when considering whether a particular action ought to have been brought, or brought first before a Belgian court, the Communities' Court declared:

> The Treaties are based upon the principle of the rigorous separation of the jurisdiction of the Court on the one hand and the national jurisdictions on the other. It follows that any overlap between the powers possessed by these various jurisdictions has been excluded.[61]

It follows, therefore, it is submitted, that because by Article 178 the Communities' Court possesses jurisdiction in respect of tortious acts committed by the Community, or by its employees acting in the performance of their duties, no municipal court can hear such a case.[62]

CRIMINAL ACTION AGAINST THE COMMUNITY

Although it is unlikely that the Community would in any way fall foul of the criminal law of a country, it is possible that the Community, even inadvertently, might violate such laws as those relating to Town and Country Planning, or Building Regulations. In such a situation, it is submitted that nothing in the Treaty prevents legal action being taken against the Community, but such action would be sterile by virtue of the provision in the Protocol on the Privileges and Immunities of the Community Act, that:

> The property and assets of the Community shall not be the subject of any administrative or legal measure of constraint without the authorisation of the Court of Justice.[63]

---

[60] Arts. 177, 178, 179, 180, 181 and 182.

[61] *Humblet* v. *The Belgian State* (Case 6–60), Vol. II.

[62] If a municipal court attempted to assume jurisdiction in such a case, it would appear that the Commission would refuse to take any part or to submit any pleadings. If the defendant in the action were an employee of the Community he would not be immune from suit—Protocol on Privileges and Immunities, Art. 11 (a)—but would be able to request the municipal court to apply under Art. 177 for a preliminary ruling concerning the interpretation of the relevant articles of the Treaty, see p. 303, above. The Commission could also take action against the Member State concerned under Art. 169, see p. 274, above.

[63] Art. 1. Whether the municipal court or the prosecuting party could apply to the Communities' Court for such authorisation is not stated, but it would appear that someone must apply, and the Community appears inherently unlikely to do so itself.

ARTICLE 184

Notwithstanding the expiration of the time limit set out in Article 173, paragraph 3, any party in an action bringing into issue a Regulation of the Council or of the Commission may rely upon the grounds set out in Article 173, paragraph 1, in order to allege before the Court of Justice the inapplicability of this Regulation.[64]

This Article has to be read with Article 173, above, and some aspects of it have been considered together with that Article.[65] This provision, however, is of value not only to enterprises and other legal or natural persons who, as considered above, wish to challenge a fine imposed upon them by virtue of a Regulation, but who have no standing to challenge that Regulation under Article 173.[66] It is also of value to Member States when, for example, they are declared [67] by the Commission to have violated one of their Treaty obligations, namely the obligation to comply with a Regulation. If, as is almost inevitable, this declaration of the Commission is made more than two months after the publication of the Regulation, the time limit of two months for appealing against the Regulation will have expired.[68] Under Article 184, however, it is still open to the State to allege that the Regulation imposed no valid legal duty upon it, or the ground that the Regulation in question is void on one or more of the grounds set out in Article 173.

DIRECTIVES OF THE COUNCIL OR THE COMMISSION

It will have been noted that Article 184 implies in terms only to " a Regulation " of the Council or of the Commission. Either of these bodies, however, may also issue Directives which are " binding, in respect of the result to be achieved, upon every Member State, but the form and manner of enforcing them shall be a matter for the national

---

[64] French:
   " *Nonobstant l'expiration du délai prévu à l'article 173, alinéa 3, toute partie peut, à l'occasion d'un litige mettant en cause un règlement du Conseil ou de la Commission, se prévaloir des moyens prévus à l'article 173, alinéa 1, pour invoquer devant la Cour de Justice l'inapplicabilité de ce règlement.*"
   Stationery Office:
   " Where a Regulation made by the Council or the Commission is the subject of legal proceedings, any of the parties concerned may, notwithstanding the expiry of the period laid down in Article 173 (3), invoke the grounds set out in Article 173 (1), in order to submit to the Court of Justice that the Regulation in question does not apply."
[65] See pp. 287–295, above.
[66] See p. 292, above.
[67] This declaration is made by an Opinion passed under Arts. 169 and 170; see pp. 274 and 277, above.
[68] Art. 173, para. 3, see p. 287, above.

authorities." [69] If a State challenges the validity of such a Directive under Article 173,[70] and the Court annuls it, the matter is clearly at an end. If, however, after the two months' time limit for challenge has expired, the State is accused of having failed to comply with the Directive, the Commission may issue an Opinion setting out the breach and the State may eventually be brought before the Court. Such State may then very well wish to allege the invalidity of the original Directive.

It might be contended, because Article 184 makes no reference at all to Directives, that this article does not cover them, and that, therefore, the State cannot challenge the Directive. Under the E.C.S.C. Treaty, however, where there is no provision equivalent to Article 184, the Court has held that:

> When, after the expiration of the time limit set out in the last paragraph of Article 33,[71] a plaintiff is challenging an individual Decision, he may avail himself of the irregularity of general Decisions *and Recommendations* upon which that particular Decision has been based.[72]

Now, general Decisions under the E.C.S.C. Treaty are equivalent to Regulations under the E.E.C. Treaty, and Recommendations are equivalent to Directives.[73] It appears, therefore, that because the law concerning the challenge of acts of the institutions of these two Communities are so similar,[74] had the E.E.C. Treaty not contained the provisions of Article 184, the above passage of the judgment of the Court given in relation to the E.C.S.C. Treaty would have been applicable to the E.E.C. Treaty, so that under the E.E.C. Treaty a State would have been allowed to allege the invalidity of the Directive. If this is so, then it is suggested, although the provisions of Article 184 have in fact been included, by which a State is granted express rights in relation to Regulations, that a State cannot be in a worse position legally, with respect to Directives, than it would have been if it had not been granted any rights in relation to this type of appeal at all. It is, therefore, submitted that a State can challenge the validity of a Directive out of time.

ARTICLE 185

Appeals brought before the Court of Justice shall not have a suspensive effect. However, the Court of Justice may, if it

---

[69] Art. 189, para. 3. In practice far more Directives than Regulations will be issued.
[70] See p. 287, above.
[71] The equivalent of the time limit under E.E.C. Treaty, Art. 173, para. 3.
[72] *Meroni & Co., S.p.A.* v. *The High Authority* (Case 9–56), Vol. II. See p. 163, above.
[73] *Cf.* E.C.S.C. Treaty, Art. 15 and E.E.C. Treaty, Art. 189, and see p. 289, above.
[74] *E.g.*, E.E.C. Treaty, Art. 173, para. 1 sets out the same four grounds of appeal as are in E.C.S.C. Treaty, Art. 33, para. 1.

considers that the circumstances require it, order the suspension of the execution of the act challenged.[75]

This Article reproduces Article 39, paragraphs 1 and 2 of the E.C.S.C. Treaty, except that it has been phrased in slightly wider terms by being made applicable to the suspension of the execution of the " act " being challenged, whereas Article 39 refers merely to " Decision or Recommendation." In the present provision, however, the term " act " appears to be applicable only to Regulations, Directives and Decisions, and not to Recommendations and Opinions because the latter are not binding in any event.[76] If this is so, then, unfortunately, the word " act " in the present Article is being used in a different sense from the same word when it appears in Article 173, paragraph 1, where reference is made to " acts . . . other than Recommendations or Opinions," from which, it is suggested, it can be inferred only that Recommendations and Opinions are acts.

For the Court's interpretation of the wording of the similar Article 39, the reader is referred to the discussion of that article.[77]

ARTICLE 186

In actions which have been referred to it, the Court of Justice may prescribe the necessary interim measures.[78]

This Article is a reproduction of the terms of Article 39, paragraph 3 of the E.C.S.C. Treaty, the terms of which have been discussed above.[79]

ARTICLE 225

If the measures taken in the cases mentioned in Articles 223 and 224 have the effect of distorting conditions of competition

---

[75] French:
" *Les recours formés devant la Cour de Justice n'ont pas d'effet suspensif. Toutefois, la Cour de Justice peut, si elle estime que les circonstances l'exigent, ordonner le sursis à l'exécution de l'acte attaqué.*"
Stationery Office:
" Proceedings instituted before the Court of Justice shall not suspend the operation of the act in question. The Court of Justice may, however, if it considers that circumstances so require, order that the operation of the act in question be suspended."

[76] Art. 189, para. 5 provides:
" Recommendations and opinions shall have no binding force."

[77] See pp. 211–217, above.

[78] French:
" *Dans les affaires dont elle est saisie, la Cour de Justice peut prescrire les mesures provisoires nécessaires.*"
Stationery Office:
" The Court of Justice may, in any cases referred to it, prescribe any necessary interim measures."

[79] See pp. 216–217, above.

within the Common Market, the Commission shall investigate with the State concerned the conditions under which these measures may be adapted to the rules established by the present Treaty.

Notwithstanding the procedure provided for in Articles 169 and 170, the Commission or any Member State may appeal directly to the Court of Justice, if it considers that another Member State is making an improper use of the powers mentioned in Articles 223 and 224. The Court of Justice shall sit *in camera*.[80]

THE SCOPE OF PARAGRAPH 1

Although the E.E.C. Treaty is intended to establish free trade throughout the Community, State interference in the market is expressly allowed under the special circumstances set out in Articles 223 and 224. By these articles, it is declared that any Member State may take whatever measures connected with the production of or trade in arms, munitions and war material it shall consider necessary for the protection of the essential interest of its security.[81] These measures, however, must not adversely affect conditions of competition in the Common Market in

---

[80] French:

" *Si des mesures prises dans les cas prévus aux articles 223 et 224 ont pour effet de fausser les conditions de la concurrence dans le marché commun, la Commission examine avec l'Etat intéressé les conditions dans lesquelles ces mesures peuvent être adaptées aux règles établies par le présent Traité.*

Par dérogation à la procédure prévue aux articles 169 et 170, la Commission ou tout Etat membre peut saisir directement la Cour de Justice, s'il estime qu'un autre Etat membre fait un usage abusif des pouvoirs prévus aux articles 223 et 224. La Cour de Justice statue à huis clos."

Stationery Office:

" If the measures taken under the conditions envisaged in Articles 223 and 224 have the effect of distorting conditions of competition in the Common Market, the Commission shall, jointly with the State concerned, investigate the conditions under which these measures may be adapted to the rules laid down by this Treaty.

Notwithstanding the procedure provided for in Articles 169 and 170, the Commission or any Member State may apply directly to the Court of Justice if it considers that another Member State is making an improper use of the powers provided for under Articles 223 and 224. The Court of Justice shall sit *in camera*."

[81] Art. 223, para. 1 provides:

" The provisions of this Treaty shall not adversely affect the following rules:

(a) No Member State shall be obliged to supply information the disclosure of which it considers contrary to the essential interests of its security;

(b) Any Member State may take whatever measures it considers necessary for the protection of the essential interests of its security, and which are connected with the production of or trade in arms, munitions and war material; such measures shall, however, not adversely affect conditions of competition in the Common Market in the case of products which are not intended for specifically military purposes."

respect to products which are not intended for specifically military purposes.[82]

It is further provided that " the Member States shall consult one another with a view to taking in common the steps necessary to prevent the operation of the Common Market being affected by measures which one Member State may be called upon to take either as a result of serious internal disturbances, affecting law and order, or as a result of war or of serious international tension, constituting a threat of war, or in order to carry out undertakings into which it has entered for the purpose of maintaining peace and international security." [83]

The present Article then declares that if any of the above measures taken by a Member State have the effect of distorting conditions of competition within the Common Market, the Commission is to conduct an investigation with the State concerned. It would appear that this consultation is of an entirely informal nature, and is not intended to be preliminary to the Commission issuing an Opinion under Article 169, paragraph 1.[84] However, because Article 225, paragraph 2, which opens with the word " notwithstanding," adds to the power of the Commission and does not curtail its existing powers, it appears that the Commission acting by virtue of its existing power under Article 169 could issue a reasoned Opinion setting out the breach of Article 223 or 224 and require the State to rectify the breach.

By paragraph 1 of this article, the power of the Commission to undertake an investigation of the measures which a State has taken is dependent upon those measures having the effect of distorting competition within the Common Market. If the measures do not have that affect, the Commission does not possess any power of investigation. Where, therefore, a State, which has taken measures under either Article 223 or 224, denies that these measures do distort competition, it will clearly refuse to undertake any examination with the Commission. In this situation it appears that the Commission can appeal to the Court directly under paragraph 2.[85]

THE SCOPE OF PARAGRAPH 2

Under paragraph 2 the Commission or any Member State may appeal directly to the Court if it considers that another Member State " is making an improper use of the powers mentioned in Articles 223 and

---

[82] *Ibid.* The Council has been required by the Treaty to draw up the list of products to which para. 1 (b) applies—*ibid.* para. 2.
[83] Art. 224.
[84] See p. 274, above.
[85] See, however, the discussion on para. 2, below.

224." This wording has to be carefully compared with that in paragraph 1, for under that paragraph the Commission is granted power to conduct an investigation with a State if measures taken in the cases mentioned in those Articles " have the effect of distorting competition within the Common Market." Now it is suggested that to use powers so as to distort competition within the meaning of paragraph 1 is also to make an improper use of those powers, within the meaning of paragraph 2. However, one of the powers mentioned in Article 223 is that of withholding information which a Member State considers is contrary to the essential interest of its security.[86] Now a State would make an improper use of this power if it withheld information which it did not believe affected the essential interests of its security.[87] It is suggested, however, that this withholding of information would not necessarily distort competition within the Common Market, so that it would not come within the terms of paragraph 1 of Article 225. It follows, therefore, that, whereas by Article 225 every distortion of the conditions of competition, by being also an improper use of the powers mentioned, founds a right of appeal to the Court, yet it is not on every occasion when the Commission can appeal to the Court that it can also undertake an investigation with the State concerned.

Where the measures taken by a Member State concerning the production of or trade in arms, munitions and war material, do distort conditions of competition, the Commission, by paragraph 1, has a duty to undertake an investigation with the State concerned. By paragraph 2, however, the Commission can also appeal to the Court directly, notwithstanding the procedure provided for in Article 169. This raises a difficulty. By Article 169,[88] the Commission can only appeal to the Court after it has requested the State to submit its observations, and after it has embodied its findings in an Opinion.[89] Because that Article does not apply here, such a request to the State does not have to be made, and such an Opinion does not have to be issued. However, it may be queried whether the Commission, without having complied with its Treaty obligation under paragraph 1 to investigate the offending measures with the State concerned, can submit the matter to the Court under paragraph 2.

---

[86] Art. 223, para. 1 (a), see note 81, above.

[87] It is not clear whether the words " information the disclosure of which [a Member State] considers contrary . . ." imply that any bona fide belief on the part of that State brings it within this provision, or whether the test of that belief is objective and the State must show that the disclosure would indeed be contrary to the essential interests of its security.

[88] See p. 274, above.

[89] For a discussion of this provision, see pp. 274–277, above.

It may be argued that just as Article 169 gives a Member State an opportunity to comply with the Commission's Opinion, so under the present Article the Member State is intended to be given the benefit of the advice of the Commission before being arraigned before the Court. Further, unless the Commission had made the required investigation with the State, the Commission would be in breach of its Treaty obligation to hold that investigation, and it would ill become it, therefore, to allege that a Member State was also in breach of the Treaty.

Alternatively, one can well contend that paragraph 2 grants a right of appeal to the Court which is expressly freed from any procedural limitations imposed by Article 169, and, therefore, to attempt to read into paragraph 2 other alternative limitations is unjustified. Further, some effect must be given to the phrase " . . . may appeal *directly* to the Court "; and it may be held that the word " directly " here means without compliance with any preliminary procedural requirements, such as those specified in paragraph 1.

It is suggested that, on balance, this alternative view is the stronger, mainly because implying terms when they are not essential is an unrewarding way of interpreting a document. However, although there is doubt about the right of appeal of the Commission, there is no doubt that a Member State, if it considers that another Member State is making an improper use of its powers, can appeal directly to the Court without prior reference to the Commission or to the defendant State.

THE TIME FOR BRINGING AN APPEAL

No time period for the bringing of appeals is specified in the present article, and none is specified under the " parent " Articles, 169 and 170. It appears, therefore, that appeals can be brought at any time.

THE POWER OF THE COURT

It will be noticed that when the Court is hearing an appeal brought under the present Article, it is required to sit *in camera*. This is clearly owing to the nature of the evidence which will have to be presented, affecting, as it may, a State's armament programme and its essential security.

The first power of the Court will naturally be to determine whether the alleged improper use of powers has occurred. If it has, the judgment of the Court must state this. However, such improper use will amount to a breach by a State of one of the obligations imposed upon it by the Treaty. By Article 171,[90] therefore, the State will be required to take

---

[90] See p. 281, above.

the measures which comprise the execution of the judgment. This will mean that it must put an end to the improper use.

Where the judgment specifies a particular improper use of powers which, besides being merely a breach of the Treaty, have, in addition, the effect of distorting competition within the Common Market, a duty, as above, is placed on the State to carry out the judgment. Where, however, the Commission up until the judgment has not been allowed by the defaulting State to undertake any investigation,[91] it appears that the Commission's duty under paragraph 1 has yet to be fulfilled. It is suggested, however, that the duty of the Court is merely to act under paragraph 2, and that it is not required in its judgment to specify whether any particular breaches in fact have the effect of distorting competition within the meaning of paragraph 1.

ARTICLE 228, Section 1

In cases where the terms of the present Treaty provide for the conclusion of agreements between the Community and one or more States or an international organisation, these agreements shall be negotiated by the Commission. Subject to the powers conferred upon the Commission in this respect, they shall be concluded by the Council after consultation with the Assembly in the cases specified in the present Treaty.

The Council, the Commission or a Member State may obtain the prior Opinion of the Court of Justice upon the compatibility of the proposed agreement with the provisions of the present Treaty. The agreement which receives an adverse Opinion of the Court of Justice may come into force only under the conditions determined in accordance with Article 236.[92]

[91] Owing to that State's denial that the measure in question did distort competition, see p. 274, above.

[92] French:

" Dans les cas où les dispositions du présent Traité prévoient la conclusion d'accords entre la Communauté et un ou plusieurs Etats ou une organisation internationale, ces accords sont négociés par la Commission. Sous réserve des compétences reconnues à la Commission dans ce domaine, ils sont conclus par le Conseil, après consultation de l'Assemblée dans les cas prévus au present Traité.

Le Conseil, la Commission ou un Etat membre peut recueillir au préalable l'avis de la Cour de Justice sur la compatibilité de l'accord envisagé avec les dispositions du présent Traité. L'accord qui a fait l'objet d'un avis négatif de la Cour de Justice ne peut entrer en vigueur que dans les conditions fixées selon le cas à l'article 236."

" Where this Treaty provides for the conclusion of agreements between the Community and one or more States or an international organisation, such agreement shall be negotiated by the Commission. Subject to the powers conferred upon the

By this provision it is the Commission which is to negotiate international agreements. Power to enter into the agreements is conferred upon the Community when it is provided that:

> The Community may conclude with a non-Member State, a union of States or an international organisation agreements creating the association embodying reciprocal rights and obligations, joint actions and appropriate forms of procedure.[93]

These agreements, if entered into, are to be concluded by the Council.[94] It is set out, however, that before the agreement is so concluded, either the Council, the Commission or a Member State may obtain the prior Opinion of the Court [95] upon the compatibility of the proposed agreement with the provisions of the Treaty. Under this Article, it is suggested, the Court will have the same wide powers as it possesses under Article 95 of the E.C.S.C. Treaty to determine whether a proposed amendment of that Treaty conforms to the specified requirements [96]; although it must be noted that under Article 95 the Court is expressly given " full jurisdiction to consider all matters of fact and law " and such power is not set out in the present Article.

If the Court gives an adverse opinion, the agreement in question can come into force only provided that it is ratified by all the Member States in accordance with their respective constitutional requirements.[97] There is no obligation, however, upon anyone to obtain the Opinion of the Court, nor, it appears, is there any means by which action can be taken after an agreement which is not compatible with the Treaty has, in fact, been concluded.

Commission in this respect, such agreements shall be concluded by the Council after the Assembly has been consulted where required by the Treaty.

The Council, the Commission or a Member State may, as a preliminary, obtain the opinion of the Court of Justice as to the extent to which the agreements contemplated are compatible with the provisions of this Treaty. An agreement which has been the subject of an adverse opinion of the Court of Justice shall only come into force under the conditions laid down in Article 236."

[93] Art. 238, para. 1.

[94] It may be noted that the Council of Ministers is not itself specifically created a legal entity capable of entering into agreements on its own behalf: it is not stated that the Council signs as agent for the Community. However, this and kindred problems are outside the scope of the present work.

[95] The wording " may *request* the prior Opinion of the Court " might better have conveyed the drafter's intention.

[96] See p. 260, above.

[97] Art. 228.1, para. 2 and Art. 236, para. 3. It might be argued that the agreement when ratified had been made with the Member States and not with the Community.

CHAPTER
6

THE JURISDICTION OF THE COURT UNDER THE EURATOM TREATY

ARTICLE 12, Para. 4

In default of agreement on the fixing of the conditions set out in paragraph 3, the licensees may refer the matter to the Court of Justice with a view to having appropriate conditions fixed.[1]

In order to spread information and technical know-how it is provided by the Treaty[2] that any person or enterprise may apply for a non-exclusive licence relating to patents or patent rights or patent applications which are owned by the Community, provided that the applicant is able to make effective use of the inventions to which these patents, and so on, relate.

When such an application is made, the Commission is required to grant the licence requested[3] or to grant sub-licences where the Community holds contractual licences enabling it to grant them.[4] In addition the Commission is under a duty to supply all the information required for the use of these patents.[5]

It is then provided[6] that the Commission is to agree the conditions for the grant of these licences and sub-licences, and these conditions are to be concerned in particular with what payment is appropriate and with the right of the licensee to grant sub-licences to third parties as well as with the obligation to treat the information given to it by the Commission as a trade secret.

---

[1] French:
> " A défaut d'accord sur la fixation des conditions prévues à l'alinéa 3, les bénéficiaires peuvent saisir la Cour de Justice en vue de faire fixer les conditions appropriées."

Stationery Office:
> " If no agreement is reached on the conditions referred to in paragraph 3, the licensees may refer the matter to the Court of Justice so that appropriate conditions may be determined."

[2] Art. 12, para. 1.
[3] Art. 12, para. 3.
[4] Art. 12, para. 2.
[5] Art. 12, para. 3.
[6] *Ibid.*

338

Paragraph 4 of Article 12, set out above, then provides that in default of such agreement, the licensees [7] may refer the matter to the Court with a view to having appropriate conditions fixed. In determining these conditions the Court acts with *pleine juridiction*,[8] so that it possesses unhampered power to consider all relevant matters. There are no special rules of procedure laid down for the referring of this matter to the Court, so that it appears that the normal provisions apply.[9]

ARTICLE 18, Para. 2

Within a period of one month calculated from their notification, the Decisions of the Arbitration Committee may be the subject of an appeal, which shall be suspensive, brought by the parties before the Court of Justice. The control of the Court of Justice may extend only to the regularity of the decision in point of form, and to the interpretation given by the Arbitration Committee to the provisions of the present Treaty.[10]

By the Treaty,[11] an Arbitration Committee [12] is to be established and its members are to be appointed by the Council of Ministers. The function of this Committee is exclusively in relation to the granting of patent licences. Where the Commission does not itself own patents in relation to nuclear matters, so that Article 12 cannot apply,[13] the Commission is required to obtain the communication of information concerning nuclear patents so that this information may be used by the Community itself, and it is also to obtain the granting of licences in respect of such patents.[14]

[7] This term in the provision is incorrect. The parties concerned will only be prospective licensees.
[8] Art. 144 (a), see p. 357, below. As to the meaning of *pleine juridiction,* see p. 195, above.
[9] The action will thus be commenced by a Request addressed to the Registrar—Euratom Statute, Art. 19, followed by the normal stages of the written and oral procedures, as to which see pp. 50–56 and 72–74, above.
[10] French:
" *Dans un délai d'un mois, à compter de leur notification, les décisions du Comité d'arbitrage peuvent faire l'objet d'un recours suspensif des parties devant la Cour de Justice. Le contrôle de la Cour de Justice ne peut porter que sur la régularité formelle de la décision, et sur l'interprétation donnée par le Comité d'arbitrage aux disposition du présent Traité.*"
Stationery Office:
" Within a period of one month from their notification, the decisions of the Arbitration Committee may be the subject of an appeal by the parties to the Court of Justice involving suspension of their operation. The Court of Justice shall only examine the formal legality of the decision and the Arbitration Committee's interpretation of the provisions of this Treaty."
[11] Art. 10, para. 1.
[12] As to this Arbitration Committee, see p. 442, below.
[13] As to Art. 12, see p. 338, above.   [14] Art. 14.

As soon as an application for a patent relating to a specifically nuclear subject is filed with a Member State, that State is required to ask the applicant to agree that the contents of the application should be immediately communicated to the Commission.[15] If the applicant agrees to this, then this communication is made within three months from the date of the filing of the application.[16] However, if the applicant does not agree to this communication, the Member State merely notifies the Commission that the application has been made.[17] Following this, the Commission may request the Member State to communicate the contents of this application to it and if the Commission does so, the Member State again asks the applicant whether he consents. If he does, the communication is made; if he does not, then nonetheless the Member State still makes this communication to the Commission at the end of a period of eighteen months from the date of its filing of the patent application.[18]

Where a person owns a patent, provisionally protected claim or utility model relating to inventions directly connected with nuclear matters, that person may, of course, grant a licence to anyone to exploit his invention, and if he does he can lay down his own terms for such a licence. In order, however, to prevent nuclear research being impeded by the existence of some patent where the owner will not grant any licences, the Treaty lays down certain provisions.

Thus, if no amicable agreement is reached between the owner and the Commission concerning the grant of one or more non-exclusive licences, the Commission may propose to the owner that a licence shall be granted to it, in any case where the granting of such a licence is necessary to the Commission's own research or indispensable to carrying out its duties.[19] Similarly, if the owner has refused to grant a non-exclusive licence to a person or enterprise, the Commission may take up the case and propose to the owner that a licence should be granted.[20] Following such a proposal the owner may propose to the

---

[15] Art. 16, section 1, para. 1.
[16] Art. 16, section 1, para. 2.
[17] *Ibid.*
[18] Art. 16, section 1, para. 6.
[19] Art. 14 and Art. 17.1, para. 1 (a). As to the duty of the Commission to carry out research, see p. 437, below.
[20] Art. 19 and Art. 17.1, para. 1 (b). This proposal of the Commission may only be made, however, provided:
    (i) that a period of at least four years has elapsed since the filing of the application for the patent, save in the case of an invention relating to the specifically nuclear subject;
    (ii) that the needs arising from the development of nuclear energy in the territories of a Member State where an invention is protected are not met in respect of that invention;

Commission,[21] and where necessary to the person or enterprise concerned that they should agree to submit the question to the Arbitration Committee.[22]

In this submission to it, the Arbitration Committee's duty is, in broad terms, to see whether the patents etc. in question are directly connected with nuclear matters, and that, in respect of proposals on behalf of persons or enterprises the four requirements set out above have been satisfied.[23] If the Committee is satisfied on these points, it is required to give a reasoned decision ordering the granting of the licence to the Commission or to the person or enterprise concerned, as the case may be, and this decision must set out the conditions to be observed and the compensation to be paid, in so far as the parties have not already reached agreement on this.

Article 18, paragraph 3 then states that:

> within a period of one month calculated from their notification, the decisions of the Arbitration Committee may be the subject of an appeal, which shall be suspensive, brought by the parties [24] before the Court of Justice.[25]

This reference to the Court must be commenced by means of an appeal addressed to the Registrar,[26] and the subsequent stages of the action must comply with the special procedure set out.[27] It will be noticed that this appeal to the Court is suspensive and that it is thus an exception to the general rule.[28]

    (iii) that the owner, having been asked to satisfy these needs either personally or through his licensees, has not done so; and

    (iv) that the person or enterprises applying for licences are in a position effectively to meet these needs by exploiting the licences—Art. 17.1, para. 1 (b).

[21] At the request of the Commission, the granting of such a licence shall include the right of the Commission to authorise third parties to use the invention in so far as they are carrying out work or orders for the Community or for joint enterprises—Art. 17, para. 1 (a).

[22] Art. 20, para. 3. If either the Commission, or in the second case, the person or enterprise, refuse to sign this arbitration agreement, there is no obligation upon the owner to grant any licence at all—Art. 20, para. 2.

[23] Art. 20, para. 3, and Art. 17.1, para. 2 (b). The Arbitration Committee must also ensure that the owner has not established a legitimate reason for refusing to grant the licence, and in particular whether he has had an adequate period of time at his disposal—Art. 20, para. 3, and Art. 17.2—and that the Paris Convention of 1883 for the Protection of Industrial Property has not been infringed—Art. 20, para. 3, and Art. 17.4. In interpreting the Euratom Treaty and in applying the general principles of law common to the Member States, the Committee is expressly required to act *ex aequo et bono*—as also in the matter of costs—Regulation 7–63 of the Euratom Council of Ministers, Arts. 23 and 26, para. 1.

[24] This presumably means " by any one of the parties."

[25] See p. 339, above.

[26] Euratom Statute, Art. 20, para. 1, and Rules, Art. 101, para. 1, see pp. 87 above and 536, below.

[27] Statute, Art. 20, and Rules, Art. 101, see pp. 479 and 536, below.

[28] For the general rule, see Art. 157, discussed p. 85, above.

THE COURT'S JURISDICTION

It should be noted that under Article 18, the power of the Court to review the decision of the Arbitration Committee is limited in terms to two matters. First, to considering the regularity of the decision in point of form, and secondly, to reviewing the interpretation given by the Committee to the provisions of the Treaty. It is clear from this that the Court is not to act as a court of appeal and is not to review the merits of the Committee's decision, but merely to ensure that that decision has been given in accordance with law. However, when the Court is empowered to review other administrative action, four grounds of appeal are granted to it.[29] Because the Court is here merely to examine the regularity of the *decision* in point of form, it might be contended that the Court was not to examine the regularity of the procedure of the Arbitration Committee leading up to that decision, and which, of course, is distinct from the decision itself. Therefore, if the contention were that the Committee had failed to comply with its rules of procedure,[30] it might be contended that the irregularity was in a matter of procedure, and that *in point of form* there was no irregularity in the decision itself. However, it is suggested that this is a distinction which should not be pressed, because in the Treaty the only requirement *in point of form* which is expressly provided for the decision is that it should be reasoned.[31] A decision which, although reasoned, has been reached by the Committee in violation of its rules is, it is submitted, a decision which is not regular in point of form. Other administrative decisions can be challenged on the ground of the violation of a substantial procedural requirement, whereas this ground of appeal is not included in Article 18. It is suggested that the reason for this omission is that the jurisdiction of the Court under Article 18 is intended to be wider than merely to consider the various procedural matters as is the limit of the Court's power in other cases.

Because under Article 18 the Court does not expressly possess any power to annul a decision of the Arbitration Committee on the grounds of incompetence or of a *détournement de pouvoir* it must be considered whether a decision of that Committee which is vitiated by one of these defects is nevertheless able to be annulled.

If the Arbitration Committee gives a reasoned decision in a matter over which it possesses no jurisdiction, that decision is vitiated by

---

[29] See Art. 146, para. 1, p. 362, below.
[30] The rules of procedure were to be determined by the Council of Ministers upon a proposal of the Court of Justice—Art. 18, para. 1. As to their rules, see p. 442, below.
[31] Art. 20, para. 3.

342

incompetence, and because the jurisdiction of the Arbitration Committee is set out in the Treaty it is suggested that if the Committee acted beyond its powers it would have failed correctly to interpret the provisions of the Treaty, so that its decision could be annulled by the Court in exercise of its power under Article 18 to control the interpretation given by the Committee to the provisions of the Treaty.

However, if the decision of the Committee granting a patent licence was prompted by a desire, for example, to spite the owner of such a licence, so that the decision is vitiated by a *détournement de pouvoir,* there appears to be no means by which this decision can be set aside by the Court. The decision in point of form would be valid; it would only be the subjective motives lying behind that decision which would be improper. Further, a *détournement de pouvoir* in no way affects the interpretation of the provisions of the Treaty, so that this decision also falls outside the second limb of the Court's jurisdiction.

Procedure Following the Judgment of the Court

The Euratom Statute of the Court states [32] that if the Court rejects the appeal, the decision of the Arbitration Committee shall become final,[33] and it is further stated [34] that once it is final, the decision shall have the force of *res judicata* as between the parties and shall be enforceable in the normal way,[35] that is to say, in accordance with Article 164 of the Treaty.[36] Paragraph 3 of Article 164 declares that " enforcement may be suspended only by a decision of the Court of Justice." A reference to the Rules of the Court,[37] however, shows that this paragraph applies only to the suspension of the enforcement of " a decision of the Court or of an act of another institution," and the Arbitration Committee is not included in the list of institutions set out in Article 3 of the

---

[32] Art. 20, para. 3.
[33] In so far as the decision of the Committee sets out the conditions of the licence, it is annually open to review, and also when " new facts justify revision "—Art. 13, para. 1.
[34] Euratom Treaty, Art. 18, para. 3.
[35] *Ibid.*
[36] Art. 164, paras. 1 and 2, provides:
 " Enforcement shall be governed by the rules of civil procedure in force in the State in whose territory it takes place. The order for its enforcement shall be stamped on the decision, without more verification than that the document is authentic, by the municipal authority which the Government of each Member State shall designate for this purpose and which shall be notified to the Commission, to the Court of Justice and to the Arbitration Committee established under Article 18. When the formalities have been completed at his request, the party concerned may proceed to enforcement by applying directly to the authority which is competent according to municipal law."
[37] Rules, Art. 89, para. 1, see p. 527, below.

343

Euratom Treaty.[38] It appears, therefore, that the enforcement of the decisions of the Arbitration Committee cannot be suspended even by the Court itself.

If the Court annuls the decision of the Committee, the proceedings may, where appropriate, be re-opened before the Arbitration Committee at the request of one of the parties.[39] This provision, however, is in some ways in conflict with the Rules of the Court where it is provided [40] that:

> In the event of an annulment of the Committee's decision the Court shall, if necessary, refer the case back to the Committee.

It appears, therefore, that under the Statute, a reference back to the Committee was to be left to the parties themselves, while under the Rules, the Court, presumably without the consent of the parties, can refer the case back " if necessary," a phrase which is undefined. Following such a reference back, the Committee is required to act " in accordance with the points of law laid down by the Court." [41]

ARTICLE 21, Para. 3

If [the Member State] refuses to grant the licence or to cause it to be granted, or if it does not give, within a period of four months calculated from the request, any explanation with regard to granting of the licence, the Commission shall have a period of two months in which to refer the matter to the Court of Justice.[42]

---

[38] Art. 3.1 states:
    " 1. The achievement of the tasks entrusted to the Community shall be ensured by:
        an ASSEMBLY,
        a COUNCIL,
        a COMMISSION,
        a COURT OF JUSTICE.
    Each institution shall act within the limits of the powers conferred upon it by the present Treaty."
    It may be noted that Art. 4.1 of the E.E.C. Treaty uses the words " . . . shall be ensured *by the following institutions.*"
[39] Euratom Statute, Art. 20, para. 4—see p. 479, below.
[40] Rules, Art. 101, para. 5, see p. 537, below.
[41] Euratom Statute, Art. 20, para. 4, see p. 479, below. Although in terms, this provision applies only to the case where a reference back to the Committee is made by one of the parties, it must inevitably apply also to the case where that reference is made by the Court itself.
[42] French:
    " *S'il refuse de concéder ou faire concéder la licence, ou ne fournit dans un délai de quatre mois à compter de la requête aucune explication quant à la concession de*

The position has been seen [43] where the owner of a nuclear patent agrees to grant a licence of that patent to the Commission, or agrees to refer to the Arbitration Committee the question of whether that licence should be granted. The present paragraph deals with the case where the owner of the patent refuses either to grant a licence or to refer the matter to the Committee. It is provided by the Treaty [44] that in the case of this complete refusal, the Commission may require the Member State concerned, or its competent authorities, to grant the licence in question or to cause a licence to be granted. If this requirement is made to the Member State, then that State, or its competent authorities, hear the owner's case why the granting of the licence should be refused.[45] In doing this, regard is primarily had to the conditions set out which must be satisfied by the Community or by a joint undertaking or a person or enterprise before they can claim a right to a patent licence.[46] If these conditions are found to be satisfied, then it appears that the Member State is itself required to grant the licence or to cause it to be granted. If, however, as a result of these proceedings it is held that these conditions have not been satisfied, the State or the authorities notify the Commission of this and of their consequent refusal to grant the licence.[47] It is then provided in the present paragraph that the Commission within a further two months may refer the question to the Court of Justice, as it may also do if the State or the competent

---

la licence, la Commission dispose d'un délai de deux mois pour saisir la Cour de Justice."
Stationery Office:
    " If they refuse to grant the licence or to cause it to be granted, or if, within a period of four months from the date of the request they do not give any explanation with regard to the granting of the licence, the Commission shall have two months in which to refer the question to the Court of Justice."
[43] See p. 340, above.
[44] Art. 21, para. 1.
[45] Art. 21, para. 2.
[46] *Ibid.* Where the request is that the non-exclusive licence shall be in favour of the Community these conditions are:
    (a) That the patents, etc., relate to inventions directly connected with nuclear research.
    (b) That the granting of such licences is necessary to the pursuit of the Commission's own research is indispensable for the operating of its facilities.
    (c) That the owner has not established a legitimate interest, in particular the fact that he has not had an adequate period of time at his disposal.
    (d) That the provisions of the 1883 Paris Convention for the protection of industrial property are not infringed.
Where the request is that the non-exclusive licence shall be in favour of a person or enterprise, these conditions are:
    (a) that the patents, etc., relate to inventions directly connected with and essential to the development of nuclear energy within the Community.
    (b) That the requirements set out on p. 340, note 20, above, have been fulfilled.
    (c) and (d) As conditions (c) and (d) for the grant of a non-exclusive licence in favour of the Community—see above.
[47] *Ibid.*

authorities do not give any explanation within four months from the date of the request to that State as to whether they will grant the licence or not.

THE JURISDICTION OF THE COURT

No rules of procedure are laid down for this reference but two provisions roughly indicate what the jurisdiction of the Court is to be. The first of these states that the owner shall be heard in the proceedings before the Court [48]; and the second that:

> If the judgment of the Court of Justice states that the conditions referred to in Article 17 have been fulfilled, the Member State concerned, or its competent authorities, shall be required to take the measures which comprise the execution of this judgment.[49]

The action before the Court is brought by the Commission and it would appear that the request concerning it will, in effect, cite either the Member State or the authority concerned. It is not stated, however, whether, if the competent authority is cited, the relevant Member State has a right of audience, or whether it must expressly intervene.[50] It would appear, however, that the latter is the case, as it is provided that the judgment of the Court shall require " the Member State concerned *or* its competent authorities " to take the measures which comprise the execution of the judgment. That is to say, in an action relating to an authority, the State apparently need not be concerned at all.

Further, the only entities which will be parties to the action are the Commission, and either the Member State or the authority cited, unless in the latter case the Member State intervenes. This being so, the owner of the patents, etc., who is expressly to be heard in the proceedings before the Court, is not a party to the action, so that the provision of the Statute of the Court which require " parties " to be represented [51] does not here apply, and it would seem, therefore, that the owner will appear in the capacity of a witness. The Rules of Court relating to witnesses, therefore, probably apply to him.[52]

If the Court finds that the conditions laid down in Article 17 [53] have in fact been fulfilled, this will mean that the Member State or the competent authorities were wrong in finding that they had not been

---

[48] Art. 21, para. 4.

[49] Art. 21, para. 5.

[50] As to the right of intervention, see pp. 57–60, above.

[51] Art. 17, para. 2. The similar provision—Art. 30—which declares that the parties themselves may plead only through their representative, does not apply either, as the owner is not here pleading.

[52] For these rules, see p. 66, above.

[53] As to these conditions, see p. 340, note 20, above.

fulfilled.[54]   When it is stated [55] that the State or the authority is thereupon required " to take the measures required for the execution of the judgment," it is naturally assumed that this means that the licence is now to be granted.   However, it is surprising to find that it is nowhere set out that the State or the authority would previously have been under any duty to grant a licence even if these themselves had found that the conditions laid down in Article 17 had been fulfilled.   Presumably, however, such a duty is to be implied, and it is this duty which must be carried out in order to comply with the judgment.

A reference to the Court can be made not only because of a refusal of a Member State, or of an authority to grant a licence, but also because, for four months after the request of the Commission, that Member State or authority has failed to give any explanation concerning the granting of the licence.   In such a case, it is not clear what the jurisdiction of the Court is to be.

Article 21, paragraph 4, states, as set out above, that " the owner *shall be* heard in the proceedings before the Court of Justice," and this provision applies both to the case of a reference to the Court in respect of a refusal to grant a licence, and in respect of a four months' failure to give any explanation concerning the granting.   It appears, therefore, that this four months' silence is being equated to a refusal on the part of the State or of the authority so that the jurisdiction of the Court will be the same as in the case of an express refusal.[56]

ARTICLE 38, Para. 3

If this State does not comply with the Directive of the Commission within the time limit specified, the Commission or any Member State concerned may, notwithstanding Articles 141 and 142, immediately refer the matter to the Court of Justice.[57]

---

54 As " the competent authority " may well be a court of law of the Member State, the Communities Court may here be acting as a true court of appeal.

55 Art. 21, para. 5.

56 This equating of silence to an express refusal to grant a licence may be compared with the equating of silence on the part of the Council or the Commission with an express act—Art. 148, see p. 364, below—and particularly with the provision in the E.C.S.C. Treaty, Art. 35, see p. 184, above.

57 French:
  " *Si cet Etat ne se conforme pas, dans le délai imparti, à la directive de la Commission celle-ci ou tout Etat membre intéressé peut, par dérogation aux articles 141 et 142, saisir immédiatement la Cour de Justice.*"
  Stationery Office:
  " If the State in question does not comply with the Commission's directive within the period laid down, the Commission or any Member State concerned may refer the matter immediately to the Court of Justice, notwithstanding the provisions of Articles 141 and 142."

The Euratom Treaty provided that within the Community certain basic standards shall be established in order to protect the health both of workers and of the general public from the dangers arising from ionising radiation.[58] These basic standards concern the maximum doses of radiation which are compatible with adequate safety [59]; the maximum possible degree of exposure and contamination [60] and the fundamental principles governing the medical supervision of the workers.[61] In addition to this, the Commission is required to make Recommendations to Member States regarding the level of radioactivity in the atmosphere, water or soil.[62] These Recommendations, however, have no binding force upon the States [63] and are merely for their guidance. In cases of urgency, however, the Commission may issue a Directive requiring the Member State concerned, within a time limit fixed by the Commission, to take all measures necessary in order to prevent the above basic standards from being exceeded and in addition to ensure that the relevant provisions are observed in future.[64] Such a Directive is binding upon the Member State as to the result to be achieved, but it leaves to the municipal authorities the form and manner in which it shall be complied with.[65]

NON-COMPLIANCE WITH THE DIRECTIVE

It is then provided in Article 38, paragraph 3, that " if this State does not comply with the Directive of the Commission within the time limit specified, the Commission or any Member State concerned may, notwithstanding Articles 141 and 142, immediately refer the matter to the Court of Justice."

The effect of this non-compliance with the Directive is that the Member State concerned has failed to fulfil one of its obligations under the Treaty.[66] Without the present provision, therefore, it would be open to the Commission to issue a reasoned Opinion after it has required the State to submit its comments and then, if the State does not comply

---

[58] Art. 30, para. 1.
[59] Art. 30, para. 2 (a).
[60] Art. 30, para. 2 (b).
[61] Art. 30, para. 2 (c).
[62] Art. 38, para. 1.
[63] Art. 161, para. 5.
[64] Art. 38, para. 2.
[65] Art. 161, para. 3.
[66] Namely Art. 192, para. 1, which provides:
" Member States shall take all general and particular measures which are appropriate for ensuring the carrying out of the obligations arising out of the present Treaty or resulting from acts of the institutions of the Community . . . ";
and Art. 161, para. 3, which provides:
" Directives shall bind any Member State to which they are addressed as to the result to be achieved. . . ."

with the Opinion within the time limit laid down by the Commission, the whole may be referred to the Court.[67] Similarly, another Member State could have referred this breach to the Court provided that previously it had referred the matter to the Commission, which, in this case also, would be required to issue a reasoned Opinion after it has required the State to submit its comments.[68] It is expressly provided, however, that if after three months of the reference to it, the Commission has still not given its Opinion the State shall not thereby be prevented from appealing to the Court.[69]

It will thus be seen that such a procedure is totally unfitted to an urgent case where radioactivity is concerned. It is, therefore, provided that the Commission or the Member State may immediately refer the matter to the Court.

The jurisdiction possessed by the Court in this matter is considered under the relevant articles below.[70]

ARTICLE 81, Paras. 3 and 4

In the event of opposition to the carrying out of an inspection, the Commission is required to apply to the President of the Court for a warrant to enforce the carrying out of this inspection. The President of the Court of Justice shall decide within a period of three days.

If there is danger in delay, the Commission may itself issue, in the form of a Decision, a written order that the inspection shall continue. This Order must be submitted without delay to the President of the Court of Justice for subsequent approval.[71]

---

[67] Art. 141, see p. 355, below. [68] Art. 142, paras. 1–3, see p. 356, below.
[69] Art. 142, para. 4, see p. 356, below.
[70] See Arts. 141 and 142, pp. 355–356, below.
[71] French:
    " En cas d'opposition à l'exécution d'un contrôle, la Commission est tenue de demander au président de la Cour de Justice un mandat, afin d'assurer, par voie de contrainte, l'exécution de se contrôle. Le président de la Cour de Justice décide dans un délai de trois jours.
    S'il y a péril en la demeure, la Commission peut délivrer elle-même, sous forme d'une décision, un ordre écrit de procéder au contrôle. Cet ordre doit être soumis sans délai, pour approbation ultérieure, au président de la Cour de Justice."
Stationery Office:
    " Should there be opposition to the carrying out of a supervisory measure the Commission shall be bound to ask the President of the Court of Justice for a warrant to enforce the carrying out of such supervisory measure. The President of the Court of Justice shall give a decision within three days.
    If there is danger in delay, the Commission may itself issue a written order, in the form of a decision, to proceed with the supervisory measure. This order shall be submitted without delay to the President of the Court of Justice for subsequent approval."

Under the Euratom Treaty,[72] the Commission is required to ensure that within the Community none of the ores, source materials or special fissionable materials are diverted from their intended uses as stated by the users, and that agreements concerning supplies and any special undertakings concerning inspection which are entered into by the Community in an agreement concluded with a non-Member State or with an international organisation are observed. To do this the Commission is required to recruit inspectors,[73] who may be sent into the territories of the Member States,[74] who, on presenting their credentials, are at all times to have access to all places and data necessary to ensure that ores and materials are not being diverted.[75] In addition they are to have access to any person who by reason of his occupation deals with relevant materials, equipment or facilities.[76] The Council of Ministers is to approve Regulations drafted by the Commission specifying what operating records are to be kept and produced to the inspectors relating not only to the ores and materials used and produced but also to the transporting of any source materials or special fissionable materials.[77]

THE PRESIDENT'S WARRANT

Article 81, paragraph 7 then provides that " In the event of opposition to the carrying out of an inspection, the Commission is required to apply to the President of the Court for a warrant to enforce the carrying out of this inspection."

This request to the President must specify the name and address of the person or enterprise which is to be inspected, and must state the object and purpose of the inspection [78] but, strangely enough, the request does not seem to be required to set out in which way the earlier attempts at inspection have been opposed. It is assumed, therefore, that the duty of the President [79] is to satisfy himself merely that the inspection is one which falls within the powers of the Commission.

[72] Art. 77. [73] Art. 82, para. 1.
[74] Art. 81, para. 1. Prior to the first visit of an inspector the Commission shall enter into negotiations with the State concerned to agree arrangements covering all future visits of the inspector—*ibid.*
[75] Art. 81, para. 2. The inspectors are to be accompanied by representatives of the authorities of the State concerned, if that State so requests, provided that the inspectors are not thereby delayed or otherwise impeded in their duties—*ibid.* [76] *Ibid.*
[77] Inspection is not to extend to materials intended for the purposes of defence which are in course of being specially prepared for such purposes or which, after being so prepared, are installed or stocked in a military establishment in accordance with an operational plan—Art. 84, para. 3.
[78] Rules, Art. 90, para. 1, see p. 527, below.
[79] If the President is absent or unable to discharge his duties, this task shall be undertaken by the senior of the two Presidents of the Chambers—Rules, Art. 90, para. 2.2, and Art. 7, para. 2.1, see pp. 527 and 486, below. Seniority is determined in accordance with Rules, Art. 4, see p. 18, above.

The President is to give his decision within three days,[80] and this decision is to be by means of a reasoned order which is immediately to be notified to " the parties." [81] However, as the person or enterprise referred to in the original request is not a party to the reference, it appears that the order is to be notified only to the Commission.

It is provided that after service of the warrant or the decision the municipal authorities of the State concerned are to ensure that the inspectors have access to the places named in the warrant or decision.[82] A failure to comply with this duty is considered below.[83]

Although the President of the Court is required to give his decision within three days, if it is dangerous even to delay this long, it is provided that the Commission " may itself issue, in the form of a Decision, a written order that the inspection shall continue." [84] This order is then to be submitted without delay to the President of the Court for subsequent approval.[85] The Rules of the Court provide that this submission is to be made in the same way as is the Request for a warrant.[86] It would appear that the duty of the President, as in the former case, is merely to satisfy himself as to the competence of the Commission to carry out the inspections but not to concern himself with the question of whether there was in fact danger in delay so that the Commission was not able to apply for the warrant before the inspection.[87]

THE APPEAL TO THE COURT

It may be questioned whether the person or enterprise referred to in the order of the Commission may appeal against that order in an action before the Court. Under Article 146, paragraph 2,[88] any natural or legal person may bring an appeal against Decisions directed to him,

---

80 Art. 81, para. 3.
81 Rules, Art. 90, para. 2.1, and Art. 86, para. 1. It may well surprise the Commission, having applied for a warrant—*un mandat*—under Art. 81, para. 3, to receive back an order but this will occur because the Rules have not been properly tied in with the Treaty.
82 Art. 81, para. 5. As has been seen above, under the Rules there will be no warrant issued but only a decision by means of an order of the Court—see note 81, above. Further, this provision refers only to access to the place named although, as has been seen, access to individuals may also have been demanded, and the States must, surely, similarly be required to give access to them. Finally, although express reference is made only to the inspectors, it is presumed that access must also be given to the accompanying representatives.
83 See p. 352, below.
84 Art. 81, para. 4.
85 *Ibid.*
86 Rules, Art. 90, para. 1, see p. 89, above. The submission must therefore specify the name and address of the person or enterprise to be inspected although this will appear on the Commission's written order.
87 This would appear to be a subjective matter to be determined by the Commission itself.
88 See p. 363, below.

on any one of the four classic grounds set out in that article.[89]   It may, of course, be argued that the written order of the Commission here in question is not a Decision but only " in the form of a Decision," but it is suggested that this written order is not only in the form of a Decision, but because it is binding in every respect upon those to whom it is directed, that it is also in substance a Decision.[90]   If this is correct, then the person or enterprise may allege that, although the President of the Court correctly found that the inspection lay within the competence of the Commission, nevertheless the exercise of this competence amounted, for example, to a *détournement de pouvoir.*

If, following such a challenge the Court were to annul the written order of the Commission requiring the inspection to proceed, or if the President failed to approve the order when it was submitted to him, it is suggested that the inspection of the Commission might well be illegal and a question of tortious liability under the law of the Member State concerned might arise.[91]   Such matters, however, are outside the scope of the present work.

ARTICLE 82, Para. 3

If the Member State does not comply, within the time period specified, with this Directive of the Commission, the latter or any Member State concerned may, notwithstanding Articles 141 and 142, refer the matter immediately to the Court of Justice.[92]

The Directive here being referred to is one issued by the Commission in which it calls upon the Member State concerned to take, within a period of time laid down by the Commission, all necessary measures to

---

[89] For these grounds see the terms of Art. 146, para. 1, p. 362, below.

[90] The point might well be taken that because it is the State concerned which must ensure access for the inspectors—Art. 81, para. 5—the decision in question is directed to the State and not to the person or enterprise, nonetheless it still falls within the terms of Art. 146, para. 2, which gives natural or legal persons a right of action even against a Decision addressed to another person if it concerns him directly or indirectly, as this Decision assuredly does.

[91] By Art. 188, para. 2, it is provided that " in the case of non-contractual liability, the Community shall, in accordance with the general principles common to the laws of the Member States, make good any damage caused by its institutions or by its servants in the performance of their duties."

[92] French:
   " *Si l'Etat membre ne se conforme pas, dans le délai imparti, à cette directive de la Commission, celle-ci ou tout Etat membre intéressé peut, par dérogation aux articles 141 et 142, saisir immédiatement la Cour de Justice.*"
Stationery Office:
   " If the Member State does not comply, within the specified time, with the Commission's directive, the Commission or any Member State concerned may, notwithstanding the provisions of Articles 141 and 142 refer the matter immediately to the Court of Justice."

put an end to any infringement which has been discovered by the Commission's inspectors in the keeping of operating records, which are required of ores, source materials and special fissile material used or produced, or of the transport of source material and special fissile material.

The normal procedure, where a State has infringed the Treaty, is for the Commission to issue a reasoned Opinion, setting out the breach after it has given the State concerned an opportunity to submit its observations, and only upon a failure to comply with the terms of such Opinion is the matter able to be referred to the Court. In the present case, owing to the urgency of the matter, this proceeding is able to be avoided and the Commission can refer the matter immediately to the Court of Justice. It is assumed that the jurisdiction of the Court is then similar to that when it is dealing with other less urgent infringements referred to it under Articles 141 and 142,[93] and finds that the Member State has in fact as alleged failed to comply with the Treaty. It is declared that such State is bound to take the measures required for the implementation for the judgment of the Court.[94]

ARTICLE 83, Section 2, Para. 2

Notwithstanding the provisions of Article 157, appeals brought before the Court of Justice against Decisions of the Commission imposing the sanctions provided for in the preceding section, shall have a suspensive effect. However, the Court of Justice may, at the request of the Commission or of any Member State concerned, order the immediate execution of the Decision.[95]

Article 83 empowers the Commission to impose sanctions upon any persons or enterprises which violate any of the obligations imposed by Chapter 7 of the Treaty. These obligations require, for example, that

[93] As to these, see pp. 355–357, below.
[94] Art. 143, see p. 357, below.
[95] French:
   " *Par dérogation aux dispositions de l'article 157, les recours introduits devant la Cour de Justice contre les décisions de la Commission infligeant des sanctions prévues au paragraphe précédent ont un effet suspensif. Toutefois, la Cour de Justice peut, à la demande de la Commission ou de tout Etat membre intéressé, ordonner l'exécution immédiate de la décision.*"
   Stationery Office:
   " Notwithstanding the provisions of Article 157, appeals brought before the Court of Justice against decisions of the Commission which impose any of the sanctions provided for in the preceding paragraph shall suspend operation of the act in question. The Court of Justice may, however, at the request of the Commission or of any Member State concerned, order the immediate implementation of the decision."

anyone establishing or operating a plant concerned with fissile material or nuclear fuel shall be bound to declare to the Commission the basic characteristics of the plant [96] and require the keeping and production of operating records [97] and that any excess fissile material not actually being used or ready for use shall be deposited where they are or can be subject to the supervision of the Commission.[98]

The sanctions which the Commission may impose are declared to be, in order of severity:

    (1) a warning;

    (2) the withdrawal of special privileges such as financial or technical assistance;

    (3) the placing of the undertaking for a maximum period of four months under the administration of a person or board appointed by mutual agreement between the Commission and the State having jurisdiction over the undertaking;

    (4) the total or partial withdrawal of source material or special fissile material.[99]

By Article 83, section 2, paragraph 2, it is implied that the party being sanctioned may appeal against the Decision imposing the sanction. It is here pertinent to note that the warning referred to under (1) above is declared to be a sanction, so that a Decision which merely warns appears in theory to be open to challenge. The appeals are suspensive so that they are an exception to the general rule laid down in Article 157.[1]

ARTICLE 129

Any member of the Commission, if he no longer fulfils the conditions required for the performance of his duties, or if he has been guilty of serious misconduct, may be pronounced dismissed by the Court of Justice, at the request of the Council or of the Commission.

In such a case, the Council, by a unanimous vote, may provisionally suspend him from his office and provide for his replacement until the time when the Court of Justice shall

[96] Art. 78, para. 1.
[97] Art. 79, para. 1.
[98] Art. 80, para. 1.
[99] Art. 83, section 1, para. 2. Decisions of the Commission requiring the delivery of material are executory and may be enforced in accordance with Art. 164—Art. 83, section 2, para. 1.
[1] See p. 368, below.

have given its ruling. The Court of Justice may, provisionally, suspend him from his office at the request of the Council or of the Commission.[2]

This provision is identical to Article 160 of the E.E.C. Treaty.[3]

ARTICLE 136

The Court of Justice shall ensure the respect of law in the interpretation and application of the present Treaty.[4]

This provision is identical to Article 164 of the E.E.C. Treaty.[5]

ARTICLE 141

If the Commission considers that a Member State has failed in one of the obligations imposed upon it by virtue of the present Treaty, it shall issue a reasoned Opinion to this effect, after having given the State an opportunity to present its observations.

[2] French:
" *Tout membre de la Commission, s'il ne remplit plus les conditions nécessaires à l'exercice de ses fonctions ou s'il a commis une faute grave, peut être déclaré démissionnaire par la Cour de Justice, à la requête du Conseil ou de la Commission.*

En pareil cas, le Conseil statuant à l'unanimité, peut à titre provisoire, le suspendre de ses fonctions et pourvoir à son remplacement jusqu'au moment où la Cour de Justice se sera prononcée.

La Cour de Justice peut, à titre provisoire, le suspendre de ses fonctions, à la requête du Conseil ou de la Commission."

Stationery Office:
" If any member of the Commission no longer fulfils the conditions required for the performance of his duties or if he has been guilty of serious misconduct, the Court of Justice, on the application of the Council or of the Commission, may compulsorily retire him.

In such a case the Council may, by a unanimous decision, provisionally suspend the member from his duties and make provision for his replacement pending the ruling of the Court of Justice.

The Court of Justice may on the application of the Council or of the Commission provisionally suspend the member from his duties."

[3] As to which, see p. 272, above.

[4] French:
" *La Cour de Justice assure le respect du droit dans l'interprétation et l'application du présent Traité.*"

Stationery Office:
" The Court of Justice shall ensure the observance of law in the interpretation and implementation of this Treaty."

[5] As to which see p. 273, above.

355

If the State in question does not comply with this Opinion within the period specified by the Commission, the latter may appeal to the Court of Justice.[6]

This provision is identical to Article 169 of the E.E.C. Treaty.[7]

ARTICLE 142

Any of the Member States may appeal to the Court of Justice if it considers that another Member State has failed to fulfil one of the obligations incumbent upon it by virtue of the present Treaty.

Before a Member State may introduce an appeal against another Member State based upon an alleged violation of the obligations imposed upon it by virtue of the present Treaty, it shall refer the matter to the Commission.

The Commission shall issue a reasoned Opinion after the States concerned have been given an opportunity to present their own and reply to each other's written and oral observations.

If the Commission has not issued an Opinion within a period of three months from the request, the lack of an Opinion shall be no bar to the bringing of an appeal before the Court of Justice.[8]

---

[6] French:
" *Si la Commission estime qu'un Etat membre a manqué à une des obligations qui lui incombent en vertu du présent Traité, elle émet un avis motivé à ce sujet, après avoir mis cet Etat en mesure de présenter ses observations.*
Si l'Etat en cause ne se conforme pas à cet avis dans le délai déterminé par la Commission, celle-ci peut saisir la Cour de Justice."
Stationery Office:
" If the Commission considers that a Member State has failed to fulfil any of its obligations under this Treaty, it shall issue a reasoned opinion on the matter after giving the State concerned the opportunity to submit its comments.
If the State concerned does not comply with the terms of such opinion within the period laid down by the Commission, the latter may refer the matter to the Court of Justice."

[7] As to which see p. 274, above.

[8] French:
" *Chacun des Etats membres peut saisir la Cour de Justice, s'il estime qu'un autre Etat membre a manqué à une des obligations qui lui incombent en vertu du présent Traité.*
Avant qu'un Etat membre n'introduise, contre un autre Etat membre, un recours fondé sur une prétendue violation des obligations qui lui incombent en vertu du présent Traité, il doit en saisir la Commission.
La Commission émet un avis motivé après que les Etats intéressés aient été mis en mesure de présenter contradictoirement leurs observations écrites et orales.
Si la Commission n'a pas émis l'avis dans un délai de trois mois à compter de la demande, l'absence d'avis ne fait pas obstacle à la saisie de la Cour de Justice."

This provision is identical to Article 170 of the Economic Community Treaty.[9]

ARTICLE 143

If the Court of Justice finds that a Member State has failed in one of the obligations incumbent upon it by virtue of the present Treaty, this State is required to take the measures which comprise the execution of the judgment of the Court.[10]

This provision is identical to Article 171 of the E.E.C. Treaty.[11]

ARTICLE 144

The Court of Justice shall exercise competence in *pleine juridiction* **with regard to:**

   (a) proceedings instituted in application of Article 12 with a view to having fixed the appropriate conditions for the granting by the Commission of licences or sub-licences;

   (b) appeals instituted by persons or enterprises against the sanctions which have been imposed upon them by the Commission in accordance with Article 83.[12]

Stationery Office:
   " Any Member State which considers that another Member State has failed to fulfil any of its obligations under this Treaty, may refer the matter to the Court of Justice.

   Before a Member State institutes, against another Member State, proceedings relating to an alleged infringement of its obligations under the Treaty, it shall refer the matter to the Commission.

   The Commission shall deliver a reasoned opinion after the States concerned have been given the opportunity to submit their own cases and to reply to each other's cases both orally and in writing.

   If the Commission, within a period of three months from the date on which the matter was referred to it, has not given an opinion, the absence of such opinion shall not preclude reference to the Court of Justice."

[9] As to which, see p. 277, above.
[10] French:
   " *Si la Cour de Justice reconnaît qu'un Etat membre a manqué à une des obligations qui lui incombent en vertu du présent Traité, cet Etat est tenu de prendre les mesures qui comporte l'exécution de l'arrêt de la Cour de Justice.*"
Stationery Office:
   " If the Court of Justice finds that a Member State has failed to fulfil any of its obligations under this Treaty, such State is bound to take the measures required for the implementation of the judgment of the Court."
[11] As to which, see p. 281, above.
[12] French:
   " *La Cour de Justice exerce une compétence de pleine juridiction a l'égard:*
   (*a*) *des recours introduits en application de l'article 12 en vue de faire fixer les*

By this provision the Court is given the widest possible powers [13] to determine what should be the conditions under which the Commission should grant licences or sub-licences relating to patents, provisionally protected rights or patent applications, etc.[14] and also with respect to the sanctions imposed by the Commission upon persons or enterprises who have failed, for example, to keep the required records of their source material and special fissile material.[15] The sanctions referred to have been set out under Article 83 above.[16]

ARTICLE 145

If the Commission considers that a person or enterprise has committed a violation of the present Treaty to which the provisions of Article 83 are not applicable, it shall request the Member States having jurisdiction over this person or this enterprise to cause a sanction to be imposed in accordance with its municipal legislation.

If the State concerned, within a period laid down by the Commission, does not take the action required by this request, the Commission may refer the matter to the Court of Justice with a view to having the alleged violation of the person or enterprise concerned put on record.[17]

conditions appropriées de la concession par la Commission de licences ou sous-licences;
    (b) des recours introduits par des personnes ou entreprises contre les sanctions qui leur seraient infligées par la Commission en application de l'article 83."
Stationery Office:
    " The Court of Justice shall exercise full jurisdiction as to the merits with regard to:
    (a) proceedings instituted in accordance with Article 12 to determine the appropriate conditions for the granting by the Commission of licences or sub-licences;
    (b) appeals instituted by persons or undertakings against penalties imposed on them by the Commission in accordance with Article 83."
[13] For a discussion of the meaning of the term " *pleine juridiction* " see pp. 195–196, above.
[14] Art. 12, see p. 338, above.
[15] As required by Arts. 78 and 79.
[16] See p. 353, above.
[17] French:
    " *Si la Commission estime qu'une personne ou entreprise a commis une violation du présent Traité à laquelle les dispositions de l'article 83 ne sont pas applicables, elle invite l'Etat membre dont relève cette personne ou cette entreprise à faire sanctionner la violation en application de sa législation nationale.*
    Si l'Etat intéressé n'exerce pas, dans le délai déterminé par la Commission, l'action que comporte cette invitation, la Commission peut saisir la Cour de Justice en vue."
Stationery Office:
    " If the Commission considers that a person or undertaking has committed an infringement of this Treaty to which the provisions of Article 83 do not apply, it shall call upon the Member State having jurisdiction over that person or undertaking

This article presents certain difficulties of interpretation because so little is said and so much is implied.

The procedure here being dealt with starts with the Commission considering that a person or enterprise [18] has committed a violation of the Treaty. It is presumed that this finding of fault cannot, on general principles, be made without the person or enterprise being entitled to present its case. Nothing about this, however, is stated, nor whether the presentation can be oral or only in writing, or whether there can be representation.

THE COMMISSION'S REQUEST

When, however, following this, the Commission considers that a violation has been committed, it then " requests " the Member State " to cause a sanction to be imposed " upon the party concerned and this sanction is expressly to be imposed in accordance with that State's municipal legislation.[19] In the Member States, the provisions of the Treaty which are directly applicable to persons and enterprises became binding upon persons and enterprises as part of municipal law by virtue of the Treaty coming into operation.[20] A breach, therefore, of these provisions constitutes a breach of the municipal law of the Member State concerned. However, the Euratom Commission is not a judicial organ of the Member States, so that, it is suggested, the finding of the Commission of itself has no legal effect in the relevant municipal law. In other words, as far as that law is concerned, there has been no conviction.

When the Commission makes its " request " to the Member State, it is not clear whether that State comes under a duty to comply with the request. Two matters appear relevant. First, Article 161 [21] sets out that in its relations with States, the Commission may impose obligations by means of Regulations, Directives or Decisions. A " request " is none

to cause penalties to be imposed in respect of such infringement in accordance with its domestic legislation.
    If the State concerned does not comply with such a request within the period laid down by the Commission, the latter may refer the matter to the Court of Justice, in order to have the existence of the infringement of which the person or undertaking concerned is accused put on record."
[18] A " person " is defined as:
    " any natural person who carries out the whole or part of his activities in the territories of Member States within the field specified in the relevant Chapter of this Treaty ";
and an " enterprise " as:
    " any enterprise or institution which carries out the whole or part of its activities under the same conditions, whatever its public or private legal constitution and statute "—Art. 196.
[19] See, for example, the discussion in *Chemin de Fer française* [1962] C.M.L.R. 33.
[20] This differs from the position in the United Kingdom where the terms of a treaty must be incorporated into municipal law.
[21] Art. 161 provides:
    " To effect the achievement of their tasks and under the conditions provided for

of these, so that it would appear to impose no obligation. However, by Article 192:

> Member States shall take all measures, whether general or particular, appropriate to ensure the carrying out of the obligations arising out of this Treaty or resulting from formal measures taken by the institutions of the Community.[22]

If it is held that one of the obligations arising out of the Treaty is to ensure that persons and enterprises will not violate the Treaty, then it appears that by Article 192 a Member State has a duty by the Treaty to " ensure the carrying out of this obligation." The request to the Member State, therefore, does not of itself impose any obligation upon that State, but by informing it that the Commission considers that a violation has occurred, informs the State that its Treaty duty is now to be carried out. It would thus seem that the correct view, therefore, is that a failure to comply with the request is a failure for which there appears to be no legal sanction possible, but this failure is in addition a breach of the Treaty obligation which has been pointed out by the request.

" To Cause a Sanction to be Imposed "

Article 145 states that the Member State is " to cause a sanction to be imposed." Now, this sanction upon a person or enterprise will be imposed in accordance with municipal law, and it is suggested that a State cannot impose such a sanction merely because the Commission requests it to do so. A sanction can lawfully be imposed only in accordance with municipal law, following the due process of that law. This may mean a trial or similar investigation prior to the imposition of the sanction, or at the very least some method of appeal against the sanction after it has been imposed.[23] It appears, therefore, that a second trial or investigation must be undertaken, this time by the appropriate legal authority of the Member State, and unless the original survey by

---

in this Treaty, the Council and the Commission shall issue regulations and directives, take decisions and formulate recommendations or opinions.

Regulations shall be general in their ambit. They shall be binding in every respect and take direct effect in each Member State.

Directives shall be binding, as to the result to be achieved, upon each Member State to which they are directed, while leaving to national authorities the choice of form and methods.

Decisions shall be binding in every respect upon those to whom they are directed. Recommendations and opinions shall have no binding force."

22 Art. 192 continues:
" They shall abstain from any measures which could jeopardise the attainment of the objectives of this Treaty."

23 It will be noted that under Art. 145 the Commission cannot specify the amount or nature of the sanction. Some judicial decision within the relevant municipal law must be taken to determine the proper amount. This, in itself, implies a right to some form of hearing.

the Commission is to be held to render the matter *res judicata* within municipal law, the possibility cannot be ruled out of the municipal authority holding that there was no violation, and thus that the Commission was wrong in considering that there had been one.

By paragraph 2 of this article, if the Member State within the period laid down by the Commission has not caused a sanction to be imposed, the Commission may refer the matter to the Court of Justice.

If a State has started a prosecution against the person or enterprise whom the Commission considers has violated the Treaty, but that prosecution has not yet terminated in a judgment before the Commission's time period expires, and if it can be held that the Member State has not " taken the action required " by the request, the question of the existence or non-existence of the alleged violation can come before the Communities' Court. If, in order to have " taken the action," a Member State is required to have caused the sanction to be imposed, then in the present circumstances the State has clearly not " taken the action." If, however, " taken the action " means " has constituted proceedings which may lead to a sanction being imposed," or, more briefly, if it means " has commenced to take the action " then the State has complied with the Commission's request even although no sanction has been imposed, and although no sanction may ever be able lawfully to be imposed.

If the former and prima facie the more obviously correct interpretation is accepted, namely that " taken the action " requested means " has taken the action required " it appears that the Communities' Court has jurisdiction to determine upon the alleged violation concurrently with the municipal authority, be it a court or other form of tribunal. This is clearly most undesirable. It is suggested, therefore, that the alternative interpretation is to be preferred so that the Communities' Court possesses jurisdiction only if the Member State refuses to " commence to take " the action requested.

Although this solution appears workable, the case must be considered of where a Member State, by whatever means it has adopted to determine the matter, refuses to comply with the Commission's request because for its own part it considers that no violation has occurred.

The Reference to the Court

In this case, on any interpretation, the Commission must be able to refer the matter to the Communities' Court. If, therefore, the Member State has adopted some form of judicial process to review the alleged violation, the proceedings before the Court will, in effect, be an appeal from that judicial process.

No rules have been prescribed for the bringing of these proceedings before the Court, but, once again, it would appear that the person or enterprise concerned must be given a right to present its case, either itself or by the intermediary of the Member State. Thus a third trial of these matters will be held. As the Member State will be an interested party, it must be present before the Court, although whether it is to be made a defendant, so as to possess the right to submit pleadings, etc., is not stated.[24]

After the Court has reviewed the matter, acting, it would appear, in *pleine juridiction,* although this is not stated, it will reach a decision whether the alleged violation has occurred or not.

If the Court holds that there has been no violation, the State will have been correct in its refusal to cause a sanction to be imposed. Costs will presumably be paid by the Commission [25] and the matter will be at an end.

If, however, the Court holds that there has been a violation, then, in accordance with paragraph 2, it will have this violation put on record. The question then arises of what is the effect of this finding.

Clearly, Article 145 allows the Court merely to place the violation on record: the Court cannot itself impose a fine upon the party concerned. Such a fine can be imposed only in accordance with the municipal law of the State concerned. The State, therefore, must somehow incorporate into its municipal law a sanction commensurate with the gravity of the violation which has been placed on record.

The finding of the Court, it is submitted, must render the existence of a violation *res judicata,* so that, without the opportunity of any further process within municipal law, a sanction must be imposed, but there would appear to be no objection to a right of appeal, if one is granted in municipal law against the sanction imposed, on the grounds that it was out of proportion to the violation which was placed on record by the Court.

ARTICLE 146

The Court of Justice shall determine upon the legality of the acts, other than Recommendations or Opinions, of the

[24] It will be noted that the procedure under Art. 145 is distinct from an action against a State for the State's violation of the Treaty, a matter governed by Art. 141.

[25] It might be held that the Commission should also pay the costs of the innocent person or enterprise not only when it appeared before the Commission but also when the Member State instituted proceedings against it in compliance with the Commission's request.

Council and of the Commission. To this end, it is competent to pronounce upon appeals for incompetence, violation of a substantial procedural requirement, violation of the present Treaty, or of any rule of law concerning its application or for *détournement de pouvoir*, brought by a Member State, the Council or the Commission.

Any other natural or legal person may, under the same conditions, bring an appeal against Decisions directed to him and against Decisions which, although taken under the appearance of a Regulation, or of a Decision addressed to another person, concern him directly and individually.

The appeals referred to in the present article must be brought within a period of two months, calculated, according to the case, from the publication of the act, or from its notification to the plaintiff, or in default of these, from the day when he had knowledge of it.[26]

This provision is identical to Article 173 of the E.E.C. Treaty.[27]

ARTICLE 147

If the appeal is well founded, the Court of Justice shall declare the act challenged to be null and void.

[26] French:

"*La Cour de Justice contrôle la légalité des actes du Conseil et de la Commission, autres que les recommandations ou avis. A cet effet, elle est compétente pour se prononcer sur les recours pour incompétence, violation des formes substantielles, violation du présent Traité ou de toute règle de droit relative à son application, ou détournement de pouvoir formés par un Etat membre, le Conseil ou la Commission.*

Toute personne physique ou morale peut former, dans les mêmes conditions, un recours contre les décisions, dont elle est le destinataire, et contre les décisions qui, bien que prises sous l'apparence d'un règlement ou d'une décision adressée à une autre personne, la concernent directement et individuellement.

Les recours prévus au présent article doivent être formés dans un délai de deux mois à compter, suivant le cas, de la publication de l'acte, de sa notification au requérant, ou, à defaut, du jour où celui-ci en a eu connaissance."

Stationery Office:

" Supervision of the legality of the acts of the Council and the Commission other than recommendations or opinions shall be a matter for the Court of Justice. It shall for this purpose have jurisdiction in proceedings instituted by a Member State, the Council or the Commission on the grounds of lack of jurisdiction, violations of basic procedural rules, infringements of this Treaty or of any rule of law relating to its implementation, or misuse of powers.

Any natural or legal person may, under the same conditions, appeal against a decision directed to him or it, or against a decision which, although in the form of a regulation or a decision directed to another person, is of direct and individual concern to him or to it.

The proceedings provided for in this Article shall be instituted within a period of two months, dating as the case may be, either from the publication of the measure concerned or from its notification to the complainant or, in default of this, from the day on which the latter learned of the said measure."

[27] As to which, see p. 287, above.

However, as concerns Regulations, the Court of Justice shall indicate, if it considers it necessary, those effects of the Regulations annulled which may be deemed to continue in force.[28]

This provision is identical to Article 174 of the E.E.C. Treaty.[29]

ARTICLE 148

In a case where, in violation of the present Treaty, the Council or the Commission fail to pass an act, the Member States and the other institutions of the Community may appeal to the Court with a view to having this violation placed on record.

This appeal is admissible only if the institution in question has previously been requested to act. If at the expiration of two months from this request, the institution has not declared its position, the appeal can be brought within a further period of two months.

Any natural or legal person, under the conditions specified in the preceding paragraphs, may submit to the Court of Justice a complaint that one of the institutions of the Community has failed to address to him an act other than a Recommendation or an Opinion.[30]

This provision is identical to Article 175 of the E.E.C. Treaty.[31]

---

[28] French:
  " Si le recours est fondé, la Cour de Justice déclare nul et non avenu l'acte contesté.
  Toutefois, en ce qui concerne les règlements, la Cour de Justice indique, si elle l'estime nécessaire, ceux des effets du règlement annulé qui doivent être considérés comme définitifs."
  Stationery Office:
  " Should the complaint be well founded, the Court of Justice shall declare the act concerned to be null and void.
  As regards regulations, however, the Court of Justice shall, if it considers it necessary, declare which effects of the annulled decision shall be deemed to remain in force."
[29] As to which, see p. 295, above.
[30] French:
  " Dans le cas où, en violation du présent Traité, le Conseil ou la Commission s'abstient de statuer, les Etats membres et les autres institutions de la Communauté peuvent saisir la Cour de Justice en vue de faire constater cette violation.
  Ce recours n'est recevable que si l'institution en cause a été préalablement invitée à agir. Si, à l'expiration d'un délai de deux mois à compter de cette invitation, l'institution n'a pas pris position, le recours peut être formé dans un nouveau délai de deux mois.
  Toute personne physique ou morale peut saisir la Cour de Justice dans les conditions fixées aux alinéas précédents pour faire grief à l'une des institutions de la

---

[31] As to which, see p. 297, above.

ARTICLE 149

The institution from which the annulled act originated, or whose failure to take action has been declared contrary to the present Treaty, shall be required to take the measures which comprise the carrying out of the judgment of the Court of Justice.

This obligation does not affect any obligation resulting from the application of Article 188, paragraph 2.[32]

This provision is similar to Article 176 of the E.E.C. Treaty.[33]

ARTICLE 150

The Court of Justice shall have jurisdiction to give a preliminary ruling:

(a) on the interpretation of the present Treaty;

(b) on the validity and interpretation of acts passed by the institutions of the Community;

(c) on the interpretation of the statutes of bodies set up by an act of the Council, when these statutes so provide.

Communauté d'avoir manqué de lui adresser un acte autre qu'une recommandation ou un avis."
Stationery Office:
" In the event of the Council of the Commission in violation of this Treaty failing to give a decision, the Member States and the other institutions of the Community may refer the matter to the Court of Justice in order to have the said violation placed on record.

Such proceedings shall only be heard if the institution concerned has previously been called upon to act. If within two months of being so called upon, the institution has not made clear its attitude, the said proceedings may be instituted within a further period of two months.

Any natural or legal person may submit to the Court of Justice, under the conditions laid down in the preceding paragraphs, a complaint to the effect that an institution of the Community has failed to direct to him an act other than a recommendation or an opinion."

[32] French:
" L'institution dont émane l'acte annulé, ou dont l'abstention a été déclarée contraire au présent Traité, est tenue de prendre les mesures que comporte l'exécution de l'arrêt de la Cour de Justice.

Cette obligation ne préjuge pas celle qui peut résulter de l'application de l'article 188, alinéa 2."
Stationery Office:
" An institution responsible for an act subsequently declared null and void or an institution whose failure to act has been declared contrary to the provisions of this Treaty shall be required to take the measures necessary for the implementation of the judgment of the Court of Justice.

This obligation shall not affect any obligation arising from the application of the second paragraph of Article 188."

[33] As to which, see p. 301, above.

When such a question is raised before a court of one of the Member States, this court may, if it considers that a decision on this point is necessary in order to deliver its judgment, request the Court of Justice to rule on this question.

When such a question is raised in a case pending before a municipal court whose decisions are not open to appeal under municipal law, this court is required to refer the matter to the Court of Justice.[34]

This provision is identical to Article 177 of the E.E.C. Treaty.[35]

ARTICLE 151

The Court of Justice shall have jurisdiction to hear cases concerning compensation for damage as provided for in Article 188, paragraph 2.[36]

This provision is similar to Article 178 of the E.E.C. Treaty.[37]

---

[34] French:
> " *La Cour de Justice est compétente pour statuer, à titre préjudiciel,*
> (a) *sur l'interprétation du présent Traité,*
> (b) *sur la validité et l'interprétation des actes pris par les institutions de la Communauté,*
> (c) *sur l'interprétation des statuts des organismes créés par un acte du Conseil, sauf dispositions contraires de ces status.*
> *Lorsqu'une telle question est soulevée devant une juridiction d'un des Etats membres, cette juridiction peut, si elle estime qu'une décision sur ce point est nécessaire pour rendre son jugement, demander à la Cour de Justice de statuer sur cette question.*
> *Lorsqu'une telle question est soulevée dans une affaire pendante devant une juridiction nationale dont les décisions ne sont pas susceptibles d'un recours juridictionnel de droit interne, cette juridiction est tenue de saisir la Cour de Justice.*"

Stationery Office:
> " The Court of Justice shall be competent to give preliminary rulings concerning:
> (a) the interpretation of this Treaty;
> (b) the validity and interpretation of acts of the institutions of the Community;
> (c) the interpretation of the statutes of any bodies set up by an act of the Council, except where these statutes provide otherwise.
> Where any such question is raised before a court of one of the Member States, the said court may, if it considers that a decision on the question is essential to enable it to render judgment, request the Court of Justice to give a ruling thereon.
> Where any such question is raised in a case pending before a domestic court from whose decisions there is no possibility of appeal under domestic law, the said court is bound to refer the matter to the Court of Justice."

[35] As to which, see p. 303, above.

[36] French:
> " *La Cour de Justice est compétente pour connaître des litiges relatifs à la réparation des dommages visés à l'article 188, alinéa 2.*"

Stationery Office:
> " The Court of Justice shall be competent to hear cases relating to compensation for damage as provided for in the second paragraph of Article 188."

[37] As to which, see p. 310, above.

ARTICLE 152

The Court of Justice shall have jurisdiction to determine actions between the Community and its employees within the limits and under the conditions laid down in Service Regulations or arising out of the system applicable to employees.[38]

This provision is identical to Article 179 of the E.E.C. Treaty.[39]

ARTICLE 153

The Court of Justice shall have jurisdiction to determine by virtue of a clause conferring jurisdiction contained in a contract in public or private law entered into by the Community or on its benefit.[40]

This provision is identical to Article 181 of the E.E.C. Treaty.[41]

ARTICLE 154

The Court of Justice shall have jurisdiction to determine upon any difference between Member States in connection with the object of the present Treaty if this difference is referred to it by virtue of an agreement.[42]

This provision is identical to Article 182 of the E.E.C. Treaty.[43]

---

[38] French:
 " *La Cour de Justice est compétente pour statuer sur tout litige entre la Communauté et ses agents dans les limites et conditions déterminées au statut ou résultant du régime applicable à ces derniers.*"
Stationery Office:
 " The Court of Justice shall be competent to decide any dispute between the Community and its servants, within the limits and under the conditions laid down by the relevant statute of service or conditions of employment."
[39] As to which, see p. 312, above.
[40] French:
 " *La Cour de Justice est compétente pour statuer en vertu d'une clause compromissoire contenue dans un contrat de droit public ou de droit privé passé par la Communauté ou pour son compte.*"
Stationery Office:
 " The Court of Justice shall be competent to make a decision pursuant to any clause referring matters to it contained in a contract concluded, under public or private law, by or on behalf of the Community."
 " The Court of Justice shall be competent to decide any dispute between the Community and its servants, within the limits and under the conditions laid down by the relevant statute of service or conditions of employment."
[41] As to which, see p. 324, above.
[42] French:
 " *La Cour de Justice est compétente pour statuer sur tout différend entre Etats*

---

[43] As to which, see p. 325, above.

367

ARTICLE 155

Subject to the jurisdiction conferred upon the Court of Justice by the present Treaty, legal action to which the Community is a party shall not, for that reason, be excluded from the jurisdiction of municipal courts.[44]

This provision is identical to Article 183 of the E.E.C. Treaty.[45]

ARTICLE 156

Notwithstanding the expiration of the time limit set out in Article 146, paragraph 3, any party in an action bringing into issue a Regulation of the Council or of the Commission may rely upon the grounds set out in Article 146, paragraph 1, in order to allege before the Court of Justice the inapplicability of this Regulation.[46]

This provision is similar to Article 184 of the E.E.C. Treaty.[47]

ARTICLE 157

Appeals brought before the Court of Justice shall not have a suspensive effect. However, the Court of Justice may, if it

membres en connexité avec l'objet du présent Traité, si ce différend lui est soumis en vertu d'un compromis."
Stationery Office:
" The Court of Justice shall be competent to decide in any dispute between Member States connected with the subject of this Treaty, where the said dispute is submitted to it on the basis of a special agreement between the Member States."
[44] French:
" Sous réserve des compétences attribuées à la Cour de Justice par le présent Traité, les litiges auxquels la Communauté est partie ne sont pas, de ce chef, soustraits à la compétence des juridictions nationales."
Stationery Office:
" Subject to the powers conferred on the Court of Justice by this Treaty, cases to which the Community is a party shall not for that reason alone be excluded from the jurisdiction of national courts."
[45] As to which, see p. 326, above.
[46] French:
" Nonobstant l'expiration du délai prévu à l'article 146, alinéa 3, toute partie peut, à l'occasion d'un litige mettant en cause un règlement du Conseil ou de la Commission, se prévaloir des moyens prévus à l'article 146, alinéa 1, pour invoquer devant la Cour de Justice l'inapplicabilité de ce règlement."
Stationery Office:
" In any proceedings where a regulation made by the Council or the Commission is in point, any of the parties concerned may, notwithstanding the expiry of the period laid down in the third paragraph of Article 146, invoke the grounds set out in the first paragraph of Article 146, in order to submit to the Court of Justice that the regulation concerned does not apply."
[47] As to which, see p. 329, above.

considers that the circumstances require it, order the suspension of the execution of the act challenged.[48]

This provision is identical to Article 185 of the E.E.C. Treaty.[49]

ARTICLE 158

In actions which have been referred to it, the Court of Justice may prescribe the necessary interim measures.[50]

This provision is identical to Article 186 of the E.E.C. Treaty.[51]

---

[48] French:
  "*Les recours formés devant la Cour de Justice n'ont pas d'effet suspensif. Toutefois, la Cour de Justice peut, si elle estime que les circonstances l'exigent ordonner le sursis à l'exécution de l'acte attaque.*"
  Stationery Office:
  " Except where otherwise provided for in this Treaty (*sic*), proceedings instituted before the Court of Justice shall not suspend operation of the act in question. The Court of Justice may, however, if it considers that circumstances so require, order that the operation of the act contested be suspended."
[49] As to which, see p. 330, above.
[50] French:
  "*Dans les affaires dont elle est saisie, la Cour de Justice peut prescrire les mesures provisoires nécessaires.*"
  Stationery Office:
  " The Court of Justice may, in any cases referred to it, prescribe any necessary interim measures."
[51] As to which, see p. 331 and pp. 216–217, above.

CHAPTER
7

THE COURT'S METHOD OF INTERPRETING THE TREATIES

In interpreting the Community Treaties, the Court has adopted certain methods: it has also made certain assumptions which are extremely important because these are not derived from the texts of the Treaties but are a reflection of the Court's own views.

THE COURT'S METHOD OF INTERPRETATION

IN INTERPRETING A TREATY, THE DUTY OF THE COURT IS TO DISCOVER THE INTENTION OF THE AUTHORS

(A) BY THE USE OF *Travaux Préparatoires*

It is a general rule of interpretation in international law that a Court may study *travaux préparatoires* in order to establish the meaning of a particular provision. This rule has been accepted and applied without question by the Court of the Communities. The desire of the Court to find *travaux préparatoires* in order to assist it in its interpretation can well be illustrated by a case in 1961.[1] Here the Court was faced with a document which referred to an employee living at a " distance " of up to 25 kilometres from his place of employment. This document had taken the place of an earlier one which had referred to an employee living within a " radius " of 25 kilometres, and the Court was required to determine whether within a " distance " of 25 kilometres meant within a " radius " of 25 kilometres, or whether distance meant the actual distance travelled by the employee by road or rail. The Court declared:

> In the absence of *travaux préparatoires* clearly expressing the intentions of the authors of the provision, the Court can base its conclusions only upon the scope of the text in the form in which it has been drafted, and give it the meaning which flows naturally from a literal and logical interpretation.[2]

[1] *Gabriel Simon* v. *The Court of Justice of the European Communities.*
[2] *Ibid.*

370

Perhaps the best case to illustrate the extent to which the Court will go in order to discover the intention lying behind a provision of the Treaties is a case concerning the interpretation of a provision in the Protocol on Privileges and Immunities in the E.C.S.C. Treaty.[3] Article 11 of the Protocol provides:

> In the territory of each Member State, and regardless of their nationality, the members of the High Authority and officials of the Community:
>
> . . .
>
> (b) shall be exempt from any tax on salaries and emoluments paid by the Community.[4]

The point at issue was whether this provision meant that, when assessing income tax, the Belgian revenue authorities were not only unable to tax the plaintiff's salary paid to him by the High Authority, a matter which was not in dispute, but also whether, when for tax purposes they were assessing the plaintiff's joint family income, the authorities could add the plaintiff's salary to that of his wife, whose income was not exempt from tax, and thereby ascertain the correct rate of tax to be applied *to the wife's share* of that joint income. The alternative view was that the sole income able to be reckoned within the term " joint family income " was that of the wife. In the latter view, the wife would be treated as being the sole wage earner in the family: in the former view, although the husband's salary would not itself be taxed, it would be recognised that he was contributing to the joint family income.

Because the *exposés des motifs* of the Governments of the Member States prior to the ratification of the E.C.S.C. Treaty had made no mention of Article 11, the Court turned to the *exposés* submitted by the Governments in relation to the E.E.C. and Euratom Communities, notwithstanding that these *exposés* had been drawn up some five years after the E.C.S.C. Treaty had been ratified.

When considering the validity and interpretation of particular Decisions of the High Authority, the Court has also made fairly free use of *travaux préparatoires*. These *travaux* have included the minutes of meetings of the Council of Ministers and of the Consultative Committee.[5] The Court has also referred to the report of a Mixed Commission set up to consider the subsidising of the Belgian coal industry, to the High

---

[3] *Humblet* v. *The Belgian State* (Case 6–60), Vol. II.
[4] The similar provision in the other Treaties is E.E.C. Protocol on Privileges and Immunities, Art. 12, para. 2, and Euratom Protocol on Privileges and Immunities Art. 12, para. 2.
[5] *Netherlands Government* v. *The High Authority* (Case 6–54), Vol. II.

Authority's own preliminary calculations,[6] and on one occasion to the debates in the Netherlands Parliament itself.[7]

(B) BY THE COMPARISON OF ONE TREATY WITH ANOTHER

The Court has fairly readily referred to the E.E.C. and Euratom Treaties, signed in 1957, when discussing the terms of the E.C.S.C. Treaty signed in 1951. Thus in one case,[8] the Court had to consider whether under the E.C.S.C. Treaty, as part of its claim that an individual Decision of the High Authority imposing a subsidy levy was void, an enterprise could challenge the validity of the general parent Decision setting up the subsidy levy system itself. From Article 36,[9] the Court abstracted a general principle permitting this, and found support for so doing from the terms of the other two Treaties. It stated:

> The Treaties establishing the European Economic Community and Euratom expressly adopt a similar interpretation when they set out in Articles 184 and 156 respectively that:
>
>> notwithstanding the expiration of the time limit set out in Article 173, paragraph 3 (or, in the case of Euratom, Article 146, paragragh 3) any party in an action challenging a Regulation of the Council or of the Commission may rely upon the grounds set out in Article 173, paragraph 1 (or, in the case of Euratom, Article 146, paragraph 1) when challenging that Regulation before the Court of Justice.
>
> The particular Articles, *without providing a conclusive argument,* support the above reasoning by *showing that it is also accepted by the drafters of these new Treaties.*[10]

In the tax case referred to above,[11] the Court also referred to the E.E.C. and Euratom Treaties in order to interpret the terms of the E.C.S.C. Treaty,[12] but, in addition, it went much further. It compared Article 11

---

[6] *Fédération Charbonnière de Belgique* v. *The High Authority* (Case 8–55) (Final judgment), Vol. II.

[7] *Niederrheinische Bergwerks-Aktiengesellschaft und Unternehmensverband des Aachener Steinkohlenbergbaus* v. *The High Authority* (Joint Cases 2 and 3–60).

[8] *Meroni & Co. S.p.A.* v. *The High Authority* (Case 9–56), Vol. II.

[9] Art. 36, para. 3, which relates to fines and not to levies, and to an action in *pleine juridiction* and not to one for annulment provides:
" In support of this appeal [against the Decision imposing the fine] the plaintiffs, under the conditions set out in the first paragraph of Article 33 of the present Treaty, may rely upon the irregularity of the Decisions and Recommendations which they are accused of having contravened."

[10] *Ibid.* at p. 164, above. Author's italics.

[11] *Humblet* v. *The Belgian State* (Case 6–60), Vol. II.

[12] Art. 12, para. 2, of the E.E.C. and Euratom Protocols on Privileges and Immunities, provides:
" [The officials and servants of the Communities] shall be exempt from national taxes on salaries, wages and emoluments paid by the Community."

of the Protocol on Privileges and Immunities with provisions in other treaties dealing with employees' salaries, and did so although two of the treaties it referred to had been signed after the date of the signing of the E.C.S.C. Treaty [13] and although in one case the treaty had been concluded between Great Britain and Sweden,[14] neither of which is a signatory of the E.C.S.C. Treaty that was being interpreted.

(C) BY THE INTERPRETATION OF THE TREATY IN THE LIGHT OF REGULATIONS MADE UNDER IT

In a recent case,[15] the Court went very much further than to compare the provisions of one treaty with the provisions of another treaty subsequently passed: it referred to a particular Regulation passed by the E.E.C. Council of Ministers on February 21, 1962, as an aid, and virtually a decisive aid, in the interpretation of Article 85 of the E.E.C. Treaty signed in 1957, and it did so despite the fact that the reference of the case to the Court had been made on July 10, 1961, namely seven months before the Regulation was passed, and despite the fact that events giving rise to the litigation had occurred in 1959 and 1960.

The case concerned the validity of a sole agency agreement made in 1903 between Robert Bosch, a German company and van Rijn, a Dutch company. By this agreement, van Rijn was given the exclusive right to sell Bosch products in the Netherlands. During 1959, de Geus, a second Dutch company, started to import Bosch refrigerators into the Netherlands. An action was brought by Bosch in the Rotterdam court for a declaration that the importation by de Geus was illegal, and for an injunction and damages. Bosch was successful. De Geus appealed to the Hague Court of Appeal on the ground that under Article 85 of the E.E.C. Treaty the fifty years old agreement between Bosch and van Rijn was null and void.

By Article 85 (1) of the E.E.C. Treaty all agreements between enterprises which were liable to affect trade between Member States and in particular agreements limiting or sharing markets are prohibited.[16] Article 85 (2) then provides:

---

[13] Art. XVI (d) of the Treaty of March 27, 1953, between Belgium and Great Britain and Art. 18 of the Treaty of April 1, 1953, between Belgium and Sweden.
[14] The Treaty of April 1, 1953. The Court also referred to Art. XIX (i) of the Treaty of April 29, 1948, between the Netherlands and the U.S.A. and Art. 6 of the Treaty of September 25, 1948, between Belgium and the Netherlands.
[15] *Robert Bosch G.m.b.H. and others* v. *Kleding Verkoopbedrigt de Geus en Uitdenbogerd* (Case 13–61) [1962] C.M.L.R. 1.
[16] Art. 85 (1) provides:
  " The following practices shall be prohibited as incompatible with the Common Market: all agreements between enterprises, all decisions by associations of enterprises and all concerted practices which are liable to affect trade between Member States and which are designed to prevent, restrict or distort competition within the Common Market or which have this effect. . . ."

Any agreements or decisions prohibited pursuant to this Article shall automatically be null and void.

By Article 85 (3), however, the prohibition imposed by Article 85 (1) may be declared inapplicable in the case of certain agreements which either help to improve the production or distribution of goods or which promote technical or economic progress.[17] It had further been provided in the Treaty that within three years the Council of Ministers was to issue the necessary Regulations for putting into effect the principles of Article 85 [18] but until those Regulations were in force the competent authorities in the Member States were themselves to issue any necessary declarations that restrictive trade practices were not prohibited.[19]

When the Court was requested by the Hague Court of Appeal to give a preliminary ruling upon the validity of the 1903 agreement between Bosch and van Rijn,[20] it was necessary for the Court to interpret the words of Article 85 (2) " shall automatically be null and void."

The Court admitted that in principle Article 85 was effective as from the time of the coming into force of the Treaty.[21] However, the implementing Regulation of the Council of Ministers [22] published in February 1962, gave the Commission power as from March 1962, to grant the necessary declaration under Article 85 (3) that a particular agreement was not prohibited under Article 85 (1) and therefore not null and void under Article 85 (2). Two interpretations of the words " null and void " in Article 85 (2) were possible. It might either have been that agreements falling within Article 85 (1) were automatically null and void as from the date of the coming into force of the Treaty, or, alternatively, the provisions of Article 85 (2) might have been in some way suspended prior to the date of the publication of the implementing Regulation.

[17] Art. 85 (3) provides:
" The provisions of paragraph I may, however, be declared inapplicable in the case of :
—any agreement or type of agreement between enterprises,
—any decision or type of decision by associations of enterprises, and
—any concerted practice or type of concerted practice which helps to improve the production or distribution of goods or to promote technical or economic progress, whilst allowing consumers a fair share of the resulting profit and which does not :
(a) subject the concerns in question to any restrictions which are not indispensible to the achievements of the above objectives;
(b) enable such concerns to eliminate competition in respect of a substantial part of the goods concerned."
[18] Art. 87 (1).
[19] Art. 88.
[20] A Request brought under E.E.C. Treaty, Art. 177; see p. 303, above.
[21] [1962] C.M.L.R. at p. 27.
[22] Regulation 17 of 1962.

The Court noted that if, prior to 1962, restrictive agreements had been automatically null and void, but nevertheless the Commission under the implementing Regulation was enabled to authorise such agreements retrospectively, severe difficulties would arise. The Court declared:

> The . . . effect . . . of this Regulation is that the Commission is able firstly to make declarations under Article 85 (3) in respect of agreements subsisting at the time of entry into force of the said Regulation, and is empowered, secondly, to give such Regulations a retroactive effect, even to a date prior to that on which a particular agreement had been notified to the Commission.
>
> It follows that the authors of the Regulation seem to have envisaged also that at the date of its entry into force there would be subsisting agreements caught by Article 85 (1) but in respect of which decisions under Article 85 (3) had not been taken but without such agreements thereby being null and void.
>
> The opposite interpretation would lead to the inadmissible result that some agreements would have been null and void already for several years without having been so declared by any authority, and even though they might ultimately be validated subsequently with retroactive effect. In general it would be contrary to the general principle of legal certainty—a rule to be upheld in the application of the Treaty—to render agreements null and void before it is even possible to tell which ones are caught by Article 85 as a whole.[23]

A further consideration which also weighed with the Court was that by Article 7 of the Regulation, the Commission was empowered to declare that although the agreement in its present form could not be authorised under Article 85 (3), nevertheless if certain amendments were made to it, the agreement could be so authorised. This implied, the Court found, that the authors of the Regulation were again assuming that at the date of the coming into force of the Regulation, agreements, although within the terms of Article 85 (1), were nevertheless valid and not " automatically null and void " under Article 85 (2).

The Court stated this in the following terms:

> Even if the agreement or decision is not such as by Article 85 (3) can avoid being prohibited, the Commission is given a discretion under Article 7 of the Regulation to declare the prohibition imposed by Article 85—that is to say, the nullity—operative only until such time as the parties may withdraw or amend such agreement or decision.
>
> *This provision of Article 7 of the Regulation can be given its full effect only on the basis that agreements and decisions shall not be null and void unless, on being laid before the Commission, they are so declared.*[24]

[23] [1962] C.M.L.R. at p. 28.
[24] [1962] C.M.L.R. at p. 29. Author's italics.

In the light of these considerations the Court interpreted the words in Article 85 (2) " shall automatically be null and void " as meaning:

> shall automatically be null and void only as from the date of the coming into force of the Regulation, referred to in Article 87 [25] of the Treaty, to put into effect the principles of Article 85 *i.e.* March 14, 1962.

It is submitted that this interpretation is unlikely to have been reached by any English court and, indeed, the concept of interpreting a legislative provision in the light of delegated legislation made thereunder is anathema. However, it is suggested that the Court's judgment in this case is to be regarded not as the judgment of a body interpreting words in isolation from the outside world, but rather as the judgment of a body seeking to facilitate the working of the Economic Community in the way in which the Member States who set it up intended. It follows, therefore, that if a Regulation passed by the representatives of the Governments of those Member States, sitting as the Council of Ministers, reveals the assumptions and intention of those States, it is for the Court to the best of its ability to give effect to those intentions. The fact, therefore, that the Regulation implementing Article 85 was passed long after the occurrence of the facts giving rise to the litigation in question is irrelevant, and indeed from the present viewpoint it would have been wrong for the Court to have given judgment in the *Bosch* case without taking into account the only document which bore upon the vital question in issue, namely, what was Article 85 (2) intended to mean.

(D) BY GIVING EFFECT TO THE ECONOMIC OR OTHER PURPOSE OF THE PROVISION

In its very first case,[26] the Court was required to interpret the meaning of the words in the E.C.S.C. Treaty:

> the price lists . . . applied by enterprises . . . shall be published,[27]

and to determine whether the lists here being referred to were lists of exact prices, or as the High Authority contended, lists of average or approximate prices.

---

[25] Art. 87, para. 1, provides:
"Within three years of this Treaty coming into force, the Council [of Ministers] shall issue the necessary regulations or directives to put into effect the principles set out in Articles 85 and 86 [dealing with enterprises in a dominant position within the common market]."

[26] *French Government* v. *The High Authority* (Case 1–54), Vol. II.

[27] Art. 60, section 2 (a), provides:
"The price lists and conditions of sale applied by enterprises within the common market must be made public to the extent and in the form prescribed by the High Authority after consulting the Consultative Committee."

To determine this, the Court first established that the purpose of this publication was not only so that buyers could know when best to make their purchases but also so that any particular enterprise could bring its prices into line with those of its competitors. The Court stated:

> There is no doubt that the Treaty requires a publication of exact prices in the form of price lists. *This follows from the purpose which the publication of prices is intended to achieve;* information given to buyers only has value for them if it informs them of the exact prices at which they can make purchases. Likewise, publication must make alignment possible and this alignment must be made with the exact prices of the competition. Alignment is a right granted to enterprises by the Treaty, and not merely a faculty which can be exercised only if enterprises are able by either more or less fortuitous means to acquaint themselves with the prices practised by their competitors.[28]

A further example of the Court interpreting a provision of a Treaty in the light of its economic purpose is provided by a case from Luxembourg[29] in which the phrase " special financial burdens imposed by [States] " had to be interpreted.[30] The steps in the Court's reasoning are felt to be sufficiently interesting to be set out in full.

> It is necessary to determine the criteria which will enable one to define what constitutes a special financial burden abolished and prohibited by Article 4 (c), as well as by the conditions specified in Article 67, section 3.[31]
>
> The Treaty does not state what are the elements that make a financial burden a special financial burden, but, in Article 67, section 3 it gives an example of a financial burden which is treated as being special because it is imposed upon the coal and steel enterprises falling under the jurisdiction of a State and not upon other industries in the same country.
>
> This financial burden clearly becomes special from the fact that it affects only a part of all the industries which are under the jurisdiction of one and the same State, and which find themselves in a comparable situation with regard to this State.
>
> However, the comparability of situations gives only a relative and changing criterion from the fact that it depends upon the size of the area within which comparisons are being made.

28 *French Government* v. *The High Authority* (Case 1–54), Vol. II, Author's italics.
29 *Groupement des Industries Sidérurgiques Luxembourgeoises* v. *The High Authority* (Joint Cases 7–54 and 9–54), Vol. II.
30 Art. 4 provides:
" The following practices are hereby abolished and prohibited within the Community, as incompatible with the common market for coal and steel, under the conditions laid down in the present Treaty:
. . .
(c) subsidies or assistance granted by States or special financial burdens imposed by them in any form whatsoever."
31 For the terms of Art. 67, section 3, see note 36, p. 379, below.

A financial burden which is general as regards all the enterprises of a State could cease to be general and become special if one were considering all the enterprises of the Community.

Hence, it is advisable, if there is any doubt, to support the criterion of comparability *by checking the results to which it leads against those which were intended by the Treaty.*

Article 2 of the Treaty in particular specifies as an aim of the Community, the progressive establishment of conditions which will themselves ensure the most rational distribution of production at the highest possible level of productivity, while safeguarding continuity of employment and avoiding the creation of fundamental and persistent disturbances in the economies of Member States.

Article 67 makes this requirement more specific by authorising the High Authority to grant compensation for the harmful effects produced by the action of a Member State when this action is liable to provoke a serious disequilibrium by substantially increasing differences in costs of production otherwise than through variations in productivity.

It follows, conversely, that the Treaty allows action of Member States when it does not substantially increase differences in costs of production or when it increases them through variations in production.

In the light of this provision, the most rational distribution of production referred to in Article 2 is the one that is based, in particular, upon the linking of production costs to productivity, that is to say, to the physical and technical conditions peculiar to the various producers.

From a preliminary analysis, although this definition cannot in itself be considered as final, a financial burden may be held to be special, and, therefore, abolished and prohibited by the Treaty, if, by affecting unequally the costs of production of producers who find themselves in comparable positions, it introduces into the costs of production, factors which are not related to variations of productivity.[32]

In other words, because the term " special financial burden " is not defined in Article 4, the Court considered Article 67. There the High Authority can act against burdens imposed upon coal enterprises run by a Member State where these same burdens are not also imposed upon privately run coal enterprises. These burdens are seen to be " special " because they have not been imposed uniformly. The Court, however, rejected the deduction from this that a burden imposed upon all the coal enterprises within a State could not be special. It did this because, from a Community viewpoint, such a burden would still not be a uniform one on all Community coal enterprises.

The Court, therefore, sought assistance from discovering the aim of the Treaty which it found to be set out in Article 2, namely the attainment of the highest level of productivity. However, because the High

---

[32] *Groupement des Industries Sidérurgiques Luxembourgeoises* v. *The High Authority* (Joint Cases 7-54 and 9-54), Vol. II.

Authority can compensate State action which is liable to cause disequilibrium by increasing differences in costs of production otherwise than through variations in productivity, it follows, the Court deduced, that disequilibria caused by variations in productivity cannot be so compensated.

Applying this to the problem in hand, a burden which causes disequilibria by increasing differences in costs of production, otherwise than through variations in productivity, is illegal. Such burdens are, therefore, the Court held, the ones being referred to as " special " and the ones that are made illegal.

(E) BY INFERRING THAT THE AUTHORS DID NOT INTEND RESULTS
IF THESE WERE NOT CLEARLY STATED

In one case [33] the German Government intervened in an action concerning the granting of a bonus to certain coal face miners,[34] and argued that although Article 4 (c) of the E.C.S.C. Treaty prohibits " subsidies or assistance granted by States " [35] nevertheless Article 63, section 3 of the Treaty refers to what is to occur:

> If the action taken by [a Member State] reduces differences in costs of production by granting a special advantage to . . . coal or steel enterprises over which it has authority by comparison with the other industries in the same country.[36]

From this, the German Government argued that because this provision was based upon the assumption that a State would grant special advantages, it followed that the prohibition upon such advantages set out in Article 4 (c) had been modified.

On this the Court declared:

> It would hardly be compatible with the accustomed rigour of the Treaty that its authors should have wished substantially to detract from the scope of the prohibitions set out in Article 4 when dealing with entirely different matters, which is apparent as much from the title of Chapter VII (Impairment of the Conditions of Competition) as by the text of Article 67 itself. . . .

---

[33] *De Gazamenlijke Steenkolenmijnen in Limburg* v. *The High Authority* (Case 30–59).
[34] For details of this, see *De Gazamenlijke Steenkolenmijnen in Limburg* v. *The High Authority* (Case 17–57), Vol. II.
[35] For the terms of Art. 4 (c), see note 30, p. 377, above.
[36] Art. 67, section 3, provides:
" If the action taken by the said State reduces differences in costs of production by granting a special advantage to, or by imposing special burdens on, coal or steel enterprises over which it has authority by comparison with the other industries in the same country, the High Authority is empowered to make the necessary recommendations to the State in question after consulting the Consultative Committee and the Council."

It is difficult to accept that the authors of the Treaty should have wished not only to detract from, but in certain cases to annul, the abolitions and prohibitions which have been set out in Article 4 with exceptional rigour, without referring to the article whose scope they were seeking to limit.[37]

(F) BY ASSUMING THAT A DIFFERENCE OF WORDING CONNOTES A DIFFERENCE OF MEANING

In a case referred to above,[38] when the Court had to determine whether the substitution of the phrase within a " distance " of 25 kilometres, in place of the phrase " within a ' radius ' of 25 kilometres " connoted any difference of meaning, it accepted that, because the wording had been altered, effect was to be given to the alteration. It declared:

The existence of a difference in wording between the two texts in itself connotes an argument leading to the presumption that the authors of the new provision intended to modify the previous criterion, because, without evidence to the contrary, it must be presumed that every difference in wording connotes a difference in meaning . . .

The wording of the previous text leaves no room for doubt, because the term " radius " corresponds exactly to the concept of distance as the crow flies.

On the other hand, the terms used in [this provision], even in their literal sense can lead to two interpretations: a distance which may be calculated either in a direct line or on the actual distance by road or rail.

Thus, if the term " radius " had been substituted for the term " distance," the scope of the alteration would have been clear, because the authors of the new provision would plainly have intended to make the choice, from the two possible interpretations of the old text, of the one which related to the idea of distance as the crow flies.

In the present case, however, it is just the opposite which has happened.

The very fact of having replaced the word " radius " by the word " distance " plainly shows that the authors of the text wanted to reject the concept of measurement as the crow flies (a concept which was clearly expressed by the word " radius ") and that in fact they wanted to adopt the concept of " the distance covered by road or rail." [39]

THE ARTICLES OF A TREATY ARE TO BE READ TOGETHER

Referring to the E.C.S.C. Treaty, the Court has held:

Articles 2, 3 and 4 of the Treaty . . . constitute fundamental provisions establishing the common market and the common objectives of the Community.[40]

---

[37] *De Gazamenlijke Steenkolenmijnen in Limburg* v. *The High Authority* (Case 30–59).
[38] *Simon* v. *The Court of Justice of the European Communities* (Case 15–60).
[39] *Ibid.*
[40] *French Government* v. *The High Authority* (Case 1–54); Vol. II.

Later, the Court declared:

> Article 4 (b) prohibits measures "which discriminate between . . . consumers especially as regards . . . transport rates." This prohibition, which forms an essential condition for the establishment and functioning of the common market, permits of no exceptions, and exceptions from it cannot exist without express provision in the Treaty.[41]

So fundamental are these early provisions of the Treaty that when in Article 53 of the Treaty the High Authority is empowered to authorise the creation of

> any financial arrangements common to several enterprises which it considers necessary in order to carry out the duties set out in Article 3,

the Court declared:

> The express mention of Article 3 does not release the High Authority from the obligation to respect the other articles of the Treaty, and in particular Articles 2, 4 and 5 which, with Article 3, must always be respected because they set out the fundamental objectives of the Community. These provisions have equal binding force and must be read together if they are to be correctly applied.[42]

These early Articles, however, were not to be read on their own but in the light of the subsequent provisions of the Treaty. In the Court's words:

> Article 4 recognises the practices enumerated in paragraphs (a), (b), (c) and (d) as "incompatible with the common market and abolished and prohibited under the conditions laid down in the present Treaty . . ."[43]

> By Article 84 of the Treaty,[44] the expression "the present Treaty" must be understood as meaning the clauses of the Treaty and its

---

[41] *Compagnie des Hauts Fourneaux et Fonderies de Givors and others* v. *The High Authority* (Joint Cases 27–58, 28–58 and 29–58), Vol. II.

[42] *Groupement des Hauts Fourneaux et Aciéries Belges* v. *The High Authority* (Case 8–57), Vol. II.

[43] Art. 4 provides:
"The following practices are hereby abolished and prohibited within the Community, as incompatible with the common market for coal and steel under the conditions laid down in the present Treaty:
(a) import and export duties, or charges having equivalent effect, and quantitative restrictions on the movement of products;
(b) measures or practices which discriminate between producers, between purchasers and between consumers especially as regards price and delivery terms or transport rates, as well as measures or practices which hamper the purchaser in the free choice of his supplier;
(c) subsidies or assistance granted by States or special financial burdens imposed by them in any form whatsoever;
(d) restrictive practices tending towards the sharing or exploitation of markets."

[44] Art. 84 provides:
"For the purposes of the present Treaty, the words 'the present Treaty' shall include the Treaty's clauses, its Annexes, the Protocols annexed thereto and the Convention containing the Transitional Provisions."

Annexes, those of the Protocols annexed and of the Convention containing the Transitional Provisions.

Hence, the provisions contained in all of these texts have the same binding force, and there can be no question of setting one against another, but only of reading them together in order to apply them correctly.

The Court has already decided . . . that " Articles 2, 3 and 4 of the Treaty . . . constitute fundamental provisions establishing the common market and the common objectives of the Community. . . ."

For the same reason, the provisions of Article 4 are sufficient in themselves and are directly applicable when they are not modified in any other part of the Treaty.

When the provisions of Article 4 are referred to, modified or regulated by other parts of the Treaty, the texts referring to one and the same provision must be considered in their entirety and applied together.[45]

Applying this statement in practice, the Court has read Article 4 (b) [46] together with Article 65 of the Treaty.[47] It declared:

In support of their claim that there has been a misconstruction of the relationship between Article 4 (b) and Article 65, the plaintiffs contend that the provisions of Article 65, as being a *lex specialis,* exclude the fundamental provisions of Article 4 (b).

This, however, is not so.

Articles 4 (b) and 65 of the Treaty, each in their own field of application, regulate different aspects of the economic sphere.

These two articles are not exclusive, far less does the one cancel out the other. They serve to further the aims of the Community, and in this respect they are therefore complementary.[48]

[45] *Groupement des Industries Sidérurgiques Luxembourgeoises* v. *The High Authority* (Joint Cases 7–54 and 9–54), Vol. II.
[46] For the terms of Art. 4 (b), see note 43, p. 381, above.
[47] Art. 65, sections 1 and 2, provides:
   " 1. All agreements between enterprises; all decisions by associations of enterprises and all concerted practices tending, directly or indirectly, to prevent, restrict or distort the normal operation of competition within the common market are forbidden, and in particular those tending:
   (a) to fix or determine prices;
   (b) to restrict or control production, technical development or investments;
   (c) to allocate markets, products, customers or sources of supply.
   2. However, the High Authority shall authorise agreements to specialise in the production of, or to engage in the joint buying or selling of specified products if it finds:
   (a) that such specialisation or such joint buying or selling will contribute to a substantial improvement in the production or distribution of the products in question; and
   (b) that the agreement in question is essential to achieve these results, and is not more restrictive than is necessary for that purpose; and
   (c) that it is not capable of giving the enterprises concerned the power to determine prices or to control or limit the production or marketing of a substantial part of the products in question within the common market or of protecting them from effective competition by other enterprises within the common market."
[48] " *Geitling* " *and others* v. *The High Authority* (Case 2–56), Vol. II.

Similarly the Court has read Article 4 (b) [49] of the Treaty with Article 70 [50] and has held:

> The provisions of Article 4 (b) of the Treaty are amplified by Article 70, paragraph 1, which states the necessity of applying such transport rates for coal and steel as will make possible comparable price conditions to consumers placed in comparable circumstances. [51]

WHERE A TREATY IS SILENT ON A POINT:
(A) THE COURT WILL IMPLY A REASONABLE TERM

It is inevitable that the Community Treaties should not have been able to cover every situation which has arisen. Where a situation not covered by the relevant Treaty has come before the Court, the Court has proceeded to imply a reasonable term into the Treaty, and conversely it has refused to imply a term which it regarded as unreasonable. A few examples will illustrate the Court's concept of what is reasonable.

Under the system set up to subsidise imported scrap, the High Authority was empowered to impose a levy upon certain consumers of Community produced scrap, and with the funds thus raised it paid a subsidy to the consumers of imported scrap. [52] The High Authority, however, without fault on its own part paid out a subsidy to a consumer who was not entitled to it. The question thus arose [53] whether the High Authority could demand back the payment wrongly made.

The Court stated:

> In default of an express provision on this subject, the question arises of whether the repayment of a subsidy wrongly received is not the necessary corollary of compulsory contributions and of the right to receive the subsidy provided for in the Decisions concerning the subsidy system. . . .
> The subsidy arrangement to which numerous enterprises of the six countries of the Community which are consumers of scrap have been compulsorily subjected will always enable errors to be made in the payment of the amount of the subsidy and it must, therefore, be admitted that the legal basis of an obligation to contribute implies the right to enforce repayment because without this obligation the subsidy system . . . could not be operated in a reasonable manner. Thus an express authorisation was not necessary. . . . [54]

---

[49] For terms of Art. 4 (b), see note 43, p. 381, above.
[50] Art. 70, para. 1, provides:
   " It is recognised that the establishment of the common market requires the application of such transport rates for coal and steel as will make possible comparable price conditions for consumers in comparable circumstances."
[51] *Compagnie des Haut Fourneaux et Fonderies de Givors* v. *The High Authority* (Joint Cases 27–58, 28–58 and 29–58), Vol. II.
[52] As to this subsidy system, see Vol. II.
[53] *Mannesman AG and others* v. *The High Authority* (Cases 4 to 13–59), Vol. II.
[54] *Ibid.* Vol. II.

In an earlier case it had been contended that a provision should be read into Article 33 of the Treaty that only coal enterprises could appeal against a Decision of the High Authority relating to coal, and similarly only steel enterprises could appeal against Decisions relating to steel. On this the Court held:

> There is no provision in the Treaty which requires that the particular product made by the producer should be connected with the subject-matter of the dispute.
>
> The silence of the Treaty on this point cannot be interpreted in any manner which would be detrimental to enterprises and associations.

As an example of a further provision which the Court has refused to imply into the E.C.S.C. Treaty, one may refer to a case from Belgium.[55]

In the years immediately following the creation of the common market in coal and steel, the High Authority devised a system by which the price of Belgian coal was to be reduced, but coal mines were to receive a compensating subsidy, paid partly by the Belgian Government and partly by the High Authority itself.[56] Belgian coalmines sought to argue that there was to be read into the E.C.S.C. Treaty a guarantee that under the High Authority's system the total receipts of the mines would be maintained. On this the Court declared:

> Despite the silence of the Convention [containing the Transitional Provisions] upon the existence, if the case should arise, of a relationship between the equalisation levy and receipts . . . such an interpretation would be admissible only if the subsidy were necessarily and in all circumstances to cover the whole of the difference between the reduced selling price and receipts existing at the beginning of the transitional period. However, this is not so. The subsidy is only a protective measure necessary in order to avoid the results caused by a sudden and dangerous disturbance in production. . . . The subsidy must not, therefore, exceed the limits which are strictly necessary in order to neutralise to a certain extent the disadvantages resulting from these differences, and this does not imply a guarantee of the original receipts.[57]

(B) THE COURT WILL HAVE RESORT TO GENERAL PRINCIPLES OF LAW

As will be set out below,[58] when the Court had to determine whether, without any express power to that effect in the E.C.S.C. Treaty, the High Authority could fix the prices of Belgian coal, it declared:

---

[55] *Fédération Charbonnière de Belgique* v. *The High Authority* (Case 8-55) (Final judgment), Vol. II.
[56] For details of this subsidy system, see Vol. II.
[57] *Ibid.* Vol. II.
[58] See note 32, p. 400, below.

The plaintiffs contended . . . that the absence in the Treaty of an express power to fix prices by administrative action prevents the recognition of such power. . . . In the opinion of the Court, it is permissible . . . to allow a rule of interpretation that is generally admitted as much in international law as in municipal law, by which the norms established by an international treaty or by a law imply those norms without which the former would not make any sense or would not permit of a reasonable and useful application.[59]

In the same case, the plaintiffs had argued that there was no necessity for the High Authority to fix the price of coal in Belgium because in practice the High Authority could have brought down the price of coal by threatening to withdraw the subsidy payments from any mines which did not lower their prices. The Court rejected this argument, not by reference to provisions of the Treaty, but by reference to general principles of law. It stated:

The Court cannot accept this argument, because in application of a generally recognised rule of law, such indirect action of the High Authority in response to the wrongful act of enterprises [namely the refusal to lower their prices] must be proportional to the gravity of that act. For this reason, the High Authority would only be empowered to reduce the compensation to an equivalent extent to that to which the enterprises had not lowered their prices within the prescribed limits.[60]

(C) THE COURT WILL REFER TO THE MUNICIPAL LAWS OF THE MEMBER STATES [61]

In one case,[62] certain employees of the Coal and Steel Community had had their employment regulated by the terms of the Community's Statute of Service, rather than its being regulated by contracts of employment. The question arising before the Court was whether admission to the Statute could subsequently be withdrawn. On this the Court declared:

The decrees of December 12, 1955, declare the plaintiffs to be admitted to benefit under the Statute of Service, place them in certain " grades " and fix their position in the scale of seniority.

---

[59] *Fédération Charbonnière de Belgique* v. *The High Authority* (Case 8–55) (Final judgment), Vol. II.

[60] *Ibid.* (Interim judgment), Vol. II.

[61] For a discussion of the effects of municipal law upon decisions of the Court, see Rivero, Jean: " Le problème de l'influence des droits internes sur la Cour de Justice de la C.E.C.A.," in 4 *Annuaire Français du Droit International* (1958), p. 295; Donner, A. M.: " National Law and the Case Law of the Court of Justice of the European Communities," in *Common Market Law Review* (1963), p. 8, and Migliazza, A.: " La jurisprudence de la Cour de Justice des Communautés Européennes et le problème des sources du droit," in *Österreichischer Zeitung für öffentliches Recht* (1962), p. 332.

[62] *Algera and others* v. *The High Authority* (Joint Cases 7–56 and 3 to 7–57), Vol. II.

If these decrees are legal and valid in law, they amount to individual administrative acts creating substantive rights.

As for the possibility of a revocation of such acts, this involves a problem of administrative law known in the case law and theory of all the countries of the Community, but for the solution of which the Treaty does not contain any rules. The Court, lest it commit a denial of justice, is therefore compelled to solve the problem by reliance upon rules recognised by the legislation, theory and case law of the member countries.[63]

The Court then continued:

A study of comparative law reveals that in the six Member States an administrative act creating substantive rights in a particular party cannot in principle be revoked, provided that it amounted to a legal act. . . .

If on the contrary, an administrative act is illegal, the law of all the Member States recognises the possibility of revocation.[64]

In another case,[65] the question at issue was whether the plaintiffs who had their works in the small Italian village of Magliano Alpi had been notified of the contents of a letter addressed to their head office in Turin. The Court held:

---

[63] *Ibid.* Vol. II.
[64] *Ibid.* Vol. II. The Court went on to declare:
" French law requires that the revocation of the illegal act must occur before the expiration of the time limit for bringing an appeal, or if an appeal is brought, before judgment. Belgian, Luxembourg and Dutch law, with certain slight differences, appear to follow analogous rules.

On the other hand, German law does not recognise a time limit for the exercise of the right of revocation unless such a limit is provided by a special provision. Thus, the Federal law concerning public officials, by Article 13 thereof, allows the withdrawal of an appointment only within a period of six months. However, it is generally recognised that the principle of good faith (*Treu und Glauben*) is opposed to an unduly delayed withdrawal if it is made an appreciable time after the date on which the withdrawal could have been made. Precedents and doctrines on this matter rely equally upon the concept of the renunciation of the right of revocation (*Verzicht*), and of its becoming barred by the running of time (*Verwirkung*).

Italian law is particularly precise upon this question. Any administrative act vitiated by incompetence, violation of the law or *ultra vires* (*eccesso di potere*) can be annulled *ex tunc* by the administration which enacted it, independently of the substantive rights to which it might have given rise. This withdrawal can be pronounced at any time whatsoever (*in qualsiasi momento*). There is therefore no time limit fixed for the withdrawal. However, according to doctrines and precedents, an unduly delayed withdrawal might be *ultra vires*. Acts that have been in existence for a long time (*fatti avvenuti da lunga data*) ought to be upheld, even if they were contrary to law, unless higher considerations require their withdrawal in the public interest.

The revocability of an administrative act tainted with illegality is therefore recognised in all the Member States.

The Court, in agreement with the submission of the Advocate General, recognises the principle of the revocability of illegal acts, at least during a reasonable period, such as that within which the Decisions in the present action were taken."
[65] *Acciaieria Laminatoi Magliano Alpi (A.L.M.A.)* v. *The High Authority* (Case 8–56), Vol. II.

It is of little importance to know whether—as the plaintiffs allege—
the letter was not sent from Turin to Magliano Alpi. As it has been
established that it properly reached the plaintiffs' administrative office,
one must apply the rule of law generally accepted within all the
countries of the Community, by which a written document has effect
from the time when it is duly received by the administrative department
of the addressee.[66]

(D) THE COURT MAY MAKE DEDUCTIONS FROM OTHER
ARTICLES WHICH DEAL WITH THE POINT IN ISSUE

Where one article of a Treaty is silent on a particular matter, but another
article *in pari materia* includes specific provisions, the Court has been
able to infer that there was some reason why in the former articles these
specific provisions had been omitted. An example of this was illustrated
in a case concerning transport.[67]

The E.C.S.C. Treaty provides that:

> The price lists and conditions of sale applied by enterprises within
> the common market must be made public *to the extent and in the form
> prescribed by the High Authority* after consulting the Consultative
> Committee.[68]

However, when the Treaty deals with transport contracts, the wording
of the provision dealing with publication is slightly different. It
provides:

> The rates, prices, and tariff provisions of all kinds, applied to the
> transport of coal and steel within each Member State and between
> Member States *shall be published or brought to the knowledge of
> the High Authority*.[69]

It will be noted that this second provision does not state who is to be able
to regulate how these rates, etc., are to be published or brought to the
knowledge of the High Authority. When the High Authority passed a
Decision regulating this matter,[70] therefore, the Italian Government
challenged the High Authority's power to do so. On this the Court
stated:

> A comparison of Article 70, paragraph 3, and the provision of
> Article 60, section 2 (a), reveals that, in a parallel matter, the Treaty,
> when imposing the obligation to publish prices contained in Article 60,
> grants to the High Authority powers concerning its application, by
> prescribing that this publication shall be made " to the extent and
> in the form prescribed by the High Authority after consulting the
> Consultative Committee."

[66] *Ibid.* Vol. II.
[67] *Italian Government* v. *The High Authority* (Case 20–59), Vol. II.
[68] Art. 60, section 2 (a).
[69] Art. 70, para. 3.
[70] Decision 18–59; see Vol. II.

One can see from the fact that, as concerns the publication of rates, prices and conditions of sale applied on the common market, the Treaty has expressly granted a legislative power to the High Authority. . . .

The absence of any *ad hoc* provision in Article 70 indicates, conversely, that in respect of transport, the text of the Treaty denies to the High Authority any power to take an executory Decision.[71]

THE COURT'S INTERPRETATION OF ITS OWN JURISDICTION

The jurisdiction of the Court has been set out in provisions in the three Treaties.[72] In interpreting these the Court can be seen to have placed certain limits upon its own competence.

THE COURT IS EXCLUSIVELY A LEGAL FORUM

The Communities' Court is a Court concerned with interpreting and enforcing a particular system of law: it is, therefore, first, no part of its duty to comment upon the nature of the law or to criticise it. Thus, in one case [73] it was suggested that even if the system for the publication of prices as laid down by the Treaty had not been observed, the system which had in fact been followed was administratively more desirable than the Treaty system and should thus be upheld. The Court rejected this and declared:

> It is not the task of the Court to give its opinion about the appropriateness of the system imposed by the Treaty, or to suggest a revision of the Treaty, but it is required by Article 31 to ensure the respect of law in the interpretation and application of the Treaty in the form in which it has been drawn up.[74]

Secondly, the Court has had to be careful to distinguish between legal and political considerations, because the latter fall outside its purview. In one matter [75] it was contended that a proposed amendment of the powers of the High Authority so as to enable it to give assistance to displaced employees would inevitably mean a greater expenditure by the High Authority, which could only be met by an increased levy on coal. The argument went that this increased levy, the direct result of the amendment, would be invalid as violating Article 3 (d) of the

[71] *Italian Government* v. *The High Authority* (Case 20–59), Vol. II.
[72] See Chaps. 4, 5 and 6 above.
[73] *French Government* v. *The High Authority* (Case 1–54).
[74] *Ibid.* Vol. II.
[75] *Amendment Procedure under Article 95, paras. 3 and 4 of the E.C.S.C. Treaty* (Opinion 1–60), Vol. II.

Treaty[76] by which the High Authority is required to encourage enterprises to expand, so that the High Authority did not have power to restrict that expansion by taxation. Whatever may be thought of the validity of this argument, the Court refused to look at it. It declared:

> The ill-effects, if they should occur, of a possible—but not a necessary—increase in the amount of the levy is a political and not a legal consideration.[77]

Thirdly, because the duty of interpreting the law had been entrusted to the Court and to no other body, the Court has made it quite plain that it has no intention of being bound by the legal opinion of other people. Thus, in one case[78] it was brought to the Court's attention that the Commission of Presidents, a body set up to supervise the administrative side of the Coal and Steel Community,[79] had adopted a certain interpretation of its powers so as to give itself a right of decision in a particular matter relating to employees. The Court was unimpressed by this and stated:

> By Article 31 of the Treaty, the Court is required to ensure that the law is respected in the interpretation and application of the Treaty and of the regulations for its execution. It would, therefore, be bound neither by the view adopted by the Commission of Presidents nor by the text of the Statute of Service, if it should appear that a choice between the two above-mentioned contentions was necessary for a solution of the present action.[80]

THE COURT IS NOT IN GENERAL CONCERNED WITH THE MUNICIPAL LAW OF THE MEMBER STATES

The principal duty of the Court is to ensure the observance of law in the interpretation and application of the three Treaties setting up the

[76] Art. 3 provides:
"The Community's institutions shall within the limits of their respective competence and in the common interest:
. . . .
(d) seek to maintain conditions which will encourage enterprises to expand and improve their productive capacity and to promote a policy of rational exploitation of natural resources avoiding unplanned exhaustion."
[77] *Ibid.* Vol. II.
[78] *Algera and others* v. *The Common Assembly* (Joint Cases 7–56 and 3–57 to 7–57), Vol. II.
[79] Art. 78, section 3.2, provides:
"However, the number of the Community's servants and the scales of their salaries, allowances and pensions, provided that they are not fixed by another provision of the Treaty or a regulation for its implementation, as well as any extraordinary expenditure, shall be determined in advance by a Committee consisting of the President of the Court, the President of the High Authority, the President of the Assembly and the President of the Council. The President of the Court shall preside over this Committee."
[80] *Ibid.* Vol. II.

three Communities.[81] Its task is, therefore, entirely distinct from that of municipal courts whose duty is to watch over the interpretation and application of the municipal laws of the Member States.[82] The Court has, therefore, declared:

> The Treaties establishing the European Communities did not place the Court of Justice of these Communities above national judicial proceedings, in the sense that decisions taken in those proceedings could be challenged before the Court. . . .
> It follows that any overlapping of the jurisdictions entrusted to these various authorities is excluded.[83]

Several results follow immediately from this. First, as the Court has stated:

> There can be no question of a prior " exhaustion " of the local judicial remedies, which would result in submitting one and the same question to the decision first of the municipal tribunals and then of the Court.[84]

Secondly, the Court is concerned exclusively with Community law and not with municipal law. The Court has, therefore, on several occasions refused to consider what the law might be in a particular Member State. A few quotations will reveal the Court's attitude on this. Thus, in a case dealing with the extent of the immunity from Belgian income tax of the joint family salary of a Belgian employee of the High Authority, the Court declared:

> Neither Belgian legislation and case law nor the practice followed in analogous cases by the Belgian authorities can be decisive in this particular case, since they determine the problem on the basis of municipal law.[85]

In a case brought by a German enterprise concerning the validity of the trading regulations of the German sole agencies for Ruhr coal,[86] it was argued that the regulations were void by German law, and that the High Authority had acted wrongly to ignore this fact. The Court held:

> This allegation is not well founded.
> Indeed, by Article 8 of the Treaty,[87] the High Authority is only called upon to apply the law of the Community. It is not competent

---

[81] E.C.S.C. Treaty, Art. 31; E.E.C. Treaty, Art. 164; Euratom Treaty, Art. 136.
[82] This is not affected by such provisions as E.C.S.C. Treaty, Art. 41 and E.E.C. Treaty, Art. 177, which merely ensure that the European Court and not the municipal courts has the final word in the interpretation of Community law.
[83] *Humblet* v. *The Belgian State* (Case 6–60), Vol. II.
[84] *Ibid.* Vol. II.
[85] *Ibid.* Vol. II, see, however, pp. 392–394, below.
[86] *Friedrich Stork et Cie* v. *The High Authority* (Case 1–58), Vol. II.
[87] Art. 8 provides:
" The High Authority shall be charged with the duty of ensuring the attainment of the objectives set out in the present Treaty under the conditions laid down therein."

to apply the municipal law of Member States. In the same way, by Article 31 of the Treaty, the Court has merely to ensure the rule of law in the interpretation and application of the Treaty and of the regulations for its execution. Generally speaking it is not required to pronounce upon rules of municipal law. Consequently, it cannot examine the contention that the High Authority, in taking its Decision, violated the principles of German constitutional law (particularly Articles 2 and 12 of the Basic Law).[88]

In another case from Germany [89] the Court stated:

The plaintiffs base their contention upon German case law concerning the interpretation of Article 14 of the Basic Law of the Federal Republic which guarantees private property.

It is no part of the duty of the Court, which is the judge of the legality of the decisions taken by the High Authority and, therefore, of those taken in the present case . . . to ensure the respect of rules of municipal law, even constitutional law, in force within one of the Member States.[90]

The third result of the dichotomy of the legal systems is that the Communities' Court can in no way annul any muncipal law or administrative act of one of the Member States, even where this has been passed in violation of one of the Community Treaties. The Court declared:

The E.C.S.C. Treaty is based on the principle of a strict separation of the jurisdictions of the institutions of the Community and those of the organs of Member States.

Community law does not confer on institutions of the Community the right to annul the legislative or administrative acts of a Member State.

Thus, if the High Authority considers that a State has failed in one of the obligations incumbent upon it by virtue of the Treaty, by enacting or upholding provisions contrary to that Treaty, it may not itself annul or repeal those provisions, but may merely set out such failure, in accordance with Article 88 of the Treaty,[91] and then adopt the procedure which is laid down therein to lead the State in question itself to withdraw the measure it has taken.

The same applies to the Court of Justice. . . . The Court may not of its own authority, annul or repeal the municipal laws of a Member State in the administrative acts of its authorities.[92]

The Court went on to state that this position under the E.C.S.C. Treaty was identical with that under the two later Treaties [93]

---

[88] *Ibid.* Vol. II.
[89] " *Präsident,*" " *Geitling,*" " *Mausegatt,*" *Nold KG* v. *The High Authority* (Joint Cases 36, 37, 38–54 and 40–59), Vol. II.
[90] *Ibid.* Vol. II.
[91] For the terms of Art. 88, see p. 249, above.
[92] *Humblet* v. *The Belgian State* (Case 6–60), Vol. II.
[93] E.E.C. Treaty, Art. 171 and Euratom Treaty, Art. 143.

which confer only a declaratory effect upon the decisions of the Court in the case of a failure [of a Member State] to carry out the provisions of the Treaties, while obliging the States to take the measures required to carry out the judgment.[94]

THE COURT CONSIDERS MUNICIPAL LAWS IN RELATION TO FACTS FALLING WITHIN THE SPHERE OF SUCH LAWS

Although in general the Court is not concerned with municipal laws, on occasion it has given effect to them. Thus, in one case,[95] the Court had to determine whether an individual M. Erich Nold had been validly authorised to bring the action on behalf of a German financing association which was acting as liquidator of the plaintiff's enterprise. In its judgment the Court showed that German law was here the relevant law. It declared:

" Nold," a limited liability company, incorporated and established in Germany, is governed, as concerns its creation, its liquidation and its dissolution, by the rules of the municipal law of its registered office. . . .

Also, by the provisions of German law, associations financing a limited liability company when duly authorised as a liquidator may, for the purpose of the liquidation, delegate to an agent the carrying out of a particular legal act. . . .

On this matter German law, which is applicable to the present case, does not in principle require the mandate to be in writing, even if the act for the purpose of which the power is conferred must itself be in writing.

M. Erich Nold was, therefore, duly empowered to bring the action.[96]

In the same case the Court was also concerned with the question of whether a member of the Bar of Frankfurt-am-Main had effectively signed the plaintiff's request commencing the action although at the time of the filing of that request he had been prohibited from practising. The Court again looked to municipal law to determine this.

The law governing the legal profession in the *Land* of Hesse, which law regulates the professional status of Me. Klibansky and which is applicable to M. Nold, his client, declares in paragraph 107 (2) thereof that a prohibition from practising does not affect the validity of past acts of a barrister.

It follows . . . that the request commencing the action is valid in point of form.[97]

94 *Humblet* v. *The Belgian State* (Case 6–60), Vol. II.
95 *Nold KG* v. *The High Authority* (Case 18–57), Vol. II.
96 *Ibid.* Vol. II.
97 *Ibid.* Vol. II.

THE COURT HAS WIDE POWERS OF INVESTIGATION OF ITS OWN MOTION

Quite apart from the Court's power to call its own witnesses [98] or to refer certain matters for an expert report,[99] the Court on many occasions has considered matters which have not been raised in the pleadings and even matters on which the parties were not in dispute.

Thus, the Court has often of itself considered whether the action before it was admissible.[1] On one occasion the Court of its own motion considered whether a special committee had been consulted by the High Authority before it had passed a particular Decision.[2] Indeed, in one case,[3] although the text of the Decisions passed by the High Authority confirmed that consultations with the Consultative Committee and with the Council of Ministers had taken place, the Court declared that this confirmation did not release the Court from exercising its control and investigating for itself.

The Court's powers of independent examination which it has attributed to itself are, however, in no way limited to mere procedural matters. The Court has held [4] that a failure to support a particular Decision with adequate reasoning renders that Decision void for violation of a substantial procedural requirement. In one case,[5] the plaintiffs alleged such a violation, but because this allegation was made only in the plaintiffs' reply and not in their original request it was inadmissible.[6]

The High Authority, therefore, not unnaturally objected when despite this inadmissibility the Court proceeded to consider whether the Decision in question had been adequately reasoned. This objection, however, was overruled by the Court in the following terms:

> The duty to give reasons which Article 15 of the E.C.S.C. Treaty [7] imposes upon the High Authority has been prescribed not only for the benefit of the parties concerned but also with a view to placing the Court in a position freely to exercise the legal control which the Treaty confers upon it.

---

[98] See p. 66, above.

[99] See p. 69, above.

[1] See, *e.g., Groupement des Industries Sidérurgiques Luxembourgeoises* v. *The High Authority* (Joint Cases 7–54 and 9–54), Vol. II.

[2] *Italian Government* v. *The High Authority* (Case 2–54), Vol. II.

[3] *Netherlands Government* v. *The High Authority* (Case 6–54), Vol. II.

[4] See the cases discussed, pp. 126–134, above.

[5] *Nold KG* v. *The High Authority* (Case 18–57), Vol. II.

[6] Rules, Art. 42, para. 2, provides:
" The submission of fresh arguments during the proceedings shall be prohibited unless these arguments are based upon points of law or of fact which have come to light during the written proceedings."

[7] Art. 15, para. 1, provides:
" Decisions, Recommendations and Opinions of the High Authority shall include the reasons therefor, and shall refer to the advice which the High Authority is required to obtain."

In consequence, a possible failure to give reasons which prevents this legal control, may be and must be reviewed by the Court of its own motion.[8]

In this particular case, not only did the Court find itself able to exercise this legal control, but it also annulled the Decision in question on the ground of its not having been adequately supported with reasons—a ground which, as stated above, had not been validly alleged by the plaintiffs.[9]

WHERE POSSIBLE THE JURISDICTION OF THE COURT IS TO BE EXTENDED RATHER THAN REDUCED

Under each of the three Treaties, the right to determine its own jurisdiction is in the final resort vested in the Court itself. When, however, there have arisen any doubts as to the extent of the Court's jurisdiction, except in respect of one matter,[10] the Court has always sought to extend that jurisdiction and has rejected any arguments which sought to reduce it or to impose fetters upon it.

The first attempt to restrict the right of appeal to the Court was made by the Luxembourg Government when it contended that in respect of a Decision of the High Authority relating to coal, no enterprises which did not themselves produce coal or an association of such enterprises could bring an appeal. The Court in rejecting this contention declared:

> There is no provision in the Treaty which requires that the particular product made by the producer should be connected with the subject-matter of the dispute.

It then stated:

> *The silence of the Treaty on this point cannot be interpreted in any manner which would be detrimental to enterprises and associations.*[11]

Together with this refusal to restrict its jurisdiction, the Court in two most important ways has extended its jurisdiction.

First, as has been noted above,[12] the Court had not adopted a restrictive interpretation of Article 33 of the E.C.S.C. Treaty, which in terms refers only to a right of appeal against Decisions and Recommendations " of the High Authority." As a result, the Court has held admissible an appeal against a Decision of the *Caisse de Péréquation des Ferrailles Importées*, an administrative body set up in Brussels by

---

[8] *Nold KG* v. *The High Authority* (Case 18–57), Vol. II.
[9] For a further discussion of this case, see pp. 115–117, above.
[10] Namely, enterprises' right to intervene in State affairs, see pp. 401–402, below.
[11] *Groupement des Industries Sidérurgiques Luxembourgeoises* v. *The High Authority* (Joint Cases 7–54 and 9–54), Vol. II.
[12] See p. 121, above.

the High Authority to run the financial side of a subsidy system to equalise the price of imported and Community scrap.[13] The Court argued as follows:

> Article 33 of the E.C.S.C. Treaty provides only for appeals for annulment against Decisions of the High Authority. It is necessary, therefore, to consider whether decisions taken by the C.P.F.I. are equivalent to Decisions of the High Authority.
>
> In this respect, one must take into consideration the fact that C.P.F.I. was an organ of the financial mechanism established by the High Authority, and it received its powers from the latter.
>
> Further . . . the notifications by the C.P.F.I. constituted, in fact, the administrative Decision taken at final instance.[14]

In view of this, the Court declared:

> *Therefore in order not to deprive enterprises of the benefit of the protection which Article 33 of the E.C.S.C. Treaty has granted to them*, it must be admitted that the Decisions taken by the C.P.F.I. . . . are equivalent to Decisions of the High Authority and are, therefore, subject to an appeal for annulment under the conditions set out in Article 33.[15]

The second wide interpretation of its jurisdiction relates to an enterprise's right to appeal against general Decisions and Recommendations of the High Authority. It will be remembered that under Article 33, paragraph 2, of the E.C.S.C. Treaty [16] enterprises may challenge an individual Decision or Recommendation concerning them on any of the four classic grounds, but that it may only challenge a general Decision on the grounds of a *détournement de pouvoir* with respect to itself. The question arose, therefore, of whether an enterprise, when challenging an individual Decision imposing a levy upon itself, could allege, as part of its case against the validity of that individual Decision, that the general parent Decision under which the whole system of imposing levies had been set up was itself illegal. Further, if the enterprise could make this allegation, could it be made

(a) on the three classic grounds of appeal other than the ground of *détournement de pouvoir*, which was the only ground on which by

---

13 As to this *Caisse* (C.P.F.I.), see Vol. II. Author's italics.

14 *Société Nouvelle des Usines de Pontlieue-Aciéries du Temple (S.N.U.P.A.T.)* v. *The High Authority* (Joint Cases 32–58 and 33–58), Vol. II.

15 *Ibid.* see Vol. II. Similarly, where under Art. 35 a plaintiff seeking to challenge the implied Decision of the High Authority refusing to take action must show that he has requested that Authority to take action, the Court has been prepared to hold that a request to the C.P.F.I. was equivalent to a request to the High Authority and that a two months' failure on the part of the C.P.F.I. was deemed to constitute an implied Decision of the C.P.F.I. refusing to act and that an appeal was open to challenge the validity of this Decision. See *Société Nouvelle des Usines de Pontlieue-Acieries du Temple (S.N.U.P.A.T.)* v. *The High Authority* (Joint Cases 32–58 and 33–58), Vol. II.

16 See p. 152, above.

Article 33, para. 2, an enterprise could challenge the validity of a general Decision, and

(b) could this allegation be made after the expiration of the period of one month during which Decisions can be challenged?

The Court answered affirmatively to both these questions, and thereby went a long way beyond the strict reading of Article 33.

To justify this extension of its jurisdiction, the Court referred to Article 36 of the Treaty, which is an Article dealing not with levies, as was the case in issue, but with fines and daily penalty payments and, which was far more relevant, Article 36 expressly relates to a situation where the Court is empowered to act in *pleine juridiction* as distinct from its more limited power of annulment. Article 36 provides:

> . . . The pecuniary sanctions and daily penalty payments imposed by virtue of the provisions of the present Treaty may form the subject of an appeal in *pleine juridiction*.
>
> In support of this appeal, the plaintiffs, under the conditions set out in the first paragraph of Article 33 of the present Treaty, *may rely upon the irregularity of the Decisions and Recommendations which they are accused of having contravened.*

Of this provision, the Court declared:

> There is no occasion to hold this provision of Article 36 to be a special provision applicable only to the case of pecuniary sanctions and daily penalty payments, but as the application of a general principle, of which Article 36 is its application to the special case of an appeal in *pleine juridiction*.[17]

By an application of this general principle, the Court was able to declare:

> . . . when, after the expiration of the time limit set out in the last paragraph of Article 33, a plaintiff is challenging an individual Decision, he may avail himself of the irregularity of the general Decisions and Recommendations upon which that particular individual Decision has been based.[18]

ASSUMPTIONS MADE BY THE COURT

In interpreting the Treaties, the Court has worked from certain assumptions which are of supreme importance as they form the basis of the logical reasoning adopted by the Court.

[17] *Meroni & Co. S.p.A.* v. *The High Authority* (Case 9–56), Vol. II.
[18] *Ibid.* The same general principle will also apply to appeals brought under the provisions of the other two Treaties which are equivalent to Art. 33 of the E.C.S.C. Treaty, namely E.E.C. Treaty, Art. 173 and Euratom Treaty, Art. 146.

SOVEREIGNTY REMAINS WITH THE MEMBER STATES EXCEPT TO THE
EXTENT TO WHICH IT HAS BEEN RENOUNCED

By the E.C.S.C. Treaty, the High Authority was set up to run the coal
and steel industries of the six Member States. In order that it might be
able to do this, the Treaty endowed the High Authority with certain
powers which previously had been exercisable by the Member States
themselves. Questions have inevitably arisen as to the extent of these
powers and the Court has thus had to decide whether it should read the
relevant provisions transferring such power in a restrictive manner or in a
liberal one.

Before determining this, the Court has been careful to draw attention
to the fact that the E.C.S.C. Treaty creates only a very partial integration
of the Member States. Thus, it has declared:

> The Treaty does not subject to action by the High Authority those
> sectors of the economy of Member States which do not fall within
> the Community sphere.
>
> The provisions of the Treaty, for example, exclude from the Com-
> munity sphere the activities of distributive enterprises which fall outside
> the terms of Article 80 [19] and, more generally, all economic activity
> which has not been included by the Treaty within the Community
> sphere.
>
> Article 2 confirms this interpretation by declaring that the Com-
> munity " shall be charged with accomplishing tasks conferred upon it
> in harmony with the general economy of Member States. . . ."
>
> Article 26 of the Treaty [20] sets out that the Treaty has not removed
> the responsibility for their general political economy from Member
> States when it charges the Council with ". . . the actions of the High
> Authority and those of the Governments which are responsible for the
> general economic policy of their countries."
>
> These provisions clearly bring to light the partial nature of the
> integration achieved by the Treaty; the Governments of the Member
> States remaining responsible for all the sectors of their political economy
> which the Treaty has not expressly placed in the Community sector.[21]

[19] Art. 80 provides:
    " The term ' enterprise ' shall, for the purposes of the present Treaty, mean
    any enterprise engaged in production in the field of coal and steel within the
    territories mentioned in the first paragraph of Article 79; and in addition, as regards
    Articles 65 and 66, and the information required for their implementation and
    appeals based upon them, any enterprise or organisation regularly engaged in
    distribution other than sale to domestic consumers or to craft industries."
[20] Art. 26 provides:
    " The Council shall carry out its duties in the cases provided for and in the
    manner laid down by this Treaty, with a view in particular to harmonising the
    actions of the High Authority and those of the Governments which are responsible
    for the general economic policy of their countries."
[21] *De Gazamenlijke Steenkolenmijen in Limburg* v. *The High Authority* (Case 30–59).
    The Court continued:
    " In effect, the integration achieved by the Treaty is only partial and, by
    reason of the powers retained by Member States, the coal and steel enterprises

However, within that Community sector, the powers of legislation are possessed solely by the Community institutions and no longer by the Member States. Thus, for example, Article 4 (c) of the Treaty declares that subsidies or assistance granted by States are prohibited [22] whereas other articles allow the High Authority to grant assistance to enterprises.[23] On this the Court has declared:

> This distinction highlights the wish of the Treaty to reserve to the Community institutions, and to remove from States, the ability within the Community to grant subsidies or assistance or to impose . . . financial burdens in any form whatsoever.
> The very tenor of the terms of Article 4 underlines the exclusive character of the Community jurisdiction within the Community.[24]

Because certain matters remain within the jurisdiction of the Member States,[25] and other matters fall solely within the competence of the Community, there is naturally the borderline between the two. In interpreting Articles of the Treaty where it is not clear whether the Member States retain jurisdiction or whether they have lost it to the Community, the Court had adopted an interpretation in favour of the Member States.

This may be illustrated by its interpretation of an Article dealing with transport. By this Article [26] it is provided that:

> The rates, prices and tariff provisions of all kinds applied to the transport of coal and steel within each Member State and between Member States *shall be published or brought to the knowledge of the High Authority.*

Under this Article, in 1958, the High Authority wrote to the Italian Government and gave it an alternative of various methods by which it

existing within their respective territories remain subject to their legislation and to the various regulations, the terms of which may well be to the advantage or to the disadvantage of the coal or steel industry of a Member State with respect to similar industries falling under the jurisdiction of other Member States or other industries of the same State.
This situation, although it may run counter to the general aim of the Treaty, is the necessary and proper consequence of the partial character of the integration produced by the Treaty."

[22] Art. 4 provides:
" The following practices are hereby abolished and prohibited within the Community, as incompatible with the common market for coal and steel, under the conditions laid down in the present Treaty:
. . . .
(c) subsidies or assistance granted by States or special financial burdens imposed by them in any form whatsoever."

[23] *E.g.,* Art. 55, para. 2, Art. 58, para. 2, and Convention, Art. 11.

[24] *De Gazamenlijke Steenkolenmijen in Limburg* v. *The High Authority* (Case 30–59).

[25] The Court has declared:
" By the terms of Article 68 (para. 1) [the Member States] remain in full control of their wages and social benefits.
Clearly this is also true as concerns large sectors of their economic policy "— *ibid.*

[26] Art. 70, para. 3.

was required to publish or bring to the knowledge of the High Authority the rates and prices being applied by Italian hauliers. The Italian Government, however, refused to adopt any of the methods proposed, but declared that the Italian Ambassador in Luxembourg would keep in touch with the High Authority every month. The High Authority replied by passing a Decision [27] setting out that the Italian Government was in breach of one of the obligations incumbent upon it by virtue of the Treaty. In an action for the annulment of this Decision,[28] the Court held:

> The basic problem raised by the appeal for annulment of Decision 18–59 is . . . what are the regulatory powers in respect of transport which the High Authority can claim by Article 70, paragraph 3. . . .
> In effect, although it is true that, by virtue of a general principle, applied by Article 70 in regard to transport, the control of discriminations and punitive action with respect to them is entrusted to the High Authority; nevertheless it cannot be deduced from this principle that the High Authority has been granted a power of decision relating to an anticipatory control by means of prescribing the manner of the publication of price lists or prices.
> Its competence is by way of an exception *and is conditional upon a renunciation by Member States, which in this instance the Treaty does not contain, either expressly or by implication.*[29]

THE POWERS OF THE COMMUNITY INSTITUTIONS MUST BE SUFFICIENTLY WIDE TO BE EFFECTIVE

The basic assumption that State sovereignty has not been surrendered to a greater extent than has been expressly or impliedly set out in the Treaty, has in practice come up against another assumption, namely that the institutions established by the Treaties were intended to be endowed with powers which were sufficiently wide for them to carry out their tasks. On several occasions this assumption has led the Court to extend the express powers granted to the High Authority, and perhaps the clearest example of this occurred when the Court was considering the High Authority's powers of inspection.

The plaintiffs in the case in question [30] were a mixed enterprise, one section producing steel and the other piping to be used mainly in connection with hydro-electric works. When certain inspectors from the High Authority wished to examine the plaintiffs' books, they were presented with all those relating to steel production but the plaintiffs withheld all their documents concerning the production of piping on the grounds that the High Authority possessed no powers to investigate the

---

[27] Decision 18–59, see Vol. II.
[28] *Italian Government* v. *The High Authority* (Case 20–59), Vol. II.
[29] *Ibid.* Vol. II.
[30] *Acciaieria e Tubificio di Brescia* v. *The High Authority* (Case 31–59), Vol. II.

books of an enterprise, or one section of an enterprise, engaged in manufacturing goods not referred to in the E.C.S.C. Treaty.[31] Such investigation, they contended, would clearly be *ultra vires*. The Court, however, rejected this contention on the ground that only by having power to inspect the non-steel sections of the plaintiffs' enterprise could it effectively complete its control of the steel section. The Court declared:

> The High Authority's exercise of the right of verification must, in principle, be confined to the activities of enterprises within the sphere of the production of coal and steel.
> Thus, in so far as the administrative organisation, and in particular the accounting, of enterprises is based on a clear division between those sectors of production which are subject to the E.C.S.C. Treaty and other sectors of production, the High Authority, in principle, must not extend its verification beyond the coal and steel sectors.
> On the other hand, the High Authority is empowered to satisfy itself whether such a division exists in fact, and whether the partitioning has not deliberately been incorrectly produced or so produced by mistake. For these purposes it may claim the right to inspect the whole administration.
> Moreover, even if the partitioning is found to be correct, the High Authority must possess the power to complete its inquiries by also inspecting the part concerned with the production which is not subject to the Treaty, with a view to inquiring whether there exists any overlapping between the two parts of the accounting which might reveal a violation of the Treaty.[32]

A further clash between the doctrine of effectiveness and that of State sovereignty occurred in relation to matters in Belgium when the Court had to interpret a provision by which the High Authority was empowered to set up a subsidy system designed to bring the price of Belgian coal down to the level of prices in the common market generally. The provision in question then declared that price lists fixed in accordance with the specified principles " shall not be changed " without the High Authority's agreement.[33] The question arose, therefore, of whether this

---

[31] Art. 81, para 1, provides: " The terms ' coal ' and ' steel ' are defined in Annex I to the present Treaty."

[33] Convention containing the Transitional Provisions, Art. 26 (a), provides: enunciated by the Court in the following manner:
> " It is permissible, without involving a wide reading, to allow a rule of interpretation that is generally admitted as much in international law as in municipal law, by which the norms established by an international Treaty or by a law, imply those norms without which the former would not make sense or would not permit of a reasonable and useful application "—*Fédération Charbonnière de Belgique* v. *The High Authority* (Case 8–55) (Final Judgment), Vol. II.

[33] Convention containing the Transitional Provisions, Art. 26 (a), provides:
> " The equalisation system is intended from the beginning of the transitional period:
> (a) to make it possible to bring the price of Belgian coal as close as possible to its price in the Common Market generally, so as to reduce Belgian coal

provision, in addition to giving the High Authority power to allow or to prevent coal prices being charged after they had been fixed, also gave it power to fix these prices in the first place.

The plaintiffs quite naturally claimed that because before the Treaty came into force enterprises had been able to fix their own prices, their power to do so must continue after that date unless there was an express provision in the Treaty bringing that power to an end. The Court, however, rejected this claim, and went on to rule that the power to fix prices belonged to the High Authority by virtue of the assumption that its powers must be effective. The Court declared:

> Only direct intervention of the High Authority is of a nature to guarantee the immediate realisation of the lowering of prices which must of necessity accompany [the subsidy system].[34]

Because the principle of effectiveness necessitated that the High Authority should possess the power to fix coal prices for Belgian enterprises, it followed that, even without any express surrender of Belgian sovereignty in the matter, the enterprises concerned had lost their previous power.

ENTERPRISES CAN TAKE NO PART IN LEGAL ACTIONS RELATING TO STATE AFFAIRS

In recent years, the Court has given two important decisions which, however, substantially limit the right of appeal of enterprises, and associations.

In effect, the Court has declared that actions under Article 37 of the E.C.S.C. Treaty[35] which relates to economic disturbances within a Member State, and Article 88[36] which relates to the machinery for dealing with a breach of the Treaty of a Member State, can be brought only by the Member States, and, furthermore, enterprises and associations cannot intervene in those actions in so far as they relate to State affairs. Concerning Article 37, the Court declared:

> It is clear from the text of the first paragraph of Article 37 that the right to bring a matter to the attention of the High Auhority belongs exclusively to the State where the disturbances have occurred or are likely to occur.
> Indeed, only the Member State concerned is in a position to assess whether its economic situation demands the application of Article 37.

prices to a level near that of the costs of production foreseeable at the end of the transitional period. Price lists fixed in accordance with the principles shall not be changed without the High Authority's agreement."

[34] *Fédération Charbonnière de Belgique* v. *The High Authority* (Case 8–55) (Final Judgment), Vol. II.
[35] See p. 199, above.
[36] See p. 249, above.

It is clear that an appeal against the express or implied Decision refusing to recognise that disturbances have occurred *can be brought only by the Member State concerned* as it also possesses the right to bring the matter to the attention of the High Authority and it alone, therefore, can establish an interest justifying its appeal.[37]

Apart from bringing an appeal itself, an enterprise cannot ever allege that a particular Decision is likely to cause fundamental and persistent disturbances and therefore that it is void for violation of the Treaty. This has been declared in the following terms:

The plaintiffs contend that the Decision being challenged is of a kind to cause fundamental and persistent disturbances in the French economy. . . .
This contention must be rejected because the existence of such disturbances, in view of their general effect in relation to the national economy, may be invoked only by the interested State and in accordance with the procedure set out in Article 37.[38]

Further, in relation to an intervention by an enterprise in an action brought under Article 88, the Court has declared:

That intervention . . . can have as its object only the mere interpretation of the Treaty, excluding any examination directed at the question of the fixing of a time limit which the High Authority might grant to the State to provide for the fulfilment of its obligations, or even the methods of execution of a possible coercive Decision of the High Authority against that State, because in these various cases the very nature of these acts, which take effect at the level of the relations between the States, which are public powers, and the High Authority, which is a Community organ, preclude the intervention of private persons: thus, discussion of these questions must occur solely between the principal parties.[39]

THE E.E.C. TREATY CONFERS DIRECT RIGHTS UPON INDIVIDUALS WHICH MUNICIPAL COURTS MUST PROTECT

In an important judgment in 1963 [40] the Court held that where in the E.E.C. Treaty it is declared that:

Member States shall refrain from introducing, as between themselves, any new customs duties on imports or exports or any charges having equivalent effect, and from increasing those which they already levy on their trade with each other,[41]

---

[37] *Niederrheinische Bergwerks-Aktiengesellschaft, Unternehmensverband des Aachener Steinkohlenbergbaus* v. *The High Authority* (Joint Cases 2–60 and 3–60).

[38] *Compagnie des Hauts Fourneaux et Fonderies de Givors and others* v. *The High Authority* (Joint Cases 27 and 29–58), Vol. II.

[39] *Netherlands Government* v. *The High Authority* (Case 25–59), Vol. II.

[40] *N.V. Algemene Transport- en Expeditie Onderneming Van Gend en Loos* v. *Nederlandse Tariefcommissie* [1963] C.M.L.R. 105. For a note on this case, see Samkalden, I., in *Common Market Law Review* (1963), p. 88.

[41] Art. 12.

this provision confers a right upon individuals to bring a case in a municipal court requiring that court to hold as void within municipal law any new customs duties which violated this provision. In other words, the Court rejected the view urged upon it by the Advocate General, that the E.E.C. Treaty was an agreement between Member States imposing duties merely upon those States. The E.E.C. Treaty, it declared, conferred a right on an individual that its own home State should not violate the Treaty.

The Court's decision on this point is of sufficient importance to be set out in full.

> The first question posed by the *Tariefcommissie* is whether Article 12 of the Treaty has an immediate effect on internal law, in that nationals of the Member States could, on the basis of the Article, enforce rights which the national court should protect.
>
> To know whether the provisions of an international treaty have such an effect it is necessary to look at its spirit, its economic aspect, and the terms used.
>
> The purpose of the E.E.C. Treaty—to create a common market, the functioning of which directly affects the citizens of the Community—implies that this Treaty is more than an agreement creating only mutual obligations between the contracting parties. This interpretation is confirmed both by the preamble to the Treaty which, in addition to governments, affects individuals. The creation of organs institutionalising certain sovereign rights, the exercise of which affects both Member States and citizens is a particular example. In addition, the nationals of the States, united into the Community, are required to collaborate in the functioning of that Community, by means of the European Parliament and the Economic and Social Council. Furthermore, the role of the Court of Justice in the framework of Article 177,[42] the aim of which is to ensure uniformity of interpretation of the Treaty by national courts, confirms that the States recognised in Community law have an authority capable of being invoked by their nationals before those courts. We must conclude from this that the Community constitutes a new legal order in international law, for whose benefit the States have limited their sovereign rights, albeit within limited fields, and the subjects of which comprise not only the Member States, but also their nationals. Community law, therefore, apart from legislation by the Member States, not only imposes obligations on individuals but also confers on them legal rights. These latter arise not only when an explicit grant is made by the Treaty, but also through obligations imposed, in a clearly defined manner, by the Treaty on individuals as well as on Member States of the Community institutions.
>
> The text of Article 12 sets out a clear and unconditional prohibition, which is not a duty to act but a duty not to act. This duty is imposed without any power in the States to subordinate its application to a positive act of internal law. The prohibition is perfectly suited by its

[42] See p. 303, above.

nature to produce direct effects in the legal relations between the Member States and their citizens.

The carrying out of Article 12 does not require legislative intervention by the States. The fact that the Article designates the Member States as subject to the duty to abstain does not imply that their nationals may not be the beneficiaries of the duty.

The fact that the Treaty, in the aforementioned Articles allows the Commission and the Member States to bring before the Court a State which has not carried out its obligations, does not imply that individuals may not invoke these obligations, in appropriate cases, before a national court; and likewise, the fact that the Treaty puts at the disposal of the Commission means to ensure respect for the duties imposed on those subject to it does not exclude the possibility of invoking violation of these obligations in litigation between individuals before national courts. To limit the sanctions against violation of Article 12 by Member States merely to the procedures laid down in Articles 169 [43] and 170 [44] would remove all direct judicial protection of the individual rights of their nationals. Reliance on these Articles would risk being ineffective if it had to be exercised after the enforcement of a national decision which misinterpreted the requirements of the Treaty. The vigilance of individuals interested in protecting their rights creates an effective control additional to that entrusted by Articles 169 and 170 to the diligence of the Commission and the Member States.

For these reasons, according to the spirit, the economic aspect and the terms of the Treaty, Article 12 should be interpreted in such a sense as to produce direct effect and to create individual rights which internal courts should protect.[45]

This judgment, it is suggested, is unique and, together with the Court's other assumptions and interpretations, clearly points to the way in which the Court's case law will develop.

[43] See p. 274, above.
[44] See p. 277, above.
[45] [1963] C.M.L.R. at pp. 129–131.

CHAPTER
8

THE CONSTITUTIONS OF THE COMMUNITIES

THE EUROPEAN COAL AND STEEL COMMUNITY

THE AIMS OF THE COMMUNITY

The aims of the E.C.S.C. Treaty in relation to coal and steel are twofold. First, the Treaty is to prevent the Member States from interfering with normal competition in the production and sale of these materials and, secondly, it was to create special institutions which were given positive duties of promoting the development of the coal and steel industries of the Member States, not as national but as European undertakings.

To achieve this, Member States were forbidden by the Treaty to impose any import or export duties upon coal and steel, or to impose any charges which would have an equivalent effect, and were prevented from imposing any quantitative restrictions upon the movement of coal and steel.[1] Further, subsidies and State assistance and special financial burdens imposed by the State in any form whatsoever were declared to be illegal.[2]

Many of the other prohibitions contained in the Treaty are not imposed upon the States themselves but directly regulate the contractual power of enterprises within those States. Thus, all restrictive practices, a term which is not defined, are forbidden if they tend towards a sharing or exploitation of markets,[3] and so also are all measures or practices which discriminate between any producers, buyers or consumers, especially in such matters as prices, delivery terms or transport rates, or which in other ways hamper the purchaser in the free choice of his supplier.[4]

These measures on their own, of course, would have led to some anaemic form of *laissez-faire*, but this was very far from the intention of the Treaty. The Community itself is given specific duties which in many cases must involve direct interference.

The Community is to ensure that the common market is regularly supplied, but in doing this it must take into consideration the needs of

---

[1] E.C.S.C. Treaty, Art. 4 (a).
[2] Art. 4 (b).
[3] Art. 4 (d).
[4] Art. 4 (b).

those countries outside the Community [5]: it is to ensure also that all consumers who are in comparable situations within the common market have an equal access to the sources of production,[6] and that conditions are maintained which will encourage enterprises to expand and improve their productive capacity, and the Community is itself to promote regular expansion and modernisation.[7]

Together with this, the Community is to try and ensure that the prices charged by enterprises are the lowest ones possible which are compatible with good business practices.[8] It is also to foster the development of " international trade," [9] which in this context clearly means trade between the Community and non-Member States. This is based, therefore, on the assumption that trade between, say, France and Germany is no longer " international trade."

Finally, one may note that the Community is required to promote the improvement of the living and working conditions of the labour force in the industries for which it is responsible,[10] and this provision has been assumed by the Community to be wide enough to enable it to provide houses for employees in the coal and steel industries.[11]

The duties thus imposed upon the Community may perhaps best be summed up in the words of Article 2 of the Treaty which sets out that:

> The European Coal and Steel Community shall be charged with the duty of contributing to economic expansion, the growth of employment and a rising standard of living in Member States, in harmony with the general economy of Member States and through the creation of a common market . . .
>
> The Community shall progressively establish conditions which will themselves ensure the most rational distribution of production at the highest possible level of productivity, while safeguarding continuity of employment and avoiding the creation of fundamental and persistent disturbances in the economies of Member States.

---

5 Art. 3 (a).

6 Art. 3 (b).

7 Art. 3 (d) and (g).

8 Art. 3 (c). The danger is foreseen that an enforced lowering of the price of one product may merely encourage enterprises to raise prices of other products and thus achieve little or nothing—*ibid.*

9 Art. 3 (f).

10 Art. 3 (e).

11 To accomplish its mission, the Community by Art. 5, para. 2, of the E.C.S.C. Treaty shall:

" Inform and facilitate the action of the parties concerned, by gathering information, organising consultation, and defining general objectives;

Place means of financing schemes at the disposal of enterprises for their investments and participate in the expenses of re-adaptation;

Ensure the establishment, maintenance and observance of normal competitive conditions and only interfere directly with production or the operation of the market when circumstances make it imperative to do so."

The Community itself is declared to be a legal person and, in its international relationships, it is to enjoy the legal capacity necessary to exercise its functions and to achieve its purposes.[12] Further, within each of the Member States, the Community is to enjoy the most extensive legal capacity granted to other legal persons within that State.[13] It is expressly declared to be able to acquire and transfer moveable and immoveable property and to sue and be sued in its own name.[14] In its transactions the Community is to be represented by its institutions acting within the sphere of their own competence.[15]

THE INSTITUTIONS OF THE COMMUNITY

THE HIGH AUTHORITY

The High Authority is the executive organ of the Community, and its members, in effect, constitute the Board of Directors of the coal and steel industries. There are required to be nine members [16] who are all to be nationals of the Member States but no State is to have more than two members on the High Authority.[17]

The election of eight of the nine members is to be made by the Governments of the Member States, who, in default of a unanimous agreement, may act upon a five-sixths majority.[18] However, the dissentient State is granted an absolute right of veto of four candidates, and a further right of veto, subject to an appeal to the Court by the other States alleging that the right of veto has been abused.[19] The

---

[12] Art. 6, paras. 1 and 2. This provision raises the whole question of personality in International Law. It has been held by the International Court of Justice in the case concerning Reparation for Injuries suffered in the Service of the United Nations (*I.C.J. Reports*, 1949, p. 179) that the nations signing the United Nations Charter thereby brought into existence an entity possessing sufficient personality to enforce certain rights and duties in International Law. In the present case, six signatory States to a Treaty are similarly seeking to bring into existence an international person.

[13] Art. 6, para. 3.

[14] *Ibid.*

[15] Art. 6, para. 4. It was presumably under the provisions of this paragraph that the High Authority and not the Community as such signed the Agreement of Association with Great Britain.

[16] Art. 9, para. 1. The number, however, may be reduced by a unanimous decision of the Council of Ministers—*ibid.*

[17] Art. 9, para. 3, provides:
" The High Authority may not include more than two members having the nationality of the same State."
For an institution composed of nine members drawn from only six States, it is suggested that this is not the happiest of phraseology.

[18] Art. 10, para. 5. The election of the first eight members in 1952 was to be by unanimous consent—Art. 10, para. 1.

[19] Art. 10, para. 11. For this appeal, see p. 110, above.

ninth member is selected by these eight members and requires only five of their votes.[20]

One-third of the members of the High Authority are to be renewed every two years [21] : the election of members at these two-yearly intervals being made on alternative occasions by the Governments and by the remaining members of the High Authority.[22]

Members are to be independent and are not to solicit or accept instructions from any Government or from any organisation [23] : during their term of office, and for a period of three years afterwards, they are forbidden to have any business or professional activities, either paid or unpaid, and are to have no direct or indirect interest in any business related to coal or steel.[24] At the end of their period of office they are eligible for re-election.[25]

The High Authority possesses no power to enter the industrial realm itself, and is limited to directing and controlling existing enterprises, as well as the activities of the Member States themselves in matters relating to coal and steel. This control is exercised in one of three ways: first, the High Authority may pass Decisions which are binding in every respect [26] : secondly, it may make Recommendations, which are binding as respects the objectives which they specify, while they leave the means of obtaining those objectives to the parties concerned [27] : thirdly, the Treaty states that the High Authority may issue Opinions, which are in no way binding.[28] Whichever of these three means the High Authority adopts, it must set out the reasons which justify its action and it is to refer to any advice which it is required to obtain before taking action.[29]

THE CONSULTATIVE COMMITTEE

The High Authority is assisted by a Consultative Committee which is attached to it. The Committee consists of not less than thirty and not

---

[20] Art. 10, para. 1.
[21] Art. 10, para. 6.
[22] Art. 10, para. 8. Further provisions cover the election of members who die or retire or who are removed by the Court under Art. 12, para. 2—see p. 110, above.
[23] Art. 9, para. 5.
[24] Art. 9, para. 7.
[25] Art. 9, para. 2.
[26] Art. 14, para. 2. Decisions are either general or individual in character. For a definition by the Court of what amounts to a Decision, see the general discussion, p. 117, above.
[27] Art. 14, para. 3. Recommendations are either general or individual in character. For the effects of this distinction, see p. 157, above. If the High Authority is empowered to take a Decision, it may instead merely make a Recommendation—para. 5.
[28] Art. 14, para. 4. The High Authority also, on occasions, proceeds by means of *Arrêtés*, a procedure which is not referred to in the Treaty.
[29] Art. 15, para. 1.

more than fifty-one members, with equal numbers of producers, workers, consumers and merchants.[30]

The Council of Ministers designates representative organisations among which it distributes the seats to be filled.[31] These organisations then submit a list of candidates for appointment, the list containing twice as many candidates as there are seats to be filled[32]: the selection from these lists is then made by the Council.[33] The method of appointing the representatives of the consumers and merchants is not set out in the Treaty, but in practice it is done by direct appointment usually from members of existing organisations.

The members thus appointed serve for a period of two years and are not to be bound by any mandate or instruction from the organisations which proposed them as candidates.[34]

The High Authority is empowered to consult this Committee on any matters which it thinks fit[35]: it is also required to keep the Committee informed upon its general objectives and programmes concerning such matters as the development of markets, price trends, modernisation, re-employment and the improvement of conditions of the labour force,[36] as well as the broad lines of its action concerning investment and of its action to prevent price-fixing agreements and monopolies.[37] Other matters, such as the imposing of production quotas and the authorising of certain State subsidies must be referred to the Committee for their consideration and report.[38] The High Authority, however, is in no way bound by the opinion of this Committee.

THE COUNCIL OF MINISTERS

The Council of Ministers consists of one member of the Government of each of the Member States who is appointed by that State.[39] The

---

[30] Art. 18, para. 1.
[31] Art. 18, para. 3.
[32] *Ibid.*
[33] Art. 18, para. 2.
[34] Art. 18, para. 4.
[35] Art. 19, para. 1.
[36] Art. 19, para. 2, and Art. 46.
[37] Art. 19, para. 2, and Arts. 54, 65 and 66.
[38] Arts. 58 and 67. The other matters that must be referred to the Consultative Committee are: the authorisation of financial arrangements common to several enterprises —Art. 53; the financing of research projects—Art. 55; the re-employment of workers made redundant by new processes or equipment—Art. 56; the taking of action to meet a manifest crisis within the Community—Art. 59; the dealing with unfair competitive practices—Art. 60; the fixing of certain maximum and minimum prices— Art. 61; the establishment of compensation schemes for unproductive mines—Art. 62; the dealing with abnormally low wages paid by enterprises—Art. 68; the taking of Decisions or Recommendations not expressly authorised by the Treaty—Art. 95.
[39] Art. 27, para. 1.

main purpose of the Council is declared to be " to harmonise the actions of the High Authority and those of the Governments which are responsible for the general economic policy of their countries."[40] In order to assist in doing this, the High Authority is required to exchange information with the Council, and to consult with it,[41] and the Council may request the High Authority to examine any proposals and measures which the Council consider as appropriate or necessary for the realisation of the aims of the Treaty.[42]

Although the above provisions might lead one to regard the Council as being merely a means of liaison between the High Authority and the Member States, this is, in fact, far from the case. The Council of Ministers have themselves many executive powers and on some occasions can even overrule proposals of the High Authority.

To take a few examples: the Council by a unanimous vote may require the High Authority during a period of manifest crisis within the Community to establish a system of quotas specifying the amount that may be produced.[43] During such a crisis, the Council, on the basis of proposals made by the High Authority and in consultation with it, is required to establish consumption priorities and to determine the allocation of the coal and steel resources of the Community to the various industries.[44] The Council may subsequently terminate such a system of allocation.[45] Again, the export duties upon coal and steel being exported to countries outside the Community may be fixed by the Council,[46] and the Council determines the conditions under which other States are allowed to accede to the Treaty.[47]

---

[40] Art. 26, para. 1.
[41] Art. 26, para. 2.
[42] Art. 26, para. 3.
[43] Art. 58, section 1, para. 2.
[44] Art. 59, section 2, para. 1.
[45] Art. 59, section 6, para. 2.
[46] Art. 72, para. 1.
[47] Art. 98. The other executive functions of the Council consist of: increasing the number of members of the High Authority—Art. 9, para. 2; appointing the Consultative Committee—Art. 18, paras. 2, 3 and 6; determining salaries—Art. 29; terminating production quotas—Art. 58, section 3; deciding whether action to deal with a serious shortage of coal or steel shall be dealt with by the High Authority—Art. 59, section 1, para. 1; recognising the existence of such a shortage—Art. 59, para. 1.2; deciding upon restrictions of exports to third countries—Art. 59, para. 5; objecting to the High Authority terminating the system of allocating resources in short supply—Art. 59, para. 6.1; inviting the High Authority to fix maximum and minimum prices—Art. 61, para. 3; making additions to the meaning of the terms " coal " and " steel "—Art. 81; making proposals to modify the powers of the High Authority—Art. 95; approving a Conference to amend the terms of the Treaty—Art. 96. Other minor powers are contained in the Statute on the Court of Justice—Arts. 4, 5, 13, 15 and 16, and in the Convention containing the Transitional Provisions—Art. 8, para. 4.

In addition to this, the High Authority on certain occasions is required to obtain the consent of the Council before certain action may be taken. The relevant provisions mainly concern such matters as imposing levies upon the production of coal and steel [48]; the granting or guaranteeing of loans to enterprises [49]; allocating funds for research work [50] and the imposing of sanctions upon a State which has broken one of the provisions of the Treaty.[51]

Finally, the Treaty specifies several occasions on which the High Authority is required to consult with the Council of Ministers, but is not in any way bound to accept their views. Thus, before the High Authority can decide what measures it is to take to meet a situation that is likely to cause fundamental and persistent disturbances in the economy of a Member State, it must consult the Council.[52] It must also do so before it decides how the assessment and collection of levies upon coal and steel is to be made,[53] and again before it grants compensation to the most costly mine in a particular basin, so as to prevent the possibility of a rise in the price of coal which is sold by the other mines.[54] It is also provided that the High Authority is to consult the Council before making Recommendations about any abnormally low wages.[55]

---

[48] Art. 50, para. 2.
[49] Art. 54, para. 2.
[50] Art. 55, section 2.
[51] Art. 88, para. 3. Other occasions when the Council is to be consulted are: before certain financial arrangements are instituted—Art. 53, para. 1 (b); before facilitating the financing of industries not connected with coal or steel—Art. 56, section 1, para. 1 (b); before making non-reimbursable assistance dependent upon similar assistance being given by the State concerned—Art. 56, section 2, para. 1 (a); before establishing a system of production quotas—Art. 58, section 1, para. 1; before imposing restrictions upon exports to third countries—Art. 59; before determining the conditions upon which concentrations do not require prior authorisation—Art. 66, sections 1, 3 and 4; before defining the size of enterprises in respect of which Recommendations concerning their low wages do not require prior consultation with the Council—Art. 68, section 5, para. 1; before issuing Recommendations to Governments concerning imposing certain quantitative restrictions upon imports—Art. 74, para. 2; before making a Decision or Recommendation, required to fulfil the aims of the Treaty, where these are not expressly authorised by the Treaty—Art. 95, para. 1. Certain other minor occasions are contained in the Convention containing the Transitional Provisions—Art. 23, paras. 3, 6 and 8; Art. 26, para. 4.1; and Art. 29, paras. 1 and 3.
[52] Art. 37, para. 2.
[53] Art. 50, para. 2.
[54] Art. 62, para. 1.
[55] Art. 68, para. 5.1. The other occasions when consultation is required are: before requiring a Government to guarantee a loan—Art. 51, para. 1.3; before authorising certain financial measures common to several enterprises—Art. 53, para. 1 (a); before making Recommendations concerning illegal financial measures—Art. 53, para. 2; before terminating a system of allocation of materials—Art. 59, para. 6; before defining what amounts to unfair competitive practices and discriminations—Art. 60, para. 1.2; before fixing maximum and minimum prices—Art. 61, para. 1; before determining what constitutes control of an enterprise so as to bring about a concentration—Art. 66, para. 1; before requiring certain information relating to concentrations—Art. 66, para. 4; before taking measures to prevent serious disequilibrium being caused by certain increases in the differentials in the costs of production—Art. 67,

Where, as in the cases just mentioned, the High Authority is merely required to consult the Council, the Council need not proceed to a vote, it is enough if there is an expression of opinion, the minutes of the session being forwarded to the High Authority.[56]

If the actual agreement of the Council is required, this agreement can be shown in one of two ways: either by at least four out of the six members voting in favour, provided that this four includes either the member representing France or the one representing Germany.[57] Alternatively, if when the matter first comes before the Council, the voting on the matter is three-three, regardless of who votes in favour, and the High Authority re-considers the matter and again submits it to the Council, the Council's agreement can then be given by a vote of two to four—so that by normal procedure the vote would be lost—if the two States voting in favour are France and Germany.[58]

Where the unanimous consent of the Council is required, this can only be given by all the six States voting in favour.[59]

THE PARLIAMENTARY ASSEMBLY

The members of the High Authority are jointly responsible to a Parliamentary Assembly.[60] It was originally provided in the Treaty that this Assembly was to be composed of seventy-eight members.[61] This provision has now, however, been annulled and replaced by a provision contained in the Convention relating to certain Institutions common to the European Communities [62] by which the number of members is

para. 2.1; before making Recommendations to a State which has reduced these differentials—Art. 67, para. 3; before making Recommendations concerning import and export licences—Art. 73, para. 2. Other subsidiary occasions are contained in the Convention containing the Transitional Provisions, Art. 2, para. 4; Art. 11; Art. 18, para. 13; Art. 26, para. 1.2; and Art. 29, paras. 1 (a) and 2.

56 Art. 28, para. 2.

57 Art. 28, para. 3. These States are not mentioned by name in the Treaty, para. 3 merely requiring the inclusion of the vote of the representative of " one of the States which produces at least twenty per cent. of the total value of coal and steel produced in the Community." If production figures were to alter, therefore, other powers could join the Big Two.

58 Art. 28, para. 3. See also footnote 57 above.

59 Art. 28, para. 4. A normal majority decision of the Council requires the voting to be four to two with one of the States producing at least twenty per cent. of the total value of coal and steel produced in the Community voting with the four—Art. 28, para. 5.

60 Art. 24. At the constituent session of the Common Assembly of the European Economic Community on March 19-21, 1958, that Assembly decided to adopt the name of " European Parliamentary Assembly "—*First General Report on the Articles of the E.E.C.*, p. 18.

61 These seventy-eight members were made up of 18 each from France, Germany and Italy, 10 from both Belgium and the Netherlands and four from Luxembourg—Art. 21, section 2.

62 Art. 21, section 2, as re-enacted by the Convention, Section I, Art. 2.2.

increased to 142.[63]   These members are required to be appointed
annually from among their own numbers by the Parliaments of each
of the Member States.[64]   Under the original procedure set out in the
E.C.S.C. Treaty, any one of the Member States was empowered to elect
its members by direct universal suffrage,[65] whereas it is now provided
that the Assembly itself is to draw up proposals for elections by direct
universal suffrage in accordance with a uniform procedure in all
Member States.[66]

The Assembly, which is now common to the three Communities, is
required under each of the three Treaties to meet annually.[67]   As,
however, the dates for these meetings vary according to the provisions
of the Treaties, the net effect is that the Assembly must meet at least twice
a year.[68]

The main power possessed by the Assembly in relation to the Coal
and Steel Community, apart from its power to ask questions of the
High Authority and its power to approve the Budget, is to pass a motion
of censure upon the Annual Report of that Authority.   To be passed,
such a motion must be voted for by two-thirds of the votes cast at the
meeting, provided also that these two-thirds also represent a majority
of the total membership.[69]   If the motion of censure is carried, the
High Authority must resign in a body [70] and a new membership is
required to be elected by the machinery that has been set out above.[71]

THE COURT OF JUSTICE

Over these institutions, and ensuring the respect of law in the interpretation and application of the Treaty, stands the Court of Justice.[72]

---

63 This number is made up of 36 each from France, Germany and Italy, 14 from
Belgium and the Netherlands, and 6 from Luxembourg.   Thus, while the representation of France, Germany and Italy has doubled, that of the other countries has
only been increased by about fifty per cent.
64 Art. 21, section 1, as amended.
65 Art. 21, section 1.
66 Art. 21, section 3, as amended.   The Council of Ministers by a unanimous vote is
to determine the provisions which it is to recommend to Member States for adoption
in accordance with their respective constitutional rules—Art. 21, section 4, as amended.
There appears to be no obligation upon the Council to recommend the proposals
drawn up by the Assembly.   No time limit is fixed for compliance with these
provisions.
67 E.C.S.C. Treaty, Art. 22, para. 1; E.E.C. Treaty, Art. 139, para. 1; Euratom Treaty,
Art. 109, para. 1.
68 On the second Tuesday in May under the E.C.S.C. Treaty; on the third Tuesday in
October under the E.E.C. Treaty; and on the same day under the Euratom Treaty.
69 Art. 24, para. 3.   This provision means that if there are ninety-six or less members
present, the motion will be passed if seventy-two members vote in favour.   If there
are more than ninety-six members present, two out of every three additional members
must vote in favour for the motion to be passed.
70 Art. 24, para. 3.   71 See p. 109, above.
72 Art. 31.

THE EUROPEAN ECONOMIC COMMUNITY

The Treaty establishing the European Economic Community came into force on 1 January 1958. The Economic Community, which follows up the work of economic integration begun in the European Coal and Steel Community and which has as its complement, in the establishment of Euratom, a special effort in the field of atomic energy, is introducing a new form of economic organisation in Europe. Creation of the Community opens up new prospects of progress and prosperity for the peoples of the six States, now more closely bound together, and offers all Europe the picture of a union that is becoming more and more necessary, together with the means of attaining it.[73]

The concept of extending the association which had been formed by the six States signing the European Coal and Steel Community Treaty was first approved at the Conference of Venice on May 29, 1956. Within a year, the Economic Community Treaty, which runs to nearly 250 Articles, and four Annexes, together with fourteen Protocols and two Conventions had been drawn up and they were all signed in Rome on March 25, 1957. The Treaty came into effect on January 1, 1958 and the common market was instituted on January 1, 1959.

THE AIMS OF THE COMMUNITY

The E.C.S.C. Treaty sought to achieve free trade in coal and steel and to prevent any State interfering to support its own industries or to hamper those of other Member States. The Economic Community seeks to extend this freedom to all other products, including agricultural products, and also to free the movement both of workers and of capital, of inter-State transport and of the professional classes.

The common market is not to be established immediately, however, but in three stages, each stage being of four years.[74] The primary task in order to achieve the common market, as set out in the Treaty, is the elimination of all customs duties between the Member States and the ending of all quantitative restrictions, or quotas, upon the import or export of goods.[75] The States undertake from the date of entry into force of the Treaty to refrain from introducing, as between themselves, any new customs duties on any imports or exports.[76] The process, however, of abolishing all the existing customs duties upon imports is divided into three stages.

[73] The First General Report on the Activities of the European Economic Community, p. 9. The stilted translation is the product of the E.E.C., not of the author.
[74] E.E.C. Treaty, Art. 8.1. These three stages may be extended, but the transitional period may in no circumstances extend beyond fifteen years—Art. 8.6.
[75] Art. 3 (a).
[76] Art. 12.

In the First Stage, three reductions of the duty existing on January 1, 1957 [77] were to be made: the first in January 1959, the second in June 1960 and the third at the end of 1961.[78]

In the Second Stage, three further reductions were to be made: the first in June 1963, the second in December 1964 and the third in December 1965.[79]

The final reductions are to be made in the Third Stage, but the timing of these is to be left to be decided by the Council of Ministers.[80]

It was intended that after the three reductions in the First Stage, the duties upon imports as on January 1, 1957 should have been reduced by at least 25 per cent., and at the end of the Second Stage by at least 50 per cent.,[81] but the Member States undertook to proceed more rapidly with these reductions if the general economic situation allowed.[82]

The removal of customs duties upon exports, however, is required to be far more rapid and was required to have been completed by the end of the First Stage, that is to say by the end of 1961.[83]

Together with the removal of these internal restrictions, the common market is to establish a uniform customs tariff against non-Member States and a common commercial policy towards those States.[84] The basic way in which this common tariff is to be determined is to take the average of the tariffs in force on January 1, 1957, in the four customs territories of the Community.[85] Formidable lists of exceptions to this, however, are attached to the Treaty and in respect of the goods set out in those lists, the duties are to be 3, 10, 15 and 25 per cent.[86]

As with the abolition of import and export duties, so also the imposition of this common tariff is to be gradual. Where the tariff actually being applied on January 1, 1957, was not more than 15 per cent. above or below the amount of the common tariff as required by the

---

[77] Art. 14.1.
[78] Art. 14.2 (a).
[79] Art. 14.2 (b). These dates assumed that the First and Second Stages would not be extended; if they had been, these dates would have been postponed by the periods of those extensions.
[80] Art. 14.2 (c).
[81] Art. 14.6, para. 1.
[82] Art. 15.2, para. 1. The situation did so allow.
[83] Art. 16. See also footnote 79, above.
[84] Art. 3 (b).
[85] Art. 19.1 and 2, para. 1. The four customs territories are France, Germany, Italy and the Benelux, which has a unified tariff.
[86] Art. 19.3. These lists deal with such wonderful things as: mechanisms and keyboards (containing not less than 85 notes) for pianos; natural sponges, unmarked; organo-therapeutic glands or other organs, dried, whether or not powdered; acyclic alcohols and their hologenated, sulphated, nitrated or nitrosated derivatives (excluding butyl and isobutyl alcohols); roughly shaped blocks of wood or root for smoking pipes, and crayfish, crabs, oysters and prunes, dried.

Treaty, or as set out in the lists of goods attached to the Treaty, then this tariff was to be adjusted to the required amount by the end of the First Stage, that is to say, by the end of 1961.[87]

With all other tariffs, the difference between the existing [88] tariff and the required tariff was to be reduced by 30 per cent. by 1961, and by a further 30 per cent. by 1965; the common tariff being finally adopted by not later than the end of the twelve to fifteen year transitional period.[89] States are, however, free to align their tariffs at an earlier date if they so desire.[90]

The third of the prerequisites to the establishment of the common market is the abolition, as between Member States, of obstacles to the free movement of persons.[91] This is required to have been achieved by not later than the end of the transitional period.[92]

This free movement of persons is stated to involve the abolition of any discrimination based upon the nationality of the workers of the Member States in matters of employment, pay and working conditions.[93] It includes, on the other hand, the right, subject only to limitations that are justified by reasons of public order, public safety and public health,[94] to accept any offers of employment and, for this purpose, the right to move about freely within the Community. It includes also the right of an employee to stay in the Member State during the period of his employment and also to remain there after it has ceased.[95]

Further, the Council of Ministers is to ensure close collaboration between the labour administrations of the Member States,[96] and progressively to abolish not only any administrative procedures and practices which hinder this free movement of persons, but also to abolish all time limits which are required to be satisfied before a person may take up employment.[97]

On the question of insurance, the Council is to require the Member States to see that insurance policies become transferable from one State

---

[87] Art. 23.1 (a). See also note 79, p. 415, above.
[88] Art. 23.1 (b) and (c). See also note 82, p. 415, above.
[89] Art. 23.3.
[90] Art. 24.
[91] Art. 3 (c).
[92] Art. 48.1.
[93] Art. 48.2.
[94] During the transitional period the Member States' legislative and administrative provisions which deal with public order, public safety and public health are to be co-ordinated—Art. 56.2.
[95] Art. 48.3. The Protocol concerning the Grand Duchy of Luxembourg, however, requires the Commission, when laying down Regulations to ensure this free movement, to take due account, in so far as the Grand Duchy is concerned, of the particular demographic situation of that country—Art. 2.
[96] Art. 49 (a).
[97] Art. 49 (b).

The European Economic Community

to another and that a qualifying period for entitlement to benefit is not lost by taking employment in another Member State.[98]

Finally, Member States are to encourage the exchange of young workers within the Community.[99]

Apart from freeing the exchange of goods, the Treaty also makes arrangements for freeing the supply of services. The term " services " is defined as being services normally supplied for remuneration, and is declared to include activities of an industrial and commercial nature as well as artisan activities and activities of the liberal professions.[1] No detailed rules for the freeing of the supply of these services are set out in the Treaty and it is left to the Council, acting in this case by means of a unanimous vote, to lay down before the end of the First Stage,[2] a general programme for the ending of restrictions upon them.[3] In this general programme, priority is to be given to the freeing of those services which directly affect the costs of production, or whose liberalisation will assist the exchange of goods.[4]

By further provisions of the Treaty, the Member States have agreed that during the Transitional Period they will progressively abolish restrictions upon the movement of capital belonging to persons resident within the Member States, as well as end any discriminatory treatment based upon the nationality or place of residence of the parties concerned or upon the place in which such capital is invested.[5] The means by which these restrictions and discriminations are to be abolished are not set out in the Treaty—it being left to the Council to issue the necessary Directives.[6] However, even before these Directives have been issued, the Member States have undertaken to grant in " the most liberal manner possible " such exchange authorisations as are still necessary and to apply their internal regulations regarding the movement of capital in a non-discriminatory manner.[7] The Member States have further undertaken not to introduce any new restrictions upon the movement of capital.[8]

[98] Art. 51. [99] Art. 50.
[1] Art. 60, para. 1.
[2] As to this Stage, see p. 415, above. [3] Art. 63.1.
[4] Art. 63.3. Services in respect of transport are governed by Arts. 74–84, which deal with transport. Banking and insurance services are to be dealt with as part of the programme for freeing the movement of capital—Art. 61.2, as to which see immediately below. [5] Art. 67.1.
[6] Art. 69. In the First and Second Stages, the Council is to act by means of a unanimous vote, and in the Third State by means of a qualified majority. As to which see page 426, below. [7] Art. 68.1 and 2.
[8] Art. 71, para. 1. Where the movement of capital causes disturbances in the capital market of any Member State, the Commission may authorise it to take protective measures, or the State itself, in an urgent case or in order to retain secrecy, may take measures itself. If it does so, however, it may subsequently be required by the Commission to modify or rescind them—Art. 73.1 and 2.

v.—14   417

Related to the movement of capital is the right to set up businesses within other Member States. To ensure this right, the States have agreed that during the Transitional Period they will progressively abolish all restrictions upon the setting up of agencies, branches or subsidiaries.[9] Once these restrictions have been abolished there will be freedom to engage in and carry on non-wage-earning activities as well as freedom to set up and manage enterprises by merely complying with the same conditions as are applicable to nationals of the country in question.[10]

The task of determining the exact way in which existing restrictions are to be abolished has been left to the Council, which is to be assisted by the Commission, the Economic and Social Committee, and the General Assembly.[11]

The common market, set up by the Treaty, is declared to extend to agriculture and trade in agricultural products.[12] These products are listed in an Annex to the Treaty and include such objects as live animals, birds' eggs, natural honey, cut flowers, margarine, cocoa beans, wine of fresh grapes, natural cork and true hemp.[13]

In order to achieve this common market, the Member States have undertaken to set up a common organisation of agricultural markets either by adopting common rules concerning agriculture, or by means of a compulsory co-ordination of the various national market organisations that already exist, or by setting up a special European market organisation.[14] Whichever form of organisation is adopted for a particular product, that organisation is to regulate such matters as prices, subsidies, arrangements for stock-piling and carry-forward and the stabilising of imports and exports.[15]

However, until these organisations have been set up, the Member States are to conclude long-term agreements or contracts between themselves in order to guarantee to producers a sale for their products.[16] These agreements are to deal with quantities and prices and the latter are, if possible, to be approximated to those paid to home producers in the importing States.[17]

[9] Art. 52, para. 1.
[10] Art. 52, para. 2.
[11] Art. 54.1, para. 1.
[12] Art. 38.1. " Agricultural products " are defined as products of the soil, of stock breeding and of fisheries as well as products after the first processing stage which are directly connected with such products—Art. 38.1.
[13] E.E.C. Treaty, Annex II. The Council by a qualified vote may add products to this list.
[14] E.E.C. Treaty, Art. 40.2.
[15] Art. 40.3.
[16] Art. 45.1, para. 1.
[17] Art. 45.2, paras. 1 and 2.

Together with this, the Member States have agreed to adopt a common agricultural policy, having as its aims the increase of agricultural production by developing technical progress, the achievement of a fair standard of living for the agricultural population and the ensuring of stabilised markets, guaranteed supplies and reasonable prices.[18] It is recognised that such a policy may involve occupational training, research and efforts to make country life popular as well as common action to encourage the consumption of certain products.[19]

Matters concerning transport and the adoption of a common transport policy are grouped together in a special Title of the Treaty. This Title declares that any discrimination by a carrier in his transport rates in respect of similar goods conveyed in similar circumstances,[20] where these are based upon the country of origin of the goods or upon their destination, is to be abolished not later than at the end of the Second Stage.[21] Further, any support or protection given by a Member State to any transport enterprise is to be prohibited by the beginning of this Second Stage.[22] Finally, the Council, as soon as it is able, is to lay down common rules that are to be applied to international transport from or to the territory of a Member State, or which crosses the territory of one or more of such States. It is also to lay down conditions for the admission of non-resident carriers to the national transport services within a Member State, and to deal with any other appropriate matters.[23]

At the present time the Treaty applies merely to transport by rail, road and inland waterways,[24] but the Council by a unanimous vote may extend it to air and sea transport as well.[25]

In order to ensure that free trade is achieved, the Treaty has to make all restrictive agreements between enterprises illegal and has to prevent any form of State subsidy which would interfere with the free play of competition. The Treaty, therefore, prohibits and renders null and void [26] any agreements between enterprises which have as their object or result the prevention, restriction or distortion of competition, and the Treaty specifies, in particular, any fixing of purchase or selling prices, any limitation upon production, markets, technical developments or investment, any market sharing or sharing of the sources of supply, any

---

[18] Art. 39.1.
[19] Art. 41.
[20] Art. 79.1 speaks of " the *same* goods conveyed in the same circumstances." This is clearly an error.
[21] Art. 79.1. As to the timing of the Second Stage, see p. 415, above.
[22] Art. 80.1.
[23] Art. 75.1. See Regulation 11 of 1962.
[24] Art. 48.1.
[25] Art. 84.2.
[26] Art. 84.2.

imposition of unequal terms to similar transactions and any subjection of the conclusion of a contract to the acceptance of additional supplies, which have no connection with the subject of the contract.[27]

The dumping of goods—that is to say the exporting of subsidised goods and their subsequent sale at an artificially low price—is very largely prevented by a boomerang clause which provides that the dumping State cannot prevent the re-entry of these goods into its own country at their artificial price.[28] Apart from this general provision, however, particular cases of dumping are to be dealt with *ad hoc* by the Commission.[29]

To prevent State subsidies, any aid granted by a Member State, or granted by means of State resources which distorts or threatens to distort competition by favouring certain enterprises or certain productions are declared to be incompatible with the common market to the extent to which they adversely affect trade between Member States.[30]

A further aim of the Community is to co-ordinate the economic policies of the Member States and to remedy deficits in their balance of payments.[31] To achieve this, the States are to institute a collaboration between the competent services of their administrative departments and between their Central Banks.[32] Also they are to set up a Monetary Committee with consultative status, which is given the task of reviewing the monetary and financial status of the Community.[33]

In addition, it is also the aim of the Community to improve the living and working conditions of labour,[34] to ensure equal pay for men and women by the end of the First Stage [35] and, by subsequent Conventions, to ensure the free movement of workers from Colonial territories into the Member States.[36]

---

[27] Art. 85.1. This prohibition, however, does not extend to certain practices which contribute to the improvement of production or distribution of goods, or to the promotion of technical or economic progress where such practices do not impose any restrictions that are not indispensable and do not enable enterprises to eliminate competition in respect of a substantial proportion of the goods concerned—Art. 85.3. Until the Council decided otherwise, the authorities within the Member States themselves were to rule upon the legality of any agreement—Art. 88. On this see Regulation 17 of 1962.

[28] Art. 91.2.

[29] Art. 91.1.

[30] Art. 92.1. Certain aids, however, are expressly authorised, such as those intended to remedy damage caused by natural calamities, or those to promote the economic development of regions where the standard of living is abnormally low or where there exists serious under-employment—Art. 93.2 and 3.

[31] Art. 3 (g).

[32] Art. 105.1.

[33] Art. 105.2. As to this Committee, see below, p. 435.

[34] Art. 117, para. 1.

[35] Art. 119, para. 1. As to the duration of the First Stage, see p. 415, above.

[36] Art. 135.

THE FINANCING OF THE COMMUNITY

A balanced picture of the Economic Community, however, would not be given if mention were not made of the provision for dealing with employees who will be rendered unemployed when their firms are unable to meet the competition of efficient rivals. As the introduction of free trade is only to be gradual over the Transitional Period of twelve to fifteen years, the problem of temporary unemployment and of re-training is not likely to be acute at any one time, but will probably have to be met for a number of years.

EUROPEAN SOCIAL FUND

To meet this problem, the Treaty has established a European Social Fund [36a] which is to be administered by the Commission with the assistance of Government representatives, and representatives of trade unions and employers' associations.[37]

The Fund is to be used, first, to provide occupational re-training where it is impossible to employ the unemployed workers except in a new occupation [38]; secondly to provide re-settlement allowances where unemployed workers have been obliged to change their residence within the Community,[39] and thirdly to keep up to their old level the wages of employees whose employment is temporarily reduced or suspended as a result of the conversion of their enterprise to another production.[40]

EUROPEAN INVESTMENT BANK

Apart from the European Social Fund, the financing of the development of the Community is largely in the hands of the European Investment Bank.[41] This Bank obtains its capital both by calling upon the capital markets of the Community and by receiving from Member States a prescribed amount of capital which is measured in units, each unit

---

[36a] Art. 123.

[37] Art. 124, para. 1. The Treaty does not set out from where the Fund is to be derived, nor how large it is to be.

[38] Art. 125.1 (a) and Art. 125.2, para. 1. This grant from the Fund, however, will only be paid *after* the employee has continued for at least six months in the employment for which he has been re-trained—Art. 125.2, para. 1.

[39] Art. 125.1 (b) and 2. This grant from the Fund is similarly conditional upon the person concerned having been in productive employment for at least six months in his new place of residence—Art. 125.2, para. 2.

[40] Art. 125.1 (b). The grant of this subsidy is conditional upon the worker having been employed in that enterprise for at least six months and upon the Community having approved the plan of conversion—Art. 125.2, para. 3.

[41] For an outline of the constitution of this Bank, see below, p. 429.

representing the value of so many grammes of fine gold.[42]   The Bank is to use this money for granting loans and guarantees, on a non-profit-making basis, to assist projects for the development of less developed regions.[43]   It may also be used for modernising or converting enterprises, where this is required as a result of the setting up of the common market, and where, owing to the size or nature of the task, it could not be financed entirely by the Member States themselves.[44]   Further, the money may be used for projects which are of common interest to several Member States, but which also could not be financed entirely by the Member States concerned.[45]

These loans and guarantees may be made either to the Member States themselves or to public or private enterprises.[46]

THE INSTITUTIONS OF THE COMMUNITY

THE COMMISSION

The Commission in its structure is very similar to the High Authority of the European Coal and Steel Community.   It consists of nine members, who must all be nationals of the Member States, but it is provided that not more than two members are to be of the same nationality.[47]   The members are appointed by the Governments of the Member States by common agreement for a period of four years,[48] but

---

[42] Art. 130, para. 1.   One unit represents the value of 0·88867088 grammes of fine gold—Protocol on the Statute of the European Investment Bank, Art. 4.1, para. 2.   The States' contributions are:—

Germany	300 m. units.
France	300 m. units.
Italy	240 m. units.
Belgium	86·5 m. units.
Netherlands	71·5 m. units.
Luxembourg	2 m. units.—Art. 4.1, para. 1.

Member States were to pay the first 25 per cent. of their portion of the prescribed capital by five equal payments, to be made not later than two months, nine months, 16 months, 23 months and 30 months after the date of entry into force of the Treaty —Jan. 1, 1958—Art. 5.1, para. 1.   The remaining 75 per cent. is to be paid when requested by the Board of Directors of the Bank—Art. 5.2, para. 1.   In addition, States may be required by the Board of Governors of the Bank to grant special loans to the Bank so that it can finance a specific project—Art. 6.1.

[43] Art. 130 (a).

[44] Art. 130 (b).

[45] Art. 130 (c).

[46] Protocol on the Statutes of the European Investment Bank, Art. 18.1 and 4.   As a general rule these loans are only to be for investment projects which are to be carried out within the European territories of Member States, but, by the unanimous approval of the Board of Governors of the Bank, these loans may be for projects to be carried out wholly or partly overseas—Art. 18.1.   Loans and guarantees of the Bank are never to exceed 250 per cent. of the amount of the capital subscribed—Art. 18.5.

[47] Art. 157, para. 1.

[48] Art. 158, paras. 1 and 2.

there is no detailed provision, as there is with the High Authority, for partial renewal of the membership of the Commission at stated intervals —there is merely an obscure reference in Article 159 to " retirement in regular rotation " and death as being means of terminating office. The members of the Commission may also be dismissed by vote of censure passed by the Parliamentary Assembly upon the Annual Report.[49]

The members of the Commission are to be independent, and are not to seek or accept instructions from any Government or other body,[50] and during their term of office they are not to engage in any other paid or unpaid professional activity.[51] Whereas members of the High Authority are forbidden to acquire or hold any interest in any business related to coal or steel during the three years after the end of their period of office, this provision is not repeated in the E.E.C. Treaty, but instead there is the vaguer requirement that members of the Commission are to exercise honesty and discretion as regards the acceptance, after their term of office, of certain functions and advantages [52]—a phrase which is not defined.

The Treaty requires the Commission to ensure the application of the provisions of the Treaty,[53] and this it is to do by adopting Regulations, which are of general application and binding in every respect,[54] or by adopting Directives which bind any Member State to which they are addressed as to the object to be achieved, but they leave the form and manner of achieving it to the domestic agencies of the State concerned.[55] Further, the Commission may take a Decision which is binding in every respect upon the party concerned,[56] or it may issue a Recommendation or give an Opinion, neither of which is to have any binding force.[57]

Although the Treaty distinguishes between Regulations and Decisions, it is in no way clear what this distinction is intended to be. Both Regulations and Decisions are declared to be " binding in every respect," but because only Regulations are declared to have a general application, it might have been assumed that Decisions were intended to be more

---

49 See below, p. 428.
50 Art. 157.2, para. 2.
51 Art. 157.2, para. 2.
52 Art. 157.2, para. 3. A breach of this undertaking may entail a forfeiture of the member's pension or its equivalent—*ibid.*
53 Art. 155.
54 Art. 189, para. 2. These Regulations may be equated with general Decisions under the E.C.S.C. Treaty, see further, p. 289, above.
55 Art. 189, para. 3. These Directives may be equated with Recommendations to Member States under the E.C.S.C. Treaty, see further, p. 289, above.
56 Art. 189, para. 4.
57 Art. 189, para. 5.

limited in their scope.[58]   However, this assumption does not appear
to be justified when one finds that the Commission, by taking a Decision
can, for example, require a State to abolish an import quota[59] or to
abolish measures concerning the movement of capital.[60]

However, whether the Commission proceeds by Regulations, Directives or by Decisions these are required to be supported by reasons
and must refer to any proposals or opinions that were considered.[61]

Under the E.C.S.C. Treaty, the High Authority controls and directs
the Community.   It is natural to assume therefore that the Commission
is to control and direct the Economic Community.   This, however, is
not entirely so.   On nearly every important matter one finds the Commission being merely empowered to make proposals to the Council of
Ministers for them to take the necessary action.   Thus, the Commission
proposes measures concerning such matters as the prohibition of
discrimination on the grounds of nationality,[62] the reduction of duties
on imports,[63] the modification of duties,[64] and the ensuring of minimum
prices in agriculture.[65]   It makes proposals for the free movement of
workers,[66] for providing social security for migrant workers,[67] and for
co-ordinating the legislative and administrative provisions of the Member
States with respect to public order, public safety and public health.[68]
In fact there are only nine matters in the whole Treaty on which the
Commission can itself take any final action.   These include the laying
down of the conditions under which an employee may continue to live in
another Member State after he has been employed there,[69] the fixing of

[58] A comparison with the wording of the E.C.S.C. Treaty, Art. 33, para. 2, and the
E.E.C. Treaty, Art. 173, para. 2, would lead one at first sight to assume that Regulations were the equivalent of General Decisions of the High Authority, and Decisions
to individual Decisions of that Authority, but see further p. 288, above.

[59] Art. 33, para. 4. This quota was also required to be imposed by means of a Decision
—Art. 33, para. 2.2.

[60] Art. 73, para. 2.   There appears to be nothing limited in the Decisions of the Commission concerning discrimination against carriers—Art. 79, para. 4—or Decisions
addressed to Member States concerning monopolies—Art. 90, para. 3. For a further
discussion of this, see p. 288, above.

[61] Art 190. This provision may be compared with E.C.S.C. Treaty, Art. 15.

[62] Art. 7, para. 2.

[63] Art. 14, para. 2 (1).

[64] Art. 28.

[65] Art. 44, para. 3.

[66] Art. 49, para. 1.

[67] Art. 51, para. 1.

[68] Art. 56.2. Other matters on which proposals are made by the Commission concern
the freeing of capital—Art. 69; non-discrimination by transport carriers—Art. 79,
para. 3; authorisation of certain excise dutes—Art. 94, para. 1, and amending or
extending the Treaty—Arts. 235 and 236.

[69] Art. 48, para. 3 (d). This is the only Regulation that the Commission is empowered
to make.

the time for the abolition of all charges having an effect equivalent to that of customs duties upon imports,[70] and the abolition of all measures existing at the time of the coming into force of the Treaty which have an effect equivalent to that of quotas,[71] and the substitution of other temporary quotas during the Transitional Period.[72] The Commission, by means of Directives or Decisions, is to ensure that price-fixing, market-sharing and dumping, etc., are not practised or allowed by Member States.[73]

Nevertheless, although from this it appears that the Commission has none of the strength and importance of the High Authority, it is laid down that:

> When, pursuant to this Treaty, the Council acts on a proposal of the Commission, it shall, where the amendment of such proposal is involved, act only by means of a unanimous vote.[74]

Thus, the proposal may be rejected *in toto* by its failing to obtain the necessary qualified majority,[75] but it takes a unanimous vote to amend it in any way.[76]

THE COUNCIL OF MINISTERS

In the same manner as under the E.C.S.C. Treaty, the Council of the Economic Community consists of one member of the Government of each of the Member States who is appointed by that State.[77] The main purposes of the Council are " to ensure the co-ordination of the general economic policies of the Member States and to exercise a power of decision." [78]

The manner of voting in the Council differs quite widely. The basic method is by means of a majority vote of the members, every vote having the same value.[79] As the wording of the Treaty specifies a

---

70 Art. 13, para. 2.
71 Art. 33.7.
72 Art. 33.2, para. 2, and Art. 33.4.
73 Art. 90.3. The other matters are: the fixing of the means for setting the prices of certain agricultural products—Art. 45, para. 4; the abolition of restrictions upon the movement of capital—Art. 73.2; the taking of Decisions to ensure non-discrimination by carriers—Art. 79.4, and the taking of Decisions concerning subsidies granted to transport employed by enterprises—Art. 80.2.
74 Art. 149, para. 1.
75 See p. 426, below.
76 The Treaty does not specify whether, if the Council rejects a proposal of the Commission, it can proceed with its own proposals or whether the matter is to be referred back to the Commission for further proposals, the latter, however, has become the accepted practice.
77 Art. 146, para. 1.
78 Art. 145. This does not mean, of course, that the Council is limited to taking Decisions as defined in Art. 189, para. 4, for it can also issue Regulations and Directives—Art. 189, para. 1.
79 Art. 148.1.

majority vote " of the members " and not merely " of those present " it appears that at least four of the six members must vote in favour of such a motion either in person or by proxy in order for it to be passed.

In certain cases the Treaty provides that for measures to be passed they must receive a qualified majority. In such cases the votes of the members of the Council are weighted—Germany, France, and Italy being given four votes each, Belgium and the Netherlands two votes each and Luxembourg one vote. A total of twelve votes in favour, out of a possible seventeen, is required for the adoption of any measure which has been proposed to the Council by the Commission.[80] These measures include, for example, ones to prohibit any discriminations on the grounds of nationality,[81] or to add additional agricultural products to those already benefiting from the Common Market,[82] or to require a State to increase the freedom of movement of capital.[83]

Where, however, the matter being decided is not required to have been made the subject of a previous proposal of the Commission, so that the Council is acting on its own initiative, as for example, when the Council is granting mutual assistance to Member States,[84] the voting is weighted as set out above, but for a motion to be passed there is required not only twelve votes in favour, as before, but these twelve must be cast by at least four members.[85]

When the Council is voting upon the section of the budget of the Community which relates to the European Social Fund, the votes of the members are weighted [86]:

Belgium	...	... 8	Italy ...	...	... 20
Germany	...	... 32	Luxembourg		... 1
France	...	... 32	Netherlands ...	...	7

[80] Art. 148, para. 2. The only exception to this is where the Council, after the expiration of the Transitional Period, is voting upon a proposal submitted to it by the Commission dealing with the means of determining minimum prices of agricultural products. Here the Council must cast 13 affirmative votes and not 12—Art. 46.6.
[81] Art. 7, para. 2.
[82] Art. 38.3.
[83] Art. 70.2, para. 2. For other matters which the Commission may propose to the Council, see p. 424, above. The effect of this weighted voting is that the big three can force the adoption of a proposal put forward by the Commission, but no one of the big three acting alone can prevent its adoption.
[84] Art. 108.2, para. 1.
[85] Art. 148, para. 2. The effect of this is that for such a motion to be passed it must be voted for by the big three and one other State, or by two of the big three plus Belgium and The Netherlands.
[86] Art. 203.5. The rest of the Budget requires a qualified vote of the Council, see this page, above.

The Treaty declares that for the adoption of any conclusions a "majority of at least 67 votes shall be required." It is suggested, however, that this does not mean a majority of at least 67 votes but rather that 67 votes are required to be cast in favour, which implies a minimum majority of 34.[87]

Finally, in certain matters the Council is required to be unanimous, except that the abstention of a member either present or represented by the proxy of another member,[88] does not prevent the voting being unanimous. Matters requiring a unanimous vote are the more important ones, such as Directives for the approbation of legislative and administrative provisions in force in the Member States,[89] Recommendations to Member States for direct election of the members of the Parliamentary Assembly,[90] and the admission of other European States to the Community.[91]

The Council, in the same way as the Commission, is required to carry out its duties by means of adopting Regulations and Directives, by making Decisions and formulating Recommendations and Opinions.[92] However, by the Treaty there are only four occasions when the Council is empowered to issue Regulations. These concern the achieving of a common agricultural policy by the Member States,[93] the setting out of the measures necessary to ensure the free movement of workers,[94] the prevention of restrictive trade practices and cartels,[95] and the authorisation of State aids in certain circumstances.[96]

There is envisaged in the Treaty, however, a much wider use of Directives than of Regulations because Directives leave to the State concerned a choice as to the means by which it is to comply with the requirements set out. Certain Directives, those dealing with the common agricultural policy, with the movement of workers and with price-fixing, etc., may be adopted by the Council instead of Regulations.[97] However, it is strange that in the E.E.C. Treaty there is no provision similar to that in the E.C.S.C. Treaty enabling a Directive to be issued in any case where a Regulation could have been issued. Such a provision would

---

[87] In practice, the smallest effective affirmative vote is 71, which, if there are any votes against, gives possible majorities of 70, 62 and 42.
[88] Proxy voting is allowed by Art. 150.
[89] Art. 100, para. 1.
[90] Art. 138.3, para. 2.
[91] Art. 237, para. 1.
[92] Art. 189, para. 1. For the distinction between these various types of procedure, see p. 423, above.
[93] Art. 43.2, para. 3.
[94] Art. 49, para. 1.
[95] Art. 87.1.
[96] Art. 94.
[97] Art. 43.2, para. 3; Art. 49, para. 1, and Art. 87.1.

have enabled the Council on those matters to decide whether to leave the details of execution to the Member States or not.[98]

Apart from the subjects already mentioned, the main topics upon which Directives can be issued are the reduction of customs duties during the Transitional Period,[99] the co-ordination of States' laws relating to foreign nationals, public order, public safety and public health,[1] the abolition of restrictions upon the movement of capital [2] and the appropriation of the legislative and administrative provisions of the Member States.[3]

There are few matters upon which the Council is specifically empowered to take a Decision, but those that are mentioned are of a certain importance. Thus, it is by a Decision of the Council that the Second and Third Stages of the Transitional Period may be extended or curtailed,[4] that the provisions of the Treaty can be extended to sea and air transport,[5] and that a State can be allowed to continue in force any measure it has taken to meet a crisis in its balance of payments.[6]

THE PARLIAMENTARY ASSEMBLY

The constitution of the Assembly, which is common to the three Communities, has been set out above.[7] As originally conceived under the E.C.S.C. Treaty, the Assembly's functions were virtually limited to approving or rejecting the Annual Report of the High Authority. Under the E.E.C. Treaty it has wider powers and its control over the Commission is greater than that over the High Authority, for whereas it can only require the resignation of the members of the High Authority if a motion of censure is passed on the Annual Report,[8] it can require the resignation of the members of the Commission if a motion of censure is passed at any time.[9]

---

[98] E.C.S.C. Treaty, Art. 14, para. 5, provides:
   " When the High Authority is empowered to take a Decision, it may limit itself to formulating a Recommendation."
   For the meaning of " Decision " and " Recommendation " in the E.C.S.C. Treaty, see p. 117, above.

[99] Art. 14.5.

[1] Art. 56.2.

[2] Art. 69.

[3] Art. 100, para. 1. Other topics concern the mutual recognition of diplomas—Art. 57, para. 1; conditions for the granting of mutual assistance—Art. 108.2, and the harmonising of measures to aid exports to non-Member States—Art. 112.1.

[4] Art. 8.5.

[5] Art. 84.2.

[6] Art. 109.3.   [7] See p. 412, above.

[8] Art. 24, para. 2.

[9] Art. 144, para. 1. In practice, of course the most obvious time for such a motion of censure to be passed is when the Assembly meets to consider the Annual Report; however, the Assembly can be convened for an extraordinary session under Art. 139, para. 2.

The only proposals that the Assembly can itself initiate are those for the election of its members by direct universal suffrage [10] and for amendments to the draft budget of the Community.[11] However, there are many matters upon which the Council or the Commission are unable to act until they have consulted the Common Assembly. Such matters include the drafting of rules for the prohibition of discriminations,[12] the drawing up of a common agricultural policy,[13] the drafting of rules to govern inter-State transport,[14] and of provisions to prevent price-fixing and market-sharing [15] and to approximate the Member States' legislative and administrative provisions,[16] and for altering and amending the Treaty.[17] Finally, the Assembly can challenge before the Court any failure of the Commission or of the Council to carry out their duties under the Treaty.[18]

THE EUROPEAN INVESTMENT BANK

Each of the Member States of the Community is also a member of the European Investment Bank,[19] which is to be run by a Board of Governors, a Board of Directors and a Management Committee.[20]

The Board of Governors

The Board of Governors is to consist of ministers appointed by the Member States,[21] who are to lay down general Directives concerning the credit policy of the Bank.[22] Apart from this, the Board of Governors is to appoint the members of the Board of Directors,[23] and to remove

---

[10] Art. 138.3, as amended by the Convention relating to certain Institutions common to the European Communities, Art. 2.2.

[11] Art. 203.3, para. 3.

[12] Art. 7, para. 2.

[13] Art. 43.2, para. 3.

[14] Art. 75.1.

[15] Art. 87.1, para. 1.

[16] Art. 100, para. 2.

[17] Arts. 235 and 236, para. 2. Other matters on which the Assembly has to be consulted are: the timing of the reductions of customs duties—Art. 14.7; the abolition of restrictions upon freedom of establishment—Art. 54.1; the co-ordination of legislative and administrative provisions dealing with public order, public safety and public health—Art. 56.2; the abolition of restrictions upon the free supply of services —Art. 63.1, para. 1; the withdrawal of re-training and resettlement allowances, etc.— Art. 126; the conditions for the provision for the grant of money from the European Social Fund—Art. 127; the recommendation of provisions by which the Member States' contributions to the European Social Fund can be derived from a common customs tariff—Art. 201, para. 3; the conclusion of agreements between the Community and non-Member States—Art. 228.1, para. 1; and the conclusion of agreements with other legal entities so as to create an association—Art. 238, para. 2.

[18] Art. 175, para. 1. See further, p. 297, above.

[19] Protocol on the Statute of the European Investment Bank, Art. 3.

[20] Art. 8.

[21] Art. 9.1.

[22] Art. 9.2, para. 1.   [23] Art. 9.3 (c) and Art. 11.2, para. 2.

them if they are no longer competent or no longer independent.[24] Similarly, the Board of Governors is to appoint and may remove the members of the Management Committee.[25] The Board is required to approve the Annual Balance Sheet and Profit and Loss Account and the Annual Report of the Board of Directors.[26] If this Annual Report is not accepted the entire Board of Directors is required to resign.[27]

The consideration of all requests for loans or for guarantees and the subsequent financing of them is the province of the Board of Directors, but on occasions the Board of Governors have a part to play. Thus, they may request Member States to advance to the Bank special interest-bearing loans [28] in order to finance specific projects,[29] or the Board may decide to increase the subscribed capital of the Bank.[30] Further, loans to States or enterprises for investment projects to be carried out either wholly or in part outside the European territories of those States require the sanction of the Board of Governors.[31] If a State fails to fulfil any of its obligations to the Bank, and in particular if it fails to provide the capital of the Bank or to advance the special loans demanded from it, the Board of Governors may suspend all outstanding loans and guarantees which have been given to that State or to any of its nationals.[32] Finally, the Board of Governors can at any time decide to suspend the activities of the Bank and in such a case they are further required to appoint the liquidators.[33]

---

[24] Art. 9.3 (c) and Art. 11.3, para. 1. Directors may also presumably be removed if they carry on activities which, under Art. 11.5, have been declared incompatible with their office.

[25] Art. 9.3 (c) and Art. 13.1 and 2.

[26] Art. 9.3 (c) and (f).

[27] Art. 11.3, para. 2.

[28] The rate of interest is to be 4 per cent. per year unless the Board of Governors, after considering the rates of interest of the capital markets, decides on a different rate—Art. 6.4.

[29] Art. 6.1. Such loans are to be paid by the Member States in proportion to their subscription to the total capital of the Bank—Art. 6.5.

[30] Art. 4.3.

[31] Art. 18.1, para. 2.

[32] Art. 26, para. 1.

[33] Art. 9.4 and Art. 17, paras. 1 and 2. The other Decisions which may be taken by the Board of Governors concern: the repayment of the special State loans to the Bank at a date prior to that specified in the loan agreement—Art. 6.3; action to deal with the situation where the par value of the currencies of the Member States is uniformly proportionately adjusted—Art. 7.4; the fixing of the remuneration of the members of the Board of Directors and of the Management Committee and the decision upon what matters are incompatible with this membership—Art. 11.5 and Art. 13.5; the appointment of the auditors of the accounts—Art. 14.1; the interpreting or supplementing of its own Directives—Art. 17, and the approval of the rules of procedure of the Bank—Art. 9.3 (h).

The normal method by which the Board of Governors reach their Decisions is by means of a majority vote of its members.[34] Thus, the taking of general Directives, the appointment of the Board of Directors and the Management Committee, the passing of the Balance Sheet and the Directors' Annual Report all require a majority vote.

Other matters, however, expressly require a qualified majority. These include, for example, the taking of the Decision that Member States are to make a special loan to the Bank to finance a specific project,[35] the suspending of all outstanding loans and guarantees to a Member State or its nationals following upon the failure of that State to fulfil its obligations to the Bank,[36] and the removal from office of one of the Directors [37] or the dismissal of the Management Committee.[38]

Where a qualified majority is required, the votes of the members of the Board of Governors are weighted—Germany, France and Italy each have four votes, Belgium and the Netherlands two each and Luxembourg one vote. For a motion to be passed it appears from the Treaty that four members are required to have voted in favour and to have cast at least twelve votes.[39]

Finally, in four matters the Board are permitted to act only by means of a unanimous vote. These matters are an increase of the subscribed capital of the Bank,[40] the authorising of loans to be used for projects outside Europe,[41] the suspension and liquidation of the Bank,[42] and, for some reason, the far less momentous matter of what activities are to be declared to be incompatible with the position of a director of the Bank or his deputy.[43]

---

[34] Art. 10. As there are six members of the Bank—Art. 3—this provision must mean that four affirmative votes are required for a motion to be passed, regardless of the number of Governors present at the particular meeting. There is no provision for voting by proxy.

[35] Art. 6.1.

[36] Art. 26, para. 1.

[37] Art. 11.3.

[38] Art. 13.2. The approval of the repayment to a Member State of a special loan at a date prior to that set out in the loan agreement also requires a qualified majority—Art. 6.3.

[39] Art. 10 and E.E.C. Treaty, Art. 148.2. Art. 10 of the Protocol makes the voting of the Board of Directors subject to Art. 148 of the Treaty, which deals with the qualified voting of the Council of Ministers. The Article there sets out two different majorities that are needed for motions to be passed by the Council: first, where the motion requires the previous proposal of the Council, and secondly, where it does not. It is presumed that it is the second of these majorities which is to be applied to the voting of the Board of Governors.

[40] Art. 4.3.

[41] Art. 18.1, para. 2.

[42] Art. 9.4.

[43] Art. 11.5. The Decision upon which activities are to be declared to be incompatible with the position of a member of the Management Committee requires merely a simple majority—Art. 13.5.

Although these matters require a unanimous vote, it is provided that the abstention of a member, or presumably of any number of members, provided that there is a quorum, does not prevent the passing of such a motion.[44]

The Board of Directors

The Board of Directors consists of twelve directors and twelve deputy directors.[45] They are appointed for a renewable term of office of five years by the Board of Governors.[46] Three directors and three deputy directors are nominated by Germany, three by France and three by Italy; two are nominated by the Benelux countries acting jointly, and finally one director and one deputy director are nominated by the Commission.[47] As, however, there appears to be no means by which the candidates nominated can be rejected by the Board of Governors, its role appears to be entirely formal.

Each director has one vote,[48] but as directors are only to be persons of indisputable independence,[49] the voting is not necessarily weighted in favour of the big three. Ordinary Decisions of the Board require merely a simple majority of the members of the Board entitled to vote.[50] It is specified in the Statute, however, that, where provided for, a qualified majority is to mean a majority of at least eight votes.[51] The only occasion, however, when a qualified majority is provided for is when the Board of Directors is voting upon the removal from office of a member of the Management Committee.

In one case the Board is allowed to act only by means of a unanimous vote. This is when it seeks to approve a request for a loan or a guarantee which the Management Committee or the Commission has already considered unfavourably.[52] Where any other organ is similarly required to act unanimously, it is provided that abstention is not to prevent this unanimity,[53] but no such provision is included in this present case. It is

44 Art. 10 and E.E.C. Treaty, Art. 148.3.
45 Art. 11.2, para. 1.
46 Art. 11.2, paras. 2 and 3.
47 Art. 11.2, para. 2.
48 Art. 12.1. The deputies possess a vote only when they are replacing a director who is unable to carry out his duty—Art. 11.2, para. 5.
49 Art. 11.2, para. 7.
50 Art. 12.2. It is assumed that " entitled to vote " means " present and entitled to vote."
51 Art. 12.2.
52 Art. 21.5 and 6. Where the Commission have given an unfavourable opinion, the Director appointed by the Commission must abstain from voting—Art. 21.6. Where the Management Committee and the Commission both give an unfavourable opinion, the Board of Directors may not grant such a loan or guarantee—Art. 21.7.
53 For the provision referring to the Council of Ministers, see E.E.C. Treaty, Art. 148.3, and to the Board of Governors, see Protocol on the Statute of the European Investment Bank, Art. 10.

open to argument, therefore, by the maxim *expressio unius est exclusio alterius* that abstention here does prevent unanimity, or alternatively that, by analogy with the case of the Council of Ministers and of the Board of Directors, abstention does not prevent unanimity.

The function of the Board is to exercise exclusive powers of decision in respect of the granting of loans and guarantees,[54] and is to fix the relevant rate of interest. The Board must also supervise the sound administration of the Bank and ensure that it is managed in conformity with the Treaty and the Statute and with the directives laid down by the Board of Governors.[55]

The Board of Directors, that is to say, the twelve directors and the twelve deputy directors, must resign *en bloc* if their Annual Report is not accepted by the Board of Governors.[56] An individual director may be removed by the Board of Governors acting by means of a qualified majority if he no longer fulfils the conditions necessary for the exercise of his functions.[57] Strange to say, however, there are no provisions for the removal of a deputy director.

The Management Committee

The control of the day-to-day running of the Bank is vested in a Management Committee which consists of three persons—a Chairman and two Vice-Chairmen.[58] These three are appointed by the Board of Governors on the proposal of the Board of Directors.[59] As their term of office is for six years, their resignation will not often coincide with that of the Board of Directors, who, unless forced to resign *en bloc*, sit for five years, so that continuity in certain matters is preserved.[60]

The Management Committee are to prepare the Decisions of the Board of Directors, and in particular those relating to the granting of loans and guarantees.[61] Further, the Committee is itself to give an Opinion upon whether these loans and guarantees should be granted, and,

---

[54] Art. 11.1, para. 1. This provision also says that the Board of Directors has exclusive power over the raising of loans. This, however, is incorrect and the provision must be read subject to the terms of Art. 6.1, concerning the raising of loans from Member States, which requires a qualified majority of the Board of Governors.

[55] Art. 11.1, para. 1.

[56] Art. 11.3, para. 2.

[57] Art. 11.3, para. 1. This means where the director has ceased to be a person of indisputable independence and competence and also, presumably, where he has engaged in activities that have been declared incompatible with his office under Art. 11.5.

[58] Art. 13.1 and 3, para. 1.

[59] Art. 13.1.

[60] Art. 13.1 and Art. 11.2, para. 2.

[61] Art. 13.3, para. 2.

as set out above, the Board of Directors can override an unfavourable Opinion of the Management Committee only by its unanimous vote.[62]

The Management Committee are jointly responsible for carrying out the Decisions of the Board of Directors,[63] and the Chairman of the Committee is further responsible for engaging and dismissing the staff of the Bank who are all placed under his authority.[64]

The members of the Committee may be dismissed by a vote of the Board of Governors, passed by a qualified majority, following upon a proposal to that effect passed by the Board of Directors also acting by a qualified majority.[65]

THE ECONOMIC AND SOCIAL COMMITTEE

The E.E.C. Treaty sets up an Economic and Social Committee which is to be a body common to the Economic Community and to Euratom.[66] The Committee is to comprise 101 members appointed by the Council for a period of four years, but members are eligible for re-election.[67] The appointments are to be made from lists submitted by the Member States but each list is to contain twice as many candidates as there are seats allotted to that State's nationals.[68] In making its choice from these candidates, the Council may consult any European organisations which represent sectors controlled by the Community, and the persons appointed are required to represent in particular, producers, agriculturists, transport operators, workers, merchants, artisans, the liberal professions, and the general public.[69]

The Economic and Social Committee is merely a consultative body, but its opinion is to be sought before any of the more important Decisions can be taken. Thus, the Committee is to be consulted before the Council lays down the measures necessary to free the movement of workers,[70] and before the Council lays down a general programme for abolishing restrictions upon setting up enterprises in other Member States.[71] Similarly, it must be consulted before Decisions are taken concerning the

---

[62] Art. 21.5.
[63] Art. 13.3, para. 2.
[64] Art. 13.7. In the choice of staff, due account is to be taken not only of personal ability and professional qualifications but also of the equitable representation of the nationals of Member States—Art. 13.7.
[65] Art. 13.2.
[66] Art. 193, para. 1, and the Convention relating to certain Institutions common to the European Communities, section III, Art. 5.
[67] Art. 144. Of these 101 seats, 24 go to Germany, France and Italy each, 12 to both Belgium and the Netherlands and five to Luxembourg.
[68] Art. 195.1, para. 1.
[69] Art. 195.2 and Art. 193, para. 2.
[70] Art. 49.
[71] Art. 54.1, para. 1.

abolition of restrictions upon the free supply of services,[72] or the making of common rules for international transport,[73] or the prevention of discriminations by carriers on the grounds of nationality [74] or the unifying of legal and administrative provisions of the Member States affecting the common market.[75]

However, although the Committee is required to be consulted on these matters, either the Council or the Commission can specify, in relation to a particular matter, a time limit of not less than ten days within which the Committee is to give its Opinion. If within that time the Opinion has not been given, the Council or Commission may proceed without it.[76]

THE MONETARY COMMITTEE

It is one of the objects of the co-operation established by the Treaty, that the Member States should co-ordinate their economic policies so as to ensure confidence in their respective currencies and an overall balance of payments.[77] In order to assist this co-ordination, the Treaty set up a Monetary Committee with the task of keeping the monetary and financial situation of the Member States under review, as well as watching over the general payments system of the Member States and reporting regularly to the Council and to the Commission.[78] In addition, either the Council or the Commission can request the Monetary Committee to give an Opinion upon any specific matter, and the Monetary Committee of its own volition may formulate such an Opinion and submit it to these two bodies.[79]

In addition to this, the Treaty sets out a number of subjects upon which the Monetary Committee is required to be consulted before action can be taken. Thus, before proposals are drawn up for the ending of restrictions upon the movement of capital, it must have been consulted by the Commission.[80] Similarly, it is to be consulted before the Commission adopts any Recommendations to a Member State

---

[72] Art. 63.1, para. 1.
[73] Art. 75.1.
[74] Art. 79.3, para. 1.
[75] Art. 100, para. 2. The Committee is also to be consulted before the Commission issues any opinion upon such matters as working conditions, social security, industrial hygiene and the law relating to trade unions and collective bargaining—Art. 118, para. 3; before the Council decides certain matters relating to migrant workers— Art. 121; before the European Social Fund can be abolished—Art. 126; and before rules for the application of that fund are drawn up—Arts. 127 and 128.
[76] Art. 198, para. 2.
[77] Arts. 104 and 105.1.
[78] Art. 105.2.
[79] Art. 105.2.
[80] Art. 69.

concerning exchange restrictions.[81] It is to be consulted before the Community takes action to counteract disturbances caused either by movements of capital,[82] or by alterations in the exchange rate of a Member State [83] or where a State is in difficulties with its balance of payments.[84]

The Monetary Committee is composed of fourteen members, two appointed by each of the six Member States and two appointed by the Commission.[85]

THE COURT OF JUSTICE

Over these institutions, and ensuring the respect of law in the interpretation and application of the Treaty, stands the Court of Justice.[86]

THE EUROPEAN ATOMIC ENERGY COMMUNITY

THE AIMS OF THE COMMUNITY

The aims of the Euratom Community as set out in the Euratom Treaty are twofold. First, the Member States are required to establish a common market in nuclear products and to establish a common customs tariff [87] and must abolish all restrictions based on nationality governing access to skilled employment in nuclear energy.[88] Secondly, the Community itself is established, whose duty it is to contribute to the raising of the standard of living in Member States and to assist the speedy establishment and growth of nuclear industries.[89]

In order to fulfil its task, the Community is required to develop nuclear research, to establish uniform safety standards to protect the health of workers and the general public, to assist the creation of the basic facilities necessary to develop nuclear energy, to make certain that nuclear materials are not diverted to purposes for which they were

[81] Art. 71, para. 3.
[82] Art. 73.1, para. 1.
[83] Art. 107.2.
[84] Art. 108.1, para. 2, and Art. 109.3.
[85] Art. 105.2, para. 2. The Treaty does not set out any of the required qualifications of members, but as at present constituted it contains one Minister of Economics, one University Professor, one Director of the European Investment Bank, three Treasury officials, and the rest Governors, etc., of Banks within the Member States. In addition to members of the Committees, alternatives have been elected. These have not Treaty authority.
[86] Art. 164.
[87] Arts. 93 and 94.
[88] Art. 96, para. 1.
[89] Art. 1, para. 2.

not intended and to ensure wide commercial outlets for such material by establishing the free circulation of capital for investment.[90]

THE INSTITUTIONS OF THE COMMUNITY

THE COMMISSION

The Commission consists of five members, each of a different nationality, who are chosen on the grounds of their general competence in nuclear matters and whose independence can be fully guaranteed.[91] Only nationals of the Member States may be appointed.[92] Appointments are made by mutual agreement between the Governments of Member States [93]: the term of office is for four years and is renewable.[94]

The duties of the Commission are to assist in the accomplishment of the aims of the Community, and in order to do this the Commission is made responsible for permitting and facilitating nuclear research in the Member States and for complementing it by carrying out the Community's programme of research and training.[95] To assist this, the Commission is required at regular intervals to publish a list of those sectors of nuclear research which in its opinion have not been the object of sufficient study.[96] It is also to discourage unnecessary duplication in research work.[97] For the purpose of training specialists, the Commission is required to set up training colleges, particularly in the fields of prospecting for minerals, the production of nuclear materials of a high degree of purity, the processing of irradiated fuels and in similar matters including health protection.[98] The Commission is also to establish an institution at University level to carry out the above training.[99]

The next main duty of the Commission is to watch over the enforcement of this Treaty and to ensure the enforcement of the rules laid down by the Council of Ministers.[1] To do this the Commission may send out inspectors who may be armed with warrants to inspect the operating records in which enterprises are required to account for the ores, source material and special fissile material used or produced.[2]

---

[90] Art. 2.
[91] Art. 126, section 1, para. 1. [92] *Ibid.* para. 3.
[93] Art. 127, para. 1.
[94] Art. 127, para. 2.
[95] Art. 4, section 1.
[96] Art. 5, para. 4. [97] Art. 5, para. 3.
[98] Art. 9, section 1, para. 1. The Commission shall determine the details of this training—*ibid.* para. 2.
[99] This university will probably be sited in northern Italy.
[1] Art. 124.
[2] Art. 82, para. 1. If the Commission finds any irregularities, it may issue a Directive to the Member State concerned—Art. 82, para. 2—and can impose sanctions on the persons or enterprises responsible—Art. 83, section 1.

The Commission also acts as a centre through which the results of nuclear research can be pooled,[3] and the Commission is also to assist in enabling competent persons to obtain patent licences so that their work in nuclear matters may continue.[4]

A further duty of the Commission is to make proposals to the Council of Ministers for adoption by that Council. Thus, the Commission proposes the security regulations fixing the various secrecy gradings to be applied to information on nuclear matters [5]; the Commission also makes the necessary proposal for the establishing of emergency stocks of nuclear material [6]; the Commission draws up the necessary proposal upon which the Council of Ministers subsequently issues its Directives concerning the method in which the restrictions upon the movement of skilled employees in the field of nuclear energy can be removed.[7] It is for the Commission to make the necessary proposal for the setting up of joint enterprises,[8] which are international undertakings which possess their own legal personality, and on a proposal of the Commission [9] the Council of Ministers may confer on them powers of compulsory acquisition, exemption from all direct taxes and exemption from certain customs duties.[10]

To carry out its tasks the Commission is empowered to issue Regulations and Directives, to take Decisions and to formulate Recommendations or Opinions.[11] There is, however, no provision in the Treaty

---

[3] Art. 15.
[5] Art. 24, section 1.
[7] Art. 96, para. 2.
[8] Art. 46, section 2, para. 2.
[9] Art. 48, para. 1.

[4] Art. 12.
[6] Art. 72, para. 2.

[10] Art. 48 and Annex 3. The Commission is also empowered to make proposals to the Council concerning the Community's programmes of research and training—Art. 7, para. 1; concerning the functioning of the training at university level—Art. 9, section 2; concerning those persons and enterprises required to communicate their investment projects to the Commission—Art. 41; it may propose a variation of the time limit for the receipt of this information—Art. 42, para. 2; it may propose the level at which prices of ores, etc., may be fixed by the Council—Art. 69, para. 1; the amendment of the provisions of the Treaty concerning the supply of nuclear material, particularly if unforeseen circumstances create a situation of general shortage—Art. 76, para. 1; the Commission is to draw up regulations concerning the keeping and provision of operating records for approval by the Council—Art. 79, para. 3; the Commission makes proposals to the Council concerning the levies necessary for obtaining the Community's funds—Art. 173, para. 2; and the preliminary draft budgets are laid before the Council by the Commission—Art. 177, section 2, para. 2; the Commission may make a proposal concerning the imposition of the duties of the common customs tariff to specified products—Art. 95; and shall make the proposal to the Council on which it may issue its Directive concerning insurance contracts covering nuclear risks—Art. 98.

[11] Art. 161, para. 1. Regulations are binding in every respect and take effect directly in each Member State; Directives are binding as to the result to be achieved but they leave the national authorities the choice of the means of achieving those results; Decisions are binding, but Recommendations and Opinions are not—Art. 161, paras. 2, 3, 4 and 5. *Cf.* p. 423, above.

specifying a matter on which the Commission may issue any Regulations.

It may, however, issue Directives to the Member States on one matter: where the level of radio activity in the air, water, or soil rises appreciably, the Commission is required to issue a Directive to the Member State concerned to take within a period laid down by the Commission all necessary measures to prevent the basic standards from being exceeded.[12] Decisions may be issued on two occasions. By a Decision a producer may be authorised to dispose of his available production outside the Community provided that the terms offered are not more favourable than those he could obtain within the Community,[13] and the sanctions imposed upon persons or enterprises for violation of their obligations *inter alia* not to use nuclear material for improper purposes, are also described as being Decisions.[14]

The Commission may make Recommendations to the Member States on a variety of topics, such as the maximum permissible levels of exposure and contamination,[15] concerning radio activity,[16] concerning the development of prospecting for and the working of mineral deposits [17] with regard to fiscal or mining regulations,[18] concerning inspections to ensure that nuclear material is not used for improper purposes [19] and concerning the means of facilitating the movement of capital intended to finance certain types of production.[20]

On four matters the Commission is empowered to issue Opinions: namely, concerning proposed research programmes,[21] concerning particularly dangerous experiments on the territory of a Member State,[22] concerning the disposal of radio active waste,[23] and upon the development of prospecting and on mining investments within the Member State.[24]

THE COUNCIL OF MINISTERS

The Council of Ministers is composed of representatives of the Member States, and each Government is required to delegate to it one of its

12 Art. 38, para. 2.
13 Art. 59 (b). The use of the term Decision in this connection is somewhat unhappy because it is not seen how an authorisation can be " binding in every respect upon those to whom it is directed."
14 Art. 83, section 2, para. 2. As one of the sanctions referred to is a mere warning, the use of the term " Decision " in relation to this is again an incorrect use, because a warning can hardly be binding in every respect.
15 Art. 33, para. 3.   16 Art. 33, para. 1.
17 Art. 70, para. 2.
18 Art. 71.
19 Art. 83, section 3.
20 Art. 99.   21 Art. 5, para. 1.
22 Art. 34, para. 1.
23 Art. 37, para. 1.
24 Art. 70, para. 3.

ministers.[25] The main task of the Council is, as it were, to continue agreeing those parts of the Treaty which are merely in outline form at the moment. The Council almost invariably acts upon proposals submitted to it by the Commission.[26] It may adopt amendments to those proposals only if it is unanimous,[27] but until the Council has reached a Decision, the Commission may amend its original proposal.[28]

Like the Commission, the Council may issue Regulations and Directives, take Decisions and formulate Recommendations or Opinions.[29] The Treaty declares that the Council is to carry out certain specific tasks, but in respect of many of these it is not stated whether the Council is to act by Regulation or not. Thus, the Council, on the proposal of the Commission, is to adopt security Regulations fixing the various secrecy gradings to be applied to information,[30] and at any time may decide unanimously to de-classify or re-grade such information.[31] Further, the Council is to establish the basic standards of permissible exposure and contamination and the basic principles of the medical supervision of workers.[32] The Council appoints the members and determines the rules of procedure of the Arbitration Committee which the Treaty requires to be set up,[33] and determines the Communities' programmes of research and training for periods of not more than five years.[34]

---

[25] Art. 116, para. 1.

[26] As to these proposals, see p. 438, above. When the Council adopts resolutions based upon a proposal of the Commission, 12 votes are required in favour of the resolution. France, Germany and Italy each possess four votes, Belgium and the Netherlands two, and Luxembourg one—Art. 118, section 2.

[27] Art. 119, para. 1.   [28] Art. 119, para. 2.

[29] Art. 161, para. 1. For the differing effect of these acts, see note 11, p. 438, above.

[30] Art. 24, section 1.   [31] Art. 34, section 2, para. 5.

[32] Art. 31, para. 2, and Art. 30, para. 2.

[33] Art. 18, para. 1. As to this Arbitration Committee, see p. 442, below.

[34] Art. 7, paras. 1 and 2. Further tasks given to the Council are the laying down of criteria of type and size of investment projects which are to be communicated to the Commission—Art. 41—and may vary the time limits specified for this communication—Art. 42, para. 2; the Council lays down the constitutional rules of the Agency which is required to be set up for the buying and selling of ores—Art. 54, para. 2; the Council may amend the scales determining the financial contributions of Member States to the Community budgets—Art. 172, section 3; the Council may authorise expenditure in excess of one-twelfth of the appropriations—Art. 178, para. 3; the Council determines the number of auditors and their remuneration and makes the necessary appointments—Art. 180, para. 1; and gives the Commission a discharge in respect of implementation of each budget—Art. 180, para. 2; the Council determines the procedure for drawing up and implementing the budget, the methods and procedure for making the contributions of Member States available to the Commission and the rules concerning the responsibility of finance officials—Art. 183, and may apply exchange arrangements to the Agency and to joint undertakings—Art. 182, section 6—and may also amend these—Art. 54, para. 3; it may fix the prices of ores, etc.—Art. 69, para. 1; it may approve the method of financing emergency stocks of nuclear material—Art. 72, para. 2—and shall settle the draft budgets of the Community before they are forwarded to the Parliamentary Assembly—Art. 177, section 3.

Specific provisions, however, require the Council to act by means of Regulations. Thus, the nature and extent of the duty to keep and produce operating records of ores and fissile material is to be defined in Regulations of the Council.[35]

The Council is to act by means of Directives when it determines the manner by which the Member States shall facilitate the conclusion of insurance contracts covering nuclear risks.[36]

By means of Decisions the Council is to establish a joint undertaking, namely, an international public body with legal immunity and compulsory powers [37]; to advance the date for the imposition of duties of a common customs tariff to specified products,[38] and the conditions for the raising of the loans for financing research or investment.[39]

THE PARLIAMENTARY ASSEMBLY

The Assembly is composed of delegates nominated by the parliaments of the Member States from among their members in accordance with the procedure laid down by each of those States.[40]

Several powers are specifically given to the Assembly. Thus, the Assembly or its members may put questions to the Commission, which the Commission is required to answer.[41] The Assembly discusses the Annual Report submitted to it by the Commission,[42] and if a motion of censure is carried against the Report by a two-thirds majority of the votes cast, representing a majority of members of the Assembly, the members of the Commission must collectively resign their office.[43] The Assembly may propose to the Council of Ministers amendments to the draft budgets,[44] and if it does so the Council must discuss these amendments with the Commission but may adopt them only by a qualified majority vote.[45]

---

[35] Art. 79, para. 3.
[36] Art. 98, para. 2. The Council may empower the Commission to enter into agreements or conventions with a non-Member State, international organisation or nationals of a non-Member State—*ibid.*
[37] Art. 49, para. 1.
[38] Art. 95.
[39] Art. 172, section 4, para. 1.
[40] Art. 108, section 1. This Assembly is common to the three Communities and many of the provisions concerning it appear in all three Treaties. As to these see pp. 412–413, and 428–429, above.
[41] Art. 110, para. 3. In practice this is one of the most important powers of the Assembly.
[42] Art. 113.
[43] Art. 114, para. 2.
[44] Art. 177, section 3, para. 3.
[45] Art. 177, section 4, para. 2. As to qualified majority voting, see note 26, p. 440, above.

In an optimistic moment it was provided that the Assembly shall draw up proposals for elections to it by direct universal suffrage in accordance with a uniform procedure in all Member States.[46]

THE ARBITRATION COMMITTEE

The Arbitration Committee consists of fifteen persons: one President, two Vice-Presidents and twelve members, appointed for six years by the Council of Ministers.[47]

The Committee sits in committees of three members, consisting of the President, or one of the Vice-Presidents, and two ordinary members, one chosen by each of the disputing parties from the twelve members.[48] Alternatively, a dispute may be submitted for the decision of one member only of the fifteen, or submitted to the Persident and four ordinary members, two chosen by each party.[49]

The jurisdiction of the Committee relates to determining the terms to be included in the grant of a patent licence when the parties concerned are unable to agree.[50]

When the Commission intends compulsorily to acquire a licence to exploit a patent, the owner of the patent may propose to the Commission that they should conclude an agreement to refer to the Arbitration Committee the settling of the terms of such a licence.[51] If the Commission refuses to enter into this agreement, it may not require the desired licence to be granted.[52] If the Commission, however, does consent to this agreement, the Arbitration Committee considers first whether the Commission's request for the licence satisfies the Treaty requirements,[53] and if it does, the Committee in a reasoned decision grants the licence and lays down the appropriate conditions and remuneration, unless these have been agreed by the parties.[54]

Alternatively, it may be the owner himself who does not wish to refer to the Arbitration Committee the question of the terms for the compulsory acquisition of a licence to exploit his patent. In such a case,

---

[46] Art. 108, section 3, para. 1. The Council of Ministers is not required to give effect to these proposals—Art. 108, section 3, para. 2.

[47] Regulation No. 7–63 of the Euratom Council, Art. 1, para. 1.1. The Court of Justice is to submit a list of 18 names for the positions of President and Vice-President, and 36 names from which the 12 ordinary members are to be selected—Art. 1, para. 2.1. Those not selected from the list of 18 are added to the list of 36—Art. 1, para. 2.2.

[48] *Ibid.* Art. 10, para. 1.2.

[49] *Ibid.* Art. 11, para. 1. What is to occur if the parties disagree about the number of arbitrators who are to sit, is not stated.

[50] On this jurisdiction, see further, p. 339, above.

[51] Euratom Treaty, Art. 20, para. 1.

[52] Art. 20, para. 2.

[53] These requirements are set out in Art. 17, as to which see pp. 340 and 345, above.

[54] Art. 20, para. 3.

the Commission may require the relevant Member State or its competent authorities to grant the licence or cause it to be granted.[55] If a dispute arises concerning the amount of the compensation, then, by agreement between the owner and the prospective licensee, this amount may be determined by the Arbitration Committee.[56]

The decisions of the Arbitration Committee may be revised in so far as they relate to the conditions of the licence after a period of one year or if new facts justify this revision.[57]

Within one month from their notification, the decisions of the Arbitration Committee may be the subject of a suspensive appeal to the Court of Justice,[58] but, subject to this, the decisions of the Committee have the force of *res judicata* between the parties concerned and are enforceable in the normal way.[59]

THE ECONOMIC AND SOCIAL COMMITTEE

An Economic and Social Committee, composed of representatives of the various categories of economic and social activity and possessing consultative status is required to be established.[60] The members of the Committee are appointed by unanimous decision of the Council of Ministers for a renewable period of four years.[61] The members are appointed in their personal capacity and may not be bound by any instructions.[62]

The Committee must be consulted by the Council or by the Commission on certain specified matters. For example, the Committee is to give its Opinion upon the fixing of the basic standards for the maximum permissible levels of exposure and contamination and the medical supervision of workers [63]; upon the Commission's programmes for the production of nuclear energy and investments of every kind required for their achievement [64]; upon those sectors of industry which are required

---

[55] Art. 21, para. 1.
[56] Art. 22, para. 1. If the owner refused to allow the matter to go to arbitration, compensation is to be determined by the competent national authorities—Art. 22, section 2, para. 2; if the licensee refuses to go to arbitration, his licence becomes null and void—Art. 22, section 2, para. 1.
[57] Art. 23, para. 1.
[58] Art. 18, para. 2. As to this appeal, see p. 341, above.
[59] Art. 18, para. 3. As to enforcement, see p. 343, above.
[60] Art. 165.
[61] Art. 166, para. 2.
[62] Art. 166, para. 3. France, Germany and Italy each have 24 members, Belgium and the Netherlands 12, and Luxembourg five.
[63] Art. 30, para. 2.
[64] Art. 40.

to communicate their investment projects to the Commission [65]; concerning the Directives which the Council may issue to the Member States for ending the restrictions on the nationality of workers employed in nuclear energy,[66] and finally it is laid down that the Committee shall be consulted concerning the means to facilitate the conclusion of insurance contracts governing nuclear risks.[67]

THE COURT OF JUSTICE

Over these institutions, and ensuring the respect of law in the interpretation and application of the Treaty, stands the Court of Justice.[68]

---

[65] Art. 41.
[66] Art. 96.
[67] Art. 98.
[68] Art. 134.

DOCUMENTS

THE EUROPEAN COAL AND STEEL COMMUNITY TREATY PROTOCOL ON THE STATUTE OF THE COURT OF JUSTICE

THE HIGH CONTRACTING PARTIES:

DESIRING TO establish [1] the Statute of the Court of Justice provided for by Article 45 of the Treaty,

HAVE AGREED as follows:

ARTICLE 1

The Court of Justice established by Article 7 of the Treaty shall be constituted and shall perform its duties in accordance with the provisions of the Treaty and of the present Statute.

TITLE I

THE JUDGES

The Oath

ARTICLE 2

Before entering upon his duties, each judge shall in open court take an oath to discharge his duties conscientiously and with complete impartiality and to preserve the secrecy of the deliberations.[2]

Privileges and Immunities

ARTICLE 3

The judges shall enjoy immunity from legal action.[3] They shall continue to benefit from such immunities after their duties have ceased, in respect of acts done by them in their official capacity,[4] including words spoken and written.

The Court, sitting in plenary session, may suspend the immunity.[5]

In a case where, after the immunity has been suspended, criminal action is brought against a judge, this shall be justiciable in the Member

---

[1] Stationery Office: " Being desirous of establishing."
[2] French: " des délibérations."
[3] French: " Les juges jouissent de l'immunité de juridiction."
  Stationery Office: " Judges, in their official capacity, shall have immunity from suit and legal process."
[4] These four words are omitted by the Stationery Office.
[5] French: " l'immunité."
  Stationery Office: " this immunity."

States only by a court competent to judge the members of the highest municipal court.[6]

Judges, whatever their nationality, shall also enjoy, in the territory of each of the Member States, the privileges set out in paragraphs (b), (c) and (d) of Article 11 of the Protocol on the Privileges and Immunities of the Community.

Eligibility for Office [7]

ARTICLE 4

The judges [8] may not hold any political or administrative office.

They may not engage in any paid or unpaid occupation or profession except by exceptional exemption granted by a two-thirds majority of the Council.

They may not acquire or hold, directly or indirectly, any interest in any business related to coal or steel during their term of office and during a period of three years thereafter.

Remuneration

ARTICLE 5

The salaries, allowances and pensions of the President and the judges shall be fixed by the Council on the proposal of the Commission provided for in Article 78 (3) of the Treaty.

Termination of Office

ARTICLE 6

Apart from retirements in regular rotation, the duties of a judge shall be individually terminated by death or resignation.

---

[6] French:
 " *Au cas où, l'immunité ayant été levée, une action pénale est engagée contre un juge, celui n'est justiciable, dans chaque des Etats membres, que de l'instance compétente pour juger les magistrats appartenant à la plus haute juridiction nationale.*"
Stationery Office:
 " Only a Court competent to judge the members of the highest national judiciary in each Member State shall have jurisdiction in criminal proceedings against judges whose immunity has been suspended."
[7] French: " *Incompatibilités.*"
Stationery Office: " Incompatibility."
[8] Stationery Office: " Judges." In the E.E.C. Statute, this is translated as " The judges."

When a judge resigns, his letter of resignation shall be addressed to the President of the Court for transmission to the President of the Council. This [9] latter notification shall cause [10] a vacancy on the bench.

Save where Article 7 below applies, each judge shall continue to hold office until his successor enters upon his duties.

ARTICLE 7

Judges may be removed from office only if, in the unanimous opinion of the other judges, they no longer fulfil the required conditions.

The President of the Council, the President of the High Authority and the President of the Assembly shall be informed of this [11] by the Registrar.

This communication [12] shall produce a vacancy on the bench.

ARTICLE 8

The [13] judge who is appointed to replace a member [14] whose term of office has not expired, shall complete [15] his predecessor's term of office.

TITLE II

ORGANISATION

ARTICLE 9

The judges, Advocates General, and the Registrar must reside at the place where the Court has its seat.

ARTICLE 10

The Court shall be assisted by two Advocates General and one Registrar.

The Advocates General

ARTICLE 11

It shall be the duty of the Advocate General to present publicly, and with complete impartiality and independence, oral reasoned submissions upon

---

9 French: " *Cette.*"
  Stationery Office: " The."
10 Stationery Office: " shall product," a form of words which is not English.
11 French: " *en sont informés.*"
  Stationery Office: " shall be notified of this."
12 French: " *cette communication.*"
  Stationery Office: " Such notification."
13 French: " *Le juge.*"
  Stationery Office: "A judge."
14 French: " *un membre.*"
  Stationery Office: " a member of the Court."
15 French: " *achève le terme.*"
  Stationery Office: " shall be appointed for the remainder of."

Documents

the cases submitted to the Court,[16] in order to assist it[17] in the performance of its duties, as defined in Article 31 of the Treaty.

ARTICLE 12

The Advocates General shall be appointed for[18] six years in the same manner as the judges. There shall be a partial re-appointment[19] every three years. The Advocate General whose term expires at the end of the first period of three years shall be designated by lot. The provisions of the third and fourth paragraphs of Article 32 of the Treaty and those[20] of Article 6 of the present Statute shall apply to the Advocates General.

ARTICLE 13

The provisions of Articles 2 to 5 and 8 above shall apply to the Advocates General.

Advocates General may be removed from office only if they no longer fulfil the conditions required.[21] The[22] decision[23] must be unanimously reached by the Council upon the advice of the Court.

Registrar

ARTICLE 14

The Registrar shall be appointed by the Court, which shall lay down his terms of office, subject to the provisions of Article 15 below. He shall take an oath before the Court to perform[24] his duties conscientiously

[16] French:
 " *L'avocat général a pour rôle de presenter publiquement, en toute impartialité et en toute indépendance, des conclusions orales et motivées sur les affairs soumises à la Cour.*"
 Stationery Office:
 " It shall be the duty of the Advocate-General to make reasoned submissions in open court on matters referred to the Court. He shall do so with complete impartiality and independence."
[17] French: " *celle-ci.*"
 Stationery Office: " the Court."
[18] French: " *sont nommés pour.*"
 Stationery Office: " shall be appointed for a term of."
[19] French : " *Un renouvellement partiel.*"
 Stationery Office: "A partial change in membership "—the membership has not in fact ever yet changed.
[20] French: " *celles.*"
 Stationery Office: " the provisions."
[21] Stationery Office adds: " for holding such office."
[22] French: " *La.*"
 Stationery Office: "Any."
[23] Stationery Office adds: " to remove them."
[24] Stationery Office: " to discharge." When this provision is repeated in the E.E.C. and Euratom Statute the Stationery Office uses the term " to perform "—E.E.C. Statute, Art. 9; Euratom Statute, Art. 9.

and with complete impartiality and to preserve the secrecy of the deliberations.[25]

The provisions of Articles 11 and 13 of the Protocol on the Privileges and Immunities of the Community shall be applicable to the Registrar; however, the powers conferred by those Articles upon the President of the High Authority shall be exercised by the President of the Court.

ARTICLE 15

The Registrar's salary, allowances and pension shall be fixed by the Council upon the proposal of the Committee provided for in Article 78 (3) of the Treaty.

The Court's Staff

ARTICLE 16

Officials or employees shall be attached to the Court to enable it to carry out its tasks. They shall be responsible to the Registrar under the authority of the President. Their conditions of employment [26] shall be fixed by the Court. One of them shall be appointed by the Court to replace the Registrar if he is unable to carry out his duties.

Assistant Rapporteurs having the necessary qualifications, may be called upon in case of need and under the conditions to be laid down in rules of procedure provided for in Article 44 below, to take part in the instruction of cases [28] pending before the Court, and to collaborate with the *juge rapporteur*.[29] Their conditions of employment [30] shall be laid down by the Council on the proposal of the Court. They shall be appointed by the Council.[31]

The provisions of Articles [32] 11, 12 and 13 of the Protocol on Privileges and Immunities of the Community shall be applicable [33] to the officials and employees of the Court, and to the assistant rapporteurs; however, the powers conferred by these Articles on the

---

[25] French: " *des délibérations.*"
Stationery Office: " of the Court's consideration of the cases before it."
[26] French: " *Leur statut.*"
Stationery Office: " Their terms of office (or status)."
[28] French: " *l'instruction des affaires.*"
Stationery Office: " the examination of cases "—the Instruction is a distinct part of the procedure before the Court, see pp. 62 and 72, above.
[29] French: " *juge rapporteur.*"
Stationery Office: " judge acting as Rapporteur."
[30] See note 26, above.
[31] This sentence is omitted by the Stationery Office.
[32] Stationery Office: "Article."
[33] Stationery Office: " are applicable."

Documents

President of the High Authority shall be exercised by the President of the Court.

Functioning of the Court

ARTICLE 17

The Court shall sit permanently. The length of Court vacations shall be fixed by the Court subject to [35] the exigencies of its business.

Composition of the Court

ARTICLE 18

The Court shall sit in plenary session. It may, however, set up within itself two Chambers,[36] each consisting of three judges, in order either to conduct certain measures of instruction,[37] or to decide certain classes [38] of cases, under conditions to be determined by rules which it [39] shall lay down to that effect.

The Court shall be competent to act only when sitting with an uneven number.[40] The deliberations [41] of the Court sitting [42] in plenary session shall be valid if five judges are present. The deliberations [43] of the Chambers [44] shall be valid only if they are conducted by three judges; if one of the judges of the [45] Chamber [44] is unable to carry out his duties, a judge of the other Chamber [44] may be asked to sit, in accordance with conditions which shall be laid down in the rules provided for above.

Appeals by States or by the Council must in all cases be heard in plenary session.

[35] French: " *sous réserve.*"
Stationery Office: " with due regard for."
[36] French: " *deux Chambres.*"
Stationery Office: " two Sections." In the Rules of the International Court of Justice, " *Chambre* " is translated as " Chamber."
[37] French: " *certaines mesures d'instruction.*"
Stationery Office: " certain methods of investigation." A measure of instruction forms part of the Instruction itself, see p. 62, above.
[38] Stationery Office: " certain kinds."
[39] French: " *qu'elle.*"
Stationery Office: " which the Court."
[40] Stationery Office adds: " of members."
[41] French: " *Les délibérations.*"
Stationery Office: " The Decisions "—the deliberations lead to the Decisions but are distinct from them.
[42] Stationery Office: " meeting."
[43] See note 41, above.
[44] See Note 36, above
[45] French: "*la . . .*"
Stationery Office: " one."

Special Rules

ARTICLE 19

Judges and the Advocates General may not take part in [46] the settlement [47] of any case in which they have previously participated as agent of, legal adviser to, or counsel for one of the parties, or on which they have been called upon to decide as a member of a tribunal [48] of a commission of inquiry, or in any other capacity.

If, for some special reason, a [49] judge or Advocate General considers that he should not take part in the Judgment [50] or in the examination [51] of a particular case, he shall so inform the President. If the President considers that a [52] judge or Advocate General should not, for some special reason, sit or make submissions in a particular case he shall give notice thereof to the person concerned.

The Court shall decide in case of any difficulties arising as to the application [53] of the present Article.

A party may not invoke either the nationality of a judge or the absence from the Court [54] or from one of its Chambers,[55] of a judge of its own [56] nationality, in order to ask for a change in the composition of the Court [57] or of one of its Chambers.

---

[46] French: " *participer.*"
Stationery Office: " participate in." In the following line " *intervenus* " is also translated as " participate."
[47] French: " *au règlement.*"
Stationery Office: " in the hearing." " *Règlement* " is wider than " hearing " and covers the written proceedings of a case before the parties are heard.
[48] French: " *un tribunal.*"
Stationery Office: " a court of law."
[49] French: " *un.*"
Stationery Office: " any."
[50] Stationery Office: " judgement."
[51] French: " *l'examen.*"
Stationery Office: " hearing." " *Examen* " is wider than merely to cover the oral hearing: this provision relates also to the written proceedings.
[52] See note 49, above.
[53] French: " *l'application.*"
Stationery Office: " the interpretation "—this is clearly an error. The Stationery Office earlier translated " *l'interprétation ou application* " as " the interpretation or implementation "—Art. 16 of the Protocol on Privileges and Immunities.
[54] French: " *l'absence au sein de la Cour.*"
Stationery Office: " the absence from the bench." The three judges of a Chamber also constitute a bench.
[55] See note 36, p. 450, above.
[56] Stationery Office: " his own."
[57] To be consistent the Stationery Office should use the word " bench " here, but it does not.

TITLE III

PROCEDURE

Representation and Presence of Parties [58]

ARTICLE 20

The States as well as [59] the institutions of the Community shall be represented before the Court by agents [60] appointed for each case; the agent may be assisted by a counsel who is a member of a Bar of one of the Member States.[61]

Enterprises [62] and all other natural or legal persons must be represented by counsel who is a member of a Bar of one of the Member States.[63]

The agents and counsel appearing before the Court shall have the rights and guarantees necessary for the independent performance of their duties under conditions to be laid down in rules made by the Court and submitted for the approval of the Council.

The Court shall have, as regards counsel who appear before it, the powers normally accorded to courts and tribunals,[64] under conditions which shall be laid down by the same rules.

Senior university teachers of the Member States,[65] whose domestic law gives them the right of audience,[66] shall have the rights [67] before the Court as are afforded by the present article [68] to counsel.

[58] French: "*Parties.*"
  Stationery Office: "Interested parties."
[59] French: "*ainsi que.*"
  Stationery Office: "and."
[60] French: "*par des agents.*"
  Stationery Office: "by an agent." The later Statutes correct the French by stating "*par un agent*"—E.E.C. Statute, Art. 17, para. 1 and Euratom Statute, Art. 17, para. 1.
[61] French: "*un avocat inscrit à un barreau de l'un des Etats membres*": "a counsel who is a practising member of the Bar of one of the Member States." Many States however, have more than one Bar.
[62] French: "*entreprises.*"
  Stationery Office: "undertakings."
[63] See note 61, above.
[64] French: "*aux Cours et tribunaux.*"
  Stationery Office: "to courts of law."
[65] French: "*Les professeurs ressortissants des Etats membres.*"
  Stationery Office: "Senior teachers being nationals of Member States."
[66] Stationery Office adds: "before their own courts."
[67] Stationery Office: "the same rights."
[68] French: "*le présent article.*"
  Stationery Office: "this Article."

Stages of the Proceedings [69]

ARTICLE 21

The proceedings [70] before the Court shall be in two stages: one written and the other oral.

The written proceedings [70] shall consist of [71] communications to the parties, as well as to the institutions of the Community whose Decisions are in dispute, of the requests, memoranda, defence and observations, and replies,[72] if any, as well as of all supporting documentary evidence and papers or certified copies thereof.

The [73] communications shall be made under the direction of [74] the Registrar in the sequence and within the time limits fixed by the rules of procedure.

The oral proceedings [75] shall consist of [76] the reading of the report presented by the *juge rapporteur*,[77] as well as [78] the hearing by the Court [79] of the witnesses, experts, agents and counsel and of the submissions of the Advocate General.

Requests [80]

ARTICLE 22

Proceedings shall be instituted before the Court by a request [80] addressed to the Registrar. The request must contain the name and address [81]

[69] Stationery Office: " Stages of Procedure."
[70] Stationery Office: " the procedure." In the Rules of the International Court of Justice " *Procédure* " is translated as " Proceedings "—see Heading II thereof.
[71] French: " *comprend.*"
    Stationery Office: " shall include."
[72] French: " *requêtes, mémoires, défences et observations des répliques.*"
    Stationery Office: " formal requests, statements of case, defences, comments and replies "—the request of a party is its statement of case—see Rules, Art. 38, para. 1, p. 460, below.
[73] French: " *les.*"
    Stationery Office: " such."
[74] French: " *par les soins du.*"
    Stationery Office: " by."
[75] See note 70, above.
[76] See note 71, above.
[77] See note 29, p. 449, above.
[78] French: " *ainsi que.*"
    Stationery Office: " and."
[79] Stationery Office: " the hearing of the Court."
[80] French: " *Requête.*"
    Stationery Office: " Formal requests."
[81] French: " *et de la demeure.*"
    Stationery Office: " and the residence."

of the party [82] and the status [83] of the party signing it,[84] the subject matter of the action,[85] the submissions,[86] and a short summary of the grounds relied upon.[87]

It [88] must be accompanied, where appropriate, by the Decision [89] whose annulment is sought,[90] or, in the case of an appeal against an implied Decision,[91] by a document establishing the date of the making of the request for action.[92] If these documents are not annexed to [93] the request, the Registrar shall ask the party concerned to produce them within a reasonable period. However, the case may not be struck out in the event of compliance occurring after the expiration of the time limit for appealing.[94]

Transmission of Documents

ARTICLE 23

When an appeal is lodged against a Decision taken [95] by one of the Community's institutions, this institution [96] shall transmit to the Court all documents relating to the case before the Court.

[82] French: " *de la partie.*"
Stationery Office: " of the plaintiff."
[83] French: " *la qualité.*"
Stationery Office: "—the description "—in the E.E.C. Statute; the Stationery Office translate this as " the status "—*ibid.* Art. 19, para. 1.
[84] Stationery Office: " The signatory."
[85] French: " *litige.*"
Stationery Office: " dispute."
[86] French: " *les conclusions.*"
Stationery Office: " the arguments."
[87] French: " *un exposé sommaire des moyens invoqués.*"
Stationery Office: " a short summary of the grounds on which the formal Request is based."
[88] French: " *Elle.*"
Stationery Office: " The formal Request."
[89] French: " *la décision.*"
Stationery Office: " the act (*acte*)." It appears that here the Stationery Office is translating from something other than the official version of the E.C.S.C. Statute.
[90] Stationery Office: " the annulment of which is sought."
[91] Stationery Office: " implicit decision."
[92] French: " *une pièce justifiant la date du dépôt de la demande.*"
Stationery Office: " documentary evidence of the date of the filing of the Request." This is a complete misunderstanding: " *la demande* " here being referred to is the request for action submitted to the High Authority, it has nothing to do with *la requête* which instituted the relevant proceedings before the Court—see Art. 35, pp. 184–193, above.   [93] Stationery Office: " attached to."
[94] French:
" *sans qu'aucune forclusion puisse être opposée au cas où la regularisation interviendroit après l'expiration du délai de recours.*"
Stationery Office:
" in that case the rights of the party shall not lapse even if such documents are produced after the expiry of the time-limit set for the institution of proceedings."
[95] French: " *prise.*"
Stationery Office does not translate this word.
[96] French: " *cette institution.*"
Stationery Office: " it."

Measures of Instruction [97]

ARTICLE 24

The Court may request [98] the parties, their representatives or agents, as well as the Governments of the Member States, to produce all documents and to supply all information which it [99] considers desirable. In case of refusal, the Court shall take judicial notice thereof.

ARTICLE 25

The Court may at any time entrust to [1] any person, body, office, commission or organ of its own choice, an inquiry or the making of an expert's report [2]: for this purpose it [3] may draw up a list of persons or organisations qualified to serve as experts.

The Public Nature of the Sessions [4]

ARTICLE 26

The hearings shall be public, unless the Court for substantial reasons shall decide otherwise.

Records of the Sessions [5]

ARTICLE 27

Records shall be kept of each session,[6] signed by the President and the Registrar.

The Sessions [6]

ARTICLE 28

The cause list shall be settled by the President.

[97] French: " *Mesures d'Instruction.*"
Stationery Office: " Methods of Investigation."
[98] French: " *peut demander.*"
Stationery Office: " may require."
[99] French: " *elle.*"
Stationery Office: " the Court."
[1] French: " *peut confier.*"
Stationery Office: " may charge."
[2] French: " *peut confier une mission d'enquête ou une expertise à toute personne. . . .*"
Stationery Office: " charge any person . . . with the duty of making a formal inquiry or expert appraisal."
[3] See note 99, above.
[4] Stationery Office: " Publicity of the Hearings."
[5] Stationery Office: " Records of the Hearings."
[6] Stationery Office: " hearings."

Witnesses may be heard under conditions which shall be determined by the rules of procedure. They may be heard on oath.

During the sessions [6] the Court may also examine the experts and the persons entrusted to make an inquiry,[7] as well as the parties themselves; the latter, however, may address the Court only [8] through their representative or counsel.

When it is established that a witness or an expert has concealed or falsified the facts on which he has testified or been examined by the Court, the Court shall be empowered to refer such failure to the Minister of Justice of the State of which the witness or expert is a national, with a view to his seeing to [9] the enforcement of the sanctions provided for in each case by the national law.

The Court shall have as regards defaulting witnesses the powers generally accorded in such cases to courts and tribunals,[10] under the conditions which shall be laid down [11] by rules laid down by the Court and submitted for the Council's approval.

Secrecy of the Deliberations [12]

ARTICLE 29

The Court's deliberations [12] shall be and shall remain secret.

Judgments [13]

ARTICLE 30

Judgments [13] shall be reasoned. They shall state the name of the judges [14] who sat.[15]

---

[7] Stationery Office: " charged with a formal inquiry."
[8] Stationery Office: " may only address the Court."
[9] French: " *en vue de lui voir*."
   Stationery Office: " for."
[10] French: " *Cours et tribunaux*."
   Stationery Office: " Courts of law."
[11] French: " *dans les conditions qui seront déterminées*."
   Stationery Office: " under conditions determined "—in E.E.C. Statute, these same words are translated as: " as shall be laid down "—*ibid*. Art. 24.
[12] French: " *délibérations*."
   Stationery Office: " consideration of cases."
[13] Stationery Office: " Judgements."
[14] French: " *le nom des juges*."
   Stationery Office: " the names of the judges." In the later Statutes, this provision becomes " *les noms des juges*."
[15] French: " *ont siégé*."
   Stationery Office: " took part."

ARTICLE 31

Judgments [13] shall be signed by the President, the *juge rapporteur* [16] and the Registrar. They shall be read in public session.[17]

Costs

ARTICLE 32

The Court shall adjudicate upon costs.

Summary Proceedings [18]

ARTICLE 33

The President of the Court may rule [19] by means of a summary procedure, derogating,[20] to the extent necessary from certain [21] of the rules contained in the present [22] Statute, and which shall be determined [23] by the Rules of Procedure, upon submissions either for obtaining the stay of execution [24] as provided for in Article 39, paragraph 2 [25] of the [26] Treaty or for the application of provisional measures [27] pursuant to the third paragraph of the same article, or for a stay of execution,[28] in accordance with Article 92, third paragraph.

If the President is prevented from carrying out his duties, his place shall be taken by another judge under conditions laid down by the rules provided for in Article 18 of the present Statute.

[16] See note 29, p. 449, above.
[17] Stationery Office: " in open court."
[18] French : " *Déféré.*"
Stationery Office: " Summary procedure in cases of urgency."
[19] French : " *peut statuer.*"
Stationery Office: " shall have power to decide certain matters."
[20] French : " *dérogeant.*"
Stationery Office: " which shall depart."
[21] Stationery Office: " from some."
[22] French : " *le présent.*"
Stationery Office: " this."
[23] French : " *et qui sera fixée.*"
Stationery Office: " This summary procedure, the details of which shall be determined."
[24] French : " *conclusions tendant soit à l'obtention du sursis.*"
Stationery Office: " applications for suspension of operation."
[25] French : " *alinéa 2.*"
Stationery Office: " second paragraph."
[26] French : " *du.*"
Stationery Office: " of this."
[27] Stationery Office: " the prescribing of interim measures."
[28] Stationery Office: " the suspension of enforcement."

Documents

The order [29] issued by [30] the President, or by his substitute,[31] shall only [32] be provisional and shall in no way prejudice the decision of the Court in determining upon the principal action.[33]

Intervention

ARTICLE 34

Natural or legal persons who show that they have an interest [34] in the result of a case before the Court may intervene in that case.

Submissions contained in the request to intervene [35] may have as their object only the support of the submissions of one party or their rejection.[36]

Judgment in Default [37]

ARTICLE 35

When, in a case in *pleine juridiction*,[38] the defendant,[39] having been duly notified, fails to file its written submissions,[40] judgment [41] shall be given in [42] its case by default. The judgment shall be open to challenge [43]

29 French: "*l'ordonnance.*"
Stationery Office: "the ruling."
30 French: "*rendue par.*"
Stationery Office: "by."
31 French: "*son remplaçant.*"
Stationery Office: "his alternate."
32 French: "*ne . . . que.*"
Stationery Office omits this.
33 French: "*statuant au principal.*"
Stationery Office: "on the substance of the case."
34 French: "*un intérêt.*"
Stationery Office: "a valid interest."
35 French: "*la requête en intervention.*"
Stationery Office: "the application to intervene."
36 French: "*le soutien des conclusions d'une partie ou leur rejet.*"
Stationery Office: "the support or rejection of the written case of a party to the dispute."
37 Stationery Office: "Judgement by default."
38 French: "*de pleine juridiction.*"
Stationery Office: "where the Court has full jurisdiction over the subject matter of the proceedings."
39 Stationery Office: "and the defending party."
40 French: "*des conclusions écrites.*"
Stationery Office: "a written submission in defence."
41 See note 13, p. 456, above.
42 Stationery Office: "on."
43 French: "*l'arrêt est susceptible d'opposition.*"
Stationery Office: "A retrial may be claimed."

within the time limit [44] of one month calculated from its notification.[45] Unless the Court decides otherwise, the challenge shall not suspend the execution of the judgment given by default.[46]

Requests by Third Parties to Set Aside or Modify Judgment [47]

ARTICLE 36

Natural or legal persons, as well as [48] the institutions of the Community [49] may, in cases and under conditions to be fixed [50] by the Rules of Procedure, bring third party proceedings, to set aside or modify judgments given without their having been notified.[51]

Interpretation

ARTICLE 37

In case of difficulty as to the meaning or scope of a judgment,[52] it shall be for the Court to interpret it [53] upon the request of a [54] party or of an institution of the Community [55] showing an interest [56] therein.

[44] French: " *le délai.*"
Stationery Office omits these words.
[45] French: " *à compter de sa notification.*"
Stationery Office: " from the date of notification."
[46] French: " *l'opposition ne suspend pas l'exécution de l'arrêt rendu par défaut.*"
Stationery Office: " enforcement of the judgement by default shall not be suspended by a demand for retrial."
[47] French: " *Tierce opposition.*"
Stationery Office: " Requests for retrial by third parties."
[48] See note 78, p. 453, above.
[49] Stationery Office: " any of the Community's institutions."
[50] French: " *dans les cas et dans les conditions qui seront déterminés.*"
Stationery Office: " in such cases and under such conditions as shall be fixed."
The translation in the text is that of the Stationery Office when translating the identical phrase in E.E.C. Statute, Art. 39.
[51] French: " *former tierce opposition contre les arrêts rendus sans qu'elles aient été appelées.*"
Stationery Office: " may intervene as third-parties to request retrial in the case of judgements given without notification to them." The Stationery Office, unlike the French, inserts this provision before the words " in such cases and under such conditions. . . ."
[52] See note 13, p. 456, above.
[53] French: " *l'interpréter.*"
Stationery Office: " to interpret such judgement."
[54] French: " *une partie.*"
Stationery Office: " any party."
[55] See note 34, p. 458, above.
[56] French: " *justifiant d'un intérêt.*"
Stationery Office: " showing it has a valid interest."

Documents

Revision [57]

ARTICLE 38

The revision of a judgment may be requested from the Court only [58] by reason of the discovery of a fact likely to exercise a decisive influence,[59] and which was unknown both to the Court and to the party which requests the revision before judgment was delivered.

The procedure for revision shall begin by the Court delivering a judgment [60] expressly [61] finding that a new fact exists, recognising that it possesses the characteristics justifying a revision,[62] and declaring the request admissible on this ground.[63]

No request for revision [64] may be [65] brought after the expiration of a time limit of ten years from the date of the judgment.[66]

Time Limits

ARTICLE 39

The appeals provided for in Articles 36 and 37 of the Treaty must be lodged within a period of one month provided for in the last paragraph of Article 33.[67]

Time limits [68] on grounds of distance shall be determined by the rules of procedure.

[57] French: " *Révision.*"
Stationery Office: " Review."
[58] French: " *La révision de l'arrêt ne peut être demandée à la Cour que. . . .*"
Stationery Office: " Application to review a judgement shall only be made to the Court."
[59] French: " *en raison de la découverte d'un fait de nature à exercer une influence décisive.*"
Stationery Office: " if a fact becomes known which is likely to prove decisive."
[60] See note 13, p. 456, above.
[61] French: " *expressément.*"
Stationery Office omits this word.
[62] French: " *lui reconnaissant les caractères qui donnent overture à la révision.*"
Stationery Office: " that this fact comes within the definition contained in the preceding paragraph."
[63] French: " *et déclarant de ce chef la demand recevable.*"
Stationery Office: " finding . . . that the grounds for the said reconsideration have therefore been made out."
[64] French: " *aucune demande de révision.*"
Stationery Office: " No application for such reconsideration."
[65] French: " *pourra être formée.*"
Stationery Office: " shall be entertained."
[66] French: " *après l'expiration d'un délai de dix ans à dater de l'arrêt.*"
Stationery Office: " if it is made more than ten years after judgement was delivered."
[67] Stationery Office adds the words " of the Treaty."
[68] French: " *Des délais.*"
Stationery Office: " Periods of grace." In the heading to this article, " *délais* " was translated as " time limits."

There shall be no lapse of rights through the expiry of time limits if the party concerned proves the existence of an unforeseeable circumstance or *force majeure.*

Prescriptions

ARTICLE 40

Proceedings referred to in the first two paragraphs of Article 40 of the Treaty shall be time barred after five years calculated from the occurrence of the act which gives rise to them.[69] The running of time shall be interrupted [70] either by the request brought before the Court,[71] or by the preliminary demand which the injured party may send [72] to the appropriate institution of the Community.[73] In this latter case,[74] the request must be brought [75] within a period of one month [76] provided for in the last paragraph of Article 33; the provisions of the last paragraph of Article 35 shall apply where appropriate.

Special Rules Relating to Disputes between Member States

ARTICLE 41

When a dispute between Member States is submitted to the Court, under Article 89 of the Treaty, the other Member States shall be notified forthwith by the Registrar concerning the subject matter of such dispute.

[69] French:
"*Les actions prévues aux deux premiers alinéas de article 40 du Traité se prescrivant par cinq ans à compter de la survenance du fait qui y donne lieu.*"
Stationery Office:
"No proceedings in respect of the matters covered by Article 40 of the Treaty shall be brought more than five years after the circumstances giving rise to them occurred."
[70] French: "*La prescription est interrompue.*"
Stationery Office: "Time shall not run." The translation in the text is that of the Stationery Office when translating the identical phrase in E.E.C. Statute, Art. 43.
[71] French: "*la requête formé devant la Cour.*"
Stationery Office: "when proceedings were instituted."
[72] French: "*soit par la demande préalable que la victime peur adresser.*"
Stationery Office: "or when the injured party sent a preliminary demand."
[73] Stationery Office: "the Community's appropriate institution." In E.E.C. Art. 43, the Stationery Office renders this "the relevant institution of the Community."
[74] French: "*Dans ce dernier cas.*"
Stationery Office: "In the latter event."
[75] French: "*la requête doit être formée.*"
Stationery Office: "proceedings must have been instituted."
[76] French: "*un mois.*"
Stationery Office: "two months"—an almost unbelievable translation.

Documents

Each of these [77] States shall have the right to intervene in the proceedings.

The disputes referred to in the present article [78] must be judged by the Court in plenary session.

ARTICLE 42

If a State under the conditions provided for in the preceding article intervenes in a case submitted to the Court,[79] the interpretation given by the judgment [80] shall be binding upon it.[81]

Appeals [82] *by Third Parties*

ARTICLE 43

Decisions taken by [83] the High Authority under Article 63, section 2, of the Treaty, must be notified to the buyer as well as to the enterprises [84] concerned; if the Decision refers to all or an important class of the enterprises,[85] the notification to them may be replaced by publication.[86]

An appeal shall be open,[87] under the conditions laid down in Article 36 of the Treaty, to any person on whom a daily penalty [88] has been imposed in accordance with Article 66, section 5, paragraph 4.[88a]

[77] French: " *ces.*"
Stationery Office: " the."
[78] French: " *du présent article.*"
Stationery Office: " this Article."
[79] Stationery Office: " If a State intervenes in a case submitted to the Court under the conditions provided for in the preceding Article "—the conditions relate to the intervention, not to the submission.
[80] French: " *l'interprétation donnée par l'arrêt.*"
Stationery Office: "the findings contained in the judgement."
[81] French: " *à lui.*"
Stationery Office: " on that State."
[82] French: " *Recours.*"
Stationery Office: " Proceedings."
[83] French: " *des décisions prises par.*"
Stationery Office: " Decisions of."
[84] Stationery Office: " undertakings."
[85] French: " *l'ensemble ou une catégorie importante des entreprises.*"
Stationery Office: " to all undertakings or to an important class of them."
[86] French: " *la notification à leur égard peut être remplacée par une publication.*"
Stationery Office: " publication may be substituted for such individual notification."
[87] French: " *Un recours est ouvert.*"
Stationery Office: " Proceedings may be instituted."
[88] French: " *une astreinte.*"
Stationery Office: " a financial penalty."
[88a] Stationery Office: " Article 66 (5), fourth sub-paragraph."

Rules of Procedure

ARTICLE 44

The Court shall establish its own rules of procedure. These rules shall contain all the provisions necessary for giving effect to, and where necessary, completing the present Statute.

Transitional Provisions

ARTICLE 45

Immediately after the oath has been taken, the President of the Council shall proceed to choose by lot the judges and the Advocates General whose term of office is to expire at the end of the first period of three years in accordance with Article 32 of the Treaty.

Done in Paris, the eighteenth day of April, one thousand nine hundred and fifty-one.

THE EUROPEAN ECONOMIC COMMUNITY TREATY
PROTOCOL ON THE STATUTE OF THE COURT OF JUSTICE

THE HIGH CONTRACTING PARTIES:

DESIRING TO establish [1] the Statute of the Court provided for by Article 188 of this Treaty,

HAVE AGREED AS FOLLOWS:

ARTICLE 1

The Court established by Article 4 of the [2] Treaty shall be constituted and shall perform its duties in accordance with the provisions of the [2] Treaty and of the present [3] Statute.

TITLE I

THE JUDGES [4] AND THE ADVOCATES GENERAL

ARTICLE 2

[As E.C.S.C. Statute, Article 2.]

ARTICLE 3

[As E.C.S.C. Statute, Article 3, paras. 1, 2 and 3.]

ARTICLE 4

The judges may not hold any political or administrative office.

They may not engage in any paid or unpaid occupation or profession except by exceptional exemption granted by the Council.

When entering upon their duties, they shall give a solemn undertaking to respect,[5] during their term of office and after its termination,[6] the obligations resulting therefrom, in particular the duty to exercise honesty

---

[1] Stationery Office: " Being desirous of establishing."
[2] French: " *du.*"
  Stationery Office: " of this."
[3] French: " *du présent.*"
  Stationery Office: " of this."
[4] French: " *Statut des Juges.*"
  Stationery Office: " Status of the Judges."
[5] French: " *de respecter.*"
  Stationery Office: " that . . . they will respect."
[6] French: " *pendant la durée de leurs fonctions et après la cessation de celles-ci.*"
  Stationery Office: " both during and after their term of office."

E.E.C. *Statute of the Court*

and discretion as regards the acceptance, after this termination [7] of certain positions or of certain benefits.[8]

In case of doubt, the Court shall decide.[9]

ARTICLE 5

Apart from retirements in regular rotation and in the case of death, the duties of a judge shall be individually terminated [10] by resignation.

[Paragraphs 2 and 3 as E.C.S.C. Statute, Article 6, paras. 2 and 3 but with reference to Article 6 of the E.E.C. Statute in place of Article 7 of the E.C.S.C. Statute.]

ARTICLE 6

The judges may be deprived of office or declared to have forfeited their right to a pension [11] or other advantages [12] only if, in the unanimous opinion of the judges and the Advocates General of the Court, they no longer fulfil the required conditions or meet the obligations resulting from their office. The judge concerned shall not take part in these deliberations.

The Registrar [13] shall communicate the Court's decision to the Presidents of the Assembly and of the Commission [14] and shall notify the President of the Council.

In the case of a decision removing a judge from office, this last notification [15] shall produce a vacancy on the bench.

---

[7] French: " *à l'acceptation, après cette cessation.*"
Stationery Office: " accepting . . . after they have ceased to hold office."
[8] French: " *ou de certains avantages.*"
Stationery Office: " or benefits."
[9] French: " *la Cour décide.*"
Stationery Office: " a decision shall be made by the Court."
[10] French: " *fin individuellement.*"
Stationery Office: " terminated in individual cases." In E.C.S.C. Statute, Art. 6, the Stationery Office translate this as " individually terminated." The wording, but not the substance, of this paragraph differs from its equivalent in the E.C.S.C. Statute—Art. 6, para. 1.
[11] French: " *ne peuvent être relevés de leurs fonctions ni déclarés déchus de leur droit à pension . . . que si.*"
Stationery Office: " may be deprived of office and of their right to a pension."
[12] French: " *ou d'autres avantages.*"
Stationery Office: " or alternative advantages." The rights here referred to include payments to widows, etc., see pp. 561–571, below. There is no idea that these are an alternative to a pension.
[13] French : " *Le greffier.*"
Stationery Office: " The Registrar of the Court."
[14] French: " *des présidents de l'Assemblée et de la Commission.*"
Stationery Office: " to the President of the Assembly and to the President of the Commission."
[15] French: " *cette dernière notification.*"
Stationery Office: " such notification."

ARTICLE 7

The judges who cease to hold office before the expiration of their term of office shall be replaced for the duration of the term of office remaining to run.

ARTICLE 8

The provision of Articles 2 to 7 inclusive shall apply to the Advocates General.

TITLE II

ORGANISATION

ARTICLE 9

The Registrar shall take an oath before the Court to perform his duties conscientiously and with complete impartiality and to preserve the secrecy of the deliberations.[17]

ARTICLE 10

The Court shall arrange for the Registrar to be represented by an alternate if he is unable to carry out his duties.

ARTICLE 11

[As E.C.S.C. Statute, Article 16, para. 1, sentences 1 and 2.]

ARTICLE 12

On a proposal of the Court, the Council may, by a unanimous decision [18] provide for the appointment of *rapporteurs adjoints* [19] and lay down their terms of service. The *rapporteurs adjoints* [19] may be required under conditions to be laid down by the rules of procedure, to participate in the Instruction [20] of cases before the Court and to collaborate with the *juge rapporteur*.[21]

The *rapporteurs adjoints* [19] shall be chosen from among persons offering every guarantee of independence [22] and possessing [23] the necessary legal qualifications; they shall be appointed by the Council. They

---

17 French: " *du secret des délibérations.*"
  Stationery Office: " the secrecy of the Court's consideration of its judgements."
18 The Stationery Office here inserts the words " on a proposal of the Court." They are the opening words in the French.
19 Stationery Office: " assistant Rapporteurs."
20 French: " *l'instruction des affaires.*"
  Stationery Office: " the examination of cases." As to the Instruction, see pp. 62–65, above.
21 Stationery Office: " the judge who acts as rapporteur."
22 French: " *offrant toutes garanties d'indépendance.*"
  Stationery Office: " whose independence can be fully guaranteed."
23 French: " *et réunissant.*"
  Stationery Office: " and who possess."

shall take an oath before the Court to perform their duties impartially and conscientiously and to preserve the secrecy of the deliberations.[24]

ARTICLE 13

[As E.C.S.C. Statute, Article 9.]

ARTICLE 14

[As E.C.S.C. Statute, Article 17.[25]]

ARTICLE 15

[As E.C.S.C. Statute, Article 18, para. 2.[26]]

ARTICLE 16

[As E.C.S.C. Statute, Article 19.]

ARTICLE 17

The States as well as [27] the institutions of the Community shall be represented before the Court by an agent appointed for each case; the agent may be assisted by a legal adviser or counsel [28] who is a member of a Bar of one of the Member States.[29]

Other parties must be represented by counsel who is a member of a Bar of one of the Member States.[30]

The agents, legal advisers and counsel appearing before the Court shall have the rights and guarantees necessary [31] for the independent

---

[24] French: " *des délibérations.*"
Stationery Office: " the Court's deliberations."
[25] In Art. 14, the words " *compte tenu des nécessités du service* "—" taking account of the exigencies of its business "—have been substituted for " *sous réserve des nécessités du service* "—" subject to the exigencies of its business "—appearing in E.C.S.C. Statute, Art. 17.
[26] E.E.C. Art. 18, however, refers to the judges of " another " Chamber, and not to the judges of " the other " Chamber, thereby paving the way for a possible increase in the number of Chambers.
[27] French: " *ainsi que.*"
Stationery Office: " and."
[28] French: " *d'un conseil ou d'un avocat.*"
Stationery Office: " by a legal adviser." This completely fails to note that mention of a " *conseil* " has been inserted in this Article, although it is not in the similar provision in the E.C.S.C. Statute—*ibid.* Art. 20, para. 1.
[29] French: " *inscrit à un barreau de l'un des Etats membres.*"
Stationery Office: " who is a practising member of the Bar of one of the Member States."
[30] See note above.
[31] French: " *garanties necéssaires.*"
Stationery Office: " privileges required." In the E.C.S.C. Statute, this phrase is translated as " guarantees necessary "—*ibid.* Art. 20, para. 3.

performance of their duties, under conditions which will be laid down [32] by the rules of procedure.

The Court shall have, as regards the legal advisers and counsel who appear before it, the powers normally accorded to courts and tribunals [33], under conditions which shall be laid down by the same rules.
[Paragraph 5 as E.C.S.C. Statute, Article 20, para. 5.]

ARTICLE 18

[Paragraphs 1–3 as E.C.S.C. Statute, Article 21, paras. 1–3.]

The oral proceedings [34] shall consist of [35] the reading of the report presented by the *juge rapporteur*,[36] the hearing by the Court of agents, legal advisers and counsel and of the submissions of the Advocate General, as well as the hearing, if required,[37] of witnesses and experts.

ARTICLE 19

Proceedings shall be instituted before the Court by a request [38] addressed to the Registrar. The request must contain the name and address [39] of the plaintiff and the status of the party signing it,[40] the name of the party against which [41] the request is brought,[42] the subject matter of the action,[43] the submissions [44] and a short summary of the grounds relied on.[45]

[32] French: " *qui seront déterminées.*"
Stationery Office: " to be laid down."
[33] French: " *aux cours et tribunaux.*"
Stationery Office: " to courts of law."
[34] Stationery Office: " the oral procedure."
[35] French: " *comprend.*"
Stationery Office: " shall include."
[36] French: " *juge rapporteur.*"
Stationery Office: " judge acting as rapporteur."
[37] French: " *s'il y a lieu.*"
Stationery Office: " if appropriate."
[38] French: " *requête.*"
Stationery Office: " formal request."
[39] French: " *du domicile.*"
Stationery Office: " the ' *domicile* '."
[40] Stationery Office: " of the signatory."
[41] Stationery Office: " against whom."
[42] Stationery Office: " is lodged."
[43] French: " *litige.*"
Stationery Office: " dispute."
[44] French: " *les conclusions.*"
Stationery Office: " the relief sought." In the E.C.S.C. Statute, this term is translated as " arguments "—*ibid.* Art. 33, para. 1.
[45] French: " *un exposé sommaire des moyens invoqués.*"
Stationery Office: " a short summary of the main arguments on which the petition is based." In this paragraph, however, the Stationery Office has not been referring to a petition but to a request.

It [46] must be accompanied, where appropriate by the act whose annulment is sought,[47] or, in the case mentioned in Article 175 of the Treaty,[48] by a document [49] establishing the date of the request referred to in that article.[50] If these documents are not annexed to [51] the request, the Registrar shall ask the party concerned to produce them within a reasonable period. However, the case may not be struck out in the event of compliance occurring after the expiration of the time limit for appealing.[52]

ARTICLE 20

In cases provided for under Article 177 of the Treaty,[53] the decision of the municipal court [54] which suspends its proceedings and refers a case to the Court shall be notified to the Court by this municipal court.[55] This decision [56] shall then be notified by the Registrar of the Court [57] to the parties in the case, to the Member States and to the Commission, as well as [58] to the Council if the act the validity or interpretation of which is in dispute originates from the Council.

Within a time period of two months calculated from this last notification [59] the parties, the Member States, the Commission and, where

---

46 French: " *Elle.* "
   Stationery Office: " The formal request."
47 Stationery Office: " the annulment of which is sought."
48 French: " *du Traité.* "
   Stationery Office: " of this Treaty."
49 French: " *une pièce justifiant de la date.* "
   Stationery Office: " documentary evidence of the date."
50 French: " *la date de l'invitation prévue à cet article.* "
   Stationery Office: " the date on which an institution referred to in that Article was called upon to act."
51 Stationery Office: " attached to."
52 French:
   " *sans qu'aucune forclusion puisse être opposée au cas où la regularisation interviendrait après l'expiration du délai de recours.* "
   Stationery Office:
   " in that case the rights of the party shall not lapse even if such documents are produced after the expiry of the time-limit set for the bringing of proceedings."
53 French: " *du Traité.* "
   Stationery Office: " of this Treaty."
54 Stationery Office: " domestic court."
55 French: " *cette juridiction nationale.* "
   Stationery Office: " the domestic court concerned."
56 French: " *Cette decision.* "
   Stationery Office: " Such decision."
57 French: " *greffier de la Cour.* "
   Stationery Office: " the Registrar."
58 French: " *ainsi que.* "
   Stationery Office: " and also."
59 French: " *Dans un délai de deux mois à compter de cette dernière notification.* "
   Stationery Office: " Within two months of such notification." In the French this paragraph opens with these words: the Stationery Office places them at the end of the paragraph.

appropriate, the Council, shall have the right to submit statements [60] or written observations [61] to the Court.

ARTICLE 21

The Court may request [62] the parties to produce all documents and to supply all information which it [63] considers desirable. In case of refusal, the Court shall take judicial notice thereof.

The Court may also request Member States and institutions which are not [64] parties to the case to supply all information which it [65] considers necessary for the proceedings.

ARTICLE 22

The Court may at any time entrust to [66] any person, body, office, commission or organ of its choice, the making of an expert's report.[67]

ARTICLE 23

Witnesses may be heard under conditions which shall be laid down [68] by the Rules of Procedure.

ARTICLE 24

The Court shall have as regards defaulting witnesses the powers generally accorded [69] in such cases to courts and tribunals [70] and may impose

[60] French: " *des mémoires.*"
Stationery Office: " statements of Case."
[61] French: " *observations écrites.*"
Stationery Office: " written comments."
[62] French: " *peut demander.*"
Stationery Office: " may require." In para. 2, the Stationery Office translates " *peut également demander* " as " may also request."
[63] French: "*elle.*"
Stationery Office: " the Court."
[64] French: " *qui ne sont pas.*"
Stationery Office: " not being."
[65] See note 63, above.
[66] French: " *peut confier.*"
Stationery Office: " may charge."
[67] French: " *une expertise.*"
Stationery Office: " an expert examination and report."
[68] French: " *dans les conditions qui seront déterminées.*"
Stationery Office: " in the circumstances to be laid down." In the similar provision in the E.C.S.C. Statute, the Stationery Office translates this phrase as " under conditions which shall be determined."
[69] Stationery Office: " The Court shall have the powers generally possessed by courts of law as regards defaulting witnesses "—in the E.C.S.C. Statute, the Stationery Office translated the same phrase as in the text above.
[70] French: " *cours et tribunaux.*"
Stationery Office: " courts of law."

pecuniary penalties under conditions which shall be laid down [71] by the Rules of Procedure.[72]

ARTICLE 25

Witnesses and experts may be heard on oath [73] taken in the form laid down by the Rules of Procedure or in the manner prescribed [74] by the municipal law [75] of the witness or expert.

ARTICLE 26

The Court may order that a witness or an expert be heard by the judicial authority of his place of residence.

This Order shall be sent for execution to the competent judicial authority in accordance with the Rules of Procedure. The documents arising out of the execution of the *commission rogatoire* [76] shall be sent [77] to the Court under the same conditions.[78]

The Court shall defray the expenses [79] subject to charging them [80] where appropriate, to the parties.[81]

ARTICLE 27

Each Member State shall treat any violation of an oath by a witness or expert as if the similar offence [82] had been committed before a municipal court [83] dealing with a civil matter.[84] When the Court reports such a violation, it [85] shall prosecute the offender before the competent municipal court.[86]

[71] French: " *dans les conditions qui seront déterminées.*"
Stationery Office: " as shall be laid down." *Cf.* note 68, above.
[72] On this occasion only, the Stationery Office prints " Rules of Procedure " with capitals.
[73] Stationery Office: " on an oath."
[74] French: " *prévues.*"
Stationery Office: " laid down." Earlier in this Article " *déterminée* " is also translated as " laid down."
[75] Stationery Office: " domestic law."
[76] French: " *Les pièces resultant de l'exécution de la commission rogatoire.*"
Stationery Office: " The documents obtained in pursuance of these letters of request."
[77] French: " *sont renvoyées.*"
Stationery Office: " shall similarly be sent."
[78] French: " *dans les mêmes conditions.*"
Stationery Office: " in accordance with these rules."
[79] French: " *les frais.*"
Stationery Office: " the expenses incurred."
[80] French: " *sous réserve de les mettre.*"
Stationery Office: " subject to the right to charge their expenses."
[81] French: " *les parties.*"
Stationery Office: " to the parties concerned."
[82] French: " *ce délit correspondant.*"
Stationery Office: " the same offence."
[83] Stationery Office: " domestic court."
[84] French: " *statuant en matière civile.*"
Stationery Office: " dealing with a case in civil proceedings."
[85] French: " *il.*"
Stationery Office: " the Member State concerned."
[86] See note 83, above.

Documents

ARTICLE 28

The hearings shall be public,[87] unless for substantial reasons, it shall be decided otherwise by the Court, of its own motion or at the request of the parties.[88]

ARTICLE 29

During the hearings, the Court may put questions[89] to experts and witnesses, as well as[90] to the parties themselves. However,[91] the latter[92] may address the Court only[93] through their representative.

ARTICLE 30

[As E.C.S.C. Statute, Article 27.]

ARTICLE 31

The cause list shall be settled by the President.

ARTICLE 32

[As E.C.S.C. Statute, Article 29.]

ARTICLE 33

Judgments shall be reasoned. They shall state[94] the names of the judges who took part in the deliberations.[95]

---

87 Stationery Office: "Hearings shall be in public." The translation in the text is as the Stationery Office's translation in the E.C.S.C. Statute, Art. 26.
88 French:
    "*à moins qu'il n'en soit décidé outrement par la Cour d'office ou sur demande des parties, pour les motifs graves.*"
    Stationery Office:
    "Unless the Court, of its own volition or at the request of the parties, shall, for substantial reasons, decide otherwise."
89 French: "*peut interroger.*"
    Stationery Office: "may examine." It is inappropriate in this context to state that the parties are examined.
90 French: "*ainsi que.*"
    Stationery Office: "and."
91 French: "*Toutefois.*"
    Stationery Office: "Provided always that."
92 French: "*ces dernières.*"
    Stationery Office: "the parties."
93 Stationery Office: "may only address the Court."
94 Stationery Office: "They shall give." The translation in the text is as the Stationery Office's translation of the similar provision in E.C.S.C., Art. 30.
95 French: "*les noms des juges qui ont délibéré.*"
    Stationery Office: "the names of the judges responsible for them."

472

ARTICLE 34

Judgments shall be signed by the President and the Registrar. They shall be read in public session.[96]

ARTICLE 35

[As E.C.S.C. Statute, Article 32.]

ARTICLE 36

The President of the Court shall rule,[97] by means of a summary procedure, derogating,[98] to the extent necessary, from certain [99] of the rules contained in the present [1] Statute, and which shall be determined [2] by the Rules of Procedure, upon submissions either for obtaining the stay of execution,[3] as provided for in Article 185 of the [4] Treaty, or for the application of provisional measures [5] pursuant to Article 186, or for a stay of execution [6] in accordance with Article 192, last paragraph.

If the President is prevented from carrying out his duties,[7] his place shall be taken by another judge under conditions laid down [8] by the Rules of Procedure.

[Paragraph 3 as E.C.S.C. Statute, Article 33, para. 3.]

ARTICLE 37

The Member States and the institutions of the Community may intervene in cases before the Court.

[96] Stationery Office: " in open court."
[97] French: " *peut statuer.*"
  Stationery Office: " shall have power to decide certain matters."
[98] French: " *dérogeant.*"
  Stationery Office: " which shall depart."
[99] Stationery Office: " from some."
[1] French: " *le présent.*"
  Stationery Office: " this."
[2] French: " *et qui sera fixée.*"
  Stationery Office: " This summary procedure, the details of which shall be determined."
[3] French: " *conclusions tendant soit à l'obtention du sursis.*"
  Stationery Office: " applications for suspensions of operation."
[4] French: " *du.*"
  Stationery Office: " of this."
[5] Stationery Office: " the prescribing of interim measures."
[6] Stationery Office: " the suspension of enforcement."
[7] Stationery Office: " In the event of the President being prevented from carrying out his duties." The translation in the text is that of the Stationery Office when translating the identical phrase in E.C.S.C. Statute, Art. 33, para. 2.
[8] French: " *dans les conditions déterminées.*
  Stationery Office: " in accordance with." The translation in the text is that of the Stationery Office when translating the identical phrase in E.C.S.C. Statute, Art. 33, para. 2.

The same right shall belong to [9] any other person who shows he has an interest [10] in the result of a case referred to the Court, except in cases [11] between Member States, between institutions of the Community or between Member States and institutions of the Community.

Submissions in the request to intervene [12] may have as their object only [13] the support of the submissions [14] of one of the parties.[15]

ARTICLE 38

[As E.C.S.C. Statute, Article 35, but omitting the words " in a case in *pleine juridiction.*"]

ARTICLE 39

The Member States, the institutions of the Community and any other natural or legal persons may, in cases and under conditions to be fixed [16] by the Rules of Procedure, bring third party proceedings to set aside or modify judgments given without their having been notified [17] where such judgments are prejudicial to their rights.

ARTICLE 40

[As E.C.S.C. Statute, Article 37.]

ARTICLE 41

[As E.C.S.C. Statute, Article 38.]

[9] Stationery Office: " shall appertain to."
[10] French: " *un intérêt.*"
Stationery Office: " a valid interest."
[11] French: " *un litige.*"
Stationery Office: " any case."
[12] French: " *la requête en intervention.*"
Stationery Office: " the application to intervene."
[13] French: " *ne peut avoir d'autre objet que.*"
Stationery Office: " shall be limited to." The translation in the text is that of the Stationery Office when translating the identical phrase in E.C.S.C. Statute, Art. 34, para. 2.
[14] French: " *le soutien des conclusions.*"
Stationery Office: " supporting the case."
[15] French: " *de l'une des parties.*"
Stationery Office: " of one of the original parties to the case."
[16] Stationery Office: " determined."
[17] French: " *former tierce-opposition contre les arrêts rendus sans qu'ils aient été appelés.*"
Stationery Office: " claim as third parties a retrial of cases decided without their having been heard."

ARTICLE 42

[As E.C.S.C. Statute, Article 39, paras. 2 and 3.]

ARTICLE 43

Proceedings against the Community in matters arising from non-contractual responsibility shall be time barred [18] after five years [19] from the occurrence of the event [20] giving rise thereto. The running of time shall be interpreted either by the request brought before the Court [21] or by the preliminary demand [22] which the injured party may send to the appropriate institution [23] of the Community. In this latter case,[24] the request must be brought [25] within the period of two months [26] provided for in Article 173; the provisions of Article 175, second paragraph, shall apply where appropriate.

ARTICLE 44

The Rules of Procedure of the Court provided for under Article 188 of the [27] Treaty shall contain, in addition to [28] the provisions contemplated by the present [29] Statute, all other provisions necessary for its application [30] and, where necessary, for its supplementation.

ARTICLE 45

The Council may, by means of a unanimous vote, make such further amendments to the provisions of the present [31] Statute as may be required

---

[18] Stationery Office: " statute-barred."
[19] French: " *cinq ans.*"
  Stationery Office: " a period of five years."
[20] French: " *le fait.*"
  Stationery Office: " the circumstance."
[21] French: " *soit par la requête formée devant la Cour.*"
  Stationery Office: " by the institution of proceedings before the Court."
[22] French: " *la demande préalable.*"
  Stationery Office: " a prior formal demand."
[23] Stationery Office: " directed to the relevant institution."
[24] French: " *Dans ce dernier cas.*"
  Stationery Office: " In this event." In E.C.S.C. Statute, this was rendered: " In the latter event."
[25] French: " *la requête doit être formée.*"
  Stationery Office: " proceedings must be instituted."
[26] French: " *dans le délai de deux mois.*"
  Stationery Office: " within the two months." In E.C.S.C. Statute this was rendered, " within the period of . . ."—*ibid.* Art. 40.
[27] See note 4, p. 473, above.
[28] Stationery Office: " apart from."
[29] See note 1, p. 473, above.
[30] French: " *l'appliquer.*"
  Stationery Office: " the latter's implementation."
[31] See note 1, p. 473, above.

by reason of the measures which it may take[32] under the terms of the last paragraph of Article 165 of the[33] Treaty.

ARTICLE 46

[As E.C.S.C. Statute, Article 45, but with reference to Article 167, paras. 2 and 3 of the E.E.C. Treaty in place of Article 32 of the E.C.S.C. Treaty.]

---

[32] French: " *qu'il aurait prises.*"
  Stationery Office: " taken by the Council."
[33] French: " *du Traité.*"
  Stationery Office: " of this Treaty."

THE EUROPEAN ATOMIC ENERGY COMMUNITY TREATY PROTOCOL ON THE STATUTE OF THE COURT OF JUSTICE

THE HIGH CONTRACTING PARTIES:

DESIRING TO establish [1] the Statute of the Court provided for by Article 160 of this Treaty,

HAVE AGREED upon the following provisions:

ARTICLE 1

The Court established by Article 3 of the [2] Treaty shall be constituted and shall perform its duties in accordance with the provisions of the Treaty [2] and of the present Statute. [3]

TITLE I

THE JUDGES [4] AND THE ADVOCATES GENERAL

ARTICLE 2

[As E.C.S.C. Statute, Article 2.]

ARTICLE 3

[As E.C.S.C. Statute, Article 3, paras. 1, 2 and 3.]

ARTICLE 4

[As E.E.C. Statute, Article 4.]

ARTICLE 5

[As E.E.C. Statute, Article 5, para. 1.]

[Paragraphs 2 and 3 as E.C.S.C. Statute, Article 6, paras. 2 and 3 but with reference to Article 6 of the Euratom Statute in place of Article 7 of the E.C.S.C. Statute.]

ARTICLE 6

[As E.E.C. Statute, Article 6.]

---

[1] Stationery Office: " Being desirous of establishing."
[2] French: " du Traité."
Stationery Office: " of this Treaty."
[3] French: " du présent Statut."
Stationery Office: " of this Statute."
[4] French: " Statut des Juges."
Stationery Office: " Status of the Judges."

ARTICLE 7

[As E.E.C. Statute, Article 7.]

ARTICLE 8

[As E.E.C. Statute, Article 8.]

TITLE II

ORGANISATION

ARTICLE 9

[As E.E.C. Statute, Article 9.]

ARTICLE 10

[As E.E.C. Statute, Article 10.]

ARTICLE 11

[As E.C.S.C. Statute, Article 16, para. 1, sentences 1 and 2.]

ARTICLE 12

[As E.E.C. Statute, Article 12.]

ARTICLE 13

[As E.C.S.C. Statute, Article 9.]

ARTICLE 14

[As E.C.S.C. Statute, Article 17 [5]]

ARTICLE 15

[As E.C.S.C. Statute, Article 18, para. 2.]

ARTICLE 16

[As E.C.S.C. Statute, Article 19.]

TITLE III

PROCEDURE

ARTICLE 17

[As E.E.C. Statute, Article 17.]

[5] In para. 2 of this Article, the words " *compte tenu des nécessités du service,*" " taking account of the exigencies of its business," are substituted for " *sous réserve des nécessités du service,*" " subject to the exigencies of its business " appearing in E.C.S.C. Statute, Art. 17.

ARTICLE 18

[As E.E.C. Statute, Article 18.]

ARTICLE 19

[As E.E.C. Statute, Article 19.]

ARTICLE 20

In cases provided for under Article 18 of the Treaty,[6] proceedings are instituted before the Court by a request[7] addressed to the Registrar. The request shall contain the name and address[8] of the appellant, and the status[9] of the party signing it,[10] the name of the decision[11] against which the request is lodged, the names of the opposing parties,[12] the subject matter of the action,[13] the submissions[14] and a short summary of the grounds relied upon.[15]

The appeal must[16] be accompanied by a certified copy of the decision of the Arbitration Committee being challenged.[17]

If the Court rejects the appeal, the decision of the Arbitration Committee shall become final.

If the Court annuls the decision of the Arbitration Committee, the matter may be re-opened where appropriate, on the initiative of one

---

[6] French: " *du Traité.*"
Stationery Office: " of this Treaty."
[7] French: " *un recours.*"
Stationery Office: " an appeal." In the similar provision in the E.C.S.C. Statute, Art. 22, " *un recours* " is translated as " a request."
[8] French: " *domicile.*"
Stationery Office: " domicile." The domicile of the party concerned is, of course, quite irrelevant.
[9] French: " *la qualité.*"
Stationery Office: " the description."
[10] Stationery Office: " the signatory."
[11] French: " *l'indication de la décision.*"
Stationery Office: " the Decision."
[12] French: " *l'indication des parties adverses.*"
Stationery Office: " the names of the respondents." The French is wider than to cover merely the respondents, and would include third parties intervening.
[13] French: " *litige.*"
Stationery Office: " the dispute."
[14] French: " *les conclusions.*"
Stationery Office: " the relief sought." In the E.C.S.C. Statute, Art. 20, para. 1, " *les conclusions* " is translated as " the arguments."
[15] French: " *un exposé sommaire des moyens invoqués.*"
Stationery Office: " a short summary of the main arguments on which the appeal is based."
[16] French: " *doit.*"
Stationery Office: " shall." In E.C.S.C. Statute, Art. 20, para. 2 " *doit* " is translated as " must."
[17] French: " *attaquée.*"
Stationery Office: " in dispute."

of the parties in the case before the Arbitration Committee. The latter shall comply with the points of law determined [18] by the Court.

ARTICLE 21
[As E.E.C. Statute, Article 20, but with reference to Article 150 of the Euratom Treaty in place of Article 177 of the E.E.C. Treaty.]

ARTICLE 22
[As E.E.C. Statute, Article 21.]

ARTICLE 23
[As E.E.C. Statute, Article 22.]

ARTICLE 24
[As E.E.C. Statute, Article 23.]

ARTICLE 25
[As E.E.C. Statute, Article 24.]

ARTICLE 26
[As E.E.C. Statute, Article 25.]

ARTICLE 27
[As E.E.C. Statute, Article 26.]

ARTICLE 28
[As E.E.C. Statute, Article 27.]

ARTICLE 29
[As E.E.C. Statute, Article 28.]

ARTICLE 30
[As E.E.C. Statute, Article 29.]

ARTICLE 31
[As E.C.S.C. Statute, Article 27.]

[18] French: " *se conforme aux points de droit arrêtés par la Cour.*"
Stationery Office: " shall comply with decisions on points of law given by the Court."

480

ARTICLE 32

[As E.E.C. Statute, Article 31.]

ARTICLE 33

[As E.C.S.C. Statute, Article 29.]

ARTICLE 34

[As E.E.C. Statute, Article 33.]

ARTICLE 35

[As E.E.C. Statute, Article 34.]

ARTICLE 36

[As E.C.S.C. Statute, Article 32.]

ARTICLE 37

[As E.E.C. Statute, Article 36, but with reference to Article 157, Article 158 and Article 164, last paragraph, of the Euratom Treaty in place of Article 185, Article 186 and Article 192, last paragraph of the E.E.C. Treaty.]

ARTICLE 38

[As E.E.C. Statute, Article 37.]

ARTICLE 39

[As E.C.S.C. Statute, Article 35 but omitting the words " in a case in *pleine juridiction.*"]

ARTICLE 40

[As E.E.C. Statute, Article 39.]

ARTICLE 41

[As E.C.S.C. Statute, Article 37.]

ARTICLE 42

[As E.C.S.C. Statute, Article 38.]

ARTICLE 43

[As E.C.S.C. Statute, Article 39, paras. 2 and 3.]

ARTICLE 44

[As E.E.C. Statute, Article 43.]

ARTICLE 45

[As E.E.C. Statute, Article 44 but with reference to Article 160 of the Euratom Treaty in place of Article 188 of the E.E.C. Treaty.]

ARTICLE 46

[As E.E.C. Statute, Article 45 but with reference to Article 137, last paragraph of the Euratom Treaty in place of the last paragraph of Article 165 of the E.E.C. Treaty.]

ARTICLE 147

[As E.C.S.C. Statute, Article 45 but with reference to Article 193, paragraphs 2 and 3 in place of Article 32 of the E.C.S.C. Treaty.]

RULES OF PROCEDURE OF THE COURT OF JUSTICE [1]

THE COURT, having

considered the powers given to the Court of Justice by the Treaty establishing the European Coal and Steel Community, the Treaty establishing the European Economic Community and the Treaty establishing the European Atomic Energy Community (Euratom) [2];

considered Articles 3 and 4 of the Convention relating to [3] certain institutions common to the European Communities;

considered Articles 20, 28 and 44 of the Protocol on the Statute of the Court of Justice of the European Coal and Steel Community;

considered Article 44 of the Protocol on the Statute of the Court of Justice of the European Economic Community [4];

considered Article 45 of the Protocol on the Statute of the Court of Justice of the European Atomic Energy Community;

considered the letters dated December 23, 1958, by means of which the Court of Justice forwarded to the Councils the draft of the Rules of Procedure;

considered the unanimous approval given on February 2, 1959, by the Council of the European Economic Community by virtue of Article 188 of the Treaty;

considered the unanimous approval given on February 2, 1959, by the Council of the European Atomic Energy Community by virtue of Article 160 of the Treaty;

considered the approval given on March 2, 1959, by the Special Council of Ministers of the European Coal and Steel Community by virtue of Articles 20 and 28 of the Statute of the Court of Justice;

---

[1] *Journal Officiel*, January 18, 1960, p. 13. An earlier version of the Rules published in the *Journal Officiel* on March 3, 1959, p. 349, contained 27 errors and was completely superseded. For a further translation of the Rules, see *The Rules of Procedure of the Court of Justice of the European Communities*, Sythott, Leyden (1962).

[2] The Stationery Office in its translation refers to these three Treaties as " setting up " the three Communities, and is thus inconsistent with the titles of those Treaties in its own translation of them where the correct term " establishing " is used.

[3] The Stationery Office in its translation refers to the Convention " on " certain institutions: this is again inconsistent with its own translation of the Convention which was the term " relating to."

[4] The Stationery Office translation refers to " The Statute of the European Coal and Steel Community Court of Justice," etc., a translation out of line even with the translation of Art. 1 of the Rules.

LAYS DOWN the following Rules of Procedure:

PRELIMINARY PROVISION

ARTICLE 1

In the provisions of these Rules of Procedure:
the Treaty establishing the European Coal and Steel Community [2] shall be called " the E.C.S.C. Treaty ";
the Protocol on the Statute of the Court of Justice of the European Coal and Steel Community shall be called " the E.C.S.C. Statute ";
the Treaty establishing the European Economic Community [2] shall be called " the E.E.C. Treaty ";
the Protocol on the Statute of the Court of Justice of the European Economic Community shall be called " the E.E.C. Statute ";
the Treaty establishing the European Atomic Energy Community (Euratom) shall be called " the E.A.E.C. Treaty ";
the Protocol on the Statute of the Court of Justice of the European Atomic Energy Community shall be called " the E.A.E.C. Statute."

For the purposes of these Rules, the term " institutions " shall mean the institutions of the European Communities, including the European Investment Bank.

PART I

ORGANISATION OF THE COURT

CHAPTER 1

JUDGES

ARTICLE 2

The period of office of a judge shall commence from the date laid down in his appointment. If the formal document of appointment does not lay down a date, then the period shall commence from the date of the document.

ARTICLE 3

Paragraph 1

Before taking up their office, judges shall swear the following oath at the first public sitting of the Court which they attend after their appointment:

" I swear to perform my duties conscientiously and with complete impartiality: I swear to divulge nothing of the Court's consideration of its judgments."

Paragraph 2

The oath may be taken in the forms laid down by the national legislation of the judge concerned.

Paragraph 3

Immediately after having taken the oath, judges shall sign a declaration by which they solemnly undertake to respect, both during their term of office and after its termination, those obligations inherent in their position, and in particular the duty of exercising honesty and discretion as regards accepting certain positions or certain benefits after they have ceased to hold office.

ARTICLE 4

The order of precedence of judges shall be governed by their seniority of office.

The precedence of judges having the same seniority of office shall be governed by their seniority of age.

Retiring judges who are re-appointed shall retain their original precedence.

ARTICLE 5

When the Court is called upon to decide whether a judge no longer fulfils the required conditions or no longer satisfies the obligations inherent in his position, the President shall invite the person concerned to appear at a private session of the Court,[5] and present his comments, without the Registrar being present.

CHAPTER 2

PRESIDENCY OF THE COURT, AND OF ITS CHAMBERS [6]

ARTICLE 6

Paragraph 1

The judges shall elect one of their number as President of the Court for a period of three years, immediately after the partial renewal

---

5 French: *" En Chambre du conseil."*
   Stationery Office: " In the Judges' Council Chamber."
6 French: *" Chambres."*
   Stationery Office: " sections." In the Statute of the International Court of Justice (Art. 29) *" chambre "* is translated as " Chamber."

provided for in Articles 32 (3) of the E.C.S.C. Treaty,[7] 167 of the E.E.C. Treaty and 139 of the E.A.E.C. Treaty.

Paragraph 2

The Court shall elect for a period of one year Presidents of the Chambers [6] referred to in Article 24 of these Rules.

Paragraph 3

In the event of the termination of the mandate of the President of the Court or of a President of a Chamber [6] before the end of their normal period of office, the Court shall appoint a replacement for the remainder of the current period.

Paragraph 4

Voting at the elections mentioned in this Article shall be by secret ballot, the judge obtaining an absolute majority being elected. Should none of the judges obtain an absolute majority, a new ballot shall be taken and the judge obtaining the most votes shall be elected. Where voting is equal, the elder shall be elected.

ARTICLE 7

Paragraph 1

The President shall direct the work and the running of the Court; he shall preside at sittings of the Court and at the deliberations at a private session of the Court.[8]

Paragraph 2

In the event of absence or inability to attend of the President of the Court, or of the post being vacant, his functions shall be taken over by one of the Presidents of the Chambers [6] according to the order of precedence laid down in Article 4 of these Rules.

In the event of inability to attend of both the President of the Court and the Presidents of the Chambers,[6] or of all their posts being vacant at the same time, the functions of President shall be taken over by one of the other judges according to the order of precedence laid down in Article 4 of these Rules.

---

[7] French: " *Article 32 ter.*"
Stationery Office: " Article 32 (c)."

[8] French: " *ainsi que les délibérations en chambre du conseil.*"
Stationery Office: " and at the proceedings in the Judges' Council Chamber." The Rules of the International Court of Justice (Art. 30) translate " *La Cour délibère au Chambre du Conseil* " as " The Court shall sit in private to deliberate."

CHAPTER 3

ADVOCATES GENERAL

ARTICLE 8

The provisions of Articles 2, 3 and 5 of these Rules are applicable to Advocates General.

ARTICLE 9

The Advocates General follow the judges in order of precedence, according to the rules laid down in Article 4 of these Rules.

ARTICLE 10

Paragraph 1

When the Chambers [6] are set up, the Court shall decide on the assignment of an Advocate General to each Chamber.[6]

The President may, on the joint proposal [9] of the Advocates General, appoint for a particular case the Advocate General assigned to the other Chamber.[6]

Paragraph 2

In the event of one of the Advocates General being absent or unable to attend, and where there is a question of urgency, the President may call on the other Advocate General.

CHAPTER 4

REGISTRY [10]

Section 1

Registrar and Deputy Registrars

ARTICLE 11

Paragraph 1

The Registrar is appointed by the Court, after hearing the Advocates General.

[9] The Stationery Office prints " joint proposal " with a capital " J " and a small " p."
[10] French: " *Le Greffe.*"
Stationery Office: " Registrar's Office."

Documents

The President shall inform the judges and Advocates General of the candidates whose names have been submitted for the post, fourteen days before the date fixed for the appointment.

Paragraph 2

Applications shall be accompanied by full details of age, nationality, university degrees, linguistic knowledge, present and past occupations and of any experience of candidates in the judicial and international fields.

Paragraph 3

The procedure for the appointment shall be that laid down in Article 6, paragraph 4, of these Rules.

Paragraph 4

The Registrar shall be appointed for a period of six years, and shall be eligible for re-appointment.

Paragraph 5

The provisions of Article 3 of these Rules shall be applicable to the Registrar.

Paragraph 6

The Registrar may be relieved of his office only [11] if he no longer fulfils the required conditions or if he no longer fulfils the duties of his position; the Court shall reach its decision at a private session [4] after having heard the Advocates General and having given the Registrar the opportunity of presenting his comments.

Paragraph 7

Should the Registrar cease to hold office [12] before the end of his period of office, the Court shall appoint a new Registrar for a period of six years.

ARTICLE 12

The Court may, following the procedure laid down for the Registrar, appoint one or more Deputy Registrars to assist the Registrar and to take his place within the limitations specified in the instructions to the Registrar referred to in Article 14 of these Rules.

[11] Stationery Office: " may only be relieved of his office."
[12] French: " *cesse ses fonctions.*"
Stationery Office: " relinquish his post." This is inaccurate as the present provision covers the case of dismissal as well as that of retirement.

ARTICLE 13

In the event of the absence or inability to attend of the Registrar and his deputies, or in the event of their posts being vacant at the same time, the President shall appoint an official to carry out the duties of Registrar for the time being.

ARTICLE 14

The instruction to the Registrar shall be drawn up by the Court on proposals put forward by the President.[13]

ARTICLE 15

Paragraph 1

A register, initialled by the President, shall be kept in the Registry [10] and under the Registrar's responsibility, recording after [14] and in the order of their occurrence or submission all steps in the procedure and exhibits submitted in support.

Paragraph 2

The Registrar shall mark original documents to show that they have been entered in the register, and shall also, upon the demand of the parties, so mark copies submitted for this purpose.

Paragraph 3

The recording in the register and the marking specified in the foregoing paragraph shall constitute an official record.

Paragraph 4

The way in which the register is kept shall be determined by the instructions to the Registrar specified in Article 14 of these Rules.

Paragraph 5

Any interested person may consult the register in the Registry [10] and may obtain copies of extracts according to the scale of charges laid down by the Court on proposals put forward by the Registrar.[15]

All parties to a case may furthermore obtain, at the appropriate charge, copies of the written pleadings and office copies of orders and decisions.

---

13 For these Rules, see pp. 545–555, below.
14 French: " *à la suite.*"
   Stationery Office: " one after another."
15 For this scale, see Instructions to the Registrar, Art. 20, p. 552, below.

Documents

Paragraph 6

A notice shall be published in the *Journal Officiel des Communautés Européennes* [16] indicating the date of the request [17] instituting proceedings, the names and addresses [18] of the parties, the matter in dispute and the relief sought in the request.

ARTICLE 16

Paragraph 1

Subject to the directions of the President, it shall be for the Registrar to receive, send, and preserve all documents, and to effect all notifications required by these Rules.

Paragraph 2

The Registrar shall assist the Court, the Chambers,[6] the President and the judges in all their official duties.[19]

ARTICLE 17

The Registrar shall have custody of the seals. He shall be responsible for the Court Archives, and be in charge of Court publications.

ARTICLE 18

Subject to the provisions of Articles 5 and 27 of these Rules, the Registrar shall attend the sittings of the Court and the Chambers.[6]

Section 2

Court Administrative Services

ARTICLE 19

Paragraph 1

The officials and other servants of the Court shall be appointed in the manner laid down in the regulations setting out the terms of service of personnel.

---

[16] Stationery Office: " The Official Journal of the European Communities." As no English translation of the *Journal Officiel* exists, there is no publication of this name. The Stationery Office sometimes prints this title in italics and sometimes not—*cf.* Art. 80, para. 2 and Art. 112.

[17] French: " *la requête.*"
Stationery Office: " Formal request."

[18] French: " *domicile.*"
Stationery Office: " domicile."

[19] French: " *dans tous les actes de leur ministère.*"
Stationery Office: " In the carrying-out of all their duties and functions."

Paragraph 2

Before taking up their posts, officials shall take the following oath before the President and in the presence of the Registrar:
" I swear to carry out the duties assigned to me by the Court of Justice of the European Communities with complete loyalty, discretion and conscientiousness."

Paragraph 3

The oath may be taken in the form provided by the national legislation of the official concerned.

ARTICLE 20

On proposals put forward by the Registrar, the Court shall decide or amend the organisation of the Court administrative services.

ARTICLE 21

The Court shall set up a translation department [20] composed of experts having appropriate legal knowledge and extensive knowledge of several of the official languages of the Court.

ARTICLE 22

The administration of the Court, the financial management and the keeping of the Court's accounts shall, under the authority of the President, be undertaken by the Registrar with the help of an administrative assistant.

CHAPTER 5

ASSISTANT RAPPORTEURS

ARTICLE 23

Paragraph 1

Where the Court feels that it is necessary for the study of, and the Instruction [21] in, cases placed before it, it shall, pursuant to Article 16

[20] Stationery Office: " a language department."
[21] French: " *l'étude et l'instruction.*"
Stationery Office: " the study and investigation of the cases." This fails to bring out that the Instruction is a distinct procedural stage in the trial of a case—see Arts. 45–54.

of the E.C.S.C. Statute and Article 12 of the E.E.C. and E.A.E.C. Statutes, propose the appointment of assistant Rapporteurs.

Paragraph 2

The duties of assistant Rapporteurs are, in particular:
—to assist the President in the summary procedure [22];
—to assist *juges rapporteurs* [23] in their work.

Paragraph 3

In the carrying out of their functions the assistant Rapporteurs shall be responsible to the President of the Court, the President of a Chamber [24] or the *juge rapporteur*,[25] as the case may be.

Paragraph 4

Before taking up their duties, the assistant Rapporteurs shall take before the Court the oath laid down in Article 3 of these Rules of Procedure.

CHAPTER 6

THE CHAMBERS [24]

ARTICLE 24

Paragraph 1

The Court shall constitute within itself two Chambers [24] each of three judges, which shall undertake the Instruction [26] of the cases assigned to them.

Paragraph 2

As soon as a request [27] has been filed, the President shall assign the case to one of the Chambers [24] and appoint from within that Chamber [24] the *juge rapporteur*.[28]

---

[22] French: "*la procédure de référé*."
   Stationery Office: " in the summary procedure in case of urgency."
[23] See note 21, p. 466, above.
[24] See note 6, p. 485, above.
[25] See note 23, above.
[26] See note 24, above.
[27] See note 17, p. 490, above.
[28] French: "*et designe le juge rapporteur en son sein*."
   Stationery Office: " and appoint the Judge acting as Rapporteur within that Section."
   As the position of a judge acting as a rapporteur does not exist in English law, it is felt that it is preferable to retain the French term.

Unless the President decides otherwise, the *juge rapporteur* [28] shall continue to exercise that function, even though he may be appointed to the other Chamber [24] in the course of the proceedings.

CHAPTER 7

FUNCTIONING OF THE COURT

ARTICLE 25

Paragraph 1

The dates and times of the sittings of the Court shall be fixed by the President.

Paragraph 2

The dates and times of the sittings of the Chambers [24] shall be fixed by the President of each of them.

Paragraph 3

The Court and the Chambers [29] may, for one or more given sittings, choose a place other than that where the Court has its seat.

ARTICLE 26

Paragraph 1

If, by reason of absence or inability to attend or in consequence of Article 24, Paragraph 2, second Sub-paragraph, of these Rules, there is an even number of judges, then the junior judge as ascertained under Article 4 of these Rules shall abstain from taking part in the judges' consideration of their judgment.

Paragraph 2

If, when the Court has been convened, it is found that the quorum of five judges is not present, then the President shall adjourn the sitting until the quorum is present.

Paragraph 3

If, in one of the Chambers [29] the quorum of three judges is not present, the President of that Chamber [29] shall inform the President of the Court of the fact and the latter shall then appoint another judge to take the place of the judge who is unable to attend.

[29] See note 6, p. 485, above.

Documents

ARTICLE 27

Paragraph 1

Both the Court and its Chambers shall consider their judgments in private.[30]

Paragraph 2

Only those judges who have been present at the oral proceedings and, if required, the assistant Rapporteur entrusted with the study of the case, shall take part in the consideration of the judgment to be given.

Paragraph 3

Each of the judges taking part in the consideration of the judgment shall express his opinion giving his grounds therefor.

Paragraph 4

At the request of a judge, any question shall be formulated [31] in the official languages selected by him [32] and communicated in writing to the Court or the Chamber [29] before being put to the vote.

Paragraph 5

The findings reached by the majority of the judges after final discussion shall constitute the decision of the Court. Votes shall be cast in reverse order of precedence to that laid down in Article 4 of these Rules.

Paragraph 6

In the event of a difference of opinion on the purpose, purport and order of questions, or on the interpretation of the voting, the Court or the Chamber [29] shall decide.

Paragraph 7

When the Court has to decide on administrative matters,[33] the Advocates General shall take part and may vote.[34] The Registrar shall be present, unless the Court decides otherwise.

[30] See note 5, p. 485, above.
[31] Stationery Office: " shall be phrased."
[32] Stationery Office: " of his choice."
[33] Stationery Office: " administrative questions."
[34] French:
    " *Lorsque les délibérations de la Cour portent sur des questions administratives, les avocats généraux y prennent part avec voix délibérative.*"
Stationery Office:
    " When the Court has to decide on administrative questions, the Advocates General shall take part in the judgment."
The Stationery Office translation thus omits all reference to voting. The term

Paragraph 8

When the Court sits without the Registrar being present, it shall instruct the junior judge within the meaning of Article 4 of these Rules of Procedure [35] to draw up a record of the proceedings if required. This record shall be signed by this judge and by the President.

ARTICLE 28

Paragraph 1

Unless there be a special decision by the Court, the Court vacations shall be as follows:

from December 18 to January 10;
from the Sunday next before [36] Easter Sunday to the second Sunday after Easter Sunday;
from July 15 to September 15.

During the Court vacations, the functions of President shall be exercised in the place where the Court has its seat, either by the President himself, who shall keep in touch with the Registrar, or by a President of a Chamber [37] or another judge whom he asks to take his place.

Paragraph 2

During the vacations, the President may, in case of urgency, convene the judges and the Advocates General.

Paragraph 3

The Court shall observe the official public holidays of the place where it has its seat.

Paragraph 4

The Court may, where there are good reasons, grant leave of absence to judges and Advocates General.

"judgment" is inappropriate to a decision taken, *e.g.*, under Art. 20 amending the Court's administrative services.

[35] French: "*présent règlement*."
Stationery Office: "These Rules of Procedure." There is no consistency in the Stationery Office's translation of this phrase, *e.g.*, in Art. 27 para. 5 "*présent règlements*" is translated as "these Rules."
[36] Stationery Office: "The Sunday preceding Easter."
[37] See note 6, p. 485, above.

CHAPTER 8
OFFICIAL LANGUAGES

ARTICLE 29

Paragraph 1

The official languages of the Court shall be Dutch, French, German and Italian.

Only one of the official languages may be used as the procedural language.

Paragraph 2

The choice of procedural language shall be made by the Plaintiff with the following reservations:

(*a*) if the Defendant is a Member State or natural person or legal person subject to the jurisdiction of a Member State,[38] then the procedural language shall be the official language of that State; in the event of there being more than one official language, the plaintiff shall be allowed to choose whichever suits him;

(*b*) upon joint request by the parties concerned, the Court may authorise [39] the use of another official language as the procedural language;

(*c*) at the request of one of the parties, after hearing the other party and the Advocate General, the Court or the Chamber [40] may, notwithstanding sub-paragraphs (*a*) and (*b*) above, authorise the total or partial use of another official language as the procedural language; this request may not be submitted by one of the institutions of the European Communities.

In the cases provided for in Article 103 of these Rules of Procedure, the procedural language shall be that of the national court of law which lays the matter before the Court.

Paragraph 3

The procedural language shall be used in particular in the parties' written statements of case and in their pleadings,[41] including such exhibits

---

[38] French: " *ressortissant d'un État membre.*"
Stationery Office: " being a national of or constituted under the laws of a Member State."

[39] On this occasion this word is spelt by the Stationery Office with a " z." Where it appears in the next sub-para. it is spelt with an " s."

[40] See note 6, p. 485, above.

[41] French: " *et plaidoires des parties.*"
Stationery Office: " and in their Counsel's speeches." This reference to Counsel is confusing: parties may plead through an agent, or counsel—E.C.S.C. Statute, Art. 20; E.E.C. Statute, Art. 17: Euratom Statute, Art. 17.

as are annexed, and in the written record of the proceedings and decisions of the Court.

All exhibits and all documents which are produced or annexed and are drawn up in a language other than the procedural language shall be accompanied by a translation into [42] the procedural language.

However, in the case of bulky exhibits and documents, translations of extracts may be submitted. The Court or the Chamber [43] may, at any time, require a more complete or verbatim translation, either of its own motion [44] or at the request of one of the parties.

Paragraph 4

When witnesses or experts state that they are unable to express themselves properly in one of the official languages, the Court or the Chamber [43] shall authorise them to make their statements in another language. The Registrar shall ensure its translation into the procedural language.

Paragraph 5

An official language other than the procedural language may be used by the President of the Court and Presidents of the Chambers [43] in directing the proceedings, by the *juge rapporteur* [28] for his preliminary report and his report at the hearing, by judges and Advocates General when putting questions and by Advocates General when making their submissions. The Registrar shall ensure its translation into the procedural language.

ARTICLE 30

Paragraph 1

The Registrar shall ensure that at the request of one of the judges, of the Advocates General or of one of the parties, a translation into [45] the official languages of his choice is made of anything [46] said or written during the proceedings before the Court or Chamber.[43]

Paragraph 2

The Court publications shall be made in the official languages.

[42] Stationery Office: " in " ; *cf.* Art. 29, paras. 4 and 5.
[43] See note 21, p. 466, above.
[44] Stationery Office: " of its own volition."
[45] Stationery Office: " in " ; *cf.* Art. 29, paras. 4 and 5.
[46] Stationery Office: " of what is."

ARTICLE 31

Texts drawn up in the procedural language or, where necessary, in another language authorised by the Court by virtue of Article 29, Paragraph 4 of these Rules, shall be authentic.

CHAPTER 9

RIGHTS AND OBLIGATIONS OF AGENTS, LEGAL ADVISERS AND COUNSEL

ARTICLE 32

Paragraph 1

Agents representing a State or institution together with legal advisers and counsel appearing before the Court, or before a judicial authority appointed by it by virtue of a *commission rogatoire* [47] shall enjoy immunity in regard to spoken words and written documents relevant to the case or parties in question.

Paragraph 2

Agents, legal advisers and counsel shall also enjoy the following privileges and facilities:

(*a*) all papers and documents relating to the proceedings shall be exempt from search and confiscation.

In [48] case of dispute, the Customs officials or police may seal the papers and documents in question, which shall then be forwarded immediately to the Court for examination in the presence of the Registrar and of the person concerned.

(*b*) agents, legal advisers and counsel shall be entitled to such allocation of currency as may be necessary for the carrying out of their tasks.

(*c*) agents, legal advisers and counsel shall enjoy such liberty of movement as may be necessary for the carrying out of their tasks.

---

[47] French:

"*une autorité judiciaire commise par elle en vertu d'une commission rogatoire, jouissent de l'inviolabilité pour les paroles prononcées et les écrits produits relatifs à la cause ou aux parties.*"

Stationery Office:

"a judicial authority appointed by the Court by virtue of letters of request."

[48] The Stationery Office does not print this as a separate paragraph.

ARTICLE 33

In order to enjoy the privileges, immunities and facilities specified in the preceding Article, they shall first furnish the following proof of status:

(*a*) for agents, an official document issued by the State or institution which they represent; a copy of this document shall immediately be sent [49] to the Registrar by the State or institution concerned;

(*b*) for legal advisers and counsel, credentials signed by the Registrar. The validity of these credentials shall be limited to a set period, which may be extended or shortened according to the length of the proceedings.

ARTICLE 34

The privileges, immunities and facilities specified in Article 32 of these Rules are granted solely in the interest of the proceedings.

The Court may waive immunity when it considers that such waiver is not inconsistent with the interest of the proceedings.[50]

ARTICLE 35

Paragraph 1

Any legal adviser or counsel whose conduct before the Court, a Chamber [51] or a municipal judge [52] is incompatible with the dignity of the Court, or who makes use of the rights which he enjoys by reason of his position for purposes [53] other than those for which they are intended may at any time be barred from the proceedings by order of the Court or Chamber [51] after the Advocate General has been heard and the defence of the party concerned has been ensured.[54]

This order shall be enforceable immediately.

---

[49] Stationery Office: " shall be at once passed."
[50] French: " *la levée de celle-ci n'est pas contraire à l'intérêt de la procédure.*"
Stationery Office:
" such waiver of immunity is not inconsistent with the proper conduct of the proceedings."
In sub-para. 1 of this article it is stated that these privileges, etc., " are granted solely in the interest of the proceedings " (" *sont accordées exclusivement dans l'intérêt de la procédure* "), and in sub-para. 2 the French repeats the phrase " *intérêt de la procédure.*" It is suggested that it is unfortunate for the Stationery Office to introduce the new concept of " proper conduct."
[51] See note 6, p. 485, above.
[52] French: " *ou magistrat.*"
Stationery Office: " or a member of the Court." The Stationery Office is referring to a member of the Communities' Court: the French, however, is referring to a judge of the judicial authority mentioned in Art. 32, para. 1.
[53] Stationery Office: " to ends."
[54] French: " *la défense de l'intéressé assurée.*"
Stationery Office: " after giving full opportunity to the person concerned to reply to the complaint against him."

Documents

Paragraph 2

Where a legal adviser or counsel is barred from the proceedings, the proceedings shall be adjourned for a period set [55] by the President, in order to allow the party concerned to appoint another legal adviser or counsel.

Paragraph 3

Decisions taken pursuant to the provisions of this Article may be declared no longer effective.

ARTICLE 36

The provisions of this Chapter shall be applicable to senior university teachers [56] having the right to appear before the Court in accordance with Article 20 of the E.C.S.C. Statute and Article 17 of the E.E.C. and E.A.E.C. Statutes.

PART 2

THE PROCEDURE

CHAPTER 1
WRITTEN PROCEEDINGS [57]

ARTICLE 37

Paragraph 1

The original of every procedural document [58] shall be signed by the agent or counsel of the party concerned.

It shall be submitted with two copies for the Court and as many copies as there are parties in the case. These copies shall be certified by the party submitting them.

[55] French: " *jusqu'à l'expiration d'un délai fixé.*"
   Stationery Office: " for a period to be set."
[56] French: " *professeurs.*"
   Stationery Office: " senior teachers."
[57] French: " *De la procédure écrite.*"
   Stationery Office: " written procedure."
   In the Rules of the International Court of Justice, the phrase " *De la procédure écrite* " is translated as " written proceedings."
[58] French: " *l'original de tout acte de procédure.*"
   Stationery Office: " The original of every record of a step in the procedure."

Paragraph 2

Within such time as is specified by the Court, institutions [59] shall furthermore produce translations of every procedural document [60] into [61] the other official languages. The second sub-paragraph of the last preceding paragraph shall apply.

Paragraph 3

Every procedural document [62] shall be dated. For the purpose of calculating time limits, only the date of submission to the Registry [63] of the Court shall be taken into consideration.

Paragraph 4

Every procedural document [64] shall have annexed to it a file containing the supporting exhibits and documents, together with a schedule of these exhibits and documents.

Paragraph 5

If, by reason of the length of an exhibit or document, extracts only are annexed to the procedural document,[64] then the exhibit or document in its entirety, or a complete copy thereof, shall be deposited in the Registry.[65]

ARTICLE 38

Paragraph 1

The request [66] referred to in Articles 22 of the E.C.S.C. and 19 of the E.E.C. and E.A.E.C. Statutes shall contain:

(a) the name and address of the plaintiff [67];

(b) the description of the party against whom the appeal [68] is made;

---

[59] The Stationery Office here prints "Institutions" with a capital "I"; *cf.* the small "i" in, especially, Art. 1, para. 2.
[60] French: "*traductions de tout acte de procédure.*"
Stationery Office: "translations of all records of steps in the procedure."
[61] Stationery Office: "in."
[62] French: "*tout acte de procédure.*"
Stationery Office: "Every record of a step in the procedure."
[63] French: "*Le Greffe.*"
Stationery Office: "The office of the Registrar."
[64] See note 62, above.
[65] See note 63, above.
[66] French: "*La requête.*"
Stationery Office: "The formal request."
[67] French: "*Les nom et domicile du réquérant.*"
Stationery Office: "The full names and 'domicile' of the plaintiff"—in other places plaintiff is printed with a capital "P," *e.g.*, Art. 38, para. 5.
[68] French: "*La requête est formée.*"
Stationery Office: "The request is made." The request is the technical name of the document by which an appeal to the Court commenced: no request as such is being made to the defendant.

   (c) the object of the action [69] and a summary of the main arguments put forward;

   (d) the relief sought by the plaintiff;

   (e) an outline of the evidence, if any.[70]

Paragraph 2

For the purpose of the procedure, the request [71] shall specify an address for service at the place [72] where the Court has its seat. It shall also indicate the name of the person who has been authorised to accept service [73] of documents and who has agreed to do so.

Paragraph 3

Counsel assisting or representing a party shall be required to submit credentials to the Registry,[74] certifying that he is a member of the Bar [75] in one of the Member States.

Paragraph 4

The request [76] shall be accompanied, where applicable,[77] by the exhibits specified in Article 22, Second Paragraph of the E.C.S.C. Statute and in Article 19, Second Paragraph, of the E.E.C. and E.A.E.C. Statutes.

Paragraph 5

If the Plaintiff is a legal person in private law,[78] it shall attach to its request [79]:

   (a) its memorandum and articles of association [80];

   (b) proof that the powers granted to counsel have been properly conferred by a representative authorised to do so.

---

[69] French: " *L'objet du litige.*"
   Stationery Office: " the subject in dispute."
[70] French: " *Les offres de preuve s'il y a lieu.*"
   Stationery Office: " means of proof available where necessary."
[71] See note 66, p. 501, above.
[72] French: " *au lieu.*"
   Stationery Office: " in the town."
[73] French: " *à recevoir toutes significations.*"
   Stationery Office: " to receive service."
[74] See note 63, p. 501, above.
[75] French: " *un avocat inscrit à un barreau.*"
   Stationery Office: " a practising member of the Bar."
[76] See note 66, p. 501, above.
[77] French: " *s'il y a lieu.*"
   Stationery Office: " if necessary."
[78] French: " *de droit privé.*"
   Stationery Office: " constituted under private law."
[79] See note 66, p. 501, above.
[80] French: " *ses statuts.*"
   Stationery Office: " its statutes."

Paragraph 6

Requests [81] presented by virtue of Articles 42 and 89 of the E.C.S.C. Treaty, Articles 181 and 182 of the E.E.C. Treaty and Articles 153 and 154 of the E.A.E.C. Treaty shall be accompanied, as the case may be, by a copy of the clause conferring jurisdiction [82] contained in the contract made under public law or private law by the Communities or on their behalf, or by a copy of the submission agreement [83] reached between the Member States concerned.

Paragraph 7

If the request [84] does not comply with the conditions enumerated in Paragraphs 2 to 6 of the present Article, then the Registrar shall fix a reasonable period for the Plaintiff to regularise the request [84] or to produce the documents [85] mentioned above. Failing such regularisation or production within the period allowed, the Court shall decide after hearing the Advocate General, whether as a result of the non-compliance with these conditions it must refuse to entertain the request as being bad in form.

ARTICLE 39

The request shall be served on [86] the Defendant. In the case provided for in Paragraph 7 of the preceding Article, the request shall be served as soon as it has been regularised [87] or the Court has agreed to entertain it having regard to the formal requirements set out in the preceding Article.

ARTICLE 40

Paragraph 1

During the month following service [88] of the request,[89] the Defendant shall submit a defence,[90] containing:

[81] See note 66, p. 501, above.
[82] French: " *un exemplaire de la clause compromissoire.*"
Stationery Office: " copy of the arbitration clause "; under the articles cited, however, the Court does not act as an arbitrator.
[83] French: " *du compromis.*"
Stationery Office: " the special agreement."
[84] See note 66, p. 501, above.
[85] French: " *pièces.*"
Stationery Office: " the papers."
[86] French: " *signifiée.*"
Stationery Office: " notified to."
[87] French: "*la signification est faite dès la régularisation.*"
Stationery Office: " notification shall be served as soon as the request has been regularised "—the service of notification is a difficult concept.
[88] *Cf.* note 86, above.
[89] See note 66, p. 501, above.
[90] French: " *un mémoire en défense.*"
Stationery Office: " a statement of defence."

(*a*) the name and address [91] of the Defendant;
(*b*) the arguments of fact and of law which are relied upon;
(*c*) the submissions of the Defendant;
(*d*) an outline of the evidence.[92]

The provisions of Article 38, Paragraphs 2 to 5 of these Rules shall apply.

Paragraph 2

The time limit allowed by the preceding paragraph may be extended by the President at the Defendant's request and for good cause shown.

ARTICLE 41

Paragraph 1

The request [93] and the defence [94] may be supplemented by a reply from the Plaintiff and by a rejoinder from the Defendant.

Paragraph 2

The President shall set a date by which these procedural documents [95] shall be submitted.

ARTICLE 42

Paragraph 1

The parties in the reply and the rejoinder may put forward further evidence in support of their arguments.[96] They shall give reasons for the delay in the presentation of their additional evidence.[97]

---

[91] French: " *domicile.*"
  Stationery Office: " ' domicile '."
[92] French: " *Les offres de preuve.*"
  Stationery Office: " means of proof available."
[93] See note 66, p. 501, above.
[94] French: " *le mémoirs en défense.*"
  Stationery Office: " the formal statement of defence "—the translation of this term has thus varied since Art. 40, para. 1; in Art. 42 the translation becomes merely " the defence."
[95] French: " *ces actes de procédure.*"
  Stationery Office: " these formal documents." The word " formal " as used here, however, has a different meaning from the Stationery Office's use of " formal " in the phrase " formal statement of defence " in Art. 41, para. 1.
[96] French:
  " *Les parties peuvent encore faire des offres de preuve dans la réplique et la duplique à l'appui de leur argumentation.*"
  Stationery Office: " The parties may in reply to the defence and in rejoinder to that reply offer further means of proof in support of their arguments."
[97] French: " *Elles motivent le retard apporté à la présentation de leurs offres de preuve.*"
  Stationery Office: " Good reason shall be given for delay in indicating these means."

Paragraph 2

The submission of fresh arguments [98] during the proceedings shall be prohibited unless these arguments are based upon points of law and of fact which have come to light during the written proceedings.[99]

If, in the course of the written proceedings, one of the parties raises a fresh argument as mentioned in the preceding paragraph, the President may, upon expiry of the normal procedural time limits, upon the report of the *juge rapporteur* [28] and after hearing the Advocate General, grant the other party a time limit within which to reply thereto.

The decision on the admissibility of the fresh argument shall be reserved until the final judgment.

ARTICLE 43

The Court may after hearing the parties and the Advocate General and, at any time, whether for the purposes of the written or oral proceedings or for those of its final judgment, order the joinder of several pending cases which relate to the same subject, on the ground of their interconnection. The Court may separate them again.[99]

ARTICLE 44

Paragraph 1

After the submission of the rejoinder referred to in Article 41, Paragraph 1, of these Rules, the President shall fix a date on which the *juge rapporteur* [1] shall present his preliminary report on whether the case requires an Instruction.[2] The Court, having heard the Advocate General shall decide whether it will be necessary to proceed to measures of instruction.[3]

The same procedure shall be applied:

(a) if the reply or the rejoinder [4] has not been submitted within the time limit fixed in accordance with Article 41, Paragraph 2 of these Rules;

[98] French: " *moyens nouveaux.*"
Stationery Office: " fresh main arguments "—the Rules, however, make no distinction between main and subsidiary arguments.
[99] Stationery Office: " written procedure."
[1] See note 21, p. 466, above.   [2] See note 21, p. 491, above.
[3] French: " *procéder à des mésures d'instruction.*"
Stationery Office: " to take steps by way of investigation."
[4] French: " *si la réplique ou la duplique.*"
Stationery Office: " if the reply." It is this sort of omission which makes the Stationery Office translations such unreliable documents.

(*b*) if the party concerned states that it is waiving its right [5] of presenting a reply or rejoinder.

Paragraph 2

If the Court decides to hold an Instruction [6] and does not undertake this itself, it shall assign the matter to a Chamber. [7]

If the Court decides to open the oral proceedings without an Instruction, [8] the President shall set a date for the opening. [9]

CHAPTER 2

INSTRUCTION [10]

Section 1

Measure of Instruction [11]

ARTICLE 45

Paragraph 1

The Court, having heard the Advocate General, shall determine the measures [12] it considers suitable, by an order setting out the facts to be proved. This order shall be served on the parties.

Paragraph 2

Without prejudice to the provisions of Articles 24 and 25 of the E.C.S.C. Statute, Articles 21 and 22 of the E.E.C. Statute and Articles 22 and 23 of the E.A.E.C. Statute, the measures of instruction [11] shall include:

(*a*) the personal appearance of the parties;

(*b*) a request for information and the production of documents;

(*c*) evidence by witnesses;

---

[5] Stationery Office: " that he is waiving his right."
[6] French: " *ouvrir une instruction*."
Stationery Office: " to conduct an investigation."
[7] See note 6, p. 485, above.
[8] *Cf.* note 6, above.
[9] French: " *ouverture*."
Stationery Office: " the opening of the oral proceedings."
[10] See note 21, p. 491, above.
[11] French: *"Mésures d'instruction."*
Stationery Office: " Methods of Investigation." These *mésures* are listed in Rules, Art. 45, para. 2.
[12] French: " *les mésures*."
Stationery Office: " what methods of investigation "

(*d*) the expert's report [13];

(*e*) a visit to the site.[14]

Paragraph 3

The Court shall proceed to the measures of instruction [11] which it has ordered, or shall entrust them to the *juge rapporteur*.[15]

The Advocate General shall take part in the measures of instruction.[16]

Paragraph 4

Rebutting evidence and the amplification of evidence shall be reserved for a later stage.[17]

ARTICLE 46

Paragraph 1

The Chamber [18] entrusted with carrying out the Instruction [19] shall exercise the powers vested in the Court by Articles 45 and 47 to 53 of these Rules; the powers vested in the President of the Court shall be exercised by the President of the Chambers.[20]

Paragraph 2

Articles 56 and 57 of these Rules shall apply to proceedings before the Chamber.[20]

Paragraph 3

The parties may be present at the measures of instruction.[21]

---

[13] French: " *L'expertise*."
Stationery Office: " expert opinion." " *L'expertise* " is not what an English lawyer would understand by expert evidence; it is the hearing of the report ordered by the Court under Rules, Art. 49, para. 1, see p. 510, below.

[14] French: " *les lieux*."
Stationery Office: " scene."

[15] French: " *en charge le juge rapporteur*."
Stationery Office: " shall delegate this duty to the Judge acting as Rapporteur."

[16] French: " *Prend part aux mésures d'instruction*."
Stationery Office: " shall take part in this investigation." The French text makes a clear distinction between the *instruction* and the *mésures d'instruction* which form part of it—see the heading to Chapter 2 of the Rules, p. 506, above.

[17] French: " *La preuve contraire et l'amplification des offres de preuve restent réservées*."
Stationery Office: " The rights of submitting evidence and amplifying the means of proof available shall be reserved."

[18] See note 6, p. 485, above.

[19] See note 21, p. 491, above.

[20] See note 6, p. 485, above.

[21] French: " *assister aux mésures d'instruction*."
Stationery Office: " attend the investigation." See note 16, above.

Documents

Section 2

The Summoning and Hearing of Witnesses and Experts

ARTICLE 47

Paragraph 1

The Court shall order the proof of certain facts by witnesses, either of its own motion,[22] or at the request of the parties, after hearing the Advocate General. The order of the Court shall set out the facts to be established.

Witnesses shall be summoned by the Court, either of its own motion [22] or at the request of the parties or of the Advocate General.

The request by one of the parties for the hearing of a witness shall indicate precisely the facts on which he is required to be heard,[23] and the reasons justifying his being heard.[24]

Paragraph 2

Witnesses the hearing of whom is recognised as being necessary shall be subpoenaed [25] by virtue of an order of the Court which shall contain:

(*a*) the surname, Christian names, occupation [26] and address [27] of the witnesses:

(*b*) an outline [28] of the facts on which the witnesses are to be heard:

(*c*) where appropriate, mention of the arrangements made by the Court for re-imbursement of expenses claimed by the witnesses, and of the penalties to which defaulting witnesses are liable.

This order shall be served on [29] the parties and the witnesses.

22 French: " *d'office.*"
  Stationery Office: " of its own volition."
23 French: " *les faits sur lesquels il y a lieu de l'entendre.*"
  Stationery Office: " the facts on which the witness is to be heard."
24 French: " *les raisons de nature à justifier son audition.*"
  Stationery Office: " for what reasons the calling of that witness is to be registered as justified."
25 French: " *cités.*"
  Stationery Office: " summoned." The *poena* for non-appearance is contained in Rules, Art. 48, para. 2.1.
26 French: " *qualité.*"
  Stationery Office: " description."
27 Stationery Office: " place of residence."
28 French: " *indication.*"
  Stationery Office: " indication."
29 French: " *signification . . . est faite.*"
  Stationery Office: " notified to."

Paragraph 2

The expert shall receive a copy of the order together with all the documentation necessary for carrying out his task. He shall be placed under the orders of the *juge rapporteur* [43] who may be present during the investigations involved in the report [44] and shall be kept informed of the progress of the expert in the task assigned to him.

Paragraph 3

At the request of the expert, the Court may decide to hear witnesses. This shall be carried out in accordance with the provisions of Article 47 of these Rules.

Paragraph 4

The expert may give his opinion only on the points [45] which are expressly put to him.

Paragraph 5

After presentation of the report, the Court may order the hearing of the expert, after notice to the parties to attend.

Paragraph 6

After presentation of the report, the expert shall take before the Court the following oath:

" I swear that I have carried out my task conscientiously and with full impartiality."

The oath may be taken in the form laid down by the expert's national law.

The Court may, with the agreement of the parties, excuse the expert from taking the oath.

ARTICLE 50

Paragraph 1

If one of the parties should object to a witness or an expert for reasons of lack of ability, lack of qualification,[46] or for any other reason, or if a witness or expert should refuse to give evidence or to take the oath, the Court shall give a ruling thereon.

[43] See note 21, p. 466, above.
[44] French: " *opérations d'expertise.*"
  Stationery Office: " the expert's work."
[45] Stationery Office: " may only give his opinion on the points."
[46] French: " *pour incapacité, indignité.*"
  Stationery Office: " for lack of qualification, disqualification."

Paragraph 2

An objection to a witness or an expert shall be raised within 14 days of the service [47] of the order summoning the witness or nominating the expert, by means of a written statement indicating the grounds for objection and the evidence in support thereof.[48]

ARTICLE 51

Paragraph 1

Witnesses and experts shall be entitled to re-imbursement of expenses for travel and subsistence. An advance to cover these expenses [49] may be granted to them from the Court pay office.

Paragraph 2

Witnesses shall be entitled to compensation for loss of earnings, and experts to fees for their work.

This compensation shall be paid to witnesses and experts by the Court pay office after they have fulfilled their duties or tasks.

ARTICLE 52

The Court may, at the request of the parties or of its own motion,[50] issue commissions [51] for the hearing of witnesses or experts, in manner to be determined by the regulations referred to in Article 109 of these Rules.

ARTICLE 53

Paragraph 1

The Registrar shall draw up a record of every hearing. This record shall be signed by the President and by the Registrar and shall constitute an official record.

Paragraph 2

The parties may examine in the Registry [52] all such records as well as the expert's record and obtain copies at their own expense.

---

[47] French: " *signification.*"
Stationery Office: " notification."
[48] French: " *les offres de preuve.*"
Stationery Office: " means of proof available."
[49] Stationery Office: " for these expenses."
[50] See note 22, p. 508, above.
[51] French: " *commissions rogatoires.*"
Stationery Office: " letters of request."
[52] See note 10, p. 487, above.

Section 3

Closing of the Instruction [53]

ARTICLE 54

Unless the Court decides to set a time limit within which the parties may submit written observations, the President shall fix the date for the opening of the oral proceedings [54] after completion of the measures of instruction.[55]

If a time limit has been set for the submission of written observations, the President shall set the date for the opening of the oral proceedings [54] at the end of this time limit.[56]

CHAPTER 3

ORAL PROCEEDINGS [57]

ARTICLE 55

Paragraph 1

Subject to [58] the giving of priority to decisions referred to in Article 85 of these Rules, the Court shall consider [59] the cases before it in the order in which their Instruction [60] has been completed. Where there are a number of cases whose Instruction [60] is completed simultaneously, the order [61] shall be determined by the date of entry of the requests in the register.[62]

The President may, in view of special circumstances, decide to give priority of hearing to a given case.

---

[53] French: " *De la clôture de l'instruction.*"
Stationery Office: " Closure of Investigation."
[54] See note 70, p. 453, above.
[55] French: " *mésures d'instruction.*"
Stationery Office: " the investigation." See note 11, p. 506, above.
[56] French: " *Délai.*"
Stationery Office:" period." Earlier in this paragraph the Stationery Office translated " *délai* " as " time limit."
[57] See note 70, p. 453, above. The Rules of the International Court of Justice (Art. 47) translate: " *la procédure orale* " as " the oral proceedings."
[58] French: " *sans reserve.*"
Stationery Office: " without prejudice." In Art. 66, para. 1 " *sans préjudice* " also translated as " without prejudice."
[59] French: " *connaît.*"
Stationery Office: " shall take cognizance of."
[60] See note 6, p. 506, above.
[61] French: " *l'ordre.*"
Stationery Office: " the order of hearing."
[62] French: " *par la date d'inscription ou registre des requêtes.*"
Stationery Office: " by the date of entry of the formal request in the register of such requests."

Paragraph 2

If the parties in a case whose Instruction [60] has been completed, jointly request a postponement [63] the President may accede to their request. Where there is not agreement between the parties, the President shall refer to the Court for a decision.[64]

ARTICLE 56

Paragraph 1

The hearing shall be opened and directed by the President, who shall have full power over the conduct of the proceedings.

Paragraph 2

A decision to hear a case *in camera* shall involve a prohibition against publication of the proceedings.

ARTICLE 57

The President may, in the course of the hearing, put questions to the agents, legal advisers or counsel of the parties.

Each judge and the Advocate General shall also have this right.[65]

ARTICLE 58

The parties may address the Court only [66] through their agent, legal adviser or counsel.

ARTICLE 59

Paragraph 1

The Advocate General shall present his oral reasoned submissions [67] before the closing of the oral proceedings.

Paragraph 2

After the submissions [68] of the Advocate General, the President shall declare the oral proceedings [69] closed.

---

[63] French: " *demandent le renvoi d'un commun accord.*"
Stationery Office: " all agree to ask for the case to be put back." It is not sufficient for the parties merely to agree to ask, they have in fact to ask.

[64] Stationery Office: " shall refer the decision to the Court."

[65] The French original prints this article in two paragraphs: the Stationery Office prints it in one.

[66] Stationery Office: " The parties may only address the Court."

[67] French: " *présente ses conclusions orales et motivées.*"
Stationery Office: " shall present his submissions by word of mouth indicating his grounds therefor."

[68] French: "*Après les conclusions.*"
Stationery Office: " After presentation of the submission."

[69] See note 70, p. 453, above.

ARTICLE 60

The Court may at any time order a measure of instruction,[70] or require the re-opening or amplification of any part of the Instruction. It may direct the Chamber [71] or *juge rapporteur* [72] to carry out these measures.

ARTICLE 61

The Court may order the re-opening of the oral proceedings.[73]

ARTICLE 62

Paragraph 1

The Registrar shall draw up a record of every hearing. This record shall be signed by the President and the Registrar, and shall constitute an official record.

Paragraph 2

The parties may examine all such records in the Registry,[74] and may obtain copies at their own expense.

CHAPTER 4

JUDGMENTS

ARTICLE 63

The judgment shall contain:

a statement [75] that it has been delivered by the Court;
the date when it was pronounced [76];
the names of the President and the judges taking part;
the name of the Advocate General;
the name of the Registrar;

---

[70] See note 11, p. 506, above.
[71] See note 6, p. 485, above.
[72] See note 21, p. 466, above.
[73] See note 70, p. 453, above.
[74] See note 63, p. 501, above.
[75] French: " *l'indication*."
   Stationery Office: " an indication."
[76] French: " *la date du prononcé*."
   Stationery Office: " the date of the judgment." Care must be taken to distinguish between the date when a judgment is pronounced and the date when it is delivered, see note 75, p. 75, above.

Documents

particulars of the parties;
the names of agents, legal advisers and counsel for the parties;
the submissions [77] of the parties;
reference [78] that the Advocate General had been heard;
a brief summary of the facts;
the grounds on which the judgment is based;
the order of the Court, including a decision on costs.

ARTICLE 64

Paragraph 1

The judgment shall be delivered in open court, after notice to the parties to attend.

Paragraph 2

The record [79] of the judgment, signed by the President, by the judges who took part in the consideration of the judgment and by the Registrar, shall be sealed and deposited in the Registry [80]; a certified copy of it shall be sent to each of the parties.

Paragraph 3

The Registrar shall make a note on the record [81] of the judgment of the date on which it was delivered.

ARTICLE 65

The judgment shall have binding force from the date of its pronouncement.

ARTICLE 66

Paragraph 1

Without prejudice to the provisions relating to the interpretation of judgments, clerical errors and arithmetical errors [82] or obvious inaccuracies [83] may be corrected by the Court, either of its own motion [84]

---

[77] French: " *conclusion.*"
  Stationery Office: " the contentions."
[78] French: " *ia mention.*"
  Stationery Office: " a mention."
[79] French: " *La minute.*"
  Stationery Office: " the original record."
[80] See note 63, p. 501, above.
[81] French: " *la minute.*"
  Stationery Office: " the original "; *cf.* note 79 above. In Art. 66, para. 4 " *la minute* " is translated as " the record."
[82] Stationery Office: " mistakes in reckoning."
[83] Stationery Office: " patent inaccuracies."
[84] See note 22, p. 508, above.

or at the request of one of the parties within a time limit [85] of 14 days from the pronouncement of the judgment.

Paragraph 2

The parties, duly notified by the Registrar, may submit written observations [86] within a time limit fixed by the President.

Paragraph 3

The Court shall decide at a private session,[87] after hearing the Advocate General.

Paragraph 4

The record of the order making the correction shall be annexed to the record of the judgment which is corrected. A note of this order shall be made in the margin of the record of the judgment which is corrected.

ARTICLE 67

If the Court has omitted to give a ruling, either on a particular point in the submissions [88] or on the matter of costs, the party intending to rely upon this shall bring the matter before [89] the Court by means [90] of a request [91] within one month of the notification of the judgment.

The request [91] shall be served on [92] the other party, and the President shall set it a time limit in which it may submit its [93] written observations.

After presentation [94] of these observations [95] the Court, having heard the Advocate General, shall decide at one and the same time whether the request is admissible [96] and whether it is well founded.

---

[85] French: " *délai.*"
Stationery Office: " period." In para. 2 of this article " *délai* " is translated as " time limit."
[86] French: " *observations.*"
Stationery Office: " comments." In Art. 67, para. 3, " *observations* " is translated as " observations."
[87] French: " *décide en chambre du conseil.*"
Stationery Office: " shall reach a decision in the Judges' Council Chamber."
[88] French: " *sur un chef isolé des conclusions.*"
Stationery Office: " on a single point of the contentions."
[89] French: " *saisit.*"
Stationery Office: " shall approach."
[90] Stationery Office: " by way of."
[91] See note 66, p. 501, above.
[92] See note 86, p. 503, above.
[93] Stationery Office: " him," " he " and " his."
[94] French: " *Après la présentation.*"
Stationery Office: " After submission." In Art. 49, para. 6, " *après la présentation* " is translated as " after presentation."
[95] French: " *ces observations.*"
Stationery Office: " these written observations."
[96] French: " *la recevabilité.*"
Stationery Office: " shall be entertained."

ARTICLE 68

The Registrar shall be in charge of [97] the publication of official law reports of all the judgments of the Court.

CHAPTER 5

COSTS

ARTICLE 69

Paragraph 1

The Court shall give a ruling on costs in the judgment or order terminating the case.

Paragraph 2

The losing party shall pay the costs, if application is made to this effect.

If there are several losing parties the Court shall decide how the costs are to be apportioned.

Paragraph 3

The Court may order each party to pay its own costs wholly or in part if the parties fail respectively on one or more counts, or for exceptional reasons.

The Court may order one of the parties, even the winning one, to refund to the other party the costs which the former has caused the latter to incur and which the Court considers to have been thrown away [98] or vexatious.

Paragraph 4

A party who discontinues [99] shall be ordered to pay costs unless this discontinuance [1] is justified by the conduct [2] of the other party.

[97] French: " *par les soins.*"
   Stationery Office: " shall see to."
[98] French: " *frustratoires.*"
   Stationery Office: " frivolous."
[99] French: " *qui se désist.*"
   Stationery Office: " who withdraws from the case."
[1] French: " *ce désistement.*"
   Stationery Office: " withdrawal."
[2] French: " *attitude.*"
   Stationery Office: " attitude "

In the absence of an application by the other party for costs [3] the parties shall pay their own costs.

Paragraph 5

In the event of there being nothing upon which to adjudicate, costs shall be in the discretion of the Court.[4]

ARTICLE 70

In the proceedings referred to in Article 95, Paragraph 1, of these Rules, the costs incurred by the institutions shall be borne by them, without prejudice to the provisions of Article 69, Paragraph 3, second sub-paragraph of these Rules.

ARTICLE 71

The costs which one of the parties has had to incur for the purposes of enforcement shall be refunded by the other party on the scale in force in the State where the enforcement takes place.

ARTICLE 72

The proceedings before the Court shall be free of charge, subject to the following provisions:

(a) if the Court has incurred costs which might have been avoided it may, after hearing the Advocate General, order the party who has caused these costs to refund them.

(b) the cost of all copying and translation work carried out at the request of one of the parties, considered by the Registrar to have been excessive, shall be paid for by this party on the basis of the scale of charges referred to in Article 15, paragraph 5 of these Rules.[5]

ARTICLE 73

Without prejudice to the provisions of the preceding Article, the following shall be regarded as recoverable expenditure:

[3] French: " *A défaut de conclusion de l'autre partie sur ce point.*"
Stationery Office: " in the absence of written observations from the other party on this point."

[4] French: " *En cas de non-lieu à statuer, la Cour règle librement les dépens.*"
Stationery Office: " Where there is no need to proceed to judgment the Court shall award or not award costs as it thinks fit."

[5] For this scale of charges, see the Instructions to the Registrar, Art. 20, p. 552, below.

(*a*) sums due to witnesses and experts[6] by virtue of Article 51 of these Rules;

(*b*) necessary costs incurred by the parties for the purpose of the proceedings, in particular expenditure on travel and subsistence and the remuneration of an agent, legal adviser or counsel.

ARTICLE 74

Paragraph 1

If there is dispute on the recoverable costs, the Chamber[7] to which the case has been assigned shall, at the request of the party concerned, decide by making an order, which shall not be subject to appeal, after hearing the other party's observations[8] and the Advocate General's submissions.

Paragraph 2

The parties may, for the purpose of enforcement, request a copy[9] of the order.

ARTICLE 75

Paragraph 1

The Court pay office shall make payments in the currency of the country in which the Court has its seat.

At the request of the person concerned, payment shall be made in the currency of the country in which recoverable costs have been incurred or where the acts were carried out[10] which give rise to reimbursement.

Paragraph 2

Other debtors shall make their payments in the currency of their country of origin.

Paragraph 3

Exchange of currency[11] shall be effected at the official rate of exchange ruling on the day of payment in the country where the Court has its seat.

---

6 French " *experts.*"
  Stationery Office: " expert witnesses." As noted above, an expert is one who produces an expert report in accordance with Art. 49 above. An " expert witness " is classified in the Rules as a witness.
7 See note 6, p. 485, above.
8 See note 95, p. 517, above.
9 French: " *une expédition.*"
  Stationery Office: " an office copy."
10 Stationery Office: " where the steps were taken."
11 French: " *Le change des monnaies.*"
   Stationery Office: " Exchange of foreign currency."

CHAPTER 6

FREE LEGAL AID

ARTICLE 76

Paragraph 1

If one of the parties finds himself partially or wholly unable to meet the costs of the proceedings, he may at any time apply for [12] free legal aid.

The request shall be accompanied by full information showing that the party concerned is in need, such as a certificate from the competent authority certifying his lack of means.[13]

Paragraph 2

If the request is made prior to the proceedings which the party making the request intends to institute, it shall give a brief account of the object of those proceedings.

The request need not be made through the intermediary of counsel.

Paragraph 3

The President shall appoint a *juge rapporteur*. The Chamber [14] to which the latter belongs shall decide, after studying the written observations [15] of the other party and having heard the Advocate General, whether free legal aid [16] should be granted wholly or in part, or whether it should be refused. It shall consider whether the case is not clearly ill-founded.

The Chamber [17] shall decide by making an order without giving reasons, which shall not be subject to appeal.[18]

Paragraph 4

The Chamber [19] may at any time, either of its own motion [20] or on request, withdraw the grant [21] of free legal aid if the conditions which

---

[12] French: " *demander le bénéfice de.*"
  Stationery Office: " ask for the benefit of."
[13] French: " *justifiant son indigence.*"
  Stationery Office: " in support of his contention of lack of means."
[14] See note 6, p. 485, above.
[15] See note 95, p. 517, above.
[16] French: " *bénéfice de l'assistance judiciaire gratuite.*"
  Stationery Office: " the benefit of free legal aid."
[17] See note 6, p. 485, above.
[18] French: " *non susceptible de recours.*"
  Stationery Office: " which shall be final." In Art. 74, para. 1, " *non susceptible de recours* " is translated as " not be subject to appeal."
[19] See note 6, p. 485, above.
[20] See note 22, p. 508, above.
[21] French: " *la bénéfice.*"
  Stationery Office: " the benefit."

led to its being granted have changed during the course of the proceedings.

Paragraph 5

In the event of free legal aid being granted, the Court pay office shall advance the funds.[22]

The decision as to costs shall order deduction to be made in favour of the Court of the sums disbursed as free legal aid.

These sums shall be recovered under the direction of the Registrar [23] from the party ordered to pay them.

CHAPTER 7

DISCONTINUANCE [24]

ARTICLE 77

If, before the Court has given its decision, the parties come to an agreement on the solution to be adopted in the case and inform the Court that they abandon all claims,[25] the Court shall order the case to be struck out from the register.

This provision shall not apply to proceedings referred to in Articles 33 and 35 of the E.C.S.C. Treaty, Articles 173 and 175 of the E.E.C. Treaty and Articles 146 and 148 of the E.A.E.C. Treaty.

ARTICLE 78

If the Plaintiff gives written notice to the Court that he wishes to discontinue, the Court shall order the case to be struck out from the register.

CHAPTER 8

SERVICE OF DOCUMENTS [26]

ARTICLE 79

Paragraph 1

The service of documents referred to in these Rules shall be effected under the direction of the Registrar at the chosen address of the person

[22] French: " *les frais.*"
Stationery Office: " the costs."
[23] French: " *par les soins du greffier.*"
Stationery Office: " by the Registrar."
[24] French: " *Des désistements.*"
Stationery Office: " withdrawal."
[25] French: " *à toute prétention.*"
Stationery Office: " all contentions."
[26] French: " *Des significations.*"
Stationery Office: " Notifications."

concerned,[27] either by despatch by registered post of a copy of the document to be served,[28] followed by acknowledgment of its receipt, or by delivery against receipt.

Copies of the document to be served [28] shall be made and certified to be copies of the original by the Registrar, save where they come from the parties themselves in accordance with Article 37, Paragraph 1 of these Rules.

Paragraph 2

The Post Office receipt on despatch and the acknowledgment of receipt by post or by hand shall be annexed to the original of the document.

CHAPTER 9

TIME LIMITS

ARTICLE 80

Paragraph 1

The procedural time limits provided for by the E.C.S.C., E.E.C. and E.A.E.C. Treaties, the Statutes of the Court and these Rules of Procedure, shall be calculated excluding [29] the day of the date of the procedural step from which time runs.[30]

Time limits shall not be suspended during Court vacations.

Paragraph 2

If the time limit expires on a Sunday or on a public holiday, its expiry shall be postponed until [31] the end of the next working day.

The list of official public holidays drawn up by the Court shall be published in the *Journal Officiel des Communautés Européennes*.[32]

---

[27] French:
"*Les significations prévues au présent règlement sont faites par les soins du greffier au domicile élu du destinataire.*"
Stationery Office:
"It shall be for the Registrar to see that notifications required by these Rules of Procedure reach the address for service of the addressee."
[28] French: "*à signifier.*"
Stationery Office: "to be notified."
[29] Stationery Office: "calculated by excluding." Exclusion will not perform the calculation.
[30] French: "*qui en constitue le point de départ.*"
Stationery Office: "forming the starting point of the time limit."
[31] Stationery Office: "shall be put off to."
[32] See note 16, p. 490, above. A list of these holidays is to be found in Appendix I to the Rules, p. 543, below.

Documents

ARTICLE 81

Paragraph 1

The time limits fixed for the introduction[33] of proceedings against some act[34] taken by an institution shall commence, in the case of notification, from the day following that on which the person concerned has received notice of the act[34] in the *Journal Officiel des Communautés Européennes.*[32]

Paragraph 2

Periods of grace allowed on account of distance shall be determined by a Decision of the Court published in the *Journal Officiel des Communautés Européennes.*[36]

ARTICLE 82

Time limits fixed by virtue of these Rules may be extended by the authority which has laid them down.

PART 3

SPECIAL PROCEDURES

CHAPTER 1

STAYS OF EXECUTION AND OTHER INTERIM MEASURES BY WAY OF INTERLOCUTORY PROCEEDINGS[37]

ARTICLE 83

Paragraph 1

Any request for a stay of execution[38] of an act[39] taken by an institution within the terms of Article 39, paragraph 2[40] of the E.C.S.C.

---

[33] French: " *l'introduction.*"
Stationery Office: " the institution."
[34] French: " *un acte.*"
Stationery Office: " some measure."
[36] See note 16, p. 490, above. A list of these periods is to be found in Appendix II to these Rules, p. 544, below.
[37] French: " *Du sursis et des autres mesures provisoires par voie de référé.*"
Stationery Office: " Suspension of execution and other provincial measures by way of summary procedure in case of urgency."
[38] French: " *sursis à l'exécution.*"
Stationery Office: " suspension of enforcement."
[39] French: " *un acte.*"
Stationery Office: " some measure."
[40] French: " *alinéa 2.*"
Stationery Office: " second Paragraph." In Art. 39 numerals are used.

Treaty, Article 185 of the E.E.C. Treaty and Article 157 of the E.A.E.C. Treaty shall be admissible only [41] if the plaintiff has challenged this act in proceedings before the Court.[42]

Any request relating to one of the other interim measures [43] referred to in Article 39, third paragraph [44] of the E.C.S.C. Treaty, Article 186 of the E.E.C. Treaty and Article 158 of the E.A.E.C. Treaty shall be admissible [45] only if it is made by [46] one of the parties in a case before the Court and if it refers to that case.

Paragraph 2

The requests referred to in the preceding Paragraph shall specify the subject of the dispute, the circumstances giving rise to urgency and the grounds of fact and of law showing prima facie justification for the granting of the interim measure [43] requested.

Paragraph 3

The request shall be made in a separate document and in accordance with conditions laid down in Articles 37 and 38 of these Rules.

ARTICLE 84

Paragraph 1

The request shall be served on [47] the other party, and the President shall set a short time limit within which that party may make written or oral observation.[48]

Paragraph 2

The President shall decide whether there is need [49] to order the opening of an Instruction.[50]

[41] Stationery Office: " shall only be admissible."
[42] French: " *A attaqué cet acte dans un recours devant la Cour.*"
Stationery Office: " has made this measure the subject of proceedings before the Court."
[43] French: " *mésures provisoires.*"
Stationery Office: " provisional measures."
[44] French: " *alinéa 3.*"
Stationery Office: " third paragraph." In the preceding sentence, " Paragraph " is spelt with a capital " P." In Art. 92 numerals are used.
[45] French: " *n'est recevable que.*"
Stationery Office: " shall only be entertained." In the preceding sentence, " *n'est recevable que,*" is translated as " shall only be admissible."
[46] French: " *si elle émane.*"
Stationery Office: " if it comes from."
[47] See note 86, p. 503, above.   [48] Stationery Office: " comments."
[49] French: " *s'il y a lieu.*"
Stationery Office: " whether."
[50] French: " *l'ouverture d'une instruction.*"
Stationery Office: " that an investigation should be opened."

The President may grant the request even before the other party has presented its observations.[51] This ruling may be later amended or revoked, even of the President's own motion.[52]

ARTICLE 85

The President shall give a ruling himself or refer the decision to the Court.

In the event of the absence or inability to attend of the President, the provisions of Article 7, Paragraph 2 of these Rules shall apply.

If the request is referred to the Court it shall leave all other business [53] and give a ruling, after hearing the Advocate General. The provisions of the preceding Article shall apply.

ARTICLE 86

Paragraph 1

Rulings on requests shall be given by a reasoned order which shall not be open to appeal.[54] This order shall be immediately served on [55] the parties.

Paragraph 2

The enforcement of the order may be made subject to the provision of security by the person making the request, the amount and the nature of which shall be fixed having regard to the circumstances.

Paragraph 3

The order may appoint a date from which the measure will cease to be applicable. Failing this, the measure shall cease to have effect from the pronouncement of the judgment terminating the case.

---

[51] French: " *ses observations.*"
   Stationery Office: " his comments." The other party will almost certainly be one of the Communities.
[52] French: " *même d'office.*"
   Stationery Office: " even of the Court's own motion." This is clearly wrong: the Court's power of amendment is contained in Art. 85, para. 3. Art. 84, para. 2.2, is referring to the President's power.
[53] French: " *toutes affaires cessantes.*"
   Stationery Office: " adjourn all cases."
[54] French: " *non susceptible de recours.*"
   Stationery Office: " which may not be appealed against or otherwise impugned."
[55] See note 86, p. 503, above.

Paragraph 4

The order shall be only temporary in nature, and shall in no way prejudice the Court's decision on the principal action.[56]

ARTICLE 87

On the application of one of the parties, the order may at any time be amended or revoked by reason of a change in circumstances.

ARTICLE 88

Rejection of a request for interim provisional measures [57] shall not prevent the party who made it from making another request based on fresh facts.

ARTICLE 89

The provisions of the present Chapter shall apply to a request for a stay of execution [58] of a decision of the Court or of an act [59] taken by another institution, submitted by virtue of Articles 44 and 92 of the E.C.S.C. Treaty, Articles 187 and 192 of the E.E.C. Treaty and Articles 159 and 164 of the E.A.E.C. Treaty.

The order granting the request shall fix a date on which the interim measure [60] shall cease to have effect.

ARTICLE 90

Paragraph 1

The request referred to in Article 81, Paragraphs 3 and 4 of the E.A.E.C. Treaty shall contain:

(*a*) the name and address [61] of the persons or enterprises [62] subject to inspection;

(*b*) an indication of the object and aim of the inspection.

Paragraph 2

The President shall give his ruling by an order.[63] The provisions of Article 86 of these Rules shall apply.

---

[56] French: " *sur le principal.*"
  Stationery Office: " on the substance of the case."
[57] French: " *relative à une mesure provisoire.*"
  Stationery Office: " for the taking of a provisional measure."
[58] See note 38, p. 524, above.
[59] See note 39, p. 524, above.
[60] See note 43, p. 525, above.
[61] French: " *les nom et domicile.*"
  Stationery Office: " the names and domicile."
[62] French: " *entreprises.*"
  Stationery Office: " undertakings."
[63] Stationery Office: " his ruling by order."

In the event of the absence or inability to attend of the President, Article 7, Paragraph 2 of these Rules shall apply.

CHAPTER 2

POINTS ARISING DURING THE PROCEEDINGS

ARTICLE 91

Paragraph 1

If one of the parties should apply to the Court for a ruling upon a preliminary objection [64] or upon a preliminary issue of fact [65] without undertaking a consideration of the merits,[66] it shall [67] make this application in a separate document.

The application shall contain a summary of the main arguments of fact and of law on which it is based, the relief sought and, annexed thereto, documents relied upon in support.

Paragraph 2

After [68] the submission of the document [69] making the application, the President shall fix a time limit within which the other party may submit its case and its submissions [70] in writing.

Paragraph 3

Unless the Court decides otherwise, the remainder of the proceedings upon the application [71] shall be oral.

Paragraph 4

The Court shall, after hearing the Advocate General, rule on the application or join it to the merits.[72]

[64] French: " *sur une exception.*"
Stationery Office: " on a point of procedure." (The real translation, if one dare use it, is surely " upon a demurrer.")
[65] French: " *incident.*"
Stationery Office: " incidental point."
[66] French: " *sans engager le débat au fond.*"
Stationery Office: " without involving the main points at issue." In the rules of the International Court of Justice, this phrase is translated as: " Without entering upon the merits." [67] Stationery Office: " he shall."
[68] French: " *Dès.*"
Stationery Office: " Immediately after."
[69] French: " *l'acte.*"
Stationery Office: " the formal document."
[70] French: " *présenter ses moyens et conclusions.*"
Stationery Office: " his main arguments and contentions."
[71] French: " *sur la demande.*"
This is omitted by the Stationery Office.
[72] French: " *ou la joint au fond.*"
Stationery Office: " or else join it to be dealt with as part of the main issue." In

If the Court rejects the application or joins it to the merits [72] the President shall fix new time limits for the case.

ARTICLE 92

The Court may at any time of its own motion [73] consider refusal to entertain a case on grounds of public policy: it shall give its ruling following the procedure laid down in Article 91, Paragraphs 3 and 4 of these Rules.

CHAPTER 3

INTERVENTION

ARTICLE 93

Paragraph 1

A request to intervene shall be submitted at the latest before the opening of the oral proceedings.[74]

Paragraph 2

The request shall contain:

(*a*) particulars of the case;

(*b*) particulars of the parties;

(*c*) the name and address [75] of the intervening party [76];

(*d*) a summary of the reasons establishing the interest of the intervening party [76] in the outcome of the case, subject to [77] the provisions of Article 37 of the E.E.C. Statute and Article 38 of the E.A.E.C. Statute;

(*e*) submissions seeking to support [78] or oppose those of one of the parties to the case;

(*f*) an outline of its evidence [79] and documents in support attached;

---

the Rules of the International Court of Justice, this phrase is translated: " Join it to the merits."

[73] See note 22, p. 508, above.

[74] See note 70, p. 453, above.

[75] French: " *domicile.*"
Stationery Office: " domicile."

[76] French: " *intervenant.*"
Stationery Office: " the intervener."

[77] French: " *sans réserve.*"
Stationery Office: " without prejudice to."

[78] French: " *les conclusions tendant au soutien.*"
Stationery Office: " submissions tending to support."

[79] French: " *les offres de preuve.*"
Stationery Office: " means of proof available."

(g) the intervening party's chosen address at the place [80] where the Court has its seat.

The intervening party [76] shall be represented in accordance with the provisions of Article 20, paragraphs 1 and 2 [81] of the E.C.S.C. Statute and Article 17 of the E.E.C. and E.A.E.C. Statutes.

The provisions of Articles 38 and 39 of these Rules shall apply.

Paragraph 3

The request shall be served on [82] the parties to the case. After giving them an opportunity of submitting their written or oral observations [83] the Court shall, after hearing the Advocate General, make an order.

Paragraph 4

If the Court allows the intervention, the intervening party shall receive copies of all procedural documents served on the parties.[84]

Paragraph 5

The intervening party [85] shall accept the case as it finds it at the time of its [86] intervention.

The President shall fix a time limit by which the intervening party [85] shall set out [87] in writing the arguments [88] supporting its submissions [89] and also the time limit within which the original parties to the case may reply.[90]

---

[80] French: " *l'élection de domicile de l'intervenant au lieu.*"
Stationery Office: " specification by the intervener of an address for service in the town."
[81] French: " *alinéas 1 et 2.*"
Stationery Office: " first and second paragraph."
[82] See note 86, p. 503, above.
[83] See note 48, p. 525, above.
[84] French: " *l'intervenant reçoit communication de tous les actes de procédure signifiés aux parties.*"
Stationery Office: " every step in the procedure notified to the parties shall be communicated to the intervener."
[85] See note 76, p. 529, above.
[86] Stationery Office: " he " and " his."
[87] French: " *expose.*"
Stationery Office: " shall submit."
[88] French: " *moyens.*"
Stationery Office: " main arguments."
[89] Stationery Office: " his submissions."
[90] French: " *peuvent répondre.*"
Stationery Office: " may make their replies."

CHAPTER 4

JUDGMENTS IN DEFAULT [91] AND REQUESTS TO SET THEM ASIDE [92]

ARTICLE 94

Paragraph 1

If the Defendant, having been duly served [93] does not reply to the request [94] in the form and within the time limit laid down, the Plaintiff may request the Court to give judgment in its [86] favour.

This request shall be served on [95] the Defendant. The President shall fix a date for the opening of the oral proceedings. [96]

Paragraph 2

Before giving judgment by default, the Court, after hearing the Advocate General, shall consider the admissibility of the request and shall verify that the procedural formalities [97] have been properly observed and that the contentions of the Plaintiff appear to be based on good grounds. The Court may order measures of instruction [98] to be carried out.

Paragraph 3

Judgment by default shall be executory. [99] The Court may, however, stay execution [1] until it has given a ruling on an application to set aside such judgment [92] submitted by virtue of paragraph 4 below, or it may make execution conditional upon the giving of a recognisance [3] the

---

[91] Stationery Office: " Judgments by default."
[92] French: " *Opposition*."
    Stationery Office: " retrial."
[93] French: " *mis en cause*."
    Stationery Office: " notified."
[94] See note 66, p. 501, above.
[95] See note 86, p. 503, above.
[96] See note 70, p. 453, above.
[97] French: " *les formalités*."
    Stationery Office: " the formalities."
[98] See note 11, p. 506.
[99] Stationery Office: " enforceable."
[1] French: " *suspendre l'exécution*."
    Stationery Office: " suspend enforcement."
[3] French: " *la constitution d'une caution*."
    Stationery Office: " the provision of security."

531

Documents

amount and nature of which shall be fixed having regard to the circumstances; this recognisance [3] shall be released if no application is made to set aside the judgment [92] or if it is rejected.[4]

Paragraph 4

Application may be made to have a judgment by default set aside.[5]

This application to set aside [6] shall be lodged within a time limit of one month, calculated from service of the judgment [7]; it shall be submitted according to the rules laid down in Articles 37 and 38 of these Rules.

Paragraph 5

After notification of the application,[8] the President shall fix a time limit for the other party to submit [9] its written observations.[10]

The procedure shall follow the provisions of Article 44 *et seq.* of these Rules.

Paragraph 6

The Court shall give its ruling by a judgment which shall not be open to challenge.[11]

The record [12] of this judgment shall be annexed to the record [12] of the judgment by default. Reference to [13] the judgment given on the application to set aside the judgment by default [14] shall be made in the margin of the record of the judgment by default.[15]

[4] French: "*ou en cas de rejet.*"
Stationery Office: "or if the request for retrial is rejected."
[5] French: "*l'arrêt par défaut est susceptible d'opposition.*"
Stationery Office: "A judgment by default is open to objection by means of a request for retrial."
[6] French: "*l'opposition.*"
Stationery Office: "The request."
[7] French: "*dans le délai d'un mois à compter de la signification de l'arrêt.*"
Stationery Office: "within one month dating from the notification of the judgment."
[8] French "*l'opposition.*"
Stationery Office: "the request for retrial."
[9] Stationery Office: "his."
[10] French: "*ses observations écrites.*"
Stationery Office: "its written comments."
[11] French: "*non susceptible d'opposition.*"
Stationery Office: "not open to a request for retrial."
[12] French: "*la minute.*"
Stationery Office: "the original."
[13] French "*Mention de.*"
Stationery Office: "A note of."
[14] French: "*l'arrêt rendu sur opposition.*"
Stationery Office: "the judgment given on the retrial."
[15] French: "*en marge de la minute de l'arrêt par défaut.*"
Stationery Office: "in the margin of the judgment by default."

CHAPTER 5

PROCEEDINGS BY SERVANTS[16] OF THE COMMUNITIES

ARTICLE 95

Paragraph 1

Proceedings instituted by an official or other servant of an institution against the institution shall be judged by a Chamber[17] appointed each year for this purpose by the Court, unless they concern a request for interim measures.[18]

The provisions of these Rules shall apply to proceedings before a Chamber.[17] The powers of the President of the Court shall be exercised by the President of the Chamber.[17]

Paragraph 2

The Chamber[17] may remit the case to the Court.

ARTICLE 96

Paragraph 1

Where a request is made for interim measures in a case referred to in Article 95, Paragraph 1 of these Rules of Procedure[19] and the President of the Court is absent or unable to attend, he shall be replaced by the President of the competent Chamber.[17]

Paragraph 2

Without prejudice to his power of referring the matter to the Court, given in Article 85 of these Rules, the President may refer consideration of the request for interim measures[20] to the competent Chamber.[17]

---

[16] French: "*agents.*"
Stationery Office: "servants."
[17] See note 6, p. 485, above.
[18] French: "*à moins qu'il ne s'agisse d'une demande en référé.*"
Stationery Office: "unless the matter be one to be dealt with under the summary procedure in case of urgency."
[19] French: "*à moins qu'il ne s'agisse d'une demande en référé dans un litige visé à l'article 95, paragraph 1.*"
Stationery Office: "where a request has been duly made in proceedings falling within Article 95, Paragraph 1, for a matter to be dealt with under the summary procedure in case of urgency."
[20] French: "*la demande en référé.*"
Stationery Office: "the request under summary procedure."

CHAPTER 6

EXCEPTIONAL PROCEEDINGS

Section 1

Requests by Third Parties to Set Aside or Modify a Judgment [21]

ARTICLE 97

Paragraph 1

The provisions of Articles 37 and 38 of these Rules shall be applicable to a request to have a judgment set aside or modified [22] and in addition the request shall:

(*a*) specify the judgment objected to;

(*b*) indicate in what way the judgment objected to prejudices the rights of the third party making the request [23];

(*c*) indicate the reasons why the third party making the request [24] has not been able to take part in the case.

The request shall be made against all the parties in the case. If the judgment has been published in the *Journal Officiel des Communautés Européennes,* [25] the request shall be submitted within two months of that publication.

Paragraph 2

A stay of execution [26] of the judgment objected to may be ordered on application of the third party raising the objection. The provisions of Part 3, Chapter 1 of these Rules of Procedure [27] shall apply.

Paragraph 3

The judgment objected to shall be amended to the extent to which the third party's request is allowed. The record [28] of the judgment given in pursuance of the request [29] shall be annexed to the original of the

---

21 French: " *De la tierce opposition.*"
   Stationery Office: " Application for retrial by a third party."
22 French: " *la demande en tierce opposition.*"
   Stationery Office: " a request for retrial by a third party."
23 French: " *préjudice aux droits du tiers opposant.*"
   Stationery Office: " prejudices the rights of the third party raising the objection."
24 French: " *le tiers opposant.*"
   Stationery Office: " the third party making the objection."
25 See note 16, p. 490, above.
26 See note 38, p. 524, above.
27 *i.e.,* Arts. 83–90, above.
28 See note 12, p. 532, above.
29 French: " *l'arrêt rendu sur tierce opposition.*"
   Stationery Office: " judgment given on the retrial."

judgment objected to. Reference to [30] the judgment given in pursuance of the request [29] shall be made in the margin of the judgment objected to.

Section 2

Revision [31]

ARTICLE 98

Revision [31] shall be requested at the latest within three months from the day when the applicant had knowledge of the fact on which the request for revision is based.[32]

ARTICLE 99

Paragraph 1

The provisions of Articles 37 and 38 of these Rules shall apply to a request for a revision [33] which shall in addition:

(*a*) specify the judgment objected to;

(*b*) indicate the points on which the judgment is objected to;

(*c*) set out the facts on which the request is based;

(*d*) indicate the evidence showing [34] that there are facts which justify a revision [33] and showing that the time limit laid down in the preceding Article has been observed.

Paragraph 2

The request for a revision [33] shall be made against all the parties to the judgment whose revision [35] is sought.

ARTICLE 100

Paragraph 1

Without prejudice to the merits,[36] the Court shall rule on the admissibility of the request by means of a judgment delivered in private

---

[30] See note 13, p. 532, above.

[31] French: " *Révision.*"
  Stationery Office: " review."

[32] Stationery Office: " three months from the day on which the fact upon which the request for review is based came to the knowledge of the applicant."

[33] French: " *la demande en révision.*"
  Stationery Office: " request."

[34] French: " *les moyens de preuve tendent à démontrer.*"
  Stationery Office: " the means of proof tending to show."

[35] Stationery Office: " the review of which."

[36] See note 66, p. 528, above.

Documents

session [37] after hearing the Advocate General and after considering the written observations [38] of the parties.

Paragraph 2

If the Court declares the request to be admissible, then, in accordance with the provisions of these Rules,[39] it shall proceed with the consideration of the merits [36] and give its ruling by giving judgment.

Paragraph 3

The record of the revised judgment [40] shall be annexed to the record of the judgment revised.[41] Reference to [42] the revised judgment [40] shall be made in the margin of the judgment revised.[41]

CHAPTER 7
APPEALS AGAINST DECISIONS OF THE ARBITRATION COMMITTEE

ARTICLE 101

Paragraph 1

The request instituting the appeal referred to in Article 18, paragraph 2 [43] of the E.A.E.C. Treaty shall contain:

(a) the name and address [44] of the applicant;

(b) the status of the signatory [45];

(c) particulars of the Arbitration Committee's Decision against which appeal is made;

---

[37] See note 5, p. 485, above.
[38] French: " *Par voie d'arrêt rendu en chambre du conseil.*"
Stationery Office: " giving judgment in the Judges' Council Chamber," see note 8, p. 486, above.
[39] The Stationery Office place this phrase at the end of the paragraph so that it is the giving of the judgment only which is to be in accordance with the provisions of these Rules.
[40] French: " *La minute de l'arrêt portant révision.*"
Stationery Office: " The original of the reviewing judgment."
[41] French: " *la minute de l'arrêt révisé.*"
Stationery Office: " the original of the judgment reviewed."
[42] See note 13, p. 532, above.
[43] French: " *alinéa 2.*"
Stationery Office: " second Paragraph."
[44] See note 61, p. 527, above.
[45] French: " *la qualité du signatoire.*"
Stationery Office: " the description of the person signing the request."

(*d*) particulars of the parties;

(*e*) a brief summary of the facts;

(*f*) the grounds of appeal [46] and submissions of the applicant.

Paragraph 2

The provisions of Article 37, Paragraphs 3 and 4 and of Article 38, Paragraphs 2, 3 and 5 of these Rules shall apply.

In addition, a certified copy of the Decision being challenged [47] shall be annexed to the request.[48]

Paragraph 3

After [49] the request [48] has been lodged, the Registrar shall ask the Registry [50] of the Arbitration Committee to forward the file on the case to the Court.

Paragraph 4

The procedure shall continue [51] in accordance with Articles 39, 40, 55 *et seq.* of these Rules.

Paragraph 5

The Court shall give its ruling by a judgment.[52] In the event of an annulment [53] of the Committee's Decision, the Court shall, if necessary, refer the case back to the Committee.

CHAPTER 8

INTERPRETATION OF JUDGMENTS

ARTICLE 102

Paragraph 1

A request for interpretation shall be submitted in accordance with the provisions of Articles 37 and 38 of these Rules. It shall also specify:

[46] French: "*les moyens.*"
  Stationery Office: "the main arguments."
[47] French: "*la décision attaquée.*"
  Stationery Office: "the decision objected to."
[48] See note 66, p. 501, above.
[49] French: "*dès.*"
  Stationery Office: "as soon as."
[50] See note 10, p. 487, above.
[51] French: "*est poursuivie.*"
  Stationery Office: "shall be."
[52] Stationery Office: "give its ruling by judgment." In Art. 94, para. 6, the translation is "give its ruling by means of a judgment."
[53] French: "*annulation.*"
  Stationery Office: "quashing."

(*a*) the judgment in question;

(*b*) the provisions, of which interpretation is sought.[54]

The request shall be made against all the parties bound by this judgment.[55]

Paragraph 2

The Court shall give its ruling by a judgment [56] after giving the parties an opportunity to present their observation [57] and hearing the Advocate General.

The record [58] of the interpretative judgment [59] shall be annexed to the record [58] of the judgment so interpreted. Reference to [60] the interpretative judgment [59] shall be made in the margin of the record of judgment [61] so interpreted.

CHAPTER 9

PRELIMINARY RULINGS [62]

ARTICLE 103

Paragraph 1

In the case referred to in [63] Article 20 of the E.E.C. Statute and Article 21 of the E.A.E.C. Statute, the provisions of Article 44 *et seq.* of these Rules shall apply after the submission of the written statements or observations [64] referred to in the aforesaid Articles 20 and 21.

The same provisions shall apply in default of submissions within the time limit fixed by the aforesaid Articles 20 and 21, or if the parties, the Member States, the Commission or, as the case may be, the Council declare that they renounce their rights in respect thereto.[65]

---

54 Stationery Office: " the provisions, the interpretation of which is sought."
55 French: " *les parties en cause à cet arrêt.*"
   Stationery Office: " the parties involved in the judgment concerned."
56 See note 13, p. 456, above.
57 See note 48, p. 525, above.
58 See note 12, p. 532, above.
59 Stationery Office: " the interpreting judgment."
60 See note 13, p. 532, above.
61 French: " *la minute de.*"
   Stationery Office omits these words.
62 French: " *Décisions à titre préjudiciel.*"
63 French: " *Dans le cas visé aux.*"
   Stationery Office: " where the question arises which is dealt with in."
64 French: " *après le dépôt des mémoires ou observations écrites.*"
   Stationery Office: " after submission of written statements of case or written comments."
65 French: " *déclarent y renoncer.*"
   Stationery Office: " declare their intention not to make any such submissions."

Paragraph 2

In the case referred to in [63] Article 41 of the E.C.S.C. Treaty, the Decision to refer the matter shall be served [66] on the parties in the case, the Member States, the High Authority and the Special Council of Ministers.

Within a time limit of two months calculated from this service [67] the entities concerned [68] mentioned in the preceding paragraph shall have the right to submit written statements or observations.[64]

After submission of these documents,[69] or in default of submission within the time limit laid down in the preceding paragraph,[70] the provisions of Article 44 *et seq.* of these Rules shall apply.

CHAPTER 10

SPECIAL PROCEEDINGS [71] UNDER ARTICLES 103 TO 105 OF THE EUROPEAN ATOMIC ENERGY COMMUNITY TREATY

ARTICLE 104

Paragraph 1

In the case referred to in [72] Article 103, third paragraph of the E.A.E.C. Treaty, the request [73] shall be submitted in four certified copies. It shall be served on [74] the Commission.

Paragraph 2

The request shall be accompanied by the draft agreement or convention concerned, observations [75] made by the Commission to the State concerned and by all other documents in support.

The Commission shall submit its observations [75] to the Court within a time limit of ten days, which may be extended by the President after hearing the State concerned.

[66] See note 86, p. 503, above.
[67] French: "*compter de cette signification.*"
Stationery Office: "dating from the day of this notification."
[68] Stationery Office: "the interested persons."
[69] French: "*de ces pièces.*"
Stationery Office: "of these."
[70] French: "*l'alinéa précédent.*"
Stationery Office: "the preceding sub-paragraph." In para. 2.2 of this article, "*l'alinéa précédent*" is translated as "the preceding paragraph."
[71] See note 57, p. 500, above.
[72] French: "*Dans le cas visé à.*"
Stationery Office: "Where a question arises under": *cf.* note 63, p. 538, above.
[73] See note 66, p. 501, above.
[74] See note 86, p. 503, above.
[75] See note 48, p. 525, above.

Documents

A certified copy of the aforementioned observation[75] shall be served on[76] this State.

Paragraph 3

After[77] the lodging of the request,[78] the President shall appoint a *juge rapporteur*.

Paragraph 4

The Decision shall be taken at a private session[79] after hearing the Advocate General.

If they so request, the agents or legal advisers of the State concerned and of the Commission shall be heard.

ARTICLE 105

Paragraph 1

In the case referred to[80] in Article 104, last paragraph and Article 105, last paragraph of the E.A.E.C. Treaty, the provisions of Article 37 *et seq.* of these Rules shall apply.

Paragraph 2

The request[78] shall be served on[76] the State having jurisdiction over the person or enterprise[81] against whom the request is directed.[82]

CHAPTER 11

OPINIONS

ARTICLE 106

Paragraph 1

If the request for a preliminary opinion referred to in Article 228 of the E.E.C. Treaty is submitted by the Council, it shall be served on[83] the Commission. If the request is submitted by the Commission, it shall be served on[83] the Council and the Member States. If the request is

---

76 See note 86, p. 503, above.
77 See note 49, p. 573, above.
78 See note 66, p. 501, above.
79 See note 5, p. 485, above.
80 See note 63, p. 538, above.
81 French: " *l'Etat dont ressortit la personne ou l'enterprise.*"
   Stationery Office: " the State to which the person or undertaking belongs."
82 French: " *la requête est dirigée.*"
   Stationery Office: " the request is made."
83 See note 86, p. 503, above.

submitted by one of the Member States, it shall be served on the Council, the Commission and the other Member States.

The President shall fix a time limit within which the institutions and Member States on whom the request has been served [83] shall be able to submit their written observations.[84]

Paragraph 2

The opinion may deal not only [85] with the compatibility of the agreement envisaged with the provisions of the E.E.C. Treaty, but also the power of the Community or one of its institutions to enter into this agreement.

ARTICLE 107

Paragraph 1

After [86] the submission of the request for a preliminary opinion referred to in the preceding Article, the President shall appoint a *juge rapporteur*.[87]

Paragraph 2

The Court shall deliver a reasoned opinion in a private session [88] after having heard the Advocates General.

Paragraph 3

The opinion signed by the President, the judges taking part in its consideration and the Registrar shall be served on [89] the Council, the Commission and the Member States.

ARTICLE 108

When the Court is called upon to give its opinion in pursuance of Article 95, paragraph 4 of the E.C.S.C. Treaty, the matter shall be brought before it by a request introduced jointly by the High Authority and the Special Council of Ministers.

The opinion shall be given in accordance with the provisions of the preceding Article. It shall be notified to the High Authority, the Special Council of Ministers and the European Parliamentary Assembly.

[84] See note 48, p. 525, above.
[85] French: " *peut porter tant sur . . . que sur.*"
Stationery Office: " may deal with either . . . or."
[86] See note 49, p. 573, above.
[87] See note 21, p. 466, above.
[88] See note 5, p. 485, above.
[89] See note 86, p. 503, above.

Final Provisions

ARTICLE 109

Subject to the application of Article 188 of the E.E.C. Treaty and Article 160 of the E.A.E.C. Treaty and after consultation with the governments concerned, the Court shall draw up in so far as it is concerned, additional Rules [90] providing for:

(a) *commissions rogatoires* [91];

(b) request for free legal aid;

(c) formal report by the Court, in accordance with Article 28 of the E.C.S.C. and E.A.E.C. Statutes and Article 27 of the E.E.C. Statute, of perjury committed by [92] witnesses and experts.

ARTICLE 110

Upon entry into force of these Rules the following shall be repealed:

(a) The Rules of the Court of Justice of the European Coal and Steel Community, enacted on March 4, 1953, and published in the *Journal Officiel de la Communauté Européenne du Charbon et de l'Acier* [93] on March 7, 1953;

(b) The additional Rules of the Court of Justice of the European Coal and Steel Community enacted on March 31, 1954, and published in the *Journal Officiel de la Communauté Européenne du Charbon et de l'Acier* on April 7, 1954;

(c) The Rules of the European Coal and Steel Community Court of Justice on costs, enacted on May 19, 1954, and published in the *Journal Officiel de la Communauté Européenne du Charbon et de l'Acier* on May 26, 1954;

(d) The Rules of Procedure of the European Coal and Steel Community Court of Justice for disputes referred to in Article 58 of the Service Regulations for Personnel of the Community, enacted on February 21, 1957, and published in the *Journal Officiel de la Communauté Européenne du Charbon et de l'Acier* on March 11, 1957.

ARTICLE 111

The provisions of these Rules shall not apply to proceedings begun before their coming into force.

[90] For the additional Rules, see pp. 556–559.
[91] Stationery Office: " Letters of request."
[92] French: " *violation des serments des.*"
   Stationery Office: " violation of the oath by."
[93] See note 16, p. 490, above.

ARTICLE 112

These Rules, drawn up in the official languages, shall be published in the *Journal Officiel de la Communautés Européennes* [93] and all four texts shall be authentic.

Decided [94] at Luxembourg, March 3, 1959.

APPENDIX I

DECISION ON OFFICIAL HOLIDAYS

THE COURT OF JUSTICE OF THE EUROPEAN COMMUNITIES

Having regard to Article 80, paragraph 2, of the Rules of Procedure requiring the Court to fix the list of official holidays;

DECIDES:

ARTICLE 1

The list of official holidays in accordance with Article 80, paragraph 2, of the Rules of Procedure is fixed as follows:

> New Year's Day
> January 23
> Easter Monday
> May 1
> Ascension Day
> Whit Monday
> August 15
> November 1
> December 25
> December 26

ARTICLE 2

The provisions of Article 80, paragraph 2, of the Rules of Procedure refer solely to the official holidays mentioned in Article 1 of this Decision.

[94] French: " *arrêté à.*"
Stationery Office: " done at." In Appendices I and II to the Rules " *arrêté* " is translated as " Decided at."

ARTICLE 3

This Decision which shall be [95] Appendix I to the Rules of Procedure shall enter into force on the same day as the Rules of Procedure to which it is annexed.

It shall be published in the *Journal Officiel de la Communautés Européennes.*
Decided at Luxembourg, March 3, 1959.

APPENDIX II

DECISION ON PERIODS OF GRACE ALLOWED ON ACCOUNT OF DISTANCE

THE COURT OF JUSTICE OF THE EUROPEAN COMMUNITIES

Having regard to Article 81, paragraph 2, of the Rules of Procedure relating to periods of grace allowed on account of distance;

DECIDES:

ARTICLE 1

Except where the parties have their usual residence in the Grand Duchy of Luxembourg, the procedural time limits shall be increased by reason of distance as follows:

In Belgium	2 days
In Germany, Metropolitan France and the Netherlands	6 days
In Italy	10 days
In the other Countries of Europe	15 days
In other Countries	one month

ARTICLE 2

This Decision which shall be [95] Appendix II to the Rules of Procedure shall enter into force on the same day as the Rules of Procedure to which it is annexed.

It shall be published in the *Journal Officiel des Communautés Européennes.*
Decided at Luxembourg, March 3, 1959.

[95] Stationery Office: "which shall constitute."

INSTRUCTIONS TO THE REGISTRAR

Instructions to the Registrar as amended by the Decision of the Court of April 6, 1962.[27]

THE COURT OF JUSTICE OF THE EUROPEAN COMMUNITIES

Having considered Articles 14, 15 (5) and 72 of the Rules of Procedure:

On the proposal of the President of the Court [28]

On the proposal of the Registrar concerning the Registry's scale of charges [29];

Has adopted the following instructions to the Registrar:

Section 1

Duties of the Registry [30]

ARTICLE 1

Paragraph 1

The Registry [31] shall be open to the public on Mondays to Fridays from 10 a.m. to 12 noon [32] and from 3 p.m. to 6 p.m., and on Saturdays from 10 a.m. to 12 noon [32] except on those official holidays [33] listed in Appendix 1 to the Rules of Procedure.

When the Registry [31] is closed, procedural documents [34] may be properly placed in the Court's letter box, which shall be cleared daily when the Registry is opened.

---

[27] The amendments, printed in the text below, are not included in the Stationery Office translation, although they were published on the same day as the Supplementary Rules which have been translated.

[28] French: "*du Président de la Cour.*"
Stationery Office: "of the President."

[29] French: "*le tariff du greffe.*"
Stationery Office: "the fees of the Registrar's Office." Rules, Art. 15, para. 5, refers to "the scale of charges of the Registrar's Office."

[30] French: "*Des attributions du greffe.*"
Stationery Office: "Functions of the Registrar's Office."

[31] French: "*le greffe.*"
Stationery Office: "The Registrar's Office."

[32] Stationery Office: "to 12 p.m."

[33] Stationery Office: "those public holidays listed in Appendix I." Appendix I does not list public holidays.

[34] French: "*les pièces de procédure.*"
Stationery Office: "formal procedural documents."

Documents

Paragraph 2

When the Court or a Chamber [35] holds a public sitting, the Registry shall always be opened to the public 30 minutes before the sitting is due to begin.

ARTICLE 2

The Registrar shall be responsible for the keeping of the Court files relating to pending cases and shall arrange that they be constantly kept up to date.

ARTICLE 3

Paragraph 1

The originals of judgments, orders and decisions shall be drawn up under the responsibility of the Registrar who shall submit them for signature to the competent members of the Court.

Paragraph 2

The Registrar shall ensure that any service, notification or communication provided for in the E.C.S.C., the E.E.C. and the E.A.E.C. Treaties, or the E.C.S.C. the E.E.C. and the E.A.E.C. Statutes,[36] as well as in the Rules of Procedure shall be made in accordance with the provisions thereof [37]; he shall attach a registered letter signed by him, to the copy of the document to be served, notified or communicated, specifying the case number, register number and a summary statement of the nature of the document. A copy of this letter shall be attached to the original document.

Paragraph 3

Procedural documents and the documents relating thereto shall be served on the parties.[38]

If only one copy of bulky documents is deposited with the Registry,[39] the Registrar, after consulting the *juge rapporteur*,[40] shall inform the parties by registered letter that they may be seen at the Registry.[39]

[35] French : " *une chambre.*"
Stationery Office : " a Section."
[36] French : " These are all referred to by their initials.
Stationery Office : The treaties and Statutes are printed without abbreviations; but see Art. 1 of the Rules.
[37] French : " *de celui-ci.*"
Stationery Office : " of the latter."
[38] French : " *Les actes de procédure et les documents relatifs à celle-ci sont signifiés aux parties.*"
Stationery Office : " The parties shall be served with the formal records of steps in procedure and the documents relating thereto."
[39] See note 10, p. 487, above.
[40] Stationery Office : " Judge acting as Rapporteur."

ARTICLE 4

Paragraph 1

A receipt shall be given, on request by the party concerned, for any procedural document [41] lodged with the Registry.[39]

Paragraph 2

Without express authorisation [42] from the President or the Court, the Registrar shall refuse to accept, or as the case may be, shall immediately return, by registered post,[43] any record [44] or document not provided for in the Rules of Procedure or not in the procedural language.

Paragraph 3

If a procedural document [45] is deposited with the Registrar's Office on a different date to its entry in the register, mention of this shall be made on the procedural document.[45]

ARTICLE 5

Paragraph 1

The Registrar after consultation with the President and the *juge rapporteur,* shall take all necessary steps to ensure the application of Article 38 (7) of the Rules of Procedure.

He shall fix [46] the time limit provided for in the said Article by registered letter with acknowledgment of receipt.

Should the Party [47] concerned not comply with the request of the Registrar, the latter shall refer the matter to the President of the Court.

Paragraph 2

The request to the Registry [39] of the Arbitration Committee provided for in Article 101 (3) of the Rules of Procedure, shall be sent by registered letter with acknowledgment of receipt.

---

[41] French: " *pièce de procédure.*"
 Stationery Office: " formal procedural document."
[42] Stationery Office: " Failing express authorisation."
[43] Stationery Office: " by registered cover."
[44] French: " *acte.*"
 Stationery Office: " Formal Record."
[45] French: " *un acte de procédure.*"
 Stationery Office: " formal procedural document."
[46] Stationery Office: " He shall set."
[47] French: " *l'intéressé.*"
 Stationery Office: " the person."

Documents

The file shall be returned to the Registry [39] of the Arbitration Committee after the Court has pronounced judgment or after the case has been struck off [48] the Court register.

ARTICLE 6

Paragraph 1

An entry shall be made at the foot of the record that the judgment or order has been read in open Court; this entry, in the procedural language, shall be as follows:

> " Read in open Court at .... on the ....
>
> Registrar   President
>
> (Signature)   (Signature) "

Paragraph 2

Marginal entries in judgments referred to in Articles 66 (4), 94 (6), 97 (3), 100 (3) and 102 (2) of the Rules of Procedure shall be made in the procedural language; they shall be initialled by the President and the Registrar.

ARTICLE 7

Before each public sitting of the Court or Chamber [49] a cause list shall be drawn up by the Registrar in the procedural language.

This list shall contain:

the date, hour and place of the sitting;

particulars of the cases to be called;

the names of the parties;

the names and status [50] of the agents, legal advisers and counsel of the parties.

The cause list shall be put up at the entrance to the Court-room.

Paragraph 2

The Registrar shall draw up a record, in the procedural language, of each public hearing.

This record shall contain:

the date and place of the hearing;

the names of the judges, Advocates-General [51] and Registrar present [52];

---

48 Stationery Office: " struck out from."
49 See note 6, p. 485, above.
50 French: " *qualités.*"
  Stationery Office: " description."
51 In the Rules these words are printed without a hyphen.
52 Stationery Office: " in attendance."

particulars of the case;

the names of the parties;

the names and status [50] of the agents, legal advisers and counsel of the parties;

the names, forenames, status [50] and address [53] of witnesses or experts heard;

particulars of evidence produced at the hearing;

particulars of documents produced [54] by the parties during the hearing;

the decisions of the Court or Chamber [55] or of the President of the Court or Chamber [55] given at the hearing.

Should the oral proceedings [56] in one case [57] require several successive hearings, one record only need be drawn up.

ARTICLE 8

The Registrar shall ensure that the persons or bodies entrusted with an investigation or experts' report, shall, in accordance with Article 49 of the Rules of Procedure, possess [58] all necessary means for the performance of such duties entrusted to them.

ARTICLE 9

The credentials for which provision is made in Article 33 (*b*) of the Rules of Procedure shall be transmitted to the legal adviser or counsel as soon as the date for the opening of the oral proceedings [56] has been set, or, at the request of the party [59] concerned, at any other time following the filing [60] with the Registry of the authority containing his appointment [61] should this be necessary for the smooth functioning of the proceedings.

Credentials shall be drawn up by the Registrar.

---

[53] French: "*domicile*."
Stationery Office: "domicile."
[54] French: "*l'indication des pièces déposées*."
Stationery Office: "particulars of exhibits or documents filed."
[55] See note 6, p. 485, above.
[56] Stationery Office: "The oral procedure."
[57] Stationery Office: "in the same case."
[58] French: "*disposent*."
Stationery Office: "dispose of."
[59] See note 47, p. 547, above.
[60] French: "*dépôt*."
Stationery Office: "the depositing."
[61] French: "*sa nomination*."
Stationery Office: "his nomination."

Documents

ARTICLE 10

In accordance with Article 32 of the Rules of Procedure, an extract from the cause list shall be communicated in advance to the Minister for Foreign Affairs of the State in which the Court is sitting.

Section 2

Keeping the Register

ARTICLE 11

The Registrar shall be responsible for keeping up to date [61a] the register of cases submitted to the Court.

ARTICLE 12

When the request [62] commencing [63] the action is registered, a serial number shall be ascribed to the case, followed by the year and accompanied by mention either of the plaintiff's name or of the subject-matter of the request. Cases shall be referred to by this number.

Summary proceedings [64] shall be given the same number as the main proceedings followed by the letter R."

ARTICLE 13

The pages of the register shall be numbered in advance.

It shall periodically be certified and initialled by the President and the Registrar in the margin of the last entry made.

ARTICLE 14

The procedural documents [65] relating to cases submitted to the Court shall be entered in the register and, in particular, the procedural documents filed by the parties and those served by the Registrar.

The appendices to procedural documents [67] shall be entered when they are filed separately from the principal document.

[61a] The Stationery Office places these three words at the end of the sentence.
[62] French: " *la requête.*"
  Stationery Office: " the Formal Request."
[63] French " *introductive.*"
  Stationery Office: " instituting."
[64] Stationery Office: " A summary procedure."
[65] French: " *Les actes de procédure.*"
  Stationery Office: " the formal steps in procedure."
[67] French: " *les annexes aux actes de procédure.*"
  Stationery Office: " Documents accompanying formal steps in procedure."

ARTICLE 15

Paragraph 1

Entries shall be made consecutively and in the order of the presentation of the document to be entered.[68]

They shall be numbered in consecutive and continuous sequence.

Paragraph 2

Registration shall be effected immediately after the document [69] has been filed [70] with the Registry.[71]

Where the document is issued by [72] the Court, registration shall be made on the same day as the document [73] is drawn up.

Paragraph 3

The entry in the register shall contain the necessary information for identification of the document [69] and in particular:

the date of the entry [74];
particulars of the case;
the nature of the document [73];
the date of the document.[69]

It shall be made in the procedural language; numbers shall be entered in figures and standard abbreviations shall be permitted.

Paragraph 4

Where alterations are deemed necessary these shall be made in the margin and initialled by the Registrar.

ARTICLE 16

The serial number of the registration shall be shown on the first page of any document [73] issued by [75] the Court.

---

[68] French:
"*Les inscriptions sont faites à la suite et dans l'ordre de la présentation des actes à inscrire.*"
Stationery Office:
" Entries shall be made consecutively and in the order of production or performance of the formal document or step to be registered."
[69] French: "*pièce.*"
Stationery Office: "formal document."
[70] See note 60, p. 549, above.
[71] See note 10, p. 487, above.
[72] French: "*Au cas où l'acte émane de la Cour.*"
Stationery Office: "Where the formal step emanates from the Court."
[73] French: "*l'acte.*"
Stationery Office: "the record."
[74] French: "*l'inscription.*"
Stationery Office: "the date of registration."
[75] Stationery Office: "issuing from."

Documents

Reference to the entry[76] shall be made on the original copy of any document[69] filed[70] by the parties by the affixing of a stamp[77] bearing the following wording, in the procedural language:

"Entered in the register of the Court of Justice under
No..........................
Luxembourg, the.........................."

This statement shall be signed by the Registrar.

Section 3

Scale of Charges[78] of the Registry[79] and Court Fees

ARTICLE 17

Only the Registry charges[80] appearing in this Section shall be charged.

ARTICLE 18

Payment of Registry charges[80] shall be made either in cash at the Court Pay Office or by bank transfer to the Court's bank account shown in the payment advice.

ARTICLE 19

Where the party liable to pay Registry charges[80] has been granted legal aid, the provisions of Article 76 (5) of the Rules of Procedure shall apply.

ARTICLE 20

The Registry charges[80] shall be as follows:

(a) for a copy[81] of a judgment or order, a copy[81] of a procedural document[82] or of minutes of proceedings, an extract from the Court register, a copy[81] of the Court register, a copy[81] made under Article 72 (b) of the Rules of Procedure: 30 Lux. francs per page.

[76] Stationery Office: " Mention of the register entry."
[77] French: " *par apposition d'un cachet.*"
    Stationery Office: " in the form of a stamp."
[78] See note 29, p. 545, above.
[79] See note 10, p. 487, above.
[80] French: " *les droits de greffe.*"
    Stationery Office: " the Registrar's fees."
[81] French: " *une expédition.*"
    Stationery Office: " an office copy."
[82] See note 69, p. 551, above.

(*b*) For a translation made under Article 72 (*b*) of the Rules of Procedure: 200 Lux. francs per page.

One page contains a maximum of 40 lines.

These charges [81] shall be for the first copy, each subsequent copy being charged at the rate of 5 Lux. francs per page or part of a page.[83]

ARTICLE 21

Paragraph 1

Where, pursuant to Articles 47 (3), 51 (1) and 76 (5) of the Rules of Procedure, an advance is requested from the Court Pay Office, the Registrar shall require the submission of details of the expenses in respect of which the advance is requested.

Witnesses shall be required by him to provide documentary evidence of their loss of earnings and experts to provide a note of their fees.

Paragraph 2

The Registrar shall *order payment by the Court Pay Office of* [84] the sums due under the previous paragraph [85] vouched by a signed receipt or proof of transfer.

Where he considers [86] a sum requested to be excessive he may reduce it [87] on his own authority or spread payment over a period.

Paragraph 3 [87a]

The Registrar shall order payment by the Court Pay Office, against proof of transfer and in the currency of the country concerned, of the costs of the commission rogatoire incurred in accordance with Article 3 of the Supplementary Rules to the body specified by the Minister referred to in Article 2 of those Rules.

Paragraph 4 [87a]

The Registrar shall order the payment by the Court Pay Office of the advance referred to in Article 5, Paragraph 2 of the Supplementary

---

[83] Stationery Office: " or part of page."
[84] The words in italics were substituted by the amendment to the Instructions to the Registrar of April 6, 1962, for the previous wording, namely: " The Registrar shall instruct the Court Pay Office to pay the sum due . . ."—" *Le greffier ordonne le versement par la caisse de la Cour* " in place of " *Le greffier donne ordre à la caisse de la Cour.*" The amendment is omitted by the Stationery Office.
[85] French: " *au paragraph précédent.*"
Stationery Office: " the previous Article."
[86] Stationery Office: " where he deems."
[87] French: " *il peut le réduire.*"
Stationery Office: " he shall have power to reduce this sum."
[87a] This paragraph was added by the Amendment to the Instructions to the Registrar of April 6, 1962, see p. 560. It is omitted by the Stationery Office.

Documents

Rules, subject to what is specified in Paragraph 2, sub-paragraph 2, of this Article.

ARTICLE 22

Paragraph 1

When sums paid in respect of free legal aid are recoverable as provided in Article 76 (5) of the Rules of Procedure, such sums shall be claimed by registered letter signed by the Registrar. This letter shall specify, in addition to the sum to be reimbursed, the method and time limit allowed for such reimbursement.

The same provisions shall apply in cases coming within Article 72 (a) of the Rules of Procedure and of Article 21 (1) *(3) and (4)* [88] of the present Instructions.

Paragraph 2

In default of payment of the sum claimed within the time limit allowed by the Registrar, the latter shall request the Court to make an executory order [89] which he shall require to be enforced as provided in Articles 44 and 92 of the E.C.S.C. Treaty, 187 and 192 of the E.E.C. Treaty, and 159 and 164 of the E.A.E.C. Treaty.[90]

Where, by a judgment or order, a party has been ordered to pay costs into the Court Pay Office, the Registrar, in default of payment within the period fixed, shall request recovery of such costs by way of execution.

Section 4

Court Publications

ARTICLE 23

The Registrar shall be responsible for Court publications.

ARTICLE 24

Official law reports [91] shall be published in the official languages and shall consist, unless otherwise decided, of judgments of the Court with

---

[88] The numbers in italics were added by the amendment of April 6, 1962, of the Instructions to the Registrar. They are omitted by the Stationery Office.
[89] French : " *une ordonnance exécutoire*."
Stationery Office : " an immediately enforceable order."
[90] See note 36, p. 546, above.
[91] " *Recueil de la jurisprudence de la Cour*."

the submissions of the Advocates-General, and opinions given and interim orders [92] made during the course of the calendar year.

ARTICLE 25

The Registrar shall be responsible for publication in the *Journal Officiel des Communautés Européennes* [93]:

(*a*) of notices concerning Requests [94] instituting proceedings pursuant to Article 15 (6) of the Rules of Procedure;

(*b*) of notices relative to a case being struck off [94a] the register;

(*c*) unless decided otherwise by the Court, of the order contained in any judgment or interim order [92];

(*d*) of the composition of the Chambers [95];

(*e*) of the appointment of the President of the Court;

(*f*) of the appointment of the Registrar;

(*g*) of the appointment of the Assistant Registrar and of the Administrative Assistant.

Final Provisions

ARTICLE 26

The present instructions, drawn up in the official languages shall be published in the *Journal Officiel des Communautés Européennes* [93] all four texts being authentic.

Decided [96] at Luxembourg June 23, 1960.

---

[92] French: " *les ordonnances de référé.*"
   Stationery Office: " provisional orders."
[93] See note 16, p. 490, above.
[94] See note 66, p. 501, above.
[94a] Stationery Office: " struck out of."
[95] See note 6, p. 485, above.
[96] French: " *arrêté.*"
   Stationery Office: " Adopted "—see note 25, p. 559, below.

SUPPLEMENTARY RULES

THE COURT, having

considered Articles 26 and 27 of the Protocol on the Statute of the Court of Justice of the European Economic Community;

considered Articles 27 and 28 of the Protocol on the Statute of the Court of Justice of the European Atomic Energy Community;

considered Article 109 of the Rules of Procedure;

considered the letters, dated November 24, 1961, in which the Court of Justice conveyed to the Councils the Draft Supplementary Rules;

considered the unanimous approval given on February 5, 1962, by the Council of the European Economic Community pursuant to Article 188 of the Treaty;

considered the unanimous approval given on February 5, 1962, by the Council of the European Atomic Energy Community pursuant to Article 160 of the Treaty;

LAYS DOWN the following Supplementary Rules:

CHAPTER 1

TAKING EVIDENCE ON COMMISSIONS [1]

ARTICLE 1

Commissions to take evidence shall be issued by means of an Order which shall contain the names, forenames, occupations [2] and addresses of the witnesses or experts, state the facts on which the witnesses or experts are to be heard, name the parties, their agents, counsel or legal advisers together with their address for service and set out briefly the subject of the dispute.

Notice of the Order shall be served on [3] the parties by the Registrar.

ARTICLE 2

The Registrar shall forward the Order to the Minister of Justice of the Member State on whose territory the witnesses or experts are to be

---

[1] French: " *Commissions rogatoires.*"
Stationery Office: " Letters of request."
[2] French: " *qualité.*"
Stationery Office: " description."
[3] French: " *Signification de l'ordonnance est faite.*"
Stationery Office: " The Order shall be notified." In the Rules, " order " is printed without a capital " O."

heard. Where applicable the Order [4] shall be accompanied by a translation into [5] the official language or languages of the Member State to which it is sent.[6] The Minister of Justice of the Member State shall transmit the Order to the judicial authority competent under its domestic law.

The competent judicial authority shall carry out the commission [7] in accordance with the provisions of its domestic law. After having carried out the commission [8] the competent judicial authority shall forward to the Minister of Justice the Order containing the commission to take evidence,[9] the records of hearing [10] and a statement of costs.[11] The Minister of Justice shall forward these documents to the Registrar of the Court.

The Registrar shall be responsible for having the documents translated into the procedural language.

ARTICLE 3

The Court shall defray the costs of the commission to take evidence [12] subject to the right, where applicable, to order such costs to be repaid by the parties.[13]

CHAPTER II

FREE LEGAL AID

ARTICLE 4

The Court shall, in the Order in which it decides to grant [14] free legal aid, order that counsel shall be appointed to assist the party.

---

[4] French: " *l'ordonnance.*"
  Stationery Office: " it."
[5] Stationery Office: " in."   [6] Stationery Office: " addressed."
[7] French: " *exécuté la commission rogatoire.*"
  Stationery Office: " shall implement the letters of request."
[8] French: " *Après exécution.*"
  Stationery Office: "After implementation."
[9] French: " *l'ordonnance portant commission rogatoire.*"
  Stationery Office: " the Order embodying a Letter of Request."   The letters of request have not received capitals before.
[10] French: " *les pièces de l'exécution.*"
  Stationery Office: " the implementing documents."
[11] French: " *un bordereau des dépens.*"
  Stationery Office: " a detailed statement of costs."
[12] See note 1, p. 556, above.
[13] French: " *sous réserve de les mettre, le cas échéant, à la charge des parties.*"
  Stationery Office: " subject to the right to order their payment, where applicable, by the parties."   [14] Stationery Office: " deciding entitlement to."

Documents

If the party does not himself [15] indicate his choice of counsel, or if the Court considers that his choice should not be endorsed, the Registrar shall forward a copy [16] of the Order and a copy of the request for legal aid to the competent authority of the State concerned as shown in Appendix I.[17] Having regard to [18] the proposals transmitted by that authority, the Court shall itself proceed to appoint counsel to assist the party.

ARTICLE 5

The Court shall advance the costs.

It shall decide upon [19] Counsel's expenses and fees: on request,[20] the President may order that he receive an advance.

CHAPTER III

REPORTS [21] OF PERJURY ON THE PART OF WITNESSES OR EXPERTS

ARTICLE 6

The Court, after hearing the Advocate General, may decide to report to the Minister of Justice of the Member State whose courts are competent to deal with a criminal charge, any case of false testimony or false statement by an expert committed under oath before it.[22]

ARTICLE 7

The Registrar shall be responsible for transmitting the decision of the Court.

15 French: " *lui-même.*"
This is not translated by the Stationery Office.
16 French: " *une expédition.*"
Stationery Office: " an authenticated copy."
17 Stationery Office: "Annex." Two " appendices " are attached to the main Rules of the Court.
18 French: "*Au vue des propositions.*"
Stationery Office: " with the proposals before it."
19 Stationery Office: " adjudicate on."
20 French: " *sur requête.*"
Stationery Office: " on formal request."
21 French: " *De la dénonciation.*"
Stationery Office: " Formal reports."
22 French: " *devant elle.*"
Stationery Office: " before the Court."

Such decision shall set out the facts and circumstances on which the report [23] is founded.

ARTICLE 8

These Supplementary Rules shall be published in the official languages in the *Journal Officiel des Communautés Européennes* [24] all four texts being authentic.

They shall enter into force as from the date of publication.

Decided [25] at Luxembourg, March 9, 1962.

APPENDIX I [17]

LIST REFERRED TO IN ARTICLE 4,
PARAGRAPH 2 [26]

Germany

Bundesrechtsanwaltskammer
Schaumburg-Lippe-Strasse 2, Bonn.

Belgium

The Minister of Justice.

France

The Minister of Justice.

Italy

The Minister of Justice.

Luxembourg

The Minister of Justice.

Netherlands

Algemene Raad van de Nederlandse Orde van Advocaten.
Frederik Handrikplein 23, 's-Gravenhage.

---

[23] French: "*la dénonciation.*"
Stationery Office: "the formal report of perjury."

[24] Stationery Office: "*The Official Journal of the European Communities,*" see note 16, p. 490, above.

[25] French: "*arrêté.*"
Stationery Office: "given." This is the fourth different translation of this word, the others being "done," "decided" and "adopted"; see note 49, p. 543, p. 544 and note 96, p. 555, above.

[26] French: "*alinéa 2.*"
Stationery Office: "second paragraph."

AMENDMENT TO THE INSTRUCTIONS TO THE REGISTRAR

The Court of Justice of the European Communities, having considered the Instructions to the Registrar, decided at Luxembourg on June 23, 1960;

having considered the Supplementary Rules decided at Luxembourg on March 9, 1962;

considering that, by reason of the adoption of the Supplementary Rules, it is necessary to amend the Instructions to the Registrar;

Having considered Article 14 of the Rules of Procedure;

On the proposal of the President of the Court,

DECIDES:

ARTICLE I

Article 21, paragraph 2, sub-paragraph 1, shall be amended as follows except in the German text:

The Registrar shall order payment by the Court Pay Office of the sums due under the previous paragraph, vouched by a signed receipt or proof of transfer.

ARTICLE II

Article 21 shall be completed as follows:

Paragraph 3. The Registrar shall order payment by the Court Pay Office, against proof of transfer and in the currency of the country concerned, of the costs of the *commission rogatoire* incurred in accordance with Article 3 of the Supplementary Rules to the body specified by the Minister referred to in Article 2 of those Rules.

Paragraph 4. The Registrar shall order the payment by the Court Pay Office of the advance referred to in Article 5, paragraph 2 of the Supplementary Rules, subject to what is specified in paragraph 2, sub-paragraph 2 of this Article.

ARTICLE III

Article 22, paragraph 1, sub-paragraph 2 shall be amended as follows:

The same provisions shall apply in cases coming within Article 72 (a) of the Rules of Procedure and of Article 21 (1), (3) and (4) of the present Instructions.

ARTICLE IV

The present Decision, drawn up in four official languages, shall be published in the *Journal Officiel des Communautés Européennes*, the four texts being authoritative.

It shall come into force from the date of its publication.

Decided at Luxembourg, April 6, 1962.

E.E.C. REGULATION NO. 62 AND EURATOM REGULATION NO. 13

determining the emoluments of members of the Court of Justice [1]

THE COUNCIL OF THE EUROPEAN ECONOMIC COMMUNITY
THE COUNCIL OF THE EUROPEAN ATOMIC ENERGY COMMUNITY
THE SPECIAL COUNCIL OF MINISTERS OF THE EUROPEAN COAL AND STEEL COMMUNITY

HAVING REGARD to the Treaty establishing [2] the European Economic Community and in particular Article 154 thereof and to Article 20 of the Protocol on the Privileges and Immunities of the Community;

HAVING REGARD to the Treaty establishing [2] the European Atomic Energy Community and in particular Article 123 thereof and to Article 20 of the Protocol on the Privileges and Immunities of the Community;

HAVING REGARD to the Treaty establishing [2] the European Coal and Steel Community and in particular Article 29 thereof and to Articles 5, 13 and 15 of the Protocol on the Statute of the Court of Justice;

HAVING REGARD to the Decision of the Special Council of Ministers dated October 13, 1958;

HAVING REGARD to the proposal by the Commission provided for in Article 78 (3) of the Treaty setting up the European Coal and Steel Community;

HAVE ADOPTED THE PRESENT REGULATION:

ARTICLE 1

From the date of assuming office until termination of the same, members [3] of the Court shall be entitled to a basic salary and family allowances, expressed in the currency of the country where the European Coal and Steel Community has for the time being its headquarters.

---

[1] *Journal Officiel*, July 14, 1962, p. 1713/62. This Regulation is printed as amended on August 8, 1962, see p. 570, below.

[2] Stationery Office: " setting up." The title pages of the Stationery Office's own translations of these Treaties use the word " establishing."

[3] On this occasion only, the Stationery Office prints members with a capital " M."

ARTICLE 2

The monthly basic salary shall be

President	85,600 fr.
Judges and Advocates-General	68,750 fr.
Registrar	61,600 fr.

ARTICLE 3

1. Family allowances shall comprise:

    (*a*) Head of household's allowance, equal to 5 per cent. of the basic salary;

    (*b*) Dependent children's allowance, equal to 1,000 fr. per child per month;

    (*c*) School fees allowance.

2. A head of household shall be defined as being a married member of the Court or a member who has dependent children. Where the spouse is gainfully employed, the member shall not be entitled to head of household's allowance.

3. A dependent child shall be defined as being the legitimate, natural or adopted child of a member of the Court or of his spouse and actually maintained by the member of the Court.

The allowance shall be granted:

—in respect of any child under 18 years of age;

—in respect of any child between 18 and 25 years of age who is receiving formal education or vocational training.

Payment of the allowance in respect of a child incapacitated by serious illness or disablement from earning a livelihood shall continue throughout the period of such illness or disablement without regard to age limit.

4. For each dependent child within the meaning of para. 3 above who is in regular full-time attendance at an educational establishment, a member of the Court shall in addition be entitled to a school fees allowance equal to the actual school fees contracted by him up to a maximum of 900 francs [4] per month.

Entitlement to this allowance shall commence on the first day of the month in which the child reaches the age of six years and shall cease at the end of the month in which the child reaches the age of 21 years.

[4] In the French text this amount was written as " frb " but by the amendment published on August 8, 1962, " fr " was to be read for " frb " in Arts. 2, 3 para. 1 (*b*), 4 paras. 2 and 3, and Art. 6 (*c*)—see p. 570, below.

ARTICLE 4

1. Members of the Court shall be entitled to a local allowance equal to 15 per cent. of the basic salary.

2. Members of the Court shall receive monthly an entertainment allowance amounting to:

President	17,500 francs [4]
Judges and Advocates-General	7,500 „
Registrar	6,875 „

3. The Presidents of the Chambers [5] shall in addition receive during their term of office a special duty allowance of 10,000 francs [4] per month.

ARTICLE 5

On taking up his duties and on termination of the same a member of the Court shall be entitled:

(a) To an installation allowance equal to two months' basic salary on taking up his duties and a resettlement allowance equal to one month's basic salary on termination of the same;

(b) To reimbursement of the cost of removal of his personal effects and furniture, including insurance against ordinary risks (theft, breakage, fire).

In the event of renewal of his term of office he shall not be entitled to any of the allowances set out above,[7] neither shall he be so entitled in the event of appointment to the membership of another institution of the Communities, if such institution has for the time being its headquarters in the town where he was formerly required to reside by reason of his office and if at the time of such new appointment he had not already effected his resettlement.

ARTICLE 6

A member of the Court who has to travel in the course of his duties outside the place where the European Coal and Steel Community has for the time being its headquarters shall be entitled to:

(a) Reimbursement of travelling expenses;

(b) Reimbursement of hotel expenses (room, service and taxes, excluding all other expenses [8]);

(c) A subsistence allowance of 650 francs [9] for each complete day of absence or 1,250 francs [9] for journeys outside Europe.

---

[5] French: " *Les Présidents de Chambre.*"
Stationery Office: " Presiding judges of Sections of the Court."
[7] French: " *annoncées ci-dessus.*"
Stationery Office: " set out in this Article."
[8] French: " *à l'exclusion de tous autres frais.*"
Stationery Office: "" only."   [9] See note 4, p. 562, above.

ARTICLE 7

1. As from the first day of the month following termination of office and for a period of three years, an ex-member of the Court shall receive monthly a transitional allowance equal to 40 per cent. of the basic salary which he was receiving at the date of termination, if he has served for less than two years, to 45 per cent. of such basic salary if he has served for more than two but less than three years and to 50 per cent. in other cases.

2. Entitlement to this allowance shall cease if the ex-member of the Court is reappointed to office in one of the institutions of the Communities or on death. On the event of reappointment, the allowance shall be paid up to the date of assuming office; in the event of death the payment for the month in which death occurred shall be the last.

3. If during this three-year period the person concerned undertakes other duties the gross monthly remuneration (*i.e.*, before deduction of taxes) which he receives therefor shall be deducted from the allowance provided for in paragraph 1, to the extent that such remuneration plus the said allowance together exceed the amounts, before compensatory adjustment or deduction of taxes, which the person concerned was receiving as a member of the Court under Articles 2, 3 and 4 (1) above. In calculating the amount of remuneration received for the new duties, all forms of remuneration shall be reckoned, save only those representing reimbursement of expenses.

The Councils shall take all appropriate steps for enforcement of the foregoing paragraph.[10]

ARTICLE 8

1. After termination of office, members of the Court shall be entitled to a life pension payable from the date when they reach the age of 65.

2. They may, however, ask to start drawing such pension from the age of 60 years. In that case the pension shall be reduced in accordance with the following table:

Age	Coefficient
60 years	0·64271
61 „	0·69762
62 „	0·75985
63 „	0·82157
64 „	0·90554

---

10 French: " *alinéa qui précède.*"
Stationery Office: " the foregoing paragraph." (The reference, however, is not to para. 2, but to the first subdivision of Art. 7.3.)

ARTICLE 9

The amount of the pension shall be 4·5 per cent. of the basic salary last received for each full year in office and one-twelfth of that sum for each complete month, up to a maximum pension of 50 per cent. of the basic salary last received.

ARTICLE 10

A member of the Court suffering from a disability considered to be [11] total and incapacitating him from the performance of his duties and who on these grounds resigns or is compulsorily retired shall be entitled from the date of such resignation or compulsory retirement to benefits as follows:

(a) Where the disability is recognised as being permanent, he shall be entitled to a life pension, calculated in accordance with the provisions of Article 9, subject to a minimum of 25 per cent. of the basic salary last received. He shall be entitled to the maximum pension if the disability is the result of disablement or illness contracted in connection with the performance of his duties.

(b) Where the disability is temporary he shall be entitled, until his recovery [12] to a grant [13] at the rate of 50 per cent. of the basic salary last received, where the disablement or illness was contracted in the performance of his duties, and 25 per cent. in other cases. When the recipient of this grant [14] reaches the age of 65 years [14a] or the grant [15] has been in effect for seven years it shall be replaced by a life pension calculated in accordance with the provisions of Article 9.

ARTICLE 11

Members of the Court shall be entitled to the benefits of the social security scheme as provided in Articles 72 to 75 of the Service

[11] Stationery Office: " deemed to be."
[12] Stationery Office: " until cured."
[13] French: " *une rente.*"
Stationery Office: " a pension." In the next sentence the Stationery Office also translates " *une pension* " as " a pension." In the phrase " *les pensions et les rentes* " in Art. 13, a translation of " *les rentes* " is omitted altogether.
[14] French: " *cette rente.*"
Stationery Office: " such invalidity pension."
[14a] Stationery Office: " 65 completed years."
[15] French: " *il.*"
Stationery Office: " the invalidity grant."

Regulations for officials of the European Economic Community and the European Atomic Energy Community and of the Service Regulations for officials of the European Coal and Steel Community.[16]

ARTICLE 12

Where a third party is liable in respect of the invalidity or death of a member of the Court, the Communities shall as of right represent [17] the member or his dependants in any action against such third party to the extent of the Communities' obligations under the present pensions scheme.

ARTICLE 13

The transitional allowance, referred to in Article 7, the pension referred to in Article 8, and the pensions and grants referred to in Article 10, may not be cumulative.[18] Where a member of the Court is entitled to claim benefit under more than one of the above-mentioned provisions, that provision alone shall be applied which is the most favourable to the claimant.

ARTICLE 14

Where a member of the Court dies before the expiration [19] of his term of office, the surviving spouse or dependent children shall be entitled, until the end of the third month following that in which death occurred, to the salary and allowances to which the member of the Court would have been entitled under Articles 2, 3 and 4 (1).

---

[16] Under these Articles (*Journal Officiel*, June 14, 1962, pp. 1403–4/62), any member of the Court *inter alia* receives up to 80% of the cost of artificial teeth for his illegitimate children (Art. 73.3, together in the Art. 72.1 and Appendix VII, Art. 2.2), and 5,500 Belgian francs for each of his wife's miscarriages (after not less than seven months pregnancy)—Art. 74, para. 2.

[17] French: " *subrogées de plein droit.*"
Stationery Office: " delegated as of right to act in place of."

[18] French:
" *L'indemnité transitoire prévue à l'article 7, la pension prévue à l'article 8, et les pensions et rentes prévues à l'article 10, ne peuvent se cumuler.*"
Stationery Office:
" Not more than one of the pensions or allowances, namely the transitional allowance, as provided in Article 7, the pension, as provided in Article 8, and the pension as provided in Article 10, may be drawn by the same person at any one time."

[19] French: " *avant l'expiration de.*"
Stationery Office: " during."

ARTICLE 15

1. The widow and dependent children of a member or ex-member of the Court to whom pension rights have accrued at the time of his death shall be entitled to survivor's pension.

Such pension shall be equal to a percentage of the pension accruing to the member or ex-member of the Court under Article 9 above at the date of death, namely:

	Per cent.
For the widow	50
For each fatherless child	10
For each orphan	20

However,[20] where the death of the member of the Court occurred during his term of office, survivor's pension shall be calculated on the basis of a pension equal to 50 per cent. of the basic salary received at the time of death.

2. The total amount of the above survivor's pensions shall not exceed the amount of the member's or ex-member's pension on which they are calculated. The maximum total survivor's pension payable shall be divided, where applicable, between the beneficiaries in accordance with the above percentages.

3. Survivor's pensions shall be granted from the first day of the calendar month following the date of death; however,[20] where the provisions of Article 14 are applied, the date of starting benefit shall be deferred until the first day of the fourth month following that in which death occurred.

4. In the event of the death of a surviving pensioner, entitlement to pension shall cease at the end of the calendar month in which death occurred. Furthermore, entitlement to a fatherless child's or orphan's [21] pension shall cease at the end of the month in which such child or orphan [21] reaches his twenty-first birthday; however,[22] such entitlement shall be extended during the period of the child's vocational training up to a date not later than the end of the month in which he reaches his twenty-fifth birthday.

Such pension shall continue to be payable to a fatherless child or orphan [21] who is not incapacitated through sickness or disablement from earning a livelihood.

5. No right to a survivor's pension shall accrue either to a woman

---

20 French: "*Toutefois.*"
   Stationery Office: "Provided always that."
21 French: "*orphelin.*" Art. 15, para. 1, refers to "*orphelin de père*" and "*orphelin de père et de mère.*"
22 See note 20, above.

marrying an ex-member of the Court who, at the date of marriage, was entitled to pension rightly by virtue of the present Regulation, or to any children of this marriage unless the death of the ex-member of the Court occurs more than five years from the marriage.[23]

6. A widow's entitlement to survivor's pension shall cease on re-marriage. She shall then be entitled to immediate payment of a capital sum equal to double the annual amount of her survivor's pension.

ARTICLE 16

If a member of the Court is relieved of his duties or condemned to loss of pension rights he shall forfeit any right to transitional allowance. The effect of loss of pension rights pronounced against a member of the Court [24] shall not extend [25] to his dependants.

ARTICLE 17

Should the Councils decide to increase the basic salary, they shall simultaneously decide on an appropriate increase in existing pensions.

ARTICLE 18

Payment of the benefits as provided under the present pensions scheme shall constitute a charge on the budget of the European Economic Community and the European Atomic Energy Community and on the General Estimates of the European Coal and Steel Community.

ARTICLE 19

1. Payment of the sums due under Articles 2, 3, 4, 5, 11 and 14 shall be made in the currency of the country where the European Coal and Steel Community has for the time being its headquarters.

2. Beneficiaries may elect to have sums due under Articles 7, 8, 10 and 15 paid in the currency either of the country of which they are nationals or in the currency of their country of residence or in the

---

[23] French:
> "*Aucun droit à pension de suivie n'est ouvert à la femme qui a épousé un ancien membre de la Cour ayant acquis, au moment du mariage, des droits à pension au titre du présent règlement, ni aux enfants issus de cette union, sauf si le décès de l'ancien membre de la Cour survient après cinq ans de mariage.*"

Stationery Office:
> " Where an ex-member of the Court marries and at the date of marriage has pension rights accruing to him under the present Regulation, the wife and any children of such marriage shall not be entitled to survivor's pension save where the marriage precedes the death of the ex-member of the Court by five years or more."

[24] French: " *prononcée à l'encontre d'un membre de la Cour.*"
The Stationery Office omits this phrase.

[25] French: " *ne s'étendent pas.*"
Stationery Office: " shall not be extended."

currency [26] of the country where the Community has for the time being its headquarters, their choice to remain operative for not less than two years. Where neither the first nor the second of these countries is a member country of the Community, the sums due shall be paid in the currency of the country where the European Coal and Steel Community has for the time being its headquarters.

ARTICLE 20

Members of the Court who have resigned between the date when the present Regulation comes into force and the date of its adoption may at their request opt within two months from the date of publication of the present Regulation for the continued application in their entirety of the provisions on emoluments previously applicable.

ARTICLE 21

In implementation of the provisions of Article 20 of the Protocols on Privileges and Immunities of the European Economic Community and the European Atomic Energy Community and of the provisions of Article 11 (*b*) of the Protocol on Privileges and Immunities of the European Coal and Steel Community, the emoluments of members of the Court deriving from the present Regulation shall, in so far as they are covered out of the funds of the European Economic Community and the European Atomic Energy Community, be subject to the tax imposed in favour of the Community, in accordance with the Regulation determining the conditions and procedure for levying the said tax,[27] and in so far as they are covered out of the funds of the European Coal and Steel Community, be subject to compensatory adjustment to bring them to the same level as those of members of the Commissions of the European Economic Community and the European Atomic Energy Community subjected to Community tax. This calculation shall be so effected that the amount [28] of the adjustment, plus the tax, shall be equal to the amount which members of the Court would have paid as Community tax if they had been members of the Commission of the European Economic Community, or of the European Atomic Energy Community,

[26] French: " *dans la monnaie.*"
The Stationery Office omits this phrase.
[27] *i.e.* E.E.C. Regulation No. 32 and Euratom Regulation No. 12, *Journal Officiel*, June 14, 1962, p. 1461/62.
[28] French: " *le montant.*"
Stationery Office: " the sum." A few words further on " *le montant* " is translated as " the amount."

on the basis of the Regulation determining the conditions and procedure for levying the tax adopted by the Councils of the European Economic Community and the European Atomic Energy Community, and all regulations for implementing the said Regulation.

ARTICLE 22

The present Regulation shall take effect as from January 10, 1962.

As from that date all previous Decisions governing the emoluments of members of the Court shall cease to have effect. The Decision of the Special Council of Ministers [29] of the European Coal and Steel Community dated October 13 and 14, 1958 shall however remain in force.

The present Regulation shall be binding in every respect and directly applicable in each Member State.[30]

Done on June 12, 1962.

By the Councils of the European Economic Community and the European Atomic Energy Community.
M. COUVE DE MURVILLE

By the Special Council of Ministers [31] *of the European Coal and Steel Community.*
E. COLOMBO [32]

AMENDMENT [1] OF THE REGULATION OF THE COUNCILS
Determining the Emoluments of Members of the Court of Justice
(E.E.C. No. 62—E.A.E.C. No. 13) [2]

Article 2:
For: Frb
Read: Fr
Article 3, paragraph 1 (b):
For: Frb
Read: Fr

Article 4, paragraphs 2 and 3:
For: Frb
Read: Fr
Article 6 (c):
For: Frb
Read: Fr

---

29 Stationery Office: " The Special Ministerial Council." In Art. 7 of the E.C.S.C. Treaty, and throughout that Treaty this body is correctly translated as the " Special Council of Ministers."
30 Stationery Office: " shall be binding in all its parts and directly enforceable in all Member States." The Stationery Office's translation of the relevant provision in the E.E.C. Treaty reads: " [Regulations] shall be binding in every respect and directly applicable in each Member State."
31 See note 29, above.
32 The words in italics were omitted from the original regulation and were added by the amendment of August 8, 1962, see below.
1 *Journal Officiel*, August 8, 1962, p. 2062/62.
2 See p. 561, above.

Complete the Regulation as follows:

Done on June 12, 1962.

By the Councils of the European Economic Community and the European Atomic Energy Community.	*By the Special Council of Ministers* [3] *of the European Coal and Steel Community.*
M. Couve de Murville	*E. Colombo*

---

[3] Stationery Office: " Special Ministerial Council "; see note 29, p. 570, above.

BIBLIOGRAPHY

BOOKS

Arena, *L'impresa pubblica e la sua inesistenza giuridica* (Palermo, 1962).
Bächle, H.-U., *Die Rechtsstellung der Richter am Gerichtshof der Europäischen Gemeinschaften* (Duncker and Humblot, Berlin, 1961).
Bebr, Gerhard, *Judicial Control of the European Communities* (Stevens, 1962).
Bonaert, A. and others, *Fragen der Nichtigkeits-und Untätigkeitsklagen nach dem Recht der Europäischen Gemeinschaft für Kohle und Stahl* (Vittorio Klostermann, 1961).
Breitner, Franz, *Der Gerichtshof der Montangemeinschaft und Seine Anrufung bei fehlerhaften Organakten—Forschungsstelle für Völkerrecht und ausländisches öffentliches Recht der Universität Hamburg* (Hamburg, 1953).
Brinkhorst and Wittenberg (Translators), *The Rules of Procedure of the Court of Justice of the European Communities* (A. E. Sythoff, Leyden, 1962).
Delvaux, L., *La Cour de Justice de la Communauté Européenne du Charbon et de l'Acier* (L.G.D.J., Paris, 1956).
Feld, Werner, *The Court of the European Communities: New Dimension in International Adjudication* (Nijhoff, 1964).
Fikentscher, Wolfgang, *Wettbewerb und gewerblicher Rechtsschutz (Die Stellung des Rechts der Wettbewerbsbeschrankungen in der Rechtsordung)* (Ch. H. Beck, München-Berlin, 1958).
Huber, Ernst, *Wirtschaftsverwaltungrecht*—J. C. B. Mohr (Paul Siebeck) Tübingen (2nd ed. 1953–54).
Mathias, *Das Recht der Europäischen Gemeinschaft für Kohle und Stahl und die nationalen Gerechte der Mitgliedstaaten* (J.2, 1954).
Mathijsen, Pierre, *Le Droit de la Communauté Européenne du Charbon et de l'Acier: une étude des sources* (Nijhoff, 1958).
Migliazzi, *La Corte di Giustizia della Communità Europee* (Milano, 1961).
Much, *Die Amtschaftung im Recht der Europäischen Gemeinschaft für Kohle und Stahl* (Klostermann, Frankfurt, 1952).
Osterhald, *Die Vollstreckung von Entscheidungen der E.G.K.S. in der Bundesrepublik Deutschland* (Klostermann, Frankfurt, 1954).
Richemont J. De, *La Cour de Justice—Code Annoté: Librairie du Journal des Notaires et des Avocats* (Paris, 1954).
Riphagen, Charles Van, *De juridische structurer der Europene Gemeenschap voor Kohen en Staal* (Universitaire Pers, Leiden, 1955).
Reepinghan, Charles Van and Orianne, Paul, *La Procédure devant la Cour de Justice des Communautés européennes* (Bruxelles/Paris, 1961).
Reuter, Paul, *La Communauté Européenne du Charbon et de l'Acier* (L.G.D.J., Paris, 1953).
Service de Documentation de la Cour de Justice de la Communauté Européenne du Charbon et de l'Acier, *Etat actual des questions juridiques et de la Jurisprudence* (2 Vols.) (1958).
Stein, Eric and Hay, Peter, *New Legal Remedies of Enterprises: A Survey. Chapter VII in American Enterprise in the European Common Market—A Legal Profile* (University of Michigan, 1960).
Steindorff, Ernst, *Die Nichtigkeitsklage im Recht der Europäischen Gemeinschaft für Kohle und Stahl* (Vittorio Klostermann, Frankfurt/Main, 1952).

Bibliography

Strauss, Walter, Fragen der Rechtsangleichung im Rahmen der Europäischen Gemeinschaft (Vittorio Klostermann, Frankfurt/Main, 1959).
Valentine, D. G., *The Court of Justice of the European Coal and Steel Community* (Nijhoff, The Hague, 1955).
Van Der Groeben and Von Boeckh, *Kommentar zum E. W. G. Vertrag* (2 Vols), (1958 and 1960).
Vanni, Giantranco, *Il Ricorso delle imprese nel Sistema della C.E.C.A.* (Dott. A. Giuttre, Editoro, Milan 1963).

ARTICLES

Abraham, "Les entreprises commune sujets de droit dans la Communauté Charbon-Acier," *Cahiers de Bruges* (1954).
Adler, G. R., "The E.E.C. Court of Justice," 7 *Canadian Bar Journal* (1964), p. 102.
Amphoux, M. J., "La procédure de la Cour," *Revue Générale de Droit International Public* (1961), p. 546.
Antoine A., "La Cour de Justice de la C.E.C.A. et la Cour International de Justice," *Revue Générale de Droit International Public* (1953), p. 210.
Bebr, Gerhard, "The Relation of the European Coal and Steel Community to the Law of the Member States: A Peculiar Legal Symbiosis," 58 *Columbian Law Review* (1958), p. 767.
　　"The Development of a Community Law by the Court of the European Coal and Steel Community," 42 *Minnesota Law Review* (1958), p. 845.
　　"The Concept of Enterprise under the European Communities: Legal Effects of Partial Integration," 26 *Law and Contemporary Problems* (1961), p. 454.
　　"Protection of Private Interests under the European Coal and Steel Community," 42 *Virginian Law Review* (1962), p. 879.
Boulouis, J., "Cour de Justice de la C.E.C.A. Commentaires des arrêts des 21 decembre 1954, 14 fevrier 1955, 21 mars 1955, 38 juin 1955, 18 juillet 1955," *Annuaire Français de Droit International* (1955).
　　"Cour de Justice de la C.E.C.A. Commentaires des arrêts 7–54, 9–54 and 8–55," *Annuaire Français de Droit International* (1956) p. 441.
　　"Cour de Justice de la C.E.C.A.," *Annuaire Français de Droit International* (1958), p. 314.
　　"Cour de Justice des Communautés Européennes," *Annuaire Français de Droit International* (1960).
Berri, "Sulle imprese marginali nel Tratto C.E.C.A.," *Rivista Trimestrale di Diritto e Procedura Civile Milano* (1961).
Bowyer, J. M., "Legal Aspects of the European Economic Community," 5 *Business Law Review* (1958), pp. 154 and 205.
Breban, Jean, "Revue de Jurisprudence de la Cour de Justice des Communautés Européennes," *Revue de Droit Public et de la Science Politique en France et à l'Etranger* (1962), pp. 873 and 1041.
Breitner, Franz, "Der Gerichtshof der Montangemeinschaft und seine Anrufung bei fehlerhaften Ortanakten," *Forschungsstelle für Volkerrecht an der Universität Hamburg* (1954).
Brunt, K., "Het Hot van Justitie van de Europese Gemeenschappen en de vrijstelling van inkomstenbelasting voor internationale ambtenaren," *De Naamlooze Vennootschap* (1961), p. 124.
Buergenthal, T., "Appeals for Annulment by Enterprises in the European Coal and Steel Community," 10 *American Journal of Comparative Law* (1961) p. 227.

" Private appeal against illegal State activities in the European Coal and Steel Community," 11 *American Journal of Comparative Law* (1962), p. 325.

Chevallier, Roger M., " L'arrêt 30–59 de la Cour de Justice des Communautés Européennes," *Revue Générale de Droit International Public* (1962), p. 546.

Cohn, E. J., " Aspects of the Procedure before the Court of Justice of the European Communities," *The Solicitors' Quarterly,* October 1962, p. 309.

Croquet, " Prospects Juridiques du Marché Commun," 1 *Droit Européen,* p. 65.

Daig, Hans Wolfran, " Die Gerichtsbarkeit in der Europäischen Wirtschaftsgemeinschaft und der Europäischen Atomgemeinschaft," 83 *Archiv des Öffentlichen Rechts* (1958), p. 132.

" Die Rechtsprechung des Gerichtshofes der Europäischen Gemeinschaft für Kohle und Stahl in den Jahren 1956 und 1957," 13 *Juristenzeitung,* p. 204.

" Die vier ersten Urteile des Gerichtshofes des Europäischen Gemeinschaft für Kohle und Stahl," *Juristenzeitung* (1955).

" Die Gerichtsbarkeit in der Europäischen Wirtschaftsgemeinschaft und der Europäischen Atomgemeinschaft mit vergleichenden Hinweisen auf der Europäischen Gemeinschaft für Kohle und Stahl," 83, *Archiv des Öffentlichen Rechts* (1958).

" Weitere Urteile des Gerichtshofes der E.G.K.S. (Notes sous les arrêts de la Cour 6–54, 5–55, 1–55)," *Juristenzeitung* (1956).

Delvaux, L., " Le controle de la Cour de Justice sur les faits et circonstances économiques," *Annales de Droit et de Sciences Politiques* (1958).

De Nova, " Il ricorso delle imprese contro decisioni generali dell'Alta Autorità," *Acts Officiels du Congres International d'Etudes sur la C.E.C.A.* (1958), p. 105.

Deringer, Arved, " Gewerblicher Rechtsschutz und Urberrercht," *Auslandische und Internationalische Teil,* (1962), p. 283.

Donner, A. M., " The Court of Justice of the European Communities," *International and Comparative Law Quarterly Supplementary Publication No. 1* (1961), p. 68.

" The Court of Justice of the European Communities," *The Law Society's Gazette,* August 1962, p. 444.

" The Court of Justice of the European Communities," 17 *Record of the Association of the Bar of the City of New York* (1962) p. 232.

" La Justice: élément d'intégration," *Volkenrechtelijke opstellen* (1962), p. 62.

" National Law and the Case Law of the Court of Justice of the European Communities," *Common Market Law Review,* June (1963), p. 8.

Dumon, Frederic, " La Formation de la règle de droit dans les Communautés Européennes," 12 *Revue Internationale de Droit Comparé* (1960), p. 75.

Dumon, Frederic & Rigaux F., " La Cour de Justice des Communautés Européennes et les Juridictions des Etats Membres," 18 *Annales de Droit et de Sciences Politiques* (1958), p. 263.

Durante, " La Corte di Giustizia della C.E.C.A.," *Rivista di Diritto Internazionale* (1953).

" La Cour de Justice des Communautés européennes et les juridictions des Etats membres," 14 *Revue Internationale de Droit Comparé,* (1962) p. 369.

Everling, Ulrich, " Die ersten Rechtsetzungsakte der Organe der Europäischen Gemeinschaften," 14 *Betriebs-Berater,* p. 52.

Bibliography

Esch, B. van der, " Vereveningskassen in de rechtspraak van het Europese Hof," 11 *Sociaal-economische Wetgeving* (1963), p. 245.

Fayara, F., " Ancora sul ricorsi della imprese par l'annulamento di decisioni dell'alta autorità della C.E.C.A.," *Rivista di Scienza Giuridiche* (1959), p. 550.

Federal Bar Association, Institute on Legal Aspects of the European Community, (Washington 1960).

Feld, W., " The Significance of the Court of Justice of the European Communities," 39 *North Dakota Law Review* (1963), p. 35.

" The Court of Justice of the European Communities: Emerging Political Power? An examination of selected decisions of the Courts 1961–1962 term," 38 *Tulane Law Review* (1963), p. 53.

" The Judges of the Court of Justice of the European Communities," 9 *Villanova Law Review* (1963), p. 37.

Gasparri, Pietro, " Le détournement de pouvoir dans le droit de la Communauté du Charbon et de l'Acier," in 4 *Actes Officiels du Congres International d'Etudes sur la Communauté Européenne du Charbon et de l'Acier, Stresa, 1957* (1958), p. 153.

" Sulla Tutela dei privati contro, i provvedimenti delle Autorita comunitarie," *Rivista di diretto processuale* (1958), p. 29.

Gaudet, M., "Marché commun devant les juges," 21 *Annales de Droit et de Sciences Politiqués* (1961), p. 133.

" Legal Problems of the European Common Market," 15 *Record of the Association of the Bar in the City of New York* (1960), p. 218.

Gori, P., " Sul concetta di ' decisione ' nel Trattato della C.E.C.A.," *Rivista della Società* (1960), p. 1177.

Grassetti, " La Communauté et les Entreprises," *Actes Officiels du congres international d'études sur la C.E.C.A.,* Vol. IV (Milan 1958).

Heemstra, F. van and Suermondt, G., " The Court of Justice of the European Communities," 13 *Cleveland-Marshall Law Review* (1964), p. 187.

Hay, P., " European Economic Community—Res Judicata and precedent in the Court of Justice of the Common Market," 12 *American Journal of Comparative Law* (1963), p. 404.

" Federal Jurisdiction of the Common Market Court," 12 *American Journal of Comparative Law* (1963), p. 21.

Institut Legal des Relations Internationales, " Les recours en annulation et en cas de carence dans le droit de la C.E.C.A. à la lumière de la jurisprudence de la Cour de Justice des Communautés," 13 *Chronique de Politique Etrangère* (1960), p. 291.

Jeantet, Charles Fernand, " Les interêts privés devant la Cour de Justice de la Communauté Européenne du Charbon et de l'Acier," *Revue du Droit Public et de la Science Politique* (1954).

" Note doctrinale sous les arrêts de la Cour de Justice de la C.E.C.A. du 21 décembre 1954, de 11 fevrier 1955, et du 28 juin 1955," *Revue du Droit Public et de la Science Politique* (1955), p. 618.

" Les Communautés européennes—Institutions communes aux trois Communautés européennes," *Juris-Classeur de Droit International* (1960), Fascicule 161 A-D.

Jeantet, Charles Fernand, & Loesch, Jacques, " The Court of Justice of the European Coal and Steel Community," *Union Internationale des Avocats, Les Juridictions Internationales* (1958), p. 115.

" The Court of Justice of the European Communities," *Union Internationale des Avocats, Les Juridictions Internationales* (1958), p. 223.

Jerusalem, " Die Rechtslage der Unternehmen in der Montanunion," 11 *Neuw Juristische Wochenschrift* (1958), p. 410.

Kautzar-Schroeder, " Public Tort Liability under the Treaty Constituting the European Coal and Steel Community compared with the Federal Tort Claims Act," 4 *Villanova Law Review,* p. 198.

Keilin, A. D., " Iuridicheskii mekhanizm evropeiskogo ekonomicheskogo soobshchestva," 33 *Sovetskoe Gosudarstvo i Pravo* (1963), p. 84.

Lagrange, Maurice, " L'Ordre juridique de la C.E.C.A. vu à travers la jurisprudence de sa Cour de Justice," *Revue de Droit Public et de la Science Politique* (1958), p. 841.

" La Cour de Justice de la Communauté Européenne du Charbon et de L'Acier," 70 *Revue du Droit Public et de la Science Politique* (1954), p. 417.

" La protection juridique des entreprises dans la Communauté et dans les Etats Membres," 4 *Actes Officiels du Congres sur la C.E.C.A., Stresa* (1958), p. 179.

" Le rôle de la Cour de Justice des Communautés européennes," *Les Problèmes Juridiques et Economiques du Marché Commun, Colloque des Facultés de Droit de Lille* (1959), p. 41.

" Contrôle judiciaire des décisions prises par les autorités compétentes en matière d'ententes," *Kartelle und Monopole im modernen Recht*—C. F. Muller, (Karlsruhe 1961), p. 889.

" Les pouvoirs de l'Haute Autorité et l'application du Traité de Paris," *Revue de Droit Public et de la Science Politique* (Paris 1961).

" The Role of the Court of Justice as seen through its case law," 26 *Law and Contemporary Problems* (1961), p. 400.

" Le rôle de la Cour de Justice des Communautés européennes tel qu'il se dégage de sa jurisprudence," 24 *Droit Social* (1961), p. 1 and *Revue du Marché Commun* (1962) p. 33.

" Les actions en justice dans le régime des Communautés européennes," *Sociaal Economische Wetgeving* (1962), p. 81.

Laun, " Bemerkungen zum freien Ermessen und zum détournement de pouvoir im staatlichen und in Völkerrecht " *Festschrift für Herbert Kraus* (1954), p. 128.

Lecourt, Robert, " The Development of European Law," *European Community,* (June, 1963) p. 10.

Legal Problems of the E.E.C. and the E.F.T.A. Report of a Conference held in London in September 1960, (London 1961).

Lenhoff, A. I., " Jurisdictional Relationship between the Court of the European Communities and the Courts of the Member States," 12 *Buffalo Law Review* (1963), p. 296.

L'Huillier, " Une conquête du droit administratif français: le contentieux de la C.E.C.A.," *Recueil Dalloz* (1953).

Liège, Université de, " Les Aspects Juridiques du Marché Commun," 8 *Colloque Scientifique de la Faculté de Droit de l'Université de Liège* (1958).

Lloyd, D., " The Court of Justice of the European Economic Community," *English Law and The Common Market,* (Stevens 1963).

Ludovicy, " La jurisprudence de la Cour de Justice de la C.E.C.A.," *Revue Générale du Droit International Public* (1956).

Matthies, Heinrich, " Zur Nachprüfungsbefugnis des Gerichtshof der Montanunion," 16 *Zeitschrift für Auslandisches Öffentliches Recht und Völkerrecht,* p. 42.

McMahon, J. F., " The Court of the European Communities," 1 *Journal of Common Market Studies,* (1962), p. 1.

" The Court of the European Communities: Judicial Interpretation and International Organization," 37 *British Yearbook of International Law* (1961), p. 320.

Bibliography

Meibon, H., " Die Rechtsetzung durst die Organe der Europäischen Gemein-schaften," 14 *Betriebs-Berater,* p. 127.

Miaja, de la Nuela, " El recurso por deviación de poder en al tribunal de la comunidades europeas," *Problematica de la ciencia de derecho* (Bar-celona, 1962), p. 627.

Migliazza, A., " Azione della corte di giustizia nei sistemi giuridici delle Comunità europee e degli stati membri," 6 *Rivista di Scienza Giuri-diche* (1961), p. 346.

" La Corte di giustizia delle Comunità europee e il suo ambito di giurisdizione," 14 *Rivista Trimestrale Diritto e Procedura Civile* (1960), p. 495.

" Il procedimento innazi alla Corte di giustizia delle Comunità Europee," 15 *Rivista di Diritto Processuale* (1960), p. 233.

" Su alcuni caratteri della Corte di giustizia delle Comunità Europee," 43 *Rivista di Diritto Internazionale* (1960), p. 229.

" La Jurisprudence de la Cour de Justice des Communautés européennes et le problème des sources de droit," 31 *Annuaire of the Hague Academy of International Law* (1961), p. 96, and 12 *Österreich-ische Zeitschrift für Öffentliches Recht* (1962), p. 332.

Monaco, Riccardo, " I poteri dell' Alta Autorità della Communità Europee del Carbone et dell' Acciaio, in materia di disciplina dei prezzi. (Note sur l'arrêt de la Cour du 21 décembre 1954)," 10 *Rivista di Diritto Internazionale* (1955).

Morelli, Gaetano, " La Cour de Justice des Communautés Européennes en tant que juge interne,'" 19 *Zeitschrift für Ausländisches Öffentliches Recht und Völkerrecht* (1958), p. 269.

Münch, F., " Die Entwicklung der Europäischen Gerichtsbarkeit," 11 *Jahrbuch für Internationales Recht* (1962), p. 324.

Nebolsine and others, " The ' Right of Defence ' in the Control of Restric-tive Practices under the European Community Treaties," 8 *American Journal of Comparative Law* (1959), p. 433.

Neri, " Il ricorso dei privati davanti alla Corte di Guistizia della C.E.C.A.," *Rivista di Studi Politici Internazionale* (1956).

" Il ricorso di Legittimita del' privato nei trattati C.E.C.A. e C.E.E.," *Rivista di Studi Politici Internazionali* (1958), p. 236.

Ophuls, " Gerichtsbarkeit und Rechtsprechung im Schumanplan," 4 *Neue Juristische Wochenschrift,* (1952) p. 693.

Philipp, " Vom Urteil des Gerichtshofes der Montanunion von 18 Marz 1955 zu den Hochstpreisentscheidungen der Hohen Behörde von 20 Marz 1954," *Neue Juristische Wochenschrift* (1955).

Pinay, Pierre, " La Cour de Justice des Communautés Européennes," 1 *Revue du Marché Commun* (1959), p. 138.

Ratthies, Heinrich, " Das Recht der Europäischen Gemeinschaft für Kohle und Stahl und die Nationalen Gerichte der Mitgliedstaaten," *Juristen-zeitung* (1954).

" Zur Nachprüfungsbefugnis des Gerichtshofs der Montanunion,'' 16 *Zeitschrift für Auslandisches Öffentliches Recht und Völkerrecht.* p. 427.

" Der Gerichtshof der Montanunion und dritte Länder," *Österreich-ische Juristenzeitung* (1955).

Reepinghen, C. van, and Orianne, P., " La procédure devant la Cour de Justice des Communautés européennes," 76 *Journal des Tribunaux* (1961), p. 89.

Reuter, Paul, " Aspects de la Communauté Economique Européenne,' *Revue du Marché Commun* (1958), p. 161.

Riese, Otto, " Die Verfahrensordnung des Gerichtshofen der Europäischen Gemeinschaft für Kohle und Stahl," 6 *Neue Juristische Wochenschrift* (1953), p. 521.

Riesenfeld, S. A., " Decisions of the Court of Justice of the European Communities," 56 *American Journal of International Law* (1962), p. 724.

Riesenfeld, S. A. and Buxbaum, R. M., " N.V. Algemene transport—en expeditie onderneming Van Gend & Loos c. Administration Fiscale Néerlandaise: a pioneering decision of the Court of Justice of the European Communities," 58 *American Journal of International Law* (1964), p. 152.

Riphagen, " The case law of the European Coal and Steel Community Court of Justice," *Nederlands Tijdschrift voor Internationaal Recht* (1955).

Rivero, Jean, " Le problème de l'influence des droits internes sur la Cour de Justice de la C.E.C.A.," 4 *Annuaire Français du Droit International* (1958), p. 295.

Robert, Jean, " Comment on the Bosch Case " (Case 13–61), *Recueil Dalloz* (May 1962), p. 359.

Roblot, " Die Nichtigkeitsklagen in der ersten Urteilen des Gerichtshofs," *Droit Social* (1958), p. 7.

" Il contenzioso di annullamento nella prima giurisprudenza della Corte di Giustizia della C.E.C.A.," *Nuova rivista di diritto commerciale diritto dell' economia diritto sociale, Padova,* Vol. X, (1957).

Samkalden, I., " Annotation of Van Gend en Loos *v.* Nederlandse Tarief-commissie (Case 26–62)," *Common Market Law Review* (1963), p. 88.

Scamell, E. H., " The Common Market and the Legal Profession," *English Law and the Common Market* (Stevens, 1963).

Schlochauer, " Die Gerichtsbarkeit der Europäischen Gemeinschaft für Kohle und Stahl," *Archiv des Völkerrechts* (1951–52).

Schule, Adolf, " Grenzen der Klagebefugnis von dem Gerichtshof der Montanunion," 16 *Zeitschrift für ausländisches öffentliches Recht und Völkerrecht* (1955–56), p. 227.

" Gemeinsamer Markt und nationale Wirtschaft: Zur Auslegung von Artikel 37 des Vertrages über die E.G.K.S.," *Zeitschrift für ausländisches öffentliches Recht und Völkerrecht* (1962), p. 461.

Schwarzenberger, G., " Federalism and Supra-nationalism in the European Communities," *English Law and the Common Market* (Stevens, 1963).

Séché, J.-C., " La notion d'interêt à agir dans le droit de la C.E.C.A.," *Revue général du droit international public* (1962), p. 299.

Stein, Eric, " The European Coal and Steel Community: The Beginning of its Judicial Process," 55 *Columbia Law Review* (1955), p. 985.

" Court of Justice of the European Coal and Steel Community: 1954–1957," 51 *American Journal of International Law* (1957), p. 821.

Stein, Eric and Hay, Peter, " New Legal Remedies of Enterprises: A Survey," *American Enterprise in the European Common Market, A Legal Profile* (University of Michigan, 1960), p. 459.

" Legal remedies of enterprises in the European Economic Community," 9 *American Journal of Comparative Law* (1960), p. 375.

Steindorff, Ernst, " Montanfremde Unternehmen in der Europäischen Gemeinschaft für Kohle und Stahl," 8 *Juristenzeitung,* p. 718.

" Die Europäischen Gemeinschaften in der Rechtsprechung," 8 *Archiv des Völkerrechts* (1960), p. 426.

Stone, Victor J., " The Court and Anglo-Saxon Law," *European Community,* (June 1963), p. 8.

Suetens, L.-P., " Prejudiciële vragen in het E.E.G. en E.G.A. recht," 26 *Rechtskundig Weekblad* (1963), p. 1913.

Thompson, Dennis, " The Bosch Case," 11 *International and Comparative Law Quarterly* (1962), p. 721.

Tsangarides, J. B., " Nature juridique des actes émis par le conseil et la Commission de la C.E.E.," 14 *Revue Hellénique de Droit International* (1961), p. 138.

Ule, " Gerichtlicher Rechtsschutz in der Montangemeinschaft," *Der Betrieb Marz* (1952).

" Der Gerichtshof der Montanunion als europäisches Verwaltungsgericht," 67 *Deutsches Verwoltungsblatt* (1952), p. 65.

Valentine, D. G., " The First Judgments of the Court of Justice of the European Coal and Steel Community," 20 *Modern Law Review* (1957), p. 596.

" The Competence of the Court of Justice of the European Coal and Steel Community," *Symbolae Verzijl* (Nijhoff, 1958), p. 387.

" The Jurisdiction of the Court of Justice of the European Communities to Annul Executive Action," 36 *British Yearbook of International Law* (1960), p. 174.

" The Court of the European Communities," *The Law Society's Gazette* (1962), p. 523.

Van Houtte, Albert, " La Cour de Justice de la Communauté Européenne du Charbon et de l'Acier," *European Yearbook* (1956), p. 183.

Vergottini, G. de " Responsibilità aquiliana delle intituzione della C.E.C.A. nel trattato e nella giurisprudenza della corte," 13 *Rivista Trimestrale di Diritto Pubblico* (1963), p. 91.

Vezzoso, G., " Moditicazione dell'art. 56 del Trattato institutivo della Comunità del Carbone e dell'Acciaio," 5 *Rivista della Società* (1960), p. 438.

" Rasseyna di giurisprudenza della Corte di giustizia della Comunità europee sul Trattato intitutivo della C.E.C.A.," 5 *Rivista della Società* (1959–1960), p. 1140.

Vignes, " Les Recours juridictionnels des entreprises privées contre les decisions de la Haute Autorité de Plan Schuman," *Acheteurs* (1952).

" I ricorsi giurdizionali della impresse private contra le decisioni dell' Alta Autorita del Piano Schuman," *Rivista di Studi Politici Internazionali* (1952).

Weser, Martha, " Les conflits de juridictions dans le cadre du Marché Commun: Difficultés et remèdes," 48 *Revue Critique du Droit International Privé* (1959), p. 613, and 49 at pp. 21, 150 and 313.

Weyer, E., " E.W.G. Vertrag und Ausfuhrverbote," *Der Betriebsberater* (1962), p. 467.

Wilmars, J. M. de, " De rechtsbescherming in de Europese Gemeenschappen," 26 *Rechtskundig Weekblad* (1963), p. 1417.

Wohlfarth, E., " Von der Befugnis der Organe der Europäischen Wirtschaftsgemeinschaft zur Rechtsetzung," 9 *La Justicia* (1960), p. 12.

Wolf, E., " The Role of the Court of the European Communities in the Antitrust structure of the Common Market," 31 *Fordham Law Review* (1963), p. 621.

Wolters, Adrien, " Les recours en annulation devant la Cour de Justice des Communautés Européennes," 37 *Revue de Droit International et de Droit Comparé* (1960), p. 165.

Zannini, W., " La giurisdizione della Corte di Giustizia delle Comunità europee in rapporto agli ordinamenti degli Stati membri," 16 *Diritto Internazionale* (1962), p. 242.

INDEX

ACTIONS,
compromise of, 62, 522
damages for,
  non-Community enterprises by,
  224–226
discontinuance of, 62, 97, 522
joinder of, 56, 107, 522
judges, against, 27–29
municipal courts, before, *see* MUNI-
  CIPAL COURTS.
publicity of, 59, 490
re-opening of, 80
settlement of, 61, 107, 522
time limits for, *see* TIME LIMITS.
and see APPEALS.

ADVISORY OPINIONS,
amendment, E.C.S.C. Treaty, upon,
  90
Court, of, 14
international agreements, legality of,
  upon, 90, 91, 336–337
international convention, legality of,
  upon, 91, 92, 336–337
Request for, time limit for, 104–105

ADVOCATES, *see* COUNSEL.

ADVOCATES GENERAL, 30–35
absence of, 34, 487
allowances of, 561–563, 568–571
appointment of, 4, 21, 30, 448
assignment to Chamber, 487
convening of, 21, 45, 495
costs, heard concerning, 33, 519
death of, 34, 448
declaration of, 487
dismissal of, 34–35, 448, 466
disqualifications of, 31, 34, 467, 478
duties and powers of, 30, 31–34, 447–
  448, 507
hearing of, 33, 35, 46, 49, 53, 54, 56,
  60, 61, 62, 66, 68, 76, 77, 78, 79,
  87, 90, 91, 92, 97, 98, 453, 468,
  479, 487, 496, 503, 505, 517, 519,
  526, 528, 530, 531, 538, 540, 541,
  558
immunity and privileges of, 31, 466
Instruction and, 32, 506

ADVOCATES GENERAL—*cont.*
judgment, errors in, 33, 516–517
language of submissions of, 47, 497
leave of absence of, 495
number of, increase in, 30, 31, 448
oath of, 30, 487
pensions of, 31, 564–571
powers and duties of, 30, 31–34, 447–
  448, 507
precedence of, 30, 487
qualifications of, 30, 451, 466, 487
questioning by, 73, 514
re-election of, 30, 448
replacement of, 34, 487
residence of, 31, 447, 467, 478
resignation of, 34, 466
retirement of, 30, 487
salaries of, 31, 561–563, 568–571
seniority of, 30, 487
submissions of, 30, 32, 74, 514, 544–
  555
undertaking of, 30, 487
voting of, 33, 45, 494

AGENTS,
costs of, 93, 519
documents, duty to produce, 65, 455

ARBITRATION COMMITTEE,
constitution of, 442–443
decision of, 341, 479–480
  annulment of, 343–344, 443, 479–
  480
  appeal against 14–15, 339–343,
  479–480
  res judicata, 343–344
  revision of, 443
  stay of execution of, 87–89
patent licences, jurisdiction over, 345
reference back to, 344
rules of procedure of, 440

ASSEMBLY, *see* PARLIAMENTARY
ASSEMBLY.

ASSISTANT *RAPPORTEURS,*
appointment of, 40–41, 448
immunity of, 41, 42, 449–450

Index

ASSISTANT *RAPPORTEURS—cont.*
oath of, 41, 491–492
qualifications of, 41, 466–467

ASSOCIATIONS,
appeal, right of, by, 186
Commission (E.E.C.) acts of, appeal against, 287, 290–292
Council (E.C.S.C.) acts of, appeal against, 112
damages, right to claim, 181
decisions of, validity of, 242–246
(E.E.C.) acts of,
appeal against, 287, 290–292
faute de service, claim for, damages for, 229
High Authority, acts of, appeal against, 112
meaning of, 186
and see ENTERPRISES.

ATTACHÉS,
qualifications of, 42

BOARD OF DIRECTORS, 432–433
and see EUROPEAN INVESTMENT BANK.

BOARD OF GOVERNORS, 429–432
and see EUROPEAN INVESTMENT BANK.

CATALANO, Nicola, 8

CHAMBERS OF COURT, 16–17
Advocate General of, *see* ADVOCATES GENERAL.
appeals heard by, 17, 90, 533
appointment of, 17, 533
costs, dispute about, 97
Court, remission of case to, 17, 99, 533
Court, voting in, dispute concerning, 45, 494–495
creation of, 16, 492
deliberations of, 44, 450, 478
duties of, 98
employee, appeal by, assigned to, 17, 89, 533
function of, 17, 89, 90, 533
Instruction, held by, 17, 62, 64, 73
juge rapporteur of, *see* JUGE RAPPORTEUR.
language of,
and see PROCEDURAL LANGUAGE, 46–47

CHAMBERS OF COURT—*cont.*
legal aid granted by, 23, 98, 522–523
President of, 25–26, 485–486
and see PRESIDENT OF CHAMBER.
quorum of, 22, 26, 44
sittings of, 22, 26, 43, 493

COMMISSION (E.E.C.),
acts of, 284, 288–289, 423–425
annulment of, 287–295
procedure following, 301, 303
appeal against, 10, 274–277, 279, 287–295
suspensive effect of, 330–331 *and see* REQUEST
interpretation of, 303, 307–308
legality of, 287–295
suspension of execution of, 17, 330–331
validity of, 303, 307–308
agreements with international organisations, 24, 336–337
agreements with States, 24, 336–337
appeals by,
Council, against, 297–301
Member States, against, 268–269, 274–277
compensation payable by, 302, 310–312
constitution of, 422–423
Decisions of, 288–289, 423–425
and see acts of.
Directives of, 284, 289, 329–330, 423–425
and see acts of.
duties and powers of, concerning:—
aids, illegal, 12, 268–269
competition, distortions of, 12, 331–336
Member States, breaches by, 12, 274–277, 278–281
subsidies, 12, 268–269
execution of judgments by, 301–303
inaction of,
appeal against, 297–302
investigation by, 331–336
members of, 422–423
dismissal of, 270–271
obligations of, 270–271
suspension of, 272–273
and see EMPLOYEES.
non-contractual liability of, 303, 310–312
Opinions of, concerning,
competition, 333–335

COUNCIL OF MINISTERS
(EURATOM)—*cont.*
acts of—*cont.*
suspension of execution of, 368–369
appeals against, 10, 11, 362–363, 364
appeals by, against,
Commission, 362–363, 364
members of, 365–366
Commission, challenge of inaction
of, 364
compensation payable by, 366
constitution of, 439–440
Decisions of, 440–441
and see acts of.
appeals against, 10, 11, 362–363,
364
Directives of, 440–441
and see acts of.
duties and powers of, 339, 350, 354–
355, 439–441
inaction of, appeal against, 10, 11,
364
Regulations of, 440–441
annulment of, enforcement after,
364
challenge of, out of time, 368
voting in, 440

COUNSEL,
Courts'
control over, 49–50
questions to, 73, 514
credentials of, 39, 489
exclusion of, from Court, 24, 34, 49,
50, 499
expenses and fees of, 38, 93, 519–520
immunities of, 39, 48–50
legal aid cases, in, 99, 521, 553–554,
557–559
parties, pleading through, 73, 514
qualifications of, 48, 452
signing of documents, 500
speeches of, order of, 73–74

COURT OF E.C.S.C.,
establishment of, 1–5
extensions of, proposed, 5–7
judges of, 3–4
replacement of, 7–9

COURT OF EUROPEAN COM-
MUNITIES,
administration of, 21, 36, 490–491
administrative decisions of, 45, 494

COURT OF EUROPEAN COM-
MUNITIES—*cont.*
Advisory Opinions of, *see* ADVISORY
OPINIONS.
Advocates General, *see* ADVOCATES
GENERAL.
archives of, 39, 490
assistant *rapporteurs* of, *see* ASSIST-
ANT RAPPORTEURS.
assumptions made by, 396–404
attachés to, 42
camera, sittings *in,* 66, 332, 335, 514
Chambers of, *see* CHAMBERS OF
COURT.
composition of, 16, 19, 450
and see JUDGES.
Conseil d'Etats, as, 9, 123–124
convening of, 45, 495
deliberations of, 43–45, 74, 455, 456,
472, 478, 481
Deputy Registrars of, *see* REGISTRAR.
direction of, 20, 486
documents of, 36–39
and see DOCUMENTS.
employees of, *see* EMPLOYEES.
establishment of, 1–5, 7–9
fees of, 92–93, 552–554
financial management of, 21, 491
history of, 1–15
interpretation of Treaties by, *see*
INTERPRETATION OF TREATIES.
investigation of own motion by, 55,
56, 69, 113–117, 128, 393–394, 508–
509, 510
judges of, *see* JUDGES.
judgment of, *see* JUDGMENT.
judicial notice taken by, 66, 455
jurisdiction of, 9–15
and see JURISDICTION.
Instruction before, 62–64
and see INSTRUCTION.
languages, official, of, *see* OFFICIAL
LANGUAGES.
municipal courts and, 389–392.
see MUNICIPAL COURTS.
municipal laws and, *see* MUNICIPAL
LAW.
officials of, *see* EMPLOYEES.
organisation of, 16–42, 447–451, 466–
476, 478, 484–485
origins of, 1–9
own motion of, 55, 66, 69, 113–117,
128, 393–394, 508–509, 510

HIGH AUTHORITY—*cont.*
violation of professional secret by, 239–240
violation of Treaty by, *see* VIOLATION OF TREATY.
  and see DECISIONS OF HIGH AUTHORITY; RECOMMENDATIONS OF HIGH AUTHORITY.

IMMUNITY,
Advocates General, of, 31, 448, 466, 478
agents of, 39, 48–50, 498–499
assistant *rapporteurs,* of, 18, 41–42, 449–450, 491–492
Community (E.C.S.C.), of, 265–266
counsel, of, 39, 48–50, 498–499
dispute concerning, 39, 266–267, 498
documents, of, 39, 49, 498
employees and officials, of, 449–450
judges, of, 27–29, 445–446, 464, 477
legal advisers, of, 39, 48–50, 498–499
Registrar, of, 36, 449
salaries, of, 28, 266–267, 371
waiver of, 20, 29, 36, 49, 232, 445, 449–450, 464, 477, 499

INCOMPETENCE, 124–126
annulment, as grounds of, 112, 287, 363
Arbitration Committee of, 342
manifest injustice, relation to, 144
violation of Treaty, relation to, 135

INDIVIDUALS,
appeals by, against,
  Commission (E.E.C.), 287, 292, 297–301
    (Euratom), 357, 363, 364
  Council (E.E.C.), 287, 292, 297–300
    (Euratom), 363, 364
  High Authority, 246–249, 462

INJUNCTIONS, MANDATORY, 89, 350–351, 527–528

INSTRUCTION, 62–65, 455, 506–513
Advocate General heard concerning, 32, 506–507
amplification of, 73, 515
Chamber, held before, 64–65, 505–506

INSTRUCTION—*cont.*
contents of, 62, 64, 506–507
Court, held before, 62, 508
decision to hold, 22, 26, 53, 62, 64, 79, 86, 505–525
interim measures, in case for, 86, 525
juge rapporteur, part played by, in, 26, 53, 62, 64, 505–507
measures of, 62, 64, 506–507
  additional measures of, 73, 78, 515
  order for, 73, 79, 86, 515, 531
  re-opening of, 73, 78, 515
site, visit to, 62, 506
witnesses, 62, 508–512
  and see WITNESSES.
written observations of parties on, 22, 72, 107, 513

INTERIM MEASURES,
costs of, 96
President of Chamber, power of, 90, 533
President of Court, power of, 17, 86, 90, 457–458, 533
provisional measures, prescribing of, 216–217, 331, 369
Request for,
  admissibility of, 86, 524–525
  procedure following, 33, 73, 86–87, 525–526
  ruling upon, 87, 526–527
  modification of, 87, 527
stay of,
  acts of Communities,
    E.C.S.C., 211–217, 524–525
    E.E.C., 331, 524–525
    Euratom, 368–369, 524–525
  judgment, 24, 83, 84, 342, 527, 534

INTERPRETATION OF TREATIES,
assumptions, 396–404
  effectiveness, principle of, 399–401
  protection of rights, 402–404
  sovereignty of States, 397–399, 401–402
reference to, in,
  general principles of law, 384–385
  implied terms, 384–385
  intention of authors, 370–380
  municipal laws, 385–387
  other treaties, 372–373
  purpose, 376–379
  subordinate documents, 373–376

591